Lecture Notes in Computer Scie

T0238517

Commenced Publication in 1973
Founding and Former Series Editors:
Gerhard Goos, Juris Hartmanis, and Jan van Leeuwen

Mitsuko Aramaki   Mathieu Barthet
Richard Kronland-Martinet   Sølvi Ystad (Eds.)

From Sounds
to Music and Emotions

9th International Symposium, CMMR 2012
London, UK, June 19-22, 2012
Revised Selected Papers

 Springer

Volume Editors

Mitsuko Aramaki
Richard Kronland-Martinet
Sølvi Ystad
Centre National de la Recherche Scientifique
Laboratoire de Mécanique Acoustique
31 Chemin Joseph Aiguier, 13402 Marseille Cedex 20, France
E-mail: {aramaki, kronland, ystad}@lma.cnrs-mrs.fr

Mathieu Barthet
Queen Mary University of London
Centre for Digital Music
Mile End Road, London E1 4NS, UK
E-mail: mathieu.barthet@eecs.qmul.ac.uk

ISSN 0302-9743   e-ISSN 1611-3349
ISBN 978-3-642-41247-9   e-ISBN 978-3-642-41248-6
DOI 10.1007/978-3-642-41248-6
Springer Heidelberg New York Dordrecht London

Library of Congress Control Number: 2013949028

CR Subject Classification (1998): J.5, H.5, C.3, H.5.5, G.3, I.5

LNCS Sublibrary: SL 3 – Information Systems and Application, incl. Internet/Web and HCI

Typesetting: Camera-ready by author, data conversion by Scientific Publishing Services, Chennai, India

Printed on acid-free paper

Springer is part of Springer Science+Business Media (www.springer.com)

Preface

The 9th International Symposium on Computer Music Modeling and Retrieval, CMMR2012 "Music & Emotions" took place at Queen Mary University, June 19–22, 2012. This symposium, which was initiated in 2003, has been organized in several European countries as well as in the East (Bhubaneswar, India), and was this year jointly organized by the Centre for Digital Music, London, and the CNRS - Laboratoire de Mécanique et d'Acoustique, Marseille. The post proceedings of the previous CMMR conferences were all published in the Lecture Notes in Computer Sciences Series (LNCS 2771, LNCS 3310, LNCS 3902, LNCS 4969, LNCS 5493, LNCS 5954, LNCS 6684, LNCS 7172).

A total of 150 delegates from 24 different countries were gathered during the 4 days of the conference and the various contributions included oral sessions, posters, demos, panels and tutorials. In line with previous CMMR events, a multi-disciplinary approach associating traditional music information retrieval (MIR) and sound modeling topics with human perception and cognition, musicology, and philosophy was exposed.

In addition, music submissions were solicited within the framework of the CMMR2012 New Resonances music festival that was held each evening at Wilton's Music Hall. A "Cross-Disciplinary Perspectives on Expressive Performance" Workshop was also organized by Andrew McPherson (Queen Mary University) on the first day of the conference.

This year, CMMR2012 put a special emphasis on music and emotion related research topics. Music and emotion have been subject to a large number of studies in varied fields of research. For instance, within the field of cognitive science, music-induced emotions as well as the positive affect music can have on intellectual faculties have been thoroughly investigated. Various types of expressive intentions between composers, performers and listeners have also been examined by musicologists and psychologists. From a different standpoint, music informatics researchers have employed machine learning algorithms to discover relationships between objective features computed from audio recordings and subjective mood labels given by human listeners. In spite of all these investigations, the understanding of the genesis of musical emotions and the mapping between musical structures and emotional responses remain unanswered research problems.

Three prominent keynote speakers with considerably different backgrounds and links to the conference theme (i.e., Pr. Laurent Daudet from Paris Diderot University, Pr. Patrik N. Juslin from Uppsala University and film score composer and producer Simon Boswell) gave high quality presentations of their respective domains. The conference contributions were distributed in seven technical sessions, two poster sessions, one demo session, two panel sessions, three concerts, two tutorials and a workshop. Among these contributions, 28 papers were selected for the present post proceedings edition, which is divided into seven sections corresponding to the technical sessions and an 8th session in which four workshop contributions are selected.

We would first of all like to thank all the participants of CMMR2012 who strongly contributed to the success of this conference. We would also like to thank the Program Committee members for their indispensable paper reports and the Music Committee for the difficult task of selecting the artistic contributions. We are particularly grateful to the local Organizing Committee at Queen Mary University who made sure that all the practical issues were under control. Finally, we would like to thank Springer for agreeing to publish the CMMR2012 post proceedings in their LNCS series.

June 2013

Mitsuko Aramaki
Mathieu Barthet
Richard Kronland-Martinet
Sølvi Ystad

Organization

The 9th International Symposium on Computer Music Modeling and Retrieval (CMMR2012) was jointly organized by the Centre for Digital Music, London, and the CNRS - Laboratoire de Mécanique et d'Acoustique (Centre National de la Recherche Scientifique), Marseille, France.

Symposium Chairs

Mathieu Barthet	Centre for Digital Music, Queen Mary University of London, UK
Simon Dixon	Centre for Digital Music, Queen Mary University of London, UK

Proceedings Chairs

Richard Kronland-Martinet	CNRS-LMA, France
Sølvi Ystad	CNRS-LMA, France
Mitsuko Aramaki	CNRS-LMA, France
Mathieu Barthet	Centre for Digital Music, Queen Mary University of London, UK
Simon Dixon	Centre for Digital Music, Queen Mary University of London, UK

Paper and Program Chairs

Richard Kronland-Martinet	CNRS-LMA, France
Mitsuko Aramaki	CNRS-LMA, France
Sølvi Ystad	CNRS-LMA, France
Panos Kudumakis	Centre for Digital Music, Queen Mary University of London, UK

Expressive Performance Workshop Chair

Andrew McPherson	Centre for Digital Music, Queen Mary University of London, UK

Committees

Local Organizing Committee

Daniele Barchiesi	Centre for Digital Music, Queen Mary University of London, UK
Emmanouil Benetos	Centre for Digital Music, Queen Mary University of London, UK
Luis Figueira	Centre for Digital Music, Queen Mary University of London, UK
Dimitrios Giannoulis	Centre for Digital Music, Queen Mary University of London, UK
Steven Hargreaves	Centre for Digital Music, Queen Mary University of London, UK
Tom Heathcote	Queen Mary University of London, UK
Sefki Kolozali	Centre for Digital Music, Queen Mary University of London, UK
Sue White	Queen Mary University of London, UK

Program Committee

Mitsuko Aramaki	CNRS-LMA, France
Federico Avanzini	University of Padova, Italy
Isabel Barbancho	University of Málaga, Spain
Mathieu Barthet	Queen Mary University of London, UK
Roberto Bresin	KTH, Sweden
Marcelo Caetano	IRCAM, France
Antonio Camurri	University of Genoa, Italy
Kevin Dahan	University of Paris-Est Marne-La-Vallée, France
Olivier Derrien	Toulon-Var University, France
Simon Dixon	Queen Mary University of London, UK
Barry Eaglestone	University of Sheffield, UK
George Fazekas	Queen Mary University of London, UK
Cédric Févotte	CNRS-TELECOM ParisTech, France
Bruno Giordano	McGill University, Canada
Emilia Gómez	Pompeu Fabra University, Spain
Goffredo Haus	Laboratory for Computer Applications in Music, Italy
Henkjan Honing	University of Amsterdam, The Netherlands
Kristoffer Jensen	Aalborg University, Denmark
Anssi Klapuri	Queen Mary University of London, UK
Richard Kronland-Martinet	CNRS-LMA, France
Panos Kudumakis	Queen Mary University of London, UK
Mark Levy	Last.fm, UK

Sylvain Marchand   Université de Bretagne Occidentale, France
Matthias Mauch   Queen Mary University of London, UK
Eduardo Miranda   University of Plymouth, UK
Marcus Pearce   Queen Mary University of London, UK
Emery Schubert   University of New South Wales, Australia
Björn Schuller   Munich University of Technology, Germany
Bob Sturm   Aalborg University, Denmark
George Tzanetakis   University of Victoria, Canada
Thierry Voinier   CNRS-LMA, France
Geraint A. Wiggins   Queen Mary University of London, UK
Sølvi Ystad   CNRS-LMA, France

Additional Reviewers

Samer Abdallah   Queen Mary University of London, UK
Emmanouil Benetos   Queen Mary University of London, UK
Charles Gondre   CNRS-LMA, France
Bas de Haas   Universiteit Utrecht, The Netherlands
Cyril Joder   Technische Universität Munchen, Germany
Sefki Kolozali   Queen Mary University of London, UK
Andrew McPherson   Queen Mary University of London, UK
Martin Morrell   Queen Mary University of London, UK
Katy Noland   BBC, UK
Anaïk Olivero   CNRS-LMA, France
Dan Tidhar   King's College, UK
Xue Wen   Queen Mary University of London, UK
Thomas Wilmering   Queen Mary University of London, UK
Massimiliano Zanoni   Politecnico di Milano, Italy

Table of Contents

III - Computer Models of Music Perception and Cognition

IV - Music Emotion Recognition

V - Music Information Retrieval

VI - Film Soundtrack and Music Recommendation

VII - Computational Musicology and Music Education

VIII - Cross-Disciplinary Perspectives on Expressive Performance Workshop

The Six Emotion-Face Clock as a Tool for Continuously Rating Discrete Emotional Responses to Music

Emery Schubert[1], Sam Ferguson[2], Natasha Farrar[1],
David Taylor[1], and Gary E. McPherson[3]

[1] Empirical Musicology Group, University of New South Wales, Sydney, Australia
E.Schubert@unsw.edu.au,
{natashajfarrar,david.anthony.taylor}@gmail.com
[2] University of Technology, Sydney, Australia
samuel.john.ferguson@gmail.com
[3] Melbourne Conservatorium of Music, University of Melbourne, Melbourne, Australia
g.mcpherson@unimelb.edu.au

Abstract. Recent instruments measuring continuous self-reported emotion responses to music have tended to use dimensional rating scale models of emotion such as valence (happy to sad). However, numerous retrospective studies of emotion in music use checklist style responses, usually in the form of emotion words, (such as happy, angry, sad...) or facial expressions. A response interface based on six simple sketch style emotion faces aligned into a clock-like distribution was developed with the aim of allowing participants to quickly and easily rate emotions in music continuously as the music unfolded. We tested the interface using six extracts of music, one targeting each of the six faces: 'Excited' (at 1 o'clock), 'Happy' (3), 'Calm' (5), 'Sad' (7), 'Scared' (9) and 'Angry' (11). 30 participants rated the emotion expressed by these excerpts on our 'emotion-face-clock'. By demonstrating how continuous category selections (votes) changed over time, we were able to show that (1) more than one emotion-face could be expressed by music at the same time and (2) the emotion face that best portrayed the emotion the music conveyed could change over time, and (3) the change could be attributed to changes in musical structure. Implications for research on orientation time and mixed emotions are discussed.

Keywords: Emotion in music, continuous response, discrete emotions, time-series analysis, film music.

1 Introduction*

Research on continuous ratings of emotion expressed by music (that is, rating the music while it is being heard) has led to improvements in understanding and modeling music's emotional capacity. This research has produced time series models where

---

* This article is a considerably expanded version of a submission titled 'Continuous Response to Music using Discrete Emotion Faces' presented at the *International Symposium on Computer Music and Retrieval (CMMR)* held in London, UK, 19-22 June, 2012.

M. Aramaki et al. (Eds.): CMMR 2012, LNCS 7900, pp. 1–18, 2013.

musical features such as loudness, tempo, pitch profiles and so on are used as input signals which are then mapped onto emotional response data using least squares regression and various other strategies [1-4].

One of the criticisms of self-reported continuous response however, is the rating response format. During their inception in the 1980s and 1990s [5, 6] such measures have mostly consisted of participants rating one dimension of emotion (such as the happiness, or arousal, or the tension, and so on) in the music. This approach could be viewed as so reductive that a meaningful conceptualization of emotion is lost. For example, Russell's [7, 8] work on the structure of emotion demonstrated that a large amount of variance in emotion can be explained by two fairly independent dimensions, frequently labeled valence and arousal. The solution to measuring emotion continuously can therefore be achieved by rating the stimulus twice (that is, in two passes), once along a valence scale (with poles of the scale labeled positive and negative), and once along an arousal scale (with poles labeled active and sleepy) [for another multi-pass approach see 9]. In fact, some researchers have combined these scales at right angles to form an 'emotion space' so as to allow a good compromise between reductive simplicity (the rating scale), and the richness of emotional meaning (applying what were thought to be the two most important dimensions in emotional structure simultaneously and at right angles) [e.g. 10-12].

The two dimensional emotion space has provided an effective approach to help untangle some of the relations between musical features and emotional response, as well as providing a deepening understanding of how emotions ebb and flow during the unfolding of a piece of music. However, the model has been placed under scrutiny on several occasions. The most critical matter that is of concern in the present research is theory and subsequent labeling of the emotion dimensions and ratings. For example, the work of Schimmack [13, 14] has reminded the research community that there are different ways of conceptualizing the key dimensions of emotion, and one dimension may have other dimensions hidden within it. Several researchers have proposed three key dimensions of emotion [15-17]. Also, dimensions used in the 'traditional' two dimensional emotion space may be hiding one or more dimensions. Schimmack demonstrated that the arousal dimension is more aptly a combination of underlying 'energetic arousal' and 'tense arousal'. Consider, for instance, the emotion of 'sadness'. On a single 'activity' rating scale with poles labeled active and sleepy, sadness will most likely occupy low activity (one would not imagine a sad person jumping up and down). However, in a study by Schubert [12] some participants consistently rated the word 'sad' in the high arousal region of the emotion space (all rated sad as being a negative valence word). The work of Schimmack and colleagues suggests that those participants were rating sadness along a 'tense arousal' dimension, because sadness does contain conflicting information about these two kinds of arousal – high tension arousal but low activity arousal.

Some solutions to the limitation of two dimensions are to have more than two passes when performing a continuous response (e.g. valence, tense arousal and activity arousal), or to apply a three dimensional GUI with appropriate hardware (such as a three dimensional mouse). However, in this paper we take the dilemma of dimensions as a point of departure and apply what we believe is the first attempt to use a discrete emotion response interface for continuous self-reported emotion ratings.

Discrete emotions are those that we think of in day-to-day usage of emotions, such as happy, sad, calm, excited and so forth. They can each be mapped onto the emotional dimensions discussed above, but can also be presented as independent, meaningful conceptualizations of emotion [18-22]. An early continuous self-reported rating of emotion in music that demonstrated an awareness of this discrete structure was applied by Namba *et al.* [23], where a computer keyboard was labeled with fifteen different discrete emotions. As the music unfolded, participants pressed the key representing the emotion that the music was judged to be expressing at that time. The study has to our knowledge not been replicated, and we believe it is because the complexity of learning to decode a number of single letters and their intended emotion-word meaning. It seems likely that participants would have to shift focus between decoding the emotion represented on the keyboard, or finding the emotion and then finding its representative letter before pressing. And this needed to be done on the fly, meaning that by the time the response was ready to be made, the emotion in the music may have changed. The amount of training (about 30 minutes reported in the study) needed to overcome this cognitive load can be seen as an inhibiting factor.

Inspired by Namba *et al*'s pioneering work, we wanted to develop a way of measuring emotional response continuously but one which captured the benefits of discrete emotion rating, while applying a simple, intuitive user interface.

2   Using Discrete Facial Expressions as a Response Interface

By applying the work of some of the key research of emotion in music who have used discrete emotion response tools [24-26], and based on our own investigation [27], we devised a system of simple, schematic facial expressions intended to represent a range of emotions that are known to be evoked by music. Furthermore, we wanted to recover the geometry of semantic relations, such that similar emotions were positioned beside one another, whereas distant emotions were physically more distant. This approach was identified in Hevner's [28-31] adjective checklist. Her system consisted of groups of adjectives, arranged in a circle in such a way as to place clusters of words near other clusters of similar meaning. For example, the cluster of words containing 'bright, cheerful, joyous ...' was adjacent to the cluster of words containing 'graceful, humorous, light...', but distant from the cluster containing the words 'dark, depressing, doleful...'. Eventually, the clusters would form a circle, from which it derived its alternative names 'adjective clock' [32] and 'adjective circle' [31]. Modified version of this approach, using a smaller number of words, are still in use [33]. Our approach also used a circular form, but using faces instead of words. The model was similar to that used by Schlosberg [34] and Russell [35], who each placed photographs of graded facial emotional expressions on a two-dimensional space. Consequently, we named the layout an 'emotion-face clock'. Evidence suggests that cross-cultural and even non-literate cultures are adept at speedy interpretation of emotional expressions in faces [36, 37], making faces generalizable and suitable for emotion rating tasks, and therefore more so than words. Further, several emotional expressions are universal [38, 39] making the reliance on a non-verbal, non-language specific format appealing [40-42].

Selection of faces to be used for our response interface were based on the literature of commonly used emotion expressions to describe music [43, 44], the recommendations made on a review of the literature by Schubert and McPherson [45] but also such that the circular arrangement was plausible. Hence, three criteria were used: (1) that a broad range of well understood emotions were selected, (2) that they could be represented by simple comic style face sketches in an equi-distributed circular format in emotion space, and (3) that they were likely to be useful for describing music and musical experiences. To satisfy the first criterion, we used a commonly reported form of six basic emotions, happiness, sadness, anger, fear, surprise, and disgust [46]. To satisfy the second and third criteria, surprise was replaced with excited, disgust was deleted because it is considered a non-musical emotion [47] and calm was added [excited and calm being emotions considered more useful for describing music in those locations of the emotion space—1 o'clock and 5 o'clock respectively—, as according to 48]. Cartoon faces [see 49] were constructed to correspond roughly with the emotions from top moving clockwise (see Fig. 1): Excited (at 1 o'clock), Happy (3), Calm (5), Sad (7), Scared (9) and Angry (11 o'clock), with the bottom of the circle separated by Calm and Sad. The words used to describe the faces are selected for the convenience of the researchers. Although a circle arrangement was used, a small additional gap between the positive emotion faces and the negative emotion faces was imposed, namely an additional spatial gap between angry and excited, and between calm and sad, reflecting the semantic distance between these pairs of emotions (Fig. 1). Russell [35], for example, had these gaps at 12 o'clock and 6 o'clock filled with a surprise and sleepy face respectively. We did not impose our labels of the emotion-face expressions onto the participants. Pilot testing using retrospective ratings of music using the verbal expressions are reported in Schubert *et al.* [27].

3   Aim

The aim of the present research was to develop and test the emotion-face clock as a means of continuously rating the emotion expressed by extracts of music.

4   Method

4.1   Participants

Thirty participants were recruited from a music psychology course that consisted of a range of students including some specializing in music. Self-reported years of music lessons ranged from 0 to 16 years, mean 6.6 years (SD = 5.3 years) with 10 participants reporting no music lessons ('0' years). Ages ranged from 19 to 26 years (mean 21.5 years, SD = 1.7 years). Twenty participants were male.

4.2 Software Realisation

The emotion-face clock interface was prepared, and controlled by MAX/MSP software, with musical extracts selected automatically and at random from a predetermined list of pieces. Mouse movements were converted into one of eight states: Centre, one of the six emotions represented by schematic faces, and 'Elsewhere' (Fig. 1). The eight locations were then stored in a buffer that was synchronized with the music, with a sampling rate of 44.1kHz. Given the redundancy of this sampling rate for emotional responses to music [which are in the order of 1 Hz – see 50], down-sampling to 25Hz was performed prior to analysis. The facial expressions moving around the clock in a clockwise direction were Excited, Happy, Calm, Sad, Scared and Angry, as described above. Note that the verbal labels for the faces are for the convenience of the researcher, and do not have to be the same as those used by participants. The intention of the layout was that the expressions progressed sequentially around the clock such that related emotions were closer together than distant emotions, as described above. However, the quality of our labels were tested against participant data using the explicit labeling of the same stimuli in an earlier study [27].

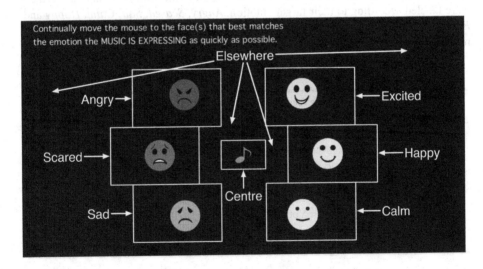

Fig. 1. Structure of six emotion-face-clock graphic user interface. Face colours were based on [27]. Crotchet icon in Centre was green when ready to play, red when excerpt was playing, and grayed out, opaque when the excerpt had completed playing. Text in top two lines provided instructions for the participant. White boxes, arrows and labels were not visible to the participants. These indicate the regions used to determine the eight response categories.

4.3 Procedure

Participants were tested one at a time. The participant sat at the computer display and wore headphones. After introductory tasks and instructions, the emotion-face clock interface was presented, with a green icon (quaver) in the centre (Fig. 1). The participant was instructed to click the green button to commence listening, and to track the emotion that the music was expressing by selecting the facial expression that best matched the response. They were asked to make their selection as quickly as possible. When the participant moved the mouse over one of the faces, the icon of the face was highlighted to provide feedback. The participant was asked to perform several other tasks between continuous the rating tasks. The focus of the present report is on continuous rating over time of emotion that six extracts of music were expressing.

4.4   Stimuli

Because the aim of this study is to examine our new continuous response instrument, we selected six musical excerpts for which we had emotion ratings made using tradition post-performance ratings scales from a previous study [27]. The pieces were taken from Pixar animated movies, based on the principle that the music would be written to stereotypically evoke a range of emotions. The excerpts selected were 11 to 21 seconds long with the intention of primarily depicting each of the emotions of the six faces on the emotion-face clock. In our reference to the stimuli in this report, they were labeled according to their target emotion: *Angry*, *Scared*, *Sad*, *Calm*, *Happy* and *Excited*. More information about the selected excerpts is shown in Table 1. When referring to a musical stimulus the emotion label is capitalized and italicised.

Table 1. Stimuli used in the study

Stimulus code (target emotion)	Film music excerpt	Start time within CD track (MM'SS elapsed)	Duration of excerpt (s)
Angry	Up: 52 Chachki Pickup	00"53	17
Calm	Finding Nemo: Wow	00"22	16
Excited	Toy Story: Infinity and Beyond	00"15	16
Happy	Cars: McQueen and Sally	00"04	16
Sad	Toy Story 3: You Got Lucky	01"00	21
Scared	Cars: McQueen's Lost	00"55	11

5   Results and Discussion

Responses were categorized into one of eight possible responses (one of the six emotions, the Centre region, and any other space on the emotion-face clock labeled 'Elsewhere' – see Fig. 1) based on mouse positions recorded during the response to each piece of music. This process was repeated for each sample (25 per second). Two main analyses were conducted. First, the relationships between the collapsed continuous ratings against rating scale results from a previous study using the same stimuli, and then an analysis of the time series responses for each of the six stimuli.

5.1   Summary Responses

In a previous study, 26 participants provided ratings of each of the six stimuli used in the present study (see [27] for details) along 11 point rating scales from '0 (not at all)' to '10 (a lot)'. The scales were labeled orthographically as Angry, Scared, Sad, Calm, Happy and Excited. No faces were used in the response interface for that study.

The continuous responses from the current study were collapsed so that the number of votes a face received as the piece unfolded was tallied, producing a proportional representation of faces that were selected as indicating the emotion expressed by each face for a particular stimulus. The plots of these results are shown in Fig. 2. Take for example the responses made to the *Angry* excerpt. All participants' first 'votes' were for the 'Centre' category because they had to click the 'play' icon at the Centre region of the emotion-face clock to commence listening. As participants decided which face represented the emotion expressed, they moved the mouse to cover the appropriate face. So, as the piece unfolded, at any given time, some of the 30 participants might have had the cursor on the Angry face, while some on the Scared face, and another who may not yet have decided remains in the Centre or has moved the mouse, but not to a face ('Elsewhere'). With a sampling rate of 25 Hz it was possible to see how these votes changes over time (the focus of the next analysis). At each sample, the votes were tallied into the eight categories. Hence each sample had a total of 30 votes (one per participant). At any sample it was possible to determine whether participants were or were not in agreement about the face that best represented the emotion expressed by the music.

The face by face tallies for each of these samples were accumulated and divided by the total number of samples for the excerpt. This provided a summary measure of the time-series to approximate the typical response profile for the stimulus in question. These profiles are reported in Fig. 2 in the right hand column. Returning to the *Angry* example we see that participants spent most time on the Angry face, followed by Scared and then the Centre. This suggests that the piece selected indeed best expressed anger according to the accumulated summary of the time series. The second highest votes belonging to the Scared face can be interpreted as a 'near miss' because of all the emotions on the clock, the scared face is semantically closest to the Angry face, despite obvious differences (for a discussion, see [27]). In fact, when comparing the accumulated summary with the post-performance rating scale profile (from the earlier study), the time series produces a profile more in line with the proposed target emotion. The post-performance ratings demonstrate that Angry is only the third highest scored scale, after Scared and Excited. The important point, however, is that Scared and Excited are located on either side of the emotion-face clock, making them the most semantically related alternatives to angry of the available faces. For each of the other stimuli, the contour of the profiles for post-performance ratings and accumulated summary of continuous response are identical.

These profile matches are evidence for the validity of the emotion-face clock because they mean that the faces are used to provide a similar meaning to the emotion words used in the post-performance verbal ratings. We can therefore be reasonably confident that at least five of the faces selected can be represented verbally by the five verbal labels we have used (the sixth – Anger, being confused occasionally with Scared, and this 'confusion' may be a consequence of the nature of the emotion expressed by the face, or the music, or both). The similarity of the profile pairs in Fig. 2 is also indicative of the reliability of the emotion-face clock because it more-or-less reproduces the emotion profile of the post-performance ratings.

Two further observations are made about the summary data. Participants spend very little time away from a face or the Centre of the emotion-face clock (the Elsewhere region is selected infrequently for all six excerpts). While there is the obvious explanation that the six faces and the screen Centre occupy the majority of the space on the response interface (see Fig. 1) the infrequent occurrence of the Elsewhere category also may indicate that participants are fairly certain about the emotion that the music is conveying. That is, when an emotion face is selected by a participant, they are likely to believe that face to be the best selection, even if it is in disagreement with the majority of votes, or with the *a priori* proposed target emotion. If this were not the case, we might expect participants to hover in 'no man's land' of the emotion-face clock—Elsewhere and Centre. The apparent 'confidence' may also be a consequence of the instruction to select a face as quickly as possible, suggesting that accuracy of face selection is not important enough to justify vacillation (a point to which we shall return).

The 'no man's land' response may be reflected by the accumulated time spent in the Centre region. As mentioned, time spent in the Centre region is biased because participants always commence their responses from that region (in order to click the play button). The Centre region votes can therefore be viewed as indicating two kinds of systematic responses: (1) initial response time and (2) response uncertainty. Initial response time is the time required for a participant to orient to the required task just as the temporally unfolding stimulus commences. The orienting process generally takes several seconds to complete, prior to ratings becoming more 'reliable' [51-53]. So stimuli in Fig. 2 with large bars for 'Centre' may require more time before an unambiguous response is made.

The *Scared* stimulus has the largest number of votes for the Centre location (on average, at any single sample, eight out of thirty participants were in the Centre region of the emotion-face clock). Without looking at the time series data (see next subsection), we may conclude that the *Scared* excerpt produced the least 'confident' rating, or that the faces provided were unable to produce satisfactory alternatives for the participants.

Using this logic (long time spent in the Centre and Elsewhere), we can conclude that the most confident responses were for those pieces where accumulated time spent in the Centre and Elsewhere were the lowest. The *Calm* stimulus had the highest 'confidence' rating (an average of about 4 participants at the Centre or Elsewhere combined). Interestingly, the *Calm* example also had the highest number of accumulated votes for any single category (the target, Calm emotion) — which was selected on average by 18 participants at any given time.

The analysis of summary data provides a useful, simple interpretation of the continuous responses. However, to appreciate the richness of the time course responses, we now examine the time-series data for each stimulus.

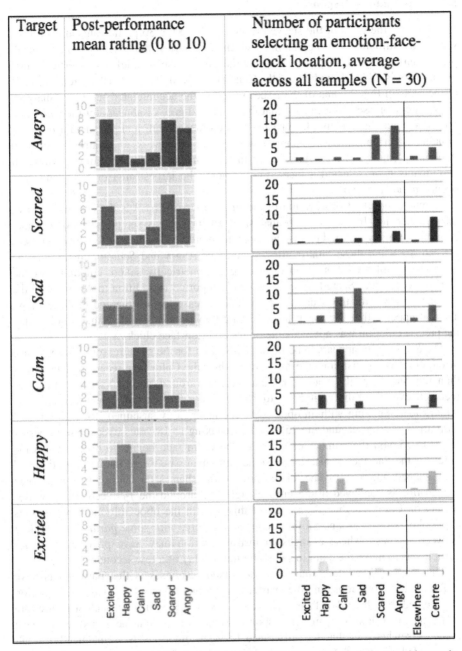

Fig. 2. Comparison of post performance ratings [from 27] (left column of charts) with sample averaged continuous response face counts for thirty participants (right column of charts) for the six stimuli, each with a target emotion shown in the leftmost column

5.2   Continuous Responses

Fig. 3 shows the plots of the stacked responses from the 30 participants at each time sample by stimulus. The beginning of each time series, thus, demonstrates that all participants commenced their response at the Centre (the first, left-most vertical 'line' of each plot is all black, indicating the Centre). By scanning for black regions for each of the plots in Fig. 3 some of the issues raised in the accumulated summary analysis, above, are addressed. We can see that the black and grey disappears for the *Calm* plot after 6 seconds have elapsed. For each of the other stimuli a small amount of doubt remains at certain times – in some cases a small amount of uncertainty is reported throughout (there are no time samples in the *Scared* and *Excited* stimuli where all participants have selected a face). Furthermore, the largest area of black and grey occurs in the *Scared* plot.

Another important observation of the time-series of Fig. 3 is the ebb and flow of face frequencies. In the summary analysis it was possible to see the selection of more than one emotion face indicating the emotion expressed by the music. However, here we can see *when* these 'ambiguities' occur. The *Angry* and *Sad* stimuli provide the clearest examples of more than one non-chronometrically salient emotion. For the *Angry* excerpt, the 'Scared' face is frequently reported in addition to Angry. And the number of votes for the Scared face slightly increase toward the end of the excerpt. Thus, it appears that the music is expressing two emotions at the same time, or that the precise emotion was not available on the emotion-face clock.

The *Sad* excerpt appears to be mixed with Calm for the same reasons (co-existence of emotions or precision of the measure). While the Calm face received fewer votes than the Sad face, the votes for Calm peak at around the 10th second (15 votes received over the time period 9.6 to 10.8s) of the *Sad* except. The excerpt is in a minor mode, opening with an oboe solo accompanied by sustained string chords and harp arpeggios. At around the 15th second (peaking at 18 votes over the time period 15.00 to 15.64s) the number of votes for the Calm face begins to decrease and the votes for the Sad face peak. Hence, some participants may find the orchestration and arch shaped melody in the oboe more calm than sad. Until some additional information is conveyed in the musical signal (at around the 14th second), responses remain on Calm. At the 10th second of this excerpt the oboe solo ends, and strings alone play, with cello and violin coming to the fore, with some *portamento* (sliding between pitches). These changes in instrumentation may have provided cues for participants to make the calm to sad shift after a delay of a few seconds [50].

Thus a plausible interpretation of the mixed responses is that participants have different interpretations of the various emotions expressed, *and* the emotion represented by the GUI faces. However, the changes in musical structure are sufficient to explain a change in response. What is important here, and as we have argued elsewhere, is that the difference between emotions is (semantically) small [27], and that musical features could be modeled to predict the overall shift away from calmness and further toward sadness in this example. The different choice of faces could be explained by the semantic similarity of the region that the two faces encompass in dimensional emotion-space.

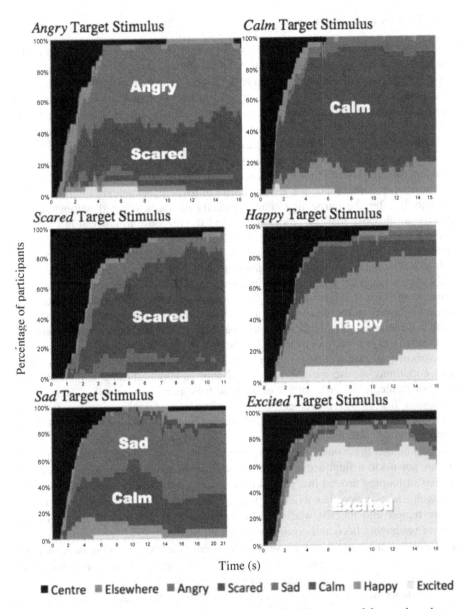

Fig. 3. Time series plots for each stimulus showing stacked frequency of faces selected over time (see Table 1 for duration on x-axis) for the 30 participants (y-axis), with face selected represented by the colour code shown. Black and grey representing Centre of emotion-face clock (where all participants commence continuous rating task) and anywhere else respectively. Note that the most dominant colour (the most frequently selected face across participants and time) match with the target emotion of the stimulus. X-axis denotes time in seconds. Y-axis denotes proportion of participants selecting a region of the emotion-face clock, expressed as a percentage of total participants.

5.3   Response Latency Issues

The time taken for 'most' participants to make a decision about the selection of a first face appears to have an identifiable range across stimuli. Inspection of Fig. 3 reveals that in the range of 0.5 seconds through to 5 seconds most participants have selected a face. This provides a rough estimate of the initial orientation time for emotional response using categorical data (for more information, see [51]). The generally shortened initial orientation time estimates (up to around 5 seconds) compared to those in previously published results (around 8 seconds) may simply be due to the task, because participants were asked to respond as quickly as possible [no instruction regarding required speed of response was cited in the studies of 51, 52].

Nevertheless, since we do not get a majority of participants quickly finding the first face shortly after the music first sounds (usually no faces selected within the first second), we propose that the processing of and the response to musical information may be taking place via three related cognitive pathways. One path begins by interpreting the audio input and making an emotion judgment [e.g. 54] which then leads to the mouse movement motor *planning*. This path continues with the execution of the actual technical portion of the required task, which is *the act of moving* the mouse to the face that best describes the emotion portrayed by the music. Once the mouse is moved to the desired position, some more processing needs to occur to check that the position is the desired emotion face. This is the ideal response path we were seeking in our study so as to satisfy the task to respond 'as quickly as possible', and is shown as Path 1 in Fig. 4. Our current, ongoing analysis suggests that under these conditions mouse movement takes a short amount of time with respect to processing time, in the order of 5% of the time from hearing to selection. Hence, Fig. 4 displays the mouse movement box as being considerably narrower than the processing box (box width representing approximate, proportional time spent on processing and mouse movement).

It may be that the mouse is moved repeatedly while the listener continues to listen but has not made a final decision. This is still represented in Fig. 4 as Path 1, but consists of looping around that path, with (usually small) mouse perturbations while processing takes place. For example, the listener may move the mouse out of the Centre region into the Elsewhere region in preparation for a quick response, but without yet having been able to decide on which face to select. This combination of indecision and mouse movements we refer to as prevarication, and continues until the listener ceases looping around Path 1 (for example, having made a decision about which face to select), or takes some other processing path.

The listener may also be undecided about which emotion face to select, but not move the mouse (leave it in the Centre region)—Path 2. This path may loop until the listener has made a decision, or commences prevaricating (Path 1).

In a study by Lucas et al [55] apparently meaningless or aimless (off-task) mouse movement were referred to as 'skywriting' — though their task required continuous response to *dimensional* emotion rating scales (specifically, valence and arousal), rather than discrete emotion faces [See also 56]. We think the differences between skywriting and prevarication may be subtly and importantly different—that the former does not employ on-task processing, but the effect is the same – systematic selection of an emotion face, is not made. Finally, although the paths shown in Fig. 4 suggest sequenced processing, the effect can be parallel – where the mouse may be in 'no man's land' while processing (and decision making) continues.

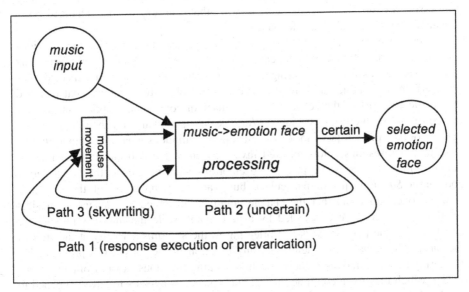

Fig. 4. Proposed cognitive processing paths as listener makes decisions about which face best matches the emotion portrayed by the incoming music as quickly as possible. Under ideal conditions, fastest response is achieved via Path 1 in a single cycle, with *processing* required to make a decision and check that the action of moving the mouse (small box of left) was accurate, However, when the decision is more complex (e.g. ambiguous musical features, insufficient data, emotion face expressions inadequate, and changing conditions of *music input*), one of two (non exclusive) possibilities may occur: The participant may take Path 2, repeatedly assessing (processing) while music input continues, but without mouse movements, or Path 1, where the mouse is moved while continuing to process the music—that is, response is uncertain, but mouse is moved in a hesitant, prevaricating way. This prevarication during processing continues while a decision is not made (looping around Path 1 continues) or switching to another path (or making a final mouse movement then exiting the loop via the 'certain' path). Finally, mouse movements might be made aimlessly without attention to the music and without task related processing. This is shown as Path 3, and is referred to as skywriting, which continues until the participant returned to more focused, task related processing. Width of boxes signifies rough proportion of response time contribution: mouse movements take a short time relative to task processing time.

6   Conclusions

In this paper we reported the development and testing of a categorical response interface consisting of a small number of salient emotional expressions upon which participants can rate emotions as a piece of music or other stimulus unfolds. We developed a small set of key emotional expression faces found in basic emotion and music research, and arranged them into a circle such that they were meaningfully positioned in space, and such that they resembled traditional valence-arousal rating scale interfaces (positive emotions toward the right, high arousal emotions toward the top). We called the response space an emotion-face clock because the faces progressed around a clock in such a way that the expressions changed in a semantically related and plausible manner.

The interface was then tested using particular pieces that expressed the emotions intended to represent the emotional expression portrayed by each of the six faces. The system was successful in measuring emotional ratings in the manner expected. The post-performance ratings used in an earlier study had profile contours that matched the profile contours of the accumulated summary of continuous response in the new device for all but the *Angry* stimulus. We took this as evidence for the reliability and validity of the emotion-face clock as a self-report continuous measure of emotion.

Continuous response plots allowed investigation of the ebb and flow of ratings, demonstrating that for some pieces two emotions were dominant (the target *Angry* and target *Sad* excerpts in particular), but that the composition of the emotions changed over time, and that the change could be attributed to changes in musical features. When no face is selected by a participant while the music is playing we conclude that the participant is (A) orienting to the stimulus—usually at the start of the piece, (B) actually not identifying any emotion in the music, (C) prevaricating (dithering between making a decision while keeping the mouse away from any of the faces), which may even continue throughout a piece, as appears to have happened to at least one participant for the *Scared* and *Excited* stimuli. Hence, the continuous, online task is complicated by the constant stream of new musical information that may be supporting or contradicting the decision that the listener is trying to make in real time.

When there were different faces selected across participants at a given moment in time (more than one emotion face receiving votes), we conclude that (1) More than one emotion is identified simultaneously, and as a one-face-at-a-time interface, different emotion selection is distributed statistically, (2) An approximate response is given because the resolution of the instrument is not sufficient, meaning, as with conclusion 1, that different faces are selected by chance, (3) The two (or more) faces selected cover a semantically similar region of emotion space that is indicative of the emotion expressed by the music, (4) Participants are responding in a staggered (lagged) manner, with some reacting quickly to the most recent part of the music, possibly even anticipating, others still responding to musical material of the recent past, and so forth [4, 53, 57]. Conclusion (3) is related to (2), except that it highlights the success of the emotion-face clock being superimposed intuitively on a two-dimensional emotion space, because the selection of adjacent faces need not be seen as errors or confusions, but as occupying a shared region that best describes the emotion being portrayed (as do the emotions represented by adjacent faces of Angry and Scared, and the adjacent faces represented by Sad and Calm).

We do not deny the possibility that listeners could hear 'conflicting' emotions simultaneously. Indeed, recent research has demonstrated how musical features can be manipulated to induce a perception of mixed, distant emotions such as sadness and happiness [58, 59]. Research will be required to see how the present instrument might explain such conflicting emotions portrayed by music (see Conclusion 1, above, for example), and may even help to resolve whether multiple emotion votes at the same point in the music are due to the poor resolution of the instrument, or because statistically some listeners select one of the two possible emotion faces, while others select the other at the same point in time.

Further analysis will reveal whether musical features can be used to predict categorical emotions in the same way that valence/arousal models do (for a review, see [4]), or whether six emotion faces is optimal. Given the widespread use of categorical emotions in music metadata [60, 61], the categorical, discrete approach to measuring continuous emotional response is bound to be a fruitful tool for researchers interested in automating emotion in music directly into categorical representations.

Acknowledgments. This research was funded by the Australian Research Council (DP1094998) held by authors ES and GEM.

References

1. Yang, Y.H., Lin, Y.C., Su, Y.F., Chen, H.H.: A regression approach to music emotion recognition. IEEE Transactions on Audio, Speech, and Language Processing 16(2), 448–457 (2008)
2. Schmidt, E.M., Turnbull, D., Kim, Y.E.: Feature selection for content-based, time-varying musical emotion regression. In: MIR 2010 Proceedings of the International Conference on Multimedia Information Retrieval. ACM, New York (2010)
3. Korhonen, M.D., Clausi, D.A., Jernigan, M.E.: Modeling emotional content of music using system identification. IEEE Transactions on Systems Man and Cybernetics Part B-Cybernetics 36(3), 588–599 (2006)
4. Schubert, E.: Continuous self-report methods. In: Juslin, P.N., Sloboda, J.A. (eds.) Handbook of Music and Emotion: Theory, Research, Applications, pp. 223–253. OUP, Oxford (2010)
5. Madsen, C.K., Frederickson, W.E.: The experience of musical tension: A replication of Nielsen's research using the continuous response digital interface. Journal of Music Therapy 30(1), 46–63 (1993)
6. Nielsen, F.V.: Musical tension and related concepts. In: Sebeok, T.A., Umiker-Sebeok, J. (eds.) The Semiotic Web 1986. An International Year-Book. Mouton de Gruyter, Berlin (1987)
7. Russell, J.A.: Affective space is bipolar. Journal of Personality and Social Psychology 37(3), 345–356 (1979)
8. Russell, J.A.: A circumplex model of affect. Journal of Social Psychology 39, 1161–1178 (1980)
9. Krumhansl, C.L.: An exploratory study of musical emotions and psychophysiology. Canadian Journal of Experimental Psychology 51(4), 336–352 (1997)
10. Cowie, R., Douglas-Cowie, E., Savvidou, S., McMahon, E., Sawey, M., Schröder, M.: FEELTRACE: An instrument for recording perceived emotion in real time. In: Cowie, R., Douglas-Cowie, E., Schroede, M. (eds.) Speech and Emotion: Proceedings of the ISCA workshop, pp. 19–24. Newcastle, Co. Down (2000)

11. Nagel, F., Kopiez, R., Grewe, O., Altenmüller, E.: EMuJoy: Software for continuous measurement of perceived emotions in music. Behavior Research Methods 39(2), 283–290 (2007)
12. Schubert, E.: Measuring emotion continuously: Validity and reliability of the two-dimensional emotion-space. Australian Journal of Psychology 51(3), 154–165 (1999)
13. Schimmack, U., Rainer, R.: Experiencing activation: Energetic arousal and tense arousal are not mixtures of valence and activation. Emotion 2(4), 412–417 (2002)
14. Schimmack, U., Grob, A.: Dimensional models of core affect: A quantitative comparison by means of structural equation modeling. European Journal of Personality 14(4), 325–345 (2000)
15. Wundt, W.: Grundzüge der physiologischen Psychologie. Engelmann, Leipzig (1905)
16. Plutchik, R.: The emotions: Facts, theories and a new model. Random House, New York (1962)
17. Russell, J.A., Mehrabian, A.: Evidence for a 3-factor theory of emotions. Journal of Research in Personality 11(3), 273–294 (1977)
18. Barrett, L.F., Wager, T.D.: The Structure of Emotion: Evidence From Neuroimaging Studies. Current Directions in Psychological Science 15(2), 79–83 (2006)
19. Barrett, L.F.: Discrete emotions or dimensions? The role of valence focus and arousal focus. Cognition & Emotion 12(4), 579–599 (1998)
20. Lewis, M., Haviland, J.M. (eds.): Handbook of emotions (1993)
21. Izard, C.E.: The psychology of emotions. Plenum Press, New York (1991)
22. Izard, C.E.: Organizational and motivational functions of discrete emotions. In: Lewis, M., Haviland, J.M. (eds.) Handbook of Emotions, pp. 631–641. The Guilford Press, New York (1993)
23. Namba, S., Kuwano, S., Hatoh, T., Kato, M.: Assessment of musical performance by using the method of continuous judgment by selected description. Music Perception 8(3), 251–275 (1991)
24. Juslin, P.N., Laukka, P.: Communication of emotions in vocal expression and music performance: Different channels, same code? Psychological Bulletin 129(5), 770–814 (2003)
25. Laukka, P., Gabrielsson, A., Juslin, P.N.: Impact of intended emotion intensity on cue utilization and decoding accuracy in vocal expression of emotion. International Journal of Psychology 35(3-4), 288 (2000)
26. Juslin, P.N.: Communicating emotion in music performance: A review and a theoretical framework. In: Juslin, P.N., Sloboda, J.A. (eds.) Music and Emotion: Theory and Research, pp. 309–337. Editors. Oxford University Press, London (2001)
27. Schubert, E., Ferguson, S., Farrar, N., McPherson, G.E.: Sonification of Emotion I: Film Music. In: The 17th International Conference on Auditory Display (ICAD-2011), International Community for Auditory Display (ICAD), Budapest (2011)
28. Hevner, K.: Expression in music: a discussion of experimental studies and theories. Psychological Review 42, 187–204 (1935)
29. Hevner, K.: The affective character of the major and minor modes in music. American Journal of Psychology 47, 103–118 (1935)
30. Hevner, K.: Experimental studies of the elements of expression in music. American Journal of Psychology 48, 246–268 (1936)
31. Hevner, K.: The affective value of pitch and tempo in music. American Journal of Psychology 49, 621–630 (1937)
32. Rigg, M.G.: The mood effects of music: A comparison of data from four investigators. The Journal of Psychology 58(2), 427–438 (1964)

33. Han, B., Rho, S., Dannenberg, R.B., Hwang, E.: SMERS: Music emotion recognition using support vector regression. In: Proceedings of the 10th International Society for Music Information Retrieval Conference (ISMIR 2009), Kobe International Conference Center, Kobe, Japan, October 26-30 (2009)

34. Schlosberg, H.: The description of facial expressions in terms of two dimensions. Journal of Experimental Psychology 44, 229–237 (1952)

35. Russell, J.A.: Reading emotion from and into faces: Resurrecting a dimensional-contextual perspective. In: Russell, J.A., Fernández-Dols, J.M. (eds.) The Psychology of Facial Expression, pp. 295–320. Cambridge University Press, Cambridge (1997)

36. Dimberg, U., Thunberg, M.: Rapid facial reactions to emotional facial expressions. Scandinavian Journal of Psychology 39(1), 39–45 (1998)

37. Britton, J.C., Taylor, S.F., Sudheimer, K.D., Liberzon, I.: Facial expressions and complex IAPS pictures: common and differential networks. Neuroimage 31(2), 906–919 (2006)

38. Waller, B.M., Cray Jr, J.J., Burrows, A.M.: Selection for universal facial emotion. Emotion 8(3), 435–439 (2008)

39. Ekman, P.: Facial expression and emotion. American Psychologist 48(4), 384–392 (1993)

40. Lang, P.J.: Behavioral treatment and bio-behavioral assessment: Computer applications. In: Sidowski, J.B., Johnson, J.H., Williams, T.A. (eds.) Technology in Mental Health Care Delivery Systems, pp. 119–137. Ablex, Norwood (1980)

41. Bradley, M.M., Lang, P.J.: Measuring emotion - the self-assessment mannequin and the semantic differential. Journal of Behavior Therapy and Experimental Psychiatry 25(1), 49–59 (1994)

42. Ekman, P., Rosenberg, E.L. (eds.): What the face reveals: Basic and applied studies of spontaneous expression using the Facial Action Coding System (FACS). Series in affective science. Oxford University Press, London (1997)

43. Eerola, T., Vuoskoski, J.K.: A comparison of the discrete and dimensional models of emotion in music. Psychology of Music 39(1), 18–49 (2011)

44. Kratus, J.: A developmental study of children's interpretation of emotion in music. Psychology of Music 21, 3–19 (1993)

45. Schubert, E., McPherson, G.E.: The perception of emotion in music. In: McPherson, G.E. (ed.) The Child as Musician: A Handbook of Musical Development, pp. 193–212. Oxford University Press, Oxford (2006)

46. Ekman, R., Friesen, W.V., Ellsworth, R.: Emotion in the human face: Guidelines jbr research and an integration of findings. Pergamon Press, New York (1972)

47. Zentner, M., Grandjean, D., Scherer, K.R.: Emotions evoked by the sound of music: characterization, classification, and measurement. Emotion 8(4), 494–521 (2008)

48. Schubert, E.: Update of the Hevner adjective checklist. Perceptual and Motor Skills 96(3), 1117–1122 (2003)

49. Kostov, V., Yanagisawa, H., Johansson, M., Fukuda, S.: Method for Face-Emotion Retrieval Using A Cartoon Emotional Expression Approach. JSME International Journal Series C 44(2), 515–526 (2001)

50. Schubert, E.: Continuous measurement of self-report emotional response to music. In: Juslin, P.N., Sloboda, J.A. (eds.) Music and Emotion: Theory and Research, pp. 393–414. Oxford University Press, Oxford (2001)

51. Schubert, E.: Reliability issues regarding the beginning, middle and end of continuous emotion ratings to music. Psychology of Music 41(3), 350–371 (2013)

52. Bachorik, J.P., Bangert, M., Loui, P., Larke, K., Berger, J., Rowe, R., Schlaug, G.: Emotion in motion: Investigating the time-course of emotional judgments of musical stimuli. Music Perception 26(4), 355–364 (2009)

53. Schubert, E., Dunsmuir, W.: Regression modelling continuous data in music psychology. In: Yi, S.W. (ed.) Music, Mind, and Science, pp. 298–352. Seoul National University, Seoul (1999)

54. Juslin, P.N., Friberg, A., Bresin, R.: Toward a computational model of expression in music performance: The GERM model. Musicae Scientiae. Special Issue: pp. 63-122 (2001)

55. Lucas, B.J., Schubert, E., Halpern, A.R.: Perception of emotion in sounded and imagined music. Music Perception 27(5), 399–412 (2010)

56. Upham, F.: Quantifying the temporal dynamics of music listening: A critical investigation of analysis techniques for collections of continuous responses to music. McGill University (2011)

57. Schubert, E., Vincs, K., Stevens, C.J.: Identifying regions of good agreement among responders in engagement with a piece of live dance. Empirical Studies of the Arts 13(1), 1–20 (2013)

58. Hunter, P.G., Schellenberg, E.G., Schimmack, U.: Mixed affective responses to music with conflicting cues. Cognition & Emotion 22(2), 327–352 (2008)

59. Hunter, P.G., Schellenberg, E.G., Schimmack, U.: Feelings and perceptions of happiness and sadness induced by music: Similarities, differences, and mixed emotions. Psychology of Aesthetics, Creativity, and the Arts 4(1), 47–56 (2010)

60. Trohidis, K., Tsoumakas, G., Kalliris, G., Vlahavas, I.: Multilabel classification of music into emotions. In: Proceedings of the 9th International Conference on Music Information Retrieval (ISMIR 2008), Philadelphia, PA (2008)

61. Levy, M., Sandler, M.: A semantic space for music derived from social tags. In: Proceedings of the 8th International Conference on Music Information Retrieval (ISMIR 2007), Vienna, Austria (2007)

Emotion in Motion:
A Study of Music and Affective Response

Javier Jaimovich[1], Niall Coghlan[1], and R. Benjamin Knapp[2]

[1] Sonic Arts Research Centre, Queen's University Belfast, UK
[2] Institute for Creativity, Arts, and Technology, Virginia Tech, USA
{javier,niall,ben}@musicsensorsemotion.com

Abstract. 'Emotion in Motion' is an experiment designed to understand the emotional responses of people to a variety of musical excerpts, via self-report questionnaires and the recording of electrodermal activity (EDA) and heart rate (HR) signals. The experiment ran for 3 months as part of a public exhibition in Dublin, having nearly 4000 participants and over 12000 listening samples. This paper presents the methodology used by the authors to approach this research, as well as preliminary results derived from the self-report data and the physiology.

Keywords: Emotion, Music, Autonomic Nervous System, ANS, Physiological Database, Electrodermal Activity, EDR, EDA, POX, Heart Rate, HR, Self-Report Questionnaire.

1 Introduction

'Emotion in Motion' is an experiment designed to understand the emotional responses of people during music listening, through self-report questionnaires and the recording of physiological data using on-body sensors. Visitors to the Science Gallery, Dublin, Ireland were asked to listen to different song excerpts while their heart rate (HR) and Electrodermal Activity (EDA) were recorded along with their responses to questions about the affective impact of the music. The songs were chosen randomly from a pool of 53 songs, which were selected to elicit positive emotions (high valence), negative emotions (low valence), high arousal and low arousal. In addition to this, special effort was made in order to include songs from different genres, styles and eras. At the end of each excerpt, subjects were asked to respond to a simple questionnaire regarding their assessment of the song, as well as how it made them feel.

Initial analysis of the dataset has focused on validation of the different measurements, as well as exploring relationships between the physiology and the self-report data, which is presented in this paper.

Following on from this initial work we intend to look for correlations between variables and sonic characteristics of the musical excerpts as well as factors such as the effect of song order on participant responses and the usefulness of the Geneva Emotional Music Scale [1] in assessing emotional responses to music listening.

M. Aramaki et al. (Eds.): CMMR 2012, LNCS 7900, pp. 19–43, 2013.
© Springer-Verlag Berlin Heidelberg 2013

1.1   Music and Emotion

Specificity of musical emotions versus 'basic' emotions. While the field of emotion research is far from new, from Tomkins theory of 'discrete' emotions [2] or Ekman's [3] studies on the 'universality' of human emotions to the fMRI enabled neuroimaging studies of today [4], there is still debate about the appropriateness of the existing 'standard' emotion models to adequately describe emotions evoked through musical or performance related experiences. It has been argued that many of the 'basic' emotions introduced by Ekman, such as anger or disgust, are rarely (if ever) evoked by music and that terms more evocative of the subtle and complex emotions engendered by music listening may be more appropriate [5]. It is also argued that the triggering of music-related emotions may be a result of complex interactions between music, cognition, semantics, memory and physiology as opposed to a direct result of audio stimulation [6, 7]. For instance a given piece of music may have a particular significance for a given listener e.g. it was their 'wedding song' or is otherwise associated with an emotionally charged memory.

While there is still widespread disagreement and confusion about the nature and causes of musically evoked emotions, recent studies involving real-time observation of brain activity seem to show that areas of the brain linked with emotion (as well as pleasure and reward) are activated by music listening [8]. Studies such as these would seem to indicate that there are undoubtedly changes in physiological state induced by music listening, with many of these correlated to changes in emotional state.

It is also important to differentiate between personal reflection of what emotions are expressed in the music, and those emotions actually felt by the listener [9]. In the study presented on this paper we specifically asked participants how the music made them feel as opposed to any cognitive judgments about the music.

During the last few decades of emotion research, several models attempting to explain the structure and causes of human emotion have been proposed. The 'discrete' model is founded on Ekman's research into 'basic' emotions, a set of discrete emotional states that he proposes are common to all humans; anger, fear, enjoyment, disgust, happiness, sadness, relief, etc. [10].

Russell developed this idea with his proposal of an emotional 'circumplex', a two or three axis space (valence, arousal and, optionally, power), into which emotional states may be placed depending on the relative strengths of each of the dimensions, i.e. states of positive valence and high arousal would lead to a categorization of 'joy'. This model allows for more subtle categorization of emotional states such as 'relaxation' [11].

The Geneva Emotional Music Scales (GEMS) [1] have been developed by Marcel Zentner's team at the University of Zurich to address the perceived issue of emotions specifically invoked by music, as opposed to the basic emotion categories found in the majority of other emotion research. He argues that musical emotions are usually a combination of complex emotions rather than easily characterised basic emotions such as happiness or sadness. The full GEMS scale consists of 45 terms chosen for their consistency in describing emotional states evoked by music, with shorter 25 point and 9 point versions of the scale. These emotional states can be condensed into

9 categories which in turn group into 3 superfactors: vitality, sublimity and unease. Zentner also argues that musically evoked emotions are rare compared to basic/day-to-day emotions and that a random selection of musical excerpts is unlikely to trigger many experiences of strong musically evoked emotions. He believes that musical emotions are evoked through a combination of factors which may include the state of the listener, the performance of the music, structures within the music, and the listening experience [5].

Lab versus Real World. Many previous studies into musically evoked emotions have noted the difficulty in inducing emotions in a lab-type setting [12, 13], far removed from any normal music listening environment. This can pose particular problems in studies including measurements of physiology as the lab environment itself may skew physiological readings [14]. While the public experiment/installation format of our experiment may also not be a 'typical' listening environment, we believe that it is informal, open and of a non-mediated nature, which at the very least provides an interesting counterpoint to lab-based studies, and potentially a more natural set of responses to the stimuli.

1.2   Physiology of Emotion

According to Bradley and Lang, emotion has "almost as many definitions as there are investigators", yet "an aspect of emotion upon which most agree, however, is that in emotional situations, the body acts. The heart pounds, flutters stops and drops; palms sweat; muscles tense and relax; blood foils; faces blush, flush, frown, and smile" [15, pp. 581]. A plausible explanation for this lack of agreement among researchers is suggested by Cacioppo et al. in [16, pp. 174]. They claim that "...language sometimes fails to capture affective experiences - so metaphors become more likely vehicles for rendering these conscious states of mind", which is coherent with the etymological meaning of the word emotion; it comes from the Latin *movere*, which means to move, as by an external force.

For more than a century, scientists have been studying the relationship between emotion and its physiological manifestation. Analysis and experimentation has given birth to systems like the polygraph, yet it has not been until the past two decades, and partly due to improvements and reduced costs in physiological sensors, that we have seen an increase in emotion recognition research in scientific publications [17]. An important factor in this growth has been responsibility of the Affective Computing field [18], interested in introducing an emotion channel of communication to human computer interaction.

One of the main problems of emotion recognition experiments using physiology is the amount of influencing factors that act on the Autonomic Nervous System (ANS) [19]. Physical activity, attention and social interaction are some of the external factors that may influence physiological measures. This has led to a multi-modal theory for physiological differentiation of emotions, where the detection of an emotional state will not depend on a single variable change, but in recognizing patterns among several signals. Another issue is the high degree of variation between subjects and low repeatability rates, which means that the same stimulus will create different reactions in different people, and furthermore, this physiological response will change over time. This suggests that any patterns among these signals will only become noticeable when dealing with large sample sizes.

2   Methodology

2.1   Experimental Design

The aim of this study is to determine what (if any) are the relationships between the properties of an excerpt of music (dynamics, rhythm, emotional intent, etc.), the self-reported emotional response, and the ANS response, as measured through features extracted from EDA and HR. In order to build a large database of physiological and self-report data, an experiment was designed and implemented as a computer work-station installation to be presented in public venues. The experiment at the Science Gallery – Dublin[1] lasted for three months (June-August 2010), having nearly 4000 participants and over 12000 listening samples. The music selection included in its 53 excerpts contains a wide variety of genres, styles and structures, which, as previously mentioned, were selected to have a balanced emotional intent between high and low valence and arousal.

To be part of the experiment, a visitor to the Science Gallery was guided by a mediator to one of the four computer workstations, and then the individual followed the on-screen instructions to progress through the experiment sections (see Fig. 1 (b)). These would first give an introduction to the experiment and explain how to wear the EDA and HR sensors. Then, the participant would be asked demographic and background questions (e.g. age, gender, musical expertise, music preferences, etc.). After completing this section, the visitor would be presented with the first song excerpt, which was followed by a brief self-report questionnaire. The audio file is selected randomly from a pool of songs divided in the four affective categories. This was repeated two more times, taking each music piece from a different affective category, so each participant had a balanced selection of music. The visitor was then asked to choose the most engaging and the most liked song from the excerpts heard. Finally, the software presented the participant plots of his or her physiological signals against the audio waveform of the selected song excerpts. This was accompanied with a brief explanation of what these signals represent.

Software. A custom Max/MSP[2] patch was developed which stepped through the different stages of the experiment (e.g. instructions, questionnaires, song selection, etc.) without the need of supervision, although a mediator from the gallery was available in case participants had any questions or problems. The software recorded the participants' questions and physiological data into files on the computer, as well as some extra information about the session (e.g. date and time, selected songs, state of

---

[1] http://www.sciencegallery.com/
[2] http://cycling74.com/products/max/

sensors, etc.). All these files were linked with a unique session ID number which was later used to build the database.

Sensors and Data Capture. Mediaid POX-OEM M15HP[3] was used to measure HR using infra-red reflectometry, which detects heart pulse and blood oxygenation. The sensor was fitted by clipping on to the participant's fingertip as shown in Fig. 1 (a).

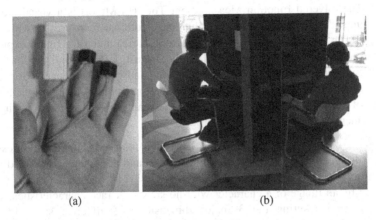

(a)   (b)

Fig. 1. (a) EDA and HR Sensors. (b) Participants during 'Emotion in Motion' experiment. To record EDA, a sensor developed by BioControl Systems was utilised.[4] This provided a continuous measurement of changes in skin conductivity. Due to the large number of participants, we had to develop a 'modular' electrode system that allowed for easy replacement of failed electrodes.

In order to acquire the data from the sensors, an Arduino[5] microcontroller was used to sample the analogue data at 250 Hz and to send via serial over USB communication to the Max/MSP patch. The code from SARCduino[6] was used for this purpose. For safety purposes the entire system was powered via an isolation transformer to eliminate any direct connection to ground. Full frequency response closed-cup headphones with a high degree of acoustic isolation were used at each terminal, with the volume set at a fixed level.

Experiment Versions. During the data collection period, variations were made to the experiment in order to correct some technical problems, add or change the songs in the pool, and test different hypothesis. All of this is annotated in the database. For example, at the beginning participants were asked to listen to four songs in each session, later this was reduced to three in order to shorten the duration of the experiment. The questionnaire varied in order to test and collect data for different questions sets (detailed below), which were selected to compare this study to other experiments in the literature (e.g. the GEMS scales), analyse the effect of the questions in the

---

[3] http://www.mediaidinc.com/Products/M15HP_Engl.htm

[4] http://infusionsystems.com/catalog/product_info.php/products_id/203

[5] http://www.arduino.cc

[6] http://www.musicsensorsemotion.com/2010/03/08/sarcduino/

physiology by running some cases without any questions, and also collect data for our own set of questions. The results presented in this paper are derived from a portion of the complete database with consistent experimental design.

Scales and Measures

LEMtool. The Layered Emotion Measurement Tool (LEMtool) is a visual measurement instrument designed for use in evaluating emotional responses to/with digital media [20]. The full set consists of eight cartoon caricatures of a figure expressing different emotional states (Joy/Sadness, Desire/Disgust, Fascination/Boredom, Satisfaction/Dissatisfaction) through facial expressions and body language. For the purposes of our experiment we used only the Fascination/Boredom images positioned at either end of a 5 point Likert item in which participants were asked to rate their levels of 'Engagement' with each musical excerpt.

SAM – Self Assessment Mannekin. The SAM is a non-verbal pictorial assessment technique, designed to measure the pleasure, arousal and dominance associated with a person's affective response to a wide range of stimuli [21]. Each point on the scale is represented by an image of a character with no gender or race characteristics, with 3 separate scales measuring the 3 major dimensions of affective state; Pleasure, Arousal, and Dominance. On the Pleasure scale the character ranges from smiling to frowning, on the Arousal scale the figure ranges from excited and wide eyed to a relaxed sleepy figure. The Dominance scale shows a figure changing in size to represent feelings of control over the emotions experienced.

After initial pilot tests we felt that it was too difficult to adequately explain the Dominance dimension to participants without a verbal explanation so we decided to use only the Pleasure and Arousal scales.

Likert Scales. Developed by the psychologist Rensis Likert [22], these are scales in which participants must give a score along a range (usually symmetrical with a midpoint) for a number of items making up a scale investigating a particular phenomenon. Essentially most of the questions we asked during the experiment were Likert items, in which participants were asked to rate the intensity of a particular emotion or experience from 1 (none) to 5 (very strong) or bipolar version i.e. 1 (positive) to 5 (negative).

GEMS – Geneva Emotional Music Scales. The 9 point GEMS scale [1] was used to ask participants to rate any instance of experiencing the following emotions: Wonder, Transcendence, Tenderness, Nostalgia, Peacefulness, Energy, Joyful activation, Tension, and Sadness. Again, they were asked to rate the intensity with which they were felt using a 5 point Likert scale.

Tension Scale. This scale was drafted by Dr. Roddy Cowie of QUB School of Psychology. It is a 5 point Likert scale with pictorial indicators at the Low and High ends of the scale depicting a SAM-type mannekin in a 'Very Relaxed' or 'Very Tense' state.

Chills Scale. This was adaptation from the SAM and featured a 5 point Likert scale with a pictorial representation of a character experiencing Chills / Shivers / Thrills / Goosebumps (CSTG), as appropriate, above the scale. The CSTG questions of the first version of the experiments were subsequently replaced with a single chills measure/question.

2.2   Song Selection and Description

The musical excerpts used in the experiment were chosen by the researchers using several criteria: most were selected on the basis of having been used in previous experiments concerning music and emotion, while some were selected by the researchers for their perceived emotional content. All excerpts were vetted by the researchers for suitability. As far as possible we tried to select excerpts without lyrics, or sections in which the lyrical content was minimal.[7]

Each musical example was edited down to approximately 90 seconds of audio. As much as possible, edits were made at 'musically sensible' points i.e. the end of a verse/chorus/bar. The excerpts then had their volume adjusted to ensure a consistent perceived level across all excerpts. Much of the previous research into music and emotion has used excerpts of music of around 30 seconds which may not be long enough to definitely attribute physiological changes to the music (as opposed to a prior stimulus). We chose 90 seconds duration to maximize the physiological changes that might be attributable to the musical excerpt heard. Each excerpt was also processed to add a short (< 0.5 seconds) fade In/Out to prevent clicks or pops, and 2 seconds of silence added to the start and end of each sound file. We also categorized each song according to the most dominant characteristic of its perceived affective content: Relaxed = Low Arousal, Tense = High Arousal, Sad=Low Valence, Happy = High Valence. Songs were randomly selected from each category pool every time the experiment was run with participants only hearing one song from any given category.

Acoustic Feature Extraction. In order to analyse the relationship between the sonic and structural features of the musical excerpts and the participants experiences whilst listening to the excerpts, it was necessary to extract these features from the excerpts, preferably via an automatic software based approach in order to ensure consistency and repeatability. There are a wide range of potential features that can be extracted but for the purposes of this analysis we chose to focus on the musical mode (Major/Minor) and dynamic range variability of the excerpts.

Key and mode information was automatically extracted using the commercial 'Mixed in Key' (MiK) software.[8] The outputs from this software were compared with information available from online sources to determine the accuracy of the automatic extraction and in most cases these matched well.

Dynamic range values were calculated using the free stand-alone Windows version of Algorhythmix TT-Dynamic Range (TT-DR) Meter.[9] This software calculates the

---

[7] The full list of songs used in the experiment is available in the Appendix.
[8] www.mixedinkey.com
[9] http://www.pleasurizemusic.com/es/es/download#menu1

average loudness of an audio file (RMS, an established loudness measurement standard) and also calculates a Dynamic Range (DR) value, the difference between the peak headroom and the top 20 average RMS measurements, to give an integer value representing the overall density, thickness or 'loudness' of the audio file analysed. With this method lower DR values represent consistently 'loud' recordings lacking dynamic range. These values were then entered into the database to be incorporated into the analysis.

2.3   Feature Extraction from Physiology and Database Built

Database Built. Once the signals and answer files were collected from the experiment terminals, the next step was to populate a database with the information of each session and listening case. This consisted in several steps, detailed below.

First, the metadata information was checked against the rest of the files with the same session ID number for consistency, dropping any files that had a wrong filename or that were corrupted. Subsequently, and because the clocks in each acquisition device and the number of samples in each recorded file can have small variations, the sample rates (SR) of each signal file were re-calculated. Moreover, some files had very different number of samples, which were detected and discarded by this process. To calculate the SR of each file, a MATLAB[10] script counted the number of samples of each file, and obtained the SR using the duration of the song excerpt used in that recording. Two conditions were tested: a) that the SR was within an acceptable range of the original programmed SR (acquisition device) and b) that the SR did not present more than 0.5% variation over time. After this stage, the calculated SR was recorded as a separate variable in the database.

Finally, the data from each song excerpt was separated from its session and copied into a new case in the database. This means that each case in the database contains variables with background information of the participant, answers to the song questionnaire, and features extracted from the physiological signals, as well as metadata about the session (experiment number, SR, order in which the song was heard, terminal number, date, etc.).

EDAtool and HRtool. Two tools developed in MATLAB were used to extract features from the physiological data: *EDAtool* and *HRtool*. Extraction of features included detection and removal of artifacts and abnormalities in the data. The output from both tools consisted of the processed features vectors and an indication of the accuracy of the input signal, which is defined as the percentage of the signal which did not present artifacts. This value can be utilized later to remove signals from the database that fall below a specified confidence threshold.[11]

EDAtool. EDAtool is a function developed to pre-process the EDA signal. Its processing includes the removal of electrical noise and the detection and measurement of

---

[10] www.mathworks.com/products/matlab/

[11] Latest versions can be found in:
http://www.musicsensorsemotion.com/tag/tools/

artifacts. Additionally, it separates the EDA signal into phasic and tonic components (please refer to [23] for a detailed description of EDA). Fig. 2 shows an example of the different stages of the *EDAtool*.

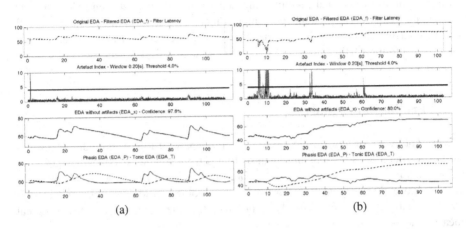

Fig. 2. Stages of the *EDAtool* on a Skin Conductance signal. The top plots show the original signal and the low-passed filtered signal (dotted), which removes any electrical noise. The next plots show the artifact detection method, which identifies abrupt changes in the signal. (a) shows a signal above the confidence threshold used in this experiment, while signal in (b) would be discarded. The third row from the top shows the filtered signals with the artifacts removed. The bottom plots show the phasic and tonic (dotted) components of the signal.

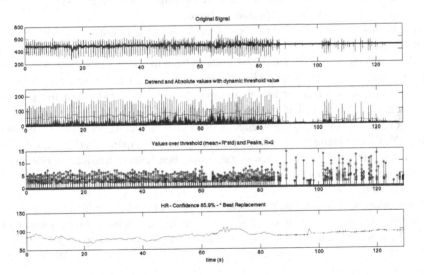

Fig. 3. Stages of the *HRtool* on an ECG signal. The top plot shows the raw ECG signal. The two middle plots show the peak detection stages, with a dynamic threshold. The bottom plot shows the final HR vector, with the resulting replacement of values that were outside the specified ranges (marked as dots in the plot). In this example, accuracy is at 85.9%, which falls below the acceptance tolerance for this experiment, and would be discarded as a valid case.

HRtool. HRtool is a function developed to convert the data from an Electrocardiogram (ECG) or Pulse Oximetry (POX) signal into an HR vector. This involves three main stages (see Fig. 3), which are the detection of peaks in the signal (which is different for a POX or an ECG signal), the measurement of the interval between pulses and the calculation of the corresponding HR value. Finally, the algorithm evaluates the HR vector replacing any values that are outside the ranges entered by the user (e.g. maximum and minimum HR values and maximum change ratio between two consequent pulses).

3   Preliminary Analysis

We are not aware of any similar study with a database of this magnitude, which has made it difficult to apply existing methodologies from smaller sized studies [17, 19]. Consequently, a large portion of the research presented in this paper has been dedicated to do exploratory analysis on the results; looking to identify relationships between variables and to evaluate the validity of the questionnaire and physiological measurements.

3.1   Preliminary Results from Questionnaire

General Demographic Information. After removing all data with artifacts, as described previously, an overall sample size of 3343 participants representing 11041 individual song listens was obtained. The remaining files were checked for consistency and accuracy and no other problems found.

The mean DOB was 1980 (Std. Dev. 13.147) with the oldest participants born in 1930 (22 participants, 0.2%). 47% of the participants were Male, 53% Female, with 62.2% identifying as 'Irish', and 37.8% coming from the 'Rest of the World'.

In the first version of the experiment participants heard four songs (1012 participants) with the subsequent versions consisting of three songs (2331 participants).

Participants were asked if they considered themselves to have a musical background or specialist musical knowledge, with 60.7% indicating 'No' and 39.3% indicating 'Yes'. Interestingly, despite the majority of participants stating they had no specialist musical knowledge, when asked to rate their level of musical expertise from '1= No Musical Expertise' to '5= Professional Musician' 41.3% rated their level of musical expertise as '3'.

Participants were also asked to indicate the styles of music to which they regularly listen (by selecting one or more categories from the list below). From a sample of N=3343 cases, preferences broke down as follows: Rock 68.1%, Pop 60.3%, Classical 35%, Jazz 24.9%, Dance 34.2%, Hip Hop 27%, Traditional Irish 17%, World 27.9%, and None 1.2%.

Self-Report Data. An initial analysis was run to determine the song excerpts identified as most enjoyed and engaging. At the end of each experiment session, participants were asked which of the 3 or 4 (depending on experiment version) excerpts they had heard was the most enjoyable and which they had found most engaging. These questions were asked in all 5 versions of the experiment, making them the only ones to appear in all versions (other than the background or demographic questions).

The excerpts rated as 'Most Enjoyed' were James Brown 'Get Up (I Feel Like being a) Sex Machine' and Juan Luis Guerra 'A Pedir Su Mano' with these excerpts chosen by participants in 55% of the cases where they were one of the excerpts heard. At the other end of the scale, the excerpts rated lowest (fewest percentage of 'Most Enjoyed') were Slayer 'Raining Blood' and Dimitri Shostakovich 'Symphony 11, Op. 103 − 2nd Movement' with these excerpts chosen by participants in 13% of the cases where they were one of the songs heard.

Participants were also asked to rate their 'Liking' of each excerpt (in experiment versions 1-3). Having analysed the mean values for 'Liking' on a per-song basis, the songs with the highest means were Jeff Buckley 'Hallelujah' (4.07/5) and The Verve 'Bittersweet Symphony' (4.03/5). The songs with the lowest mean values for 'Liking' were Slayer 'Raining Blood' (2.66/5) and Vengaboys 'We like to party!' (2.93/5).

The excerpt rated most often as 'Most Engaging' was Clint Mansell's 'Requiem for a Dream Theme' with this excerpt chosen by participants in 53% of the cases where it was one of the excerpts heard. At the other end of the scale, the excerpt rated lowest (fewest percentage of 'Most Engaging') was Ceoltóirí Chualann 'Marbhna Luimnigh' with this excerpt chosen by participants in 11% of the cases where it was one of the excerpts heard.

Interestingly, when the mean values for 'Engagement' for each excerpt were calculated, Clint Mansell's 'Requiem for a Dream Theme' was only rated in 10th place (3.74/5), with Nirvana 'Smells Like Teen Spirit' rated highest (3.99/5), closely followed by The Verve 'Bittersweet Symphony' (3.95/5) and Jeff Buckley 'Hallelujah' (3.94/5). It was observed that while mean values for engagement are all within the 3-4 point range, there are much more significant differences between songs when participants were asked to rate the excerpt which they found 'Most Engaging', with participants clearly indicating a preference for one song over another.

The excerpts with the lowest mean values for 'Engagement' were Primal Scream 'Higher Than The Sun' (3.05/5) and Ceoltóirí Chualann 'Marbhna Luimigh' (3.09/5). The excerpts with the highest mean values for Chills / Shivers / Thrills / Goosebumps (CSTG) were Jeff Buckley 'Hallelujah' (2.24/5), Mussorgsky 'A Night on the Bare Mountain' (2.23/5) and G.A. Rossini 'William Tell Overture' (2.23/5). The excerpts with the lowest mean values for CSTG were Providence 'J.O. Forbes of Course' (1.4/5), Paul Brady 'Paddys Green Shamrock Shore' (1.43/5) and Neil Young 'Only Love Can Break Your Heart' (1.5/5).

An analysis was also run to attempt to determine the overall frequency of participants experiencing the sensation of CSTG. The number of instances where CSTG were reported as a 4 or 5 after a musical excerpt was tallied, giving 872 reports of a 4 or 5 from 9062 listens, meaning that significant CSTGs were experienced in around 10% of cases.

A selection of the musical excerpts used (some of which were outliers in the above analyses) were mapped on to an emotional circumplex (as per Russell 1980), with Arousal and Valence (as measured using the SAM) as the Y and X axes respectively. An overall tendency of participants to report positive experiences during music listening was observed, even for songs which might be categorised as 'Sad' e.g. Nina Simone. Arousal responses were a little more evenly distributed but still with a slight positive skew. It seems that while some songs may be perceived as being of negative affect or 'sad', these songs do not in the majority of cases induce feelings of sadness. It may therefore be more appropriate to rescale songs to fit the circumplex from 'saddest' to 'happiest' (lowest Valence to highest Valence) and 'most relaxing' to 'most exciting' (lowest Arousal to highest Arousal) rather than using the absolute values reported (as seen on Fig. 4). This 'positive' skew indicating the rewarding nature of music listening corroborates previous findings as documented in Juslin and Sloboda 2001 [24]. In future versions of this experiment we hope to identify songs that extend this mapping and are reported as even 'sadder' than Nina Simone.

Fig. 4. Circumplex mapping of selected excerpts after a normalisation process to rescale the values 0 -1 with the lowest scoring excerpt in each axis as '0' and the highest as '1'

In addition we mapped all the excerpts on to the circumplex and identified each according to which of the initial affective categories the development team had placed them in e.g. Happy, Sad, Tense or Relaxed. As seen in Fig. 5 the self-reported Valence and Arousal scores for the Happy and Sad categories were for the most part remarkably consistent, clustering in the upper right and lower left quadrants of the circumplex respectively (happiness usually being characterised as a state of positive valence and medium to high arousal, sadness as negatively valence and with low arousal). Participant responses for the Tense and Relaxed categories were less clearly defined yet still tended to group above and below the median line for Arousal respectively. This may be due to greater ambiguity as to what defines a 'tense' song versus a song that induces high arousal and also positive valence, indeed examining

Fig. 5 one can see that the excerpts positioned in the extreme of the upper right quadrant all belong to the Tense category. Fig. 4 shows the outliers in all categories as well as typical examples in each group.

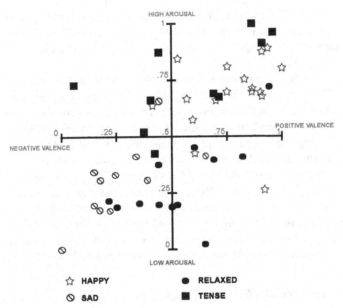

Fig. 5. Circumplex mapping of all normalised excerpts to show position of excerpts from Happy/Sad/Tense/Relaxed categories

MODE. A Mann-Whitney U test was used to examine significant differences between songs in Major and Minor modes in how they affected the listeners self-reports of Valence (negativity/positivity) and Arousal (drowsy/lively) as measured with the SAM. Songs in Major modes (N = 4428, mean rank = 4530.28) were found to score significantly higher (U = 10254, 255.00, p <.05) than Minor modes (N = 4501, mean rank = 4400.78) in terms of how they affected self-reports of valence.

This appears to indicate that increased levels of positive affect (as evaluated using the SAM) are associated with songs in a Major mode.

Songs in Major modes (N = 4428, mean rank = 4551.80) were found to score significantly higher (U = 10349, 563.00, p < .01) than Minor keys (N = 4501, mean rank = 4379.61) in terms of how they affected self-reports of arousal. This appears to indicate that increased levels of arousal may be associated with songs in a Major mode.

Songs in Major modes were also found to have a relationship with the listeners engagement with the music (p < .01), indicating that listeners' were more engaged with music in a major mode.

There did not however appear to be any relationship between listeners' 'liking' of the music (as measured with a 5 point Likert item) and whether the music was in a major or minor mode.

Dynamic Range. A Spearman's rho correlation was used to examine the relationship between the participants' self-reported Valence and Arousal (as measured with the SAM) and the Dynamic Range of the excerpt they had listened to (as measured with the TT-DR Meter). A significant negative correlation was found between Valence and Dynamic Range (r[8927] = - 0.119, p <.01). The negative correlation would appear to indicate that excerpts with less variable dynamic range (usually those that have undergone dynamic range compression, an audio production technique) are associated with positive valence.

A significant negative correlation was also found between Arousal and Dynamic Range (r[8927] = - 0.211, p <.01). The negative correlation would appear to indicate that excerpts with less variable dynamic range are associated with high arousal.

A Spearman's rho correlation was used to examine the relationship between the participants self-reported Engagement (as measured with the LEMtool) and the Dynamic Range of the excerpt they had listened to (as measured with the TT-DR Meter). A significant negative correlation was found between Engagement and Dynamic Range (r[8927] = - 0.053, p <.01). The negative correlation would appear to indicate that excerpts with less variable dynamic range are associated with high Engagement.

A significant negative correlation was found between Liking and Dynamic Range (r[8927] = - 0.029, p <.01). The negative correlation would appear to indicate that excerpts with less variable dynamic are associated with increased liking of the excerpt.

3.2   Preliminary Results from Physiology

Features Extracted from Physiology. Due to the scope and nature of the experiment, the statistical analysis of the physiological signals has been approached as a continuous iteration, extracting a few basic features from the physiology, running statistical tests and using the results to extract new features. For this reason, the results from the physiology presented in this paper are still in a preliminary stage. Table 1 shows the features that have been extracted from the 3 physiological vectors recorded in each case of the database (Phasic EDA, Tonic EDA and HR).

Evaluation of Measurements
Dry Skin Issue. Originally, the accuracy level given by the *EDAtool* was calculated only from the amount of artifacts presented during the duration of the EDA signal, without considering the measured samples values' relationship to the range of the sensor. Preliminary analysis of the features extracted from EDA, filtering for signals that presented less than 10% of artifacts, resulted in an overwhelming amount of signals with variances close or equal to zero, which did not correlate with any of the variables measured or changed during the experiment. At first, these participants were considered to simply have a flat EDA response, yet further analysis proved differently.

In order to analyse the effect that the initial impedance of each subject might have on the EDA response, the mean of the first 10 EDA samples was calculated and added to the database as a new variable (*Init_EDA*). Fig. 6 shows the distribution of this initial impedance, for EDA signals with confidence levels above 90% (calculated only for motion artifacts).

Table 1. Summary of statistical features extracted from physiological vectors

Abbreviation	Description
SD_EDAP	Standard Deviation of phasic EDA
mean_EDAP	Mean of phasic EDA
RMS_EDAP	Root Mean Square of phasic EDA
End_EDAT	Tonic EDA end value*
Area_EDAT	Trapezoidal numerical integration of tonic EDA
SD_EDAT	Standard Deviation of tonic EDA
Lin_EDAT	Linearity (difference between tonic EDA and linear regression)
RMS_EDAT	Root Mean Square of tonic EDA
Init_EDA	Initial value of tonic EDA (average of 1st 10 samples)
Range_EDAP	Range of phasic EDA
Range_EDAT	Range of tonic EDA
HR	Average HR during recording
mean_HRV	Mean of normalised* HR vector
End_HRV	End value of normalised* HR vector
SDNN	Standard Deviation of NN intervals
RMSSD	Square Root of the Mean Squared Difference of successive NN
LF_HRV	Low Frequency HRV (0.04-0.15[Hz])
HF_HRV	High Frequency HRV (0.15-0.4[Hz])
LtoH_HRV	Low to High HRV frequency Ratio
pNN50	Fraction of NN > 50ms
pNN20	Fraction of NN > 20ms
TSP	Total Spectral Power up to 0.04[Hz]

* These results are obtained after removing the initial offset from the vector.

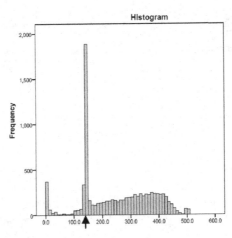

Fig. 6. Histogram of the mean of the 1st 10 samples of the EDA signal; equivalent to the initial conductivity. The histogram shows a large group of participants with an initial conductivity around the 160 mark (high impedance).

The distribution shows a clear predominance of a group of participants that presented very high initial impedance (around the 160 mark, with over 1700 participants). Although the origin of this irregularity is not clear, it is equivalent to the measurement of the EDA sensor when it has an open circuit (e.g. no skin connection). Due to the decision to use dry-skin electrodes (avoiding the application of conductive gel prior to the experiment), it is possible that this abnormality corresponds to a large group of participants in which the sensor did not make a good connection with the skin, probably due to them having a drier skin than the rest of the participants. It is also interesting to point out that there were a few hundred cases in which the sensor failed to work correctly (e.g. cases with conductivity near zero). For these reasons, the number of cases used for the analysis was filtered by the *Init_EDA* variable, looking for values that had normal impedance (above open-circuit value and below short-circuit value), at the cost of significantly reducing the valid cases in the database by approximately 37%.

EDA Level Dependence. While doing preliminary analysis on the EiM database, an inverse proportional relationship was found between the EDA level and the amplitude of changes in the EDA signal. Originally this was thought as being caused by a non-linearity of the sensor utilised, which was observed and corrected, although the EDA level still presented an influence on all features extracted from EDA. Fig. 7 shows an example of valid EDA signals for one excerpt, showing the phasic component of EDA. When analysing the amplitude of each phasic signal compared to its baseline EDL, the inverse relationship is apparent. This relationship is better illustrated in Fig. 8, by dividing participants in 10 groups of equidistant EDA starting levels against their phasic standard deviation. EDA initial level correlation coefficients with EDA features range from .35 (*mean_EDAP*) to .62 (*RMS_EDAP*), all with p-values < .001.

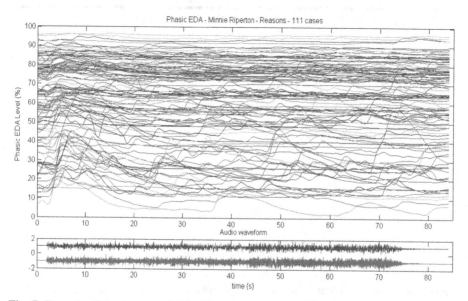

Fig. 7. Example of the inverse relationship of EDA level on the phasic response variability. Excerpt corresponds to Minnie Riperton 'Reasons', N=111.

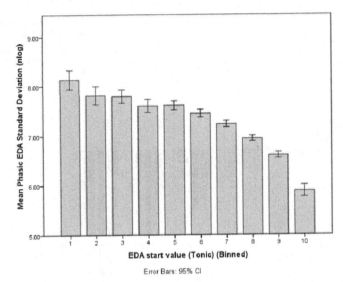

Fig. 8. Phasic SD versus EDA level, split into ten equidistance bins, in ascending order (N=2013)

Even though the EDA level dependence has been discussed in the psychophysiology literature for over 4 decades [23, see 25], it is surprisingly not considered when processing EDA signals in numerous publications [see 26–28, and 7 to name a few]. The origin of this relationship has been attributed to the Law of Initial Values (LIV) [29], in which the amplitude of ANS responses is reciprocal to their baselines, as well as to the "ceiling and bottom effects" [23]. This means that a very high or very low baseline limits the range in which an EDA signal can vary (as seen in Fig. 7). Some baseline correction methods have been suggested, such as using Autonomic Liability Scores [30] or performing data transformations. Yet, an empirical elucidation of the relationship between EDA level and phasic changes is still to be provided, and baseline corrections remain to be problematic [23].

Effect of Age and Gender on Physiological Measures. Age and gender have been related to influence changes in HRV and EDA. HRV decreases with age [31], and variation is greater for females than males [32], this includes both spectral and temporal measures of HRV [33, 34]. The influence of gender and age on EDA features is less reported, yet Boucsein [23] cites studies in which both EDL and SCR amplitudes decrease for older participants. He also summarises several studies in which females present higher levels of EDA, and male subjects having higher amplitude of SCRs.

Correlation analyses revealed significant relationships (p<.001) between age groups and several HR features, including: *mean_HR, SDNN, RMSSD, LF_HRV, HF_HRV, pNN50, pNN20,* and *TSP* features. A closer look at these sets of features per age group can be seen in Fig. 9. The plot of standard scores shows a clear decrease of HRV for older age groups, in agreement with the literature. The correlation

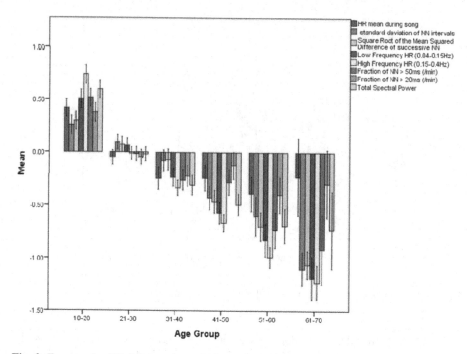

Fig. 9. Z-scores for HR features that correlate with age. Error bars correspond to 95% confidence intervals.

between average HR and age can be explained mainly by the group of younger participants (aged between 10 and 20), which have a tendency to higher mean HR values [35]. Another plausible non-exclusive explanation is the effect of heart conditions, more frequent in older participants, causing higher average heart rates with age [36, 37]. With regard to gender, females do not show higher variability than males (except for a non-significant increase for ages 51-70), yet they do have higher *HF_HRV* values, and lower *LtoH_HRV* ratio [31].

EDA level per age group and gender are shown in Fig. 10. Even though EDL shows a slight decrease between the age groups of 10-20 and 41-50, these stabilise for older groups. Conversely, female participants show significantly lower EDA levels than male participants. Additionally, no other EDA feature shows significant differences between age groups.

It is important to state that many of the averages and trends described in the literature are measured in resting and un-stimulated environments, whereas the correlations presented in this experiment are measured with musical stimulus (except for *Init_EDA*), and are not necessarily comparable to these criterions.

Effect of Average HR on HRV Features. Mean HR value, calculated during the duration of the musical excerpt, showed significant correlations (p<.001) with several HRV features, including large effect sizes with *pNN20*, *TSP* and *RMSSD*. The relationship between the average HR and HRV is not broadly mentioned in the literature, although Tsuji et al. [38] indicate it as being the "strongest clinical determinant of HRV", having an inverse association with HRV [39].

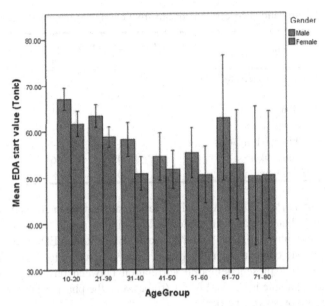

Fig. 10. EDA level before listening to the excerpt per age group, for male and female participants. Error bars correspond to 95% confidence intervals.

Factor Analysis of Physiological Features. Principal Component Analysis (PCA) was performed on a selection of features, excluding features with high degrees of correlation (it is important to state that all physiological features are derived from only two channels, EDA and HR, which can produce problems of multi-collinearity between features. This needs to be addressed prior to running a PCA). Principal Component Analysis shows three salient factors after rotation. These indicate a clear distinction between frequency-related features from HR vector (Component 1: *SDNN, HF_HRV, LF_HRV,* Age and *RMSSD*), features from EDA (Component 2: *Area_EDAT, End_EDAT* and *SD_EDAP*) and secondary features from HRV (Component 3: *mean_HRV* and *End_HRV*).

Correlation between Factors and Questionnaire. The three salient components from PCA were correlated against a selection of the self-report questionnaire: Song Engagement, Song Positivity, Song Activity, Song Tension, Song CSTG, Song Likeness and Song Familiarity. Results show a relationship between components 1 and 2 with the self-report questionnaire (see Table 2).

   It is important to point out that the correlation coefficients presented below explain only a small portion of the variation in the questionnaire results. Furthermore, it is interesting that there was no significant correlation between CSTG and the 2nd

component, taking into account that 10% of the participants reported to experience CSTG. Nevertheless, it is fascinating to see a relationship between physiological features and self-reports such as song likeness, positivity, activity and tension.

Table 2. Correlation between components from physiology and questionnaire

Question	Correlation by component (p<.001)		
	1	**2**	**3**
Song Engagement	-.081	.075	-
Song Positivity	-	.097	-
Song Activity	-	.110	-
Song Tension	-	.044	-
Song Chills/Shivers/Thrills/Goosebumps	-	-	-
Song Likeness	-.052	.061	-
Song Familiarity	-.060	.083	-

Music Events versus Physiology. Analysis of temporal changes in correlation with the excerpt's musical changes has been explored. Preliminary results show a relationship between the three physiological vectors; phasic EDA, tonic EDA and HR, with changes in the music content, such as dynamics and structure. Fig. 11 shows two examples of pieces that present temporal correlation between physiology and music dynamic (a clear example is shown Fig. 11 (b) between the phasic EDA and the audio waveform after the 60 second mark).

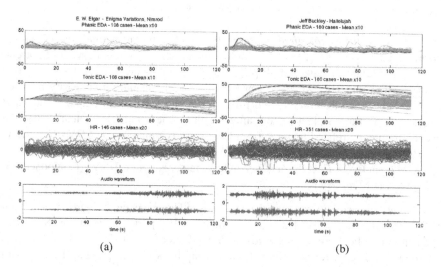

Fig. 11. Plots of changes in Phasic EDA, Tonic EDA, HR and audio waveform (top to bottom) during the duration of the song excerpt. Physiological plots show multiple individual responses overlapped, with the mean overlaid on top (dotted). (a) plots are for Elgar's 'Enigma Variations', and plots in (b) are for an excerpt of Jeff Buckley's 'Hallelujah'.

4   Discussion

Due to the public gallery nature of this study, work has mainly been focused in improving the acquisition of signals, and the algorithms that correctly identify and remove noise and artifacts. Any unaccounted variation at this stage can impact the validity of the statistical tests that use physiological measurements. It is important to point out that with the current sensor design, which requires no assistance and can be used by participants briefed with short instructions; we are obtaining approximately 65% valid signals (with a confidence threshold of 90%). This has to be taken into account when calculating group sizes for experiments that require physiological sensing of audiences.

The analysis of the physiological measures shows high levels of dispersion between participants for the same feature, which seems to indicate that large sample sizes need to be maintained for future experiments. Nonetheless, the preliminary results presented in this paper are a significant indication of the possible relationships that explain the way we react to musical stimuli. Correlations between physiology and self-report questionnaire, in groups of this size, are a statement that this relationship undoubtedly exists. Our findings relating to the frequency of 'chill' responses to musical excerpts in around 10% of participants are also broadly consistent with the findings of previous studies [40–42]. We are yet to further define the precise musical cues and variables that influence changes.

In examining the relationship between acoustic features and induced affective responses one must pay particular attention to the complex nature of musical stimuli. While there do appear to be relationships between musical/acoustic features such as mode and changes in Valence and Arousal, it is more difficult to define a piece of music as having a specific affective character based on these features alone. For instance an excerpt may be in a minor key, have a high tempo and little dynamic range variation (such as Slayer – Raining Blood) and be associated with tension or negative valence, yet another excerpt bearing similar acoustic features (such as Nirvana – Smells Like Teen Spirit) may be associated with elation and positive valence (see Fig. 4). It is clear that perception of the affective content of a piece of music is more than the sum of its acoustic or musical features.

Next steps in the analysis will be focusing on additional physiological descriptors, multimodal analysis of the dataset, looking at temporal changes (versus the current whole song approach) and measures of correlation and entrainment with musical features. After the implementation in Dublin, 'Emotion in Motion' has been installed in public spaces in the cities of New York, Genoa and Bergen. Each implementation of the experiment has been enhanced and new songs have been added to the pool. We believe augmenting the sample size of these kinds of studies is a requirement to start elucidating the complex relationship between music and our affective response to it.

Acknowledgements. The authors would like to thank Dr. Miguel Ortiz-Perez for his invaluable contribution to the software design for this experiment, as well as Dr. Rodderick Cowie and Cian Doherty from QUB for their help with the questionnaire design. Finally, we would like to express our appreciation to the Science Gallery, Dublin for their support and funding of this experiment.

The project SIEMPRE acknowledges the financial support of the Future and Emerging Technologies (FET) programme within the Seventh Framework Programme for Research of the European Commission, under FET-Open grant number: 250026-2.

References

1. The Geneva Emotional Music Scales (GEMS) | zentnerlab.com, http://www.zentnerlab.com/psychological-tests/geneva-emotional-music-scales (retrieved January 20, 2013)
2. Tomkins, S.S.: Affect Imagery Consciousness - Volume II The Negative Affects. Springer Publishing Company (1963)
3. Ekman, P., Friesen, W.V.: The repertoire of nonverbal behavior: Categories, origins, usage, and coding. Semiotica I, 49–98 (1969)
4. Salimpoor, V.N., Benovoy, M., Larcher, K., Dagher, A., Zatorre, R.J.: Anatomically distinct dopamine release during anticipation and experience of peak emotion to music. Nature Neuroscience 14, 257–262 (2011)
5. Zentner, M., Grandjean, D., Scherer, K.R.: Emotions evoked by the sound of music: Characterization, classification, and measurement. Emotion 8, 494–521 (2008)
6. Juslin, P.N., Västfjäll, D.: Emotional responses to music: the need to consider underlying mechanisms. Behav Brain Sci. 31, 559–575; discussion 575–621 (2008)
7. Balteş, F.R., Avram, J., Miclea, M., Miu, A.C.: Emotions induced by operatic music: Psychophysiological effects of music, plot, and acting: A scientist's tribute to Maria Callas. Brain and Cognition 76, 146–157 (2011)
8. Trost, W., Ethofer, T., Zentner, M., Vuilleumier, P.: Mapping Aesthetic Musical Emotions in the Brain. Cerebral Cortex (2011)
9. Gabrielsson, A., Juslin, P.N.: Emotional Expression in Music Performance: Between the Performer's Intention and the Listener's Experience. Psychology of Music 24, 68–91 (1996)
10. Ekman, P.: An argument for basic emotions. Cognition & Emotion 6, 169–200 (1992)
11. Russell, J.A.: A circumplex model of affect. Journal of Personality and Social Psychology 39, 1161–1178 (1980)
12. Villon, O., Lisetti, C.: Toward Recognizing Individual's Subjective Emotion from Physiological Signals in Practical Application. In: Twentieth IEEE International Symposium on Computer-Based Medical Systems, 2007, pp. 357–362. IEEE (2007)
13. Wilhelm, F.H., Grossman, P.: Emotions beyond the laboratory: Theoretical fundaments, study design, and analytic strategies for advanced ambulatory assessment. Biological Psychology 84, 552–569 (2010)
14. Lantelme, P., Milon, H., Gharib, C., Gayet, C., Fortrat, J.O.: White Coat Effect and Reactivity to Stress: Cardiovascular and Autonomic Nervous System Responses. Hypertension 31, 1021–1029 (1998)
15. Bradley, M.M., Lang, P.J.: Emotion and Motivation. In: Handbook of Psychophysiology, pp. 581–607 (2007)
16. Cacioppo, J.T., Bernston, G.G., Larsen, J.T., Poehlmann, K.M., Ito, T.A.: The Psychophysiology of Emotion, pp. 173–191. Guilford Press (2000)

17. Kreibig, S.D., Wilhelm, F.H., Roth, W.T., Gross, J.J.: Cardiovascular, electrodermal, and respiratory response patterns to fear- and sadness-inducing films. Psychophysiology 44, 787–806 (2007)
18. Picard, R.W.: Affective Computing, M.I.T Media Laboratory, Cambridge, MA (1997)
19. Kim, J., André, E.: Emotion Recognition Based on Physiological Changes in Music Listening. IEEE Transactions on Pattern Analysis and Machine Intelligence 30, 2067–2083 (2008)
20. Huisman, G., Van Hout, M.: Using induction and multimodal assessment to understand the role of emotion in musical performance. In: Emotion in HCI – Designing for People, Liverpool, pp. 5–7 (2008)
21. Bradley, M.M., Lang, P.J.: Measuring emotion: The self-assessment manikin and the semantic differential. Journal of Behavior Therapy and Experimental Psychiatry 25, 49–59 (1994)
22. Likert, R.: A technique for the measurement of attitudes. Archives of Psychology; Archives of Psychology 22(140), 55 (1932)
23. Boucsein, W.: Electrodermal Activity. Springer, New York (2012)
24. Juslin, P.N., Sloboda, J.A.: Music and Emotion: Theory and Research. Oxford University Press (2001)
25. Lykken, D.T., Venables, P.H.: Direct Measurement of Skin Conductance: A Proposal for Standardization. Psychophysiology 8, 656–672 (1971)
26. Healey, J., Picard, R.W.: Digital processing of affective signals. In: Proceedings of the IEEE International Conference on Acoustics, Speech and Signal Processing, vol. 6, pp. 3749–3752. Media Lab., MIT, Cambridge (1998)
27. Bechara, A., Damasio, H., Damasio, A.R., Lee, G.P.: Different Contributions of the Human Amygdala and Ventromedial Prefrontal Cortex to Decision-Making. J. Neurosci. 19, 5473–5481 (1999)
28. Haag, A., Goronzy, S., Schaich, P., Williams, J.: Emotion Recognition Using Bio-Sensors: First Steps Towards an Automatic System. In: André, E., Dybkjær, L., Minker, W., Heisterkamp, P. (eds.) ADS 2004. LNCS (LNAI), vol. 3068, pp. 36–48. Springer, Heidelberg (2004)
29. Wilder, J.: The "law of initial values," a neglected biological law and its significance for research and practice. Zeitschrift für die gesammte Neurologie und Psychiatrie 137, 317–324 (1931)
30. Lacey, J.I.: The Evaluation of Autonomic Responses: Toward a General Solution. Annals of the New York Academy of Sciences 67, 125–163 (1956)
31. Agelink, M., Malessa, R., Baumann, B., Majewski, T., Akila, F., Zeit, T., Ziegler, D.: Standardized tests of heart rate variability: normal ranges obtained from 309 healthy humans, and effects of age, gender, and heart rate. Clinical Autonomic Research 11, 99–108 (2001)
32. Rajendra Acharya, U., Paul Joseph, K., Kannathal, N., Lim, C., Suri, J.: Heart rate variability: a review. Medical and Biological Engineering and Computing 44, 1031–1051 (2006)
33. Liao, D., Barnes, R.W., Chambless, L.E., Simpson Jr., R.J., Sorlie, P., Heiss, G.: The ARIC Investigators: Age, race, and sex differences in autonomic cardiac function measured by spectral analysis of heart rate variability—The ARIC study. The American Journal of Cardiology 76, 906–912 (1995)
34. Jensen-Urstad, K., Storck, N., Bouvier, F., Ericson, M., Lindblad, L.E., Jensen-Urstad, M.: Heart rate variability in healthy subjects is related to age and gender. Acta Physiol. Scand. 160, 235–241 (1997)

35. Ostchega, Y., Porter, K.S., Hughes, J., Dillon, C.F., Nwankwo, T.: Resting Pulse Rate Reference Data for Children, Adolescents, and Adults: United States, 1999–2008. National Health Statistics Report 41, 1–16 (2011)
36. Kannel, W.B., Kannel, C., Paffenbarger Jr., R.S., Cupples, L.A.: Heart rate and cardiovascular mortality: The Framingham study. American Heart Journal 113, 1489–1494 (1987)
37. Kostis, J.B., Moreyra, A.E., Amendo, M.T., Di Pietro, J., Cosgrove, N., Kuo, P.T.: The effect of age on heart rate in subjects free of heart disease. Studies by Ambulatory Electro-Cardiography and Maximal Exercise Stress Test. Circulation 65, 141–145 (1982)
38. Tsuji, H., Venditti, F.J., Manders, E.S., Evans, J.C., Larson, M.G., Feldman, C.L., Levy, D.: Reduced heart rate variability and mortality risk in an elderly cohort. The Framingham Heart Study. Circulation. 90, 878–883 (1994)
39. Kuch, B., Hense, H.W., Sinnreich, R., Kark, J.D., Von Eckardstein, A., Sapoznikov, D., Bolte, H.D.: Determinants of short-period heart rate variability in the general population. Cardiology 95, 131–138 (2001)
40. Sloboda, J.A.: Music Structure and Emotional Response: Some Empirical Findings. Psychology of Music 19, 110–120 (1991)
41. Panksepp, J.: The Emotional Sources of "Chills" Induced by Music. Music Perception 13, 171–207 (1995)
42. Grewe, O., Nagel, F., Kopiez, R., Altenmüller, E.: How Does Music Arouse "Chills"? Investigating Strong Emotions, Combining Psychological, Physiological, and Psychoacoustical Methods. Annals of the New York Academy of Sciences 1060, 446–449 (2005)

Appendix: List of Music Pieces in Emotion in Motion (Dublin)

Artist	Title
Anton Bruckner	Te Deum
Aphex Twin	Digeridoo
Arvo Pärt	Spiegel Im Spiegel For Violin And Piano
Bing Crosby	White Christmas
Black Eyed Peas	I gotta Feeling
Ceoltóirí Chualann	Marbhna Luimnigh
Ceoltóirí Chualann	Marcshlua Ui Neill
Clint Mansell	Requiem For A Dream (Theme)
Dimitri Shostakovich	Symphony 11, op. 103, 2nd Movement
E. W. Elgar	Enigma Variations, Nimrod
G. A. Rossini	William Tell Overture
G. F. Handel	The Arrival Of The Queen Of Sheba from Solomon
G. T. Holst	Jupiter, the Bringer of Jollity
Grainne Hambley	Eleanor Plunkett
J. S. Bach	Cello Suite No 1 in G major I. Prelude
James Brown	Get Up (I feel like being a) Sex Machine
Jeff Buckley	Hallelujah
Johan Strauss	Chit Chat Polka
John McSherry	An Bhean Chaointe

Artist	Title
John Williams	Schindlers List
Journey	Dont Stop Believin
Juan Luis Guerra	A Pedir Su Mano
Louis Armstrong	What a wonderful world
M. P. Mussorgsky	A Night On The Bare Mountain
Max Bruch	Kol Nidrei
Mazzy Star	Into Dust
Minnie Riperton	Reasons
Neil Young	Only Love can break your heart
Nina Simone	I get along without you very well
Nirvana	Smells Like Teen Spirit
Paul Brady	Gleantainn Glas Ghaoth Dobhair
Paul Brady	Paddys Green Shamrock Shore
Planxty	Cunla (with lyrics)
Planxty	Cunla (without lyrics)
Primal Scream	Higher Than The Sun
Providence	J. O. Forbes of Corse
Richard Addinsell	Warsaw Concerto
Saint Saens	Carnival of the Animals (Finale)
Sean O Riada	Mise Eire Muscailt
Sharon Shannon	Blackbird
Shaun Davey	Water Under The Keel
Silvio Rodríguez	Coda Te Conozco
Sinead O Connor	Nothing Compares 2 U
Slayer	Raining Blood
The Beach Boys	Good Vibrations
The Commodores with Lionel Richie	Easy like Sunday Morning
The Ronettes	Be My Baby
The Undertones	Teenage Kicks
The Verve	Bittersweet Symphony
U2	One
Vengaboys	We like to party!
Vinnie Kilduff	Sean Sa Cheo
W. A. Mozart	Eine Kleine Nachtmusik

Psychophysiological Measures of Emotional Response to Romantic Orchestral Music and Their Musical and Acoustic Correlates

Konstantinos Trochidis, David Sears, Diêu-Ly Trân, and Stephen McAdams

Schulich School of Music, MGill University
{Konstantinos.Trochidis,David.Sears,
Dieu-Ly.Tran}@mail.mcgill.ca, smc@music.mgill.ca

Abstract. This paper examines the induction of emotions while listening to Romantic orchestral music. The study seeks to explore the relationship between subjective ratings of felt emotion and acoustic and physiological features. We employed 75 musical excerpts as stimuli to gather responses of excitement and pleasantness from 20 participants. During the experiments, physiological responses of the participants were measured, including blood volume pulse (BVP), skin conductance (SC), respiration rate (RR) and facial electromyography (EMG). A set of acoustic features was derived related to dynamics, harmony, timbre and rhythmic properties of the music stimuli. Based on the measured physiological signals, a set of physiological features was also extracted. The feature extraction process is discussed with particular emphasis on the interaction between acoustical and physiological parameters. Statistical relations among audio, physiological features and emotional ratings from psychological experiments were systematically investigated. Finally, a forward step-wise multiple linear regression model (MLR) was employed using the best features, and its prediction efficiency was evaluated and discussed. The results indicate that merging acoustic and physiological modalities substantially improves prediction of participants' ratings of felt emotion compared to the results using the modalities in isolation.

1 Introduction

With the recent advances in diverse fields of technology there is an emerging interest in recognizing and understanding the emotional content of music. Music emotion recognition plays an important role in music retrieval, mood detection, health care, and human-machine interfaces. Moreover, the entire body of music collections available to humans is increasing rapidly, and there is a need to intelligently classify and retrieve music according to the emotions they elicit from listeners. Indeed, emotion recognition is considered a key issue in integrating emotional intelligence within advanced human-machine interaction. Thus, there is strong motivation for developing systems that can recognize music-evoked emotions. In the following, we briefly review some of the work related to music emotion recognition based on acoustical and physiological features.

M. Aramaki et al. (Eds.): CMMR 2012, LNCS 7900, pp. 44–57, 2013.
© Springer-Verlag Berlin Heidelberg 2013

The emotions elicited during music listening are influenced by a number of structural music characteristics, including tempo, mode, timbre, harmony and loudness [1, 2]. In a pioneering publication [3], Li and Ogihara used acoustic features to classify music into mood categories. They achieved an accuracy of 45% using a database of 499 music clips selected from different genres annotated by a subject. They used a SVM-based multilabel classification method and determined the accuracy of their model using micro and macro-averaged precision. In [4] the authors used a similar variety of acoustic features for 800 classical music clips and achieved a recognition accuracy of 85%. Within the framework of Music Information Research Evaluation eXchange (MIREX), Tzanetakis reported an accuracy of 63.5% using a limited number of acoustic features [5]. Within the same framework, Peeters used a larger number of acoustic features and reported only a slight improvement [6], whereas in the next year Kim et al. proposed a system that reached a recognition accuracy of 65.7% [7].

Music emotion recognition has employed a number of approaches. In [8] the automatic detection of emotion in music was modeled as a multi-label classification task. A series of multi-label classification algorithms were tested and compared, with the predictive power of different audio features reaching an average precision of 81%. However, recent research in music emotion recognition from audio has shown that regression approaches can outperform existing classification techniques. In [12] the effectiveness of emotion prediction using different musical datasets (classical, film and popular music) was investigated. Their model had low generalizability between genres for valence (16%) and moderate generalizability between genres for arousal (43%), suggesting that valence operates differently depending on the musical genre. In [9] the authors used multiple acoustic features to predict pleasure and arousal ratings for music excerpts. They found that audio features are better for predicting arousal than valence and that the best prediction results are obtained for a combination of different features. In [10] a regression approach with combinations of audio features was employed in music emotion prediction. They found that the best performing features were spectral contrast and Mel-frequency cepstral coefficients (MFCC). The best performance, however, was achieved by a combination of features. In a recent publication [11], audio-based acoustical features for emotion classification were evaluated. A data set of 2090 songs was used, different audio features were extracted, and their predictive performance was evaluated. The results suggest that a combination of spectral, rhythmic and harmonic features yields the best results.

Despite the progress achieved on emotion recognition using audio features alone, the success of these various models has reached a glass ceiling. In order to improve the recognition accuracy of audio-based approaches, many studies have exploited the advantages of using additional information from other domains. This approach has led to the development of methods combining audio and lyrics [13-16], audio and tags [17], and audio and images [18], all of which result in moderate increases in recognition accuracy. There is a large body of studies establishing the relationship between physiological responses and musical emotions during music listening. Several studies have attempted to demonstrate whether the basic emotions induced by music are related to specific physiological patterns [19-23]. The relation between discrete emotions and emotion-specific physiological response patterns predicted by theorists, however, still remains an open problem.

Indeed, the attempt to provide robust, incontrovertible evidence of emotional induction during music listening remains a tremendous challenge. The adoption of psychophysiological measures provides one possible solution, as they offer direct, objective evidence of autonomic and somato-visceral activation. Physiological responses during music listening include variations in heart rate, respiration electrodermal activity, finger temperature, and surface electromyography. Little attention, however, has been paid to the effect of physiological signals in music emotion recognition. The main problem of using physiological signals is the difficulty of mapping physiological patterns to specific emotional states. Furthermore, recording physiological signals requires the use of sensors and the analysis of signals that often reflect innervation by distinct branches of the autonomic nervous system (ANS). On the other hand, physiological signals have certain advantages, as they provide an objective measure of the listener's emotional state without relying on participant self-reports.

In [24] the authors used movie clips to induce emotions in 29 subjects, and combining physiological measures and subjective ratings achieved 83% recognition accuracy. In [25] the authors recorded four biosignals from subjects listening to songs and reached a recognition accuracy of 92%. Kim [26] used music excerpts to spontaneously induce emotions, measured electromyogram, electrocardiogram, skin conductivity and respiration changes, and then extracted the best features, achieving a classification accuracy of 70% and 90% for subject-independent and subject-dependent classification, respectively. Recently, in [27] a multimodal approach was based on physiological signals for emotion recognition, using music video clips as stimuli. They recorded EEG signals, peripheral physiological signals and frontal video. A variety of features was extracted and used for emotion recognition by using different fusion techniques. The results, however, demonstrated only a modest increase in recognition performance, indicating limited complementarity of the different modalities.

An important issue in musical emotion recognition is the modeling of perceived musical emotions. The two main approaches to modeling emotions in music-related studies are the categorical and the dimensional approach. According to the categorical approach, emotions are conceptualized as discrete entities, and there are a certain number of basic emotions, such as happiness, sadness, anger, fear and disgust, from which all subsequent emotional states are ultimately derived [28]. In music-related studies, emotion researchers often employ music-specific emotion labels (awe, frisson), or they use emotion terms that are more suitable to everyday musical experience (peacefulness, tenderness). Whereas the categorical model often employs these apparently distinct labels, in the dimensional approach all of the emotions experienced in everyday life are characterized (or supported) by two underlying dimensions: valence, which is related to pleasure-displeasure, and arousal, which is related to activation-deactivation. Thus, all emotions can be characterized in terms of varying degrees of valence and arousal [29, 30]. Both approaches have been recently investigated in relation to musical emotions [31], and their limitations were analyzed and discussed. In our study, the dimensional approach was employed because existing research in psychophysiology can find little evidence to suggest that there are emotion-specific physiological descriptors [21]. Rather, psychophysiological responses appear to be related to the underlying dimensions of arousal and valence [32].

To the best of our knowledge, a combination of audio and physiological features has not been used in music emotion recognition research. There are, however, studies combining speech and physiological features for emotion recognition. In [33] and [34] the authors used combined voice data and physiological signals for emotion recognition. By fusing the features from both modalities, they achieved higher recognition accuracy compared with recognition results using the individual modalities.

The primary aim of the present work is to investigate the acoustic and physiological effects on the induction of emotions by combining audio and physiological features for music emotion recognition. Following [35] and [36], we argue that there is a possible route of emotion elicitation by peripheral feedback, and thus, that physiological arousal may influence the intensity and valence of emotions. In our study, we want to investigate the possibility of increasing the prediction rate of felt emotion through peripheral feedback by using acoustic and physiological features. The emotion recognition task is formulated as a regression problem, in which the arousal and valence ratings for each musical excerpt are predicted using a forward step-wise multiple linear regression model. During the experiment, music excerpts were employed as stimuli and the physiological responses of the listeners were measured, which included blood volume pulse, respiration rate, skin conductivity, and facial electromyographic activity. Both audio and physiological features were extracted, and the best features were combined and used for emotion recognition.

To combine the two modalities, it is important to determine at which stage in the model the individual modalities should be combined, or *fused*. A straightforward approach is to simply merge the features from each modality, called *feature-level fusion*. The alternative is to fuse the features at the decision level based on the outputs of separate single classifiers, called *decision-level fusion*. The existing literature on bimodal emotion recognition using speech features and physiological changes [34] demonstrates that feature-level fusion provides higher recognition accuracies compared to decision-level fusion. Therefore, in our study we employed feature-level fusion.

2   Methods

Participants. Twenty non-musicians (10 females) were recruited as participants (mean age = 26 years). The participants reported less than one year of training on an instrument over the past five years and less than two years of training in early childhood. In addition, all participants reported that they liked listening to Classical and Romantic music. The participants also filled out a demographic questionnaire and passed an audiometric test in order to verify that their hearing was normal.

Stimuli. Seventy-five music excerpts from the late Romantic period were selected for the stimulus set. The excerpts were 35 to 45 seconds in duration and selected by a music theorist from the Romantic, late Romantic, or Neo-classical period (from 1815 to 1900). These genres were selected under the assumption that music from this time period would elicit a variety of emotional reactions along both dimensions of the emotion model. Moreover, each excerpt was selected to clearly represent one of the four quadrants of the two-dimensional emotion space formed by the dimensions of arousal and valence. Ten excerpts were chosen from a previous study [37] and 65 excerpts from our own personal collection. Aside from the high-arousal/negative-valence quadrant, which had 18 excerpts, the other three quadrants contained 19 excerpts each.

Procedure. During the experiment, five physiological signals were measured, including facial electromyography (EMG) of the smiling (zygomaticus major) and frowning (corrugator supercilii) muscles, skin conductance (SC), respiration rate (RR), and blood volume pulse (BVP). EMG measures the muscle activity through surface voltages generated when muscles contract. It is often employed to index emotional valence [38]. EMG sensors were placed above the zygomaticus major and corrugator supercilli muscles. SC is typically employed to index the physiological arousal of participants [38]. It measures the skin's ability to conduct electricity as a result of variations in sweat-gland activity. To measure SC, we positioned electrodes on the index and ring fingers of the non-dominant hand. RR is one of the characteristics of respiration change. A stretch sensor attached around the torso was used to record the breathing activity of the listeners. Heart rate variability (HRV) is the corresponding characteristic of heart rate activity derived from blood volume (BVP) pulse, which is measured with a plethysmograph attached to the middle finger of the non-dominant hand.

During the experiment the participants were asked to sit in a comfortable and relaxed position. They were told that it was crucial not to move during the baseline recordings and while the excerpts were playing. Following a practice trial to familiarize the participants with the experimental task, there was a two-minute baseline period in which their physiological measurements were taken. To remove inter-individual variability, seven additional one-minute baselines were recorded after each block of ten excerpts. Following each excerpt, participants rated their level of experienced excitement and pleasantness on 7-point continuous-categorical Likert scales.

3   Audio Feature Extraction

A theoretical selection of musical features following [12] was made based on musical characteristics such as dynamics, timbre, pitch, harmony, rhythm and structure using the MIR Toolbox for MATLAB [40]. For all features a series of statistical descriptors was computed, such as the mean, the standard deviation and the linear slope of the trend across frames. A total of 58 descriptors related to these features was thus extracted from the musical excerpts. Table 1 lists the various acoustic features and statistical descriptors extracted.

Table 1. The acoustic feature set extracted from the audio signals

Domain	No.	Name
Dynamics	1-3	RMS[1,2,3]
Timbre	4-18	Spectral Centroid[1,2,3] Spectral Flux[1,2,3] Spectral Spread[1,2,3] Spectral Entropy[1,2,3] Roughness[1,2,3]
Pitch	19-24	Chromagram[1,2,3] Pitch[1,2,3]
Tonality	25-36	Key Clarity[1,2,3] Key Strength[1,2,3] Harmonic Change Detection Function[1,2,3] Mode[1,2,3]
Rhythm	37-49	Fluctuation Pattern[1] Attack Times[1,2,3] Event Density[1,2,3] Tempo[1,2,3] Pulse Clarity[1,2,3]
Structure	50-58	Spectral Novelty[1,2,3], Rhythmic Novelty[1,2,3], Tonal Novelty[1,2,3]

Mean[1] Standard deviation[2] Slope[3]

3.1 Dynamics

We computed the RMS amplitude to examine whether the energy is evenly distributed throughout the signals, or to determine whether certain frames are more contrasted than others.

3.2 Timbre

A set of 5 features related to musical timbre were extracted from the Short-term Fourier Transform: Spectral Centroid, Spectral Flux, Spectral Spread and Spectral Entropy. Spectral Centroid represents the degree of timbre brightness. Spectral Flux is related to the degree of temporal evolution of the spectral envelope. Spectral Spread indicates the breadth of the spectral envelope. Spectral Entropy is used to capture the formants and the "peakedness" of the spectral distribution. Roughness was also derived from the peaks in the spectrogram based on the model in [41] and represents the sensory dissonance of the sound.

3.3 Pitch

Two pitch features were derived. The Chromagram represents the energy distribution of the signals wrapped around the 12 pitch classes. The Pitch was also computed using an advanced pitch extraction method which divides the audio signal into two channels below and above 1000 Hz and computes the autocorrelation of the low channel, the envelope of the high channel, and sums the autocorrelation functions [45].

3.4 Tonality

The signals were also analyzed according to their harmonic characteristics. A Chromagram representing the distribution of pitch-classes is created. Key Strength computes the cross-correlation of the Chromagram with each possible major or minor key. The Key Clarity is the Key Strength of the key with the highest Key Strength out of all 24 keys [42]. The Harmonic Change Detection Function is a measure of the flux of the Tonal Centroid, and it captures the tonal diversity across time [43]. Finally, to model the Mode of each piece, a computational model that distinguishes major and minor excerpts was employed. It calculates an overall output that continuously ranges from zero (minor mode) to one (major mode) [44].

3.5   Rhythm

Fluctuation Pattern represents the rhythmic periodicity along auditory frequency channels) [46], and Attack Times refers to the estimation of note onset times. The Event Density measures the overall amount of simultaneous events in a musical excerpt. The tempo of each excerpt in beats per minute (BPM) was estimated by first computing a spectral decomposition of the onset detection curve. Next, the autocorrelation function was translated into the frequency domain in order to be compared to the spectrum curve, and the two curves were subsequently multiplied. Then a peak-picking algorithm was applied to the spectrum representation to select the best candidate tempo. The Pulse Clarity, a measure of the rhythmical and repetitive nature of a piece, was finally estimated by the autocorrelation of the amplitude envelope.

3.6   Structure

A degree of repetition was estimated through the computation of novelty curves [47] based on the spectrogram, the autocorrelation function, the key profiles and the Chromagram, each representing a different aspect of the novelty or static temporal nature of the music, such as Spectral, Rhythmic, and Tonal Novelty.

4   Physiological Feature Extraction

From the five psychophysiological signals, we calculated a total of 44 features, including conventional statistics in both the time and frequency domains. Table 2 lists the various physiological features extracted.

Table 2. The feature set extracted from the physiological signals

Domain	No	Name
Blood volume pulse	1-6	BVP[1,2,3,4,5,6]
Heart-rate	7-21	Heart-rate[1,2,3,4,5,6,7,8,9] SDNN[1,2,3,4,5,6]
Respiration-rate	22-26	BRV[1,2,3,4,5]
Skin conductivity	27-32	Skin conductivity[1,2,3,4,5,6]
Electromyography (Corrugator-Zygomaticus)	33-44	EMGc[1,2,3,4,5,6] EMGz[1,2,3,4,5,6]

Mean[1] Standard deviation[2] Median[3] Maximum[4] Minimum[5] Derivative[6] SpecVLF[7] SpecLF[8] SpecHF[9]

4.1 · Blood Volume Pulse (BVP)

First, we normalized the blood volume pulse (BVP) signal by subtracting the preceding baseline from the signal. From the normalized BVP we computed time-series statistics, such as the mean, standard deviation, median, max, min and the derivative. To obtain HRV (heart rate variability) from the initial BVP signal, each signal was filtered, the QRS complex was detected, and finally the RR intervals (all intervals between adjacent R waves) or the normal-to-normal (NN) intervals (all intervals between adjacent QRS complexes resulting from sinus node depolarization) were determined. In the time-domain representation of the HRV time series, we calculated statistical features, including the mean, the standard deviation of all NN intervals (SDNN), the standard deviation of the first derivative of the HRV, the number of pairs of successive NN intervals differing by greater than 50 ms (NN50), and the proportion derived by dividing NN50 by the total number of NN intervals. In the frequency-domain representation of the HRV time series, three frequency bands are typically of interest: the very-low frequency (VLF) band (0.003-0.04 Hz), the low frequency (LF) band (0.04-0.15 Hz), and the high frequency (HF) band (0.15-0.4 Hz) [26]. From these sub-band spectra, we computed the dominant frequency and mean power of each band by integrating the power spectral densities (PSD) obtained using Welch's algorithm.

4.2 Respiration Rate

After detrending with the mean value of the entire signal and low-pass filtering with a cut-off frequency of 2.2 Hz, we calculated the Breath Rate Variability (BRV) by detecting the peaks in the signal. From the BRV time series, we computed the mean, standard deviation, median, max, min and derivative values.

4.3 Skin Conductivity (SC)

The mean, median, standard deviation, max, min, and derivative were extracted as features from the normalized SC signal and the low-passed SC signal, which used a 0.3 Hz cut-off frequency. In order to remove DC drift caused by physical processes like sweat evaporation off the surface of the skin, the SC signal was detrended by removing continuous, piecewise linear trends in the two low-passed signals: the very low-passed (VLP) signal was filtered with a 0.08 Hz cutoff frequency, and the low-passed (LP) signal was filtered with a 0.2 Hz cutoff frequency.

4.4 Electromyography (EMG)

From the EMG signals we took a similar approach to the one we employed for the SC signal. From the normalized and low-passed signals, the mean, median, max, min, and derivative of the signal were extracted as features.

5   Results

For the 75 excerpts a forward step-wise multiple linear regression (MLR) model between the acoustical and physiological descriptors and participant ratings was computed to gain insight into the importance of features for the arousal and valence dimensions of the emotion space. Table 3 provides the regression estimates and variance inflation factors (VIF) for each of the excitement and pleasantness ratings. The VIF quantifies the severity of multicollinearity in an ordinary least squares regression analysis. Table 4 shows the outcome of the corresponding analysis of the physiological features. Finally, Table 5 shows the outcome of the analysis of the combined acoustic and physiological features.

Table 3. Mean audio features and standardized beta weights of the regression analysis for excitement and pleasantness

Excitement	β	VIF	Pleasantness	β	VIF
RMS **	.17	2.30	Key Clarity **	.51	1.06
Spectral Novelty **	-.21	1.56	Pitch **	.32	1.06
Spectral Spread **	-.41	2.10	Key Mode **	-.30	1.00
Spectral Entropy **	.24	1.15	Attack Times *	-.19	1.00
Spectral Centroid **	.25	1.13			
Pulse Clarity **	.18	2.00			

$R^2 = .84$ for Excitement. $R^2 = .42$ for Pleasantness. $* p < .05, ** p < .01$

Table 4. Physiological features and standardized beta weights of the regression analysis for excitement and pleasantness

Excitement	β	VIF	Pleasantness	β	VIF
SDNN[1]**	-.42	1.32			
Bvp[3]**	-.27	1.08	Heart-rate[2]**	-.37	1.00
Skin C[4]**	-.31	1.17	EMGc[4]**	-.28	1.00
EMGz[1]**	.25	1.11			
Skin C[1]*	.21	1.07			
Heart-rate[5]*	.20	1.08			

Mean[1] Standard deviation[2] Maximum[3] Minimum[4] SpecHF[5]
$R^2 = .55$ for Excitement. $R^2 = .21$ for Pleasantness. $* p<.05, ** p<.01$

Shown in Table 3, the regression model provides a good account of excitement ($R^2 = .84$) using only acoustic features (means of RMS energy, spectral centroid, spread, entropy and pulse clarity). Four features significantly predicted the pleasantness ratings ($R^2 =.42$): the means of Key Clarity, Mode, Pitch and Attack Times. Thus the results show that features related to characteristics of harmony, pitch, and articulation contribute most to pleasantness.

Table 5. Combined audio and physiological features and standardized beta weights of the regression analysis for excitement and pleasantness

Excitement	β	VIF	Pleasantness	β	VIF
RMS[1] **	.16	2.28	Key clarity[1] **	.46	1.00
Spectrum Novelty[1] **	-.21	1.59	Pitch[1] **	.23	1.06
Spectral Spread[1] **	-.34	2.29	Key mode[1] **	-.41	1.07
Spectral Entropy[1] **	.23	2.24	EMGZ[3] **	.36	1.06
Spectral Centroid[1] **	.26	1.40	Attack Time[1]**	-.24	1.06
SDNN[2]**	-.21	1.21	Heart-rate[4]**	-.22	1.13
Pulse clarity[1]**	.19	1.57			

Mean[1] Minimum[2] Derivative[3] SpecLF[4]

$R^2 = .87$ for Excitement. $R^2 = .56$ for Pleasantness. * p<.05, ** p<.01

Using only physiological features, the model provides an account of excitement with $R^2 = .55$ (see Table 4). The standard deviation of the NN intervals (SDNN) in the heart rate signals contributes most to excitement, along with the max value of the BVP and the mean and minimum of the skin conductance and EMGz signals. The power spectrum of the heart rate in the high frequency band (0.15-0.4 Hz) also contributes to this dimension. For the pleasantness dimension the model provides $R^2 = .21$ using the standard deviation of the heart rate signals and the minimum of the EMGc signals. Finally, using combined acoustical and physiological information (means of RMS energy, Spectral Centroid, Spread, Entropy, Pulse Clarity and the maximum value of SDNN), the model provides an account of excitement with $R^2 = .87$. The corresponding estimates for pleasantness use acoustic features related to Key Clarity, Mode, Pitch and the attack slope, and physiological features related to the EMGz and heart rate ($R^2 = .56$).

6 Discussion

In the present paper, the relationships among acoustic features and physiological features in emotional reactions to Romantic music were investigated. Our goal was to determine the importance of acoustic features in predicting the global emotional experience with music as measured with subjective ratings provided after each stimulus, and to explore the extent to which physiological activity may increase the prediction rate of emotion felt through peripheral feedback. A regression model based on a set of acoustic parameters and physiological features was systematically explored. The correlation analysis demonstrates that low- and mid-level acoustic features, such as RMS energy, Spectral Centroid, Spectral Spread, Spectral Entropy, and Pulse Clarity, significantly predict emotional excitement. The corresponding best features for the prediction of pleasantness are Key Clarity, Mode, Pitch and Attack Times. This result is in agreement with existing work on acoustic feature selection for emotion classification [10]. As far as the physiological features are concerned, the results indicate that features obtained from time and frequency analysis of the HRV series (SDNN, BVP), along with features of skin conductance, are decisive in the prediction of participant ratings of excitement. Furthermore, features such as heart rate and corrugator EMG are important for pleasantness prediction. These findings are in agreement with previous research on music emotion recognition using physiological signals [26] and also support the findings of previous studies, according to which SC is linearly correlated to the intensity of arousal [22].

To the best of our knowledge a combination of audio and physiological features has not been employed in music emotion recognition tasks, and thus, we cannot compare our results with existing studies. There are, however, previous studies combining speech features and physiological responses for emotion recognition [33, 34]. The results of these studies show that the combination of speech and physiological features results in a moderate improvement of 3% for both valence and arousal. In our case the corresponding improvements are 3% and 14%, respectively, suggesting that the combination of acoustic and physiological features can provide more complementary information compared to the combination of speech and physiological features.

Existing results show that combined acoustic features provide better prediction for arousal than for valence [11, 10]. Therefore, the significant increase of pleasantness prediction by employing both acoustic and physiological features in our study is noteworthy here. It seems that EMG measures and spectral features of HRV play a significant role for the correct differentiation of positive and negative valence, and thus contribute substantially to improved valence prediction. This result is of particular importance, as valence is an otherwise elusive and opaque dimension in music emotion research. Moreover, MIR approaches thus far have only considered objective acoustical/musical features in an emotion recognition task, thereby failing to account for the role of physiological responses in the evocation of subjective feelings. Thus, any attempt to model a listener's affective state must also account for how subjective ratings of emotional experience may interact with the internal physiological state of the listening individual. Indeed, we hypothesize that our autonomic and somato-visceral reactions during music listening may influence the intensity and valence of our emotions through a process of peripheral feedback.

7   Future Work

There are several aspects in the work presented here that need to be addressed in future research. It remains to be investigated whether this particular model can be applied to other music-listening populations using other musical styles. Indeed, we believe that this approach could lead to fundamental advances in different areas of research because it may provide consistent descriptions of the emotional effects of particular musical stimuli. This, in turn, will have important implications for a number of disciplines, such as psychology and music therapy. In our study, feature-level fusion was employed. However, it appears that simply combining modalities with equal weighting does not always result in improved recognition accuracy. An alternative approach would be to decompose an emotion recognition problem into sub-problems, treating valence and arousal separately. For valence recognition, audio features could be used, whereas for arousal recognition physiological changes could be used.

Acknowledgments. Konstantinos Trochidis was supported by a post-doctoral fellowship by the ACN Erasmus Mundus network. This research was funded by grants to Stephen McAdams from the Social Sciences and Humanities Research Council of Canada and the Canada Research Chairs program. David Sears was supported by a Richard H. Tomlinson fellowship and a Quebec doctoral fellowship from the Programme de Bourses d'Excellence pour Étudiants Étrangers. The authors thank Bennett K. Smith for valuable technical assistance during the experiments.

References

1. Gabrielsson, A., Lindström, E.: The role of structure in the musical expression of emotions. In: Juslin, P.N., Sloboda, J.A. (eds.) Music and Emotion: Theory, Research, Applications. Oxford University Press, Oxford (2010)
2. Gomez, P., Danuser, B.: Relationships between musical structure and physiological measures of emotion. Emotion 7(2), 377–387 (2004)
3. Li, T., Ogihara, M.: Detecting emotion in music. In: Proceedings of the International Conference for Music Information Retrieval (ISMIR), Baltimore (2003)
4. Lu, L., Lu, D., Zhang, H.J.: Automatic mood detection and tracking of music audio signal. IEEE Transactions on Audio, Speech and Language Processing 14(1), 5–18 (2006)
5. Tzanetakis, G.: Marsyas submission to MIREX 2007. MIREX (2007)
6. Peeters, G.: A generic training and classification system for MIREX08 classification tasks: Audio music mood, audio genre, audio artist, audio tag. MIREX (2008)
7. Kim, Y.E., Schmidt, E.M., Migneco, R., Morton, B.G., Richardson, P., Scott, J., Speck, J.A., Turnbull, D.: Music emotion recognition: a state of the art review. In: Proceedings of the International Conference for Music Information Retrieval (ISMIR), pp. 255–266 (2010)
8. Trochidis, K., Tsoumakas, G., Kalliris, G., Vlahavas, I.: Multi-label classification of music into emotions. In: Proceedings of the International Conference for Music Information Retrieval, ISMIR (2008)
9. Song, Y., Simon, D., Pears, M.: Evaluation of musical features for emotion classification. In: Proceedings of the International Conference for Music Information Retrieval (ISMIR), pp. 523–528 (2012)
10. Schmidt, E.M., Turnbull, D., Kim, Y.E.: Feature selection for content-based, time-varying musical emotion regression. In: Proceedings of the International Conference for Music Information Retrieval (ISMIR), pp. 267–274 (2010)
11. Mc Dornan, K.F., Ough, S., Ho, C.C.: Automatic emotion prediction of song excerpts: Index construction, algorithm design and empirical comparison. Journal of New Music Research 36(4), 281–299 (2007)
12. Eerola, T.: Are the Emotions Expressed in Music Genre-specific? An Audio-based Evaluation of Datasets Spanning Classical, Film, Pop and Mixed Genres. Journal of New Music Research 40(4), 349–366 (2011)
13. Yang, Y.-H., Lin, Y.-C., Cheng, H.-T., Liao, I.-B., Ho, Y.-C., Chen, H.H.: Toward multi-modal music emotion classification. In: Huang, Y.-M.R., Xu, C., Cheng, K.-S., Yang, J.-F.K., Swamy, M.N.S., Li, S., Ding, J.-W. (eds.) PCM 2008. LNCS, vol. 5353, pp. 70–79. Springer, Heidelberg (2008)
14. Laurier, C., Sordo, M., Serra, J., Herrera, P.: Music mood representation from social tags. In: Proceedings of the International Conference for Music Information Retrieval, ISMIR (2009)

15. Hu, Y., Chen, X., Yang, D.: Lyrics based song emotion detection with affective lexicon and fuzzy clustering method. In: Proceedings of the International Conference for Music Information Retrieval, ISMIR (2009)

16. Schuller, B., Dorfner, J., Rigoll, D.: Determination of non-prototypical valence and arousal in popular music: features and performances. EURASIP Journal on Audio, Speech and Music Processing 2010, 1–20 (2010)

17. Turnbull, D., Barrington, L., Torres, D., Lanckiert, G.: Semantic annotation and retrieval of music and sound effects. IEEE Transactions on Audio, Speech and Language Processing 16(2), 455–462 (2010)

18. Biscoff, K., Firan, C.S., Paiu, R., Nejdl, W., Laurier, C., Sodo, M.: Proceedings of the International Conference for Music Information Retrieval, ISMIR (2009)

19. Dunker, P., Nowak, S., Begau, N., Lanz, C.: Content-based mood classification framework and evaluation approach. In: Proceedings of ACM, New York (2008)

20. Nyklicek, I., Thayer, J., Van Doornen, L.: Cardiorespiratory differentiation of musically-induced emotion. Journal of Psychophysiology 11, 304–321 (1997)

21. Krumhansl, C.: An explanatory study of musical emotion and psychophysiology. Canadian Journal of Experimental Psychology 51, 336–352 (1997)

22. Khalfa, S., Peretz, I., Blondin, J., Manon, R.: Event-related skin conductance responses to music al emotion in humans. Neuroscience Letters 328, 145–149 (2002)

23. Lundquist, L., Carlsson, F., Hilmersson, P.: Facial electromyography, autonomic activity and emotional experience to happy and sad music. Paper Presented at the International Congress of Psychology (2002)

24. Nasoz, F., Lisetti, C.L., Alvarez, K., Finkelstein, N.: Emotional Recognition from Physiological Signals for User Modeling of Affect. In: Proceedings of the 3rd Workshop on Affective and Attitude User Modeling (2003)

25. Wagner, J., Kim, J., Andre, E.: From physiological signals to emotion. In: International Conference on Multimedia and Expo, pp. 940–943 (2005)

26. Kim, J.: Emotion recognition based on physiological changes in music listening. IEEE Transactions on Pattern Analysis and Machine Intelligence 30(12), 2067–2083 (2008)

27. Koelstra, S., Muehl, C., Soleymani, M., Lee, J.D., Yazdani, A., Ebrahimi, T., Pun, T., Nijholt, A., Patras, I.: DEAP: A database for emotion analysis using physiological signals. IEEE Transactions on Affective Computing 3(1), 18–31 (2011)

28. Ekman, P.: Are there basic emotions? Physiological Review 99(3), 550–553 (1992)

29. Russel, J.A.: A circumplex model of affect. Journal of Personality and Social Psychology 39(6), 1161–1178 (1980)

30. Withvliet, C.V., Vrana, S.R.: Play it again Sam: repeated exposure to emotionally evocative music polarizes liking and smiling responses and influences the affective reports, facial EMG and heart rate. Cognition & Emotion 21(1), 1–23 (2006)

31. Eerola, T., Vuoskoski, J.K.: A comparison of discrete and dimensional models of emotion in music. Psychology of Music 31(1), 18–49 (2010)

32. Bradley, M.M., Lang, P.J.: Emotion and Motivation. In: Cacioppo, J.T., Tassinary, L.G., Berntson, G.G. (eds.) Handbook of Psychophysiology, 3rd edn., pp. 581–607. Cambridge University Press, New York (2008)

33. Kim, J., Andre, E., Rehm, M., Vogt, T., Wagner, J.: Integrating information from speech and physiological signals to achieve emotion sensitivity. INTERSPEECH 2005, 809–812 (2005)

34. Kim, J., Andre, E.: Emotion recognition using physiological and speech signals in short term observation. In: ICGI 2006. LNCS (LNAI), vol. 4201, pp. 53–64. Springer, Heidelberg (2006)

35. Dibben, N.: The role of peripheral feedback in emotional experience with music. Music Perception 22(1), 79–115 (2002)
36. Scherer, K., Zentner, M.: Emotional effects of music: Production rules. In: Juslin, P., Sloboda, J. (eds.) Music and Emotion: Theory and Research, Oxford University Press, Oxford (2001)
37. Bigand, E., Vieillard, S., Madurell, F., Marozeau, J., Dacquet, A.: Multidimensional scaling of emotional responses to music: The effect of musical expertise and of the duration of the excerpts. Cognition & Emotion 19(8), 1113–1139 (2005)
38. Dimberg, U.: Facial electromyography and emotional reactions. Psychophysiology 27(5), 481–494 (1990)
39. Rickard, N.: Intense emotional responses to music: a test of the physiological arousal hypothesis. Psychology of Music 32(4), 371–399 (2004)
40. Lartillot, O., Toiviainen, P.: MIR in Matlab (II): A Toolbox for Musical Feature Extraction From Audio. In: International Conference on Music Information Retrieval, Vienna (2007)
41. Sethares, W.: Tuning, Timbre, Spectrum, Scale. Springer, Berlin (1998)
42. Gomez, E.: Tonal description of polyphonic audio for music content processing. INFORMS Journal on Computing 18(3), 294–304 (2006)
43. Harte, C., Sandler, M., Gasser, M.: Detecting harmonic change in musical audio. In: Proceedings of the 1st ACM Workshop on Audio and Music Computing Multimedia, Santa Barbara, CA, pp. 26–31 (2006)
44. Saari, P., Eerola, T., Lartillot, O.: Generalizability and simplicity as criteria in feature selection: Application to mood classification in music. IEEE Transactions in Audio, Language, and Speech Processing 19(6), 1802–1812 (2011)
45. Tolonen, T., Karjalainen, M.: A computationally efficient multipitch analysis model. IEEE Transactions on Speech and Audio Processing 8(6), 708–716 (2000)
46. Pampalk, E., Rauber, A., Merkl, D.: Content based organization and visualization of music archives. In: Proceedings of the 10th ACM International Conference on Multimedia, Juan les Pins, France, pp. 579–585 (2002)
47. Foote, J., Cooper, M.: Media segmentation using self-similarity decomposition. In: Proceedings of SPIE Storage and Retrieval for Multimedia Databases, vol. 5021, pp. 167–175 (2003)

Two-Dimensional Hybrid Spatial Audio Systems with User Variable Controls of Sound Source Attributes

Martin J. Morrell and Joshua D. Reiss

Centre for Digital Music, Queen Mary University of London, London, UK
martin.morrell@eecs.qmul.ac.uk

Abstract. This paper presents two novel hybrid spatial audio systems demonstrated for use in two-dimensional applications with their scalability to three-dimensions. The emphasis of these hybrid systems is to give further creative freedom to a composer, sound engineer or sound designer. The systems are principally based on the end result of Ambisonics spatial audio reproduction systems. Since Ambisonics systems are used primarily for temporary sound installations and exhibits, the use of B-Format can be unnecessary. Therefore these systems revert to producing channel based content rather than sound field content that is later separately decoded. The presented systems use the decoder as a real-time sound manipulation feature on a per sound source basis. A comparison is drawn between the two systems and each method is described as to how it can be used as part of a standard music production workflow.

Keywords: Ambisonics, variable-order, variable-decoder, polar pattern, octagon, spatial audio, surround sound, 2D, 3D.

1 Ambsionics Background

The work in this paper is based on Higher Order Ambisonics systems. Michael Gerzon led the original Ambsionics development team in the 1970s and wrote papers on the subject throughout his career [11–13]. Further work has been done to expand Ambisonics into Higher Order Ambisonics [3–5, 15] and to develop decoders, speaker layouts and evaluation of systems [1, 9, 10, 14, 17, 18, 31]. The basis of Ambisonics is to represent a three-dimensional auditory scene as a sound field representation that can later be reconstructed for any user speaker layout. An Ambisonics representation is based on a fixed order that is linked to the localisation attributes of sound sources. Ambisonics theory is based on spherical harmonics calculated from legendre polynomials.

$$Y_{mn}(N2D)(\theta, \phi) = \sqrt{2}\hat{P}_{mn}(\sin \phi) = \begin{cases} \cos n\theta & n \geq 0 \\ \sin n\theta & n < 0 \end{cases}. \tag{1}$$

$$\hat{P}_{mn}(\sin \phi) = \sqrt{(2 - \phi_{0,n})\frac{(m-n)!}{(m+n)!}} P_{mn}(\sin \phi). \tag{2}$$

M. Aramaki et al. (Eds.): CMMR 2012, LNCS 7900, pp. 58–81, 2013.

Where Y_{mn} is the spherical harmonic, n is the degree, m is the order and $\hat{P}_{mn}$ the associated Legendre polynomial.

The above equations use the N2D normalisation scheme. Several schemes exist for Ambisonics and affect the maximum gain of each spherical harmonic. When these are applied to a monaural sound source a sound field representation is created and is known as B-Format. The 2D representation is based only on the angular value θ as $\phi = 0°$. The spherical harmonic expansion of the sound field is truncated to a finite representation known as the Ambisonic order M and each prior order m is included, $0 \leq m \leq M$. For each included order m the degrees calculated are $n = \mp m$. The total amount of harmonics in the sound field representation is $2M + 1$.

Once encoded, Ambisonics material can be played back over various speaker layouts using a suitable decoder. The minimum number of speakers to correctly reproduce 2D Ambisonics is $2M + 2$ [22]. For a regular layout, i.e. one that has the speakers equally spaced, the angular separation is simply $360°/L$ where L is the number of speakers for 2D reproduction. For a regular layout the decoder matrix can be calculated by using the Moore-Penrose pseudo-inverse matrix of the spherical harmonics at each speaker position.

$$\begin{pmatrix} Y_{(0,0)}(spk1) & Y_{(1,-1)}(spk1) & Y_{(1,1)}(spk1) & \dots & Y_{(M,m)}(spk1) \\ \vdots & \vdots & \vdots & \ddots & \vdots \\ Y_{(0,0)}(spkN) & Y_{(1,-1)}(spkN) & Y_{(1,1)}(spkN) & \dots & Y_{(M,m)}(spkN) \end{pmatrix}^{\dagger} . \tag{3}$$

Gerzon specified criteria for low and high frequencies reproduction known as rV and rE vectors [11, 12, 14]. The given pseudo-inverse decoder results in the standard, rV, decoder matrix. To create a decoder that maximises the rE vector the decoder is then multiplied with gains g_{rE} based on each component's order and the system order.

$$g_{rE} = P_m(\text{largest root of } P_{M+1}) . \tag{4}$$

Furthermore the decoding can be changed to what is known as In-Phase decoding, using the $g_{In-Phase}$ coefficients, so that there are no negative gains used to create the sound's directionality.

$$g_{In-Phase} = \frac{M!}{(M+m)!(M-m)!} . \tag{5}$$

Ambisonics can be seen as creating a polar pattern of Mth order in the direction of the sound source where the polar pattern is sampled by discrete speaker positions. By increasing the amount of speakers the resolution of the polar pattern is increased. In turn, by increasing the order, the directionality is increased and by using different decoders as described above, the rear-lobe is altered.

2   Variable-Order, Variable-Decoder Ambisonics

This section presents the novel idea of Variable-Order, Variable-Decoder Ambisonics. The concept allows for varying the reproduced polar pattern, and therefore the sharpness of localisation, by setting the order used to a non-integer value. Further to this, the idea of a variable-decoder is discussed that can alter the amount of rear lobe of the sampled polar pattern. The two variables are linked but not interchangeable. The order alters the width of the main lobe, whilst altering the amount and gain of, the rear lobes. The decoder alters the gain of rear lobes whilst consequently altering the width and gain of the main lobe.

2.1   Variable-Order

The result of encoding a monaural sound source to Ambisonics B-Format and then decoding it for a speaker layout is equivalent to applying a gain to the monaural sound and sending it to each speaker. Therefore in this described approach, the audio signal is not converted to B-Format. Instead, the gains are calculated numerically and applied based on the octagonal layout.

The variable-order is created by calculating the decoders of the identical type, for each order. Since we are dealing with an octagonal layout the orders used are 0 through 3. The spherical harmonic values are calculated for all included orders for the sound source location θ and speaker gains obtained. By using

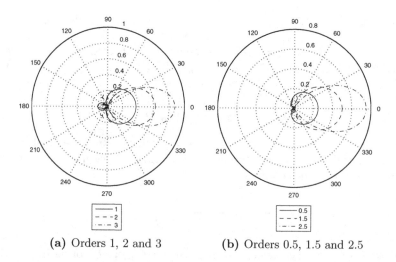

(a) Orders 1, 2 and 3   (b) Orders 0.5, 1.5 and 2.5

Fig. 1. The reproduced polar pattern of a sound source at $\theta = 0°$ for Ambisonics orders 1 through 3 are shown in (a). The half orders of 0.5, 1.5 and 2.5 are shown in (b).

interpolation the variable-order can be created by a mixture of 0th and 1st, 1st and 2nd, and 2nd and 3rd speaker gains. Figure 1 (a) shows the sampled polar pattern for the whole orders. Figure 1 (b) shows the half orders using the variable-order approach. As can be expected, the polar pattern of half orders are directly between the whole orders. The variable-order approach can be used to create the polar pattern of any decimal value order representation. For an Ambisonics representation the gain of all speakers must equal one. This fact is important so that a sound source does not experience an overall gain boost when the variable-order is used as a creative feature.

2.2   Variable-Decoder

Three types of Ambisonics decoders have been presented in section 1 where each is used for a specific purpose. However, these decoders offer an aspect of creativity in being able to manipulate the rear lobe of the polar pattern, thus altering the shape of the sound source's polar pattern.

The variable-decoder can be calculated in the same manner as for the variable-order concept. By using a weighted ratio that equals 1 of two types of decoder, a variable pattern can be created. The weightings are calculated between rV and rE decoders and the rE and In-Phase decoders. This is because the rE polar pattern lies between the basic and In-Phase patterns.

Figure 3 shows the three decoders for order 1.5 on the left and the decoders half way between the rV and rE decoders and the rE and In-Phase decoders. The variable-decoder lies at the given ratio between the standard decoders.

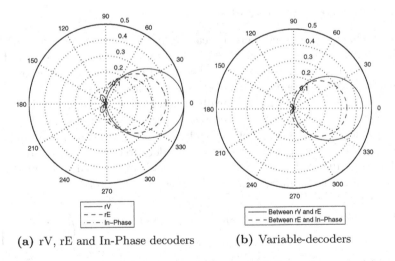

(a) rV, rE and In-Phase decoders   (b) Variable-decoders

Fig. 2. The three standard decoder types for order 1.5 are shown in (a) and the intermediate decoders in (b)

2.3 Observations

The proposed methodology creates a set of variable-order, variable-decoder speaker signals for an octagonal arrangement of speakers. The end result is sampling the sound scene at regular intervals of a third order polar pattern [6]. The resultant gain G_L for the speaker at position θ_L can be calculated by eq. (6). The sum of the gain of the orders must equal one; that is $\sum_{L=1}^{N} G_L = 1$.

$$G_L = a_0 + a_1 \cos(\theta + \theta_L) + a_2 \cos(2(\theta + \theta_L)) + a_3 \cos(3(\theta + \theta_L)) . \quad (6)$$

Therefore the variable-order is equivalent to increasing the next order gain whilst the ratio of the prior orders' gains remain the same. The variable-decoder, is like altering the ratio between the a_0 and a_1 gain coefficients thus changing the base polar pattern, as well as altering the ratio between higher orders.

2.4 Test Case

Figure 3 shows the plots for both second and third order using a variable-decoder of 0.8 rV and 0.2 rE for a sound source at $\theta = 93°$. The lower plot (c) shows 2.2 variable-order. The resultant variable-order has a maximum point between the two whole orders and the other lobes are smoothed out. The secondary lobes become more like an In-Phase decoder. The sum of the speakers for the variable-order, variable-decoder remains 1. Hence no normalisation of the speaker signals is needed. Due to the changing of the secondary lobe gains, the decoder type attributes associated to integer orders are lost.

2.5 Calculating in the Decoder

The methodology presented here to calculate the Variable-Order, Variable-Decoder Ambisonics has been to use a lookup table approach. First, all of the values between the two decoders for the lower and higher integer order are interpolated. Then the resultant variable-decoders for both orders are interpolated to produce the final signals. This has involved no creation of B-Format due to the speaker feeds directly being produced by multiplying the sound source by the resultant speaker gains. The same effect can be obtained by means of manipulating the decoder. To calculate a variable-order decoder directly, the $n = \mp m$ components for individual order $m = \lceil M \rceil$ of the variable order need to be multiplied by a factor, ν as shown in eq. (7), that is chosen by the user.

$$\begin{pmatrix} Y_{(0,0)}(spk1) \dots Y_{(\lceil M \rceil, -\lceil M \rceil)}(spk1) \; Y_{(\lceil M \rceil, \lceil M \rceil)}(spk1) \\ \vdots \qquad \ddots \qquad \vdots \qquad\qquad \vdots \\ Y_{(0,0)}(spkN) \dots Y_{(\lceil M \rceil, -\lceil M \rceil)}(spk1) \; Y_{(\lceil M \rceil, \lceil M \rceil)}(spkN) \end{pmatrix}^{\dagger} \begin{pmatrix} 1 \dots \nu \; \nu \\ \vdots \dots \ddots \vdots \\ 1 \dots \nu \; \nu \end{pmatrix} .$$

$$(7)$$

The decoder type gains can then be multiplied to eq. (7) by use of a further matrix. This uses the variable κ as the interpolation factor between the normal

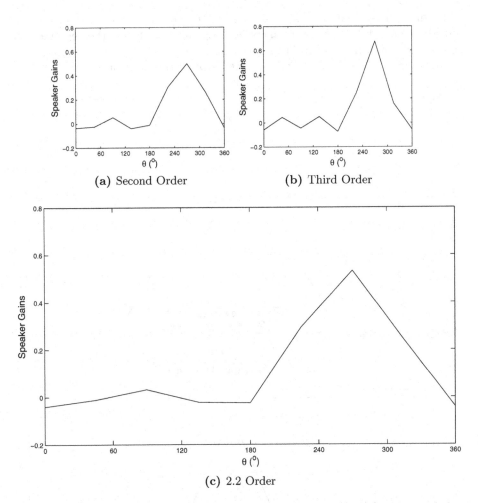

(a) Second Order

(b) Third Order

(c) 2.2 Order

Fig. 3. The speaker gains of $\theta = 93^o$ for second (a) and third (b) order and the gains for 2.2 order (c) using a variable-decoder as presented in section 2.2 with rV of 0.8 and rE of 0.2.

and g_{rE} or g_{rE} and $g_{In-Phase}$ gains as presented in section 1. The matrix to change the decoder type is given as:

$$\begin{pmatrix} 1 - \kappa_{(0,0)}(spk1) & \dots & 1 - \kappa_{(\lceil M \rceil, -\lceil M \rceil)}(spk1) & 1 - \kappa_{(\lceil M \rceil, \lceil M \rceil)}(spk1) \\ \vdots & \ddots & \vdots & \vdots \\ 1 - \kappa_{(0,0)}(spkN) & \dots & 1 - \kappa_{(\lceil M \rceil, -\lceil M \rceil)}(spkN) & 1 - \kappa_{(\lceil M \rceil, \lceil M \rceil)}(spkN) \end{pmatrix} \dots$$

$$\begin{pmatrix} \kappa g'_{(0,0)}(spk1) & \dots & \kappa g'_{(\lceil M \rceil, -\lceil M \rceil)}(spk1) & \kappa g'_{(\lceil M \rceil, \lceil M \rceil)}(spk1) \\ \vdots & \ddots & \vdots & \vdots \\ \kappa g'_{(0,0)}(spkN) & \dots & \kappa g'_{(\lceil M \rceil, \lceil M \rceil)}(spkN) & \kappa g'_{(\lceil M \rceil, \lceil M \rceil)}(spkN) \end{pmatrix} . \qquad (8)$$

The use of eqs. (7) and (8) are compared to the initial interpolation, or lookup table method in fig. 4. The original methodology as described in the beginning of this paper is shown in (a) and the direct manipulation of the decoder approach in (b). It can be seen that they do in fact result in the same outcome.

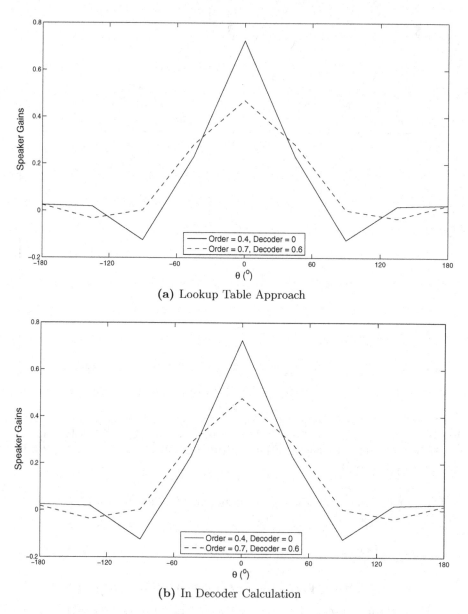

(a) Lookup Table Approach

(b) In Decoder Calculation

Fig. 4. This figure shows the identically produced speakers' gains for a sound source placed at $\theta = 0^o$ using both the lookup table approach and calculating the variable-order and variable-decoder within the decoder.

2.6   rV, rE, Power and Energy of Variable-Ambisonics

widt To further examine this system's behaviour as a result of the variable-order and variabe-decoder, the rV and rE vectors proposed by Gerzon [3, 11, 12, 14, 31] will be evaluated, as well as the power and energy values upon which those metrics are based. The results are displayed in fig. 5. Between zeroth and first order the rV linearly goes between zero and one. This is a somewhat obvious result as zeroth order has no directionality and first order is the minimum for a directional response. The power for which is the denominator for calculating rV, resulting in a constant value of one for each value of θ. This is to be expected since the speakers are regularly spaced and meet the minimum N criterion of $N > 2M + 1$. Although an expected result, it does determine that variable-order is valid for rV cues and that the power is constant irrespective of variable-order. The rE result however is an interesting one. We can see that the rE is maximised at approximately $m + 0.6$ orders, not at the whole integer orders. This can be attributed to the polar pattern produced becoming more like an rE decoder polar pattern than an rV decoder. The response of rE is not linear to the $m + 0.6$ points but curved either side. Conversely the energy is not maximised at $m + 0.6$ orders. The energy between integer orders shows an exponential growth. These results indicate that the variable-order effect should be examined for the variable-decoders.

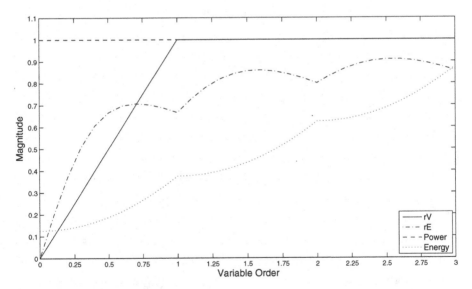

Fig. 5. The rV and rE vector, power and energy values for zeroth through to third order for Variable-Order, Variable-Decoder Ambisonics. The decoder used is the regular rV decoder from the pseudo-inverse function. The values are independent of θ since in a regular speaker array the rV, rE, power and energy are constant for $N > 2M + 1$.

Figure 6 shows the rV vector (a), rE vector (b) and energy (c) values for variable-orders of variable-decoder. The power is not shown in this figure as for all cases it has a value of one. Thus for power the Variable-Order, Variable-Decoder Ambisonics satisfies the constant power condition. The rV plot shows that the

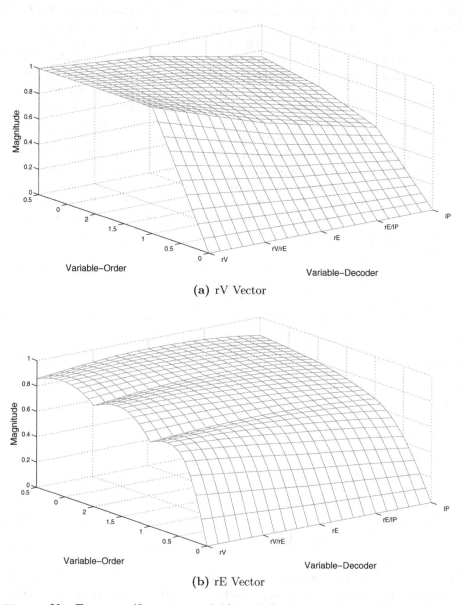

(a) rV Vector

(b) rE Vector

Fig. 6. rV, rE vector (figures a and b) and Energy attributes (figure c) of Variable-Order, Variable-Decoder Ambisonics. Under various conditions the intermediate order values are not linear between the normal integer orders.

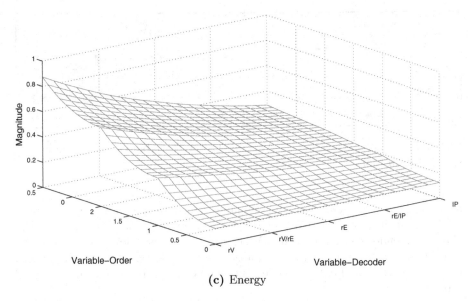

(c) Energy

Fig. 6. (*Continued*)

rV vector is reduced as the variable-decoder increases from zero. For all variable-decoder values the rV linearly increases between integer order values. For the same variable-order the rV value is linear between rV and rE decoders, and then the rE and In-Phase decoders. The rE values show that the curved nature of the rV decoder for variable-order is smoothed out as the variable-decoder increases above one. The rE decoder shows a slight curve between the integer orders in rE value, but for the In-Phase decoder the increase is linear between integer orders. The results show that for the $m + 0.6$ order the rV decoder now performs similarly to the In-Phase decoder for rE value. Finally, the energy plot shows the reduction of the curvature of energy value as the variable-decoder is increased from zero order. It shows that the energy is always greatest for variable-decoder of zero, rV decoder, and falls in value as the variable-decoder is increased. The maximum energy values for a variable-order are for the rV decoder. It can be determined that the greater energy value does not result in the best rE vector value.

To conclude, using variable-order can result in a heightened rE vector value for Variable-Order, Variable-Decoder Ambisonics and is better than the next highest integer order. This is where the rE value is maximised around the $m + 0.6$ point.

2.7   Composition/Production Tool Implementation

The tool to use the variable-order and variable-decoder methodology has been implemented in the Max/MSP 5 software environment for Mac OSX. The tool is designed to receive audio signals from digital audio workstations (DAW), e.g. via Jack or Soundflower, for a total of 16 monaural and 4 stereo signals. The controls

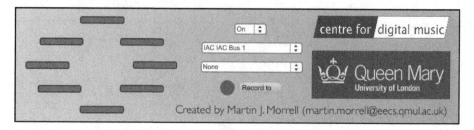

Fig. 7. The user interface for the Variable-Order, Variable-Decoder Ambisonics spatialisation tool

for each channel are sent via midi commands which are stored in a digital audio workstation project. User Control Panels were built for this function for the Cubase/Nuendo environment, but VSTs, AUs or other midi capable software can be used to control the settings for each sound source. The premise for this is that no extra saved data is needed that cannot be stored in a common DAW project.

Figure 7 shows the user interface for the tool. The user definable parameters on the interface are On/Off, midi driver, audio driver and where to save a recorded file. The interface has eight LED style meters for monitoring the signal level going to each speaker so that distortion can be avoided. Since users may not always have an eight speaker layout available, a binaural (over headphones) mix is simultaneously available.

2.8   Distance

Distance is a user definable parameter and is accomplished by gain attenuation only. No delay has been included since for music purposes pitch shifting of sound sources will affect the overall tonal effect and harmonicity of the work, alter the speed and therefore ensemble timing of the music and finally can include zipper noise. The $1/r$ inverse law is used to implement the gain change at sources greater than 1.0 where the maximum value is 10. Since the roll off of $1/r$ simulates anechoic conditions, the feature is given as a creative and not real-world application. For sources that are placed inside the speaker layout the distance calculation changes to $1 + \cos(90^\circ r)$ so that infinite gain is not reached. The maximum gain at the central position is 2.0, or approximately +6dB.

2.9   Inside Panning

Sound sources that have a distance of less than 1.0 are placed inside the speaker array. This is done by altering the reproduced polar pattern. If the order of reproduction is 1 then this is the same as cancelling out the 1st order spherical harmonics and doubling the zeroth order spherical harmonics. This methodology was first presented in [19]. For the case of third order two-dimensional Ambisonics, the maximum allowed in this tool, the inside-panning function is expanded.

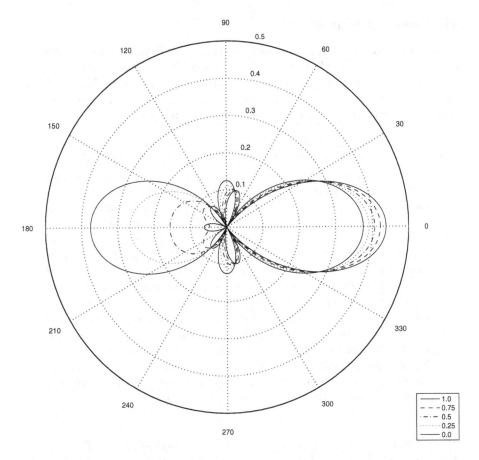

Fig. 8. The change in polar pattern exerted by a third order sound source as it is moved from a distance of 1.0 to 0.0 to be placed in the middle of the speaker array

The result is that even orders are doubled and odd orders are cancelled out. This again is all done as numerical and not audio calculations. Figure 8 shows the polar pattern change going from 1.0 to 0.0. The result is strong lobes from opposite poles giving the psychoacoustic illusion of the sound source being at the centre of the array.

2.10   Reverberation

Reverberation is produced in the tool by transforming the sound source into B-Format and processing it through either the Wigware VST (Virtual Studio Technology) reverberation plugin [31] based on the freeverb algorithm or by using a convolution plugin using B-Format impulse responses, such as those available [20, 30].

2.11   Original Composition

The authors commissioned a composer to create a multimedia piece that used the creative aspects of the Variable-Order, Variable-Decoder tool and technology. The piece was originally written for speakers and video projection. The work has subsequently been shown at various events and is available as a binaural version online. The following describes the work in the composer's words:

> *The composition was written with the intention of being realised through the use of the Variable-Order, Variable-Decoder Ambisonics two-dimensional tool for an octagonal speaker arrangement (ed. as described in section 2.7). This allowed for a greater creativity in conveying layers within the musical scene at varying distances, widths and positions across a horizontal plane. The tool helped create a greater sense of foreground and background. Placing the 'mechanical' elements in the distance and wide when in city surroundings for example, but brought to the centre and narrowed when portraying a specific man-made character/element such as the record player, horse, dog and heart. The cello and violin parts were generally placed in the stereo field in accordance with their on-screen presence but the distance feature was employed to convey the strength of the character's emotions, getting closer at climax points to create intensity for the listener. The tool was used most creatively in trying to achieve a sense of movement through swirling musical layers around the full range of the eight speakers for example in the rapid bustling city and spiral staircase scene, equally in the slow panning of the opening and pier scenes.*

When working with the composer on the mixing stage of the work, the effect of the source width could be clearly heard, as well as the distance change. The aspect of width helped enhance the use of the space surrounding the listener and the use of distance emphasised the busy nature of the world being portrayed by objects coming and going. The use of rotating the sound field was successfully used to indicate character movement and disorientation. The use of the variable-decoder was sparse, partly due to overlapping of the variable-order control where both alter the sound source width, but where the variable-order is far more intuitive to the user, in this case, the composer.

3   Variable-Polar Pattern Reproduction

Since the final output of an Ambisonics reproduction to the speakers is the same as sampling a polar pattern [3] exhibited by the audio source material, a new method is created whereby the intermediary B-Format and decoding is omitted.

Eargle [6, 21] gives two formulations for calculating higher order polar patterns. The first is given for calculating cardioid patterns in the form of $G = (0.5 + 0.5\cos(\theta))cos^{(M-1)}(\theta)$ for the Mth order, which is expanded for any base polar pattern in eq. (9) below. We define a base polar pattern as that created as a mixture of zeroth, A, and first, B, order components to calculate a gain G at horizontal angular position θ. Where $A + B = 1$ is constant.

$$G = (A + B \cos(\theta)) \cos^{(M-1)}(\theta) . \tag{9}$$

The second equation for a higher order pattern is given as the product of two or more first order microphone patterns:

$$G = (A_1 + B_1 \cos(\theta)) (A_2 + B_2 \cos(\theta)) \ldots (A_M + B_M \cos(\theta)) . \tag{10}$$

where $A_{1\ldots M}$ and $B_{1\ldots M}$ are the zeroth and first order terms for each order. To keep controls to a minimum we can limit the possible polar patterns so that $[A_1, B_1] = [A_2, B_2] = [A_M, B_M]$. By using this identity we can use a variable order for M below:

$$G = \begin{cases} (A + B \cos(\theta))^M & M \text{ is odd} \\ -(|A + B \cos(\theta)|^M) & M \text{ is even} \end{cases} . \tag{11}$$

Figure 9 shows the differences for calculating omni-directional, cardioid and figure-of-eight polar patterns using eq. (9) method and eq. (11) method. It can be seen for method A that for the omni-directional above first order the pattern changes to a figure-of-eight pattern of order $M - 1$. When looking at higher order cardioid for method A, we see that rear lobes are formed on the cardioid pattern. Finally the figure-of-eight pattern for method A behaves as expected and so are not shown; as the order increases the angular distance between the -3dB points decreases, giving a narrower polar pattern around the maxima and minima points. In the results of eq. (11) method, the omni-directional pattern remains omni-directional at all orders. The cardioid pattern for eq. (11) method does not develop rear lobes, but becomes a beam like pattern. Finally the figure-of-eight pattern for eq. (11) method behaves like that of method A, as we expect; a tighter figure-of-eight with greater side rejection. From these findings eq. (11) method will be used as it produces the most useful higher order polar patterns.

The gain applied to the Lth speaker is given as:

$$G_L = \begin{cases} (A + B \cos(\theta - \theta_L))^M & M \text{ is odd} \\ -(|A + B \cos(\theta - \theta_L)|^M) & M \text{ is even} \end{cases} . \tag{12}$$

To maintain a constant level whilst varying the order and/or polar pattern, like in the variable-Ambisonics method, a factor C is needed to scale the speaker gains:

$$C = \frac{1}{\sum\limits_{L=1}^{N} G_L} . \tag{13}$$

where the maximum order is based on N number of speakers being used, $M = (N - 2)/2$. Note that this will give a variable order and using the $\lfloor \rfloor$ function will give the highest integer order available.

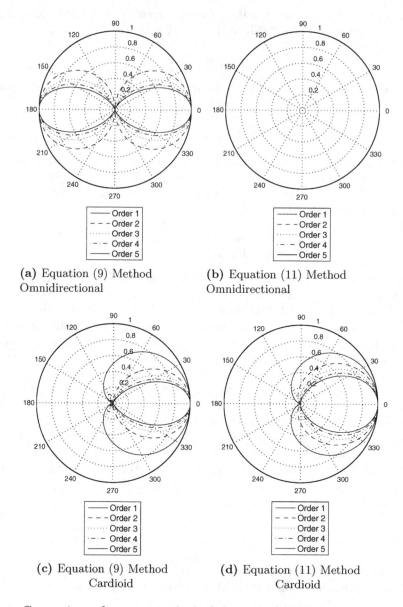

(a) Equation (9) Method
Omnidirectional

(b) Equation (11) Method
Omnidirectional

(c) Equation (9) Method
Cardioid

(d) Equation (11) Method
Cardioid

Fig. 9. Comparison of pattern methods A from eq. (9) and B from eq. (11) for omni-directional (a and b) and cardioid (c and d) as discussed in section 3

The produced gains for $\theta - \theta_L$ are shown in fig. 10. The sub-cardioid reproduction increases directivity with variable-order whilst the rear and side of the pattern is reduced in gain. The cardioid pattern has a constant zero point at the anti-pole, where the directivity and gain of the single positive lobe increases

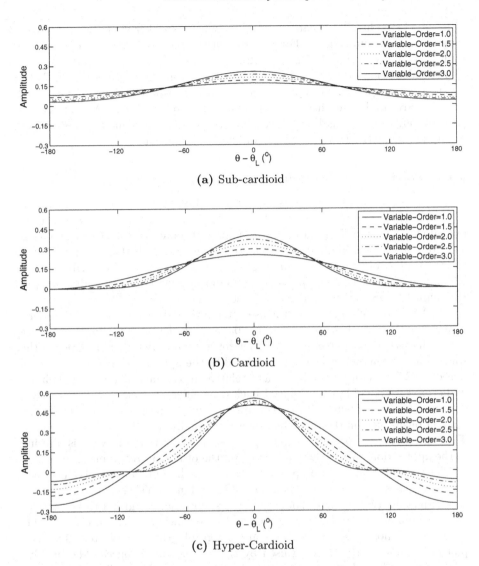

Fig. 10. Variable orders 1.0 to 3.0 for sub-cardioid (a), cardioid (b) and hyper-cardioid (c) polar patterns

with order. The hyper-cardioid pattern has a single negative lobe at the anti-pole of the main positive lobe. With an increase in order the directivity and gain of the main lobe increases whilst the negative lobe decreases in gain. Since this method uses a base polar pattern, of which the order can be changed variably, a user of a system can see the change in polar pattern easily. The figure-of-eight polar pattern poses a problem. Due to the equal gain of opposite polarities at anti-poles, the gains tend to infinity because of the cancellation when calculating

C in eq. (13). This also creates a problem since a speaker signal would have a maximum above unity gain. For this reason the base polar pattern should be limited so that $0 \leq A \lesssim 0.75$ in eq. (12).

The calculation of speaker gains in this way is similar to 3DVMS [2, 7, 16, 29], three dimensional virtual microphone synthesis, where higher order cardioid patterns are used. This has been compared to Ambisonics by Manola et. al. [16], although in their findings there were errors of localisation circa 180° which questions the methods used and the validity of the results.

3.1   Real-Time Application

A demonstration application was built using Max/MSP that is controlled and fed audio by a digital audio workstation. Audio is sent from each track using outputs via Jack OS X audio router as monaural sound sources. Control data is sent from a VST audio plugin on each audio track using the OSC (Open Sound Control) protocol [32] using a similar, but reverse, idea to that described in [8]. The audio plug-in does not process the audio in any way as its only use is to communicate OSC commands in this system environment.

The VST presents controls to the user; Azimuth, Pattern, Order and Speakers. The Azimuth control is ranged [-180 180]^o anti-clockwise. The Pattern control varies the base polar pattern. The Order control alters the variable order of the sound source. This control's range is altered by the Speakers control as described in section 3. Therefore it can be set as a relative maximum order, especially if the audio mixture is going to be played back over different speaker configurations. The Speaker control has the range [4 12] in whole integers to represent the amount of speakers in the reproduction array. Finally the VST has 20 programs. These programs are presets to change the audio track that the VST is altering in the application. When changing program the other controls remain the same.

The Max/MSP application presents the user with minimal controls since they are for the most part received from the VSTs within the DAW project. The user can turn audio processing on/off, select the sound source's graph to be plotted, view the number of speakers being used and see output meters for the 12 possible speakers. Of most interest to a user are the graphs that are plotted. This is a plot of the polar pattern being used by the chosen sound source. The positive lobe is shown in red and the negative in blue within the applications display window. This is plotted on top of up to twelve black circles representing the speaker positions. This gives the user visual feedback of how the controls of the VST are affecting the sound source reproduction. The graph to make things clear is normalised, meaning eq. (13) is ignored for plotting purposes to avoid confusion to the user.

3.2   Vector Driven Variable-Polar Pattern Reproduction

Vector Base Amplitude Panning [23–28] in two dimensions gives the same result as the cosine/sine power panning law resulting between the two speakers neighbouring the sound source. This fact can be exploited to calculate the highest order reproducible by the neighbouring speakers. If the sound source is assumed to be directly inbetween the speakers and that the polar pattern reproduced is that of a cardioid, where the most highly directional sound source is desired, then the highest order can be calculated. The differing cardioid patterns are shown for different speaker separation in fig. 11. Equation (14) shows the calculated highest order, M_V, under these assumptions.

$$M_V = \frac{\log\left(\frac{1}{\sqrt{2}}\right)}{\log\left(0.5 + 0.5\cos\left(\theta_{ML}\right)\right)} .\tag{14}$$

Where θ_{ML} is the angle between the mid-point of the neighbouring speakers and one of the speakers, or put another way; the angular separation between the neighbouring speakers divided by two.

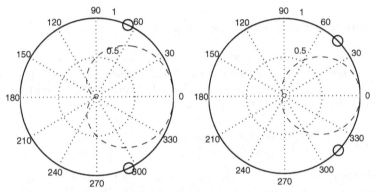

(a) Speaker separation θ_{ML} of 65.53°.

(b) Speaker separation θ_{ML} of 45°.

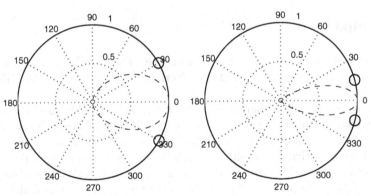

(c) Speaker separation θ_{ML} of 30°.

(d) Speaker separation θ_{ML} of 15°.

Fig. 11. The cardioid patterns calculated for four different speaker separations; 65.53°, 45°, 30° and 15°. The respective M_V values are 1.00, 2.19, 5.00 and 20.17.

This could be expanded for any polar pattern by taking the logarithm of eq. (11) in the denominator of eq. (14). Caution has to be taken when using polar patterns with negative lobes. It is not guaranteed, due to the speaker placement, that the negative gains will be reproduced at all. This could result in the exhibited polar pattern varying with the source position as M_V is changing.

It is, however, not guaranteed that the sound source will be in the middle of the two neighbouring speakers. When at a speaker's location the sound source is only reproduced by that speaker alone and therefore the calculated order would be infinite as there is no directional truncation. To overcome this problem the two neighbouring midpoints between the closest three speaker are found. The highest order of both midpoints is found using eq. (14) and then interpolated based on the angular distance between the sound source and the speaker midpoints. Finally the interpolated M_V is used in eq. (12) to find the initial speaker gains and the power kept constant by eq. (13). This procedure is shown in the flow diagram in fig. 12.

3.3   Expanding to Three-Dimensions

Expansion from the two-dimensional formulae used so far to three-dimensions is trivial. Expanding this theory to the three-dimensional case requires replacing the $\cos(\theta)$ terms to $\cos(\theta)\sin(\phi)$ in eqs. (10), (11) and (12). The resulting three-dimensional polar pattern is thus given as:

$$G_L = \begin{cases} (A + B\cos(\theta - \theta_L)\sin(\phi - \phi_L))^M & M \text{ is odd} \\ -\left(|A + B\cos(\theta - \theta_L)\sin(\phi - \phi_L)|^M\right) & M \text{ is even} \end{cases}. \quad (15)$$

where ϕ is the elevation angle of the sound source and ϕ_L the elevation angle of the speaker gain being calculated. The speaker gains will need normalising after calculation using eq. (13).

4   Comparison

In this section we present a comparison between the Variable-Order, Variable-Decoder Ambisonics system and the Variable-Polar Pattern Reproduction system.

It can be seen in the difference between the speaker gains shown in figs. 1, 3 and 10 that the former system gives a higher degree of directionality due to higher gain at the main lobe position. However, it does also introduce more rear lobes of both negative and positive gain, whereas the latter system retains the amount of rear lobes throughout the change of variable-order. The controls of altering a base polar pattern and variable-order are intuitive to an end user and have a clear distinction when looking at the plots of altering one or another of the parameters. With the first system this is not the case and the two variable controls both alter the same attributes of the polar pattern, although in different ways.

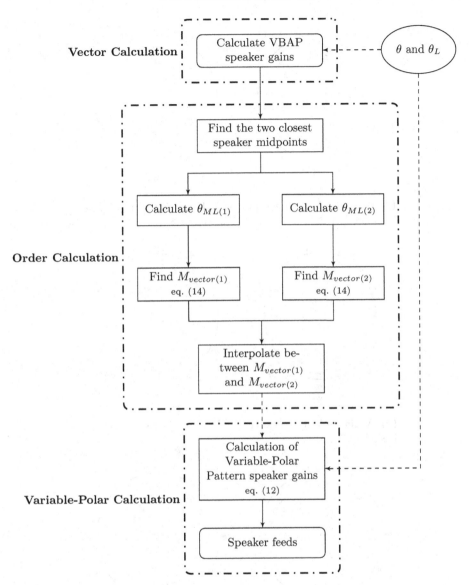

Fig. 12. Block diagram of the calculation of the Vector Driven Variable-Polar Pattern Reproduction. The Variable-Polar Pattern block could be exchanged for Variable-Order, Variable-Decoder Ambisonics or other spatialisation method.

A comparison between the two methods can be drawn using the rV and rE vectors. Figure 13 shows this comparison using 2.5 order. The left column shows the results for the Variable-Order, Variable-Decoder Ambisonics system and the right column the results for the Variable-Polar Pattern Reproduction system. The In-Phase decoder and cardioid pattern both produce identical polar patterns

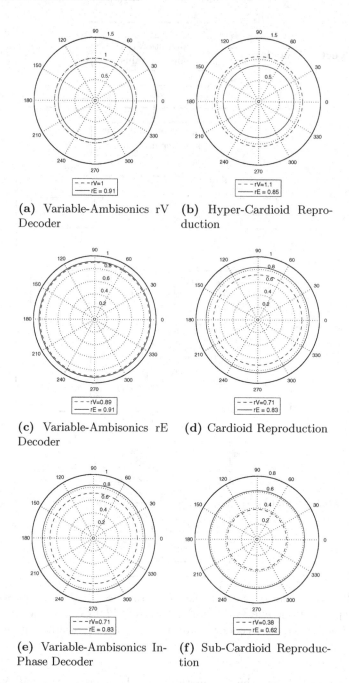

(a) Variable-Ambisonics rV Decoder

(b) Hyper-Cardioid Reproduction

(c) Variable-Ambisonics rE Decoder

(d) Cardioid Reproduction

(e) Variable-Ambisonics In-Phase Decoder

(f) Sub-Cardioid Reproduction

Fig. 13. Comparison of variable-ambisonics and variable source pattern using rV and rE vectors to represent low and high frequency directional cues presented in section 4 for order 2.5

and so have the same rV and rE values. High frequencies are localised better than lower frequencies. The rV decoder and hyper-cardioid are similar in that they both have rear negative lobe(s). The hyper-cardioid has an rV above 1.1 which is unseen in Ambisonics unless the decoding is done for an order that the speakers cannot be replayed on and in that case is an error. The rV decoder however has better high frequency localisation than the hyper cardioid. The sub-cardioid, as one might expect, has poor localisation for both high and low frequencies.

5   Conclusion

Two novel spatial audio systems have been presented and used in real applications that give end users, such as composers, musicians, sound engineers or sound designers, further creative freedom of spatial audio reproduction other than angular position and distance attenuation. The systems have been based on the theoretical underpinnings of Higher Order Ambisonics, however, by eliminating the use of B-Format as a sound scene representation results in a channel based approach like that of stereo, 5.1 and 7.1. It could be argued that by removing the sound field representation format that it has lost one of the best traits of Ambisonics, although in many situations such spatial audio systems are designed for a particular exhibition or speaker reproduction environment where the B-Format signal is not published or shared.

The first system presented here has been used to produce an animation sound track exploring the creative use of the system. From this experience and the composer's feedback the second system was developed. Overall the second system offers intuitive user controls and a wider degree of freedom.

Examples of both these systems are available as binaural sound tracks for playback over headphones and can be seen at:
www.elec.qmul.ac.uk/digitalmusic/audioengineering/spatialaudio/index.html.

Acknowledgments. This research was supported by the Engineering and Physical Sciences Research Council [grant number EP/P503426/1].

References

1. Benjamin, E.: Ambisonic loudspeaker arrays. Audio Engineering Society Convention 125 (October 2008)
2. Capra, A., Chiesi, L., Farina, A., Scopece, L.: A spherical microphone array for synthesizing virtual directive microphones in live broadcasting and in postproduction. In: Proceedings of 40th AES International Conference, Spatial Audio: Sense of the Sound of Space, Tokyo, Japan, October 8-10 (2010)
3. Daniel, J.: Représentation de champs acoustiques, application à la transmission et à la reproduction de scènes sonores complexes dans un contexte multimèdia. Ph.D. thesis, l'Universite Paris 6 (2000)
4. Daniel, J.: Spatial sound encoding including near field effect: Introducing distance coding filters and a viable, new ambisonic format. In: Audio Engineering Society Conference: 23rd International Conference: Signal Processing in Audio Recording and Reproduction (May 2003)

5. Daniel, J., Moreau, S.: Further study of sound field coding with higher order ambisonics. Audio Engineering Society Convention 116 (May 2004)
6. Eargle, J.: The Microphone Book. Focal Press (2001)
7. Farina, A., Binelli, M., Capra, A., Armelloni, E., Campanini, S., Amendola, A.: Recording, simulation and reproduction of spatial soundfields by spatial pcm sampling (sps). In: International Seminar on Virtual Acoustics, Valencia, Spain, November 24-25 (2011)
8. Freed, A., Zbyszynski, M.: Osc control of vst plug-ins. In: Open Sound Control Conference, July 30 (2004)
9. Furness, R.K.: Ambisonics-an overview. In: Audio Engineering Society Conference: 8th International Conference: The Sound of Audio (May 1990)
10. Furse, R.W.: Building an openal implementation using ambisonics. In: Audio Engineering Society Conference: 35th International Conference: Audio for Games (February 2009)
11. Gerzon, M.A.: Periphony: With-height sound reproduction. J. Audio Eng. Soc. 21(1), 2–10 (1973)
12. Gerzon, M.A.: Practical periphony: The reproduction of full-sphere sound. Audio Engineering Society Convention 65 (February 1980)
13. Gerzon, M.A., Barton, G.J.: Ambisonic decoders for hdtv. Audio Engineering Society Convention 92 (March 1992)
14. Heller, A., Lee, R., Benjamin, E.: Is my decoder ambisonic? Audio Engineering Society Convention 125 (October 2008)
15. Käsbach, J., Favrot, S.: Evaluation of a mixed-order planar and periphonic ambisonics playback implementation. Forum Acusticum 2011 (2011)
16. Manola, F., Genovese, A., Farina, A.: A comparison of different surround sound recording and reproduction techniques based on the use of a 32 capsules microphone array, including the influence of panoramic video. In: AES 25th UK Conference: Spatial Audio in Today's 3D World, York, UK, March 25-27 (2012)
17. Menzies, D.: W-panning and o-format, tools for object spatialization. In: 22nd International Conference on Virtual, Synthetic and Entertainment Audio (June 2002)
18. Moore, D., Wakefield, J.: The design of ambisonic decoders for the itu 5.1 layout with even performance characteristics. Audio Engineering Society Convention 124 (May 2008)
19. Morrell, M.J., Baume, C., Reiss, J.D.: Vambu sound: A mixed-technique 4-d reproduction system with a heightened frontal localisation area. In: AES 25th UK Conference: Spatial Audio in Today's 3D World, York, UK, March 25-27 (2012)
20. Murphy, D.T., Shelley, S.: Openair: An interactive auralization web resource and database. Audio Engineering Society Convention 129 (November 2010)
21. Olson, H.F.: Elements of Acoustical Engineering, 2nd edn. D. Van Nostrand Comapny, Inc. (1957)
22. Poletti, M.A.: Three-dimensional surround sound systems based on spherical harmonics. J. Audio Eng. Soc. 53(11), 1004–1025 (2005)
23. Pulkki, V.: Virtual sound source positioning using vector base amplitude panning. J. Audio Eng. Soc. 45(6), 456–466 (1997)
24. Pulkki, V.: Creating generic soundscapes in multichannel loudspeaker systems using vector base amplitude panning in csound synthesis software. Organised Sound 3(2), 129–134 (1998)
25. Pulkki, V.: Uniform spreading of amplitude panned virtual sources. In: Proceedings of the 1999 IEEE Workshop on Applications of Signal Processing to Audio and Acoustics, pp. 187–190. Mohonk Mountain House, New Paltz (1999)

26. Pulkki, V.: Generic panning tools for max/msp. In: The International Computer Music Conference, Berlin, Germany, pp. 304–307 (August 2000)
27. Pulkki, V.: Spatial Sound Generation and Perception By Amplitude Panning Techniques. Ph.D. thesis, Helsinki University of Technology (2001)
28. Pulkki, V., Karjalainen, M.: Directional quality of 3-d amplitude-panned virtual sources. In: The 7th International Conference on Auditory Display, Espoo, Finland, pp. 239–244 (July 2001)
29. Scopece, L., Farina, A., Capra, A.: 360 degrees video and audio recording and broadcasting employing a parabolic mirror camera and a spherical 32-capsules microphone array. In: IBC 2011, Amsterdam, September 8-11 (2011)
30. Stewart, R., Sandler, M.: Database of omnidirectional and b-format room impulse responses. In: ICASSP 2010 (2010)
31. Wiggins, B.: Has ambisonics come of age? Proceedings of the Institute of Acoustics 30(pt. 6) (2008)
32. Wright, M., Freed, A., Momeni, A.: Opensound control: State of the art 2003. In: Proceedings of the 2003 Conference on New Interfaces for Musical Expression (NIME 2003), Montreal, Canada (2003)

Perceptual Characteristic and Compression Research in 3D Audio Technology

Ruimin Hu, Shi Dong, Heng Wang, Maosheng Zhang, Song Wang, and Dengshi Li

National Engineering Research Center for Multimedia Software
School of Computer Science, Wuhan University, Wuhan, 430072, China
{hrm1964,wh825554,eterou,wangsongf117}@163.com,
edisonds@gmail.com, reallds@126.com

Abstract. The 3D audio coding forms a competitive research area due to the standardization of both international standards (i.e. MPEG) and localized standards (i.e. Audio and Video Coding Standard workgroup of China, AVS). Perception of 3D audio is a key issue for standardization and remains a challenging problem. Besides current solutions adopted from traditional audio engineering, we are working for an original 3D audio solution for compression. This paper represents our initial results about 3D audio perception include directional measurement of Just Noticeable Difference (JND) and Perceptual Entropy (PE). We also represent the possible applications of these results in our future researches.

Keywords: 3D audio, perceptual audio processing, audio compression.

1   Introduction

With the current trend of 3D movies and the popularization of 3DTV, 3D audio and video technology has become a research topic in multimedia technology. To provide the audience with a more immersive and integrated audio-visual experience, audio must work collaboratively with 3D video to provide three dimensional sound effects. However, existing 3DTV and 3D movie systems usually adopt conventional stereo audio and surround sound technology, which only provides very limited sound localization ability and envelopment in horizontal plane. Although there is not a generally acknowledged definition for 3D audio, it is widely accepted that 3D audio must have the following characteristics; localization of sound image in arbitrary direction in 3D space, realizing the distance perception of sound and giving a improved feeling of audio scene. Nowadays two types of technology are able to satisfy the requirement of 3D audio, one is based on physical principles and aims at reconstructing the original sound field, the other is based on principle of human perception and aims at giving the listener a virtual sound image. Wave Field Synthesis (WFS), Ambisonics and 22.2 multichannel systems are three typical 3D audio systems following those principles.

This paper is arranged as follows. In Sect. 2 an introduction to the three 3D audio systems is presented and the existing problems are discussed, where we conclude the complexity of the 3D systems and efficiency of the signal compression will be two problems for the popularization of 3D audio. In Sect. 3 we present our related work in

M. Aramaki et al. (Eds.): CMMR 2012, LNCS 7900, pp. 82–98, 2013.
© Springer-Verlag Berlin Heidelberg 2013

3D audio technology, including hearing mechanism and signal compression research. More specifically, we investigate the JND of the direction perception cues for human in horizon plane. This is useful in simplification the 3D audio recording and playback systems, and removing the redundant perceptual information in 3D audio signals. In Sect. 4 the development trends of 3D audio and our future work are discussed.

2   Brief View of Typical 3D Audio Systems

2.1   Wave Field Synthesis (WFS)

a. The Principle of Wave Field Synthesis
The concept of WFS was introduced by Berkhout in 1988 [1], its physical theory can date back to Huygens principle which suggests that a wave which propagates from a given wave front can be considered as emitted either by the original sound source or by a secondary source distribution along the wave front [2]. To reconstruct the primary sound field, the distribution of secondary source can replace primary source. The concept was later developed by Kirchhoff and Rayleigh, and the Kirchhoff-Helmholtz integral they proposed can be interpreted as follows: if appropriately secondary sources are driven by the values of the sound pressure and the directional pressure gradient caused by the virtual source on the boundary of a closed area, then the wave field within the region is equivalent to the original wave field [3]. By adding a degree of freedom to the secondary source distribution, Kirchhoff-Helmholtz generalized Huygens principle.

b. Realization of WFS
According to the above theory, WFS reproduces the primary sound field in time and space by making using of small and individually driven loudspeakers array, and can recover the spatial image precisely in the half space of receiving end from loudspeaker arrays [4].

But there is some limit for WFS in application. WFS needs a continuous, closed surface and a large number of idealized loudspeakers, but in practice there is only a discontinuous loudspeaker array. According to spatial nyquist sampling Theorem, if the interval between loudspeakers is less than half the wavelength of a sound wave, aliasing will not occur [5].

So according to spatial nyquist sampling Theorem, WFS can be realized by limited and discrete loudspeakers within a certain frequency range. For example, limited line loudspeaker with even intervals can reconstruct sound field in 2D horizontal plane [6]. In the recording stage, the listening area is surrounded by a microphone array. The microphone array consists of pressure and velocity microphones, which record the primary sound field of external sound sources. In the reconstruction stage, the microphones will be replaced by the loudspeakers. Each loudspeaker is driven by signal recorded by the corresponding microphone. The geometric shape of the microphone array and loudspeaker are the same [7].

2.2   Ambisonics

a. The Principle of Ambisonics

Ambisonics emerged in the 1970's and the main contributor is Gerzon [8]. The principles of Ambisonics are as follows. A certain wave (sound field) can be expanded on a sphere in sphere coordinate system by spherical harmonic functions. At the opposite end, superposition of spherical harmonic functions can rebuild a wave (sound field). There are n=2m+1 spherical harmonic functions at every order m of Ambisonics, a 3D system of M order consists of all spherical harmonic functions at every order m ($0{\leq}m{\leq}M$), total channel number N satisfies N=(M+1)2.

b. Two Simple Format of Ambisonics

The first format of Ambisonics proposed by Gerzon is B format, which displays an omnidirectional sound field by four channels: W, X, Y, Z [9]. Traditional monophony and stereophony can be seen as the subsystems of Ambisonics [10]. Sound location in horizontal plane is realized using three channels W, X, Y, and the fourth channel Z is used for reconstructing height information. Channel W is a pressure signal, and X, Y, Z are directional signal. B-format is used in studio and professional application.

The second format of Ambisonics is UHJ system which can convert directional sound into two or more channels and solve the incompatibility problem of four channels Ambisonics with monophony, stereophony [11, 12]. The coding scheme provided by UHJ can be used in broadcasting, digital audio recording [13].

c. Playback Technology of Ambisonics

According to the principle of Ambisonics, the decomposition of a sound field requires the expansion of infinite order spherical harmonic functions. But in practical application, limited order truncation of spherical harmonic functions expansion is necessary. B-format is one order expansion. Ambisonics was expanded to high order in the 1990's, the sweet point was enlarged to an area. High order Ambisonics promotes sound location with the price of more channels and loudspeakers. We can get better reconstruction quality using higher order Ambisonics. The encoding process of Ambisonics is to preserve the result of spherical harmonic functions multiplying the signal picked up by microphones. The decoding process is to calculate a group of loudspeaker signals according to the rebuilt sound field that must be equal to the primary sound field at listening point. This can be done by solving the inverse matrix which consists of spherical harmonic functions that are associated with locations of loudspeakers.

2.3   22.2 Multichannel Sound Systems

a. Fundamentals of Multichannel Sound Systems

The research of spatial hearing and sound source localization indicates that there are slight time and level differences between two ears when spatial sound signals arrive at the ears. For the estimation of direction and distance of sound source, the difference between the two ears signals is most relevant. Actually these differences, called binaural cues, are Interaural Time Difference (ITD) and Interaural Level Difference (ILD). ILD and ITD indicate the level difference and time difference between left and right ears respectively [14].

b. Stereo, 5.1 Surround Sound and 22.2 Multichannel System

The binaural localization theory is utilized in stereo system, i.e. time and level differences between signals from two loudspeakers are utilized in sound reproduction in order to reconstruct the spatial perception of the audience.

Traditional stereo cannot provide the sense of encirclement and immersion because the perception of the sound environment mainly relies on the lateral reflected sound. Surround sound, which constitutes an extension of stereophony, provides full spatial immersion by using reverberation and reflection. The most typical multichannel surround systems are the Dolby surround system, DTS Digital Surround.

Since loudspeakers in Dolby 5.1 are arranged in the same horizontal plane, the reproduction sound image cannot be extended to three dimensions. In 2009, Dolby laboratory presented ProLogic IIz, which extended Dolby 7.1 with height channels (7.1+2). By reproducing early and late reflections and reverberation, ProLogic IIz provide a much wider range of spatial sound effects such as spatial depth and spatial impression [15]. The ProLogic IIz configuration is showed in Fig. 1. Audyssey Dynamic Surround Expansion (DSX) is a scalable technology that expands auditory perception by adding height channels, which is in a similar way to Dolby 9.1.

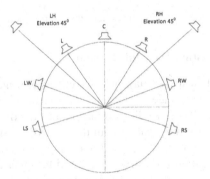

Fig. 1. Dolby IIz configuration

NHK laboratory developed the 22.2 multichannel prototype system in 2003. The system consists of three layers of loudspeakers and overcome the lack of height perception with 3D immersion and sound image localization. K. Hiyama and Keiichi Kubota evaluated the minimum number of loudspeakers and its arrangement for reproducing the spatial impression of diffuse sound field respectively [16]. The results showed that if the interval between adjacent loudspeakers is 45° in both horizontal and vertical plane, there is sufficient horizontal sound envelopment and a good sense of spatial impression. Therefore, the 22.2 multichannel system consists of loudspeakers with a middle layer of ten channels, an upper layer of nine channels, and a lower layer of three regular channels and two Low Frequency Effects (LFE) channels. Fig. 2

shows detailed arrangement of loudspeakers [17]. The vertical loudspeaker interval of the 22.2 multichannel is around 45°, which can induce the vertical spatial uniformity [18]. The 22.2 multichannel system reproduces sound images in all three dimensional directions around a listener and stable sound localization over the entire screen area. Subjective evaluations shows that subjects have better impressions using Ultrahigh-Definition TV (UHDTV) contents with 22.2 multichannel sound system than with Dolby5.1 system [19].

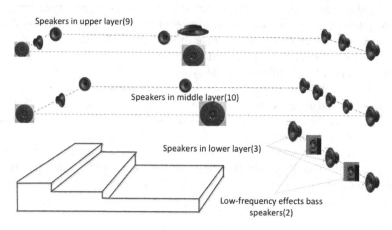

Fig. 2. 22.2 multichannel system layout

2.4   Problems of Existing 3D Audio Systems

Not need to know the loudspeaker layout at the encoding stage is the main advantage of Ambisonics, at decoding stage the loudspeaker signal can be counted according to the loudspeaker layout. The encoding format is an effective reconstruction of 3D sound field, allowing for direct dealing with the three dimensional space characteristics of the sound field such as rotation and mirroring. But along with the increase of order, more precise direction information is carried by spherical harmonic functions, which provides a more accurate location. But data quantity increases rapidly, which requires higher CPU processing power. In addition, the hypothesis that the location of the listener is known may lead to a limit listening area.

The character of WFS is that Kirchhoff-Helmholtz integral can ensure the rebuilt sound field synthesized by secondary sources is the same as the primary source, preserving time and space characteristics of primary source. So listeners can receive and locate the sound source as if it were a real listening space, and walk in the listening area at will while sound image remains unchanged. But WFS needs more loudspeakers and has a higher requirement for site and equipment which is expensive.

The research on compression of Ambisonics and WFS is limited, although recently some progress [20,21,22] has been made. But the compression efficiency cannot meet the requirement of real-time broadcasting and transmitting.

The 22.2 multichannel system, which is based on conventional surround systems plus high and low channels to produce three dimensional sound images, can be easily downmixed for 5.1 system reproduction. It is likely to become a popular 3D system since terminals can be set up with little cost using simplified configuration (10.1 and 8.1 channels), especially when the 5.1 system has already been installed. In 2011, ITU (Report BS.2159-2) pointed out that the 22.2 multichannel system has some problems to be solved: The method to localize more efficiently by using the upper and lower layers and how to reproduce three dimensional sound image movements. In addition, although it is not difficult to downmix 22.2 channel signals to 5.1 channel signals, the 3D spatial audio effects are discarded. Hence, producing three dimensional effects in home entertainment environments with limited loudspeakers is a problem. Furthermore, without compression, the data rate of 22.2 system can reach 28Mbps and the size of an one-hour audio file is about 100Gb. As a result, it is not possible for the current storage device and transmission channel to adapt to this enormous data. The application and development of 22.2 multichannel systems are constrained by the technology of compression.

3   Hearing Mechanism and Compression Research in 3D Audio

3.1   The Research of Hearing Mechanism

From mono, stereo, surround sound, and then to the 3D audio, the main line of development in audio systems is to extend the range of the sound image. Audiences are able to locate the sound which is any position around them in order to bring them a better sense of encirclement and immersion. The positioning of spatial orientation for sound sources is an important content of 3D audio, while the study of perceptual characteristics is an important research field of 3D audio. For example, the arrangement position of the 24 speakers in 22.2-channel system is based on the test and analysis of the angle resolution of sound in horizontal and vertical plane by human ear. In addition, the perceptual research of spatial orientation parameters for sound source is also important for the efficient encoding of the multi-channel audio signal. Therefore, the perceptual characteristics of sound source localization parameters in the 3D sound field are an important way to solve the problems of 3D audio systems.

The perceptual sensitivity of the sound source in the horizontal plane is significantly better than that of the vertical plane or distance by the human auditory system. In the horizontal plane, the positioning of the sound source is dependent on the two binaural cues: ITD and ILD. The human ear can perceive a change in sound image orientation only when the difference of binaural cues reaches a certain threshold value. This threshold value is known as Just Noticeable Difference (JND). The influencing factors of JND for binaural cues are various, including frequency and orientation of the sound source. A wide range of measurements and analysis of these factors has been performed.

Hershkowitz in 1969 [23] and Mossop in 1998 [24] have been researching the influence of sound source position on the perceptual threshold JND of ITD and ILD. The results show that the greater the difference of left and right channels in intensity and time, the larger the JND value of the human perception. This shows that the human ear is less sensitive when the sound source is closer to the left and right sides.

Millers in 1960 measured JNDs of ILD on the midline with pure tones and there were 5 Normal-Hearing (NH) subjects took part in the experiment [25]. The result is as follows: JNDs were around 1dB for 1000Hz, around 0.5dB for frequencies higher than 1000Hz and somewhat smaller than 1dB for frequencies lower than 1000Hz. The test data showed worse sensitivity of ILD at 1000Hz than at either higher or lower frequencies. Larisa in 2011 has been researching the influence of the frequency of the signal on the JND of ITD. The results showed that the perceptual threshold of ITD has a strong dependence on the frequency [26].

The measurement data of JND for binaural cues were fragmented and the conclusions were generally described qualitatively for perceptual threshold of binaural cues. It is difficult to perform mathematical analysis and model accurately and cannot fully reveal the principal of the perceptual threshold of binaural cues. So the JND measurement of binaural cues in all-round, full-band and the mathematical analysis are important issues to reveal the perceptual characteristics of binaural cues. In order to solve the above problem, we have undertaken the research of perceptual characteristics for binaural cues:

In order to study the impact of the frequency and direction on binaural cues JND, our team measured full band JND of binaural cues and analyzed its statistics and distribution characteristics.

a. Subjects. 12 NH subjects participated in this study, 7 males and 5 females, all subjects were aged between 19 and 25 years.

b. Stimuli. The method in this article used a two-alternative-forced-choice paradigm to measure the JND. Both reference and test signals were 250 ms in duration including 10 ms raised-cosine onset and offset ramps. They were randomly combined into stimulus and separated by 500 ms duration. The stimuli were create by personal computer and presented to the subjects over headphones (Sennheiser HDA 215) at a level of 70 dB SPL. In order to exclude other factors influence on this experiment, the environment of the entire testing process should be consistent and the intensity of test sound must remain around 70 dB SPL. Meanwhile the ITD should be zero in the whole experiment in order to remove the effect on the result caused by other binaural cues and the sum of energy of left and right channels should remain unchanged.

The reference values of ILD in these experiments were 0, 1, 3, 5, 8 and 12 dB, which respond to 6 azimuths (about 0~60°) in the horizontal plane from midline to the direction of the left ear.

The whole frequency domain was divided into 20 sub-bands, each frequency sub-band satisfied the same perceptual characteristics of human ear.

The stimuli are pure tones whose frequencies are the center frequencies of sub-bands, these frequencies are 75, 150, 225, 300, 450, 600, 750, 900, 1200, 1500, 1800, 2100, 2400, 2700, 3300, 4200, 5400, 6900, 10500, 15500 Hz.

c. Method. Discrimination thresholds were estimated with an adaptive procedure. During any given trial, subjects would listen to two stimuli by activating a button on a computer screen by mouse-click, with a free number of repeats but the order of two stimulus were changed. The subjects should indicate which one was lateralized to the left relatively by means of an appropriate radio button response in 1.5 s.

An adaptive, 1-up-3-down method was also used in this article. The difference of ILD in dB was increased in every one wrong or decreased in every three consecutive correct judgments. The difference between reference and test signals in first trials was the initial variable, which was much larger than the target JND, it was changed by an given step according to previous test results.

The step was changed adaptively, it was adjusted by 50% for the first two reversals, 30% for the next two reversals, then linear changed in a small step size for the next three reversals, until the final step size reach the expected accuracy for the last three reversals. In a transformed-up-down experiment, the stimulus variable and its direction of change depend on the subjects' responses. The direction alternates back and forth between "down" and "up". Every transform between "down" and "up" was defined as a reversal.

Because of heavy workload of these experiments, adaptive test software was designed to simplify the experiments and the process of data collection and analysis. The software automatically generated test sequences and played one after another. According to the listener's choice, the software changed ILD values of test stimulus properly, and saved the results to excel sheet until listener hardly distinguished the orientation differences between two sequences. And the value of ILD at this time was the JND value.

d. Results. After a subjective listening test for half a year, we got 120 groups (six azimuths and twenty frequencies) of data, each group containing 12 JNDs corresponding to 12 subjects. For every group, we select the data that has the confidence degree of 75% to be JND in that condition. Some JND curves in different reference of ILD were plotted in Fig. 3:

- The curves vary with the reference ILD, the larger the reference ILD, the higher the corresponding curve. The JND is the most sensitive in the central plane for human perception, and the least sensitive at lateral.
- Human ear is most sensitive to the middle frequency bands except 1000 Hz and less sensitive to the high frequency bands and low frequency bands.

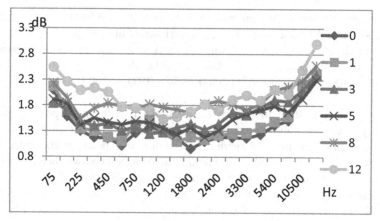

Fig. 3. JND curve of ILD with different frequencies and reference ILD

A binaural perceptual model is established and used in quantisation of ILD. It solves the problem of the perceptual redundancy removal of spatial parameters. Experimental results show that this method can reduce the bitrate by about 15% compared with parametric stereo, while maintaining the subjective sound quality.

3.2   Perceptual Information Measurement for Multichannel Audio Signal

Multimedia contents abound with subjective irrelevancy—objective information we cannot sense. For audio signals, this means lossless to the extent that the distortion after decompression is imperceptible to normal human ears (usually called transparent coding). The bitrate can be much lower than for true lossless coding. Perceptual audio coding [27] by removing the irrelevancy greatly reduces communication bandwidth or storage space. Psychoacoustics provides a quantitative theory on this irrelevancy: the limits of auditory perception, such as the audible frequency range (20–20000 Hz), the Absolute Threshold of Hearing (ATH), and masking effect [28]. In state-of-the-art perceptual audio coders, such as MPEG-2/4 Advanced Audio Coding (AAC), 64 kbps is enough for transparent coding [29]. The Shannon entropy cannot measure the perceptible information or give the bitrate bound in this case.

For perceptual audio coding technology, determining the lower limit bitrate for transparent audio coding is an important question. Perceptual Entropy (PE) gives an answer to this question [30], which shows that a large amount of audio with CD quality can be compressed with 2.1 bit per sample. PE indicates the least number of bits for quantising mono audio channel without perceptual distortion. This is widely used in the design of quantisers and fast bit allocation algorithm.

Nevertheless, PE has significant limitations when measuring perceptual information. This limitation primarily comes from the underlying monaural hearing model. Humans have two ears to receive sound waves in a 3D space: not only is the time and frequency information perceived— needing just individual ears—but also spatial information or localization information—needing both ears for spatial sampling. Due to the unawareness of binaural hearing, PE of multichannel audio signals is simplified to the supposition of PE of individual channels. This is significantly larger than real quantity of information received because multichannel audio signals usually correlate.

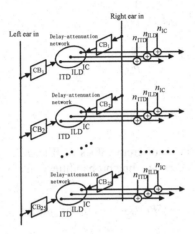

Fig. 4. Binaural Cue Physiological PerceptionModel (BCPPM)

Following the concept of PE, we establish a Binaural Cue Physiological Processing Model (BCPPM, Fig. 4). Based on MCPPM, we using EBR filter to simulate the human cochlea filter effect, and the JND of binaural cues to estimate the absolute threshold of spatial cues.

a. SPE Definition. From the information theory viewpoint, we see BCPPM as a double-in-multiple-out system (Fig. 4). The double-in is the left ear entrance sound and the right ear entrance sound. The multiple-out consists of 75 effective ITDs, ILDs, and ICs (25 CBs, each with a tuple of ITD, ILD, and IC). Like in computing PE, we view each path that leads to an output as a lossy subchannel. Then there are 75 such subchannels. Unlike PE, what a subchannel conveys is not a subband spectrum but one of ITD, ILD, and IC of the subband corresponding to the sub-channel. In each sub-channel, there are intrinsic channel noises (resolution of spatial hearing), and among sub-channels, there are interchannel interferences (interaction of binaural cues). Then there is an effective noise for each sub-channel. Under this setting, each sub-channel will have a channel capacity. We denote SPE(c), SPE(t), and SPE(l) for the capacity of IC, ITD, and ILD sub-channels respectively. Then SPE is defined as the overall capacity of these sub-channels, or the sum of capacities of all the sub-channels:

$$SPE = \sum_{all\ subbands} SPE(c) + SPE(t) + SPE(l) \qquad (1)$$

To derive SPE(c), SPE(t), and SPE(l), we need probability models for IC, ITD, and ILD. Although the binaural cues are continuous, the effective noise quantizes them into discrete values. Let [L·P], [T·P], and [C·P] denote the discrete ILD, ITD, and IC source probability spaces:

$$
\begin{aligned}
&[\mathbf{L}\cdot P] \begin{cases} \mathbf{L}: l_1, \ l_2, \ ..., \ l_i, \ ..., \ l_N \\ P(\mathbf{L}): \ P(l_1), \ \ P(l_2), \ \ ..., \ \ P(l_i), \ \ ..., \ \ P(l_N) \end{cases} \\[2mm]
&[\mathbf{T}\cdot P] \begin{cases} \mathbf{T}: t_1, \ t_2, \ ..., \ t_i, \ ..., \ t_N \\ P(\mathbf{T}): \ P(t_1), \ \ P(t_2), \ \ ..., \ \ P(t_i), \ \ ..., \ \ P(t_N) \end{cases} \\[2mm]
&[\mathbf{C}\cdot P] \begin{cases} \mathbf{C}: c_1, \ c_2, \ ..., \ c_i, \ ..., \ c_N \\ P(\mathbf{C}): \ P(c_1), \ \ P(c_2), \ \ ..., \ \ P(c_i), \ \ ..., \ \ P(c_N) \end{cases}
\end{aligned} \tag{2}
$$

where l_i, t_i, and c_i are the ith discrete values of ILD, ITD, and IC, respectively, and $P(l_i)$, $P(t_i)$, and $P(c_i)$ the corresponding probabilities. Then we have

$$
\begin{aligned}
SPE(l) &= -\sum_{i=1}^{N_L} p(l_i)\log_2 p(l_i) \\
SPE(t) &= -\sum_{i=1}^{N_T} p(t_i)\log_2 p(t_i) \\
SPE(c) &= -\sum_{i=1}^{N_C} p(c_i)\log_2 p(c_i)
\end{aligned} \tag{3}
$$

b. CB Filterbank. We use the same method as that in PE to implement the CB filterbank. Audio signals are first transformed to the frequency domain by DFT of 2048 points with 50% overlap between adjacent transform blocks. Then a DFT spectrum is partitioned into 25 CBs.

c. Binaural Cues Computation. ILD, ITD, IC are computed in the DFT domain as described in [31].

d. Effective Spatial Perception Data. The resolutions or quantization steps of the binaural cues can be determined by JND experiments. Denote by $\Delta\tau$, $\Delta\lambda$, and $\Delta\eta$ the resolutions of ITD, ILD, and IC, respectively. Generally, they are signal dependent and frequency dependent. For simplicity, we use constant values: $\Delta\tau = 0.02$ ms, $\Delta\lambda = 1$dB, and $\Delta\eta = 0.1$.

We ignore the effect of IC on ILD and only consider the effect of IC on ITD for SPE computation. Lower IC leads to lower resolution of ITD. This is equivalent to higher JND of ITD. Then the effective JND on subband b, denoted as $\Delta\tau'$ (b), can be formulated as the following:

$$
\Delta\tau'(b) = \frac{\Delta\tau(b)}{\text{IC}(b)} \tag{4}
$$

Then we have the following effective perception data $q_{ILD}(b)$, $q_{ITD}(b)$, and $q_{IC}(b)$ of ILD, ITD, and IC, respectively by quantization, where $\lfloor \cdot \rfloor$ represents the round down function:

$$q_{ILD}(b) = 2 \left\lfloor \left| \frac{ILD(b)}{\Delta\lambda(b)} \right| \right\rfloor$$

$$q_{ITD}(b) = 2 \left\lfloor \left| \frac{ITD(b)}{\Delta\tau(b) / IC(b)} \right| \right\rfloor \tag{5}$$

$$q_{IC}(b) = \left\lfloor \left| \frac{1 - IC(b)}{\Delta\eta(b)} \right| \right\rfloor$$

Suppose that $q_{ILD}(b)$, $q_{ITD}(b)$, and $q_{IC}(b)$ are uniformly distributed by (3), the SPE are expressed as

$$SPE = \frac{1}{N} \sum_{b=1}^{25} \alpha \log_2 \left(\text{int}\left(\frac{1 - IC(b)}{\Delta\eta(b)} \right) + 1 \right) + \alpha \log_2 \left(2 \, \text{int}\left(\left| \frac{ITD(b)}{\Delta\tau(b) / IC(b)} \right| \right) + 1 \right)$$
$$+ \alpha \log_2 \left(2 \, \text{int}\left(\left| \frac{ILD(b)}{\Delta\lambda(b)} \right| \right) + 1 \right) \tag{6}$$

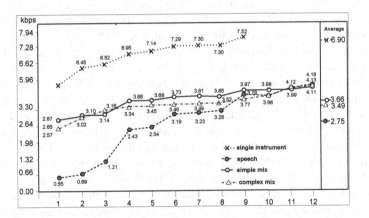

Fig. 5. Perceptual spatial information of stereo sequences sampled at 44.1 kHz. Four curves are speech, simple mixed audio, complex mixed audio and single instrument.

e. Results. Fig. 5 shows the SPE of four different stereo signals from MPEG test sequences. The experiment suggests that SPE of speech signal is very low. This is because the human voice is often recorded with fixed position without change. So coding this kind of stereo audio signals requires a low bit rate. The average SPE for speech signals is 2.75kbps, for simple mixed audio is 3.66kbps, for complex mixed audio is 3.49kbps and for a single instrument is 6.90kbps. In other words, to achieve transparent stereo effect, audio signals required more than 7kbps, which is close to the bitrate 7.7kbps of PS. So the proposed SPE can reflect the amount of perceptual spatial information that is ignored by PE. Experiments on stereo signals of different types have confirmed that SPE is compatible with the spatial parameter bitrate of PS.

Using PE to evaluate the perceptual information, only interchannel redundancy and irrelevancy are exploited; the overall PE is simply the sum of PE of the left and right channels. Using SPE based on BCPPM, interchannel redundancy and irrelevancy are also exploited; the overall perceptual information is about one normal audio channel plus some spatial parameters, which has significantly lower bitrate. For the above reason, PE gives much higher bitrate bound than SPE. PE is compatible with the traditional perceptual coding schemes, such as MP3 and AAC, in which channels are basically processed individually (except the mid/side stereo and the intensity stereo). So PE gives meaningful bitrate bound for them. But in Spatial Audio Coding (SAC), multichannel audio signals are processed as one or two core channels plus spatial parameters. SPE is necessary in this case and generally gives much lower bitrate bound ($\sim$1/2). This agrees to the sharp bitrate reduction of SAC.

4   Tendency of 3D Audio Technology and Our Future Work

4.1   Hearing Mechanism Research on 3D Audio

The spatial orientation cues of sound include three aspects: azimuth angle, elevation angle and distance. There are many acoustic factors to perceive the distance of a sound source, such as the source of the sound (sound pressure level and spectrum), the transmission environment (reflected sound, high-frequency losses and environmental noise) as well as listening factors. So the current research focuses on the expression and extraction of distance cues. Hence, the perceptual characteristic of the 3D spatial orientation is an important research direction for 3D audio technology.

Our future work will focus on the perceptual characteristics of 3D spatial orientation. The main work will include: design experiments to obtain perceptual threshold of 3D spatial position, mathematical analysis to establish representation model of perceptual sensitivity in 3D spatial orientation, get the perceptual distortion of sound image in the different offset of spatial orientation, obtain the equivalent distortion curve of azimuth angle and elevation angle in 3D spatial orientation, and to establish a position distortion model of 3D spatial position. Through the above research, we expect to establish the basic theory of perceptual mechanism for 3D audio systems and provide theoretical support for 3D audio collection, processing, reconstruction, playback and evaluation.

4.2   High Efficiency Compression for 3D Audio Signal

Existing 3D audio compression technology has exploited the perceptual redundancy within each individual channel. From the same sound field and same sound source, 3D audio signals of different channels intrinsically exhibit strong correlation. Parametric coding is able to extract the cues of sound image direction, width and scene information to reduce the interchannel redundancy, and achieve high compression efficiency using fewer channels with side information. Parametric coding for 3D audio is able to fulfill the compression requirement of transmission and storage while keep 3D effect meantime, so it is a strong direction in 3D audio compression research.

Since the compression is highly efficient, the reconstructed 3D effect strongly depends on the cues that described corresponding spatial information. The existing 3D audio parameter coding quantises those cues uniformly and reconstruction error in every direction is the same. However, according to human perceptual characteristic in 3D space, the JND to sound direction exists and varies widely in all directions. If reconstruction error for direction cues exceed corresponding threshold, perceptible 3D effect distortion is produced. So how to utilize human perceptual characteristics in 3D space for 3D audio parametric coding will be included in our future work. Our goal is to develop the 3D spatial perception information measurement and establish a computational model of 3D audio orientation perception for effective representation of 3D audio parameterization

4.3   The Evaluation of 3D Audio Quality

Along with the developments of the 3D audio technology, research institutions such as NHK [32] and Deutsche Telekom Laboratorie [33], are carrying out the subjective evaluation of the 3D audio system. Because the subjective evaluation is based on the human who is the main body directly involved in the evaluation, the result is more explicit and reasonable in spite of spending a lot of time and manpower during the period of the assessments. So, more and more scholars [34-36] are trying to establish the objective evaluation model for the 3D audio system, hoping to look for an objective evaluation model based on the human perception of the audio quality to assess the effects of a 3D sound field. The performance of the proposed model is comparable with the subjective evaluation method.

However, the current methods used to establish an objective evaluation model do not introduce the spectral cues related to the elevation perception of sound events, the envelopment or immersion in diffuse sounds, or the proximity and distance of sound events as the acoustic characteristic parameters. Research of the objective evaluation methods of the 3D audio is occuring on to investigate the spectral cues of the elevation, envelopment and distance perception of the 3D sound field.

In the study of the objective evaluation method of the 3D audio quality, we draw up an objective evaluation model, based on the acoustic characteristic parameters of a 3D audio signal, to predict the perceptual acoustic attributes of the 3D sound field. Including the Basic Audio Quality (BAQ), the Timbral Fidelity (TF), the 3D Frontal Spatial Fidelity (3DFSF) and the 3D Surround Spatial Fidelity (3DSSF). The study includes establishing the acoustic characteristic parameter set related to the 3D perceptual sound field, obtaining a predictable mapping of the perceptual acoustic attributes and the acoustic characteristic parameters of a 3D audio quality, and building up an objective evaluation model of the 3D perceptual sound field by fitting the performances of the subjective evaluation and objective evaluation. Because the main aim of this study is to express the spectral cues related to the elevation perception of a 3D sound field, we should try to analyze the duplex spectral effects of the pinna to further improve the technology of the 3D audio objective evaluation.

5   Conclusion

The complexity and large capacity limit the promotion and application of 3D audio. To solve these problems, the National Natural Science Foundation of China, Tsinghua University, Wuhan University and other colleges organized the Second International Symposium of 3D video and audio. In the 3D audio workshop, basic theory and research on the recording, compression and reconstruction for 3D audio was emphasized. We also hope to promote the research work to become part of the next generation standard for the audio and video coding (AVS2) of China. This paper gives a brief introduction on current 3D audio systems. At the same time, our research work on the hearing mechanism and compression coding are presented. Finally our future work is introduced, which includes the research of perception characteristic, compression coding and the quality evaluation.

Acknowledgments. This work is supported by National Natural Science Foundation of China (No.60832002, No.61102127), Major national science and technology special projects (2010ZX03004-003-03), Nature Science Foundation of Hubei Province (2010CDB08602, 2011CDB451), Wuhan ChenGuang Science and Technology Plan (201150431104), and the Fundamental Research Funds for the Central Universities.

References

1. Berkhout, A.J.: A holographic approach to acoustic control. Journal of the Audio Engineering Society 36, 977–995 (1988)
2. Berkhout, A., De Vries, D., Vogel, P.: Acoustic control by wave field synthesis. J. Acoust. Soc. Am. 93, 2764–2778 (1993)
3. Rabenstein, R., Spors, S.: Wave field synthesis techniques for spatial sound reproduction. In: Topics in Acoustic Echo and Noise Control, pp. 517–545. Springer, Heidelberg (2006)
4. De Vries, D.: Wave Field Synthesis: History, State-of-the-Art and Future (Invited Paper). In: ISUC 2008. Second International Symposium on Universal Communication, vol. 2008, pp. 31–35 (2008)
5. De Bruijn, W.: Application of wave field synthesis in videoconferencing, Delft University of Technology (2004)
6. Vogel, P.: Application of Wave Field Synthesis in Room Acoustics, Delft University of Technology (1993)
7. Daniel, J., Nicol, R., Moreau, S.: Further Investigations of High-Order Ambisonics and Wavefield Synthesis for Holophonic Sound Imaging. In: Audio Engineering Society Convention 114, Convention Paper 5788, Amsterdam, The Netherlands (2003)
8. Gerzon, M.A.: Ambisonics: Part two: Studio techniques. Studio Sound (1975)
9. Malham, D.G.: Spatial hearing mechanisms and sound reproduction. University of York (1998)
10. Furness, R.K.: Ambisonics-an overview. In: 8th International Conference: The Sound of Audio, pp. 181–189 (1990)
11. Keating, D.: The generation of virtual acoustic environments for blind people. In: Proc.1st Euro. Conf: Disability, Virtual Reality & Assoc. Tech., pp. 201-207. Maidenhead, UK (1996)

12. Elen, R.: Whatever happened to Ambisonics? AudioMedia Magazine (November 1991)
13. Gerzon, M.A.: Ambisonics in multichannel broadcasting and video. J. Audio Eng. Soc. 33, 859–871 (1985)
14. Strutt, J.W.: On our perception of sound direction. Philosophical Magazine 13, 214–232 (1907)
15. Theile, G., Wittek, H.: Principles in Surround Recordings with Height. Audio Engineering Society Convention, 130 (2011)
16. Hiyama, K., Komiyama, S., Hamasaki, K.: The minimum number of loudspeakers and its arrangement for reproducing the spatial impression of diffuse sound field. Audio Engineering Society Convention, 113 (2002)
17. Ando, A.: Home Reproduction of 22.2 Multichannel Sound. In: 5th International Universal Communication Symposium (2011)
18. Oode, S., Sawaya, I., Ando, A., Hamasaki, K., Ozawa, K.: Vertical Loudspeaker Arrangement for Reproducing Spatially Uniform Sound. Audio Engineering Society Convention, 131 (2011)
19. Hamasaki, K., Nishiguchi, T., Okumura, R., Nakayama, Y., Ando, A.: A 22.2 multichannel sound system for ultrahigh-definition TV (UHDTV). Smpte Motion Imaging Journal 117, 40–49 (2008)
20. Cheng, B., Ritz, C., Burnett, I.: A Spatial Squeezing approach to Ambisonic audio compression. In: IEEE International Conference on Acoustics, Speech and Signal Processing (ICASSP), pp. 369–372. IEEE (2008)
21. Hellerud, E., Solvang, A., Svensson, U.P.: Spatial redundancy in Higher Order Ambisonics and its use for lowdelay lossless compression. In: IEEE International Conference on Acoustics, Speech and Signal Processing 2009 (ICASSP 2009), pp. 269–272 (2009)
22. Pinto, F., Vetterli, M.: Space-Time-Frequency Processing of Acoustic Wave Fields: Theory, Algorithms, and Applications. IEEE Transactions on Signal Processing 58, 4608–4620 (2010)
23. Hershkowitz, R., Durlach, N.: Interaural Time and Amplitude JNDs for a 500 - Hz Tone. The Journal of the Acoustical Society of America 46, 1464–1465 (1969)
24. Mossop, J.E., Culling, J.F.: Lateralization of large interaural delays. The Journal of the Acoustical Society of America 104, 1574–1579 (1998)
25. Mills, A.W.: Lateralization of High - Frequency Tones. The Journal of the Acoustical Society of America 32, 132–134 (1960)
26. Dunai, L., Hartmann, W.M.: Frequency dependence of the interaural time difference thresholds in human listeners. The Journal of the Acoustical Society of America 129, 2485–2485 (2011)
27. Painter, T., Spanias, A.: Perceptual coding of digital audio. Proceedings of the IEEE 88, 451–515 (2000)
28. Moore, B.C.J.: Masking in the Human Auditory System. In: Audio Engineering Society Conference: Collected Papers on Digital Audio Bit-Rate Reduction. Audio Engineering Society, New York (1996)
29. Bosi, M., Goldberg, R.E.: Introduction to digital audio coding and standards. Kluwer Academic Publishers, Boston (2003)
30. Johnston, J.D.: Transform coding of audio signals using perceptual noise criteria. IEEE Journal on Selected Areas in Communications 6, 314–323 (1988)
31. Faller, C., Baumgarte, F.: Binaural cue coding—part II: schemes and applications. IEEE Transactions on Speech and Audio Processing 11(6), 520–531 (2003)

32. Hamasaki, K., Hiyama, K., Nishiguchi, T., Okumura, R.: Effectiveness of Height Information for Reproducing the Presence and Reality in Multichannel Audio System. In: Audio Engineering Society Convention, Paris, France, vol. 120 (2006)
33. Geier, M., Wierstorf, H., Ahrens, J., Wechsung, I., Raake, A., Spors, S.: Perceptual evaluation of focused sources in wave field synthesis. In: AES 128th Convention, pp. 22–25 (2010)
34. George, S.: Objective models for predicting selected multichannel audio quality attributes, Department of Music and Sound Recording, University of Surrey (2009)
35. Epain, N., Guillon, P., Kan, A., Kosobrodov, R., Sun, D., Jin, C., Van Schaik, A.: Objective evaluation of a three-dimensional sound field reproduction system. In: Proceedings of 20th International Congress on Acoustics, Sydney, Australia (2010)
36. Song, W., Ellermeier, W., Hald, J.: Psychoacoustic evaluation of multichannel reproduced sounds using binaural synthesis and spherical beamforming. The Journal of the Acoustical Society of America 130, 2063–2075 (2011)

Intuitive Control of Rolling Sound Synthesis

Simon Conan, Mitsuko Aramaki, Richard Kronland-Martinet, and Sølvi Ystad

Laboratoire de Mécanique et d'Acoustique (LMA), CNRS UPR 7051,
Aix-Marseille Université, Centrale Marseille,
31 Chemin Joseph Aiguier, 13402 Marseille Cedex 20, France
{conan,aramaki,kronland,ystad}@lma.cnrs-mrs.fr

Abstract. This paper presents a rolling sound synthesis model which can be intuitively controlled. For that purpose, different aspects of the rolling phenomenon are explored: physical modeling, perceptual studies and signal morphology. Based on these approaches, we propose a synthesis model that reproduces the main perceptual features responsible for the evocation of rolling action. Finally, a control strategy based on ball's properties (perceived size, asymmetry, speed, trajectory) and the irregularity of the surface is proposed.

Keywords: Rolling Sounds, Sound Synthesis and Control, Environmental Sound Synthesis, Sound Invariants, Physically Informed Synthesis, Rolling ball.

1 Introduction

This study is part of a larger project (*MétaSon*[1]) which aim is to build a realtime sound synthesis platform that offers intuitive controls of sounds to end users. In fact nowadays almost any everyday sound can be realistically synthesized, but the question of intuitive control of sound synthesis processes is still a substantial challenge. For instance, an impact sound can be represented and synthesized by a sum of exponentially decayed sinusoids [38]. However, obtaining a specific impact sound reflecting for instance the material, size or shape of the impacted object by acting directly on the synthesis parameters (amplitudes, frequencies and damping coefficients of the sinusoidal components) is quite impossible, even for expert users. To cope with this problem, perceptually relevant signal structures have to be identified through listening tests to define mapping strategies that enable such intuitive controls.

One aim of the *MétaSon* project is to propose a sound synthesizer with associated high-level (or intuitive) controls. To achieve this, we assume that the sound (signal) contains so-called sound *invariants*, *i.e.* signal morphologies that are responsible for the recognition of particular sound events [15,27]. These *invariants* can be either *structural invariants* or *transformational invariants*. Structural invariants reflect the intrinsic properties of an object and enable us to recognize it, whereas *transformational invariants* are linked to external interactions with

---

[1] http://metason.cnrs-mrs.fr/

M. Aramaki et al. (Eds.): CMMR 2012, LNCS 7900, pp. 99–109, 2013.

this object and enable us to recognize the actions that produced the sound. For instance a string produces a sound with a particular spectro-temporal structure that is recognized by the listener, even if it is bowed (violin), plucked (guitar) or hit (piano). Likewise, it is possible to recognize that a cylinder bounces even if it is made of glass, wood or metal [25]. Hence, "if an event is something happening to a thing, the *something happening* is presumed to be specified by *transformational invariants* while the *thing* that it is happening to is presumed to be described by *structural invariants*"[28].

For instance, Warren and Verbrugge studied auditory *transformational invariants* with recorded bouncing and breaking glass sounds [39]. They first showed listeners' ability to differentiate these sounds, then they identified the specific patterns responsible for the recognition of the interaction and then validated the identified *transformational invariants* by synthesis. Concerning the object, listening tests revealed that the evocation of a specific material is correlated to the damping of spectral components [37,21,16] and to the roughness [2], while the hardness of the striking mallet is related to the characteristics of the time attack [13]. Aramaki *et al.* used the results of such studies to propose an impact sound synthesizer with high-level controls [3] that enables the user to directly control perceived attributes of sound sources such as the object's material or size. These previous studies confirm that these *invariants* are strong enough to evoke both the object an the interaction with this object.

On the basis of these *structural* and *transformational invariants*, we propose a sound synthesis *action/object* paradigm in which the sound is defined as the result of an action on an object. In this paradigm, the object's properties are separated from the interactions it is subjected to. From a synthesis point of view, we used subtractive synthesis models based on a source-filter structure. This kind of model originally came from speech analysis and synthesis [4], but has also been studied in the context of musical sounds [31] and in the context of continuous interaction sound synthesis [38,22]. The source-filter model is an approximation of physical modeling : it stands that in an interaction, the physical exciter (for instance the vocal folds in the case of speech production) is decoupled from the resonator (the vocal tract). In the case of voiced vowel synthesis, the excitation (source) is a pulse train which is passed through a filter bank that simulates the vocal tract resonance for a particular vowel. In the case of rubbing sounds for instance, the interaction (source) can be represented by an adequate excitation signal while the object's modes (filter) can be represented by an adequate resonant filter bank [14].

This paper is devoted to a particular type of interaction, the rolling action. In the next section we will present the literature on rolling sounds, then in the 3 we will propose a sound synthesis model for rolling sounds. Section 4 will be devoted to the control strategy, and in the last section we will conclude and propose some perspectives for this work.

2   Previous Studies on Rolling Sounds

Different approaches to the synthesis of rolling sounds can be found in the literature. Physical modeling of the phenomenon and the computation of equations with finite difference scheme has been proposed. Stoelinga et al. derived a physical model that produces rolling sounds [32] from previous studies on impact sounds on damped plates [10,23]. This model can reproduce phenomena like the Doppler effect, which is also found in the measures. However, sound examples are not fully convincing, i.e. the sounds do not clearly evoke rolling objects. This can be explained by the lack of amplitude modulation, as the model considers the rolling object as a perfect sphere (i.e. the mass center is the geometrical center), which is never the case in reality. It is important to note that these models cannot be computed in real time.

Another approach is the physically informed modeling. In [17], Hermes proposed a synthesis model that consisted of simulating the excitation by a series of impacts following a Poisson law amplitude modulated to account for the asymmetry of the ball. This pattern was further convolved with the impulse response of the object (represented by a sum of gamma-tones) on which the ball rolled. The author justified the shape of the impulse response by the fact that the collisions between the ball and the plate are "softer" than in a classical representation that uses a sum of exponentially decaying sinusoids. Otherwise, in order to feed the source-filter model with parameters from real recorded sounds, Lagrange et al. [22] and Lee et al. [24] proposed an analysis/synthesis scheme. This scheme consists in extracting the excitation pattern (considered as a series of micro impacts) and the object's resonances (the resonance of the rolling object and the surface on which it rolls are not separated). Van den Doel et al. [38] proposed a model where modal resonators were fed with a noise whose spectral envelope was defined by $\sqrt{1/(\omega - \rho)^2 + d^2}$ where ρ and d are respectively the frequency and the damping of the resonance, in order to enhance the resonance near the rolling object's modes. The authors also proposed a similar source-filter model to generate rubbing sounds. In both of these models, the velocity is conveyed by filtering the signal with a lowpass filter whose cutoff frequency is tuned according to the motion's speed. Rath proposed a model for rolling sounds which is between physical modeling and physically informed considerations [30]. Based on a nonlinear contact model for impact sound synthesis [5], Rath added a supplementary physically inspired control layer to produce rolling sounds. More details concerning this model will be given later (Sect. 3.1).

As far as sound "invariants" related to the evocation of rolling objects are concerned, several studies can be found in the literature. For instance, Houben et al. studied the auditory ability to distinguish the largest or the fastest ball between two recorded sounds. They showed that at constant velocity (respectively at constant size) listeners can distinguish the largest (respectively the fastest) rolling ball with good accuracy. The performance is impaired when the two factors (i.e. velocity and size) are crossed [19]. They also attempted to identify acoustic cues that characterize the size and speed of rolling balls, like auditory roughness or spectral structure. The influence of spectral and temporal properties was studied in [20] by crossing the temporal content of a stimulus with the spectral content of another stimulus and using the obtained sound (the obtained stimulus had its spectrum very close to one stimulus and its temporal envelope very close to the other stimulus) in a perceptual experiment. It was shown that only the spectral structure was used to determine the fastest or largest ball and that results were better for the size judgement than for the speed judgement. However only recordings without clear amplitude modulations (due to an unbalanced ball or a deviation from perfect sphericity) were used in the experiment. This can explain why no temporal cues were found. The authors further investigated the influence of this amplitude modulation in [18]. Artificial amplitude modulations were added to the recordings used in the previous experiments. Perceptual experiments showed that amplitude modulations clearly influence the perceived size and speed.

Another important perceptual effect is caused by the influence of the modes of the support on which the ball rolls. These modes are excited differently along the ball's trajectory, depending on the excitation point. This effect can be observed as varying ripples in the time-frequency representation of rolling sounds and is due to the interference between the sound generated at the point of contact between the ball and the plate and the sound reflected at the edges of the plate [33]. Murphy *et al.* [29] performed a series of perceptual experiments to judge the quality of the analysis-synthesis algorithm described in [22]. In a first experiment, the listeners described the rolling sounds as "static". Then they simulated the ball's displacement with a time-varying comb filter, which resulted in rolling sounds that were perceived as more realistic.

Based on those previous studies on synthesis and perception of rolling sounds, we will propose a sound synthesis scheme in the next section.

3   Sound Synthesis Model

The proposed synthesis model aims at reproducing the main perceptual features behind the evocation of rolling actions. For that, we explored different aspects of the rolling phenomenon (physical, perceptual and signal morphology) and we concluded on the relevance of the following attributes: the nonlinear interaction force between the rolling ball and the plate, the amplitude modulation due to the imperfect sphericity of the ball, the timbre variation induced by the displacement of the contact point along the trajectory and the timbre variation induced by the ball's velocity. In the proposed synthesis scheme, each of these attributes are reproduced by separate processes. Hence, we here propose a modular approach to synthesize rolling sounds. Each step of this sound synthesis model will be detailed in this section.

3.1   Nonlinear Interaction Force

From our point of view, the model proposed by Rath [30] produces the most convincing sounds. This model consists in transforming a physical model of colliding objects into a rolling sounds model. Basically, the model proposed by

Avanzini *et al.* [5] allows to produce bouncing sounds. This model couples an exciter (a hammer or a ball for instance) to a resonant object (which is defined by its modes, each of them represented by a mass-spring-damper system) with a nonlinear interaction force that takes into account the compression and the velocity of compression between the two colliding objects [26] as described in the equations below:

$$\begin{cases} x = x_e - x_r \\ \ddot{x}_r + g_r \dot{x}_r + \omega_r x_r = \frac{1}{m_r} f(x, \dot{x}) \\ \ddot{x}_e = -\frac{1}{m_e} f(x, \dot{x}) + g \end{cases} \tag{1}$$

with

$$f(x, \dot{x}) = \begin{cases} kx^\alpha + \lambda x^\alpha \dot{x} & , x > 0 \\ 0 & , x \le 0 \end{cases} \tag{2}$$

The terms labeled with an r stands for the resonant object and those labeled with an e for the exciter (for further information on the physics or on the implementation, refer to [5,30]). The term x represents the compression between the two objects, and f is the nonlinear interaction force between the exciter and the surface that depends on the compression x. By adding a time-varying signal that captures the fact that a rolling ball "scans" the rough surface on which it rolls in a particular way to the compression term, this model produces sounds that clearly evoke a ball rolling on a rough surface. As one can note in Fig. 1, this interaction force is a series of impacts. Moreover, this force has a particular structure, *i.e.* it evolves over time in a particular way and the impacts are related in a specific manner.

It is possible to synthesize a signal that captures the main characteristics of this nonlinear interaction force (paper in preparation). Indeed, we can simulate

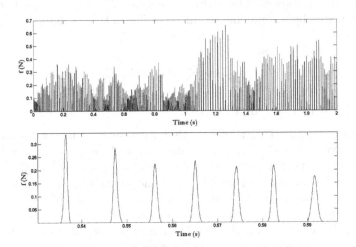

Fig. 1. Interaction force between the ball and the surface resulting from a simulation of the synthesis model proposed by [30] *(top)* and a zoom on this force *(bottom)*

the behavior of the two time series by the amplitudes of the impacts (A^n) and the intervals between each impact (Δ_T^n). Thus, our model allows to reproduce series of Dirac pulses with specific statistics.

Then, each Dirac pulse is shaped by an impact model. A simple and efficient impact model is the raised cosine (see [8]). Moreover, as the interaction force is nonlinear, the impact's duration varies with its amplitude [9,6]. This effect is taken into account. The sharpness of the pulses, which affect the sound's brightness, can also be controlled by empirically using an additional exponent ξ in the original raised cosine model. The used pulse model is then :

$$F_{\text{exc}}(n) = \begin{cases} \frac{F_{\max}}{2^\xi} \left[1 - \cos\left(\frac{2\pi n}{N_{\text{exc}}}\right)\right]^\xi & , n \in [\![0, N_{\text{exc}}]\!] \\ 0 & , \text{otherwise} \end{cases} \tag{3}$$

with $F_{\max}$ the impact's amplitude and N_{exc} the impact duration.

From a perceptual point of view, we observed that it is the nonlinear interaction force between the rolling ball and the plate that carries the main relevant information that characterizes the action *to roll*. This force can be considered as a transformational invariant related to the rolling action and, in the proposed synthesis paradigm {source/resonance}, as the source signal. Indeed, by convolving the computed force resulting from the interaction of a rolling ball and a rough surface with an impulse response of a resonant object, a realistic rolling sound is produced.

3.2 Amplitude Modulation

As exposed in Sect. 2, Houben showed that modulating the amplitude of rolling sounds influence the perceived size and speed [18]. Such an amplitude modulation can be due to imperfect sphericity of the rolling marble, or to the asymmetry of its mass center. As proposed by multiple authors [17,18,30], the modulation can be approximated by a sinusoidal modulation. Thus, the incoming signal $f(t)$ is modulated as :

$$y(t) = [1 + m \cos(2\pi\nu_m t)] f(t) \tag{4}$$

with $\nu_m \propto \dot{x}/r$, $\dot{x}$ and r are respectively the ball's velocity and radius.

3.3 Position Dependent Filtering

As previously pointed out, a marble that rolls on a plate excites its modes differently along its trajectories, depending on its location on the plate. This effect is due to the interference between the sound generated at the point of contact between the ball and the plate and the sound reflected at the edges of the plate [33]. Each reflected source is the delayed version of the sound, and the delay time of each comb filter can be calculated thanks to an image source method [1]. Hence, we simulate the reflection of the four first order images for a square plate, depending on a chosen listening point on the plate, on the ball's position and on the first natural frequency of the plate. As already pointed out by Murphy *et al.* [29], this effect enhance the sensation of the ball's displacement.

3.4   Velocity Dependent Filtering

In the synthesis model for rubbing sounds proposed by Van den Doel *et al.* [38], the transversal velocity of the contact point controls the cutoff frequency of a lowpass filter. This is important for the rendering of the gesture velocity sensation. As we found that using this lowpass filtering step in the rolling sound synthesis model also convey information about velocity of the rolling ball, this effect is added to our rolling model.

The whole synthesis scheme is presented in Fig. 2. The associated controls will be presented in the next section.

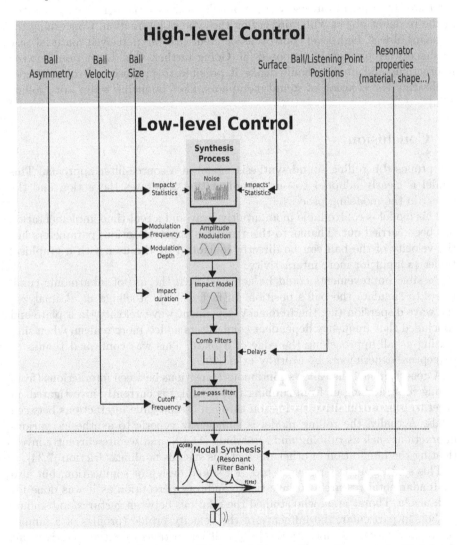

Fig. 2. General framework of the synthesis model to produce rolling sounds. High-level controls associated with the resonant surface were proposed in [3].

4   Control Strategy

Intuitive controls that are adapted to non-expert users are displayed in the upper part of Fig. 2. The proposed controls on the ball's properties are its perceived size, asymmetry, speed and trajectory. The irregularity of the surface can also be controlled. The mapping between high- and low-level controls (*i.e.* synthesis parameters defined in Sect. 3) are also presented in Fig. 2.

As one can note, the action is clearly separated from the resonant object (the surface on which the ball rolls) according to our paradigm. This means that the source part of the model can be modified to evoke interactions, independently of the resonant object. Conversely, it is possible to change the perceived properties of the resonant object while preserving the type of interaction. Concerning the resonant object, high-level controls associated with the perceived material, size or shape were previously proposed [3]. Going further, this distinction between interactions and object should make it possible to propose control strategies facilitating the creation of sound metaphors, like "bouncing water" or "rolling wind".

5   Conclusion

We proposed a rolling sound synthesis model in a source-filter approach. This model is clearly adapted to our paradigm that separates the action and the object in the modeling process.

This model is controllable in an intuitive way and a real-time implementation has been carried out. Thanks to this real-time implementation, parameters like the velocity of the ball can be directly controlled by the user with a graphical tablet as input for more interactivity.

Possible improvements could be achieved with the use of inharmonic comb filters to simulate the ball's position. In fact in [33], Stoelinga *et al.* analyzed the wave dispersion (i.e. the frequency dependent wave velocity) in a plate and concluded that frequency dependent comb filters added more realism when simulating a ball approaching the edge of a plate. This was confirmed thanks to perceptual experiments by Murphy *et al.* [29].

A generic model that allows continuous transitions between interactions (from rolling to scratching or from rubbing to squealing) is currently investigated, in order to propose intuitive navigation through the possible interactions between solids. Actually, the rolling model is sufficiently generic to synthesize various interactions such as rubbing and scratching [11,12], and we are currently investigating the integration of other interactions such as nonlinear friction [7,34].

This synthesizer is a powerful tool, for sound design or sonification, but also for fundamental research, to investigate auditory perception as it was done for instance by Thoret *et al.* who studied the relations between gestures and sounds [35,36]. In particular, the influence of the velocity profile (profiles of a human gesture versus the profiles of a rolling ball for instance) on the perceived interaction could be precisely investigated since the velocity is one of the control parameters of the synthesizer.

Acknowledgements. The authors would like to thank the French National Research Agency (ANR) which supports the *MetaSon* Project - CONTINT 2010: ANR-10-CORD-0003.

References

1. Allen, J., Berkley, D.: Image method for efficiently simulating small-room acoustics. J. Acoust. Soc. Am. 65(4), 943–950 (1978)
2. Aramaki, M., Besson, M., Kronland-Martinet, R., Ystad, S.: Timbre perception of sounds from impacted materials: behavioral, electrophysiological and acoustic approaches. Computer Music Modeling and Retrieval. In: Genesis of Meaning in Sound and Music, pp. 1–17 (2009)
3. Aramaki, M., Gondre, C., Kronland-Martinet, R., Voinier, T., Ystad, S.: Imagine the sounds: An intuitive control of an impact sound synthesizer. In: Ystad, S., Aramaki, M., Kronland-Martinet, R., Jensen, K. (eds.) CMMR/ICAD 2009. LNCS, vol. 5954, pp. 408–421. Springer, Heidelberg (2010)
4. Atal, B., Hanauer, S.: Speech analysis and synthesis by linear prediction of the speech wave. The Journal of the Acoustical Society of America 50(2B), 637–655 (1971)
5. Avanzini, F., Rocchesso, D.: Modeling collision sounds: Non-linear contact force. In: Proceedings of the COST-G6 Conference Digital Audio Effects (DAFx-01), pp. 61–66 (2001)
6. Avanzini, F., Rocchesso, D.: Physical modeling of impacts: theory and experiments on contact time and spectral centroid. In: Proceedings of the Conference on Sound and Music Computing, pp. 287–293 (2004)
7. Avanzini, F., Serafin, S., Rocchesso, D.: Interactive simulation of rigid body interaction with friction-induced sound generation. IEEE Transactions on Speech and Audio Processing 13(5), 1073–1081 (2005)
8. Bilbao, S.: Numerical Sound Synthesis: Finite Difference Schemes and Simulation in Musical Acoustics. John Wiley & Sons (2009)
9. Chaigne, A., Doutaut, V.: Numerical simulations of xylophones. i. time-domain modeling of the vibrating bars. Journal of the Acoustical Society of America 101(1), 539–557 (1997)
10. Chaigne, A., Lambourg, C.: Time-domain simulation of damped impacted plates. i. theory and experiments. The Journal of the Acoustical Society of America 109, 1422–1432 (2001)
11. Conan, S., Aramaki, M., Kronland-Martinet, R., Thoret, E., Ystad, S.: Perceptual differences between sounds produced by different continuous interactions. In: Acoustics 2012, April 23-27 (2012)
12. Conan, S., Thoret, E., Aramaki, M., Derrien, O., Gondre, C., Kronland-Martinet, R., Ystad, S.: Navigating in a space of synthesized interaction-sounds: Rubbing, scratching and rolling sounds. To appear in Proc. of the 16th International Conference on Digital Audio Effects (DAFx 2013), Maynooth, Ireland (September 2013)
13. Freed, D.: Auditory correlates of perceived mallet hardness for a set of recorded percussive sound events. The Journal of the Acoustical Society of America 87, 311–322 (1990)
14. Gaver, W.: How do we hear in the world? explorations in ecological acoustics. Ecological psychology 5(4), 285–313 (1993)

15. Gaver, W.: What in the world do we hear?: An ecological approach to auditory event perception. Ecological Psychology 5(1), 1–29 (1993)
16. Giordano, B., McAdams, S.: Material identification of real impact sounds: Effects of size variation in steel, glass, wood, and plexiglass plates. The Journal of the Acoustical Society of America 119, 1171–1181 (2006)
17. Hermes, D.: Synthesis of the sounds produced by rolling balls. Internal IPO report no. 1226, IPO, Center for User-System Interaction, Eindhoven, The Netherlands (September 1998)
18. Houben, M.: The sound of rolling objects, perception of size and speed (2002)
19. Houben, M., Kohlrausch, A., Hermes, D.: Perception of the size and speed of rolling balls by sound. Speech communication 43(4), 331–345 (2004)
20. Houben, M., Kohlrausch, A., Hermes, D.: The contribution of spectral and temporal information to the auditory perception of the size and speed of rolling balls. Acta Acustica United with Acustica 91(6), 1007–1015 (2005)
21. Klatzky, R., Pai, D., Krotkov, E.: Perception of material from contact sounds. Presence: Teleoperators & Virtual Environments 9(4), 399–410 (2000)
22. Lagrange, M., Scavone, G., Depalle, P.: Analysis/synthesis of sounds generated by sustained contact between rigid objects. IEEE Transactions on Audio, Speech, and Language Processing 18(3), 509–518 (2010)
23. Lambourg, C., Chaigne, A., Matignon, D.: Time-domain simulation of damped impacted plates. ii. numerical model and results. The Journal of the Acoustical Society of America 109, 1433–1447 (2001)
24. Lee, J., Depalle, P., Scavone, G.: Analysis/synthesis of rolling sounds using a source-filter approach. In: 13th Int. Conference on Digital Audio Effects (DAFx 2010), Graz, Austria (2010)
25. Lemaitre, G., Heller, L.: Auditory perception of material is fragile while action is strikingly robust. Journal of the Acoustical Society of America 131, 1337–1348 (2012)
26. Marhefka, D., Orin, D.: A compliant contact model with nonlinear damping for simulation of robotic systems. IEEE Transactions on Systems, Man and Cybernetics, Part A: Systems and Humans 29(6), 566–572 (1999)
27. McAdams, S., Bigand, E.: Thinking in sound: The cognitive psychology of human audition. Oxford Science Publications (1993)
28. Michaels, C., Carello, C.: Direct perception. Prentice-Hall, Englewood Cliffs (1981)
29. Murphy, E., Lagrange, M., Scavone, G., Depalle, P., Guastavino, C.: Perceptual evaluation of rolling sound synthesis. Acta Acustica united with Acustica 97(5), 840–851 (2011)
30. Rath, M.: An expressive real-time sound model of rolling. In: Proceedings of the 6th International Conference on Digital Audio Effects(DAFx 2003). Citeseer (2003)
31. Rodet, X., Depalle, P., Poirot, G.: Diphone sound synthesis based on spectral envelopes and harmonic/noise excitation functions. In: Proc. 1988 Int. Computer Music Conf., pp. 313–321 (1988)
32. Stoelinga, C., Chaigne, A.: Time-domain modeling and simulation of rolling objects. Acta Acustica united with Acustica 93(2), 290–304 (2007)
33. Stoelinga, C., Hermes, D., Hirschberg, A., Houtsma, A.: Temporal aspects of rolling sounds: A smooth ball approaching the edge of a plate. Acta Acustica united with Acustica 89(5), 809–817 (2003)
34. Thoret, E., Aramaki, M., Gondre, C., Kronland-Martinet, R., Ystad, S.: Controlling a non linear friction model for evocative sound synthesis applications. To appear in Proc. of the 16th International Conference on Digital Audio Effects (DAFx 2013), Maynooth, Ireland (September 2013)

35. Thoret, E., Aramaki, M., Kronland-Martinet, R., Velay, J., Ystad, S.: From shape to sound: sonification of two dimensional curves by reenaction of biological movements. In: 9th International Symposium on Computer Music Modeling and Retrieval, London (2012)

36. Thoret, E., Aramaki, M., Kronland-Martinet, R., Velay, J.-L., Ystad, S.: Reenacting sensorimotor features of drawing movements from friction sounds. In: Aramaki, M., Barthet, M., Kronland-Martinet, R., Ystad, S. (eds.) CMMR 2012. LNCS, vol. 7900, pp. 130–153. Springer, Heidelberg (2013)

37. Tucker, S., Brown, G.: Investigating the perception of the size, shape and material of damped and free vibrating plates. University of Sheffield, Department of Computer Science Technical Report CS-02-10 (2002)

38. Van Den Doel, K., Kry, P., Pai, D.: Foleyautomatic: physically-based sound effects for interactive simulation and animation. In: Proceedings of the 28th Annual Conference on Computer Graphics and Interactive Techniques, pp. 537–544. ACM (2001)

39. Warren, W., Verbrugge, R.: Auditory perception of breaking and bouncing events: A case study in ecological acoustics. Journal of Experimental Psychology: Human Perception and Performance 10(5), 704–712 (1984)

EarGram: An Application for Interactive Exploration of Concatenative Sound Synthesis in Pure Data

Gilberto Bernardes[1], Carlos Guedes[2], and Bruce Pennycook[3]

[1] Faculty of Engineering of the University of Porto, Portugal
g.bernardes@fe.up.pt
[2] School of Music and Performing Arts, Polytechnic of Porto, Portugal
carlosguedes@esmae-ipp.pt
[3] University of Texas at Austin, USA
bpennycook@mail.utexas.edu

Abstract. This paper describes the creative and technical processes behind earGram, an application created with Pure Data for real-time concatenative sound synthesis. The system encompasses four generative music strategies that automatically rearrange and explore a database of descriptor-analyzed sound snippets (corpus) by rules other than their original temporal order into musically coherent outputs. Of note are the system's machine-learning capabilities as well as its visualization strategies, which constitute a valuable aid for decision-making during performance by revealing musical patterns and temporal organizations of the corpus.

Keywords: Concatenative sound synthesis, recombination, and generative music.

1   Introduction

In electronic music, sampling is the act of taking a portion or sample of a particular recording and reusing it in a different piece. Apart from some previous minor and isolated experiments, the technique started to be largely explored in the late 1940s, namely by the group of composers and researchers working at the home of French Radio in Paris. Since then, we have witnessed a proliferation of sampling techniques that explore two main lines of research: the use of different musical time scales, namely the composition with micro-temporal scales, i.e. micromontage; and the development of software and algorithmic strategies that automate components of the technique, such as the segmentation and assemblage processes, as explored, for instance, in granular synthesis.

Although many strategies for composing with audio samples towards a higher level of automation have been presented in recent decades, the manipulation of such musical structures is still a very laborious and time-consuming task. Commonly, it demands the use of digital audio workstations to analyze, manipulate and render audio data, whose processing paradigm is still highly attached to analog means of working with audio.

M. Aramaki et al. (Eds.): CMMR 2012, LNCS 7900, pp. 110–129, 2013.

Concatenative sound synthesis (hereafter, CSS) is a technique for synthesizing sounds by concatenating short audio segments (called *units*). It relies on a large database of segmented and descriptor-analyzed sound snippets (called *corpus*) to assemble a given target phrase by selecting the units that best match the target specification according to a distance measure in the descriptors space. CSS is grounded in the sampling techniques mentioned in the previous paragraphs and can be seen as an extension of granular synthesis towards a higher level of automation by adopting a finer description and representation of the grains, enhancing the selection and assemblage processes through audio-content based analysis. The technical basis of this synthesis method was devised in the context of speech synthesis in the late-1980s [1]. CSS began to find its way in musical composition and performance in 2000 [2, 3]. However, even if the musical community has largely adopted this technique, the vast majority of the literature in this domain is mainly focused on solving technical problems that enhance the efficiency of these systems, paying very little attention to its musical applications.

The application detailed here, i.e. earGram, is a Pure Data[1] (hereafter, PD) patch that implements a CSS engine and several exploratory tools for musical creative practices. The major motivation behind earGram is to design software that could creatively explore a corpus of segmented and descriptor-analyzed units in an interactive and intuitive fashion. Four generative music strategies that recombine the corpus into musically coherent outputs are detailed here. The recombination strategies rely on two different approaches: the first uses the corpus to synthesize targets defined by imposed (metric and harmonic) templates selected by the user beforehand, and the second creates a novel music output while retaining the time-varying acoustic morphologies of the audio source(s). The system encompasses both the analysis and synthesis of soundscapes and polyphonic music and targets an audience more familiarized with music theory than with music technology. This is particularly evident in the devised description scheme used to characterize the units of the corpus, which utilizes a terminology derived from musical theory and practice, instead of the common low-level audio features. The need to develop this set of descriptors also emerged from several collaborations that the first author established with various composers, namely because of the difficulties experienced by these last in dealing with low-level audio descriptions of the corpus [4]. Similar approaches that devise a scheme of descriptors based on theoretical or practical musical knowledge can be found in the work of Julian Ricard [5] and Norbert Schnell [6].

EarGram not only allows the rapid prototyping of generative music processes (i.e. the implementation of unit selection strategies), but also offers several built-in algorithms that rearrange the corpus according to simple and intuitive instructions that can be manipulated by the user in real time. The recombination strategies implemented in earGram result from the adaptation of existing strategies from computer algorithmic assisted composition (hereafter, CAAC) to audio content-based processing. These strategies are suitable for interactively composing soundscapes,

---

[1] http://puredata.info/

infinitely extending a particular monophonic or polyphonic music sample without using mere repetitions, altering the meter of a song, or even synchronizing different layers of units.

Of note is the system's ability to group units into representative clusters, which, in combination with various visualization strategies, provide a valuable and intuitive representation of the audio source(s) content. These representations were designed with the purpose of being a decisive decision-making aid during performance.

Our approach to CSS is inspired by Tristan Jehan's Skeleton [7] and Diemo Schwarz's cataRT [8]. The architecture and the conceptual approach of the two systems is our fundamental basis. The analysis-synthesis models presented by Jehan [7] and implemented in Skeleton, especially the perceptual and structural modeling of the music surface, was of seminal importance for the development of the machine listening and learning in earGram. Schwarz's cataRT was equally important due to the similarities of the programing environment used and its real-time capabilities.

2   System Design

In this section, we provide an overview of the design scheme of earGram (see Fig. 1), which is composed of four modules: (1) machine listening, (2) machine learning, (3) database, and (4) composing.

The first block, machine listening is responsible for segmentation of the audio source provided initially by the user into representative units and for providing an analysis of the their content by referring to machine listening strategies.

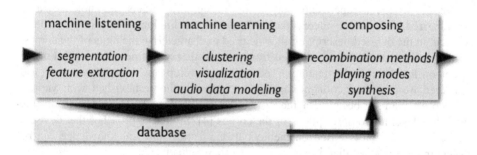

Fig. 1. Design scheme of earGram

The second block of the system covers several machine learning algorithms to: (1) cluster the corpus into representative groups of units, (2) provide intuitive and interactive visualizations of the corpus, and (3) deduce the meter and build statistical models that convey a representation of the temporal evolution of the harmonic, timbre and noisiness characteristics of the audio source(s). At this stage, a list of pointers to audio segments, their respective feature vector and the harmonic, timbre and metric models are stored in a database.

While the first two blocks are rather analytical, the last is operational. It encompasses four generative music strategies, referred to as recombination methods or playing modes. Synthesis, the last operation of the algorithm chain, is not only responsible for concatenating selected units from the corpus but also for some signal processing techniques. These techniques, which include adaptive filtering, reverberation, chorus, and spectral shift, enhance the concatenation quality between adjacent units and constitute a mean of artistic expression. Referring to CSS terminology, this last block is responsible for defining a target phrase and retrieving the best matching units according to the selection procedure.

3   Initialization of the System and General User Preferences

Initially, the user must select the type of project he/she wants to create, depending on the type of audio source(s) used: (1) single audio track, (2) folder comprising multiple audio files, or (3) live signal input. Instead of creating a new project, the user may also open a previously saved one.

During the creation of a new project the user must also feed the system with audio data that will serve as a basis to construct the corpus. This data will be commonly addressed as audio source(s). The source(s) constitutes the raw material that is concatenated during synthesis for creating new sonic structures thereby directly affecting the quality of the resulting output.

As mentioned earlier, earGram targets an audience more familiarized with music theory and practice than music technology. It demands very little knowledge of MIR-related terminology, which is commonly abundant in CSS software. The system design, and especially its interface, conveys a usability that allows the rapid creation of consistent musical results. Taking that into consideration, the system assumes by default a configuration that needs little or no fine-tuning in order to start generating some consistent results. However, expert users can also alter most settings to convey their needs via the preferences panel accessible through the main interface. In the following sections we will describe the system in detail and point out relevant differences between the auto-assigned preferences and the user-definable settings.

4   Machine Listening

The machine listening module in earGram is responsible for creating a corpus of labeled sound snippets. It encompasses two operations: (1) the segmentation of the audio source(s) into units and (2) the creation of a feature vector that characterizes the content of each unit.

4.1   Segmentation

The current implementation of earGram has three strategies that automatically segment the audio source(s) into units: (1) uniform size, (2) onset, and (3) beat. The first mode, uniform size, segments the audio source(s) at regular intervals according to a user-defined length. Onset, the second segmentation mode, defines units by slicing the audio continuum at the beginning of a musical note or other sound in which the amplitude surpasses an assigned threshold (amplitude peaks) or at sudden changes in the spectrum. The last segmentation strategy is beat, which defines units at the beginning of beats (if a regular pulse is found). The beat-tracker algorithm used in earGram is largely based on S. Dixon [9].

The system also incorporates an auto-segmentation mode that automatically chooses between onset or beat segmentation modes depending on the characteristics of the audio signal. This mode is activated by default so that less experienced users can utilize it more easily. If a clear pulse is found, the auto-mode segmentation will select beat segmentation instead of onset. In order to inspect the presence of a regular pulse, the system attempts to find clear peaks with harmonic relationships to the spectral flux autocorrelation function. If no such peaks are found, the system will segment the audio at each onset.

4.2   Morphological Analysis of the Units

The machine listening block comprises a second task: to assign a feature vector to each unit. It aims at describing relevant characteristics of the unit's content, which will represent them throughout the system. Each feature vector can be seen as a signature of the unit by significantly reducing its digital audio representation to a minimal yet meaningful collection of numerical features. Relevant perceptual features of the unit's content are described according to a descriptors scheme presented in Table 1. Pierre Schaeffer's morphological criteria of sound perception [10] and the later extensions of his work by Dennis Smalley [11] and Lasse Thoresen [12] inspired the construction of the descriptors scheme.

The top horizontal layer of the descriptor's scheme relates to two seminal concepts from Schaeffer's morphology: matter and form. Matter corresponds to "what we would hear if we could freeze the sound" [10]. Form describes the temporal evolution of a particular criterion over the length of the units.

The criteria under matter are represented by a numerical value on a limited and infinite topological space whose limits correspond to typological musical categories. In other words, each descriptor or criterion represents a sound feature by a numerical value that is meaningful in relation to a finite space whose limits correspond to specific types of sound. For example, the noisiness criterion is definable according to a space whose limits are 0 and 1, which represent two types of sound (noise and a sinusoid). Within these limits, the noisiness of the units is defined by a numerical value. The criterion of matter is further divided in two other categories, main and complementary. These categories distinguish between descriptors that produce meaningful results for the entire database and those that are only valid for a smaller part of it. The criteria under the main category encompass the totality of the units of the corpus, while the complementary category only considers part of the database of units.

The criteria under form offer a representation of the temporal evolution of a particular audio descriptor. It is represented either by a curve that exposes the descriptors' evolution or by basic statistical properties of the curve, such as mean or the standard deviation. The amplitude envelope curve is a clear example that falls under this category.

Two important properties have guided the implementation of our descriptors scheme. The first is to provide a set of descriptors that are definable according to the same finite space (whose limits are specific musical types), avoiding and consequently, dealing with the normalization of the feature vectors. The second property that guided the descriptors scheme's implementation is the invariability of the descriptors in relation to the units' length. In other words, the set of descriptors used in earGram allow meaningful comparisons between units with different lengths.

Table 1. Description scheme used in earGram to characterize the unit's content according to morphological criteria of sound perception

	Matter		Form
	Main	**Complementary**	
Mass	Noisiness	Pitch	Noisiness profile
		Fundamental bass (root relationship)	
			Spectral variability
Harmonic timbre	Brightness		
	Spectral width		
	Sensory dissonance (roughness)		
Dynamic	Loudness		Dynamic profile

The following sub-section will inspect all descriptors used and will be organized according to the three perceptual criteria (topmost vertical layer of the scheme): (1) mass, (2) harmonic timbre, and (3) dynamic, which unfold into twelve descriptors. Below we provide a conceptual and technical description of each descriptor. Its computational implementation relies on the use of individual low-level audio features or combinations of them. If not specified, William Brent's library *timbreID* is used to provide the low-level feature extraction in PD [13]. We chose this library for its robustness, efficiency, and ability to work in both real time and non-real time.

Criteria of Mass. The criteria of mass encompass four descriptors: (1) noisiness, (2) pitch, (3) fundamental bass, and (4) noisiness profile. The first is a main descriptor of matter, the middle ones are secondary descriptors of matter, and the last descriptor falls under the form category.

Measures of noisiness estimate the amount of noisy components in the signal as opposed to tonal components. Alternatives to this feature are the measure of pitchness, tonalness, or harmonicity, which offer a very similar and "inverse" description of the noisiness of a sound. Related research presents two common approaches to compute such criterion such as the use of low-level descriptors (e.g. spectral flatness [14] or zero-crossing rate [1, 15]) or by applying pattern matching techniques to compare between the spectral distribution of a sound and the expected distribution of partials according to an induced fundamental frequency [5, 6]. While the first approach is relatively poor and crude since it does not know any information about musical signals with harmonic relations, the last approach is not consistent to describe polyphonic audio signals because it is not feasible for a polyphonic signal transcription to estimate the fundamental frequencies and environmental sounds since it only consistently characterizes pitched sounds.

We decided to adopt a combination of low-level spectral descriptors to determine the noisiness of a sound since earGram deals with both polyphonic audio signals and environmental sounds. After several empirical tests we decided to calculate the noisiness criterion as the weighted sum of the following four descriptors: (1) spectral flatness, (2) spectral kurtosis, (3) spectral skewness, and (4) spectral irregularity. Through empirical tests we assigned the following weights to the aforementioned descriptors: spectral flatness 0.5, spectral kurtosis 0.2, spectral skewness 0.1, and spectral irregularity 0.2. These values make spectral flatness the most significant factor with spectral kurtosis, spectral skewness and spectral irregularity being useful to primarily balance the descriptor into an even distribution of noisy and pitched sounds. These values may also be used to enhance the detail of estimation pitched sounds (i.e., spectral kurtosis reveals the "peakedness" of the spectra and spectral irregularity enhances the difference between jagged and smooth spectra). The noisiness descriptor ranges between 0 and 1 where 0 represents a full saturated (noisy) spectrum and 1 represents a pure sinusoidal without partials. Within these two extremes we cover the totality of audible sounds including instrumental, vocal or environmental sounds.

Pitch or fundamental frequency is a secondary criterion of mass as it only conveys meaningful results for pitched sounds, and thus may reduce the corpus to a smaller collection of units. There are several robust algorithms to estimate the fundamental frequency of monophonic audio signals, however, algorithms for polyphonic pitch detection are not reliable yet. Therefore, this descriptor is confined for the characterization of monophonic audio signals. The estimation of the fundamental frequency is done by *sigmund~* a PD built-in object by M. Puckette.

The fundamental bass descriptor reports the root of a chord. Similar to the pitch criterion, it is a secondary criterion as it may reduce the corpus to a smaller number of units. We implemented this descriptor as a method for overcoming the problem of characterizing the pitch content of polyphonic audio signals. The fundamental bass is computed by an altered version of a PD object from the Dissonance Model Toolbox by Alexandre Porres [16].

The temporal evolution of the mass is expressed by two descriptors: (1) noisiness profile and (2) spectral variability. The noisiness profile describes the development of the noisiness at uniform and overlapping intervals throughout the unit's length. This is expressed in two ways: the first provides a curve of the features evolution and the second reduces the evolution to a series of single values that carry substantial information concerning its temporal dimension, such as maximum, minimum, mean, and standard deviation.

Spectral variability describes the amount of change in the spectrum of a signal by comparing the spectrum of consecutive frames. It is computed by the low-level audio descriptor spectral flux and is calculated as the Euclidean distance between two (non-normalized) spectra or the mean value between various analyzed windows. The use of non-normalized spectra not only accounts for spectral differences, but also denotes sudden changes in the overall power. The output of this descriptor is twofold: a curve denoting the spectral variability of the unit and a single numerical value that expresses the overall spectral variability throughout the unit duration.

Criteria of Harmonic Timbre. The perceptual criteria under harmonic timbre presented in Schaeffer's morphology [10] as well as the further reconsiderations by Smalley [11] and Thoresen [12] are very misleading, inconsistent, and fail at presenting a concise set of descriptors for this category. In order to define a set of systematic and computationally reliable descriptors, we base ourselves on psychoacoustic models of dissonance, implemented in PD by Alexandre Porres [16], to characterize harmonic timbre, namely a set of brightness, spectral width, and sensory dissonance (roughness).

Brightness, also referred to as sharpness, is an important perceptual attribute of sound and closely correlates with the centroid of the spectrum. In linguistics, it provides a clear distinction between the sounds of vowels and consonants (e.g. the sound 'i' is considered brighter than 'u' and 't' brighter than 'd'). In music it helps to discern and further categorize the sound (e.g. the spectrum of the various instruments). Brightness is computationally expressed by the centroid of the spectra. The resulting value is expressed in Hertz and we decided to constrain its range to the human audible frequency range which is roughly 20 Hz-20 kHz. This is further scaled between 0 and 1 to convey the same range as the other descriptors.

Spectral width expresses the interval between the extremities of the sound spectral components and it may help in distinguishing between saturated spectra and sparse distributions. For instance if we have a corpus of instrumental samples, we may distinguish between chords or tones with many partials and sinusoidal sounds or poor spectral distributions. An exact computational model of such criterion poses a few issues because we shall consider that the spectral representation of the computed audio signal may encompass noise even if the ideal conditions during recording were met. Instead of considering a solution for this problem, which has been subject to many publications and research, we adopted a simpler yet effective workaround. In order to increase both the robustness and reliability of the value expressed by this descriptor, we used a common low-level audio feature, spectral spread, which describes the concentration of the power spectrum around the spectral centroid.

In psychoacoustics, the roughness of a sound is the most relevant perceptual phenomenon to characterize sensory dissonance. Roughness depends on the distance between the partials measured in critical bandwidths, and it creates an audible phenomenon that is normally addressed as "fast beats" (i.e. amplitude fluctuations that occur at a rate over 20Hz up to a Critical Bandwidth).

Criteria of Dynamic. The loudness criterion expresses the amplitude of a unit by a single value and is defined by the square root of the sum of the squared sample values, commonly addressed as root-mean-square (RMS), which provides an approximate idea of loudness. If the units have a considerably long duration, the value expressed by the loudness criterion may be relatively crude since it is a temporal criterion by nature. However, even if the reduction of the loudness criterion to a unitary value may be seen as oversimplifying or too loose a description of this perceptual phenomenon, it may constitute a reliable source for many applications in comparison with a full detailed description of the envelope curve over the length of the event.

The dynamic profile is a form criterion of dynamic since it represents the evolution of the amplitude of the units. It is expressed in two different ways: (1) by the amplitude envelope curve or (2) by the characteristics of its shape (maximum, minimum, mean, and standard deviation).

5   Machine Learning

The second module of the system aims at (1) clustering the collection of units from the database, (2) creating visual representations of the corpus, and (3) modeling the harmonic, timbre and metric structure of the audio source(s) over time.

5.1   Clustering

Clustering intends to group similar segments to form collections of units. It aims at revealing musical patterns and particular temporal organizations of the music structure that can be applied differently during performance. The current implementation comprises three non-hierarchical clustering algorithms: k-means, quality-threshold clustering (QT-clustering) [17], and DBSCAN [18].

Our choice fell on this set of clustering algorithms because they form a good collection of tools to explore and automatically organize the corpus into distinctive groups. If the user wants to have a concise number of clusters defined a priori and consider all units in the corpus in order to create distinct corpus for different layers or sections the choice should fall on k-means. On the other hand, if the user wants to define the quality of the clusters based on threshold of similarity or neighborhood proximity between units, he/she should choose either QT-clustering or DBSCAN. On the last two clustering algorithms the user may also define the minimum number of elements per cluster. Another important property of these algorithms in relation to *k*-means is their ability to detect outliers that can be treated differently during performance namely by excluding them from the corpus as they may require special attention. Euclidian distance is the distance metric used to calculate the similarity amongst units in all clustering methods.

K-means partitions the corpus into clusters by allocating each unit to the cluster with the nearest centroid. The total number of clusters *k* needs to be defined a priori. However, the *k*-means implementation in earGram may suggest to the user the optimum number of clusters for a particular corpus by applying a technique known as 'elbow method'. Our implementation of the technique follows two steps. First, we calculate the distortion (i.e. sum of the squared distances between each unit and its allocated centroid) for each different value of *k*, ranging from 2 to 9 clusters; and subsequently, the algorithm assign the parameter *k* to the number of clusters at the point which a higher number of clusters does not offer a much better modeling of the data.

QT-clustering was developed by L. Heyer, S. Kruglyak, and S. Yooseph [17] to cluster gene expression patterns. Quality is defined by the cluster diameter and the minimum number of units contained in each cluster. Initially, the user assigns the two parameters. However, the user does not need to define the number of clusters a priori. All possible clusters are considered and a candidate cluster is generated with respect to every unit and tested in order of size against the quality criteria. In addition, it identifies outliers that should be treated differently (notably excluded) at runtime.

DBSCAN defines the clusters based on the neighborhood proximity and the density of the units in a cluster. Our implementation follows the algorithm described by M. Ester, H. Kriegel, J. Sander, and X. Xu [18]. The user must initially define two parameters: (1) the neighborhood proximity threshold and (2) the minimum density within the radius of each unit. Similarly to the QT-clustering algorithm, DBSCAN avoids defining a priori the number of clusters. However, the algorithm finds arbitrarily shaped clusters very diverse from the ones found by the QT-clustering. It can even find clusters surrounded by (but not connected to) a different cluster.

5.2   Visualization

The visualizations strategies implemented in earGram were designed for three main purposes: (1) give the user a better understanding of the corpus and similarity between units, (2) allow interactive and guided exploration of the corpus, and (3) assist in the decision-making processes during performance.

The visual representations implemented in earGram can be divided in four groups, which depict different hierarchical levels of the music structure: (1) waveform is the lowest representation level and one of the most common visualizations of audio data (the boundaries of the segments are provided on top of the waveform and below the waveform is a representation of the bark spectrum of the units), (2) 2d-plots and star coordinates [19], reveals the similarity between units by their representation on a two dimensional plane, (3) similarity matrix and arc diagram [20] aims to present the long-term (temporal) structure of the corpus, and (4) parallel coordinates [21] examines the high-dimension descriptors space.

Besides depicting relevant information of the corpus, most visualization strategies are interactive and allow the user to define regions of the audio source(s) that may be used distinctively during performance.

The waveform representation (see Fig. 2, Image 1) helps the user to examine the segmentation of the audio source(s) and browse the collection of units in their original order.

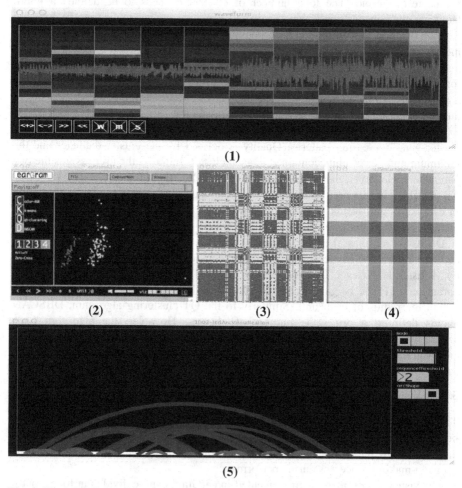

Fig. 2. Five visualizations of a corpus comprising a single-track audio source – *4* by Aphex Twin. From top to bottom and left to right: (1) waveform representation, (2) main interface of earGram that incorporates a 2d-plot representation of the corpus, (3) similarity matrix encompassing all available descriptors, (4) similarity matrix that uses the color scheme gathered from the cluster representation depicted in 2, and finally (5) visualization of the corpus by the arc diagram algorithm.

The 2D-plot representation (see Fig. 2, Image 2) is one of the most common visualizations of the corpus adopted in CSS software. To each axis is assigned a particular feature (from the collection of descriptors available), which causes units with similar characteristics to be closely plotted. It is especially suitable for browsing and exploring the corpus by navigating its representation. The units' color offers another layer of information. The color of each unit is defined by a list with three elements that correspond to the red, green, and blue values of an additive (RGB) color model. The R, G, and B values represent audio features from the available set of descriptors.

Star coordinates is a dimensionality reduction algorithm implemented in earGram that allows visualization of high-dimensional data on a 2D representation. The algorithm was formulated by E. Kandogan [19] and it maps high-dimensional data linearly to 2D or 3D using the vector sum. The choice of this algorithm over other popular dimensionality reduction algorithms such as multidimensional scaling or principal component analysis (PCA) was due to its understandability (each dimension still preserves the same meaning). A clear disadvantage of star coordinates is the need to explore the representation by weighing the variables and assigning different angles to each axis to find interesting patterns.

By depicting pairwise similarity between the units of the corpus, both self-similarity matrix and arc diagram reveal analogous patterns of the audio source(s), which ultimately expose the long-term structure of the data (see Fig. 2, Images 3, 4, and 5). The user can interact with these representations by grouping and selecting collections of units that can be addressed differently during performance.

Parallel coordinates [21] is a known algorithm used to visualize high-dimensional data and analyze multivariate data. It indicates the tendencies and the distribution of the descriptors.

5.3   Modeling the Descriptions of the Units over Time

Machine learning block encompasses a third operation module that is responsible for creating probabilistic models that represent the temporal evolution of the harmonic, timbre and noisiness content of the audio source(s) after segmentation and induce the meter of the audio source(s) if the beat segmentation mode was applied.

Harmony, timbre, and noisiness are modeled by transition probability tables that represent the probability between the different variables of each characteristic (states). The set of all states and their transition probabilities characterizes a Markov chain, which later allows the generation of new sequences based on stochastic processes.

In order to create a transition probability table, each feature needs to characterize the unit's content according to a finite number of predefined classes or states. We will further detail the used states to represent harmony, timbre, and noisiness, respectively. The unit's harmonic content is characterized by the pitch class profile (0-11) of the fundamental bass. Timbre is characterized by a single integer that represents the three highest bark spectrum bins out of a total of 24 bins. The compound value is achieved by following three operations: (1) the three highest bins numbers are sorted from the lowest to the highest and converted into binary representation; then (2) the second and the third bins numbers are shifted to the left by 5 and 10 cases, respectively; and finally (3) the three numbers are reconverted to decimal representation and added. Noisiness is represented by 10 states that are devised by dividing the descriptor's range in ten equal parts and assigning to each interval a numerical label from 0 to 9.

Whenever the audio is segmented on a pulse basis (if a regular beat is found), earGram attempts to induce the most regular pattern on the autocorrelation function of the spectral variability (spectral flux) description of the units in their original temporal order (each unit is defined by a single numerical value). It constitutes a naïve meter induction algorithm, which provides uniquely the number of pulses per measure. The autocorrelation function examines periods from 2 to 12 units, and picks the highest value of the autocorrelation function. Even it is a bit inadequate to call the technique meter induction, it satisfies our purpose of finding uniform patterns (number of pulses that expose regularities over time) on the surface of the unit's descriptions.

6   Database

The database stores most of the data produced in the machine listening and learning modules including pointers to the beginning and end of each unit in samples, feature vectors, probability transition tables, and various other details concerning the audio source(s).

Particular attention is given to the storage of the feature vectors since they need to be easily accessed in real-time. The descriptors (audio features) are implemented in PD as a collection of arrays. Each individual array stores the data correspondent to a particular feature to allow an effective and rapid search within a particular feature without compromising the retrieval of all features that characterize a particular unit.

The database and several variables used for segmentation, analysis, and audio data modeling can be saved in a text file and opened at a later stage. This saves a considerable amount of time in future uses of the same sound source(s) since the construction of the database is quite time-consuming, especially if we are dealing with hundreds or thousands of units.

7   Composing

In earGram, the main drive behind the analysis of the audio source(s), covered in the machine listening and learning blocks, is primarily synthesis. This section will start by detailing four recombination methods that automatically re-arrange the corpus by means differing from the units' original temporal order into musically coherent outputs (Sect. 7.1.1–7.1.4) and the synthesis method responsible for concatenating the selected units from the corpus (Sect. 7.2). Using CSS terminology, the following recombination strategies are used for defining a target phrase and retrieving the units from the corpus that best match the target specification, which are further concatenated in the last operation of the algorithm chain.

The methods for recombination convey the creation of three different musical results: (1) sonic textures or soundscapes (*spaceMap* and *soundscapeMode*), (2) infinitely extending the length of a particular audio sample without recurring to simple repetitions of the material (*infiniteMode*), and (3) defining targets that reflect a particular pre-assigned meter (*shuffMeter*).

7.1   Recombination Methods

SpaceMap. This method allows the interactive exploration of the corpus by the navigation of a 2D-visual representation. It can be seen as an extended granular synthesis engine where grains are organized in a meaningful visual representation. It aims at creating sonic textures with controllable nuances. It is a very powerful method to use in performance and with improvisation in particular, not only because of the automatic and meaningful segmentation that the software produces. Additionally, after a segment is defined it is consequently plotted in the interface, creating an almost instantaneous representation of the input signal during performance.

Several parameters, such as gain, density of events, pitch deviations, and stereo panning can be changed during performance and can affect each unit separately. All parameters can have a certain degree of random variability. The software also allows the creation of several bus-channels that may incorporate audio effects. At runtime, the representation of the units in the interface can be changed without affecting the synthesis, except when dealing with a live input signal.

SpaceMap has three playing modes: (1) *mouseOver* – continuously plays units at a specified density according to the mouse position on the screen; (2) *pointerClick* – plays units according to the pointer position but uniquely when the mouse button is pressed; and (3) *colorPicker* – same procedure as point 1, but the selection of the units is based on their RGB color values that are retrieved from a navigable grid of colors.

InfiniteMode. The second recombination method implemented in earGram, aims at generating an arbitrarily long musical excerpt, given a relatively short audio source(s) by scrambling the units' original temporal order. The output of this mode never repeats, nor loops the synthesized material, yet keeps playing by reconstructing the time-varying acoustic morphologies of the audio source(s). It gives better results in projects that comprise a corpus assembled from a single audio track and covers the generation of both soundscapes and polyphonic music.

Both the definition of the target and the selection of the unit that best matches the target specification are done on a unit basis. The target specification for a new unit is defined according to the characteristics of the previously selected and played unit. The resulting sequence of concatenated units conveys the metric structure and the representation of the models that encapsulate the temporal evolution of the harmonic, timbre and noisiness of the audio source(s) (detailed in Sect. 5.3). The user needs to select the characteristics that will guide the target definition, because some may not apply to the audio source(s) used. The interface of infiniteMode allows the user to select up to three of the four available characteristics (meter, harmony, timbre and noisiness). On the interface, there are two buttons that automatically assign characteristics for composing soundscapes (timbre and noisiness) and polyphonic music (meter, harmony and timbre).

The following paragraphs will first succinctly describe the characteristics used to evolve the generation of new music structures, and then address the algorithm design.

The timbre qualities and noisiness of the units' spectra, as well as the harmonic content (fundamental bass) of the audio source(s) are preserved if the characteristics timbre, noisiness and harmony are selected in the interface. Three distinct transition probability (previously described in Sect. 5.3) represent the temporal evolution of these characteristics. Relying on these tables and the previously selected units, a target specification for a future event is defined.

To preserve the distribution of metrical accents in the audio source(s), the algorithm retrieves the units that were previously labeled at each metrical accent. For example, all units in the machine learning modules are labeled with their position in the metric grid in a sequence that goes from 1 to number of pulses per measure. If the meter characteristic is selected at runtime, the algorithm attempts to preserve the metrical distribution previously devised by sequencing units with consecutive pulse labels.

The chain of operations of infiniteMode can be described in three steps: (1) define a target specification, (2) pick the unit or collection of units that satisfies the target specification, and finally, (3) from the collection of units selected in point 2, select the unit with the most similar spectra to the previously played unit in order to avoid discontinuities between adjacent (concatenated) units.

The definition of a target specification relies on the characteristics of the previously played units. The target covers the characteristics selected by the user in the interface according to the abstract models of the characteristics. When a new unit is triggered, the algorithm examines all selected characteristics, and defines a group of units that match the target for each of them. It then finds the units that are common to all groups of characteristics. From the remaining units, it selects the one that minimizes the distance on the bark spectrum representation to the previous selected unit.

If the algorithm does not find any unit that satisfies all the assigned characteristics, the algorithm will sequentially ignore characteristics until it finds suitable candidates. The selected characteristics on the upper slots will have priority over the lower ones. If we have three selected characteristics and the algorithm does not find any common units for a specific query, it will eliminate the third characteristic and again examine the number of units that satisfy the query. If it still cannot retrieve any units it will eliminate the second characteristic and so on.

SuffMetter. Clarence Barlow's metric indispensability principle [22] has been successfully applied as a metrical supervision procedure to automatically generate drum patterns in a particular style [23], as well as a model for constraining a stochastic algorithm that generates rhythmic patterns in a particular time signature [24]. Both of the aforementioned generative algorithms operate with symbolic music representations. ShuffMeter uses Barlow's principle to define a template that is translated to a target specification in order to synthesize musical phrases that reflect the use of a particular meter that is defined in advance by the user.

Given the scope of this paper and space restrictions, we cannot detail all the implementation of Barlow's metric indispensability. However, we follow the implementation described in [23]. After assigning a meter and a specific metrical level, the algorithm defines a template that represents the probabilistic weight each accent should have in order to perceive that particular meter, as well as a hierarchical organization of the strong and weak beats of the meter. We translate this template representation into two audio descriptors: loudness and spectral variability (spectral flux), by assuming that spectral and loudness changes are most likely to occur on the stronger metrical accents. Also, to simplify the computation we merged both descriptors into a single integer per unit by a function that defines each unit by the mean of both descriptors values. At each query the algorithm gathers the indispensability weight for that specific accent, and retrieves all units from the corpus that fall on the range that comprehends the value plus an additional range of 0.1 that is subtracted and added to it, respectively.

We can apply this principle either on the totality of the corpus or on separate clusters, allowing as many layers as there are existing clusters. The user can navigate in real time on a squared map, which adapts the definition of the targets by regulating the indispensability's weights (see Fig. 3). Two pairs of variables mapped to each of the vertices of the square will adapt the configuration of the weights. Rough-smooth, will adjust the variability between all accents and loud-soft will scale the weights proportionally (Fig. 4 depicts the indispensability weights' distribution conveying the mapping adjustment according to the clusters position in Fig. 3).

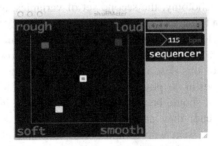

Fig. 3. Interface of shuffMeter

Each concatenated unit is triggered by a timer assigned to the duration of each pulse according to the induced beats per minute (bpm). The user may also alter the bpm manually. SchuffMeter adopts a static temporal grid in order to synchronize several units that may present slight differences in length. If the units' length does not match the specified duration, they are consequently stretched in time, which changes the playing speed of the audio signal without affecting the pitch.

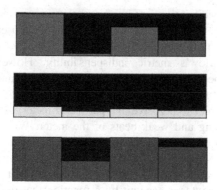

Fig. 4. Indispensability weights' distribution for four pulses of a 4/4 bar given by C. Barlow's formula [22]. The 3 graphs have a color correspondence to the clusters depicted on Fig. 3 and each configuration was scaled and conveys a percentage of variance according to their position on the navigable map.

SoundscapeMode. As the name implies, the last recombination mode implemented in earGram was designed to synthesize soundscapes in real time. It may be a valuable tool in sound design for movies or installations, because it maps segments onto a navigable squared space according to perceptual audio qualities. The navigable space is divided in four regions arranged in pairs of interconnected variables, similar to the interface of shuffMeter (see Fig. 3). The first set of variables controls the density of events (dense and sparse) and the second controls the roughness of the events (smooth and sharp).

Density defines the number of units played simultaneously, and ranges from 1 to 5 events. Smooth-sharp dichotomy, the second set of variables, aims at regulating and organizing the corpus in terms of diversity and stability. This last expressive quality is assigned to the audio feature given by the spectral variability descriptor (single numeric value per unit), which measures how quickly the power spectrum changes over time. The choice of this descriptor was due to its strong property for denoting onsets and sudden changes in the power spectrum and thus revealing how stable is the spectrum of the unit is. It should be noted that the terms used in the interface are not fixed sound types; instead, they are highly dependent on the source file(s). For instance, if we feed the system with samples with very smooth spectral shapes, the difference between smooth and sharp will be almost imperceptible.

Similarly to infiniteMode, we added a module at the end of the unit selection procedure that intends to maintain the best possible continuation between concatenated units by avoiding loudness and spectral discontinuities. This is done by gathering all candidates for a specific query within a unit and finding the one that minimizes the distance to the previously selected unit on the non-normalized bark spectrum.

7.2   Synthesis

Synthesis is done by concatenating units with a slight overlap. Each unit is played with a with Gaussian amplitude envelope. Most recombination methods incorporate strategies to avoid spectral discontinuities between adjacent units. However, in order to improve the concatenation quality, an additional feature is added at the end of the algorithm chain as a means to filter remaining transition discontinuities in the audio flow. This is done by smoothing the unit's transitions by spectral interpolation with the help of an object from the Soundhack plugins bundle [25] named +spectralcompand~, which is a spectral version of the standard expander/compressor, commonly known as compander. It divides the spectrum in 513 bands and processes each of them individually. The algorithm computes an average of the spectrum over the last 50 ms iteratively and applies it as a mask during synthesis.

8   Musical Applications

Four recombination algorithms that synthesize a novel music output based on given audio examples were detailed in this paper. These algorithms are suitable for a variety of music situations spanning from installations to concert music. The design of the system does not reflect any particular musical style. Our main purpose was to design an agnostic music system that could learn from the music it draws its database from and define coherent target phrases to be synthesized. Thus, the music output is highly dependent on the sound source(s) assigned by the user. Also, some guidance must be expected from the user to select certain recombination methods over others given the nature of the sound source(s). In other words, if we fill the database with polyphonic music signals segmented on a beat basis, it will be highly implausible that this collection of units will produce a consistent result when using soundscapeMode, which is mainly intended for synthesizing soundscapes.

The system is easily adjustable to the context of interactive performance. All recombination methods have some degree of variability that can be easily controlled on the GUI by a computer operator in real time or mapped to data extracted in real time such as motion or audio characteristics. The interface of all recombination methods is intuitive and built as navigable maps that are almost self-explainable.

The main purpose behind the machine listening and learning techniques implemented in earGram is to drive synthesis. However, the software may be useful for other application domains outside this realm. The machine listening and learning blocks combined with the visualization strategies of the corpus may constitute a valuable resource for the purpose of analyzing music in various fields such as computational musicology and cognitive musicology.

9   Conclusions and Discussion

This paper presented earGram, a novel CSS application built in Pure Data that comprises four generative strategies for interactive music contexts focusing on usability problems of CSS and filling the gap between computer algorithmic assisted composition strategies and audio content-based processing strategies.

Major differences from similar software include the focus on data-driven or rule-based generative music strategies that re-assign the original temporal order of the units into targets that: (1) arbitrarily extend a particular audio excerpt while retaining the source morphology (like being on hold), (2) dynamically change the meter of the audio source(s), and (3) organize the raw material into interactive, navigable maps suitable for creating soundscapes and/or browsing and exploring the corpus.

A particular concern that guided system implementation was to avoid the need for the user to deal with MIR-related terminology, particularly by devising a description scheme for the characterization of the units based on theoretical and practical musical knowledge.

The use of Barlow's indispensability algorithm proved to be an efficient method for assuring metrical coherence in the recombination process as well as the Markov chain algorithm for modeling the time varying morphologies of the audio source(s).

The machine learning strategies used, notably the clustering algorithms, enhance most of the visualizations revealing more clearly the long-term structure of the piece.

Both the software, several sound examples for all playing modes described in this paper, and the project template used to create each example are available at: `https://sites.google.com/site/eargram/`.

10   Future Work

A better understanding of the nature of the audio source(s) is seminal for refining many features of the system and providing increased usability. CSS is highly dependent on the quality of the database from which it draws its units. By recognizing in more detail particular qualities of the audio source(s), we could constrain a particular corpus to specific applications or playing modes thereby avoiding incoherent musical results.

Sequencing various playing modes in the same performance or using concurrent and synchronous recombination methods at runtime is still a very arduous process in the current software implementation. However, a set of objects that allows a more flexible use of the corpus adapted for the easy implementation of concurrent or sequenced playing modes is under development.

Acknowledgments. This work was supported in part by the Portuguese Foundation for Science and Technology and the European Commission, FP7 (Seventh Framework Programme), ICT-2011.1.5 Networked Media and Search Systems, grant agreement No 287711 (MIReS).

References

1. Schwarz, D.: Data-driven Concatenative Sound Synthesis. Université Paris 6 – Pierre et Marie Curie, PhD thesis (2004)
2. Zils, A., Pachet, F.: Musical mosaicking. In: Proceedings of the COST G-6 Conference on Digital Audio Effects, Limerick, Ireland (December 2001)

3. Schwarz, D.: A System for Data-driven Concatenative Sound Synthesis. In: Proceedings of the COST G-6 Conference on Digital Audio Effects (DAFX-00), Verona, Italy, pp. 97–102 (2000)

4. Bernardes, G., Peixoto de Pinho, N., Lourenço, S., Guedes, C., Pennycook, B., Oña, E.: The Creative Process Behind Dialogismos I: Theoretical and Technical Considerations. In: Proceedings of the ARTECH 2012 - 6th International Conference on Digital Arts, Faro, Portugal, pp. 2012–2016 (2012)

5. Ricard, J.: Towards computational morphological description of sound. PhD Thesis, Universitat Pompeu Fabra, Barcelona, Spain (2004)

6. Schnell, N., Cifuentes, M., Lambert, J.P.: First Steps in Relaxed Real-time Typo-morphological Audio Analysis/Synthesis. In: Proceedings of the Sound and Music Computing Conference, Barcelona (2010)

7. Jehan, T.: Creating Music by Listening. Ph.D. Thesis, M.I.T., MA (2005)

8. Schwarz, D., Cahen, R., Britton, S.: Principles and Applications of Interactive Corpus-based Concatenative Synthesis. In: Journées d'Informatique Musicale (2008)

9. Dixon, S.: An interactive beat tracking and visualization system. In: Proceedings International Computer Music Conference (2001)

10. Schaeffer, P.: Traité des objets musicaux. Le Seuil, Paris (1966)

11. Smalley, D.: Spectro-morphology and Structuring Processes. In: Emmerson, S. (ed.) The Language of Electroacoustic Music, pp. 61–93. Macmillan, London (1986)

12. Thoresen, L., Hedman, A.: Spectromorphological Analysis of Sound Objects: An Adaptation of Pierre Schaeffer's Typomorphology. Organised Sound 12, 129–141 (2007)

13. Brent, W.: A Timbre Analysis and Classification Toolkit for Pure Data. In: Proceedings of the International Computer Music Conference (2010)

14. Frisson, C., Picard, C., Tardieu, D.: Audiogarden: Towards a Usable Tool for Composite Audio Creation. QPSR of the Numediart Research Program 3(2) (2010)

15. Sturm, B.: Adaptive Concatenative Sound Synthesis and Its Application to Micromontage Composition. Computer Music Journal 30(3), 46–66 (2006)

16. Porres, A.T.: Dissonance Model Toolbox in Pure Data. In: Proceedings of the 4th Pure Data Convention, Weimar, Germany (2011)

17. Heyer, L., Kruglyak, S., Yooseph, S.: Exploring Expression Data: Identification and Analysis of Coexpressed Genes. Genome Research 9, 1106–1115 (1999)

18. Ester, M., Kriegel, H., Sander, J., Xu, X.: A density-based Algorithm for Discovering Clusters in Large Spatial Databases with Noise. In: Proceedings of the Knowledge Discovery and Data Mining, pp. 226–231. AAAI Press (1996)

19. Kandogan, E.: Visualizing Multi-dimensional Clusters, Trends, and Outliers using Star Coordinates. In: Proceedings of the Knowledge and Data Mining (2001)

20. Wattenberg, M.: Arc Diagrams: Visualizing Structure in Strings. In: Proceedings of the IEEE Information Visualization Conference (2002)

21. Inselberg, A.: Parallel Coordinates: Visual Multidimensional Geometry and Its Applications. Springer (2009)

22. Barlow, C.: Two essays on theory. Computer Music Journal 11, 44–60 (1987)

23. Bernardes, G., Guedes, C., Pennycook, B.: Style Emulation of Drum Patterns by Means of Evolutionary Methods and Statistical Analysis. In: Proceedings of the Sound and Music Computing Conference, Barcelona, Spain (2010)

24. Sioros, G., Guedes, C.: Automatic Rhythmic Performance in Max/MSP: the kin.rhythmicator. In: Proceedings of the International Conference on New Interfaces for Musical Expression, Oslo, Norway (2011)

25. SoundHack Plugins Bundle, http://soundhack.henfast.com/

Reenacting Sensorimotor Features of Drawing Movements from Friction Sounds

Etienne Thoret[1], Mitsuko Aramaki[1], Richard Kronland-Martinet[1],
Jean-Luc Velay[2], and Sølvi Ystad[1]

[1] Laboratoire de Mécanique et d'Acoustique (LMA), CNRS UPR 7051,
Aix-Marseille Université, Centrale Marseille,
31 Chemin Joseph Aiguier, 13402 Marseille Cedex 20, France
{thoret,aramaki,kronland,ystad}@lma.cnrs-mrs.fr
[2] Laboratoire de Neurosciences Cognitives - CNRS - UMR 7291,
Aix-Marseille Université
3, place Victor-Hugo 13331 Marseille cedex 3
jean-luc.velay@univ-amu.fr

Abstract. Even though we generally don't pay attention to the friction sounds produced when we are writing or drawing, these sounds are recordable, and can even evoke the underlying gesture. In this paper, auditory perception of such sounds, and the internal representations they evoke when we listen to them, is considered from the sensorimotor learning point of view. The use of synthesis processes of friction sounds makes it possible to investigate the perceptual influence of each gestures parameter separately. Here, the influence of the velocity profile on the mental representation of the gesture induced by a friction sound was investigated through 3 experiments. The results reveal the perceptual relevance of this parameter, and particularly a specific morphology corresponding to biological movements, the so-called 1/3-power law. The experiments are discussed according to the sensorimotor theory and the invariant taxonomy of the ecological approach.

Keywords: Sensorimotor Approach of Auditory Perception, Friction Sounds, 1/3 power law, Biological Movement.

1 Introduction

The relation between sound and movement is a very wide field of research. In this article we will focus on a particular topic related to this field namely the relation between a sound and a specific movement: the human drawing movement. Evoking a movement with a monophonic source only by acting on timbre variations of the sound is a process often used by electroacoustic musicians and sound engineers. Musicology analyses proposed semiotic descriptions of perceived movements in musical pieces [10]. Moreover, the general relations between intrinsic sound properties and movements have been tackled in previous studies by Adrien Merer in [27] and [28]. The motions evoked by monophonic sounds were

M. Aramaki et al. (Eds.): CMMR 2012, LNCS 7900, pp. 130–153, 2013.
© Springer-Verlag Berlin Heidelberg 2013

investigated from two angles, first by using a free categorization task, with so-called abstract sounds, that is, sounds which source was not easily identifiable. And secondly with a perceptual characterization of these evoked motions by studying the drawings produced by a group of subjects using a purpose graphical user interface. These studies had a very interesting approach which enabled to extract relevant perceptual features of relations between timbre variations of a sound and the evoked movements, and led to a sound synthesizer of evoked movements based on semantic and graphics controls.

Different psychological studies tackled the problem of sound event recognition. They principally based on the ecological approach of visual perception introduced by Gibson [15] which supports the idea that perception emerges from the extraction of invariant features in a sensory flow, and moreover from the organization of the perceptual system itself. This approach has been formalized for the auditory perception in different studies [46,12,13]. Opposed to this view, the information theory proposed that the perception is the result of a process with multiple steps which enables the association between a memorized abstract representation, and its identity and signification. In [29], McAdams has an intermediate position, he proposed to adopt the point of view of the information theory, and the notion of auditory representation, but keeping the terminology of invariants features which comes from ecological approach. It is well adapted to the description of the material world, and particularly in highlighting that some properties are perceived as invariant when others can change without changing the perception and signification of the stimulus. Moreover, we can argue that as it essentially concerns the recognition of sound events, it is adapted to adopt a representationalist view with this terminology to describe the information which is used to compare a representation of a stimulus with memorized representations. It is therefore proposed that the acoustic properties that carry information that enables the recognition of a sound event can be defined as structural and transformational invariants. The information that enables to identify the nature of the sound source was defined as a structural invariant. For instance, it has been shown that impact sounds contain sufficient information to enable the discrimination between the materials of impacted objects [47,18,2]. The information that specifies the type of change is known as a transformational invariant. For instance, a study revealed that the rhythm of a series of impacts enables to predict if a glass will break or bounce [46].

In the following study, we will focus on a particular type of sound event, the sound produced by the friction between a pen and a paper when we are drawing. This sound is audible but we did not necessary pay attention to it. The timbre variations contained in it may enable to imagine a movement and therefore a gesture. Are we able to recognize the gesture from the friction sound? If yes, can we imagine the shape which has been drawn? A graphical gesture can be mainly defined as a couple of velocity and pressure profiles which induce changes in the produced friction sound. In the following we will focus on the velocity profile of the gestures. We will investigate whether this information is sufficient to recognize a gesture and if it can be considered as a transformational invariant concerning human graphical gestures.

The relation between sound and gesture can be approached regarding a general theory at the edge between philosophy and cognitive sciences, called *enaction*, which was introduced by Francisco J. Varela [37,38]. This theory proposed a new approach of cognition distinct from the classical top down and bottom up models coming from cognitivist and connectionist approaches. He reintroduced actions and intentions at the center of our conception of cognitive processes involved in the perception of a stimulus. Varela defined the notion of *incarned/embodied actions* which can be summed up by the main idea that our perceptual processes are modeled by our actions and intentions, and that actions are central and cannot be separated from perception. Regarding the invariant taxonomy, it can be hypothesized that invariants which are used by the perceptual processes to identify a sound event refer to embodied properties of these actions [37]. As mentioned before, it should still be noted that invariant taxonomy comes from the ecological approach which is not consistent in many points with the enactive theory, but in this study, we will consider the notion of invariant as the information used by perceptual processes to identify and to recognize an event. The low level coding of embodied action has been supported by functional imagery observations in monkeys which revealed the existence of specific neurons in the ventral premotor cortex, the *so-called* mirror neurons, which fired either when the monkeys make an action or when they just observe it [32,11]. These observations have also been done in monkeys in the case of the auditory modality [19]. Finally, other electrophysiological and anatomical observations have been done with musicians whose brain area involved in the practice of their instrument was activated when they just listened to the instrument. Moreover, it has been shown that the intensity of activation is higher according to the musician's degree of expertise [3]. These last observations highlighted the importance of the perception–action coupling, also called the sensorimotor loop, in the perceptual processes and particularly in the case of auditory perception.

In this paper, we will investigate the relation between a friction sound produced by someones drawing and the evoked movement with the previous embodied action approach. It enables to make strong hypothesis about the dynamic features which can be imagined from a friction sound. We will aim at highlighting which parameters of the gesture can be evoked through a friction sound. Here we focus on the velocity profile, to set up experiments which investigate this question, we need friction sounds produced by a specific velocity profile. A graphic tablet and a microphone can be used for this purpose. This solution enables the analysis of the sound regarding the gesture properties but doesn't provide the possibility to control precisely the velocity of the writer. For control purposes, it would be more interesting to create synthetic friction sounds from given velocity profiles. A synthesis process of friction sounds which enables to synthesize such friction sounds will be present in a following section.

Finally, we will investigate the representation of a gesture from a friction sound in three experiments in which both recorded and synthesized friction sounds are used. In the first two, friction sounds produced when a writer draws different shapes will have to be associated to static visual shapes to identify if friction sounds can evoke a specific gesture, and furthermore a geometric shape. A third experiment investigates the relevance of a biological relation which links the velocity of a human gesture to the curvature of the trajectory from the auditory point of view. The results of these experiments will be discussed according to the sensorimotor theoretical background finally.

2   A Synthesis Model of Friction Sounds

In the three experiments which will be presented, a part of the stimuli will be generated with a sound synthesis process. The main goal will be to evaluate the relevance of the velocity profile in the representation of a gesture underlying

(A) Phenomenological Model

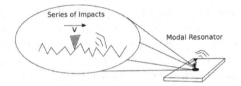

(B) Source-Filter Approach

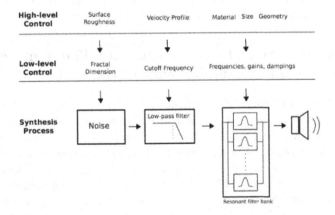

Fig. 1. Panel A: Physically Informed Friction Sound Synthesis Model - The friction sound is assumed as a series of impact of a plectrum, in our study the pen, on the asperities of a modal resonator – Panel B: Implementation of the phenomenological model with a source-filter approach that enables to separate the action, here the gesture, the object, here a paper on a table. The different levels of control are presented. The high level one corresponds to the intuitive control proposed to a user which enables to define an object from a semantic control of its perceived material and shape, while the low level corresponds to the synthesis parameters.

a friction sound: Are we able to imagine the gesture made only by listening the friction sound? Can we even recognized the shape which is drawn from the sound? And at last, is there morphologies, *so-called* invariants, linked to the velocity profile which enable the recognition of a human gesture from an auditory point of view?

From a synthesis point of view, a paradigm well adapted to the invariant's taxonomy is the *action/object* paradigm. It consists in defining the sound as the result of an action on an object (e.g. "rubbing on a metal plate"). A natural way to implement the action/object paradigm is to use subtractive synthesis, also called a source filter approach. This method enables to separate synthesis of the action, the exciter, *e.g. the transformational invariant*, and the object, the resonator, *e.g. the structural invariant*. To synthesize friction sounds with this approach, we used physically informed model, also called, phenomenological model presented by Gaver in [12] and improved by Van den Doel in [36]. It aims at reproducing the perceptual effect rather than the real physical behavior.

This approach considers a friction sound as the result of a series of impacts produced by the interaction between the pencil mine and the asperities of the surface, see Fig. 1. With a source-resonator model, it is possible to synthesize friction sounds by reading a noise wavetable with a velocity linked to the velocity of the gesture and filtered by a resonant filter bank adjusted to model the characteristics of the object which is rubbed or scratched (see Fig. 1) [7,8]. The noise wavetable represents the profile of the surface which is rubbed. Resonant filter bank simulates the resonances of the rubbed object and is characterized by a set of frequency and bandwidth values [1,2]. This synthesis model is particularly well tuned for our study, it indeed enables to generate a synthetic friction sound which varies only according to the velocity of the gesture.

3   A Relevant Acoustical Information: The Timbre Variations due to the Velocity of the Pen

Graphical tablets henceforth allowed to accurately record dynamical information like velocity and pressure, and to use it for comparing two shapes according to the kinematics which have produced them. As evoked before, many studies have highlighted the importance of the velocity profile in the production of a movement, and in particular, of graphical movements. Moreover, the friction sound synthesis previously presented enables to synthesize the friction sounds produced when someone is drawing based on the velocity profile only. As mentioned in the introduction, the velocity profile is a very important characteristic of a gesture, which may be involved at different levels of perception of a biological movement both in the visual system [41,43] and in the kinesthetic one [45]. Here we aim at investigating if this parameter is also a relevant cue to identify a drawn shape from a friction sound.

Recording Session. We asked someone to draw six different shapes on a paper, see Figure 3. While the velocity profile of the drawing movement was recorded

Fig. 2. Experimental recording set-up

thanks to a graphic tablet[1], the friction sound produced by the pen on the paper was also recorded with a microphone, see Fig. 2 for the experimental set up. The writer was asked to draw each shape as fluidly and as naturally as possible. Empirical observations were made just by listening to the recorded friction sounds. The circle seems to be a very particular shape. It indeed has a very uniform friction sound, with little timbre variations, while the ellipse, arches, line and loops have more important ones. The lemniscate seems intermediate between the other shapes, it indeed has a sound which contains more variations than the circle, but less than the loops, the arches and the line. Among the shapes which have a lot of timbre variations like ellipse, loops, line and arches, it should be noted that the line and the arches are distinct from the loops and the ellipse actually. They contain cusps, which imply silences in the friction sounds which are very audible and provide important perceptual cues linked to the geometry of the drawn shape.

Dealing with these empirical considerations, we chose to establish two corpuses of four shapes, one composed of shapes that are *a priori* distinct, the ellipse, the circle, the line and the arches. The second one of shapes which are *a priori* closer, i.e. the ellipse, the loops, the lemniscate and the circle. In particular, the first one has shapes which contain cusps: line and arches. A period of the velocity profile for each shape is presented in Fig. 4, for the arches and the loops, only one period of the four shapes is presented. The circle has a specific velocity profile

---

[1] Wacom Intuos 3.

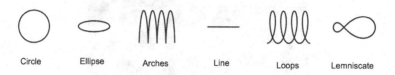

Fig. 3. The six shapes chosen for the experiments

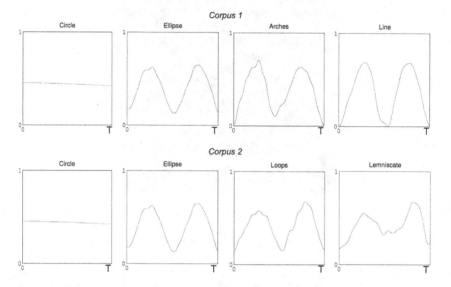

Fig. 4. Periods of the velocity profiles normalized and resampled on 512 samples used to compute the clustering

with a velocity almost constant during the whole drawing process. Otherwise, the durations of one period vary considerably according to the different shapes. To avoid this problem, the stimuli which have been chosen in the following contained four periods for the ellipse, the lemniscate and the line (one could say four *round trips* for this one). For the circle, only two periods were chosen, since the global duration for one period was indeed longer than for the other shapes. The whole durations of the chosen stimuli are summarized in Table 1.

A way to formally compare shapes of the two corpuses according to a dynamical dimension is to compare the proximity of the recorded velocity profiles with

Table 1. Durations of the Performances Chosen for the Recorded Velocity Profiles and Friction Sounds (in Seconds)

Circle	Ellipse	Arches	Line	Lemniscate	Loops
5.2	5.8	5.1	5.2	5.6	5.4

a metric. Thus, in a second time, to set up listening tests with friction sounds as stimuli to establish a perceptual distance between pairs of shapes. At last, the classifications computed from these mathematical and perceptual distances can be compared to evaluate if the velocity profile provides a relevant information from an auditory point of view.

3.1   Clustering of Geometrical Shapes from the Velocity Profile

Practically, recorded velocity profiles correspond to series of N measurements v_i at the sample frequency of the graphic tablet (here 200 Hz). A velocity profile is then defined as an array of N points according to the duration of the drawing. Finally, to compare two velocity profiles v and w it is necessary to be able to compare two vectors of different lengths. The durations of two drawings is indeed most of the time different for different shapes.

Euclidean Distance between Two Velocity Profiles. A common mathematical tool used to compare two vectors is the inner scaler product that enables to define a distance according to a metric. The choice of the metric is crucial. It indeed defines the way the distance between shapes will be calculated, and it defines an objective measure between two shapes in terms of velocity profiles. The most classical metric is the euclidean one which corresponds to the following inner product between two vectors v_i and w_i, of the same length:

$$\langle v|w \rangle = \sum_{k=1}^{N} v_k w_k \tag{1}$$

The distance between two velocity profiles can then be obtained from the Euclidean distance, $d(v, w) = \|v - w\| = \sqrt{\langle v - w|v - w \rangle}$, which is minimal when $v = w$ and increases as the difference between v and w increases. In the case of velocity profiles, since arrays are of different lengths. It has been chosen to resample each velocity profile in 512 samples and to normalize them according to their mean value. The rationale is that the recordings are about the same duration, see Table 1. Thus, this normalization does not introduce a bias in the calculus of the distance. More complex algorithms exist to compute a distance between two arrays of different lengths, such as Dynamic Time Warping [20]. This last one is effective but very expensive in computing time and provide no significant advantages here from the resampling.

Dissimilarity Matrix and Clustering. The Euclidean distance enables to compute a distance between each pair of shape for each corpus (6 pairs for each corpus). And moreover, to create a dissimilarity matrix D in which each cell represents the distance between the two velocity profiles associated to two shapes. The diagonal values of this matrix are equal to 0, indeed the distance between two equal velocity profiles is null. Two hierarchical clustering analysis of D, with complete linkage, were then effectuated from the dissimilarity matrices

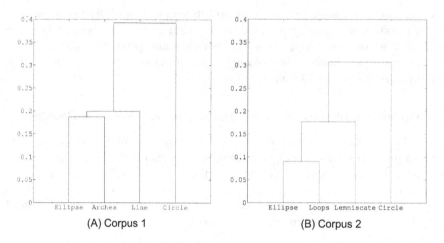

Fig. 5. Panel A and B: Ascending hierarchical clustering computed from the dissimilarity matrices computed from the corpus 1 and 2 respectively

of each corpus. The dendrograms corresponding to this matrices are presented in Fig. 5. A dendrogram corresponds to a hierarchical tree which represents a classification of different objects, here the velocity profiles. The height of each U-shape represents the distance between two objects or two clusters. For the two corpuses, the clusterings confirm the empirical observations, the circle is the shape that is most different from the others in the two sets of shapes. This could be explained by its velocity profile that is almost constant. In the first corpus, it is noticeable that the arches seem to be about equally distant from the ellipse and the line. In the second corpus, as expected, the ellipse and the loops are very close while the lemniscate is intermediate between the circle and the other two shapes. In order to determine if the previous classification obtained from the velocity profiles is relevant from an auditory perceptual point of view, two listening tests have been set up.

3.2 Clustering of Geometrical Shapes from Perceptual Comparisons of Friction Sounds

The previous mathematical clustering based on the velocity of the gesture made to draw the shapes enables to evaluate the proximity between the shapes of the two corpuses from an *objective* point of view. Our aim is to evaluate if the velocity profile is also a relevant information to compare two shapes *from the perception of friction sounds.* In other words, to investigate if the velocity profile conveys information about a gesture from the auditory point of view.

In the following, two listening tests with recorded and synthesized sounds produced during the drawing that were to be associated to the four shapes of each corpus are presented. Clusterings can then be obtained from the results of the listening tests and compared with the mathematical ones obtained previously.

In order to establish a perceptual clustering of the shapes, the two listening tests consist in a association test where subjects have to associate the friction sounds to the correct shapes.

Experiment 1 – Distinct Shapes

Subjects. Twenty participants took part in the experiment: 9 women and 11 men. The average age was 30.65 years (SD=13.11). None of the subjects were familiar with the topic of the study before the test.

Stimuli. The first listening test deals with the shapes of the corpus 1 which contains the most distinct shapes with regard to the velocity profile. The auditory stimuli are composed of eight friction sounds, four recorded and four synthesized, obtained from the shapes of corpus 1 collected during the recording sessions presented previously. The synthesized sounds were generated with the friction sound synthesis model previously presented.

Task. The subjects were asked to univocally associate four friction sounds – among the four available – to the four shapes. The test was composed by eight trials: 2 types of sound x 4 repetitions.

Results and Short Discussion. For each subject and each type of sound – synthesized vs. recorded – sixteen scores of association between a sound and a shape were averaged across the four trials. All the results were stored in confusion matrices. The global averaged scores of success of the four shapes for recorded and synthesized stimuli are presented in Table 2. The results are clear, each friction sound has been properly associated to the corresponding shape above a random level[2]. Moreover the synthesized stimuli provide results which are not significantly different from the recorded ones which confirms the hypothesis about the perceptual relevance of the velocity profile.

Table 2. Scores of success for recorded and synthesized stimuli of corpus 1 averaged across subjects – Mean and Standard Error in Percentages – Scores higher than statistical chance are bolded

	Circle	Ellipse	Arches	Line
Recorded	**98.75**	**81.25**	**80.**	**87.5**
	1.25	6.25	6.44	1.72
Synthesized	**98.75**	**87.5**	**82.5**	**97.5**
	1.25	4.97	5.76	3.08

---

[2] The random level is defined at a 25% sound to shape association rate.

Experiment 2 – Close Shapes

Subjects. Eighteen participants took part in the experiment, 8 women and 10 men. Their average age was 31.56 years (SD=13.73). None of the subjects were familiar with the topic of the study prior to the test.

Stimuli. The second listening test deals with the shapes of corpus 2 which have shapes with closer geometries. Auditory stimuli are composed by eight friction sounds obtained from the shapes of corpus 2, four recorded and four synthesized, collected during the recording sessions presented previously. As for the experiment 1, the synthesized stimuli are generated with the friction sound synthesis model presented previously.

Task. The task was the same as in Experiment 1.

Results and Short Discussion. The data analysis is the same as in the previous experiment. The results reveal that, except for the loops, each sound was associated with the correct shape with a success rate above random level. Only the recorded loops were not recognized above chance. The scores of success are summarized in Table 3. Confusions appear between the ellipse and the loops, the score of association between these two shapes is not significantly different which means that they were confounded, see Table 3.

Clustering Analysis. The two previous listening tests revealed that when shapes are sufficiently different, it is possible to discriminate them simply from friction sounds. To valid entirely this statement, an additional analysis is necessary. A perceptual distance matrix between shapes was therefore computed from the confusion matrices obtained in the two experiments. They were firstly symmetrized, to implicitly merge the rate of association of sound i to shape j with the rate of association of sound j to shape i into one value representing the perceptual distance between the two shapes. The symmetrized confusion matrix $\tilde{C}$ is obtained by:

$$\tilde{C} = \frac{C + C^t}{2} \tag{2}$$

with C^t the transposed version of matrix C. Then a discrimination matrix $\tilde{D}$ was obtained by $\tilde{D} = 1 - \tilde{C}$. At last a pairwise distance matrix D is computed with the Euclidean metric.

For each corpus, two discrimination matrices are computed: one for the recorded sounds, and one for the synthesized one. Like for the mathematical dissimilarity matrix, an ascending hierarchical clustering are computed from these discrimination matrices and provide dendrograms. Four clusterings are made from the whole results, see Fig. 5 and 7. A global observation of the dendrograms lead us to hypothesize that, for the two corpuses, the two perceptual shapes classifications, synthesized vs. recorded, are equivalent. Indeed, in each case, the relative rank of proximity between whole shapes are the same.

Table 3. Scores of success for recorded and synthesized stimuli of corpus 2 (A) — Scores of association between loops and ellipse for recorded and synthesized stimuli (B). All the scores are averaged across the subjects. Mean and standard error are presented in percentages. Scores higher than statistical chance are bolded.

(A)

	Circle	Ellipse	Lemniscate	Loops
Recorded	**97.22**	**41.67**	**68.06**	29.17
	2.78	7.29	8.04	7.36
Synthesized	**100.**	**50.**	**81.94**	**43.06**
	0.	4.52	6.00	6.00

(B)

	Ellipse Sound ↔ Loops Sound	Loops Sound ↔ Ellipse Sound
Recorded	**51.39**	**45.83**
	6.22	7.89
Synthesized	**45.83**	**43.06**
	5.05	4.87

To statistically validate this, it is necessary to introduce the notion of cophenetic distances.

The problem of comparing two dendrograms has already been studied in phylogenetics. One goal of this field of biology is to understand the evolution of living beings according to molecular sequencing and morphological data which are collected into dissimilarity matrices and presented with dendrograms. Thus, the comparison of dendrograms has been tackled to compare morphological and molecular observations. As previously presented, a dendrogram is a representation of distances between different objects, and the composition of the clusters of the dendrogram is made according to a specific metric. A dendrogram is then characterized by distances between clusters, in which a specific distance has been defined and is called the cophenetic distance[3] [35].

---

[3] According to the help of the function *cophenet* in Matlab©, the cophenetic distance can be defined as:

The [...] *distance between two observations is represented in a dendrogram by the height of the link at which those two observations are first joined. That height is the distance between the two subclusters that are merged by that link.*

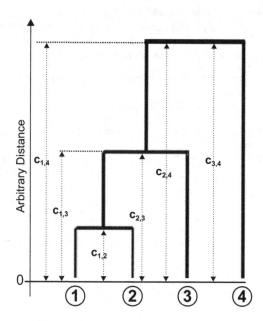

Fig. 6. An example of dendrogram and the associated cophenetic distances $c_{i,j}$ between the different objects – The cophenetic distances are summed up in an array: $C = [c_{1,2}, c_{1,3}, c_{1,4}, c_{2,3}, c_{2,4}, c_{3,4}]$ – and can be compared with cophenetic distances of others dendrograms with Pearson's and Spearman's correlation coefficients

An example of dendrogram and the associated cophenetic distances are presented in Fig. 6. The cophenetic distances are sorted in an array for each dendrogram. To determine whether two dendrograms are statistically equivalent, it has been proposed to compute the Pearson's and Spearman's correlation coefficients between the two arrays of cophenetic distances. The Pearson's correlation coefficient r corresponds to a quantitative comparison of the linear correlation between shapes. And the Spearman's correlation coefficient ρ, corresponds to a qualitative comparison of the clusterings which takes into account of the ranks of the cophenetic distances between shapes.

We wanted to compare the two dendrograms obtained in each listening test. With the statistical method presented here, no significant differences are observed both for the experiment 1 and 2. The correlation coefficients are presented in Fig. 7.

3.3   Comparison between Clusterings

Previous comparisons revealed that from a perceptual point of view, the synthesized friction sounds generated from recorded velocity profiles contained the same relevant information than the recorded ones, which seems to confirm that the velocity profile is the information which is perceptually relevant to recover a

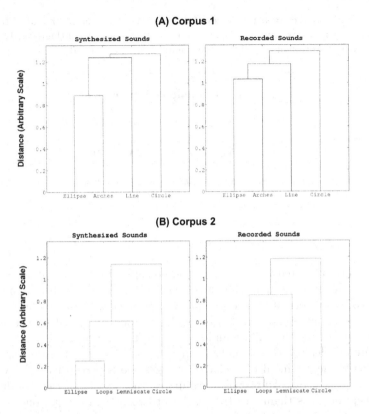

Fig. 7. Panel A: Ascending hierarchical clustering computed from the confusion matrices of the experiment 1 - Significant correlations were found between cophenetic distances of the two clusterings ($r = .89$ and $\rho = 1.$) — Panel B: Ascending hierarchical clustering computed from the confusion matrices of the experiment 2 - Significant correlations were found between cophenetic distances of the two clusterings ($r = .94$ and $\rho = 1.$) — All correlation coefficients are significant

gesture through a friction sound. To completely validate this initial hypothesis, the perceptual and the *mathematical* dendrograms have been compared using the statistical method of cophenetic distances presented in the previous paragraph. The comparison reveals that for each corpus, except for the Pearson's correlation coefficient obtained for the recorded sounds of the experiment 1, the comparisons between the perceptual clusterings are not significantly different from the mathematical ones (see Table 4 for the Pearson's and Spearman's correlation coefficient). This result reinforces the importance of the velocity profile in the perceptual process underlying the sound to shape association task, which was already suggested with the correlation between the perceptual dendrograms obtained from the listening tests.

Table 4. Pearson's and Spearman's correlations, respectively noted r and ρ, between the cophenetic distances obtained from the perceptual and the mathematical clusterings of the two experiments — Significant comparisons are bolded

	Experiment 1		Experiment 2	
	r	ρ	r	ρ
Recorded	.58	**.93**	**.98**	**.93**
Synthesized	**.89**	**.93**	**.94**	**.93**

3.4 Discussion

The clusterings reported here highlight the perceptual relevance of the velocity profile to evoke a graphical human movement. We firstly established an *objective* classification of shapes of two corpuses from the velocity recorded on a person drawing them. Shapes expected to have a close geometries are also close according to this metric like the ellipse and the loops for instance.

Our interest dealt with the auditory perception of gestural movements, and particularly to determine if the velocity of a gesture is perceptually relevant to characterize a gesture. We therefore compared the mathematical classification with perceptual ones thanks to the results of two listening tests, one for each corpus. The tests were composed of friction sounds recorded when the same person draws the shapes. Synthetic sounds generated only from the velocity were also used, which made it possible to investigate the perceptual relevance of the velocity. The variation of timbre involved in the recorded and in the synthesized sounds enabled the shape recognition. Finally, the comparisons between the perceptual and the mathematical classifications confirmed that the velocity profile of a gesture contains relevant information about the gesture underlying a friction sound. In particular that a sound can evoke a gesture. And even, to evoke a geometrical shape although the relation between a velocity profile and a shape is not bijective, i.e. one velocity profile can be the cause of the drawing movement of several geometrical shapes.

Henceforth we know that the velocity profile transmits sufficient information about the gesture, sufficient, to a certain extent, to discriminate different shapes from sounds. This implies that the kinematics of the gesture and the geometrical characteristics of the drawn shape are correlated and gives an invariant information which enables subjects to extract a common representation of the gesture evoked by the sound, a *so-called* transformational invariant.

4   An Acoustical Characterization of a Human Gesture

When someone draws a shape on a paper, the final trace is static and all the dynamic information is lost *a priori*. The previous experiments pointed out that from an acoustical point of view, the velocity profile of a gesture was a relevant information to recognize a gesture from the friction sound produced when someone is drawing. It indeed enabled the discrimination of shapes when they were distinct. Conversely, when the shapes had close geometries, perceptual confusions between sounds (both for recorded and synthesized ones) appeared in particular for the ellipse and the loops. This result reveals that the gesture made to draw a shape is closely linked to its geometry and particularly to its kinematics.

4.1   The 1/3-Power Law

Many studies have already focused on this relation between the kinematics of a movement and the geometry of a trajectory. In particular, studies led by Paolo Viviani and his colleagues since the eighties highlighted that a biomechanics constraint implies the velocity of a gesture to depend on the curvature of the traveled trajectory [39]. Besides, they proposed a power law relation between the angular velocity of the pen and the curvature of the drawn trajectory [22,40]. In terms of tangential velocity v_t and curvature C, it can be written:

$$v_t(s) = KC(s)^\beta \tag{3}$$

K is called the velocity gain factor and is almost constant during a movement. s is the curvilinear abscissa. The exponent β is close to 1/3 for adults' drawing [42] and the law has therefore been called the 1/3-power law. Possible description of this relation is that when we draw a shape, we accelerate in the flattest parts and we slow down in the most curved ones. This general principle constrains the production of biological movements but has also consequences in other sensorimotor modalities. Visual experiments revealed that a dot moving along a curved shape was perceived as the most constant when the relation between its velocity and the curvature of the traveled trajectory followed the 1/3-power law, even when the velocity variations exceeded 200% [43]. The relevance of this law has also been studied in the kinesthetic modality and revealed the same perceptual constraint [45].

This law can partly explain why the ellipse and the loops from the previous experiment were confounded. As their geometries were close, the velocities were also close, and as the produced friction sounds mainly depend on the velocity, they were not different enough to be distinguishable from an acoustical point of view. This law has therefore audible consequences, and it is legitimate to wonder if this biological invariant can be calibrated in the auditory modality.

4.2   Auditory Calibration

We adapted the protocol of visual calibration of the power law proposed in [43] to investigate the auditory perception of biological motion.

Subjects. Twenty participants took part in this experiment. Their average age was 29.42 years (SD=12.54).

Stimuli. While in the visual case studied in [43] the stimuli which were adjusted by subjects were moving visual dots, in the acoustical case, they were friction sounds. The previous synthesis model of friction sounds was used to generate a sound only from the kinematics (i.e. the velocity profile). These velocity profiles were computed by using the β-power law with a fixed mean velocity K. To avoid evoking specific known shapes, the curvature profiles were computed from pseudo-random shapes, see Fig. 8 for an example.

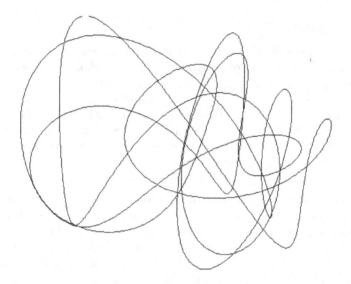

Fig. 8. An Example of Pseudo-Random Shape

Task. Each subject effectuated 6 trials and a pseudo-random shape was generated for each trial. The subjects listened to the corresponding friction sound and were asked to adjust the sound until they perceived a sound which evoked the most fluid/natural movement. They could act on the timbre variations with two buttons which modified the β value. The subjects were unaware of the parameter on which they were acting. The initial value of β was randomized at each trial and the shape was not shown to the subjects to make them focus on the sound only.

Results and Short Discussion. The subjects adjusted the exponent value with a mean value of β=0.36 (SD=0.08), it is therefore not significantly different from the 1/3-power law (p=0.10). This indicates that to produce a sound which evoked a fluid and natural gesture, the velocity profiles from which a friction sound is generated should follow the 1/3-power law. This result reinforces the importance of kinematics in the perception and representation of gestures from a cognitive viewpoint. The sensorimotor relations between auditory and other modalities have more or less been investigated regarding the mental representation of gestures.

To conclude, one of our motivations was to control a friction sound synthesis model with intuitive controls. The research perspectives that we can expect made it possible to imagine a sound synthesis platform which enables to synthesize sounds from intuitive controls based on the 1/3-power law. The scope of such a platform is presented in Fig. 9. An interesting perspective of experiment 3 would be to ask the subject to adjust the sound (implicitly the exponent of the power law) evoking an aggressive and jerky gesture, or conversely the sound evoking a sweet caress, which are two gestures evoking different intentions. Intentions are closely linked to emotions and could be classified according to the classic valence-arousal scale [5]. Intuitively, the high parameter values of the power law would correspond to an aggressive and jerky gesture, i.e. to strong accelerations and strong decelerations at a high velocity. And conversely, for the caress, which involves *a priori* a slower and smoother gesture, the power law corresponding values would be small. Not especially null for the exponent, which corresponds to a uniform and constant movement and which has therefore no audible variations, but for values high enough to perceive a smooth and sweet gesture.

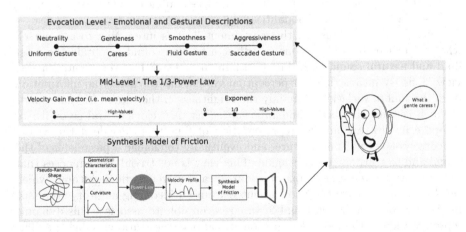

Fig. 9. Architecture of the friction sound synthesis platform with intuitive controls of the evocation. The controls discussed in the conclusion such as, aggressiveness and gentleness, have been proposed. A formal calibration of the velocity gain factor and the exponent with respect to the gestural and emotional descriptors will be conducted in future works.

5   General Discussion

The starting point of this study was to investigate the relation between sounds and gestures, more specifically to understand whether a sound can evoked a gesture, and which characteristics could be conveyed by sound. In a general context, in the previous studies by Adrien Merer [27,28], concerning the relation between an abstract sound and the evoked movements, the following questions were evoked: Why a sound evoke a specific movement? For instance, why does a sound evoke something oscillating or rotating? We therefore found it interesting to tackle this question in the case of human drawing movement regarding the sensorimotor considerations presented before.

By adopting the invariant's taxonomy, the results of the three previous experiments gave important cues about one *transformational invariant* which characterizes a gesture: its kinematic. Henceforth we know that the velocity transmits relevant information about the gesture, which moreover can be associated to a geometric shape to a certain extent. At last, the third experiment brings to light the relevance of a biological relation between the velocity and the curvature from the auditory point of view, which has never been investigated before. This last experiment also showed the interesting result that, to evoke a fluid and natural gesture through a friction sound, the velocity profile should follow the 1/3-power law, which means that friction sounds could directly informed about the naturalness and the fluidity of a gesture. This point has to be discussed because it opens the possibility to recognize qualities of a human gesture through sounds, which provides new perspectives in the understanding of auditory perception and its relation with other modalities.

Going back to the task of the experiment 3, it is interesting to ask ourself what it involves to ask someone to adjust a friction sound to obtain the most fluid and natural sound according to a human gesture? In a representationalist view, it firstly means that our perceptual system has to extract an information from the timbre variations – mainly the brightness in the case of friction sounds – which is then abstracted and *internalized* as the velocity. And secondly, to compare it with an internal representation of fluidity to decide if this velocity corresponds to a fluid gesture, and eventually to change a parameter of the sound and to start the process again. This view is not trivial and supposes that we have internal representations of gestures – and moreover fluid gesture – which can be compared with the one computed from an incoming auditory stimulus. In the case of experiment 1 and 2, we are even able to associate this dynamic representation of the gesture to a geometrical one, the static visual shape. The problem of representations in perception has been widely discussed in the visual modality to understand how a physical system, such as the brain, can makes the feeling of seeing, which is not *a priori* a physical state. The enactive approach of Varela presented in the introduction placed the action in the center of the perceptual processes. The sensorimotor theory of perception of Kevin O'Regan [31] proposed an interesting approach of this assumption. It is argued that *seeing is not making an internal representation of the outside world from the visual input,* in other words to make a mirror in the brain of the world from a visual stimulus. It is proposed that *seeing is knowing about things to do* with the outside world, i.e. knowing the actions you can make with the outside world and their consequences on your sensory input. For instance, seeing a wine glass is not having a picture of it in the head, but it is projecting what you can do with it, filling it or drinking it for example. Based on behavioral and neurophysiological observations, Marc Jeannerod and Alain Berthoz respectively introduced the notion of *Simulated Action – the perception is a simulated action*, [16,4,17]. It sums up the idea that perceiving, whatever the modality, is extracting the relevant information to interact with the objects of perception, e.g. grasping the glass to drink it. It is therefore making hypothesis about what and how I can interact with it according to my motor competences. For example, when we see a tea cup on a table, we are able to say which hand is the most adapted to grasp it according to the position of the handle, the right hand if the handle turn to right and conversely. Simulated action seems to involve the same processes as the one proposed in the sensorimotor theory of O'Regan.

If we apply the sensorimotor approach to the auditory perception in the case of the sounds produced by drawing movements, the same distinction as in the visual case can be made. Listening to the friction sounds produced by someone who is drawing is not making an internal representation of the sound produced by the gesture, but it is imagining executing the corresponding gesture to which the acoustical consequences are the perceived sound with the same timbre variations. All the action planning is involved in this task, from the intention to the proactive simulation of the execution of the movement. Finally, according to the sensorimotor paradigm, to perceive a friction sound it is almost already doing the gesture which has produced the sound. This distinction is interesting because it gives a relevant approach to make hypothesis about the invariant features which enable the auditory recognition of acoustical events. Regarding the previous definition of a simulated action, the third experiment reinforces this notion from the auditory point of view. The subjects have been able to take the place of the writer and to adjust the sound by mentally simulating the gesture they would have executed and to compare it with the internal reference of fluid gestures. Understanding the behavior of human beings involves understanding their actions, intentions, and even emotions, to react and to behave appropriately. The main difference between humans and animals is definitely the existence of a highly developed language, which enables sharing of actions, intentions and emotions through a common channel of communication among individuals. An hypothesis widely accepted now is that our verbal language derived from a gestural one, in which actual words were screams and contortions [33]. Nowadays, the ability of humans to speak articulately enables to use quasi exclusively the vocal channel rather than the gestural one. But we have not completely abandoned the gestures, and it is commonly observed that when we speak, we make a lot of gestures with a very important signification according to the context to supply our speech [30]. Another observation about gestural language and more generally about corporeal language, is related to the postural communication in animals. Darwin studied the dog postures and their significations, and remarked that posture can either evoke hostile intents or humble and affectionate mood [9]. Hence gestures and more generally corporeal articulations have a lot of perceptual significations, in line with the third experiment previously presented from the auditory modality which will be discussed.

In experiment 3, we proposed a perspective of intuitive controls based on emotional and gestural descriptions. The close relation between intention, emotion and gesture was addressed in a musical context, this question has been addressed by Marc Leman [23], a proposition to explain interpretations and emotions involved by musical and aesthetic experiences by considering the *corporeal engagement*, and the *corporeal resonances*, which are non linguistic descriptions of music and involved emotions. Such corporeal engagement has been suggest in the case of the emotions we feel when we see a painting. It could be due to the fact that we try to imagine the gestures, and therefore the underlying intentions of the artist. This question has been already discussed in [26] regarding functional imagery studies which revealed that our motor areas involved in drawing were also activated when we see passively a letter we are able to trace [24,25]. These results suggest that the visual perception of a stimulus involved all the processes implied in the motor planning, and could be the basis of emotions engaged when we perceive an artistic performance. Jeannerod suggests it in the case of the perception of a dance performance [17]. He proposed that we may perceptually take the place of the dancer in order to feel his sensorial state, so the emotions we can feel from a dance performance could be explained by such a perceptual process coupling perception to simulated action. By analogies with such processes involved in vision and according to the results of the experiment 3, we could imagine that such simulated actions should also be involved in the case of the perception of a musical piece, but more experiments, either behavioral or from functional imagery should be done to confirm such a strong hypothesis.

Finally, the enactive theory and the notion *simulated action* are a well adapted framework for studying the perception of auditory objects which involved a human action like the friction sounds produced when someone is drawing. Moreover, the invariant taxonomy seems also well adapted to this. But to extend these approaches to environmental sounds. which do not necessary involved an embodied action, we have to define a general concept of *action* and to take into account our interaction with the surrounding world with an holistic point of view. For instance, the sound of a river flowing does not involve a human action, in the sense of producing a motor act such as drawing or making a movement. And finally, what is simulated when we listen such sound? It is maybe more generally linked to experience rather than a simulated motor action. And maybe it would be interesting to define a notion which could be named a simulated situation, which englobes embodied active actions but also contains more general experiences. This point will not be discussed here but have to be clarified to establish a general ontology of sound perception based on the sensorimotor and phenomenal contingencies. It would also be interesting to discuss and to contextualize the invariants taxonomy regarding this more general framework.

Acknowledgments. This work was funded by the French National Research Agency (ANR) under the MetaSon: Métaphores Sonores (Sound Metaphors) project (ANR-10-CORD-0003) in the CONTINT 2010 framework. The authors are grateful to Charles Gondre for his precious help for the development of the listening test interfaces.

References

1. Aramaki, M., Gondre, C., Kronland-Martinet, R., Voinier, T., Ystad, S.: Thinking the sounds: an intuitive control of an impact sound synthesizer. In: Proceedings of ICAD 2009 – 15th International Conference on Auditory Display (2009)
2. Aramaki, M., Besson, M., Kronland-Martinet, R., Ystad, S.: Controlling the Perceived Material in an Impact Sound Synthesizer. IEEE Transactions on Speech and Audio Processing 19(2), 301–314 (2011)
3. Bangert, M., Peschel, T., Schlaug, G., Rotte, M., Drescher, D., Hinrichs, H., Heinze, H.J., Altenmüller, E.: Shared network for auditory and motor processing in professional pianists: evidence from fMRI conjunction. Neuroimage 30(3), 917–926 (2006)
4. Berthoz, A.: Le sens du mouvement. Odile Jacob (1997)
5. Bigand, E., Vieillard, S., Madurell, F., Marozeau, J., Dacquet, A.: Multidimensional scaling of emotional responses to music: The effect of musical expertise and of the duration of the excerpts. Cognition & Emotion 19(8), 1113–1139 (2005)
6. Carello, C., Anderson, K.L., Kunkler-Peck, A.J.: Perception of object length by sound. Psychological Science 9(3), 211–214 (2008)
7. Conan, S., Aramaki, M., Kronland-Martinet, R., Thoret, E., Ystad, S.: Perceptual Differences Between Sounds Produced by Different Continuous Interactions. Acoustics 2012, Nantes (2012)
8. Conan, S., Aramaki, M., Kronland-Martinet, R., Ystad, S.: Intuitive Control of Rolling Sound Synthesis. In: Aramaki, M., Barthet, M., Kronland-Martinet, R., Ystad, S. (eds.) CMMR 2012, vol. 7900, pp. 99–109. Springer, Heidelberg (2013)
9. Darwin, C.: The expression of the emotions in man and animals. The American Journal of the Medical Sciences 232(4), 477 (1956)
10. Frémiot, M., Mandelbrojt, J., Formosa, M., Delalande, G., Pedler, E., Malbosc, P., Gobin, P.: Les Unités Sémiotiques Temporelles: éléments nouveaux dánalyse musicale. Diffusion ESKA. MIM Laboratoire Musique et Informatique de Marseille (MIM), documents musurgia édition. 13 (1996)
11. Gallese, V., Fadiga, L., Fogassi, L., Rizzolatti, G.: Action recognition in the premotor cortex. Brain 119(2), 593–609 (1996)
12. Gaver, W.W.: What in the world do we hear?: an ecological approach to auditory event perception. Ecological psychology 5(1), 1–29 (1993)
13. Gaver, W.W.: How do we hear in the world? Explorations in ecological acoustics. Journal of Ecological Psychology 5(4), 285–313 (1993)
14. Griffiths, T.D., Warren, J.D.: What is an auditory object? Nature Reviews Neuroscience 5(11), 887–892 (2004)
15. Gibson, J.J.: The Senses Considered as Perceptual Systems. Houghton-Mifflin, Boston (1966)
16. Jeannerod, M.: The representing brain: Neural correlates of motor intention and imagery. Behavioral and Brain Sciences 17(2), 187–202 (1994)
17. Jeannerod, M.: La fabrique des idées, Odile Jacob (2011)

18. Klatzky, R.L., Pai, D.K., Krotkov, E.P.: Perception of material from contact sounds. Presence: Teleoperators & Virtual Environments 9(4), 399–410 (2000)
19. Kohler, E., Keysers, C., Umilta, M.A., Fogassi, L., Gallese, V., Rizzolatti, G.: Hearing sounds, understanding actions: action representation in mirror neurons. Science 297(5582), 846–848 (2002)
20. Keogh, E., Ratanamahatana, C.A.: Exact indexing of dynamic time warping. Knowledge and Information Systems 7(3), 358–386 (2005)
21. Kronland-Martinet, R., Voinier, T.: Real-time perceptual simulation of moving sources: application to the Leslie cabinet and 3D sound immersion. EURASIP Journal on Audio, Speech, and Music Processing (2008)
22. Lacquaniti, F., Terzuolo, C.A., Viviani, P.: The law relating kinematic and figural aspects of drawing movements. Acta Psychologica 54, 115–130 (1983)
23. Leman, M.: Embodied music cognition and mediation technology. MIT Press (2007)
24. Longcamp, M., Anton, J.L., Roth, M., Velay, J.L.: Visual presentation of single letters activates a premotor area involved in writing. Neuroimage 19(4), 1492–1500 (2003)
25. Longcamp, M., Tanskanen, T., Hari, R.: The imprint of action: Motor cortex involvement in visual perception of handwritten letters. Neuroimage 33(2), 681–688 (2006)
26. Longcamp, M., Velay, J.L.: Connaissances motrices, perception visuelle et jugements esthétiques: l'exemple des formes graphiques. In: Dans l'atelier de l'art Expériences Cognitives by Mario Borillo, Champ Vallon, Seyssel, France, p. 284. MIT Press (2010)
27. Merer, A., Ystad, S., Kronland-Martinet, R., Aramaki, M.: Semiotics of sounds evoking motions: Categorization and acoustic features. In: Kronland-Martinet, R., Ystad, S., Jensen, K. (eds.) CMMR 2007. LNCS, vol. 4969, pp. 139–158. Springer, Heidelberg (2008)
28. Merer, A., Aramaki, M., Ystad, S., Kronland-Martinet, R.: Perceptual characterization of motion evoked by sounds for synthesis control purposes. ACM Transaction on Applied Perception 10(1) (February 2013)
29. McAdams, S.: Recognition of sound sources and events. In: McAdams, S., Bigand, E. (eds.) Thinking in Sound: The Cognitive Psychology of Human Audition, pp. 146–198 (1993)
30. McNeil, D.: So you think gestures are nonverbal? Psychological Review 92(3), 350–371 (1985)
31. O'Regan, J.K., Noë, A.: A sensorimotor account of vision and visual consciousness. Behavioral and Brain Sciences 24(5), 939–972 (2001)
32. Rizzolatti, G., Fadiga, L., Gallese, V., Fogassi, L.: Premotor cortex and the recognition of motor actions. Cognitive Brain Research 3(2), 131–141 (1996)
33. Rizzolatti, G., Sinigaglia, C.: Les neurones miroirs. Odile Jacob (2008)
34. Rosenblum, L.D., Carello, C., Pastore, R.E.: Relative effectiveness of three stimulus variables for locating a moving sound source. Perception 16, 175–186 (1987)
35. Sokal, R.R., Rohlf, F.J.: The comparison of dendrograms by objective methods. Taxon 11(2), 33–40 (1962)
36. Van Den Doel, K., Kry, P.G., Pai, D.K.: FoleyAutomatic : physically-based sound effects for interactive simulation and animation. In: Proceedings of the 28th Annual Conference on Computer Graphics and Interactive Techniques, pp. 537–544. ACM (2001)
37. Varela, F.J.: Invitation aux sciences cognitives. Eds. Le Seuil (1988)
38. Varela, F.J., Thompson, E.T., Evan, T., Rosch, E.: The embodied mind: Cognitive science and human experience. MIT Press (1992)

39. Viviani, P., Terzuolo, C.: Trajectory determines movement dynamics. Neuroscience 7(2), 431–437 (1982)
40. Viviani, P., McCollum, G.: The relation between linear extent and velocity in drawing movements. Neuroscience 10(1), 211–218 (1983)
41. Viviani, P., Stucchi, N.: The effect of movement velocity on form perception: Geometric illusions in dynamic displays. Attention, Perception, & Psychophysics 46(3), 266–274 (1989)
42. Viviani, P., Schneider, R.: A developmental study of the relationship between geometry and kinematics in drawing movements. Journal of Experimental Psychology: Human Perception and Performance 17, 198–218 (1991)
43. Viviani, P., Stucchi, N.: Biological movements look uniform: Evidence of motor-perceptual interactions. Journal of Experimental Psychology: Human Perception and Performance 18, 603–623 (1992)
44. Viviani, P., Flash, T.: Minimum-jerk, two-thirds power law and isochrony: Converging approaches to movement planning. Journal of Experimental Psychology: Human Perception and Performance 21, 32–53 (1995)
45. Viviani, P., Baud-Bovy, G., Redolfi, M.: Perceiving and tracking kinesthetic stimuli: Further evidence of motor–perceptual interactions. Journal of Experimental Psychology: Human Perception and Performance 23(4), 1232–1252 (1997)
46. Warren, W.H., Verbrugge, R.R.: Auditory perception of breaking and bouncing events: a case study in ecological acoustics. Journal of Experimental Psychology: Human Perception and Performance 10(5), 704 (1984)
47. Wildes, R.P., Richards, W.A.: Recovering material properties from sound. In: Richards, W.A. (ed.) Natural Computation, pp. 356–363 (1988)

Auditory Sketches: Sparse Representations of Sounds Based on Perceptual Models

Clara Suied[1,3,*], Angélique Drémeau[2,4,*],
Daniel Pressnitzer[1], and Laurent Daudet[2]

[1] Laboratoire Psychologie de la Perception, CNRS - Université Paris Descartes &
Ecole Normale Supérieure, 29 rue d'Ulm, 75230 Paris Cedex 5, France
clara.suied@irba.fr, Daniel.Pressnitzer@ens.fr
[2] Institut Langevin, ESPCI ParisTech and CNRS UMR 7587, Université Paris
Diderot, 1 rue Jussieu, 75005 Paris France
angelique.dremeau@telecom-paristech.fr, laurent.daudet@espci.fr
[3] Institut de Recherche Biomédicale des Armées (IRBA), Département Action et
Cognition en Situation Opérationnelle, 91223 Brétigny sur Orge, France
[4] Institut Mines-Telecom - Telecom ParisTech - CNRS/LTCI UMR 5141, 75014 Paris

Abstract. An important question for both signal processing and auditory science is to understand which features of a sound carry the most
important information for the listener. Here we approach the issue by
introducing the idea of "auditory sketches": sparse representations of
sounds, severely impoverished compared to the original, which nevertheless afford good performance on a given perceptual task. Starting from
biologically-grounded representations (auditory models), a sketch is obtained by reconstructing a highly under-sampled selection of elementary
atoms. Then, the sketch is evaluated with a psychophysical experiment
involving human listeners. The process can be repeated iteratively. As a
proof of concept, we present data for an emotion recognition task with
short non-verbal sounds. We investigate 1/ the type of auditory representation that can be used for sketches 2/ the selection procedure to
sparsify such representations 3/ the smallest number of atoms that can
be kept 4/ the robustness to noise. Results indicate that it is possible
to produce recognizable sketches with a very small number of atoms
per second. Furthermore, at least in our experimental setup, a simple
and fast under-sampling method based on selecting local maxima of the
representation seems to perform as well or better than a more traditional algorithm aimed at minimizing the reconstruction error. Thus,
auditory sketches may be a useful tool for choosing sparse dictionaries,
and also for identifying the minimal set of features required in a specific
perceptual task.

1 Introduction

Sound signals are one-dimensional time series, reflecting the variation of acoustic
pressure in the air. There is a variety of ways to represent such time-series,

---

* These authors contributed equally to this work.

M. Aramaki et al. (Eds.): CMMR 2012, LNCS 7900, pp. 154–170, 2013.

starting with Fourier transforms or wavelet analyses [1]. Each representation is defined in a set of basis functions on which the time-series are projected: complex exponentials for the Fourier analysis, or dilated and translated versions of a mother wavelet for wavelets. In an "atomistic" view of this analysis process [2], the set of basis functions is often called the "dictionary", and its elements the "atoms". Desirable properties for a dictionary may be the orthogonality between elements, or its completeness and invertibility (*i.e.*, it is possible to represent any signal and transform it back without any loss of information). More recently, for applications such as source separation or denoising, further properties have been shown to be useful, such as sparsity (see [3] for a review), where only a few non-zeros coefficients can be used to represent a signal. In practice, exact sparsity is never achieved for sound signals, but still most of them can be well approximated by sparse representations (the approximation error decays quickly as the number of terms increases), a property often referred to as *compressibility*. Such sparse representations are usually computed through some non-linear algorithms, optimizing a balance between sparsity and data fidelity [4].

The size and nature of the (possibly over-complete) dictionary must be carefully chosen, as larger dictionaries tend to provide sparser representations, but the computational cost of the associated estimation algorithms may become prohibitive, and high coherence in the dictionary elements may result in identifiability issues. The choice of the dictionary elements, or "atoms", is also of prime importance, as these must be designed to fit local features of the signals under study ; they can be chosen *a priori* or learnt on the data itself [5].

In this paper, we outline an original method for investigating sparse representations of sound signals, based on perceptual considerations. The underlying idea is simple: sounds are not just any time-series, they are time-series that are being perceived by listeners. As a consequence, not all information in sound is relevant for a given listening task. For instance, speech content is remarkably resilient to large acoustic distortions [6], showing that a massive information-loss can be tolerated for tasks like speech intelligibility in quiet. The key is that the distortion should preserve a small but sufficient set of features for the task. Here we introduce the metaphor of an "auditory sketch": a sketch is a signal that has been severely impoverished compared to the original sound, and thus is clearly distinguishable from it, but that still retains enough of the original critical features to afford good performance on a target task.

A schematic of the work flow we suggest to obtain auditory sketches is presented on Fig. 1. The method is iterative, and places the listener at the centre of the design loop. The first proposal is to use auditory models. Auditory models refer to a class of signal-processing algorithms trying to mimic the way the acoustic signal is transformed along the human auditory pathways. For instance, the cochlea performs a time-frequency decomposition, which can be approximated to a first degree by a bank of overlapping band-pass filters [7]. The resulting representation is often termed an "auditory spectrogram". Subsequent stages of processing in the auditory pathways display more complex processes, which are

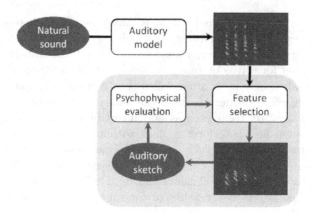

Fig. 1. Overview of the sketch design method. An auditory representation of a natural sound is generated (in this example, an auditory spectrogram) and only a few features are retained. The auditory model is then inverted for re-synthesis of the candidate sketch. Psychophysical experiments involving human listeners are then used to evaluate the efficiency of the selected features. The process is repeated iteratively to discover a sparse set of features that afford good performance with sound class and task at hand.

currently only poorly understood. For instance, neurons in the primary auditory cortex exhibit a variety of selectivity to spectro-temporal features such as spectral, temporal, or joint-spectral temporal modulations. Models nevertheless exist to idealise such a processing as a bank of 2-D wavelets operating on the auditory spectrogram [8]. Such schematic "cortical" representations have been shown, for instance, to be sufficiently rich to be an efficient front-end for timbre classification [9].

It is hoped that, because they are inspired by the physiology of the human ear, such auditory representations will contain the features that are relevant to perception. However, these representations are massively over-complete, so it is not obvious to assess which part of the representation is relevant for a given task. This is where we use a second step in the sketches method: the representations are sparsified by keeping only a small set of non-zero coefficients. A variety of selection algorithms can be envisioned, as discussed below.

Finally, to check that the relevant features have been preserved, we invert the sparse representations back into sound signals. The resulting sounds are then used in psychophysical tests with human listeners. The process should be repeated iteratively until the selection of sparse features affords good performance on the target perceptual task.

In this paper, we present preliminary data as a proof of concept for the sketches process. We compare two different auditory models, aimed at representing two distinct stages of auditory processing: the auditory spectrogram and the cortical representation [8]. The selection of non-zero coefficients from the models is obviously a central issue, and here we compare two potential candidates: a simple peak-picking algorithm, and an analysis-based iterative thresholding method

[10]. Finally, the psychophysical task chosen is that of recognition of emotion in short sound snippets. Sounds are extracted from a calibrated database of natural emotional signals [11], transformed as sketches, and then listeners have to identify the original emotion in a forced-choice task (happiness, anger, sadness, disgust). Only the first iteration in the method is tested.

2   Sparse Representations of Sounds: Dictionaries and Algorithms

The "sketching" problem we are interested in can be formalized as follows. We look for the sketch $\mathbf{x} \in \mathbb{R}^N$, representation of the audio signal $\mathbf{y}$ such as

$$\mathbf{y} = \mathbf{x} + \epsilon, \tag{1}$$

where ϵ stands for the difference between the original audio signal $\mathbf{y}$ and its sketch $\mathbf{x}$. Within our study, the sketch $\mathbf{x}$ is then assumed to have a sparse representation in a given dictionary.

Traditionally, the quality of the sparse representation is measured both in terms of sparsity and approximation (*i.e.*, the fidelity to the original signal). It depends on the dictionary in which the decomposition is performed, and the procedure for the selection of sparse features (and the corresponding algorithms). Here, an additional stage is considered. Following the algorithmic procedure implementing the sparse decomposition, the appropriateness of the resulting sketch to the target task is further tested through a psychophysical evaluation (see Fig. 1). Ideally, the whole procedure is then iterated to refine both the dictionary and the procedure for the selection of sparse features (in terms of objective functions, sparsity levels and algorithms). In this section, we discuss *a priori* choices for the dictionary, in Subsect. 2.1, and the decomposition procedures, in Subsect. 2.2. These can be thought of as reasonable initial conditions for the sketches process. In the context of this paper, they also serve to illustrate the potential of the method.

2.1   Auditory-Motivated Dictionaries

The choice of the dictionary is deeply related to the targeted application. In denoising tasks, for example, emphasis may be put on the match to the characteristics of the signal itself. Here, we will favour biologically-inspired dictionaries that take into account the ear physiology. The underlying hypothesis is that perception is shaped by the neural processing of sound. For instance, the frequency selectivity observed in auditory masking (which part of the sound will effectively be detected by a listener) is thought to be linked to frequency selectivity on the cochlea.

We chose to use the auditory model described by Chi *et al.* [8] and freely available as the "NSL toolbox"[1]. As mentioned in the introduction, the model

---

[1] http://www.isr.umd.edu/Labs/NSL/Software.htm

includes both an auditory spectrogram and a "cortical" spectro-temporal analysis of the spectrogram. It has proved successful for several signal-processing applications, such speech intelligibility assessment [12], or computational modeling of timbre perception [9].

The model consists of two major auditory transformations:

i) The *early stage* transforms the one-dimensional acoustic waveform to a two-dimensional pattern obtained with a bank of constant-Q filters, followed by spectral sharpening (lateral inhibition) and compression. Fig. 2 illustrates the result of such a transformation, producing what is termed an *auditory spectrogram*.

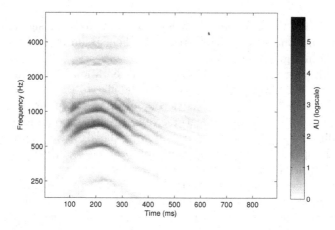

Fig. 2. Example of an auditory spectrogram (AU: arbitrary units, log scale). The sound analyzed is a short affect burst expressing anger [11]. The voiced quality of the sound is visible in the harmonic structure of the frequency components, which are themselves shaped by the vocal formants. A continuous glide of the fundamental frequency (up then down) is also salient.

ii) The *cortical stage* implements then a more complex spectrotemporal analysis, presumed to take place in the mammalian primary auditory cortex. The transformation relies on a bank of filters, selective to different spectrotemporal modulation parameters which range from slow to fast rates temporally and from narrow to broad scales spectrally. It results in a four-dimensional, time-frequency-scale-rate representation, referred to as the *cortical representation* of the signal. A detailed description of such a representation is beyond the scope of the paper, the reader is refered to [8]. Fig. 3 nevertheless illustrates some features of the cortical representation.

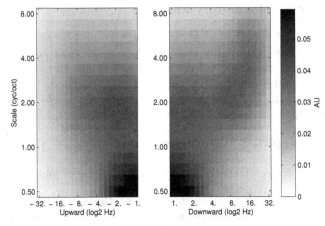

Fig. 3. Example of a cortical representation (AU: arbitrary units). The sound is the same as in Fig. 2. We only illustrate the projection of the 4-D cortical representation on the "rate" and "scale" dimensions (the cortical representation was averaged over time and over frequency channels). The pattern of rate and scale coefficients describe the spectro-temporal evolution of the sound. For instance, because the fundamental frequency glide induces temporal amplitude modulations in many frequency channels, there is a range of non-zero modulation rates in the representation. The left and right panels are for upward and downward spectro-temporal modulations, respectively (see [8] for details).

Because our method relies on a listening test, an important issue is the invertibility of the representations used. If phases are preserved, the (standard or auditory) spectrograms are easily invertible, akin to the overlap-add resynthesis procedure of the standard spectrogram. However, if non-linear processing makes phase information meaningless, as is the case here (lateral inhibition, thresholding, compression), perfect reconstruction cannot be achieved.

In order to obtain time-domain signals that are compatible with the spectrogram, one can resort to phase estimation algorithms that exploit the intrinsic redundancy of the transforms, such as the Griffin and Lim [13] phase reconstruction iterative procedure, or improvements thereof (see [14] for a review). It should be noted that this algorithm reconstructs a set of phases that are consistent, but that may be completely different from the original phases, thus precluding any time-domain sample-by-sample comparison. Here, we use the method of [15], developed for auditory spectrograms and which provides reconstructions that are highly perceptually similar to the original signal, whenever the auditory spectrogram is not modified.

The parameters chosen for the model of [8] were as follows. The audio signals were sampled at 16kHz. The auditory spectrogram was obtained with a bank of 128 bandpass filters and 8-ms time windows. The cortical stage had 5 rate channels for temporal modulations (from 1 to 32Hz) and 6 scale channels for spectral modulation (from 0.5 to 8 cycles/octave), resulting in a redundant representation 60-times larger than the original signal.

2.2   Sparsification of Auditory Models

The next step in the design of sketches is the choice of a selection procedure for the features. Here again many choices are possible. Note that the iterative method of Fig. 1 is conceived precisely as a way to refine the selection process. As a first step, to gain some insight into the kind of methods that could serve as initial choices in the iterative process, we compare two selection procedures contrasting two different approaches:

- Algorithm IHT (iterative hard thresholding), based on a sparse analysis scheme
- Algorithm PP (peak-picking), based on peak-picking of local maxima

It is important to stress that, as we shall discuss, these two procedures are not just different from an algorithmic point of view. More importantly, one of them aims at optimizing the quadratic reconstruction error (IHT), while the other (PP) is purely feedforward and does not include any optimization step. In both cases, the ultimate success of the selection or otherwise is estimated by means of the perceptual task.

Algorithm IHT: Sparse Analysis by Iterative Hard Thresholding. Two mathematical sparsity formalisms are possible, according to the adopted – *analysis* or *synthesis* – approach. On the one hand, from the analysis point of view and within our sketching problem, the sketch $\mathbf{x}$ is assumed to produce a sparse output, which can be expressed under a matrix formulation as

$$\mathbf{z} = \mathbf{A}\mathbf{x}, \tag{2}$$

where $\mathbf{z} \in \mathbb{R}^M$ is sparse, *i.e.*, contains few non-zero elements, and $\mathbf{A}$ is a $(M \times N)$-matrix with $M \geq N$ representing the analysis operator. On the other hand, from the synthesis point of view, the sketch $\mathbf{x}$ is seen as the sparse combination of atoms, namely

$$\mathbf{x} = \mathbf{D}\mathbf{z}, \tag{3}$$

where $\mathbf{D}$ is a $(N \times M)$-matrix with $M \geq N$ representing the dictionary, and $\mathbf{z}$ is sparse.

Within the sparse-representation framework, the synthesis approach constitutes the most common formalism, being the subject of numerous contributions (see *e.g.*, [16] for a review of the algorithms dealing with synthesis sparsity). However, as described above, the representations we chose rely on a sequence of filters applied to the signal and analyzing their outputs, which tends to favor the analysis point of view.

Furthermore, the sparsity constraint in which we are interested in is not taken into account in the same way within both formalisms. The synthesis formulation, by its generative nature, leads potentially to a greater compactness of the signal. But, with this formulation, the choice of the atoms to represent the signal has huge implications: a wrong decision may cause the selection of additional wrong atoms as compensation. This is not the case with the analysis formulation, where all atoms contribute equally to the representation of the signal [17]. We will thus adopt the analysis point of view in the remain of the paper. Hence, depending on the processing level, a sketch $\mathbf{x}$ of the audio signal $\mathbf{y}$ is built from a sparse auditory spectrogram or a sparse cortical representation of the signal $\mathbf{y}$.

Considering the analysis formulation (2), the estimation of the sketch $\mathbf{x}$ can then be expressed as

$$\mathbf{x}^* = \operatorname*{argmin}_{\mathbf{x}} ||\mathbf{y} - \mathbf{x}||_2^2 \text{ subject to } ||\mathbf{A}\mathbf{x}||_0 \leq L, \qquad (4)$$

where $||.||_0$ denotes the ℓ_0 pseudo-norm, counting the number of non-zero elements, and L is a parameter specifying the maximum number of non-zero elements in $\mathbf{z}$.

Finding the exact solution of (4) is an NP-hard problem, *i.e.*, it generally requires a combinatorial search over the entire solution space. Here, we use a suboptimal (but tractable) algorithm based on the iterative hard thresholding procedure introduced in [10]. This algorithm presents indeed several desirable properties:

i) Its implementation is very simple, in accordance with a filter-bank procedure, as considered within our model (see Subsect. 2.1).

ii) Its complexity is low, in $\mathcal{O}(N \log N)$, N being the number of iterations. This property is very valuable since the considered biologically inspired model involves complex mathematical computations, requiring thus a light integration procedure.

Note that the analysis-based IHT algorithm is different from the most standard synthesis-based iterative hard thresholding algorithms in the literature [18], often used in the framework of compressed sensing.

Algorithm PP: Peak-Picking of Local Maxima. The second algorithm considered in this paper is based on a simple local maxima detection.

The procedure, with variants already used in the literature (see *e.g.*, [19,20]), is based on a local gradient evaluation. In our case, the peak-picking was done on either the auditory spectrogram (finding 2-D local maxima) or the cortical representation (finding 4-D local maxima). The algorithm proceeds as follows : first, all local maxima (on the magnitude of the coefficients) are selected. Then, they are sorted by decreasing order and only the L largest are kept, L being related to the desired degree of sparsity. Note that this algorithm is not iterative, without any optimization procedure, and therefore is very fast.

It should also be noted that, as opposed to the vast majority of sparse decomposition/analysis algorithms, such as IHT described above, the goal of this analysis scheme is not to achieve the best approximation (in a least-squares sense) of the signal for a given number of coefficients. Instead, the rationale is that, if the representation itself is efficient, the selection mechanism can be rather crude: within a zone of the parameters space, local maxima should express salient features.

3 Psychophysical Experiments

The core idea of the sketches process is to put the listener at the centre of the design procedure. Thus, as candidate sketches are obtained, they are used in a perceptual task where a performance measure can be obtained. If a high performance is observed, then this indicates that the set of features that have been selected in the sparsification process is sufficient for the task, even though the sketch itself may sound very different from the original signal.

We now report two experiments using a perceptual task of emotion recognition. We asked listeners to report whether a short vocal sound expressed happiness, sadness, anger, or disgust. Each emotion was represented by several sound samples, selected from a calibrated database [11]. The main aim was to provide a first test of the sketches approach: could listeners perform the task on sounds that were severely impoverished compared to the original? More precise questions as to the nature of the sketching process were asked in each experiment.

3.1 Experiment 1: Comparison of Two Auditory Representations

Rationale. Here we wanted to investigate the influence of the basic representation used to produce sketches. We used auditory models, but contrasted auditory spectrograms with spectro-temporal "cortical" representations. The robustness of sketches to the presence or absence of noise was also tested. Indeed, if we assume that the goal of the sketches is to identify perceptually-important features of sounds, a certain robustness to noise is desirable. Robustness to noise is thus one indication that the representation is well-suited to the sound class of interest. Finally, the sparsity that can be achieved with the method was evaluated: a better representation should produce a sparser code.

Material and Methods

Participants. There were 10 participants (6 men and 4 women), aged between 19 and 39 years ($M = 25.8$ years). All listeners had self-reported normal-hearing. They all provided informed consent to participate in the study, which was conducted in accordance with the guidelines of the declaration of Helsinki.

Stimuli. All sounds were derived from the Montreal Affective Voices database [11]. They consisted of recorded nonverbal emotional interjections (on the French vowel /a/). Among the available stimuli, we selected four emotions that were easily recognized (see [11]): anger, disgust, happiness, and sadness. Each emotional interjection was uttered by 10 different actors (5 male and 5 female). The original sounds had very different durations (from 0.4 s to 1.2 s), so we shortened some of the stimuli (happiness and sadness, mainly) to avoid recognition cues linked to duration. The modified versions of the sounds were still easily recognized, as confirmed by an informal experiment. The modified sounds had an average duration of 0.99 s (std= 0.2). A repeated-measures ANOVA performed on the 40 sounds (4 emotions for the 10 speakers) revealed no significant differences between the mean duration of each emotion $[F(3, 27) = 0.95; p = 0.4]$. These 40 sounds constituted the baseline stimuli.

For the "noise" conditions, pink noise was added to the original sounds, with a signal-to-noise ratio of -6 dB.

The sketch process was performed either on the original sound or on the noise version of the sound. In this first experiment, it was only performed using the PP algorithm. Two auditory representations were compared: the auditory spectrogram and the cortical representation (see above). Three degrees of sparsity were also compared: 10, 100, and 1000 features/second were retained from the auditory representations. The measure of features/second, which we refer to as the degree of sketch, is only indirectly related to the quantity of information retained from the original signal (as for instance it ignores the size and nature of the dictionnary). However, it serves here as a first approximation of sparsity.

Apparatus. Stimuli were presented through an RME Fireface digital-to-analog converter at a 16-bit resolution and a 44.1 kHz sample-rate. They were presented to both ears simultaneously through Sennheiser HD 250 Linear II headphones. Presentation level was at 70 dB(A), as calibrated with a Bruel & Kjaer (2250) sound level meter and ear simulator (B&K 4153). Listeners were tested individually in a double-walled Industrial Acoustics (IAC) sound booth.

Procedure. A 4-AFC (Alternative Forced Choice) paradigm was used. In each trial, participants heard a single sound, which could be one of the 4 target emotions. They had to indicate whether the sound they just heard was a representative sound of happiness, sadness, anger, and disgust. Visual feedback was provided after each response.

14 conditions were presented in a randomized fashion to each participant, for a total of 1120 stimuli in total: original sounds vs. sketches and no noise vs. noise. For the sketches, we compared the auditory spectrogram vs. cortical representation and the degree of sketch (10, 100, or 1000 feat/s). The experiment lasted approximately 1 hour. The experiment was divided into small blocks, to allow time for breaks.

Results. Results are illustrated on Fig. 4. A first important observation is the overall good performance, well above the chance level (i.e. 25%), with a mean percent correct of 93% for the original sounds, and of 55% for the sketches sounds. A second key result rests upon the comparison of the two auditory models used to create the sketches: overall, the auditory spectrogram outperformed the cortical representation. Data were analyzed with a repeated-measures analysis of variance (ANOVA). We first evaluated the overall difference between the original sounds and the sketches, in the two noise conditions. A repeated-measure ANOVA revealed main significant effects for the type of sound (original

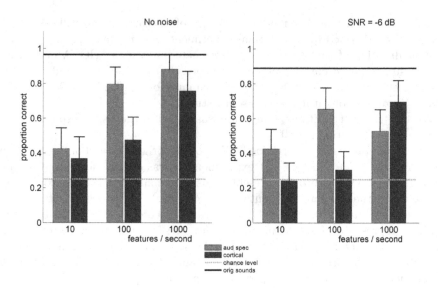

Fig. 4. Results for Experiment 1. Recognition performance of the sketches sounds corresponding to two different auditory models (aud spec for the auditory spectrogram, and cortical model), without (left panel) and with (right panel) noise. Error bars correspond to the standard error of the mean. Performance was overall higher for the auditory spectrogram than for the cortical model. These recognition data for the sketches sounds are compared to an upper baseline : the average recognition performance for the original sounds (black line). They are also compared to a lower baseline: the chance level, i.e. 25% here (dotted gray line).

vs. sketch) $[F(1,8) = 1172.55; p < 0.0001]$ and for the noise condition (silence vs. noise) $[F(1,8) = 441.81; p < 0.0001]$, as well as a significant interaction between these two variables $[F(1,8) = 21.66; p < 0.005]$. These results show that the overall recognition performance was better for the original sounds than for the sketches, and that, as expected, noise had a detrimental effect on performance; the influence of noise was more pronounced for the sketches than for the original sounds.

We then analyzed in more details data for the sketches sounds only. We performed a repeated-measure ANOVA with noise (silence vs. noise), model (auditory spectrogram vs. cortical), and features (10, 100, and 1000 feat/s) as within-subjects variables. It revealed main significant effects of noise $[F(1,8) = 582,23; p < 0.0001]$, model $[F(1,8) = 101,44; p < 0.0001]$, and features $[F(2,16) = 138,01; p < 0.0001]$. It also revealed significant interaction between features and model $[F(2,16) = 89,80; p < 0.0001]$, features and noise $[F(1,8) = 21,09; p < 0.0001]$, as well as a significant third-order interaction between features, model, and noise $[F(1,8) = 37,81; p < 0.0001]$. These results highlight that: performance was better in silence than in noise; performance increased as the number of features per second increased; the auditory spectrogram model led to better performance than the cortical model (with one notable exception, that was responsible for the significant third-order interaction: in the noise condition, for 1000 feat/s, the cortical model led to better performances than the auditory spectrogram model).

3.2   Experiment 2: Comparison of Two Sparsification Algorithms

Rationale. Experiment 1 served as a first proof of concept of the sketches process: the overall recognition performance for sketches sounds was good (55%, i.e. well above the chance level). This was the case even though the selection algorithm, PP, was extremely crude and did not contain any optimization. Here, we compare the PP algorithm with a more traditional signal-processing approach, the IHT algorithm, that minimizes the reconstruction error (see Sect. 2.2).

Material and Methods

Participants. There were 10 participants (5 men and 5 women), aged between 19 and 34 years (M = 23.2 years). All listeners had self-reported normal-hearing. They all provided informed consent to participate in the study, which was conducted in accordance with the guidelines of the declaration of Helsinki.

Stimuli. Stimuli were very similar to Experiment 1, the only differences here being that: (i) only the auditory spectrogram was used as an auditory representation for the computation of the sketches; (ii) two sparsification algorithms were used to produce the sketches: IHT and PP (see Subsect. 2.2 for details).

Apparatus and Procedure. The apparatus was the same as in Experiment 1. The procedure was also very similar. Here, the 12 conditions that were presented in a randomized fashion to the participant were a combination of 3 parameters: type of algorithm (IHT vs. PP), noise (with or without), and degree of sketch (10, 100, and 1000 feature/second).

Results. Results of this second experiment are illustrated on Fig. 5. This second experiment confirms and reproduces some important results of Experiment 1: an overall good recognition performance, with a mean percent correct of 93% for the original sounds, and of 60% for the sketches sounds. It also shows that the PP algorithm generally outperformed the IHT algorithm. Similar analyses as for the Experiment 1 were conducted. Firstly, the overall ANOVA reproduced results of Experiment 1: performance was better for the original sounds than for the sketches $[F(1,9) = 708.77; p < 0.0001]$; performance was also better in silence that in the noise $[F(1,9) = 119.44; p < 0.0001]$. For this experiment as well, the detrimental effect of the noise was more pronounced for the sketches than for the original sounds [significant interaction between the type of sound and the noise condition: $[F(1,9) = 12 : 90; p < 0 : 006]$.
Secondly, a detailed repeated-measures ANOVA on the sketches only revealed that: as expected, performance was better in silence than in noise $[F(1,9) = 148.98; p < 0.0001]$; performance increased as the number of features per second increased $[F(2,18) = 283.89; p < 0.0001]$.

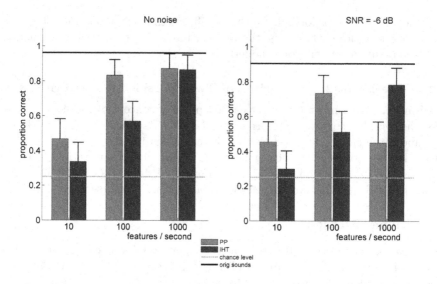

Fig. 5. Results for Experiment 2. Recognition performance of the sketches sounds corresponding to two different sparsifying algorithms (PP for peak-picking, and IHT for iterative hard thresholding), without (left panel) and with (right panel) noise. Error bars correspond to the standard error of the mean. Performance was overall higher for the PP than for the IHT algorithm. These recognition data for the sketches sounds are compared to an upper baseline: the average recognition performance for the original sounds (black line). They are also compared to a lower baseline: the chance level, i.e. 25% here (dotted gray line).

It also showed that performance was overall better for the PP algorithm than for the IHT algorithm [$F(1, 9) = 54.72; p < 0.0001$]. All second-order interactions were also significant:
[features $\times$ algorithm : $F(2, 18) = 85.92; p < 0.0001$.
features $\times$ noise : $F(2, 18) = 32.39; p < 0.0001$.
algorithm $\times$ noise : $F(1, 9) = 49.46;\ \ p < 0.0001$]. Finally, the third-order interaction was also significant [$F(1, 9) = 28.07; p < 0.0001$], and highlighted that the only exception for which the IHT algorithm outperformed the PP algorithm was in the noise condition, with 1000 feat/s.

4   Discussion

The main aim of this study was to investigate the feasibility of the auditory sketches idea. From the results, it seems that the sketches design method outlined in Fig. 1 has some potential. In the experiments, even though the vast majority of the parameters was omitted, the perceptual task (emotion recognition for nonverbal interjections) was performed well above chance: sketches retained some of the relevant information with as little as 10 features/seconds. More information-theoritic work remains to be done on quantifying the sparsity that was actually achieved, because features/second is an imperfect measure, but the results nevertheless strongly suggest that sparse representations of sounds based on biologically-motivated models produce perceptually relevant results.

Further observations can be made by comparing the variants we tested for the sketches process. Perhaps surprisingly, a state-of-the-art sparse decomposition algorithm minimizing reconstruction error (IHT) did not lead to better results than a simple peak-picking and thresholding (PP) without any optimization. In fact, in general, the reverse was true, and PP largely outperformed IHT. These preliminary results need to be extended with a larger variety of stimuli and perceptual tasks, but still, we can speculate on such an outcome. Because auditory models are inspired by the physiology of the human hearing system, they may be particularly relevant as an auditory representation. A simple algorithm like PP, although not optimal (in the least-square sense for the approximation), may be enough to capture important features by sampling some of the important landmarks of the representations.

Fig. 6 illustrates this point, by highlighting an important difference between the two selection algorithms. The PP algorithm tends to select relatively distant atoms (see Fig. 6(a)) as an extended high-energy patch in the representation can be summarized with a single peak. In contrast, the IHT algorithm will attempt to capture accurately such high-energy patches and will use several atoms to do so (see Fig. 6(c)). These opposite behaviors lead to different reconstructions: whereas IHT achieves a highly precise reconstruction of some particular parts of the original spectrogram (see Fig. 2 and Fig. 6(d)), this is done at the expense of smaller coverage of the whole parameter space.

However, we should point out that it is probably too early to generalize the superiority of a local maxima detection over a least-squares approach. The IHT algorithm constitutes one possible way to solve problem (4) amongst a large number of possibilities. We chose IHT for implementation and complexity reasons (see Subsect. 2.2) but other algorithms could potentially improve the results (see e.g., approaches based on a problem relaxation [21,22], or greedy algorithms [23]). The *sparsity-at-analysis* point of view can also be questioned, and could be compared to more standard synthesis approaches. Further experiments could finally investigate some other sparsifying procedures, intermediate between peak-picking and energy-maximizing, for instance iterative procedures based on a time-frequency masking model [24].

Another surprising result is the overall better performance for the auditory spectrogram representation compared to the cortical one. One of the limitations of the sounds we used was their short duration (around 1s). The cortical model contains filters tuned to longer modulations, so it is possible that any potential benefit of the spectro-temporal analysis only becomes apparent for longer sounds.

Finally, we found that the recognition of sketches was robust to a moderate amount of noise, but less so than for the original signal. This is in line with many psychophysical observations showing that degraded signals are more susceptible to noise. Nevertheless, one hypothesis for the sketches was that sparsification would lead to some denoising. Our results suggest that either the representations

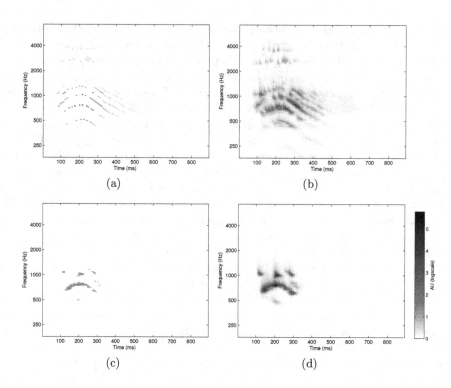

Fig. 6. Sparse auditory spectrograms obtained by means of the PP algorithm ((a) and (b)) and the IHT algorithm ((c) and (d)), directly after the decomposition ((a) and (c)) and after resynthesis of the audio signal ((b) and (d)). Here, we keep 100 feat./s. AU: arbitrary units, log scale.

failed at this goal, or that, more likely, the selection procedure could be improved. Such an approach has proven successful for denoising of speech signals, with the cortical model [25]: by increasing the dimensionality of the representation, noise and signal get mapped into different parts of the parameter space.

5   Perspectives

This preliminary study already shows that only a few features extracted from an auditory-based representation can produce a sound with recognizable perceptual traits. Even though the resulting sketch may be highly distorted compared to the original, under certain constraints, the selected features can be sufficient for recognition of complex properties such as emotional content. Obviously, more work remains to be done on each stage of the sketching process, and in particular, the iterative nature of the algorithm needs to be put to the test.

In addition, a few ideas emerge on how sound features should be combined in order to build recognizable auditory sketches. For a task of sound recognition, it seems that it is more important to have some cues on how energy is spread in the time-frequency plane, rather than a precise description of the most energetic components. Interestingly, this is similar to what is being done in state-of-the-art audio fingerprinting techniques, that choose salient points as local maxima in large blocks on the time-frequency plane. More precisely, it seems that the right way to select atoms is not purely based on energy criteria, but also their information content: we need to select a set of atoms that carry energy but also whose mutual information is minimal. In other words, we shift from the standard paradigm of sparsity justified by Occam's razor (amongst 2 explanations, prefer the one that is simplest) to an "informed" version (amongst 2 explanations, prefer the one that brings you more information on top of a prior model). This brings us close to the original sketches metaphor: to sketch a visual object, an artist will usually not attempt photographic realism. Rather, in a few pencil lines, an attempt will be made to capture what makes this object unique. It is our hypothesis that such an approach may have interesting implications for signal processing, but also for understanding how human listeners perform recognition tasks (see e.g. [26]).

Acknowledgements. This work was partly funded by the Fondation Pierre-Gilles de Gennes pour la Recherche. Laurent Daudet is on a joint position with Institut Universitaire de France. We thank Florence Bouhali for collecting the psychophysical data. We also thank Shihab Shamma and Nima Mesgarani for their input at various stages of the project. Some of these ideas were developed in the Telluride Neuromorphic Engineering workshop.

References

1. Mallat, S.: A Wavelet Tour of Signal Processing - The Sparse Way, 3rd edn. Academic Press (December 2008)
2. Gabor, D.: Acoustical quanta and the theory of hearing. Nature 159, 591–594 (1947)
3. Plumbley, M., Blumensath, T., Daudet, L., Gribonval, R., Davies, M.: Sparse representations in audio and music: From coding to source separation. Proceedings of IEEE 98(6), 995–1005 (2010)
4. Elad, M.: Sparse and Redundant Representations: From Theory to Applications in Signal and Image Processing. Springer (2010)
5. Aharon, M., Elad, M., Bruckstein, A.: K-svd: An algorithm for designing overcomplete dictionaries for sparse representation. IEEE Trans. on Signal Processing 54(11), 4311–4322 (2006)
6. Shannon, R., Zeng, F., Kamath, V., Wygonski, J., Ekelid, M.: Speech recognition with primarily temporal cues. Science 270(5234), 303–304 (1995)
7. Patterson, R., Allerhand, M., Giguére, C.: Time-domain modeling of peripheral auditory processing: A modular architecture and a software platform. Journal of the Acoustical Society of America 98(4), 1890–1894 (1995)
8. Chi, T., Ru, P., Shamma, S.A.: Multiresolution spectrotemporal analysis of complex sounds. Journal of the Acoustical Society of America 118(2), 887–906 (2005)
9. Patil, K., Pressnitzer, D., Shamma, S., Elhilali, M.: Music in our ears: the biological bases of musical timbre perception. PLoS Comp. Biol. 8(11), e1002759 (2012)

10. Portilla, J.: Image restoration through l0 analysis-based sparse optimization in tight frames. In: Proc. IEEE Int'l Conference on Image Processing (ICIP), pp. 3865–3868 (2009)

11. Belin, P., Fillion-Bilosdeau, S., Gosselin, F.: The montreal affective voices: A validated set of nonverbal affect bursts for research on auditory affective processing. Behavior Research Methods 40(2), 531–539 (2008)

12. Elhiliali, M., Chi, T., Shamma, S.A.: A spectro-temporal modulatio index (stmi) for assessment of speech intelligibility. Speech Communication 41(2-3), 331–348 (2003)

13. Griffin, D., Lim, J.: Signal reconstruction from short-time fourier transform magnitude. IEEE Trans. Acoust., Speech, and Signal Proc. 32(2), 236–243 (1984)

14. Sturmel, N., Daudet, L.: Signal reconstruction from its STFT magnitude: a state of the art. In: Proc. International Conference on Digital Audio Effects, DAFx 2011 (2011)

15. Yang, X., Wang, K., Shamma, S.A.: Auditory representations of acoustic signals. IEEE Trans. on Information Theory 38(2), 824–839 (1992)

16. Drémeau, A., Herzet, C., Daudet, L.: Boltzmann machine and mean-field approximation for structured sparse decompositions. IEEE Trans. on Signal Processing 60(7), 3425–3438 (2012)

17. Elad, M., Milanfar, P., Rubinstein, R.: Analysis versus synthesis in signal priors. Inverse problems 23(3), 947–968 (2007)

18. Blumensath, T., Davies, M.E.: Iterative thresholding for sparse approximations. Journal of Fourier Analysis and Applications 14(5-6), 629–654 (2008)

19. Hoogenboom, R., Lew, M.: Face detection using local maxima. In: Proc. Int'l Conference on Automatic Face and Gesture Recognition, 334–339 (1996)

20. Schwartzman, A., Gavrilov, Y., Adler, R.J.: Multiple testing of local maxima for detection of peaks in 1d. Annals of Statistics 39(6), 3290–3319 (2011)

21. Chambolle, A.: An algorithm for total variation minimization and application. Journal of Mathematical Imaging and Vision 20(1-2), 89–97 (2004)

22. Peyré, G., Fadili, J.: Learning analysis sparsity priors. In: Int'l Conference on Sampling Theory and Applications, SAMPTA (2011)

23. Nam, S., Davies, M., Elad, M., Gribonval, R.: Cosparse analysis modeling - uniqueness and algorithms. In: Proc. IEEE Int'l Conference on Acoustics, Speech and Signal Processing (ICASSP), pp. 5804–5807 (2011)

24. Balazs, P., Laback, B., Eckel, G., Deutsch, W.: Time-frequency sparsity by removing perceptually irrelevant components using a simple model of simultaneous masking. IEEE Transactions on Audio, Speech and Language Processing 18(1), 34–39 (2010)

25. Mesgarani, N., Shamma, S.A.: Speech enhancement using spectro-temporal modulations. EURASIP Journal on Audio, Speech, and Music Processing V, ID 42357 (2007)

26. Agus, T.A., Suied, C., Thorpe, S.J., Pressnitzer, D.: Fast recognition of musical sounds based on timbre. Journal of the Acoustical Society of America 131(5), 4124–4133 (2012)

The Role of Time in Music Emotion Recognition: Modeling Musical Emotions from Time-Varying Music Features

Marcelo Caetano[1], Athanasios Mouchtaris[1,2], and Frans Wiering[3]

[1] Institute of Computer Science, Foundation for Research and Technology
Hellas FORTH-ICS, Heraklion, Crete, Greece
{caetano,mouchtar}@ics.forth.gr
[2] University of Crete, Department of Computer Science,
Heraklion, Crete, Greece, GR-71409
[3] Department of Information and Computing Sciences,
Utrecht University, Utrecht, Netherlands
f.wiering@uu.nl

Abstract. Music is widely perceived as expressive of emotion. However, there is no consensus on which factors in music contribute to the expression of emotions, making it difficult to find robust objective predictors for music emotion recognition (MER). Currently, MER systems use supervised learning to map non time-varying feature vectors into regions of an emotion space guided by human annotations. In this work, we argue that time is neglected in MER even though musical experience is intrinsically temporal. We advance that the temporal variation of music features rather than feature values should be used as predictors in MER because the temporal evolution of musical sounds lies at the core of the cognitive processes that regulate the emotional response to music. We criticize the traditional machine learning approach to MER, then we review recent proposals to exploit the temporal variation of music features to predict time-varying ratings of emotions over the course of the music. Finally, we discuss the representation of musical time as the flow of musical information rather than clock time. Musical time is experienced through auditory memory, so music emotion recognition should exploit cognitive properties of music listening such as repetitions and expectations.

Keywords: Music, Time, Emotions, Mood, Automatic Mood Classification, Music Emotion Recognition.

1 Introduction

One of the recurring themes in treatises of music is that music both evokes emotions in listeners (emotion induction) and expresses emotions that listeners perceive, recognize, or are moved by, without necessarily feeling the emotion (emotion perception) [14]. The emotional impact of music on people and the association of music with particular emotions or 'moods' have been used in certain

M. Aramaki et al. (Eds.): CMMR 2012, LNCS 7900, pp. 171–196, 2013.

contexts to convey meaning, such as in movies, musicals, advertising, games, music recommendation systems, and even music therapy, music education, and music composition, among others. Empirical research on emotional expression started about one hundred years ago, mainly from a music psychology perspective [9], and has successively increased in scope up to today's computational models. Research on music and emotions usually investigates listeners' response to music by associating certain emotions to particular pieces, genres, styles, performances, among many others.

The mechanisms whereby music elicits emotions in listeners are not well understood. A central question in the study of music and emotions is "Which attributes or musical qualities, if any, elicit emotional reactions in listeners? [14,31]" At first, we should identify factors in the listener, in the music, and in the context that influence musical emotions (i.e., emotional reactions to music). Only then can we proceed to develop a theory about specific mechanisms that mediate among musical events and experienced emotions.

Among the causal factors that potentially affect listeners' emotional response to music are *personal, situational,* and *musical.* Personal factors include age, gender, personality, musical training, music preference, and current mood. Situational factors can be physical such as acoustic and visual conditions, time and place, or social such as type of audience, and occasion. Musical factors include genre, style, key, tuning, orchestration, among many others.

Juslin and Västfjäll [14] sustain that there is evidence of emotional reactions to music in terms of various subcomponents, such as *subjective feeling, psychophysiology, brain activation, emotional expression, action tendency, emotion regulation* and these, in turn, feature different psychological mechanisms like *brain stem reflexes, evaluative conditioning, emotional contagion, visual imagery, episodic memory, rhythmic entrainment,* and *musical expectancy.* They state that "none of the mechanisms evolved for the sake of music, but they may all be recruited in interesting (and unique) ways by musical events. Each mechanism is responsive to its own combination of information in the music, the listener, and the situation."

The literature on the emotional effects of music [15,9] has accumulated evidence that listeners often agree about the emotions expressed (or elicited) by a particular piece, suggesting that there are aspects in music that can be associated with similar emotional responses across cultures, personal bias or preferences. Several researchers imply that there is a causal relationship between music features and emotional response [9], giving evidence that certain music dimensions and qualities communicate similar affective experiences to many listeners.

An emerging field is the automatic recognition of emotions (or 'mood') in music, also called music emotion recognition (MER) [17]. The aim of MER is to design systems to automatically estimate listeners' emotional reactions to music. A typical approach to MER categorizes emotions into a number of classes and applies machine learning techniques to train a classifier and compare the results against human annotations [17,49,23]. The 'automatic mood classification' task in MIREX epitomizes the machine learning approach to MER, presenting systems whose performance range from 22 to 65 percent [11]. Some researchers speculate that musical sounds can effectively cause emotional reactions (via *brain stem reflex*, for example). Researchers are currently investigating [12,17] how to improve the performance of MER systems. Interestingly, the role of time in the automatic recognition of emotions in music is seldom discussed in MER research.

Musical experience is inherently tied to time. Studies [19,24,13,36] suggest that the temporal evolution of the musical features is intrinsically linked to listeners' emotional response to music, that is, emotions expressed or aroused by music. Among the cognitive processes involved in listening to music, memory and expectations play a major role. In this article, we argue that time lies at the core of the complex link between music and emotions, and should be brought to the foreground of MER systems.

The next section presents a brief review of the classic machine learning approach to MER. We present the traditional representation of musical features and the model of emotions to motivate the incorporation of temporal information in the next section. Then, we discuss an important drawback of this approach, the lack of temporal information. The main contribution of this work is the detailed presentation of models that exploit temporal representations of music and emotions. We also discuss modeling the relationship between the temporal evolution of musical features and emotional changes. Finally, we speculate on different representations of time that better capture the experience of musical time before presenting the conclusions and discussing future perspectives.

2   Machine Learning and Music Emotion Recognition

Traditionally, computational systems that automatically estimate the listener's emotional response to music use *supervised learning* to train the system to map a feature space representing the music onto a model of emotion according to annotated examples [17,49,23,11]. The system can perform classification [21] or regression [48], depending on the nature of the representation of emotions (see Sec. 2.2). After training, the system can be used to predict listeners' emotional responses to music that was not present in the training phase, assuming that it belongs to the same data set and therefore can be classified under the same underlying rules. System performance is measured comparing the output of the system with the annotation for the track.

Independently of the specific algorithm used, the investigator that chooses this approach must decide how to represent the two spaces, the music features and the emotions. On the one hand, we should choose music features that capture information about the expression of emotions. Some features such as tempo and loudness have been shown to bear a close relationship with the perception of emotions in music [38]. On the other hand, the model of emotion should reflect listeners' emotional response because emotions are very subjective and may change according to musical genre, cultural background, musical training and exposure, mood, physiological state, personal disposition and taste [9]. We argue that the current approach misrepresents both music and listeners' emotional experience by neglecting the role of time. In this article, we advance that

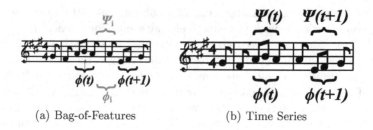

(a) Bag-of-Features   (b) Time Series

Fig. 1. Illustration of feature extraction. Part a) shows the bag-of-features approach, where the music piece is represented by a non time-varying vector of features Φ_i averaged from successive frames. Notice that there is only one global emotion Ψ_i associated with the entire piece as well. In part b), Both music features Φ and emotion annotations Ψ are kept as a time series.

the temporal variation of music features rather than the feature values should be used as predictors of musical emotions.

2.1   Music Features

Typically, MER systems represent music with a vector of features. The features can be extracted from different representations of music, such as the audio, lyrics, the score, social tags, among others [17]. Most machine learning methods described in the literature use the audio to extract the music features [17,49,23,11]. Music features such as root mean square (RMS) energy, mel frequency cepstral coefficients (MFCCs), attack time, spectral centroid, spectral rolloff, fundamental frequency, and chromagram, among many others, are calculated from the audio by means of signal processing algorithms [27,12,48]. The number and type of features dictates the dimensionality of the input space (some features such as MFCCs are multidimensional). Therefore, there usually is a feature selection or dimensionality reduction step to determine a set of uncorrelated features. A common choice for dimensionality reduction is principal component analysis (PCA)[26,12,21]. Huq *et al* [12] investigate four different feature selection algorithms and their effect on the performance of a traditional MER system. Kim *et al* [17] presented a thorough state-of-the-art review of MER in 2010, exploring a wide range of research in MER systems, particularly focusing on methods that use textual information (e.g., websites, tags, and lyrics) and content-based approaches, as well as systems combining multiple feature domains (e.g., features plus text). Their review is evidence that MER systems rarely exploit temporal information.

The term 'semantic gap' has been coined to refer to perceived musical information that does not seem to be contained in the acoustic patterns present in the audio, even though listeners agree about its existence [47]. Music happens essentially in the brain, so we need to take the cognitive mechanisms involved in processing musical information into account if we want to be able to model people's emotional response to music. Low-level audio features give rise to high-level musical features in the brain, and these, in turn, influence emotion recognition (and experience). This is where we argue that time has a major role, still neglected in most approaches found in the literature. However, only very recently have researchers started to investigate the role of time in MER. On the one hand, the different time scales in musical experience should be respected [42]. On the other hand, the temporal changes of some features are more relevant than feature values isolated from the musical context [3].

Usually, MER systems use a "bag of features" approach, where all the features are stacked together [12]. However, these features are associated with different levels of music experience, namely, the *perceptual*, the *rhythmic*, and the *formal* levels. These levels, in turn, are associated with different time scales [42]. Music features such as *pitch*, *loudness*, and *duration* are extracted early in the processing chain that converts sound waves reaching the ear into sound perception in the brain. Rhythm and melody depend hierarchically on the features from the previous level. For example, melody depends on temporal variations of pitch. Subsequently, the formal level is comprised of structural blocks from the melodic and harmonic level.

Fig. 1 illustrates the music feature extraction step in MER. Typically, these features are calculated from successive frames taken from excerpts of the audio that last a few seconds [17,49,23,11,12] and then averaged like seen in part a) of Fig. 1, losing the temporal correlation [23]. Consequently, the whole piece (or track) is represented by a static (non time-varying) vector, intrinsically assuming that musical experience is static and that the listener's emotional response can be estimated from the audio alone. Notice that, typically, each music piece (or excerpt) is associated with only one emotion, represented by Ψ_i in Fig. 1. The next section explores the representation of emotions in more detail.

2.2   Representation of Emotions

The classification paradigm of MER research uses categorical descriptions of emotions where the investigator selects a set of "emotional labels" (usually mutually exclusive). Part a) of Fig. 2 illustrates these emotional labels (Hevner's adjective circle [10]) clustered in eight classes. The annotation task typically consists of asking listeners to choose a label from one of the classes for each track. The choice of the emotional labels is important and might even affect the results. For example, the terms associated with music usually depend on genre (pop music is much more likely than classical music to be described as "cool"). As Yang [49] points out, the categorical representation of emotions faces a granularity issue because the number of classes might be too small to span the rich range of emotions perceived by humans. Increasing the number of classes does not necessarily solve the problem because the language used to categorize emotions is ambiguous and subjective [9]. Therefore, some authors [17,49] have proposed to adopt a parametric model from psychology research [30] known as the circumplex model of affect (CMA). The CMA consists of two independent dimensions whose axes represent continuous values of valence (positive or negative semantic meaning) and arousal (activity or excitation). Part b) of Fig. 2 shows the CMA

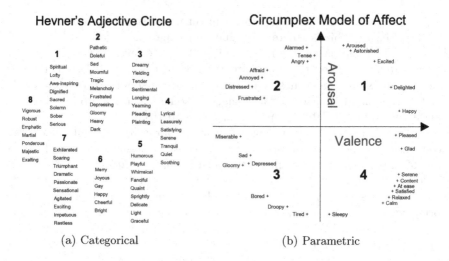

(a) Categorical   (b) Parametric

Fig. 2. Examples of models of emotion. The left-hand side shows Hevner's adjective circle [10], a categorical description. On the right, we see the circumplex model of affect [30], a parametric model.

and the position of some adjectives used to describe emotions associated with music in the plane. An interesting aspect of parametric representations such as the CMA lies in the continuous nature of the model and the possibility to pin-point where specific emotions are located. Systems based on this approach train a model to compute the valence and arousal values and represent each music piece as a point in the two-dimensional emotion space [49].

One common criticism of the CMA is that the representation does not seem to be metric. That is, emotions that are very different in terms of semantic mean-ing (and psychological and cognitive mechanisms involved) can be close in the plane. In this article, we argue that the lack of temporal information is a much bigger problem because music happens over time and the way listeners associate emotions with music is intrinsically linked to the temporal evolution of the mu-sical features. Also, emotions are dynamic and have distinctive temporal profiles (boredom is very different from astonishment in this respect, for example).

2.3   Mathematical Notation

In mathematical terms, the traditional approach to MER models the relationship between music Φ and emotions Ψ according to the following

$$\Psi = f(\Phi, A, \epsilon) \tag{2.1}$$

where Ψ represents the emotion space, Φ represents the music, f models the functional relationship between Φ and Ψ parameterized by A with error ϵ. Therefore, in this approach, MER becomes finding the values for the parameters $A = \{a_0, a_1, ..., a_N\}$ that minimize the error $\{\epsilon\}$ and correctly map each $\Phi_i \in \Phi$

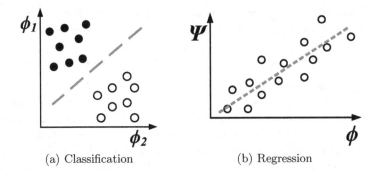

(a) Classification   (b) Regression

Fig. 3. Simple examples of machine learning applied to music emotion recognition. Part a) shows an example of classification. In part b), we see an example of regression.

onto their corresponding $\Psi_i \in \mathbf{\Psi}$. Notice that subscript i means an instance of the pair $\{\Psi, \Phi\}$ (an annotated music track). Here, $\Phi_i = [\phi_1, \phi_2, ..., \phi_N]$ is an N dimensional vector of music features and Ψ_i can be a semantic label representing an emotion for the classification case or continuous values of psychological models such as a valence/arousal pair $\Psi_i = \{v, \alpha\}$.

Fig. 3 shows a simple example of classification and regression to illustrate Eq. (2.1). Part a) illustrates linear classification into two classes, while part b) shows linear regression. In part a), the black dots represent instances of the first class, while the white dots represent the other class. The dashed line is the linear classifier (i.e., the MER system) that separates the input parameter space $\mathbf{\Phi} = \{\phi_1, \phi_2\}$ into two regions that correspond to the classes $\mathbf{\Psi} = \{black, white\}$. For example, a MER system that takes chords as input and outputs the label *happy* for major chords and *sad* for minor chords. In this case, $\mathbf{\Phi}$ is *major* or *minor* and could be encoded as ϕ_1 the first interval and ϕ_2 the second interval in cents, f is a binary classifier (such as a straight line with parameters $A = \{a_0, a_1\}$), and $\mathbf{\Psi} = \{happy, sad\}$. The error ϵ would be associated with misclassification, that is, points associated with one class by the system but labeled with the other. The system could be then used to classify inputs (music) that were not a part of the training data into "happy" or "sad" depending on which category (region) it falls into.

Part b) shows Ψ as a linear function of a single variable ϕ as $\Psi = a_0 + a_1\phi$. In this case, the dots are values of the independent variable or predictor ϕ associated with Ψ. For instance, ϕ represents loudness values positively correlated with arousal, represented by Ψ. Notice that both ϕ and Ψ are real-valued, and the MER system f modeling the relationship between them is the straight dashed line with parameters $A = \{a_0, a_1\}$ obtained by regression (expectation maximization or least-squares). The modeling error ϵ being minimized is the difference between the measures (the dots in the figure) and the model (the dashed line). The MER system can estimate *arousal* for new music tracks solely based on *loudness* values.

A more general MER system following the same approach would model Ψ as a linear combination of predictors Φ using multiple regression as follows

$$\Psi_i = a_0 + a_1\phi_{i,1} + ... + a_N\phi_{i,N} + ... + \epsilon \qquad (2.2)$$

where Ψ_i is the representation of emotion and $\Phi_i = \{\phi_{i,n}\}$ are the music features. This model assumes that emotions can be estimated as a linear combination of the music features, such as $\Phi_i = \{\text{loud}, \text{fast}\}$ music is considered $\Psi = \{\text{upbeat}\}$. Generally, the errors ϵ are supposed uncorrelated with one another (additive error) and with Φ, whose underlying *probability distribution* has a major influence on the parameters A. Naturally, fitting a straight line to the data is not the only option. Sophisticated machine learning algorithms are usually applied to MER, such as support vector machines [12,17]. However, these algorithms are seldom appropriate to deal with the temporal nature of music and the subjective nature of musical emotions.

2.4   Where Does the Traditional Approach Fail?

The traditional machine learning approach to MER assumes that the music features are good predictors of musical emotions due to a causal relationship between Φ and Ψ. The map from feature space to emotion space is assumed to implicitly capture the underlying psychological mechanisms leading to an emotional response in the form of a one-to-one relationship. However, psychological mechanisms of emotional reactions to music are usually regarded as information processing devices at various levels of the brain, using distinctive types of information to guide future behavior. Therefore, even when the map f explains most of the correlation between between Φ and Ψ, it does not necessarily mean that it captures the underlying psychological mechanism responsible for the emotional reaction (i.e., correlation does not imply causation). In other words, while Eq. (2.1) can be used to model the relationship between music features and emotional response, it does not imply the existence of causal relations between them.

Eq. (2.1) models the relationship between music features and emotional response from a behavioral viewpoint, supposing that the emotional response is consistent across listeners, irrespective of cultural and personal context. Currently, MER systems rely on self-reported annotations of emotions using a model such as Hevner's adjective circle or the CMA. On the one hand, this approach supposes that the model of emotion allows the expression of a broad palette of musical emotions. On the other hand, it supposes that self-reports are enough to describe the outcome of several different psychological mechanisms responsible for musical emotions [14]. Finally, the listener's input is only provided in the form of annotations and only used when comparing these annotations to the emotional labels output by the system, neglecting *personal* and *situational* factors. The terms 'semantic gap' [47,4] and 'glass ceiling' [1] have been coined to refer to perceived musical information that does not seem to be contained in the audio even though listeners agree about its existence. MER research needs to bridge the gap between the purely acoustic patterns of musical sounds and the emotional impact they have on listeners by modeling the generation of musical meaning [15]. Musical experience is greater than auditory impression [22]. The so called 'semantic gap' is a mere reflection of how the current typical approach misrepresents both the listener and musical experience.

Here we argue that the current approach misrepresents both music and listeners' emotional experience by neglecting the role of time. Currently, MER research ignores evidence [19,24,13,14] suggesting the existence of complex relationships between the dynamics of musical emotions and the response to how musical structure unfolds in time. The examples given in Fig. 3 illustrate this point (although in a very simplified way). Neither system uses temporal information at all. In part a), the input music is classified as "happy" or "sad" based solely on whether it uses major or minor chords, ignoring chord progression, inversions, etc. Part b) supposes a rigid association between *loudness* and *arousal* (loud music is arousing), ignoring temporal variations (like sudden changes from soft to loud).

Krumhansl [20] suggests that music is an important part of the link between emotions and cognition. More specifically, Krumhansl investigated how the dynamic aspect of musical emotion relates to the cognition of musical structure. According to Krumhansl, musical emotions change over time in intensity and quality, and these emotional changes covary with changes in psycho-physiological measures [20]. Musical meaning and emotion depend on how the actual events in the music play against this background of expectations. David Huron [13] wrote that humans use a general principle in the cognitive system that regulates our expectations to make predictions. According to Huron, music (among other stimuli) influences this principle, modulating our emotions. Time is a very important aspect of musical cognitive processes. Music is intrinsically temporal and we need to take into account the role of human memory when experiencing music. In other words, musical experience is learned. As the music unfolds, the learned model is used to generate expectations, which are implicated in the experience of listening to music. Meyer [25,24] proposed that expectations play the central psychological role in musical emotions.

3   Time and Music Emotion Recognition

We can incorporate temporal information into the representation of the music features and into the emotional response. In the first case we calculate the music features sequentially as a time-series, while the last case consists of recording listeners' annotations of emotional responses over time and keeping the information as a time-series. Fig. 1(b) illustrates the music features and emotions associated with music (represented by the score) over time. Thus $\phi(t)$ is the current value of a music feature, and $\phi(t+1)$ is the subsequent value. Similarly, $\Psi(t)$ and $\Psi(t+1)$ follow each other.

There are several ways of exploiting the information from the temporal variation of music features and emotions. A very straightforward way would be to use time-series analysis and prediction techniques, such as using previous values to predict future values of the series. In this case, the investigator could use past values of a series of valence/arousal $\{v, \alpha\}$ annotations over time to predict the next $\{v, \alpha\}$ value. A somewhat more complex approach is to use the temporal behavior of one time series as predictors of the next value of another series. In this case, the temporal variation of the music features would be used as predictors in regression. Thus variations in *loudness* rather than *loudness* values are used to predict the *arousal* associated. Several techniques can be employed, such as regression analysis, dynamical system theory, as well as machine learning algorithms developed to model the dynamic behavior of time series. Thus the next section reviews approaches to MER that use the temporal variation of music features as predictors of musical emotions.

3.1   Time Series and Prediction

The feature vector should be calculated for every frame of the audio signal and kept as a time series as shown in Fig. 1(b). In other words, the music features Φ_i are now represented by a time-varying vector $\Phi_i(t) = \{\phi_i(t), \phi_i(t-1), \phi_i(t-2), ..., \phi_i(t-N)\}$. The temporal correlation of the features must be exploited and fed into the model of emotions to estimate listeners' response to the repetitions and the degree of "surprise" that certain elements might have [38]. The simplest way to incorporate temporal information from the music features is to include time differences, such as *loudness* values and also *loudness* variations (from the previous value). This MER system uses information about how loud a certain passage sounds and also if the music is getting louder (building up tension, for example), using previous values of features to predict the next (is *loudness* going to increase or decrease?) and compare these predictions against how the same features are unfolding in the music as follows

$$\phi_i(t+1) = a_1\phi_i(t) + a_2\phi_i(t-1) + a_3\phi_i(t-2) + ... + \epsilon \qquad (3.1)$$

where $\phi_i(t+1)$ represents the next value for the feature ϕ_i, $\phi_i(t)$ the present value, $\phi_i(t-1)$ the previous, and so forth. The predictions $\phi_i(t+1)$ can be used to estimate listeners' emotional responses. Listeners have expectations about how the music is unfolding in time. For instance, expectations about the next term in a sequence (the next chord in chord progression or the next pitch in melodic contour) or expectations about continuous parameters (become louder or brighter). Whenever listeners' expectations are correct it is rewarding (fulfillment) and when they are not it is unrewarding (tension).

3.2   Emotional Trajectories

A very simple way of recording information about the temporal variation of emotional perception of music would be to ask listeners to write down the emotional label and a time stamp as the music unfolds. The result is illustrated in Fig. 4(a). However, this approach suffers from the granularity and ambiguity

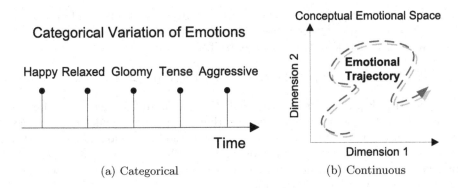

Fig. 4. Temporal variation of emotions. The left-hand side shows emotional labels recorded over time. On the right, we see a continuous conceptual emotional space with an emotional trajectory (time is represented by the arrow).

issues inherent of using a categorical description of emotions. Ideally, we would like to have an estimate of how much a certain emotion is present at a particular time. Krumhansl [19] proposes to collect listener's responses continuously while the music is played, recognizing that retrospective judgments are not sensitive to unfolding processes. However, in this study [19], listeners assessed only one emotional dimension at a time. Each listener was instructed to adjust the position of a computer indicator to reflect how the amount of a specific emotion (for example, sadness) they perceived changed over time while listening to excerpts of pieces chosen to represent the emotions [19].

Recently, there have been proposals to collect self-report of emotional reactions to music [39], including software such as EmotionSpace Lab [35], EmuJoy [28], and MoodSwings [16]. EmotionSpace Lab [35] allows listeners to continuously rate emotions while listening to music as points on the $\{v, \alpha\}$ (valence-arousal) plane (CMA), giving rise to an *emotional trajectory* on a two-dimensional model of emotion like the one shown in Fig. 4(b) (time is represented by the arrow). Use of the CMA accommodates a wide range of emotional states in a compact representation. Similarly, EmuJoy[28] allows continuous self-report of emotions over time in two-dimensional space (CMA). MoodSwings [16] is an online collaborative game designed to collect second-by-second labels for music using the CMA as model of emotion. The game was designed to capture $\{v, \alpha\}$ pairs dynamically (over time) to reflect emotion changes in synchrony with music and also to collect a distribution of labels across multiple players for a given song or even a moment within a song. Kim *et al.* state that the method provides quantitative labels that are well-suited to computational methods for parameter estimation.

A straightforward way of using information from the sequence of emotional labels $\Psi_i(t)$ to predict future values would be to use the underlying dynamics of the temporal variation of the sequence itself, like expressed below

$$\Psi_i(t+1) = a_0 + a_1\Psi_i(t) + a_2\Psi_i(t-1) + a_3\Psi_i(t-2) + \dots + \epsilon. \tag{3.2}$$

Notice that Eq. (3.2) fits a linear prediction model to the time series of emotional labels $\Psi_i(t)$ under the assumption that the previous values in the series can be used to predict future values, indicating trends and modeling the inertia of the system. In other words, the model assumes that increasing values of $\Psi_i(t)$ indicate that the next value will continue to increase by a rate estimated from previous rates of growth, for example.

3.3   Modeling Musical Emotions from Time-Varying Music Features

Finally, we should investigate the relationship between the temporal variation of musical features and the emotional trajectories. MER systems should include information about the rate of temporal change of musical features. For example, we should investigate how changes in loudness correlate with the expression of emotions. Early studies used time series analysis techniques to investigate musical structure. Vos et al [46] tested the structural and perceptual validity of notated meter applying autocorrelation to to the flow of melodic internals between notes from thirty fragments of compositions for solo instruments by J. S. Bach.

Recently, researchers started exploring the temporal evolution of music by treating the sequence of music features as a time series modeled by ordinary least squares [36,38], linear dynamical systems such as Kalman filters [32,33,34], dynamic texture mixtures (DTM) [8,44], auto-regressive models (linear prediction) [18], neural networks [5,6,7,45], among others. Notice that these techniques are intimately related. For example, the Kalman filter is based on linear dynamical systems discretized in the time domain and modeled as a Markov chain, whereas the hidden Markov model can be viewed as a specific instance of the state space model in which the latent variables are discrete.

First of all, it is important to distinguish between stationary and nonstationary sequential distributions. In the stationary case, the data evolves in time, but the distribution from which it is generated remains the same. For the more complex nonstationary situation, the generative distribution itself is evolving in time.

Ordinary Least Squares. Schubert [36,38] studied the relationship between music features and perceived emotion using continuous response methodology and time-series analysis. In these studies, both the music features $\Phi_n(t)$ and the emotional responses $\Psi_m(t)$ are multidimensional time series. For example, $\Phi_1(t) = \left[\phi_1(t)\ \phi_1(t-1)\ \dots\ \phi_1(t-N)\right]^T$ are *loudness* values over time and $\Psi_\alpha(t) = \left[\alpha(t)\ \alpha(t-1)\ \dots\ \alpha(t-N)\right]^T$ are arousal ratings annotated over time.

Schubert [36,38] proposes to model each component of $\Psi(t)$ as a linear combination of features $\Phi(t)$ plus a residual error $\epsilon(t)$ as follows

$$
\begin{bmatrix} v(t) \\ v(t-1) \\ \vdots \\ v(t-M) \end{bmatrix} = \begin{bmatrix} \phi_1(t) & \phi_2(t) & \cdots & \phi_N(t) \\ \phi_1(t-1) & \phi_2(t-1) & \cdots & \phi_N(t-1) \\ \vdots & \vdots & & \vdots \\ \phi_1(t-M) & \phi_2(t-M) & \cdots & \phi_N(t-M) \end{bmatrix} \begin{bmatrix} a_1 \\ a_2 \\ \vdots \\ a_N \end{bmatrix} + \begin{bmatrix} \epsilon(t) \\ \epsilon(t-1) \\ \vdots \\ \epsilon(t-N) \end{bmatrix} \quad (3.3)
$$

where the model parameters $A = \{a_j\}$ are fit so as to best explain variability in $\Psi(t)$. The error term $\epsilon(t)$ is included to account for discrepancies between the deterministic component of the equation and the actual data value. Two fundamental premises of this model are that the error term be reasonably small and that it fluctuate randomly. Notice that the error term $\epsilon(t)$ is simply

$$
\epsilon(t) = \Psi(t) - A\Phi(t). \quad (3.4)
$$

Thus the coefficients $A = \{a_i\}$ can be estimated using standard squared-error minimization techniques, such as ordinary least squares (OLS). OLS can be interpreted as the decomposition of $\Psi(t)$ onto the subspace spanned by $\Phi_i(t)$.

Notice that Eq. (3.3) considers the music features and the emotions as non-causal time series because information about the past (previous times) and about the future (all succeeding times) is used. Eq. (3.3) simply models $\Psi(t)$ as a linear combination of a set of feature vectors $\Phi(t)$ where time is treated as vector dimensions. Mathematically, $\Psi(t)$ is projected onto the subspace that $\Phi(t)$ spans, which is usually not orthogonal. This means that the music features used might be linearly dependent. In other words, if one of the features can be expressed as a linear combination of the others, then it is redundant in the feature set because it is correlated (colinear) with the other features.

More importantly, information about the rate of change of musical features is not exploited. The temporal correlation between successive values of features also plays an important role in listeners' emotional experience. The model in Eq. (3.3) supposes that listeners' emotional responses over time depend on *loudness* values over time, but not on *loudness* "variations". A straightforward way to consider variations in time series is to create a new sequence of values with the first order differences as follows

$$
\Delta\Psi(t) = A\Delta\Phi(t) + \ldots + \epsilon \quad (3.5)
$$

where Δ is the first order difference operator $\Delta\Psi(t) = \Psi(t) - \Psi(t-1)$. Difference time series answer questions like "how much does Ψ change when Φ changes"? [36].

Schubert [36] proposed to use music features (loudness, tempo, melodic contour, texture, and spectral centroid) as predictors in linear regression models of valence and arousal. This study found that changes in loudness and tempo were associated positively with changes in arousal, and melodic contour varied positively with valence. When Schubert [38] discussed modeling emotion as a continuous, statistical function of musical parameters, he argued that the statistical modeling of memory is a significant step forward in understanding aesthetic responses to music. In simple terms, the current system output depends on its previous values. Another interpretation is that the system exhibits "inertia", i.e., no sudden changes occur. Naturally, the input variables (music features) are also likely to exhibit autocorrelation.

Finally, Schubert [37] studied the causal connections between resting points and emotional responses using interrupted time series analysis. This study is related to a hypothesis proposed by Leonard Meyer [25] that "arousal of affect" results from musical expectations being temporarily suspended. Meyer suggests that there is a relationship between musical expectations, tension, and arousal. Schubert concluded that resting points are associated with increased *valence*.

The approach proposed by Schubert implicitly assumes that the relationship between the temporal evolution of music features and the emotional trajectories is linear and mutually independent, discarding interactions between music features. The interactions between musical variables are a prominent factor in music perception and call for joint estimation of coupled music features and modeling of said interactions. Finally, Schubert's approach does not generalize, applying to each piece analyzed.

Linear Dynamical System. A linear system models a process where the output can be described as a linear combination of the inputs as in Eq. (2.2). When the input is a stationary signal corrupted by noise, a *Wiener filter* can be used to filter out the noise that has corrupted the signal. The Wiener filter uses the autocorrelation of input signal and crosscorrelation between input and output to estimate the filter, which can be later used to predict future values of the input.

Linear dynamical systems also model the behavior of the input variable $\Phi(t)$, usually from its past values. The *Kalman Filter* gives the solution to generic *linear state space models* of the form

$$\Phi(t) = A\Phi(t-1) + q(t) \tag{3.6}$$
$$\Psi(t) = H\Phi(t) + r(t) \tag{3.7}$$

where vector $\Phi(t)$ is the state and $\Psi(t)$ is the measurement. In other words, the Kalman filter extends the Wiener filter to nonstationary processes, where the adaptive coefficients of the filter are iteratively (recursively) estimated.

Schmidt and Kim [32,33,34] have worked on the prediction of time-varying arousal-valence pairs as *probability distributions* using *multiple linear regression, conditional random fields,* and *Kalman filtering.* Each music track is described by a time-varying probability distribution from a corpus of annotations they have collected with an online collaborative game [16] from several users. Their first effort [33] to predict the emotion distribution over time simply uses multiple linear regression (MLR) to regress multiple feature windows to these annotations collected at different times without exploiting the time order or the temporal correlation of the features or the emotions.

Then, Schmidt and Kim [32] modeled the temporal evolution of the music features and the emotions as a linear dynamical system (LDS) such as Eq. (3.6).

The model considers the labels $\Psi(t)$ as noisy observations of the observed music features $\Phi(t)$ and uses a Kalman filter approach to fit the parameters. They compare the results against their previous MLR approach, which considers that each pair feature Φ_i annotation Ψ_i is statistically independent and therefore neglects the time-varying nature of music and emotions. Interestingly, they conclude that a single Kalman filter models well the temporal dependence in music emotion prediction for each music track. However, a mixture of Kalman filters must be employed to represent the dynamics of a music collection.

Later, Schmidt and Kim [34] propose to apply conditional random fields (CRF) to investigate how the relationship between music features and emotions evolve in time. They state that CRF models both the relationships between acoustic data (the music features) and emotion space parameters and also how those relationships evolve over time. CRF is a fully connected graphical model of the transition probabilities from each class to all others, thus representing the link between music features and the annotated labels as a set of transition probabilities, similarly to hidden Markov models (HMM). An interesting finding of this work is that the best performing feature for CRF prediction was MFCC rather than spectral contrast as reported earlier [32]. Schmidt and Kim conclude by speculating that this might be an indication that MFCC provides more information than spectral contrast when modeling the temporal evolution of emotion.

Dynamic Texture Mixture. A dynamic texture (DT) is a generative model that takes into account both the instantaneous acoustics and the temporal dynamics of audio sequences [8]. The texture is assumed to be a stationary second-order process with arbitrary covariance driven by white Gaussian noise (i.e., a first-order ARMA model). The model consists of two random variables, an *observed variable* $\Psi(t)$ that encodes the musical emotions, and a *hidden state variable* $\Phi(t)$ that encodes the dynamics (temporal evolution) of the music features. The two variables are modeled as a *linear dynamical system*.

$$\Phi(t) = A\Phi(t-1) + v(t) \tag{3.8}$$
$$\Psi(t) = C\Phi(t) + w(t) \tag{3.9}$$

While the DT in Eq. (3.8) models a single observed sequence, a *mixture of dynamic textures* (DTM) models a collection of sequences such as different musical features. DTM has been applied in automatic segmentation [2] and annotation [8] of music, as well as MER [44].

Vaizman *et al* [44] propose to use dynamic texture mixtures (DTM) to "investigate how informative the dynamics of the audio is for emotional content". They created a data set of 76 recordings of piano and vocal performances where "the performer was instructed to improvise a short musical segment that will *convey to listeners in a clear manner a single emotion*, one from the set of $\{happy, sad, angry, fearful\}$ [44]." These instructions were then used as ground truth labels. Vaizman *et al* claim that they "obtained a relatively wide variety of acoustic manifestations for each emotional category, which presumably capture the various strategies and aspects of how these specific emotions can be conveyed in Western music." Finally, they model the dynamics of acoustic properties of the music applying DTM to a temporal sequence of MFCCs extracted from their recordings. A different DTM model must be trained for each class (emotional label) using an iterative expectation maximization (EM) algorithm. After training, we can calculate the likelihood that a new music track was "generated" by a given DTM (i.e., the track belongs to that class). Notice that the model in Eq. (3.8) is equivalent to a first-order state space model.

Auto Regressive Model. Korhonen *et al.* [18] assume that, since music changes over time, musical emotions can also change dynamically. Therefore, they propose to measure emotion as a function of time over the course of a piece and subsequently model the time-varying emotional trajectory as a function of music features. More specifically, their model assumes that musical emotions depend on present and past feature values, including information about the rate of change or dynamics of the features. Mathematically, the model has the general form

$$\Psi_i(t, A) = f\left[\Phi_i(t), \Phi_i(t-1), ..., \epsilon_i(t), \epsilon_i(t-1)\right] \qquad (3.10)$$

where $\Psi_i(t, A)$ represents the emotions as a function of time t, A are the parameters of the function f that maps the music features $\Phi_i(t)$ and its past values $\Phi_i(t-1), ...$ with approximation error $\epsilon(t)$. Notice that the model does not include dependence on past values of $\Psi_i(t, A)$.

In this work, Korhonen *et al.* [18] adopt linear models, assuming that f can be estimated as a linear combination of current and past music features Φ given an estimation error ϵ to be minimized via least-squares and validated by K-fold cross-validation and statistical properties of the residual error ϵ [18]. The models they consider are the auto-regressive with exogenous inputs (ARX) shown in Eq. (3.11) and a state-space representation shown in Eq. (3.12) and (3.13) following.

$$\Psi(t) + A_1(\theta)\Psi(t-1) + ... + A_m(\theta)\Psi(t-m) = \\ B_0(\theta)\Phi(t) + ... + B_n(\theta)\Phi(t-n) + e(t) \qquad (3.11)$$

where $\Phi(t)$ is the N-dimensional music feature vector (N is the number of features), $\Psi(t)$ is an M-dimensional musical emotion vector (M is the dimension of the emotion representation), A_k is a matrix of coefficients (zeros) and B_k is the matrix of coefficients (poles).

$$\Phi(t+1) = A(\theta)\Phi(t) + B(\theta)u(t) + K(\theta)\epsilon(t) \qquad (3.12)$$
$$\Psi(t) = C(\theta)\Phi(t) + D(\theta)u(t) + \epsilon(t) \qquad (3.13)$$

where $\Phi(t)$ is the N-dimensional music feature vector (N is the number of features), $A(\theta)$ is a matrix representing the dynamics of the state vector, $B(\theta)$ is a matrix describing how the inputs (music features) affect the state variables Φ,

$C(\theta)$ is a matrix describing how the state variables Φ affect the outputs (emotion), $D(\theta)$ is a matrix describing how the current inputs (music features) affect the current outputs, and $K(\theta)$ is a matrix that models the noise in the state vector Φ. They used a dataset of 6 pieces "to limit the scope," while the total duration was 20 min. They report that the best model structure was ARX using 16 music features and 38 parameters, whose performance was 21.9% for valence and 78.4% for arousal. An interesting conclusion is that previous valence appraisals can be used to estimate arousal, but not the other way around.

Artificial Neural Networks. Coutinho and Cangelosi [5,6,7] propose to use recurrent neural networks to model continuous measurements of emotional response to music. Their approach assumes "that the spatio-temporal patterns of sound convey information about the nature of human affective experience with music" [6]. The temporal dimension accounts for the dynamics of music features and emotional trajectories and the spatial component accounts for the parallel contribution of various musical and psycho-acoustic factors to model continuous measurements of musical emotions.

Artificial neural networks (ANN) are nonlinear adaptive systems consisting of interconnected groups of "artificial neurons" that model complex relationships between inputs and outputs. ANNs can be viewed as nonlinear connectionist approaches to machine learning, implementing both supervised and unsupervised learning. Generally, each "artificial neuron" implements a nonlinear mathematical function $\Psi = f(\Phi)$, such that the output of each neuron is represented as a function of the weighted sum of the inputs as follows

$$\Psi_i = f\left[\sum_j^N w_{ij} g(\Phi_j)\right] \tag{3.14}$$

where Ψ_i is the ith output, Φ_j is the jth input, f is the map between input and output, and g is called *activation function*, usually nonlinear.

There are feed-forward and recurrent networks. Feed-forward networks only use information from the inputs to "learn" the implicit relationship between input and output in the form of connection weights, which act as long-term memory because once the feed-forward network has been trained, the map remains fixed. Recurrent networks use information from past outputs and from the present inputs in a feedback loop. Therefore, recurrent networks can process patterns that vary across time and space, where the feedback connections act as short-term memory (or memory of the immediate past)[3,6].

Coutinho and Cangelosi [5,6,7] sustain that the structure of emotion elicited by music is largely dependent on dynamic temporal patterns in low-level music structural parameters. Therefore, they propose to use the Elman neural network (ENN), an extension of feed-forward networks (such as the multi-layer perceptron) that include "context" units to remember past activity by storing and using past computations of the network to influence the present processing.

Mathematically,

$$\Phi(t) = f_i\left[\Phi(t-1), u(t)\right] = f\left[\sum_j w_{i,j}\Phi_j(t-1) + \sum_j w_{i,j}u_j(t)\right] \quad (3.15)$$

$$\Psi(t) = h_i\left[\Phi(t)\right] = h\left[\sum_j w_{i,j}\Phi_j(t)\right] \quad (3.16)$$

where Eq. (3.15) is the *next state function* and Eq. (3.16) is the *output function*. In these equations, Φ is the musical features, Ψ is the emotion pair $\{v, \alpha\}$, w are the connection weights (the network long-term memory), and u are the internal states of the network that encode the temporal properties of the sequential input at different levels. The recursive nature of the representation endows the network with the capability of detecting temporal relationships of sequences of features and combinations of features at different time lags [6].

This study used the dataset from Korhonen *et al.* [18]. They concluded that the spatio-temporal relationships learned fro the training set were successfully applied to a new set if stimuli and interpret this as long-term memory, as opposed to the dynamics of the system (associated with short-term memory). The result of canonical correlation analysis revealed that *loudness* is positively correlated with *arousal* and negatively with *valence*, *spectral centroid* is positively correlated with both *arousal* and *valence*, *spectral flux* correlated positively with *arousal*, *sharpness* correlated positively with both *arousal* and *valence*, *tempo* is correlated with high *arousal* and positive *valence*, and finally *texture* is positively correlated with *arousal*. Later, Vempala and Russo [45] compared the performance of a feed-forward network and an Elman network for predicting $\{v, \alpha\}$ ratings of listeners recorded over time for musical excerpts. They found similar correlations between music features and $\{v, \alpha\}$ values.

3.4   Overview

This section presents a brief overview of the techniques discussed previously. Table 1 summarizes features of the models for each approach, providing comments on aspects such as limitations and applicability.

4   Discussion

Most approaches that treat emotional responses to music as a time-varying function of the temporal variation of music features implicitly assume that time presents certain deterministic properties. In the models discussed above, time is modeled as clock time. However, musical time can be very subjective as music is experienced by the listener. Naturally, listeners' emotional reactions to music are closely related to the subjective experience of time rather than objective clock time. An interesting analogy is perception of frequencies and the Mel scale [43].

Table 1. Overview of the proposals to model musical emotions from time-varying music features. The table briefly summarizes model features with general comments for each of the approaches reviewed in Sec. 3.3.

Approach	Model Features	Comments
Ordinary Least Squares	• Linear • Stationary • Noncausal • Independent estimation • Memoryless	• Does not model temporal system dynamics • Does not model interactions between music features • Models arousal and valence separately • Models each piece separately • Least-squares error minimization
Linear Dynamical System	• Linear • Stationary (Wiener, CRF) • Nonstationary (Kalman) • Causal • Independent estimation (Wiener, Kalman) • Joint estimation (CRF) • Memoryless	• Models temporal system dynamics • Does not model interactions between music features (Wiener, Kalman) • Models each piece separately • Least-squares error minimization • Underlying filtering model is hardly musical
Dynamic Texture Mixture	• Linear • Stationary • Causal • Independent estimation • memoryless	• Models temporal system dynamics • Does not model interactions between music features • Borrowed from video • Models each piece separately • Expectation maximization parameter fit
Auto Regressive Model	• Linear • Stationary • Causal • Independent estimation • Memoryless	• Models temporal system dynamics • Does not model interactions between music features • Borrowed from statistics • Models each piece separately • Least-squares error minimization
Artificial Neural Network	• Nonlinear • Nonstationary • Causal • Joint estimation • Memory	• Models temporal system dynamics • Models interactions between music features • Many parameters • Difficult interpretation

Human auditory perception of frequencies is closer to logarithmic rather than linear, thus linear frequency representations such as the Fourier transform present a distorted picture of the information that is used to interpret the sounds that reach the ear. Therefore, in what follows, this article discusses modeling time in MER as subjective musical time rather than objective clock time.

Time. *Conceptually*, time can be seen from an objective or subjective point of view. Clocks are evidence of the objective interpretation of time as independent of anyone to experience it. Subjectively, the notion of time comes from the experience of change, sensory or otherwise [29]. Pressing [29] states that "Time is not a stimulus but a construction, an inference." Scientifically, the concept of time can be incorporated into measurements of physical quantities. In this case, time is a measure of change that involves expenditure of energy and therefore increase in entropy. Thus physical time is directly linked to the tendency of macroscopic physical systems to disorder. As a consequence, physical time involves irreversibility on macroscopic scales.

However, musical time differs from scientific time in many respects. Possible procedures to establish the nature of musical time are mathematical formalism and cognitive psychology. Mathematical formalism usually addresses objective clock time, which may be used to model the temporal processes used by composers. Cognitive psychology is concerned with subjective time, studying the mental representation of time.

Newton constructed a deterministic set of mathematical relations that allowed prediction of the future behavior of moving objects and allowed deduction of the past behavior of the moving objects. All that one needed in order to do this was data in the present regarding these moving objects. Isaac Newton believed in absolute space and absolute time. According to the Newtonian view, time is a dimension in which events and objects "move through" or an entity that "flows". Gottfried Leibniz and Immanuel Kant, among others, believed that time and space "do not exist in and of themselves, but ... are the product of the way we represent things", because we can know objects only as they appear to us.

Scientific Properties of Time. Usually, objective time presents some properties as follows [29]

1. *Time provides an ordering for events.* In classical physics and ordinary experience, this ordering is unique for any given set of events and chosen observer.
2. *This ordering has a unique direction.* This unique direction gives rise to the irreversibility of some macroscopic phenomena and is related to the rise in entropy (or disorder) of isolated systems.
3. *Time separates events into three distinct categories: past, present, future.*
4. *Time is measurable.* The existence of clocks that agree to high accuracy (in non-relativistic surroundings) provides the utility of this notion. Clock time is virtually synonymous with scientific time. Time's measurability means that in mathematical terms it acts as a metric space, i.e. a space with a function that defines distance.

5. *Time is continuous (but also discrete)*. In classical physics, time is continuous. Quantum mechanics provides a discrete interpretation of time based on the principle of uncertainty.

Musical Properties of Time. The properties of scientific time have parallels in music [29]. For example, the musical events have a unique time ordering and the unique *direction* of time is usually "accepted." Also, past, present, and future remain useful concepts, and all musical events are subject to clock measurability. Finally, the continuity or arbitrary divisibility of time applies to sound perception. Most of these properties are associated with objective clock time, such as measured by a metronome or marked on scores. However, when it comes to listening to music, musical time has a subjective, experienced, psychological component. The composer Dennis Smalley [40,41] wrote that "spectrum is perceived through time and time is perceived as spectral motion", suggesting that sound perception is inherently linked to the auditory perception of change.

Some properties of objective time listed above are modified in musical time. The most affected are 1, 2, and 4. Musically, time is inferred from ordered events. Thus time perception can only be approximately modeled as clock time because we ignore timing differences (and even tempo differences) to a substantial degree. The directionality of time is first of all a property of short-term memory. As for long-term memory, we have a memory of duration, but our memory of time order is rather imprecise once things are in the past. Redundancy is in an interesting way related to the temporal order of musical events and directionality of musical time. Recycling a theme is not just a way of improving long-term memory storage, it is also a musical way of making the time order less important.

The dichotomy between clock (objective) time and experienced (subjective) time has been the subject of considerable debate in music [29]. Snyder [42] views time as linked to the rate of change of incoming information. In this discussion, Snyder wrote that information refers to novelty and the removal of uncertainty. Habituation occurs at many levels of consciousness, cognitive as well as perceptual, and on many different time scales, from seconds to years. Thus we may not notice or remember experiences that keep repeating. However, the limitation of the capacity of memory is a limitation on how much novelty (i.e., *information*) it can handle. To be coherent and memorable, a message must have a certain amount of *non-informative repetition* or *redundancy*, which produces a certain amount of invariance or regularity. The redundancy in messages acts as a kind of implicit memory rehearsal, allowing us to have certain expectations about the messages we perceive and making them predictable to some extent.

In relation to music, we can find redundancy at different levels of music experience. Repetition of similar waveforms create pitch perception. The concepts of rhythm, tempo, and meter rely on repetition. The constraints of tuning systems and scales limit the number of elements used in a melody, creating redundancy in melodic patterns. At the formal level, redundancy includes symmetries and repetition of entire sections. Snyder suggests that this repetition, in addition to being a memory retrieval cue, is a *metaphor* for the process of remembering itself. When a pattern that appeared earlier in a piece of music reappears, it is like a recollection - an image of the past reappearing in the present, and its familiarity gives stability. Therefore, Snyder proposes that these associative repetitions are a factor in establishing closure, and points that introduce new and unfamiliar material (higher information content), such as transitions, are less stable and have a higher tension value. Snyder concludes that information can be related to tension in music. Musical tension, in turn, is associated with emotional experience. As stated before, the patterns of repetition and expectations in music are directly related to listeners' emotional reactions. One could argue that information measures over time are more suitable to bear a causal relation with *arousal/valence* ratings than music features. But what is the link between the flow of information in music and the perception of time?

Time is often thought of as existing independently of human experience. This objective notion of time is closely related to scientific concept of irreversibility of certain phenomena. Another possible interpretation is that time is an abstract construction of the human mind based on certain aspects of memory. The subjective notion of time is *constructed from* our perceptions of objects and events, and its qualities at a given moment depend on the relationships between these perceptions. In this sense, what we perceive in a given amount of time to some extent determines our sense of the length of that time. In other words, *subjective time* perception is a measure of the flow of information.

The concepts of information and redundancy are intrinsically related to musical form especially because they have a profound effect on our perception and memory of *lengths of time*. Our judgment of the length of a time period longer than the limits of short-term memory depends on the nature of the events that "fill" it. At first, it might seem reasonable to assume that how long a length of time appears to take depends on how many events happen within it, but in reality it seems to depend also on *how much information* we process from those events. Thus a time period filled with novel and unexpected events will be remembered as longer than an identical (in clock time) period filled with redundant or expected events. This implies that our expectations affect our sense of duration. Novel events take up more memory space and are usually remembered as having taken longer. On the other hand, ordinary events, which fit comfortably within our predefined schemas and require little attention and processing, are described as taking up little memory space and in retrospect seem to have taken less time to happen.

Note, however, that the above are descriptions of duration as *remembered*, not as *experienced*. Indeed, duration as experienced tend to be the opposite of duration remembered. "Boring" time periods with little information are experienced as being long, but *remembered as shorter*. Conversely, time periods filled with unusual, informative sequences of events, can seem to flow very rapidly while occurring, but are *remembered as longer*. Thus a musical passage filled with repetitive events can seem, in retrospect, shorter than one filled with unpredictable events. In other words, proportional relations of clock time do not necessarily establish similar relations of proportional *experienced time* or *remembered time* lengths. However, this effect seems to diminish with repeated listening. In addition, regular pulse and metrical frameworks seem to make it easier to get a more accurate sense of larger durational proportions.

Musical time is designed by composer and articulated by performer, shaping the perceptual processes of the listener. Systematic repetition of patterns can dull time perception, stretch or even eliminate the parallels between objective and subjective time. Continuity can be undermined by many traditional musical procedures, such as *staccato*. The hierarchical nature of time is intrinsically related to the three levels of time perception, such that "horizontal" aspects of time focus on on succession of events whereas "vertical" aspects focus on coordination between parts, synchrony, overlay, among others.

5 Conclusions

Research on automatic recognition of emotion in music, still in its infancy, has focused on comparing "emotional labels" automatically calculated from different representations of music with those of human annotators. MER systems commonly use supervised learning techniques to map non time-varying music feature vectors into regions of the emotion space. The music features are typically extracted from short audio clips and the system associates one emotion to each piece. The performance of MER systems using machine learning has been stagnant. Studies in music psychology suggest that time is essential in emotional expression. In this article, we argue that MER has neglected the temporal nature of music. We advocate the incorporation of time in both the representation of musical features and the model of emotions. This article reviews recent proposals in the literature to model musical emotions from time-varying music features. Finally, we discussed the representation of musical time as subjective time, rather than clock time.

The drawbacks of applying supervised learning to non time-varying representations of music and emotions are widely recognized by MER researchers. However, there is no standard way of representing temporal information in MER. This article urges MER researchers to model musical emotions from time-varying music features. The main point we make is that the temporal dynamics of music features are better predictors of musical emotions than feature values. However, we argue that currently, the models that take temporal dynamics into consideration are not appropriate to deal with music because they were originally developed for other purposes. Currently, we have the means to model the relevant features over scientific (clock) time. However, musical time is not in the equation.

Future perspectives include the development of computational models that exploit the temporal dynamics of music features as predictors of musical emotions. Only by including temporal information in automatic recognition of emotions can we advance MER systems to cope with the complexity of human emotions in one of its canonical means of expression, music.

Acknowledgements. This work is funded by the Marie Curie IAPP "AVID MODE" grant within the European Commission FP7.

References

1. Aucouturier, J.J., Pachet, F.: Improving Timbre Similarity: How High is the Sky? Journal of Negative Results in Speech and Audio Sciences 1(1) (2004)
2. Barrington, L., Chan, A.B., Lanckriet, G.: Dynamic texture models of music. In: Proc. ICASSP (2009)
3. Caetano, M., Wiering, F.: The Role of Time in Music Emotion Recognition. In: Proceedings of the International Symposium on Computer Music Modeling and Retrieval (2012)
4. Celma, O., Serra, X.: FOAFing the Music: Bridging the Semantic Gap in Music Recommendation. Journal of Web Semantics 6(4) (2008)
5. Coutinho, E., Cangelosi, A.: The use of spatio-temporal connectionist models in psychological studies of musical emotions. Music Perception: An Interdisciplinary Journal 27(1), 1–15 (2009)
6. Coutinho, E., Cangelosi, A.: A Neural Network Model for the Prediction of Musical Emotions. In: Nefti-Meziani, S., Grey, J.G. (eds.) Advances in Cognitive Systems, pp. 331–368. IET Publisher, London (2010) ISBN: 978-1849190756
7. Coutinho, E., Cangelosi, A.: Musical emotions: predicting second-by-second subjective feelings of emotion from low-level psychoacoustic features and physiological measurements. Emotion 11(4), 921–937 (2011)
8. Coviello, E., Chan, A.B., Lanckriet, G.: Time Series Models for Semantic Music Annotation. IEEE Transactions on Audio, Speech, and Language Processing 19(5), 1343–1359 (2011)
9. Gabrielsson, A., Lindström, E.: The Role of Structure in the Musical Expression of Emotions. In: Juslin, P.N., Sloboda, J. (eds.) Handbook of Music and Emotion: Theory, Research, Applications, pp. 367–400 (2011)
10. Hevner, K.: Experimental Studies of the Elements of Expression in Music. The Am. Journ. Psychology 48(2), 246–268 (1936)
11. Hu, X., Downie, J.S., Laurier, C., Bay, M., Ehmann, A.F.: The 2007 MIREX Audio Mood Classification Task: Lessons Learned. In: Proc. ISMIR (2008)
12. Huq, A., Bello, J.P., Rowe, R.: Automated Music Emotion Recognition: A Systematic Evaluation. Journal of New Music Research 39(4), 227–244 (2010)
13. Huron, D.: Sweet Anticipation: Music and the Psychology of Expectation. MIT Press (2006)
14. Juslin, P.N., Västfjäll, D.: Emotional Responses to Music: The Need to Consider Underlying Mechanisms. Behavioral and Brain Sciences 31(5), 559–621 (2008)
15. Juslin, P., Timmers, R.: Expression and Communication of Emotion in Music Performance. In: Juslin, P.N., Sloboda, J. (eds.) Handbook of Music and Emotion: Theory, Research, Applications, pp. 453–489 (2011)
16. Kim, Y., Schmidt, E., Emelle, L.: MoodSwings: A Collaborative Game for Music Mood Label Collection. In: Proceedings of the 9th International Conference on Music Information Retrieval, ISMIR (2008)
17. Kim, Y., Schmidt, E., Migneco, R., Morton, B., Richardson, P., Scott, J., Speck, J., Turnbull, D.: Music Emotion Recognition: A State of the Art Review. In: Proc. ISMIR (2010)
18. Korhonen, M.D., Clausi, D.A., Jernigan, M.E.: Modeling Emotional Content of Music Using System Identification. IEEE Transactions on Systems, Man, and Cybernetics, Part B, Cybernetics 36(3), 588–599 (2005)
19. Krumhansl, C.L.: An Exploratory Study of Musical Emotions and Psychophysiology. Canadian Journal of Experimental Psychology 51, 336–352 (1997)

20. Krumhansl, C.L.: Music: A Link Between Cognition and Emotion. Current Directions in Psychological Science 11, 45–50 (2002)
21. Lu, L., Liu, D., Zhang, H.J.: Automatic Mood Detection and Tracking of Music Audio Signals. IEEE Trans. Audio, Speech, Lang. Proc. 14(1) (2006)
22. McAlpin, C.: Is Music the Language of Emotions? The Musical Quarterly 11(3), 427–443 (1925)
23. MacDorman, K.F., Ough, S., Ho, C.C.: Automatic Emotion Prediction of Song Excerpts: Index Construction, Algorithm Design, and Empirical Comparison. Journal of New Music Research 36, 283–301 (2007)
24. Meyer, L.B.: Music, the Arts, and Ideas. University of Chicago Press, Chicago (1967)
25. Meyer, L.B.: Emotion and Meaning in Music. University of Chicago Press, Chicago (1956)
26. Mion, L., Poli, G.: Score-Independent Audio Features for Description of Music Expression. IEEE Transactions on Audio, Speech, and Language Processing 16(2), 458–466 (2008)
27. Müller, M., Ellis, D.P.W., Klapuri, A., Richard, G.: Signal Processing for Music Analysis. IEEE Journal of Selected Topics in Sig. Proc. 5(6), 1088–1110 (2011)
28. Nagel, F., Kopiez, R., Grewe, O., Altenmüller, E.: EMuJoy. Software for the Continuous Measurement of Emotions in Music. Behavior Research Methods 39(2), 283–290 (2007)
29. Pressing, J.: Relations Between Musical and Scientific Properties of Time. Contemporary Music Review 7(2), 105–122 (1993)
30. Russell, J.A.: A Circumplex Model of Affect. Journ. Personality and Social Psychology 39, 1161–1178 (1980)
31. Scherer, K.R.: Which Emotions Can be Induced by Music? What are the Underlying Mechanisms? and How can We Measure Them? Journal of New Music Research 33(3), 239–251 (2005)
32. Schmidt, E., Kim, Y.: Prediction of Time-Varying Musical Mood Distributions Using Kalman Filtering. In: Proc. Ninth International Conference on Machine Learning and Applications (ICMLA), pp. 655–660 (2010)
33. Schmidt, E., Kim, Y.: Prediction of Time-Varying Musical Mood Distributions from Audio. In: Proc. ISMIR (2010)
34. Schmidt, E., Kim, Y.: Modeling Musical Emotion Dynamics with Conditional Random Fields. In: Proc. ISMIR (2011)
35. Schubert, E.: Measuring Emotion Continuously: Validity and Reliability of the Two-Dimensional Emotion Space. Australian Journal of Psychology 51(3), 154–165 (1999)
36. Schubert, E.: Modeling Perceived Emotion with Continuous Musical Features. Music Perception 21(4), 561–585 (2004)
37. Schubert, E.: Introduction to Interrupted Time Series Analysis of Emotion in Music: The Case of Arousal, Valence and Points of Rest. In: Proc. International Conference on Music Perception and Cognition (2004)
38. Schubert, E.: Analysis of Emotional Dimensions in Music Using Time Series Techniques. Journ. Music Research 31, 65–80 (2006)
39. Schubert, E.: Continuous Self-Report Methods. In: Juslin, P.N., Sloboda, J. (eds.) Handbook of Music and Emotion: Theory, Research, Applications, pp. 223–254 (2011)
40. Smalley, D.: Spectro-morphology and Structuring Processes. In: Emmerson, S. (ed.) The Language of Electroacoustic Music, pp. 61–93. Macmillan, London (1986)

41. Smalley, D.: Spectromorphology: Explaining Sound-Shapes. Organised Sound 2(2), 107–126 (1997)
42. Snyder, B.: Music and Memory: An Introduction. MIT Press, Cambridge (2001)
43. Stevens, S.S., Volkman, J., Newman, E.B.: A scale for the measurement of the psychological magnitude pitch. Journal of the Acoustical Society of America 8(3), 185–190 (1937)
44. Vaizman, Y., Granot, R.Y., Lanckriet, G.: Modeling Dynamic Patterns for Emotional Content in Music. In: Proc. ISMIR (2011)
45. Vempala, N., Russo, F.A.: Predicting Emotion from Music Audio Features Using Neural Networks. In: Proceedings of the 9th International Symposium on Computer Music Modeling and Retrieval, CMMR (2012)
46. Vos, P.G., van Dijk, A., Schomaker, L.: Melodic Cues for Metre. Perception 23(8), 965–976 (1994)
47. Wiggins, G.A.: Semantic Gap?? Schemantic Schmap!! Methodological Considerations in the Scientific Study of Music. In: IEEE International Symposium on Multimedia, pp. 477–482 (2009)
48. Yang, Y.H., Lin, Y., Su, Y.F., Chen, H.H.: A regression approach to music emotion recognition. IEEE Trans. Audio, Speech, Lang. Proc. 16(2), 448–457 (2008)
49. Yang, Y., Chen, H.: Ranking-Based Emotion Recognition for Music Organization and Retrieval. IEEE Trans. Audio, Speech, Lang. Proc. 19(4) (2011)

The Intervalgram: An Audio Feature for Large-Scale Cover-Song Recognition

Thomas C. Walters, David A. Ross, and Richard F. Lyon

Google, Brandschenkestrasse 110, 8002 Zurich, Switzerland
tomwalters@google.com

Abstract. We present a system for representing the musical content of short pieces of audio using a novel chroma-based representation known as the 'intervalgram', which is a summary of the local pattern of musical intervals in a segment of music. The intervalgram is based on a chroma representation derived from the temporal profile of the stabilized auditory image [10] and is made locally pitch invariant by means of a 'soft' pitch transposition to a local reference. Intervalgrams are generated for a piece of music using multiple overlapping windows. These sets of intervalgrams are used as the basis of a system for detection of identical melodic and harmonic progressions in a database of music. Using a dynamic-programming approach for comparisons between a reference and the song database, performance is evaluated on the 'covers80' dataset [4]. A first test of an intervalgram-based system on this dataset yields a precision at top-1 of 53.8%, with an ROC curve that shows very high precision up to moderate recall, suggesting that the intervalgram is adept at identifying the easier-to-match cover songs in the dataset with high robustness. The intervalgram is designed to support locality-sensitive hashing, such that an index lookup from each single intervalgram feature has a moderate probability of retrieving a match, with few false matches. With this indexing approach, a large reference database can be quickly pruned before more detailed matching, as in previous content-identification systems.

Keywords: Cover Song Recognition, Auditory Image Model, Machine Hearing.

1 Introduction

We are interested in solving the problem of cover song detection at very large scale. In particular, given a piece of audio, we wish to identify another piece of audio representing the same underlying composition, from a potentially very large reference set. Though our approach aims at the large-scale problem, the representation developed is compared in this paper on a small-scale problem for which other results are available.

There can be many differences between performances with identical melodies. The performer may sing or play at a different speed, in a different key or on a different instrument. However, these changes in performance do not, in general, prevent a human from identifying the same melody, or pattern of notes. Thus,

M. Aramaki et al. (Eds.): CMMR 2012, LNCS 7900, pp. 197–213, 2013.
© Springer-Verlag Berlin Heidelberg 2013

given a performance of a piece of music, we wish to find a representation that is to the largest extent possible invariant to such changes in instrumentation, key, and tempo.

Serra [12] gives a thorough overview of the existing work in the field of melody identification, and breaks down the problem of creating a system for identifying versions of a musical composition into a number of discrete steps. To go from audio signals for pieces of music to a similarity measure, the proposed process is:

- Feature extraction
- Key invariance (invariance to transposition)
- Tempo invariance (invariance to a faster or slower performance)
- Structure invariance (invariance to changes in long-term structure of a piece of music)
- Similarity computation

In this study, we concentrate on the first three of these steps: the extraction of an audio feature for a signal, the problem of invariance to pitch shift (both locally and globally) and the problem of invariance to changes in tempo between performances of a piece of music. For the first stage, we present a system for generating a pitch representation from an audio signal, using the stabilized auditory image (SAI) [10] as an alternative to standard spectrogram-based approaches. Key invariance is achieved locally (per feature), rather than globally (per song). Individual intervalgrams are key normalized relative to a reference chroma vector, but no guarantees are made that the reference chroma vector will be identical across consecutive features. This local pitch invariance allows for a feature that can track poor-quality performances in which, for example, a singer changes key gradually over the course of a song. It also allows the feature to be calculated in a streaming fashion, without having to wait to process all the audio for a song before making a decision on transposition. Other approaches to this problem have included shift-invariant transforms [9], the use of all possible transpositions [5] or finding the best transposition as a function of time in a symbolic system [13]. Finally, tempo invariance is achieved by the use of variable-length time bins to summarize both local and longer-term structure. This approach is in contrast to other systems [5,9] which use explicit beat tracking to achieve tempo invariance.

While the features are designed for use in a large-scale retrieval system when coupled with a hashing technique [1], in this study we test the baseline performance of the features by using a Euclidean distance measure. A dynamic-programming alignment is performed to find the smallest-cost path through the map of distances between a probe song and a reference song; partial costs, averaged over good paths of reasonable duration, are used to compute a similarity score for a each probe-reference pair.

We evaluate performance of the intervalgam (using both SAI-based chroma and spectrogram-based chroma) using the 'covers80' dataset [4]. This is a set of 160 songs, in 80 pairs that share an underlying composition. There is no explicit notion of a 'cover' versus an 'original' in this set, just an 'A' version and a 'B' version of a given composition, randomly selected. While it is a small corpus, several researchers have made use of this dataset for development of audio features, and report results on it. Ellis [5] reports performance in terms of absolute classification accuracy for the LabRosa 2006 and 2007 music information retrieval evaluation exchange (MIREX) competition, and these results are extended by, amongst others, Ravuri and Ellis [11], who present detection error tradeoff curves for a number of systems.

Since we are ultimately interested in the use of the intervalgram in a large-scale system, it is worth briefly considering the requirements of such a system. In order to perform completely automated detection of cover songs from a large reference collection, it is necessary to tune a system to have extremely low false hit rate on each reference. For such a system, we are interested less in high absolute recall and more in finding the best possible recall given a very low threshold for false positives. Such systems have previously been reported for nearly-exact-match content identification [1]. The intervalgram has been developed for and tested with a similar large-scale back end based on indexing, but there is no large accessible data set on which performance can be reported. It is hard to estimate recall on such undocumented data sets, but the system identifies a large number of covers even when tuned for less than 1% false matches.

2   Algorithm

2.1   The Stabilized Auditory Image

The stabilized auditory image (SAI) is a correlogram-like representation of the output of an auditory filterbank. In this implementation, a 64-channel pole-zero filter cascade [8] is used. The output of the filterbank is half-wave rectified and a process of 'strobe detection' is carried out. In this process, large peaks in the waveform in each channel are identified. The original waveform is then cross-correlated with a sparsified version of itself which is zero everywhere apart from at the identified strobe points. This process of 'strobed temporal integration' [10,14] is very similar to performing autocorrelation in each channel, but is considerably cheaper to compute due to the sparsity of points in the strobe signal. The upper panels of Fig. 1 show a waveform (upper panel) and stabilized auditory image (middle panel) for a sung note. The pitch of the voice is visible as a series of vertical ridges at lags corresponding to multiples of the repetition period of the waveform, and the formant structure is visible in the pattern of horizontal resonances following each large pulse.

2.2   Chroma from the Auditory Image

To generate a chroma representation from the SAI, the 'temporal profile' is first computed by summing over the frequency dimension; this gives a single vector of values which correspond to the strength of temporally-repeating patterns in the waveform at different lags. The temporal profile gives a representation of

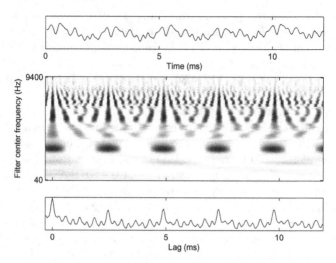

Fig. 1. Waveform (top panel), stabilized auditory image (SAI) (middle panel) and SAI temporal profile (bottom panel) for a human voice singing a note

the time intervals associated with strong temporal repetition rates, or possible pitches, in the incoming waveform. This SAI temporal profile closely models human pitch perception [6]; for example, in the case of stimuli with a missing fundamental, there may be no energy in the spectrogram at the frequency of the pitch perceived by a human, but the temporal profile will show a peak at the time interval associated with the missing fundamental.

The lower panel of Fig. 1 shows the temporal profile of the stabilized auditory image for a sung vowel. The pitch is visible as a set of strong peaks at lags corresponding to integer multiples of the pulse rate of the waveform. Fig. 2 shows a series of temporal profiles stacked in time, a 'pitch-o-gram', for a piece of music with a strong singing voice in the foreground. The dark areas correspond to lags associated with strong repetition rates in the signal, and the evolving melody is visible as a sequence of horizontal stripes corresponding to notes; for example in the first second of the clip there are four strong notes, followed by a break of around 1 second during which there are some weaker note onsets.

The temporal profile is then processed to map lag values to pitch chromas in a set of discrete bins, to yield a representation as chroma vectors, also known as 'pitch class profiles' (PCPs) [12]. In our standard implementation, we use 32 pitch bins per octave. Having more bins than the standard 12 semitones in the Western scale allows the final feature to accurately track the pitch in recordings where the performer is either mistuned or changes key gradually over the course of the performance; it also enables more accurate tracking of pitch sweeps, vibrato, and other non-quantized changes in pitch. Additionally, using an integer power of two for the dimensions of the final representation lends itself to easy use of a wavelet decomposition for hashing, which is discussed below. The chroma bin assignment is done using a weighting matrix, by which the temporal profile is multiplied to map individual samples from the lag dimension of the temporal profile into chroma bins. The weighting matrix is designed to map the linear time-interval axis to a wrapped logarithmic note pitch axis, and to provide a smooth transition between chroma bins. An example weighting matrix is shown in Fig. 3. The chroma vectors for the same piece of music as in Fig. 2 are shown in Fig. 4.

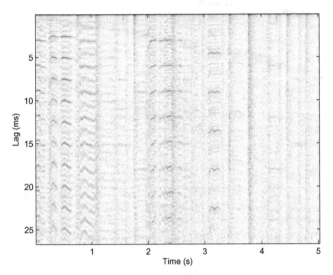

Fig. 2. A 'pitch-o-gram' created by stacking a number of SAI temporal profiles in time. The lag dimension of the auditory image is now on the vertical axis. Dark ridges are associated with strong repetition rates in the signal.

2.3   Chroma from the Spectrogram

In addition to the SAI-based chroma representation described above, a more standard spectrogram-based chroma representation was tested as the basis for the intervalgram. In this case, chroma vectors were generated using the `chromagram_E` function distributed with the covers80 [4] dataset, with a modified step size to generate chroma vectors at the rate of 50 per second, and 32 pitch bins per octave for compatibility with the SAI-based features above. This function uses a Gaussian weighting function to map FFT bins to chroma, and weights the entire spectrum with a Gaussian weighting function to emphasize octaves in the middle of the range of musical pitches.

2.4   Intervalgram Generation

A stream of chroma vectors is generated at a rate of 50 per second. From this chromagram, a stream of 'intervalgrams' is constructed at the rate of around 4 per second. The intervalgram is a matrix with dimensions of chroma and

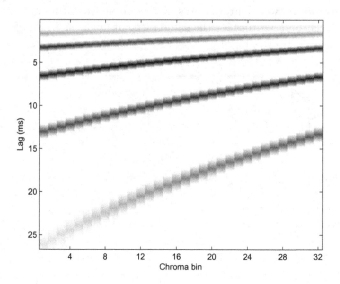

Fig. 3. Weighting matrix to map from the time-lag axis of the SAI to chroma bins

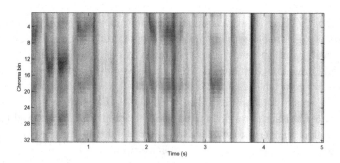

Fig. 4. Chroma vectors generated from the pitch-o-gram vectors shown in Fig. 2

time offset; however, depending on the exact design the time-offset axis may be nonlinear.

For each time-offset bin in the intervalgram, a sequence of individual chroma vectors are averaged together to summarize the chroma in some time window, before or after a central reference time. It takes several contiguous notes to effectively discern the structure of a melody, and for any given melody the stream of notes may be played a range of speeds. In order to take into account both short- and longer-term structure in the melody, a variable-length time-averaging process is used to provide a fine-grained view of the local structure, and simultaneously give a coarser view of longer timescales, to accommodate a moderate amount of tempo variation; that is, small absolute time offsets use narrow time bin widths, while larger absolute offsets use larger bin widths. Fig. 5 shows how chroma vectors are averaged together to make the intervalgram. In the examples below, the widths of the bins increase from the center of the intervalgram, and are proportional to the sum of a forward and reverse exponential $w_b = f\left(w_f^p + w_f^{-p}\right)$, where p is an integer between 0 and 15 (for the positive bins) and between 0 and -15 (for the negative bins), f is the central bin width, and w_f is the width factor which determines the speed with which the bin width increases as a function of distance from the center of the intervalgram.

In the best-performing implementation, the temporal axis of the intervalgram is 32 bins wide and spans a total time window of around 30 seconds. The central two slices along the time axis of the intervalgram are the average of 18 chroma vectors each (360ms each), moving away from the centre of the intervalgram, the outer temporal bins summarize longer time-scales before and after the central time. The number of chroma vectors averaged in each bin increases up to 99 (1.98s) in the outermost bins leading to a total temporal span of 26 seconds for each intervalgram.

A 'reference' chroma vector is also generated from the stream of incoming chroma vectors at the same rate as the intervalgrams. The reference chroma vector is computed by averaging together nine adjacent chroma vectors using a triangular window. The temporal center of the reference chroma vector corresponds to the temporal center of the intervalgram. In order to achieve local pitch invariance, this reference vector is then circularly cross-correlated with each of the surrounding intervalgram bins. This cross-correlation process implements a 'soft' normalization of the surrounding chroma vectors to a prominent pitch or pitches in the reference chroma vector. Given a single pitch peak in the reference chroma vector, the process corresponds exactly to a simple transposition of all chroma vectors to be relative to the single pitch peak. In the case where there are multiple strong peaks in the reference chroma vector, the process corresponds to a simultaneous shifting to multiple reference pitches, followed by a weighted average based on the individual pitch strengths. This process leads to a blurry and more ambiguous interval representation but, crucially, never leads to a hard decision being made about the 'correct' pitch at any point. Making only 'soft' decisions at each stage means that there is less need for either heuristics or tuning of parameters in building the system. With standard parameters the intervalgram is a 32 by 32 pixel feature vector generated at the rate of one every 240ms and spanning a 26 second window. Since there are many overlapping intervalgrams generated, there are many different pitch reference slices used, some making crisp intervalgrams, and some making fuzzy intervalgrams.

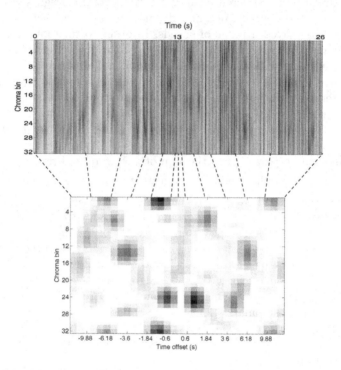

Fig. 5. The intervalgram is generated from the chromagram using variable-width time bins and cross-correlation with a reference chroma vector to normalize chroma within the individual intervalgram

2.5   Similarity Scoring

Dynamic programming is a standard approach for aligning two audio representations, and has been used for version identification by many authors (for example [16]; Serra [12] provides a representative list of example implementations). To compare sets of features from two recordings, each feature vector from the probe recording is compared to each feature vector from the reference recording, using some distance measure, for example Euclidean distance, correlation, or Hamming distance over a locality-sensitive hash of the feature. This comparison yields a distance matrix with samples from the probe on one axis and samples from the reference on the other. We then find a minimum-cost path through this matrix using a dynamic programming algorithm that is configured to allow jumping over poorly-matching pairs. Starting at the corner corresponding to the beginning of the two recordings the path can continue by jumping forward a certain number of pixels in both the horizontal and vertical dimensions. The total cost for any particular jump is a function of the similarity of the two samples to be jumped to, the cost of the jump direction and the cost of the jump distance. If two versions are exactly time-aligned, we would expect that the minimum-cost path through the distance matrix would be a straight line along the leading diagonal. Since we expect the probe and reference to be roughly aligned, the cost of a diagonal jump is set to be smaller than the cost of an off-diagonal jump.

The minimum and maximum allowed jump lengths in samples can be selected to allow the algorithm to find similar intervalgrams that are more sparsely distributed, interleaved with poorly matching ones, and to constrain the maximum and minimum deviation from the leading diagonal. Values that work well are a minimum jump of 3 and maximum of 4, with a cost factor equal to the longer of the jump dimensions (so a move of 3 steps in the reference and 4 in the probe costs as much as 4,4 even though it uses up less reference time, while jumps of 3,3 and 4,4 along the diagonal can be freely intermixed without affecting the score as long as enough good matching pairs are found to jump between). These lengths, along with the cost penalty for an off-diagonal jump and the difference in cost for long jumps over short jumps, are parameters of the algorithm. Fig. 6 shows a distance matrix for a probe and reference pair.

In the following section we test the performance of the raw intervalgrams, combined with the dynamic programming approach described above, in finding similarity between cover songs.

3   Experiments

3.1   Intervalgram Similarity

We tested performance of the similarity-scoring system based on the intervalgram, as described above, using the standard paradigm for the covers80 dataset, which is to compute a distance matrix for all query songs against all reference songs, and report the percentage of query songs for which the correct reference song has the highest similarity score.

Intervalgrams were computed from the SAI using the parameters outlined in Table 1, and scoring of probe-reference pairs was performed using the dynamic programming approach described above. Fig. 7 shows the matrix of scores for the comparison of each probe with all reference tracks. Darker pixels denote lower score, and lighter pixels denote higher scores. The white crosses show the highest-scoring reference for a given probe. 43 of the 80 probe tracks in the covers80 dataset were correctly matched to their associated reference track leading to a score of 53.8% on the dataset. For comparison, Ellis [5] reports a score of 42.5% for his MIREX2006 entry, and 67.5% for his MIREX2007 entry (the latter had the advantage of using covers80 as a development set, so is less directly comparable).

In addition to the SAI-based chroma features, standard spectrogram-based chroma features were computed from all tracks in the 'covers80' dataset. These features used 32 chroma bins, and were computed at 50 frames per second, to

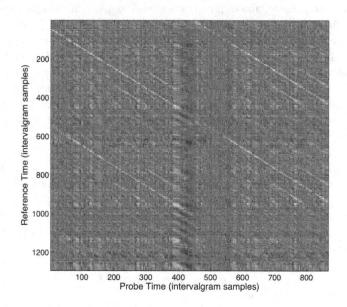

Fig. 6. Example distance matrix for a pair of songs which share an underlying composition. The lighter pixels show the regions where the intervalgrams match closely.

Table 1. Parameters used for intervalgram computation

Parameter	Value
Chromagram step size (ms)	20
Chroma bins per octave	32
Total intervalgram width (s)	26.04
Intervalgram step size (ms)	240
Reference chroma vector width (chroma vectors)	4

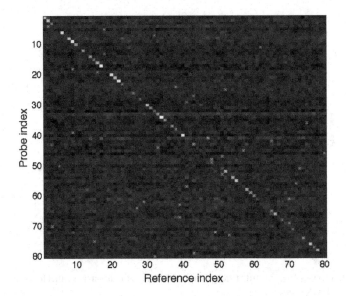

Fig. 7. Scores matrix for comparing all probes and references in the 'covers80' dataset. Lighter pixels denote higher scores, indicating a more likely match. White crosses denote the best-matching reference for each probe.

provide a drop-in replacement for the SAI-based features. Intervalgrams were computed from these features using the parameters in Table 1.

In order to generate detection error tradeoff curves for the dataset, the scores matrix from Fig. 7 was dynamically thresholded to determine the number of true and false positives for a given threshold level. The results were compared against the reference system supplied with the covers80 dataset, which is essentially the same as the system entered by LabRosa for the 2006 MIREX competition, as documented by Ellis [5]. Fig. 8 shows ROC curves the Elllis MIREX'06 entry and for the intervalgram-based system, both with SAI chroma features and spectrogram chroma features. Re-plotting the ROC curve as a DET curve to compare results with Ravuri and Ellis [11], performance of the intervalgram-based features is seen to consistently lie between that of the LabRosa MIREX 2006 entry and their 2007 entry.

Of particular interest is the performance of the features at high precision. The SAI-based intervalgram can achieve 47.5% recall at 99% precision, whereas the Ellis MIREX '06 system achieves 35% recall at 99% precision. These early results suggest that the intervalgram shows good robustness to interference. The intervalgram also stands up well to testing on larger, internal, datasets in combination with hashing techniques, as discussed below.

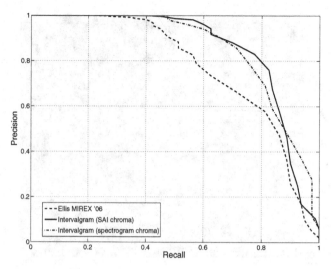

Fig. 8. ROC curves for the intervalgram-based system described in this paper and the LabROSA MIREX 2006 entry [5]

3.2   Scaling-Up with Hashing

In order to perform cover version detection on a large database of content, it is necessary to find a cheaper and more efficient way of matching a probe song against many references. The brute-force approach of computing a full distance map for the probe against every possible reference scales as the product of the number of probes and the number of references; thus a system which makes it cheap to find a set of matching segments in all references for a given probe would be of great value. Bertin-Mahieux and Ellis [2] presented a system using hashed chroma landmarks as keys for a linear-time database lookup. Their system showed promise, and demonstrated a possible approach to large-scale cover-song detection but the reported performance numbers would not make for a practically-viable system. While landmark or 'interest point' detection has been extremely successful in the context of exact audio matching in noise [15] its effectiveness in such applications is largely due to the absolute invariance in the location of strong peaks in the spectrogram. For cover version identification the variability in performances, both in timing and in pitch, means that descriptors summarizing small constellations of interest points will necessarily be less discriminative than descriptors summarizing more complete features over a long time span. With this in mind, we explore some options for generating compact hashes of full intervalgrams for indexing and retrieval purposes.

Hashing Techniques. Using the process outlined above, 32×32 pixel intervalgrams are generated from a signal at the rate of one per 240ms. To effectively find alternative performances of a piece of music in a large-scale database, it must be possible to do efficient lookup to find sequences of potentially matching intervalgrams. The use of locality-sensitive-hashing (LSH) techniques over long-timescale features for music information retrieval has previously been investigated and found to be useful for large datasets [3]. Various techniques based on locality-sensitive hashing (LSH) may be employed to generate a set of compact hashes which summarize the intervalgram, and which can be used as keys to look up likely matches in a key-value lookup system.

An effective technique for summarizing small images with a combination of wavelet analysis and Min-Hash was presented by Baluja and Covell [1] in the context of hashing spectrograms for exact audio matching. A similar system of wavelet decomposition was previously applied to image analysis [7].

Hashing of the Intervalgram. In order to test the effectiveness of such techniques on intervalgrams, the system described in [1] was adapted to produce a compact locality-sensitive hash of the intervalgram features and tested at small scale using the framework and dataset above. To generate hashes, four consecutive 32×32 intervalgram frames are temporally averaged using a moving window, and the resulting summary intervalgram is decomposed into a set of wavelet coefficients using a Haar kernel. The top $t\%$ of the wavelet coefficients with the highest magnitude values are retained, and are represented by the sign of their value. In this way, a sparse bit-vector can be produced, with two bits per wavelet coefficient. The bit pattern 00 is used to represent an unused wavelet coefficient, and the patterns 10 and 01 are used to represent a retained positive and negative coefficient respectively. This sparse bit-vector is then hashed using the min-hash techniques described in [1].

A search of the parameter space over a large internal dataset led to the optimal values for the wavelet decomposition and min-hash as detailed in Table 2. In addition the choice of random permutations was optimised using the same dataset.

Table 2. Optimal parameters for the wavelet decomposition and min-hash

Parameter	Value
Top-wavelets used (%)	5
Hash bands	100
Number of permutations	255

In this way, a 1024 element floating-point intervalgram matrix, costing 4096 bytes in storage, can be compactly summarised by a 100 byte min-hash representation. This reduction by a factor of 40 in the size of the representation comes with a cost in matching ability, which can be quantified using the same framework as was used above for intervalgram matching. To compare hashes, similarity matrices were generated for each pair of songs in the covers80 dataset, as above but this time using the bytewise Hamming similarity between hashes. The dynamic programming technique described above was again employed to

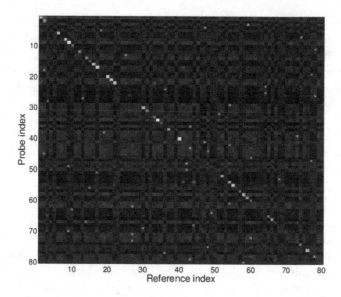

Fig. 9. Scores matrix for comparing all probes and references in the 'covers80' dataset using Hamming similarity over min-hashes. Lighter pixels denote higher scores, indicating a more likely match. White crosses denote the best-matching reference for each probe.

find the best path through the similarity matrix, and to provide a direct comparison with the raw intervalgram representation.

Fig. 9 shows the overall scores matrix for the covers80 dataset computed using the hashes. Fig. 10 shows the ROC curve computed from hashed intervalgrams. Performance is reduced from the full intervalgram case, and the ROC curve shows faster fall-off in precision with increasing recall, but recall at 99% precision is around 37.5%, reduced from 47.5% with full intervalgrams. Since this is the area of the curve which we wish to focus on for large-scale applications, it is gratifying to note that the massive decrease in fingerprint size does not lead to a correspondingly massive fall in achievable recall at high precision. In fact the recall at 99% precision is still higher after hashing than that of the unmodified Ellis MIREX 2006 features where recall was 35%.

4   Discussion

We have introduced a new chroma-based feature for summarizing musical melodies, which does not require either beat tracking or exhaustive search for transposition invariance, and have demonstrated a good baseline performance on a standard dataset. However, we developed the intervalgram representation to be a suitable candidate for large-scale, highly robust cover-song detection. In the following sections we discuss some approaches to the application of the intervalgram in such a system.

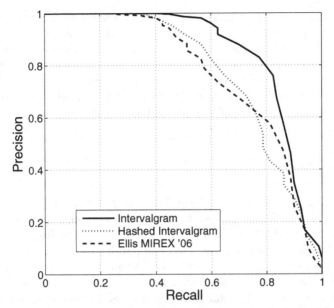

Fig. 10. ROC curves as in 8 with the addition of a curve for the hashed intervalgrams

4.1   SAI and Spectrogram-Based Chroma

There was no great difference in performance between intervalgrams generated using the temporal profile of the SAI and intervalgrams generated using
a spectrogram-based chroma feature. However, there are some small differences
in different regions of the ROC curve. Recall at high precision is very similar
for both forms of chroma features; as precision is allowed to fall, the SAI-based
features lead to slightly higher recall for a given precision, but the trend is reversed in the lower-precision end of the curve. This may suggest that there would
be a benefit in combining both SAI-based and spectrogram-based chroma into a
feature which makes use of both. There is some evidence to suggest that the temporal profile of the SAI may be robust to stimuli in which the pitch is ambiguous
[6], but this result may be less relevant in the context of music.

4.2   Hashing Results

Compared to exact-match audio identification, this system is much more challenging, since the individual hash codes are noisier and less discriminative. The
indexing stage necessarily has many false hits when it is tuned to get any reasonable recall, so there are still many (at least thousands out of a reference set
of millions) of potential matches to score in detail before deciding whether there
is a match. However, experiments with this small test set show that existing
hashing techniques can be extremely effective at retaining the important detail
in the full feature representation.

While the bytewise Hamming similarity is a reasonable measure for comparing fingerprints in the evaluation scheme described in this paper, it would not scale to very large libraries of reference content. In such a larger-scale system the matching could be implemented by grouping multiple bytes of the fingerprint and using these groups of bytes as keys into a lookup table storing candidate chunks of reference content which match the given key. A full discussion of such a system is beyond the scope of this paper, but this is the intended application of the hashing techniques describe here.

5   Conclusions

The intervalgram is a pitch-shift-independent feature for musical version recognition tasks. Like other features for such tasks, it is based on chroma features, but we have demonstrated that a chroma representation derived from the temporal profile of a stabilized auditory image gives comparable results to features derived from a spectrogram, and may provide complementary information. To achieve pitch-shift invariance, individual intervalgrams are shifted relative to a reference chroma vector, but no global shift invariance is used. Finally, to achieve some degree of tempo-invariance, variable-width time-offset bins are used to capture both local and longer-term features.

In this study, the performance of the intervalgram was tested by using dynamic-programming techniques to find the cheapest path through similarity matrices comparing a cover song to all references in the 'covers80' dataset. Intervalgrams, followed by dynamic-programming alignment and scoring, gave a precision at top-1 of 53.8%. This performance value, and the associated ROC curve, lies between the performance of the Ellis 2006 and Ellis 2007 MIREX entries (the latter of which was developed using the covers80 dataset).

The intervalgram has shown itself to be a promising feature for musical version recognition. It has good performance characteristics for high-precision matching with a low false-positive rate. Furthermore the algorithm is fairly simple and fully 'feed-forward', with no need for beat tracking or computation of global statistics. This means that it can be run in a streaming fashion, requiring only buffering of enough data to produce the first intervalgram before a stream of intervalgrams can be generated. This feature could make it suitable for applications like query-by-example in which absolute latency is an important factor.

In this study, we have also reported results which suggest that the intervalgram representation will lend itself well to large scale application when coupled with locality-sensitive hashing techniques such as wavelet-decomposition followed by minhash. The high precision at moderate recall which can be achieved with such techniques would allow for querying of a large database with a low false-positive rate, and our preliminary experiments have shown promise in this area.

References

1. Baluja, S., Covell, M.: Waveprint: Efficient wavelet-based audio fingerprinting. Pattern Recognition 41(11), 3467–3480 (2008)
2. Bertin-Mahieux, T., Ellis, D.: Large-scale cover song recognition using hashed chroma landmarks. In: Proceedings of the International Symposium on Music Information Retrieval, ISMIR (2011)
3. Casey, M., Rhodes, C., Slaney, M.: Analysis of minimum distances in high-dimensional musical spaces. IEEE Transactions on Audio, Speech, and Language Processing 16(5), 1015–1028 (2008)
4. Ellis, D.: The 'covers80' cover song data set (2007),
   `http://labrosa.ee.columbia.edu/projects/coversongs/covers80/`
5. Ellis, D., Cotton, C.: The 2007 LabROSA cover song detection system. In: MIREX 2007 Audio Cover Song Evaluation System Description (2007)
6. Ives, D., Patterson, R.: Pitch strength decreases as f0 and harmonic resolution increase in complex tones composed exclusively of high harmonics. The Journal of the Acoustical Society of America 123, 2670 (2008)
7. Jacobs, C., Finkelstein, A., Salesin, D.: Fast multiresolution image querying. In: Proceedings of the 22nd Annual Conference on Computer Graphics and Interactive Techniques, pp. 277–286. ACM (1995)
8. Lyon, R.: Cascades of two-pole-two-zero asymmetric resonators are good models of peripheral auditory function. Journal of the Acoustical Society of America 130(6), 3893 (2011)
9. Marolt, M.: A mid-level representation for melody-based retrieval in audio collections. IEEE Transactions on Multimedia 10(8), 1617–1625 (2008)
10. Patterson, R., Robinson, K., Holdsworth, J., McKeown, D., Zhang, C., Allerhand, M.: Complex sounds and auditory images. In: Auditory Physiology and Perception, Proceedings of the 9th International Symposium on Hearing, pp. 429–446. Pergamon (1992)
11. Ravuri, S., Ellis, D.: Cover song detection: from high scores to general classification. In: 2010 IEEE International Conference on Acoustics Speech and Signal Processing (ICASSP), pp. 65–68. IEEE (2010)
12. Serra Julia, J.: Identification of versions of the same musical composition by processing audio descriptions. Ph.D. thesis, Universitat Pompeu Fabra (2011)
13. Tsai, W., Yu, H., Wang, H.: Using the similarity of main melodies to identify cover versions of popular songs for music document retrieval. Journal of Information Science and Engineering 24(6), 1669–1687 (2008)
14. Walters, T.: Auditory-based processing of communication sounds. Ph.D. thesis, University of Cambridge (2011)
15. Wang, A.: An industrial strength audio search algorithm. Proceedings of the International Symposium on Music Information Retrieval (ISMIR) 2 (2003)
16. Yang, C.: Music database retrieval based on spectral similarity. In: Proceedings of the International Symposium on Music Information Retrieval, ISMIR (2001)

Perceptual Dimensions of Short Audio Clips and Corresponding Timbre Features

Jason Jiří Musil, Budr Elnusairi, and Daniel Müllensiefen

Goldsmiths, University of London
j.musil@gold.ac.uk

Abstract. This study applied a multi-dimensional scaling approach to isolating a number of perceptual dimensions from a dataset of human similarity judgements for short excerpts of recorded popular music (800-ms). Two dimensions were well identified by two of the twelve timbral coefficients from the Echo Nest's Analyze service. One of these was also identified by MFCC features from the Queen Mary Vamp plugin set, however a third dimension could not be mapped by either feature set and may represent a musical feature other than timbre. Implications are discussed within the context of existing research into music cognition and suggestions for further research regarding individual differences in sound perception are given.

Keywords: Timbre perception, short audio clips, similarity perception, sorting paradigm, MDS.

1   Introduction

Many application systems in music information retrieval rely on some kind of timbral representation of music [2, 26]. Timbre, or the surface quality of sound, seems to be a core aspect of computational systems which compare, classify, organise, search, and retrieve music. This dominance of timbre and sound representations in modern user-targeted audio application systems might be partly explained by the importance of the perceptual qualities of sound in popular music; writing about pop music in 1987, sociomusicologist Simon Frith already noted that "The interest today (...) is in constantly dealing with new textures" [8]. Whilst musical textures can contain a lot of musical structure, they also depend on surface features separate from any musical syntax or structure. These include the harmonicity of sound, the timbral and acoustical qualities of instruments and spaces, and changes introduced by various recording or post-production techniques. The precision with which many features of sound can be defined and implemented through modern signal processing has surely also contributed to their popularity in the music information retrieval community. Acoustic and timbral features have been defined as part of the MPEG4 and MPEG7 standards and are easily implemented where not already available from one of many software libraries.

M. Aramaki et al. (Eds.): CMMR 2012, LNCS 7900, pp. 214–227, 2013.

Timbral features are popular in research and commercial music information retrieval applications, yet there is surprisingly little rigorous research into perceptual principles explaining how certain timbral features can deliver results which are largely compatible with human music processing. The psychological and perceptual discourse around auditory processing often seems to be out of touch with parts of the audio engineering community. For example, an often-cited validation of mel-frequency cepstral coefficients (MFCCs) as corresponding to human perceptual processing of sound is a brief engineering paper, rather than a psychological or psycho-acoustical study [20]. Conversely, some studies of human timbre perception (e.g. [33]) may have been unfairly overlooked by the psychological music research community due to their use of 'artificial' stimuli. Also, psychological studies of musical timbre have traditionally focused on the acoustics of musical instruments, or timbral qualities imparted by individual performers (e.g. vibrato, alteration of instrumental attack and decay). These are often studied in isolation and usually with reference to styles of Western art music (e.g. [3]; see [23] for an overview). Thus there is something of a discrepancy between the scope of psychological inquiries and the broader, data-driven goals of music information retrieval (MIR) as applied to finished recordings of popular music. This may exacerbate the relative ignorance between both fields.

The current study aims to bridge this gap, at least to some extent, by presenting data from a psychological experiment on human perception of timbral similarity, using short excerpts of Western commercial pop music as stimuli. In addition, this study also tries to identify the perceptual dimensions that Western listeners use when making similarity judgements based on timbre cues and to relate these to sets of timbral features that are well known to both music information researchers and software engineers: firstly, the 12 timbre feature coefficients provided through the Echo Nest Analyze API[1], and also a set of both standard and customised MFCC and other spectral coefficients implemented by the Queen Mary Vamp plugin set. As the first set of features involve considerable auditory modeling and dimensional reduction motivated to approximate human perception [15], we assume that in this case the human and machine feature extractors under comparison are at least notionally parallel processes.

In this study, participants listen to very short excerpts of recorded commercial popular music and sort them into homogeneous groups. The paradigm is inspired by recent studies on genre [10] and song identification [17], which demonstrated that listeners are able to perform highly demanding tasks on the basis of musical information that is present in sub-second audio clips. Gjerdingen and Perrott found that 44% of participants' genre classifications of 250ms excerpts of commercially available music agreed with classifications they made of the same extracts when they were played for 3 seconds [10]. Krumhansl found that listeners could even identify the artists and titles of 25% of a series of 400ms clips of popular music spanning four decades [17]. At this timescale there are few, if any discernible melodic, rhythmic, harmonic or metric relationships to base judgements on. However, timbral information can be high even in perceptual

---

[1] http://developer.echonest.com/

situations where musical-structural information is minimal. It is also worth noting that task performance increased monotonically with longer exposures in both of the aforementioned studies, probably indicating that timbral information processing is complemented by other types of musical information as they become available in longer excerpts.

Many kinds of timbral information can be extracted from musical excerpts. The presence of typical instrumental sounds can undoubtedly help to identify a particular genre [10] and perception of key spectral and dynamic features is robust even for incomplete instrumental tones [14]. However, if timbre is defined more broadly as the spectro-temporal quality of sound, many surface features of polyphonic music could potentially be seen as coefficients in a timbre space. Indeed, the expression of musical emotion can be ascertained from 250ms of exposure, and familiarity with a piece from 500ms [6]. Spectral coefficients also join metric cues as predictors of surface judgements of musical complexity [30]. Different recording and production techniques can give rise to a plethora of perceptual timbral dimensions [16, 22].

The aim of the present research is to establish how non-expert listeners make use of musical surface features in a similarity sorting task, by applying multidimensional scaling (MDS) to extract a small number of perceptual dimensions, and then relating these to coefficients in a timbre space. The timbral coefficients returned by the Echo Nest's Analyze service were chosen as the initial pool, as they have been usefully applied in a number of real-world applications (e.g. autotagging and machine storage of music information [4, 34], creative musical re-editing [19]). The same procedure was then applied with MFCCs and other spectral coefficients from the Queen Mary Vamp Plugin set [1]. This research paradigm of identifying acoustic features to match data from perceptual experiments has a precedent in classic studies on timbral perceptual dimensions for instrumental tones [11, 35], and is sensitive to subtle processing differences not picked up by traditional discrimination paradigms [29]. The study was also motivated by a wider effort to rigorously test and understand human musical ability: the Goldsmiths Musical Sophistication Index. The procedure reported here forms a part of a test battery which is freely available and includes the musical excerpts used in this study. The project is documented and hosted at http://www.gold.ac.uk/music-mind-brain/gold-msi.

2   Method

131 participants (59 male, with a mean age of 30.8, $SD=11.8$) sorted 16 randomly ordered excerpt test-items into four equally sized bins by dragging and dropping visually identical icons representing each item via a computer interface. Sorts were unconstrained (other than the need for solutions to have exactly four items per bin) and participants could audition items repeatedly at will and with no time constraints. The set contained four items from each of four genres (jazz, rock, pop and hip-hop), taken from 16 different songs identified on the http://www.allmusic.com website as being genre-typical but not universally known (i.e. through not having achieved the highest pop chart ratings).

Genres were chosen on the basis of Rentfrow and Gosling's high-level categories of musical genre: reflective/complex (jazz), energetic/rhythmic (hip-hop), upbeat/conventional (pop), and intense/aggressive (rock) [27]. Genre-category ratings for these are stable over time and appear to correlate somewhat with stable personality traits [28]. It was therefore assumed that participants should be able to solve the task implicitly (by perceived similarity) even if they possessed no genre-specific knowledge. By focusing on these categories, we also avoided the inherent instability and fluidity of industry genre boundaries. Gjerdingen and Perrott also found that the presence of vocals in extracts reduced genre rating performance [10]. Although vocal features are important for recognising musical styles (and this is reflected in the technologies used in MIR) we chose stimuli without vocals to avoid making the already short excerpts too difficult to classify. Excerpts were chosen to be as representative of the typical instrumentation of the song as possible. 400ms and 800ms excerpts were taken at each of two different locations within each song, creating four sets of 16 extracts (see Appendix A for details of the source songs and extract beginning times), however results from only one of the 800ms item-sets are analysed here, following piloting which suggested this set to have desirable psychometric properties. A floor effect on test scores observed for 400ms stimuli was absent for 800ms stimuli from this particular set (identified in Appendix A as "B"). Per-item mean correct pairing scores (from 0 to 3 possible correct pairings) for this set were well distributed in a pilot dataset with 117 participants (800ms per-item successful pairs out of a maximum of 3: $M=1.22$, $SD=0.44$; 400ms: $M=1.05$, $SD=0.37$; $t_{(31)}=4.87$, $p<.001$). Vectors of timbral features for the same items were extracted through the Echo Nest's Analyze service and the Queen Mary Vamp plugin set for use as predictors of item-placement on perceptual dimensions arising from analysis of participants' sorting solutions.

3 Analyses and Results

The score for each bin of four clips could range from 0 correct pairs (each clip belonging to a different genre) to 6 correct pairs (each clip belonging to the same genre), giving a score from 0 to 24 for the whole solution (some scores in this range are not observed due to the fact that scores in any given bin were not orthogonal to scores in other bins). Scores for participants' grouping solutions suggested that they had some difficulty with correctly completing the task. Mean total scores were 10.145 (42.3% of 24), with 5.3% of participants below chance level (4.799 out of 24) and 1.5% of participants at ceiling.

Each possible pair of clips in the whole dataset received a score based on the number of participants assigning both clips in the pair to the same group. Complete linkage agglomerative hierarchical clustering was carried out on the resulting similarity matrix. A four-cluster solution generated the initial genre classification that was used for selecting the clips perfectly (see Fig. 1). Thus, despite a wide range of deviant sorting solutions at the level of individual participants, the result of the cluster analysis demonstrates that the general

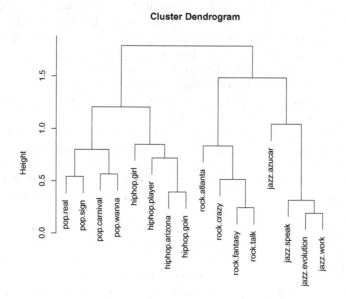

Fig. 1. Complete linkage agglomerative hierarchical clustering of pairwise similarity scores

sorting tendency of 131 participants agrees with the experimenter-chosen similarity groupings by genre category.

A distance matrix was derived from the same pairwise similarity values and taken as an input to the non-metric multi-dimensional scaling procedure as implemented in the R-function isoMDS (from package MASS). Computing a 2- as well as a 3-dimensional solution we obtained stress values of 12.05 and 6.52 respectively, indicating a much better fit of the 3-dimensional solution to the data, with the 3-dimensional solution also satisfying the elbow criterion in a stress plot (not reproduced here). As a rule of thumb, Kruskal considers MDS solutions with a stress of 5 or lower a good fit while solutions with a stress value of 10 are still fair [18]. Thus, it seems that 3 dimensions are sufficient to describe the participants' perceptual judgements. The 3-dimensional solution is shown in Fig. 2. Clustering of clips by genre in the MDS space is clearly visible.

As a subsequent step we tried to identify the 3 perceptual dimensions identified by MDS with any of the Echo Nest's 12 timbre coefficients. The Echo Nest Analyze service divides audio into segments with stable tonal content, i.e. roughly per note or chord. For each audio clip we obtained 2 to 5 segments with 12 timbre coefficients each. In order to obtain a homogeneous set of timbral features to compare to the 3 MDS dimensions we used a simple first-order linear model of the time series values of each coefficient for each clip. From each linear model we used the intercept (mean value) and the variance across the number of segments as an indicator of variability of the coefficient in the given clip.

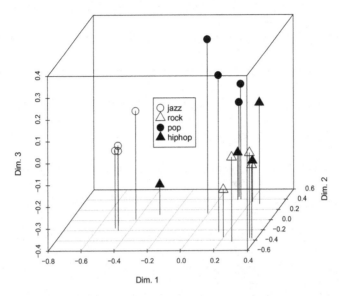

Fig. 2. The 3-dimensional solution of pairwise item distances. Points are differentiated by genre.

In addition, we used the number of segments per coefficient and clip as another indicator of tonal variability.

Inspecting the bivariate distributions and correlations between each MDS-dimension and the means and variances of the 12 coefficients suggested that the relationships between the perceptual dimensions and the timbral coefficients are mainly non-linear and distributions are far from normal. We therefore chose a random forest as an analysis technique (for a discussion of this technique, see [5]), as it is able to model non-linear relationships and can additionally deal with a relatively high number of predictors (means and variances for each of the 12 coefficients plus the number of segments resulted in 25 predictor variables) compared to the low number of observations (16 audio clips; for a discussion of random forests as a classification and regression technique see chapter 15 in [12]). More specifically, we chose the conditional random forest model as implemented in the R package `party` [13], which is assumed to deliver more reliable estimates of variable importance when predictors are highly correlated and represent different measurement levels [32].

Fitting a random forest model yielded a list of variable-importance values based on the usefulness of individual predictors for accurately predicting the so-called 'out-of-the-bag' (i.e. cross-validation) sample. The intercept (i.e. the mean) of the Echo Nest's timbral coefficient 5 was found to be of high importance as a predictor of perceptual dimension 1 (see Fig. 3). A similarly clear picture was

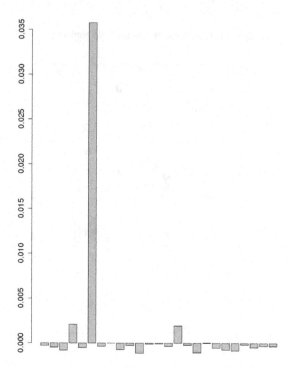

Fig. 3. Predictor importance for perceptual similarity dimension 1. The tall bar is the intercept of Echo Nest Analyze service timbre coefficient 5.

found for the intercept of coefficient 9, being highly important as a predictor of perceptual dimension 2 (see Fig. 4). However, the picture was less clear for perceptual dimension 3, where all importance values for all variables remained within the margin of error around 0, indicating that perceptual dimension 3 cannot be closely associated with any (studied) timbral coefficient (see Fig. 5).

A further analysis was undertaken to determine whether any of the three perceptual dimensions would be predicted by 51 spectral feature coefficients provided by the Queen Mary Vamp plugin set, including two sets of MFCC coefficients as well as spectral centroid, spectral irregularity, spectral spread, amongst others. Partial least squares regression (PLSR) was used to regress separately the values of the three perceptual dimensions of each clip onto the spectral feature coefficients. PLSR was chosen for its suitability in situations where the number of predictors is greater than the number of observations (the $k > n$ problem; see [36]). The PLSR model explained 27% of variance in dimension 1 after cross-validation. However, the proportion of variance explained by PLSR models for the two other perceptual dimensions was minimal. Predicted versus observed values for perceptual dimension 1 are plotted against each other in Fig. 6 .

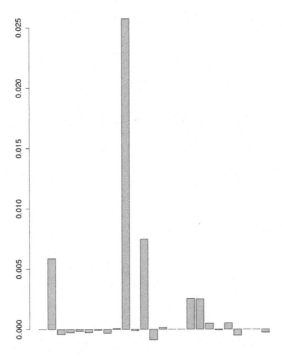

Fig. 4. Predictor importance for perceptual similarity dimension 2. The tallest bar is the intercept of Echo Nest Analyze service timbre coefficient 9.

4   Discussion

Three perceptual dimensions derived from multi-dimensional scaling were sufficient to explain listeners' similarity judgements of short musical clips. Two of these dimensions were predicted by distinct surface features from the first set which was tested (Echo Nest Analyze service). Mean values but not variances of coefficients were selected as important predictors, which is interesting because the excerpts were long enough to contain some note- and beat-like temporal variations, which we anticipated would be reflected in the time-series variation of the returned timbre vector. Unfortunately, only a few timbral features returned by the Echo Nest are publicly documented, so it is difficult to ascertain what the features correspond to. A scale-less spectrogram in the existing documentation[2] suggests that coefficient 5, which was important for predicting the coordinates of the 16 clips in perceptual dimension 1, might be a kind of mid-range filter. This would not be surprising, as spectral and dynamic effects are used to add low-end power and high-end presence to recordings. This could reduce the amount of useful information contained in those frequency bands, whilst the mid-range could become the most informative for clip discrimination and

---

[2] See http://developer.echonest.com/docs/v4/_static/
AnalyzeDocumentation.pdf

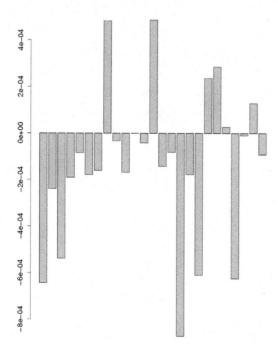

Fig. 5. Predictor importance for perceptual similarity dimension 3. Note that values which do not escape the trend of both positive and negative values around zero are generally not considered to be informative in this kind of analysis. Hence this plot suggests that no variable is important in predicting dimension 3.

classification. Indeed, the most distant cluster on this dimension was jazz, which tends towards mid-range mastering and emphasises distinctive instrumental timbres. The distribution of clips along perceptual dimension 2, as well as incomplete information from the Echo Nest documentation for coefficient 9, suggested that this dimension may represent a similar filtering function to coefficient 5, albeit shifted higher or polarised more strongly to high and low frequency bands. Despite this evidence for possible commonality between the human and machine feature extractors under study, dimension 3 is not predicted by any of the 12 Echo Nest timbral coefficients.

Applying the same procedure with a set of MFCC and other spectral feature coefficients was also deemed to be useful, partly because these features do not suffer from the same lack of documentation as those considered above. More importantly, despite the sparseness of evidence linking MFCCs directly to human music perception, MFCCs are commonly used to carry out machine-based tasks with results which are compatible with those yielded by human perceptual processes (e.g. indexing of similar music [7, 21], recognition of vocal emotion [25]). It was somewhat surprising that only one human perceptual dimension invoked by this task was predicted by the feature set, giving some grounds to question

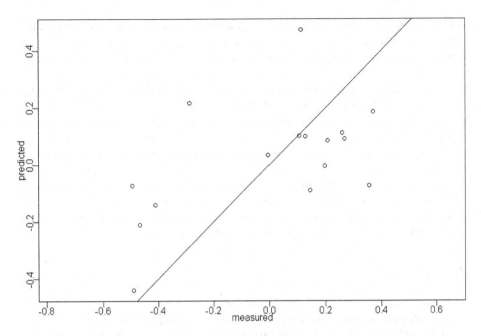

Fig. 6. Predicted versus observed values for perceptual dimension 1, from a partial least squares regression model with 51 acoustic feature coefficient predictors

the initial assumption that timbral information itself is sufficient for solving the task. However, the partial least squares regression analysis does not account for possible interactions between feature coefficients. Moreover, the latter analysis did not benefit from the pre-processing stage of the Echo Nest analysis, which arguably models the response and limitations of the human auditory system more extensively and could have a decisive effect over the short timescale of the stimulus clips.

At 800ms, the stimuli we used contain rudimentary information about tempo, chord changes, rhythm, and instrumentation. It is possible that dimension 3 represents the influence of such abstracted structures. The results obtained from studies with shorter stimuli might not suggest the presence of these particular perceptual dimensions, or may indicate reliance on more than these timbral features if they were masked by the availability of musical structure information in the current stimuli. Additionally, the discrete sorting groups could invite top-down strategies based on retrieving explicit genre information from memory, and open subjective experience responses should be taken in future studies to establish whether such information is cued by the clips. Nevertheless, the task is known to yield useful similarity data in a shorter and more easily administered experiment than would be possible with the more conventional pairwise similarity rating paradigm [24].

Scheirer and colleagues proposed that listeners may differ in the weight they give to a common set of perceived sound features when judging surface musical sound, or that different listeners may choose different features altogether [30]. Although they lacked enough data to explore these hypotheses, they were able to conclude that individual (participant) models explained complexity rating data better than a common model. Therefore, whilst we found some evidence of common feature-based perceptual dimensions, it is possible that further study with this paradigm will uncover individual strategy differences for this task. The IND-SCAL variant of MDS may be helpful in exploring this hypothesis. The reverse is also possible, given that we used far shorter stimuli (800ms versus Scheirer et al.'s 5000) and may have measured a more constrained phenomenon. Individual differences are nonetheless plausible, as task-based measures of timbral perception can be improved by training [9,31]. Indeed, because timbral perception does not require formalised musical knowledge, individuals could be expected to vary in terms of the the information they can access for this task purely on the basis of what they have previously listened to, and to what extent.

References

1. Vamp plugins: Mel-frequency cepstral coefficients,
   http://vamp-plugins.org/rdf/plugins/qm-vamp-plugins#qm-mfcc
2. Aucouturier, J., Pachet, F.: Improving timbre similarity: How high is the sky? Journal of Negative Results in Speech and Audio Sciences 1(1), 1–13 (2004)
3. Barthet, M., Depalle, P., Kronland-Martinet, R., Ystad, S.: Analysis-by-synthesis of timbre, timing, and dynamics in expressive clarinet performance. Music Perception 28(3), 265–278 (2011)
4. Bertin-Mahieux, T., Ellis, D.P.W., Whitman, B., Lamere, P.: The million song dataset. In: Klapuri, A., Leider, C. (eds.) Proceedings of the 12th International Society for Music Information Retrieval Conference (ISMIR 2011), pp. 591–597. University of Miami, Miami (2011)
5. Breiman, L.: Random forests. Machine Learning 45(1), 5–32 (2001)
6. Filipic, S., Tillmann, B., Bigand, E.: Judging familiarity and emotion from very brief musical excerpts. Psychonomic Bulletin & Review 17(3), 335–341 (2010)
7. Foote, J.T.: Content-based retrieval of music and audio. In: Kuo, C.C.J., Chang, S.F., Gudivada, V.N. (eds.) Proceedings of SPIE, Multimedia Storage and Archiving Systems II, Dallas, Texas, USA, vol. 3229, pp. 138–147 (1997)
8. Frith, C., Horne, H.: Art into Pop. Methuen Young Books, London (1987)
9. Gfeller, K., Witt, S., Adamek, M., Mehr, M., Rogers, J., Stordahl, J., Ringgenberg, S.: Effects of training on timbre recognition and appraisal by postlingually deafened cochlear implant recipients. Journal of the American Academy of Audiology 13(3), 132–145 (2002)
10. Gjerdingen, R.O., Perrott, D.: Scanning the dial: The rapid recognition of music genres. Journal of New Music Research 37(2), 93–100 (2008)
11. Grey, J.M.: Timbre discrimination in musical patterns. The Journal of the Acoustical Society of America 64, 467–478 (1978)
12. Hastie, T., Tibshirani, R., Friedman, J.: Random forests. In: The Elements of Statistical Learning. Springer Series in Statistics, pp. 1–18. Springer, New York (2009)
13. Hothorn, T., Hornik, K., Zeileis, A.: Model-based recursive partitioning. Journal of Computational and Graphical Statistics 17(2), 492–514 (2008)

14. Iverson, P., Krumhansl, C.L.: Isolating the dynamic attributes of musical timbre. The Journal of the Acoustical Society of America 94, 2595–2606 (1993)
15. Jehan, T.: Creating music by listening. Ph.D. thesis, Massachusetts Institute of Technology (2005)
16. Karadogan, C.: A comparison of kanun recording techniques as they relate to turkish makam music perception. In: Proceedings of the 130th Audio Engineering Society Convention, Audio Engineering Society (2011)
17. Krumhansl, C.L.: Plink: "Thin slices" of music. Music Perception: An Interdisciplinary Journal 27, 337–354 (2010)
18. Kruskal, J.: Nonmetric multidimensional scaling: A numerical method. Psychometrika 29(1), 115–129 (1964)
19. Lindsay, A.T., Hutchinson, D.: Fluently remixing musical objects with higher-order functions. In: Proceedings of the 12th International Conference on Digital Audio Effects (DAFx 2009), Como, Italy, pp. 429–436 (2009)
20. Logan, B.: Mel frequency cepstral coefficients for music modeling. In: International Symposium on Music Information Retrieval, vol. 28, pp. 5–11 (2000)
21. Logan, B., Salomon, A.: A music similarity function based on signal analysis. In: Proceedings of the 2001 IEEE International Conference on Multimedia and Expo. (ICME 2001), Tokyo, Japan, pp. 745–748 (2001)
22. Marui, A., Martens, W.L.: Timbre of nonlinear distortion effects: Perceptual attributes beyond sharpness. In: Proceedings of the Conference on Interdisciplinary Musicology (2005)
23. McAdams, S., Giordano, B.L.: The perception of musical timbre. In: Hallam, S., Cross, I., Thaut, M. (eds.) The Oxford Handbook of Music Psychology, pp. 72–80. Oxford University Press (2009)
24. Müllensiefen, D., Gingras, B., Stewart, L., Musil, J.J.: Goldsmiths musical sophistication index (gold-msi) v1.0: Technical report and documentation revision 0.3. Tech. rep., Goldsmiths, University of London, London (2012), http://www.gold.ac.uk/music-mind-brain/gold-msi
25. Neiberg, D., Elenius, K., Laskowski, K.: Emotion recognition in spontaneous speech using gmms. In: Proceedings of Interspeech 2006 and 9th International Conference on Spoken Language Processing, Baixas, pp. 809–812 (2006)
26. Pachet, F., Roy, P.: Exploring billions of audio features. In: CBMI, pp. 227–235 (2007)
27. Rentfrow, P.J., Gosling, S.D.: The do re mi's of everyday life: The structure and personality correlates of music preferences. Journal of Personality and Social Psychology 84, 1236–1256 (2003)
28. Rentfrow, P.J., Gosling, S.D.: Message in a ballad. Psychological Science 17(3), 236–242 (2006)
29. Samson, S., Zatorre, R.J., Ramsay, J.O.: Deficits of musical timbre perception after unilateral temporal-lobe lesion revealed with multidimensional scaling. Brain 125(3), 511–522 (2002)
30. Scheirer, E.D., Watson, R.B., Vercoe, B.L.: On the perceived complexity of short musical segments. In: Proceedings of the 2000 International Conference on Music Perception and Cognition. Citeseer (2000)
31. Shahin, A.J., Roberts, L.E., Chau, W., Trainor, L.J., Miller, L.M.: Music training leads to the development of timbre-specific gamma band activity. NeuroImage 41(1), 113–122 (2008)
32. Strobl, C., Boulesteiz, A., Kneib, T., Augustin, T., Zeileis, A.: Conditional variable importance for random forests. Bioinformatics 9, 307–327 (2008)

33. Terasawa, H., Slaney, M., Berger, J.: A statistical model of timbre perception. In: ISCA Tutorial and Research Workshop on Statistical And Perceptual Audition (SAPA 2006), Pittsburgh, pp. 18–23 (2006)

34. Tingle, D., Youngmoo, E.K., Turnbull, D.: Exploring automatic music annotation with "acoustically-objective" tags. In: Wang, J.Z., Boujemaa, N., Ramirez, N.O., Natsev, A. (eds.) Proceedings of the 11th ACM SIGMM International Conference on Multimedia Information Retrieval (MIR 2010), Philadelphia, Pennsylvania, USA, pp. 55–62. ACM (2010)

35. Wedin, L., Goude, G.: Dimension analysis of the perception of instrumental timbre. Scandinavian Journal of Psychology 13(1), 228–240 (1972)

36. Wold, H.: Soft modelling by latent variables: The non-linear iterative partial least squares (NIPALS) approach. In: Gani, J. (ed.) Perspectives in Probability and Statistics, Papers in Honour of M. S. Bartlett, pp. 117–142. Academic Press, London (1975)

A   Appendix: Stimulus Clip Attributes

Table 1. Source files and starting positions of "A" and "B" version stimulus clips

No.	Genre	Song	Artist	Album	"A" min.sec.ms	"B" min.sec.ms
1	Jazz	Work Song	Nat Adderley	Work Song/Movin' Along	3.38.005	4.02.855
2	Jazz	Speak No Evil	Wayne Shorter	Speak No Evil	0.05.505	7.06.700
3	Jazz	Azucar	Eddie Palmieri	Azucar Pa' Ti (Sugar For You)	1.13.500	5.32.500
4	Jazz	Evolution	Roy Ayers	Mystic Voyage	1.44.880	1.49.975
5	Rock	Oh Atlanta	Little Feat	Feats' Don't Fail Me Now	3.07.045	4.03.645
6	Rock	Talk To Ya Later	The Tubes	The Completion Backward Principle	2.17.220	3.16.470
7	Rock	Crazy On You	Heart	Dreamboat Annie	0.55.000	3.48.900
8	Rock	Rock & Roll Fantasy	Bad Company	Desolation Angels	1.23.100	2.23.310
9	Pop	I Wanna Love You Forever	Jessica Simpson	I Wanna Love You Forever	0.04.620	3.40.500
10	Pop	So Real	Mandy Moore	So Real	1.42.480	2.04.150
11	Pop	Carnival	The Cardigans	Life	3.06.200	3.10.385
12	Pop	The Sign	Ace of Base	The Sign	2.11.365	0.29.145
13	Hip-hop	Still Not A Player	Big Punisher	Capital Punishment	2.41.900	3.08.300
14	Hip-hop	I Ain't Goin' Out Like That	Cypress Hill	Black Sunday	3.45.000	3.56.670
15	Hip-hop	Who's That Girl	Eve	Scorpion	0.10.720	4.10.310
16	Hip-hop	By The Time I Get To Arizona	Public Enemy	Apocalypse 91: The Enemy Strikes Black	2.49.340	4.20.150

Music Emotion Recognition:
From Content- to Context-Based Models

Mathieu Barthet, György Fazekas, and Mark Sandler

Centre for Digital Music
Queen Mary University of London
{mathieu.barthet,gyorgy.fazekas,mark.sandler}@eecs.qmul.ac.uk

Abstract. The striking ability of music to elicit emotions assures its prominent status in human culture and every day life. Music is often enjoyed and sought for its ability to induce or convey emotions, which may manifest in anything from a slight variation in mood, to changes in our physical condition and actions. Consequently, research on how we might associate musical pieces with emotions and, more generally, how music brings about an emotional response is attracting ever increasing attention. First, this paper provides a thorough review of studies on the relation of music and emotions from different disciplines. We then propose new insights to enhance automated music emotion recognition models using recent results from psychology, musicology, affective computing, semantic technologies and music information retrieval.

Keywords: music emotion, mood, recognition, retrieval, metadata, model, arousal, valence, multi-modal, ontology, appraisal, review, state of the art.

1   Introduction

Since the first empirical works on the relationships between music and emotions [25,46] a large body of research studies has given strong evidence towards the fact that - depending on contextual information - music can either (i) elicit/induce/evoke emotions in listeners (*felt* emotions), or (ii) express/suggest emotions to listeners (*perceived* emotions) [71]. As pointed out by Krumhansl [33], the distinction between *felt* and *perceived* emotions is important both from the theoretical and methodological points of views since the models of representations may differ. Felt emotions relate to the observation that listeners may experience an emotional response to music, whereas perceived emotions relate to the fact that music can communicate qualities associated with emotions [73]. [91] devised a scale to analyse music-induced emotions - the Geneva emotional music scale (GEMS) - and showed that the underlying taxonomic model of emotions differed from the models which were devised in studies investigating the representations of perceived music emotions (e.g. [25]). One may argue whether music can communicate and trigger emotions in listeners and this has been the subject of numerous debates [46]. However a demonstration of the latter does not

M. Aramaki et al. (Eds.): CMMR 2012, LNCS 7900, pp. 228–252, 2013.

require a controlled laboratory setting and can be undertaken while watching films. In the documentary about film score composer Bernard Hermann [79], the motion picture editor Paul Hirsch (e.g. Star Wars, Carrie) discusses the effect of music in a scene from Alfred Hitchcock's well-known horror movie *Psycho*, the soundtrack of which was composed by Hermann: *"I was home one night and Psycho was on and I saw a scene in which Janet Lee had stolen some money. [...] The scene consisted of three very simple shots, there was a close up of her driving, there was a point of view of the road in front of her and there was a point of view of the police car behind her that was reflected in the rear mirror. The material was so simple and yet the scene was absolutely gripping. And I reached over and I turned off the sound to the television set and I realised that the extreme emotional duress I was experiencing was due almost entirely to the music."*. Such effect is in line with Chion's theory that music, by "adding value" to the image, causes the filmgoer to construe the image differently [11][1].

With regard to music retrieval, several studies on music information needs and user behaviors have highlighted an interest in developing models for the automatic classification of music pieces according to the emotions or mood they suggest[2]. In [37], the responses of 427 participants to the question *"When you search for music or music information, how likely are you to use the following search/browse options?"* showed that, where possible, emotional/mood states would be used in every third song query. The importance of musical mood metadata was further confirmed in the investigations by [39] which give high importance to affective/emotive descriptors and indicate that users enjoy discovering new music by entering mood-based queries, as well as those by [8] which showed that 15% of the song queries on the web music service Last.fm were made using mood tags. As part of our project Making Musical Mood Metadata (M4) - in partnership with the BBC and I Like Music - the present study aims to (i) review the current trends in music emotion recognition (MER) and (ii) provide insights to improve MER models. The analysis of human annotations of music emotions on editorial resources such as `AllMusicGuide.com` (AMG) showed that emotion recognition can be viewed as a multi-class (different classes of emotions) and multi-label (different mood tags for each track) classification or regression problem in which a music piece is associated with a set of emotions [31] (e.g. a track can be described as being "soft", "tender" and "peaceful"). In a generic way, music emotion recognition models can be described as the combination of two components: a detection component (feature extraction and feature selection), and an inference component (machine learning, fusion of results). If MER studies were still sparse in 2006 [43], MER has since become a burgeoning

---

[1] The analysis of the effects of music on emotion perceived in film goes beyond the scope of this article, and we refer the reader to [12] and [53] for thoughtful discussions and investigations on this subject.

[2] We will employ the words music emotion and mood interchangeably since their distinctions are out of the scope of this article. If not specified otherwise, they will refer to emotions suggested by music, rather than felt emotions. We refer the reader to the work of Meyer [46] for a discussion on the differences between emotion ("temporary and evanescent") and mood ("relatively permanent and stable").

field, as highlighted by the growing number of publications on this topic within the music information retrieval community (see Sect. 3). In parallel to MIR research, psychologists improved emotion/mood representation models, as well as measurement techniques (see Sect. 2). The two main types of computational models in MIR (content- and context-based) are closely linked with the distinctions of music meaning formulated by Meyer [46]. On one hand, content-based approaches may be associated with the "absolutist" point of view which sees "the meaning of music as being essentially intramusical (non-referential)" [46], a facet coined as *intrinsic sources* of emotions by Sloboda and Juslin [71]. On the other hand, context-based approaches may be associated with the "referentialist" point of view which contends that "music also communicates meanings which in some way refer to the extramusical world of concepts, actions, emotional states, and character", facet later coined as *extrinsic sources* of emotions in [71]. Meyer also put forward that absolute and referential meanings are not mutually exclusive and "can and do coexist in one and the same piece of music". This point of view corresponds well with the paradigm underlying hybrid approaches to the MER problem which combine content- and context-based models and are by essence multi-modal (mixing together audio, symbolic notations, lyrics, social tags, etc.). The annual evaluation campaign Music Information Retrieval Evaluation eXchange (MIREX) collocated with the International Society for Music Information Retrieval (ISMIR) conference launched a task on audio mood classification (AMC) in 2007. The reported F-measures of MIREX state-of-the arts' MER models rose from 62% in 2007 to 66% in 2009. Although great improvements have been made in pattern recognition systems, the analysis of the 2007-2009 MIREX results and that of studies published between 2009 and 2011, reviewed in Sect. 3, suggest the existence of a "glass ceiling" for MER at F-measure around 65%. Such bottleneck for MIR machine learning models was highlighted by the systematic evaluations performed in the experiments from [4], in the context of music similarity measures. In order to overcome these limitations, hybrid and multi-modal approaches have been proposed, by taking advantage of social metadata, web-mined tags, semantic reasoning [6,80], music symbolic notations [92], and/or lyrics [35]. The recent developments of such multi-modal MER approaches are not unrelated to the ever growing amount of music resources on the web, data management infrastructures and application programming interfaces (APIs), as well as the advances in the closely related field of social media retrieval. As argued in [80] "combining information from sources like web-based, text and other sorts of multi-modal information with content-based features in an efficient way could be one of the solutions to break the bottleneck of pure content-based method".

The remainder of this article is organised as follows. In Sect. 2, we present the three main types of (music) emotion representations (categorical, dimensional and appraisal), before discussing aspects related to taxonomy and ontology. In Sect. 3, we review MER studies by focusing on those published between 2009 and 2011, and discuss aspects linked with databases, features, feature selection frameworks, and emotion variation across time. Sect. 4 presents state of the art machine learning techniques for MER. Throughout the article and in Sect. 5,

Table 1. Categorical and dimensional models of music emotions used in MER

Notation	Description	Approach	Ref.
UHM9	Update of Hevner's adjective Model (UHM) in nine categories	Cat.	[68]
AMC5C	5 MIREX audio mood classification (AMC) clusters ("Passionate","Rollicking", "Literate", "Humorous", "Aggressive")	Cat.	[27] [14] [9] [75] [80]
5BE	5 basic emotions ("Happy", "Sad", "Tender", "Scary", "Angry")	Cat.	[18] [58]
AV4Q	4 quadrants of the Thayer-Russell AV space ("Exuberance", "Anxious/Frantic", "Depression", "Contentment")	Cat.	[9] [81]
AV11C	11 subdivision categories of the Thayer-Russell AV space	Cat.	[24]
AMG12C	12 clusters based on AMG tags	Cat.	[42]
72TCAL500	72 tags from the CAL-500 dataset (genres, instruments, emotions, etc.)	Cat.	[6]
AV4Q-UHM9	Categorisation of UHM9 in Thayer-Russell's quadrants (AV4Q)	Cat.	[49]
AV8C	8 subdivision categories of the Thayer-Russell AV space	Cat.	[29]
4BE	4 basic emotions ("Happy", "Sad", "Angry", "Fearful")	Cat.	[77]
4BE-AV	4 basic emotions based on the AV space ("Happy", "Sad", "Angry", "Relaxing")	Cat.	[81]
9AD	Nine affective dimensions from Asmus	Dim.	[3]
AV	Arousal/Valence (Thayer-Russell model)	Dim.	[24]
EPA	Evaluation, potency, and activity (Osgood model)	Dim.	
6D-EPA	6 dim. correlates with the EPA model	Dim.	[44]
AVT	Arousal, valence, and tension	Dim.	[18]

we discuss some of the findings in MER and highlight the main implications to improve content- and context-based MER models.

2 Representation of Emotions

Table 1 presents the main categorical and dimensional emotion models employed in the MER studies reviewed in Sect. 3 and 4, and gives the associated notations used throughout the article.

2.1 Categorical Model

According to the categorial approach, emotions can be represented as a set of categories that are distinct from each others. Ekman's categorical emotion theory [19] was formulated a century after that proposed by Darwin [15], centred on *basic* or universal emotions that are expected to have prototypical facial expressions and emotion-specific physiological signatures. Ekman developed the facial action coding system (FACS), a system to taxonomize human facial expressions. The facial action coding system affect interpretation dictionary (FACSAID) relates an emotion category (e.g. happy) to action units (AU), coding the contraction or relaxation of one or more muscles (e.g. 6+12).

The scientific study of emotions in music has often been conducted in conjunction with the analysis of musical expression [25]. In order to secure the responses of individual listeners to music in a simple and objective way while leaving them enough freedom not to force their judgements, Hevner devised a list of 66 emotion-related adjectives, arranged in 14 groups. Listeners were asked to check all the adjectives they found appropriate to describe the music [26]. The meanings or affective characteristics of music pieces were further ascertained by comparing the numbers of votes for different adjectives. Hevner proposed an arrangement of eight adjective groups organised around a circle in order to simplify the selection task, so that "any two adjacent groups should have some characteristics in common, and that the groups at the extremities of any diameter of the circle should be as unlike each other as possible". This study was seminal since it highlighted (i) the bipolar nature of music emotions (e.g. happy/sad), (ii) a possible way of representing them spatially across a circle (on which Thayer-Russell's model is based [57]; see Sect. 2.2), as well as (iii) the multi-class and multi-label nature of music emotion classification. Schubert proposed a new taxonomy, the updated Hevner model (UHM) [68], which refined the set of adjectives proposed by Hevner, based on a survey conducted by 133 musically experienced participants. Based on Hevner's list, Russell's circumplex of emotion [57], and Whissell's dictionary of affect [83], the UHM consists in 46 words grouped into nine clusters.

Some categorical approaches have emerged from dimensional approaches based on the organisation of the Thayer-Russell Arousal/Valence (AV) space (see Sect. 2.2) into a set of "landmark" or "family" areas. This procedure has been followed for instance in [9] and [81] where the Thayer/Russel space was divided into four quadrants (AV4Q). [9] considered the following four quadrants (Q): Q1 - high energy/high stress ("anxious, frantic"), Q2 - high energy/low stress ("exuberance"), Q3 - low energy/low stress ("contentment"), and Q4 - low energy/high stress ("depression"). Similarly, [81] proposed: Q1 - high energy/low stress ("happy, exciting"), Q2 - high energy/high stress ("angry, anxious"), Q3 - low energy/high stress ("sad, bored"), and Q4 - low energy/low stress ("relaxing, serene"). The results from [9] report classification confusions between the quadrants 1 and 4 which, according to the authors, come from the fact that both quadrants are associated with emotional states involving high stress (negative valence), and that the arousal dimension did not ease the differentiation between them. [24] proposed subdivisions of the four AV space quadrants into a larger set composed of 11 categories (AV11C: "pleased", "happy", "excited", "angry", "nervous", "bored", "sad", "sleepy", "peaceful", "relaxed", and "calm") associated with the middle of the space. Their model, assessed on a prototypical database, led to high MER performance (see Table 3).

[27] and [42] proposed mood taxonomies based on the (semi-)automatic analysis of mood tags with clustering techniques. In a study exploring the relationships between mood, genre, artist, and usage metadata, [27] applied an agglomerative hierarchical clustering procedure (Ward's criterion) on similarity data between mood labels mined from the AllMusicGuide.com (AMG) website presenting annotations made by professional editors. The procedure led to a set of five clusters which further served as a mood representation model (denoted AMC5C, here) in the MIREX audio mood classification task and has been widely used since (e.g. in [27,14,9], and [80]). In this model, the similarity between emotion labels is computed based on the frequency of their co-occurence in the dataset. Consequently some of the mood tag clusters may comprise tags which suggest

different emotions: e.g. "literate" and "bittersweet" in cluster 3, "witty", "humorous", and "whimsical" in cluster 4. In contrast, some of the terms belonging to different clusters present close semantic associations: e.g. "literate" and "witty" (cluster 3 and 4, respectively). Training MER models on these clusters may be misleading for inference systems, as shown in [9] where prominent confusion patterns between clusters were reported (between clusters 1 and 2, as well as between clusters 4 and 3).

By combining findings from categorical and dimensional approaches, [49] proposed a mood taxonomy model by grouping the eight clusters associated with Schubert's UHM across the four quadrants (Q) of the AV space: Q1 (UHM groups I, II, IX: "exuberance"), Q2 (UHM group VIII: "anxious"), Q3 (UHM groups V, VII: "depression"), and Q4 (UHM groups III, IV, and VI: "contentment"). However, the resulting classification accuracies have shown to be good only for the first quadrant (68% of correct classifications). [29] proposed a new categorical model by collecting 4460 mood tags and AV values from 10 music clip annotators and by further grouping them relying on unsupervised classification techniques. The collected mood tags were processed to get rid of synonymous and ambiguous terms. Based on the frequency distribution of the 115 remaining mood tags, the 32 most frequently used tags were retained. The AV values associated with the tags were processed using K-means clustering which led to a configuration of eight clusters (AV8C). The results show that some regions can be identified by the same representative mood tags as in previous models, but that some of the mood tags present overlap between regions. Categorical approaches have been criticized for their restrictions due to the discretization of the problem into a set of "families" [48], or "landmarks" [13], which prevent consideration of emotions which differ from these landmarks. However, for music retrieval applications based on language queries, such landmarks (keywords/tags) have shown to be useful.

2.2 Dimensional Model

In contrast with the categorical approach, the dimensional approach to emotion representation consists in characterising emotions based on a small number of dimensions intended to correspond to the internal human representation of emotions.

The psychologist Osgood [52] devised a technique for measuring the connotative meaning of concepts, called the *semantic differential technique (SDT)*. It involves the rating of words on a set of bipolar adjectives (e.g. happy/sad). Experiments were conducted with 200 undergraduate students who were asked to rate 20 concepts using 50 descriptive scales (7-point Likert scales whose poles were bipolar adjectives) [52]. Factor analyses accounted for almost 70% of the common variance in a three-dimensional configuration (50% of the total variance remained unexplained). The first factor was clearly identifiable as *evaluative*, for instance representing adjective pairs such as *good/bad, beautiful/ugly* (dimension also called *valence*), the second factor identified fairly well as *potency*, for instance related to bipolar adjectives like *large/small, strong/weak, heavy/light* (dimension also called *dominance*), and the third factor appeared to be mainly an *activity* variable, related to adjectives such as *fast/slow, active/passive, hot/cold* (dimension also called *arousal*). The SDT was later applied by Osgood [51] in thirty different cultures for 620 concepts validating the evaluation, potency, activity (EPA) model of representation of emotions, and the results were formulated in an *Atlas of affective meaning*. Osgood's EPA model was used for instance in the study [16] investigating how well music (theme tune) can aid automatic classification of TV programmes from BBC Information & Archives. A slight variation of the EPA model was used in [17] with the *potency* dimension being replaced by one related to *tension*. Although Osgood's model has been shown to be relevant to classify affective concepts, its adaptability to music emotions is not straightforward. In other words, it is reasonable to make the assumption that music emotions may be represented by a different set of dimensions than that uncovered for affective concepts, in general. Asmus [3] replicated Osgood's semantic differential technique in the context of music emotions classification. Measures were developed from 2057 participants on 99 affect terms in response to musical excerpts and then factor analysed. Nine affective dimensions (9AD) were found to best represent the measures, two of which (potency and activity) were found to be common to the EPA model: "evil", "sensual", "potency", "humor", "pastoral", "longing", "depression", "sedative", and "activity". Probably because it is harder to visually represent nine dimensions, and because it complicates the classification problem, this model has not been used yet in the MIR domain, to our knowledge.

The works that have had the most influence on the choice of emotion representations in MER so far are those of Russell [57] and Thayer [72]. Russell devised a *circumplex model of affect* which consists of a two-dimensional, circular structure involving the dimensions of *arousal* and *valence* (denoted AV and called the *core affect dimensions* following Russell's terminology). As in Hevner's circular representation of emotion-related adjectives, and Schlosberg's proposal that emotions are organised in a circular arrangement [62], within the AV model, emotions that are across a circle from one another correlate inversely (e.g. sadness/happiness). This characteristic is also in line with the semantic differential approach and the bipolar adjectives proposed by Osgood. Thayer's findings confirmed the relevance of the AV model in the musical domain where emotion classes can be defined in terms of arousal or energy (how exciting/calming musical pieces are) and valence or stress (how positive/negative musical pieces are). Schubert [67] developed a measurement interface called the "two-dimensional emotional space" (2DES) using Russell's core affect dimensions and proved the validity of the methodology, experimentally. However, results obtained in [90] suggest that arousal and valence are not fully independent, even though they are two axes in the 2D Thayer-Russell space.

While the AV space stood out amongst other models for its simplicity and robustness, higher dimensionality has shown to be needed when seeking completeness. The potency or dominance dimension related to power and control proposed by Osgood is necessary to make important distinctions between fear and anger, for instance, which are both active and negative states. Fontaine et al. [22] advocated the use of a fourth dimension related to the expectedness or unexpectedness of events, which to our knowledge has not been used in the MIR domain so far. It is worth mentioning that none of these dimensions can represent more complex and subtle emotional states such as *pride/shame* or *shy/extroverted* in a straightforward manner. As to whether such emotional states can be musically-induced requires investigation. Following the dimensional approach to emotion representation, several teams have focused on obtaining continuous representations of emotions from human labelers across time, both in the domains of affective computing for audiovisual recordings (e.g. FEELtrace [13]), and music (e.g. 2DES [67], MoodSwings [63]).

2.3   Comparison between Categorical and Dimensional Models

A comparison between the categorical, or discrete, and dimensional models has been conducted in [17]. Linear mapping techniques revealed a high correspondence along the core affect dimensions (arousal and valence), and the three obtained dimensions could be reduced to two without significantly reducing the goodness of fit. The major difference between the discrete and categorical models concerned the poorer resolution of the discrete model in characterizing emotionally ambiguous examples. [78] compared the applicability of music-specific and general emotion models, the Geneva emotional music scale (GEMS), and the discrete and dimensional AV emotion models, in the assessment of music-induced emotions. The AV model outperformed the other two models in the discrimination of music excerpts, and principal component analysis revealed that 89.9% of the variance in the mean ratings of all the scales (in all three models) was accounted for by two principal components that could be labelled as valence and arousal. The results also revealed that personality-related differences were the most pronounced in the case of the discrete emotion model, an aspect which seems to contradict the findings obtained in [17].

2.4   Appraisal Model

As described in [48], *"appraisal models are a third alternative perspective on emotion: they combine elements of dimensional models - emotions as emergent results of underlying dimensions - with elements of discrete theories - emotions have different subjective qualities - and add a definition of the cognitive mechanisms at the basis of emotions"*. The appraisal approach was first advocated by Arnold [2] who defined appraisal as a cognitive evaluation able to distinguish qualitatively among different emotions. The theory of appraisal therefore accounts for individual differences and variations to responses across time [56], as well as for some cultural differences [60]. Appraisal models attempt to explain the differentiation of emotional states with different configurations of the underlying appraisal dimensions which are then mapped to emotion labels. The component process appraisal model (CPM) [61] describes an emotion as a process involving five functional components: cognitive, peripheral efference, motivational, motor expression, and subjective feeling. Banse and Scherer [5] proved the relevance of CPM predictions based on acoustical features of vocal expressions of emotions. The acoustic features characterising 100 vocal affect bursts, representing five emotions, were successfully related to the power and control parts of the appraisal component of coping potential. Significant correlations between appraisals and acoustic features were also reported in [34] showing that inferred appraisals were in line with the theoretical predictions.

Mortillaro et al. [48] advocate that the appraisal framework would help to address the following concerns in automatic emotion recognition: (i) how to establish a link between models of emotion recognition and emotion production? (ii) how to add contextual information to systems of emotion recognition? (iii) how to increase the sensitivity with which weak, subtle, or complex emotion states can be detected? All these points are highly significant for MER whereas appraisal models such as the CPM have not yet been applied in the MIR field, to our knowledge. The appraisal framework is especially promising for the development of context-sensitive automatic emotion recognition systems taking into account the environment (e.g. work, or home), the situation (relaxing, performing a task), or the subject (personality traits), for instance [48]. This comes from the fact that appraisals themselves represent abstractions of contextual information. By inferring appraisals (e.g. obstruction) from behaviors (e.g. frowning), information about the causes of emotions (e.g. anger) can be uncovered [10].

2.5   Ontology

Despite the promising applications of semantic web ontologies in the field of MIR (see e.g. [32]), the ontology approach has been scarcely used in MER. [80] proposed a music-mood specific ontology grounded in the Music Ontology (see [54,55]), in order to develop a multi-modal MER model relying on audio content extraction and semantic association reasoning. Such an approach is promising since the system from [80] achieved a performance increase of approximately 20% points (60.6%) in comparison with the system by Feng, Cheng and Yang (FCY1), proposed at MIREX 2009 [47].

3   Acoustical and Contextual Analysis of Emotions

3.1   Databases

Several music emotion annotation databases produced by the MIR research community have been made publicly available to facilitate the training, assessment and systematic comparison of music emotion recognition models. Developing musical mood annotation databases is a challenge for several reasons: as discussed in the previous section, the choice of emotion representation is not obvious, the task can be very time-consuming, ground truth annotations remain subjective, and often several labelers are required to reach for consistency. The CAL500 dataset comprises emotion labels for 500 songs by 500 unique artists [76]. Each song was annotated by three (non expert) reviewers using a set of 174 music tags, from which 18 were mood tags. The labellers annotated songs as a whole, rather than over time, a choice justified by the fact that mood is believed to be less prone to changes over time in popular music as opposed to classical music. The popular online music streaming service Last.fm has built up a "folksonomy" of 960 000 tags [31] (analytics from 2007) from which between 13% [80] and 20% [9], depending on the set of considered songs/artists, have been estimated to be related to mood. [80] published a dataset of 1804 tracks covering about 21 genres, with labels from the AMC5C mood tag clusters, derived from the AMG classification. [30] devised an online collaborative music mood annotation game, MoodSwings, where players annotate 30s-long music clips from the uspop2002 database [7], across time in the AV space. [70] built the "Now That's What I Call Music!" (NTWICM) database containing 2648 tracks from over five different genres (e.g. pop, rock, rap, R&B, electronic). Arousal and valence emotion annotations were conducted on 5-point Likert scales by four labelers. Eerola et al. [18,17] established a set of stimuli for the study of music-mediated emotions. A large pilot study established a set of 110 film music excerpts, half of which were moderately and highly representative examples of five discrete emotions ("anger", "fear", "sadness", "happiness", and "tenderness"), and the other half were moderate and high examples of the six extremes of three bipolar dimensions (valence, energy arousal and tension arousal).

3.2   Content- and Context-Based Features

Finding the acoustical clues predicting music emotions is one of the most challenging aspect in the development of music emotion recognition systems. Studies in music psychology [71], musicology [23] and music information retrieval [31] have shown that music emotions were related to different musical variables. Table 2 lists the content- and context-based features used in the studies reviewed hereby, while Tables 3 and 4 present the architectures of the associated content-based and multimodal MER models, respectively. Various acoustical correlates of articulation, dynamics, harmony, instrumentation, key, mode, pitch, register, rhythm, tempo, musical structure and timbre have been used in MER models. It can be seen from Table 2 that timbre features are the most commonly used in MER models. This is due to the fact that they have shown to provide the best performance in MER systems when used as individual features [66,93]. Indeed, Schmidt et al. investigated the use of multiple audio content-based features both individually and in combination in a feature fusion system [66,63]. They tested timbre descriptors (mel frequency cepstral coefficients, spectral centroid, spectral rolloff, spectral flux, octave-based spectral contrast, modeling peaks and gaps between harmonics), and chroma descriptors. The best individual features were octave-based spectral contrast and MFCCs. However, the best overall results were achieved using a combination of features, as in [93] (combination of rhythm, timbre and pitch features). Eerola et al. [18] extracted features representing six different musical variables (dynamics, timbre, harmony, register, rhythm and articulation) to further apply statistical feature selection (FS) methods: multiple linear regression (MLR) with a stepwise FS principle, principal component analysis (PCA) followed by the selection of an optimal

Table 2. Content (audio and lyrics) and context-based features used in MER (studies between 2009 and 2011)

Type	Notation	Description	References
		Content-based features	
Articulation	EVENTD	Event density	[18]
Articulation/Timbre	ATTACS	Attack slope	[18]
Articulation/Timbre	ATTACT	Attack time	[18]
Dynamics	AVGENER	Average energy	[24]
Dynamics	INT	Intensity	[49]
Dynamics	INTR	Intensity ratio	[49]
Dynamics	DYN	Dynamics features	[58]
Dynamics	RMS	Root mean square energy	[18] [44] [58]
Dynamics	LOWENER	Low energy	[44]
Dynamics	ENER	Energy features	[45]
Harmony	OSPECENT	Octave spectrum entropy	[18]
Harmony	HARMC	Harmonic change	[18]
Harmony	CHROM	Chroma features	[66]
Harmony	HARMF	Harmony features	[58]
Harmony	RCHORDF	Relative chord frequency	[70]
Harmony	WCHORDD	Weighted chord differential	[44]
Instrum./Rhythm	PERCTO	Percussion template occurrence	[75]
Instrumentation	BASSTD	Bass-line template distance	[75]
Key/Mode	KEY	Key	[24]
Key/Mode	KEYC	Key clarity	[18]
Key/Mode	MAJ	Majorness	[18]
Key/Mode	SPITCH	Salient pitch	[18]
Key/Mode	WTON	Weighted tonality	[44]
Key/Mode	WTOND	Weighted tonality differential	[44]
Pitch/Melody	PITCHMIDI	Pitch MIDI features	[93]
Pitch/Melody	MELOMIDI	Melody MIDI features	[93]
Pitch/Melody	PITCH	Pitch features	[58]
Pitch/Timbre	ZCR	Zero-crossing rate	[93] [92]
Register	CHROMD	Chromagram deviation	[18]
Register	CHROMC	Chromagram centroid	[18]
Rhythm/Tempo	BEATINT	Beat interval	[24]
Rhythm/Tempo	SPECFLUCT	Spectrum fluctuation	[18]
Rhythm/Tempo	TEMP	Tempo	[18]
Rhythm/Tempo	PULSC	Pulse clarity	[18]
Rhythm/Tempo	RHYCONT	Rhythm content features	[93]
Rhythm/Tempo	RHYSTR	Rhythm strength	[49]
Rhythm/Tempo	CORRPEA	Correlation peak	[49]
Rhythm/Tempo	ONSF	Onset frequency	[49]
Rhythm/Tempo	RHYT	Rhythm features	[58]
Rhythm/Tempo	SCHERHYT	Scheirer rhythm features	[70]
Rhythm/Tempo	PERCF	Percussive features	[45]
Structure	MSTRUCT	Multidimensional structure features	[18]
Structure	STRUCT	Structure features	[58]
Timbre	HARMSTR	Harmonic strength	[24]
Timbre	MFCC	Mel frequency cepstral coefficient	[9] [6] [75] [93] [80] [58] [66] [63] [92] [77] [65] [58]
Timbre	SPECC	Spectral centroid	[9] [18] [93] [92] [64] [66] [49] [44] [70]
Timbre	SPECS	Spectral spread	[18]
Timbre	SPECENT	Spectral entropy	[18]
Timbre	SPECR	Spectral rolloff	[18] [93] [92] [64] [66] [49] [70]
Timbre	SF	Spectral flux	[93] [92] [64] [66] [49] [70]
Timbre	OBSC	Octave-based spectral contrast	[64] [66] [63] [65] [49] [38]
Timbre	RPEAKVAL	Ratio between average peak and valley strength	[49]
Timbre	ROUG	Roughness	[18]
Timbre	TIM	Timbre features	[58]
Timbre	SPEC	Spectral features	[45]
Timbre	ECNTT	Echo Nest timbre features	[65] [45]
Lyrics	SENTIWORD	Occurence of sentiment word	[14]
Lyrics	NEG-SENTIW	Occurrence of sentiment word with negation	[14]
Lyrics	MOD-SENTIW	Occurrence of sentiment word with modifier	[14]
Lyrics	WORDW	Word weight	[14]
Lyrics	LYRIC	Lyrics feature	[93]
Lyrics	RSTEMFR	Relative stem frequency	[70]
Lyrics	TF-IDF	Term frequency - Inverse document frequency	[14] [45]
Lyrics	RHYME	Rhyme feature	[81]
		Context-based features	
Social tags	TAGS	Tag relevance score	[6]
Web-mined tags	DOCRS	Document relevance score	[6]
Metadata	ARTISTW	Artist weight	[14]
Metadata	META	Metadata features (e.g. artist's name, title)	[70]

Table 3. Content-based music emotion recognition (MER) models (studies between 2009 and 2011). [a]: *F-measure*; [b]: *Accuracy*; [c]: r^2; [d]: *Average Kullback-Leibler divergence*; [e]: *Average distance*; [f]: *Mean l^2 error*. SSD: statistical spectrum descriptors. BAYN: Bayesian network. ACORR: Autocorrelation. Feature notations are given in Table 2. Best reported configurations are indicated in bold.

Reference	Modalities	Db (# songs)	Model (notation)	Decision hor.	Features (no.)	Machine learn.	Perf.
Lin et al. (2009) [42]	Audio	AMG (1535)	Cat. (AMG12C)	track	MARSYAS (436)	SVM	56.00%[a]
Han et al. (2009) [24]	Audio	AMG (165)	Cat. (AV11C)	track	KEY, AVGENER, TEMP, σ(BEATINT), σ(HARMSTR)	**SVR**, SVM, GMM	94.55%[b]
Eerola et al. (2009) [18]	Audio	Soundtrack110 (110)	Cat. (5BE) & Dim. (AV & AVT)	15.3 s (avg)	RMS, SPECC, SPECS, SPECENT, ROUG, OS-PECENT, HARMC, KEYC, MAJ, CHROMC, CHROMD, SPITCH, SPECFLUCT, TEMP, PULSC, EVENTD, ATTACS, ATTACT, MSTRUCT (29)	MLR + STEPS, PCA + FS, **PLSR + DT**	70%[c] (avg)
Tsunoo et al. (2010) [75]	Audio	CAL500 (240)	Cat. (AMC5C)	track	PERCTO (4), BASSTD (80), 26 M,σ MFCCs, 12 M,σ corr(Chroma)	**TEML + SVM**	56.4%[d]
Zhao et al. (2010) [93]	Audio	Chin. & West. (24)	Cat. (AV4Q)	30s	**PITCH (5)**, **RHYT (6)**, **MFCCs (10)**, SSDs (9)	**BAYN**	74.9%[b]
Schmidt et al. (2010) [64]	Audio	MoodSwings Lite (240)	Dim. (AV)	1s	OBSC	MLR, LDS Kalman, LDS KALF, **LDS KALFM**	2.88[d]
Schmidt et al. (2010) [66]	Audio	MoodSwings Lite (240)	Cat. (AV4Q) & Dim. (AV)	1s	**MFCCs**, CHROM (12), SSDs, OBSC	SVM / PLSR, **SVR**	0.137[e]
Schmidt & Kim (2010) [63]	Audio	MoodSwings Lite (240)	Dim. (AV)	15s / 1s	**MFCCs**, ACORR(CHROM), SSDs, **OBSC**	MLR, PLSR, **SVR**	3.186 / 13.61[d]
Myint & Pwint (2010) [49]	Audio	Western pop (100)	Cat. (AV4Q-UHM9)	segment	INT, INTR, SSD, OBSC, RHYSTR, CORRPEA, RPEAKVAL, M(TEMP), M(ONSF)	OAO FSVM	37%[b]
Lee et al. (2011) [38]	Audio	Clips (1000)	Dim. 2 (AV)	20s	OBSC	**SVM**	67.5%[b]
Mann et al. (2011) [44]	Audio	TV theme tunes (144)	Dim. (6D-EPA)	track	RMS, LOWENER, SPECC, WTON, WTOND, WCHORDD, TEMP	**SVM**	80-94%[b]
Vaizman et al. (2011) [77]	Audio	Piano, Vocal (76)	Cat. (4BE)	track	34 MFCCs	DTM	60%[a]
Schmidt & Kim (2011) [65]	Audio	MoodSwings Lite (240)	Dim. (AV)	15s / 1s	**MFCCs (20)**, OBSC, ECNTTs (12)	MLR, **CRF**	0.122[f]
Saari et al. (2011) [58]	Audio	Film soundtrack (104)	Cat. (5BE)	track	52 (DYN, RHY, PITCH, HARM, TIM, STRUCT) + MFCCs (14)	**NB**, k-NN, SVM, SMO	59.4%[b]
Wang et al. (2011) [81]	Lyrics	Chinese songs (500)	Cat. (4BE-AV)	track	TF-IDF, RHYME	MLR, NB, SVM-SMO, DECT (J48)	61.5%[a]

Table 4. Multi-modal music emotion recognition (MER) models (studies between 2009 and 2011). ^{a}: F-measure; ^{b}: Accuracy; ^{c}: Mean average precision; ^{d}: r^2. FSS: Feature subset selection. Feature notations are given in Table 2.

Reference	Modalities	Dtb (# songs)	Model (notation)	Decision hor.	Features (no.)	Machine learn.	Perf.
Dang & Shirai (2009) [14]	Lyrics, Web-mined Tags	LiveJournal, LyricWiki (6000)	Cat. (AMC5C)	track	TF/IDF, SENTIWORD, NEG-SENTIW, MOD-SENTIW, WORDW, ARTISTW	SVM, NB, Graph-based	57.44%^{b}
Bischoff et al. (2009) [9]	Audio, Social tags	Last.fm, (1192) AMG	Cat. (AMC5C) & AV4Q	30s	MFCCs, TEMP, CHROM (12), SPECC, ... / log(TF)	SVM (RBF), LOGR, RANF, GMM, K-NN, DECT, NB	57.2%^{a}
Barrington et al. (2009) [6]	Audio, Social tags, Web-mined tags	Last.fm, (500) CAL500	Cat. (72TCAL500)	30s	MFCCs (39), Δ MFCCs, ΔΔ MFCCs, CHROM (12) / + 8-GMM, TAGRS, DOCRS	CSA, RANB, KC-SVM	53.8%^{c}
Wang et al. (2010) [80]	Audio, Social tags	Last.fm, WordNet, AMG (1804)	Cat. (AMC5C)	track	MARSYAS (138) & PSYSOUND3 + FSS / MFCCs + GMM	SVM PPK-RBF / NRQL	60.6%^{b}
Zhao et al. (2010) [93]	Audio, Lyrics, MIDI	Chinese songs (500)	Cat. (AV4Q)	track	MFCCs, LPC, SPECC, SPECR, SPECF, ZCR, ... (113) / N-GRAM LYRIC (2000) / PITCH-MIDI, MELOMIDI (101)	SVM, NB, DECT	61.6%^{b}
Schuller et al. (2011) [70]	Audio, Lyrics, Metadata	NTWICM, lyricsDB, LyricWiki (2648)	Dim. (AV)	track	RCHORDF (22), SCHERHYT (87), SPECC,... (24) / RSTEMFr (393), META (152)	ConceptNet, Porter stemming, UREPT	.60 (A) & .74 (V)^d
McVicar et al. (2011) [45]	Audio, Lyrics	EchoNest API, lyric-smode.com, ANEW (119 664)	Dim. (AV)	track	TF-IDF, ECNT (65)	CCA	N/A

number of components, and partial least square regression (PLSR) with a Bayesian information criterion (BIC) to select the optimal number of features. PCA showed to be too sensitive to the covariance between the features and the predicted data. In contrast, PLSR simultaneously allowed to reduce the data while maximising the covariance between the features and the predicted data, providing the highest prediction rate ($r^2 = .7$) with only two components. However, feature selection frameworks operating by considering all the emotion categories or dimensions at the same time may not be optimal; for instance, features explaining why a song expresses "anger" or why another sounds "innocent" may not be the same. Pairwise classification strategies have been successfully applied to musical instrument recognition [20] showing the interest of adapting the feature sets to discriminate two specific instruments. It would be worth investigating if music emotion recognition could benefit from pairwise feature selection strategies as well.

In addition to audio content features, lyrics have also been used in MER, either individually, or in combination with features belonging to different domains (see multi-modal approaches in Sect. 4.6). Lyrics can indeed be semantically rich and expressive and have been shown to impact the way we perceive music [1]. Access to lyrics has been facilitated by the emergence of lyrics databases on the web (e.g. lyricwiki.org, musixmatch.com), some of them providing APIs to retrieve the data. Lyrics can be analysed using natural language processing (NLP) techniques. A standard way to represent text is to use a bag-of-words approach which characterises documents as vectors of words. To characterise the importance of a given word in a song given the corpus it belongs to, authors have used term frequency - inverse document frequency (TF-IDF) measure [14,45]. Methods to analyse emotions in lyrics have been developed using lexical resources for opinion and sentiment mining such as SentiWordNet (measures of positivity, negativity, objectivity) [14] and the affective norm for English words (measures of arousal, valence, and dominance) [45]. Since meaning emerges from subtle word combinations and sentence structure, research is still needed to develop new features characterising emotional meanings in lyrics. [81] proposed a feature to characterise rhymes whose patterns are relevant to emotion expression, as poems exemplify.

To attempt to improve the performance of MER systems only relying on content-based features, and in order to bridge the semantic gap between the raw data (signals) and high-level semantics (meanings), several studies introduced context-based features. [14,9,6,80] used music tags mined from websites known to have good quality information about songs, albums or artists (e.g. bbc.co.uk, rollingstone.com), social music platform (e.g. last.fm), or web blogs (e.g. livejournal.com). Social tags are generally fused with audio features to improve overall performance of the classication task [9,6,80].

3.3   Temporal Aspects

MER models are also influenced by the duration of the audio segments chosen to make the classification decisions. Research on music emotions has shown that the fastest emotion-related responses take less than a second [13]. In [69], the author recommends a sampling rate of at least 2 Hz when collecting trace measurements. However, it is not clear yet to what extent such results depend on the material and dimension which are traced since some visual stimuli have been shown to evoke fear-related responses in the amygdala in about 12 ms [36]. However, most MER models rely on long term decision horizon (e.g. whole track [42,24,14,75,80,93,44,77,58,81,70,45], or 30-s long segment [9,6,93]). Algorithms identifying emotions on long term decision horizons are not bound to predict only a single emotion category per song since they may be associated with multi-label classification schemes, i.e. several emotion labels per decision (see Sect. 4). Other MER models use short-term decision horizons (e.g. 1 s [63,64,65,66]), in order to take into account the effects of music across time. Such an approach led to the development of methods for music emotion variation detection (see Sect. 4.5).

4   Machine Learning for Music Emotion Recognition

In most music information systems, emotion is seen as a high-level semantic feature. Thus the first step in utilising emotion-related information is devising a method that associates features from one or more of the above sources with mood categories or alternatively an emotion state in a continuous space. Machine learning techniques have become predominant for bridging this semantic gap. Initial approaches in MER were grounded on emotion recognition techniques developed for speech, or previous work within the MIR community on genre classification. Noting the similarity in architectural requirements, the first methods include the works of Feng et al. [21] and Li et al. [40]. Subsequently developed techniques can be characterised by their training method and expected outputs as follows: *multi-class single-label classification* (training samples are assigned a discrete emotion category, and the best estimate is chosen as output), *multi-label classification* (estimate multiple emotion categories simultaneously), *fuzzy classification* (probability estimates in each possible category), and *regression* (an estimate of emotion state in a continuous space).

From a high-level perspective, the first three approaches rely on a categorical model (Sect. 2.1) while regression relies on a dimensional model (Sect. 2.2). Given articles already covering early approaches to MER in detail (e.g. [31,50,86]), more emphasis is placed on state of the art and recent regression-based techniques in the following review.

4.1   Early Categorical Approaches

Associating music with discrete emotion categories was demonstrated by the first works that used an audio-based approach. Li et al. [40] used a song database hand-labelled with adjectives belonging to one of 13 categories and trained Support Vector Machines (SVM) on timbral, rhythmic and pitch features. The authors report large variation in the accuracy of estimating the different mood categories with the overall accuracy (F-score) remaining below 50%. Feng et al. [21] used a Backpropagation Neural Network (BPNN) to recognise to which extent music pieces belong to four emotion categories ("happiness", "sadness", "anger", and "fear"). They used features related to tempo (fast-slow) and articulation (staccato-legato), and report 66% and 67% precision and recall, respectively. However, the actual accuracy of detecting each emotion fluctuated considerably.

4.2 Multi-label Classification

Early approaches demonstrate that content-based models of musical emotion are feasible. However, the ambiguity in the results can be attributed to the difficulty in assigning music pieces to any single category and the ambiguity of mood adjectives themselves. For these reasons subsequent research have moved on to use multi-label, fuzzy or continuous (dimensional) emotion models.

In multi-label classification, training examples are assigned multiple labels from a set of disjoint categories. MER was first formulated as a multi-label classification problem by Wieczorkowska et al. [84] applying a classifier specifically adopted to this task. The first systematic evaluation comparing several multi-label classification algorithms including Binary Relevance (BR), Label Powerset (LP), Random k-label sets (RAkEL) and Multi-Label k-Nearest Neighbours (MLkNN) was performed by Trohidis et al. [74], with RAkEL reaching 79% average precision using a dataset of 593 songs and simple rhythm and timbre features. In a recent study, Sanden and Zhang [59] examined multi-label classification in the general music tagging context (emotion labelling is seen as a subset of this task). Two datasets, the CAL500 and approximately 21,000 clips from Magnatune (each associated with one or more of 188 different tags) were used in the experiments. The clips were modeled using statistical distributions of spectral, timbral and beat features. Besides the above algorithms, the authors tested Calibrated Label Ranking (CLR), Backpropagation for Multi-Label Learning (BPMLL), Hierarchy of Multi-Label Classifiers (HOMER), Instance-Based Logistic Regression (IBLR) and Binary Relevance kNN (BRkNN) models, and two separate evaluations were performed using the two datasets. In both cases, the CLR classifier using a Support Vector Machine (CLR_{SVM}) outperformed all other approaches (peak F_1 score of 0.497 and 0.642 precision on CAL500). However, CLR with Decision Trees, BPMLL, and MLkNN also performed competitively.

4.3 Fuzzy Classification

Irrespective of considering induced or attributed emotion, people do not generally feel or perceive the same emotions. Several studies conclude that accommodating subjectivity is among the primary challenges in categorical emotion recognition models, while this was also demonstrated in a systematic evaluation using a non-categorical model [28]. A possible approach to account for subjectivity is the use of fuzzy classification incorporating fuzzy logic into conventional classification strategies. The work of Yang et al. [89] was the first to take this route. As opposed to associating pieces with a single or a discrete set of emotions, fuzzy classification uses fuzzy vectors whose elements represent the likelihood of a piece belonging to each respective emotion category in a particular model. In [89], two classifiers, Fuzzy k-NN (FkNN) and Fuzzy Nearest Mean (FNM), were tested using a database of

243 popular songs and 15 acoustic features. The authors performed 10-fold cross validation and reported 68.22% and 70.88% mean accuracy for the two classifiers respectively. After applying stepwise backward feature selection, the results improved to 70.88% and 78.33%. In some sense fuzzy classification may be seen as a special case of multi-label classification, but it is also a step towards continuous non-categorical models of emotion discussed in the next section.

4.4   Emotion Regression

The techniques mentioned so far rely on the idea that emotions may be organised in a simple taxonomy consisting of a small set of universal emotions (e.g. happy or sad) and more subtle differences within these categories. Limitations of this model include *(i)* the fixed set of classes considered, *(ii)* the ambiguity in the meaning of adjectives associated with emotion categories, and *(iii)* the potential heterogeneity in the taxonomical organisation. The use of a continuous emotion space such as Thayer-Russell's Arousal-Valence (AV) space and corresponding dimensional models is a solution to these problems. In the first study that addresses these issues [88], MER was formulated as a regression problem to map high-dimensional features extracted from audio to the two-dimensional AV space directly. AV values for *induced* emotion were collected from 253 subjects for 195 popular recordings. A 114-dimensional feature space was constructed including spectral contrast features, wavelet coefficient histograms, as well as spectral (e.g. spectral centroid) and musicological (e.g. chords) features. After basic dimensionality reduction, three regressors were trained and tested: Multiple Linear Regression (MLR) as baseline, Support Vector Regression (SVR) and Adaboost.RT, a regression tree ensemble. The authors reported coefficient of determination statistics (R^2) with peak performance of 58.3% for arousal, and 28.1% for valence using SVR. These results were then improved using feature selection.

Han et al. [24] used SVR for training distinct regressors to predict arousal and valence both in terms of Cartesian and polar coordinates of the AV space. A policy for partitioning the AV space and mapping coordinates to discrete emotions was used, and an increase in accuracy from 63.03% to 94.55% was obtained when polar coordinates were used in this process. Notably Gaussian Mixture Model (GMM) classifiers performed competitively in this study. Schmidt et al. [66] show that multi-level least-squares regression (MLSR) performs comparably to SVR at a lower computational cost. An interesting observation is that combining multiple feature sets does not necessarily improve regressor performance, probably due to the curse of dimensionality. The solution was seen in the use of different fusion topologies, i.e. using separate regressors for each feature set.

Huq et al. [28] performed a systematic evaluation of content-based emotion recognition to identify a potential "glass ceiling" in the use of regression. 160 audio features were tested in four categories, timbral, loudness, harmonic, and rhythmic (with or without feature selection), as well as different regressors in three categories, Linear Regression, variants of regression trees and SVRs with Radial Basis Function (RBF) kernel (with or without parameter optimisation). Ground truth data was collected to indicate *induced* emotion, as in [88], by averaging arousal and valence scores from 50 subjects for 288 music pieces. Confirming earlier findings that arousal is easier to predict than valence, peak R^2 of 69.7% (arousal) and 25.8% (valence) were obtained using SVR-RBF. However, none of the variations in the experimental setup led to substantial improvement. The authors concluded that small database size presents a major problem, while the wide distribution of individual responses to a song spreading in the AV space was seen as another limitation. In order to overcome the subjectivity and potential nonlinearity of AV coordinates collected from users, and to ease the cognitive load during data collection, Yang et al. proposed a method to automatically determine the AV coordinates of songs using pair-wise comparison of relative emotion differences between songs using a ranking algorithm [85]. They demonstrated that the increased reliability of ground truth pays off when different learning algorithms are compared. In [87], the authors modeled emotions as probability distributions in the AV space as opposed to discrete coordinates. They developed a method to predict these distributions using *regression fusion* and reported a weighted R^2 score of 54.39%.

4.5 Methods for Music Emotion Variation Detection

The techniques discussed so far focus on detecting emotions from songs or short clips in a static manner. It can easily be argued however that emotions are not necessarily constant during the course of a piece of music, especially in classical recordings. The problem of Music Emotion Variation Detection (MEVD) can be approached from two perspectives: the detection of time-varying emotion as a continuous trajectory in the AV space, or finding music segments that are correlated with well defined emotions. The task of dividing the music into several segments which contain homogeneous emotion expression was first proposed by Lu et al. [43]. In [89], the authors also proposed MEVD but by classifying features resulting from 10-s segments with 33.3% overlap using a fuzzy approach, and then computing arousal and valence values from the fuzzy output vectors.

Building on earlier studies, Schmidt et al. [64] demonstrated that emotion distributions may be modeled as two-dimensional Gaussian distributions in the AV space, and then approached the problem of time-varying emotion tracking in two successive publications. In [64], they employed Kalman filtering in a linear dynamical system to capture the dynamics of emotions across time. While this method provided smoothed estimates over time, the authors concluded that the wide variance in emotion space dynamics could not be accommodated by the initial model, and subsequently moved on to use Conditional Random Fields (CRF), a probabilistic graphical model to approach the same problem [65]. In modeling complex emotion-space distributions as AV *heatmaps*, CRF outperformed the prediction of 2D Gaussians using MLR. However, the CRF model has higher computational cost.

4.6 Multi-modal Approaches and Fusion Policies

When trying to account for the subjectivity of music related emotions, several factors other than audio may also be taken into account. Some of these factors, such as the acculturation of the listener, are extra-musical, or present in other modalities like lyrics. The combination of multiple feature domains has become dominant in recent MER systems and a comprehensive overview of combining acoustic features with lyrics, social tags and images (e.g. album covers) is presented in [31]. In most works, the previously discussed machine learning techniques still prevail. However, different feature fusion policies may be applied ranging from concatenating normalised feature vectors (early fusion) to boosting, or ensemble methods combining the outputs of classifiers or regressors trained on different feature sets independently (late fusion). Late fusion is becoming dominant since it solves the issues related to tractability, and the curse of dimensionality affecting early fusion.

Despite the need for a complex architecture, combining multiple modalities pays off well since different feature domains are often complementary. Bischoff et al. [9] showed that classification performance can be improved by exploiting both audio features and collaborative user annotations. In this study, SVMs with RBF kernel outperformed logistic regression, random forest, GMM, K-NN, and decision trees in the case of audio features, while the Naive Bayes Multinomial classifier produced the best results in the case of tag features. An experimentally defined linear combination of the results then outperformed classifiers using individual feature domains. In a more recent study, Lin et al. [41] demonstrated that genre-based grouping complements the use of tags in a two-stage multi-label emotion classification system reporting an improvement of 55% when genre information is used. Finally, Schuller et al. [70] combined audio features with metadata and Web-mined lyrics. They used a stemmed bag-of-words approach to represent lyrics and editorial metadata, and also extracted mood concepts from lyrics using natural language processing. Ensembles of REPTrees (a variant of Decision Trees) are used in a set of regression experiments. When the domains were considered in isolation, the best performance was achieved using audio features (chords, rhythm, timbre), but taking all modalities into account improved the results. However, they were not equally reliable, which promoted late fusion with a weighted combination of unimodal predictions. The decision between late and early fusion was not always clear cut however, since finding fusion weights was subject to overfitting.

5   Discussion and Conclusions

Although approaches relying on web social data and web documents are promising, they target commercial popular music repertoires for which web resources (e.g. blogs) are available and can be mined. Such approaches can't be applied straightforwardly to production music (music used in film, television, radio and other media, and often referred to as "mood music") which don't benefit from the same media exposure as commercial music. The semantic analysis of lyrics offers promising perspectives, however it can't be applied to instrumental music, which represents a large corpus of classical and jazz music, alternative and progressive rock, and the most part of production music catalogues, for instance.

For such reasons, there is still a need to refine purely content-based methods, in addition to continuing development of hybrid approaches. [75] put forward the dominance of timbral features in music emotion recognition over pitch, and rhythmic features, for instance. As showed in Sect. 3, a large part of MER models rely on spectral timbre descriptors, such as the mel frequency cepstral coefficients, MFCCs, used in more than half of the studies reviewed hereby, as well as the octave-based spectral contrast (OBSC) and spectral descriptors, used in a third of the reviewed studies. This is related to the fact that spectral timbre descriptors have shown to provide the best correct classification rates when they were coupled with state of the art machine learning techniques in MER (see Table 3), audio music similarity (AMS) [4], as well as audio genre classification (AGC). However, as stated above, the results obtained by audio content-based systems are likely to be prone to a "glass ceiling" effect. In a recent study [58], high-level features (mode "majorness" and key "clarity") have shown to enhance emotion recognition in a more robust way than low-level features. In line with these results, we claim that in order to improve MER models, there is a need for new mid or high-level descriptors characterising musical clues, more adapted to *explain* our conditioning to musical emotions than low-level descriptors. Some of the findings in music perception and cognition [71], psycho-musicology [23], and affective computing [48] have not yet been exploited or adapted to their full potential for music information retrieval. Most of the current approaches to emotion recognition articulate on black-box models which model the relation between features and emotion components as accurately as possible without taking into account the interpretability of the relationships, which is a disadvantage when trying to understand the underlying mechanisms [82]. Other emotion representation models - the appraisal models [48] - support the development of process models (see Sect. 2.4) which attempt to predict the association between appraisal and emotion components making it possible to interpret relationships.

With regard to machine learning techniques used in MER, the relatively low performance of classification approaches was commonly attributed to the weaknesses of the categorical emotion model discussed in Sect. 2.1 and 4.4. As a result, recent research focuses on the use of regression and attempt to estimate continuous valued coordinates in some emotion space, which may then be mapped to an emotion label or a broader category. Although these approaches seem to solve some of the problems related to classification, the decision between regression and classification is not yet straightforward, as both categorical and dimensional emotion models have strengths and weaknesses with regard to specific applications. Moreover, retrieving labels or categories given the estimated coordinates is often necessary, and requires a mapping between the dimensional and categorical models. This however may not be available for a given model, may not be psychologically validated in a given application, and may also be dependent on extra-musical circumstances. With regard to the use of multiple modalities, most studies to date confirm that the strongest factors enabling emotion recognition are indeed related to the audio content, however a "glass ceiling" seems to exist which can only be vanquished if both contextual features and features from different musical modalities are also considered.

Acknowledgments. This work was partly funded by the TSB project 12033-76187 "Making Musical Mood Metadata" (TS/J002283/1). The first author wishes to thank Christopher Jack for proofreading the article.

References

1. Ali, S.O., Peynirciogu, Z.F.: Songs and emotions: are lyrics and melodies equal partners? Psychology of Music 34(4), 511–534 (2006)
2. Arnold, M.B.: Emotion and personality. Columbia University Press, New York (1960)
3. Asmus, E.P.: Nine affective dimensions. Tech. rep., University of Miami (1986)
4. Aucouturier, J.J., Pachet, F.: Improving timbre similarity: How high is the sky? Journal of Negative Results in Speech and Audio Sciences 1(1) (2004)
5. Banse, R., Scherer, K.R.: Acoustic profiles in vocal emotion expression. Journal of Personality and Social Psychology 70, 614–636 (1996)
6. Barrington, L., Turnbull, D., Yazdani, M., Lanckriet, G.: Combining audio content and social context for semantic music discovery. In: Proc. of the ACM Special Interest Group on Information Retrieval, SIGIR (2009)
7. Berenzweig, A., Logan, B., Ellis, D., Whitman, B.: A large-scale evaluation of acoustic and subjective music-similarity measures. Computer Music Journal 28(2), 63–76 (2004)
8. Bischoff, K., Firan, C.S., Nejdl, W., Paiu, R.: Can all tags be used for search? In: Proc. of the ACM Conference on Information and Knowledge Management (CIKM), pp. 193–202 (2008)
9. Bischoff, K., Firan, C.S., Paiu, R., Nejdl, W., Laurier, C., Sordo, M.: Music mood and theme classification - a hybrid approach. In: Proc. of the 12th International Society for Music Information Retrieval (ISMIR) Conference, pp. 657–662 (2011)
10. Castellano, G., Caridakis, G., Camurri, A., Karpouzis, K., Volpe, G., Kollias, S.: Body gesture and facial expression analysis for automatic affect recognition. In: Scherer, K.R., Bänziger, T., Roesch, E.B. (eds.) Blueprint for Affective Computing: A Sourcebook, pp. 245–255. Oxford University Press, New York (2010)
11. Chion, M.: Audio-Vision: Sound On Screen. Columbia University Press (1994)
12. Cohen, A.J.: Music as a source of emotion in film. In: Music and Emotion Theory and Research, pp. 249–272. Oxford University Press (2001)
13. Cowie, R., McKeown, G., Douglas-Cowie, E.: Tracing emotion: an overview. International Journal of Synthetic Emotions 3(1), 1–17 (2012)
14. Dang, T.T., Shirai, K.: Machine learning approaches for mood classification of songs toward music search engine. In: Proc. of the International Conference on Knowledge and Systems Engineering (ICKSE), pp. 144–149 (2009)
15. Darwin, C.: The expression of the emotions in man and animals, 3rd edn. HarperCollins (1998) (original work published 1872)
16. Davies, S., Allen, P., Mann, M., Cox, T.: Musical moods: a mass participation experiment for affective classification of music. In: Proc. of the 12th International Society for Music Information Retrieval (ISMIR) Conference, pp. 741–746 (2011)
17. Eerola, T.: A comparison of the discrete and dimensional models of emotion in music. Psychology of Music 39(1), 18–49 (2010)
18. Eerola, T., Lartillot, O., Toiviainen, P.: Prediction of multidimensional emotional ratings in music from audio using multivariate regression models. In: Proc. of the International Society for Music Information Retrieval (ISMIR) Conference (2009)
19. Ekman, P., Friesen, W.V.: Facial Action Coding System. Consulting Psychologists Press, Palo Alto (1978)

20. Essid, S., Richard, G., David, B.: Musical instrument recognition by pairwise classification strategies. IEEE Trans. on Audio, Speech, and Language Proc. 14(4), 1401–1412 (2006)

21. Feng, Y., Zhuang, Y., Pan, Y.: Popular music retrieval by detecting mood. In: Proc. ACM SIGIR, pp. 375–376 (2003)

22. Fontaine, J.R., Scherer, K.R., Roesch, E.B., Ellsworth, P.: The world of emotions is not two-dimensional. Psychological Science 18(2), 1050–1057 (2007)

23. Gabrielsson, A.: The influence of musical structure on emotional expression, pp. 223–248. Oxford University Press (2001)

24. Han, B.J., Dannenberg, R.B., Hwang, E.: SMERS: music emotion recognition using support vector regression. In: Proc. of the 10th International Society for Music Information Retrieval (ISMIR) Conference, pp. 651–656 (2009)

25. Hevner, K.: Expression in music: a discussion of experimental studies and theories. Psychological Review 42(2), 186–204 (1935)

26. Hevner, K.: Experimental studies of the elements of expression in music. The American Journal of Psychology 48(2), 246–268 (1936)

27. Hu, X., Downie, J.S.: Exploring mood metadata: relationships with genre, artist and usage metadata. In: Proc. of the 8th International Conference on Music Information Retrieval (ISMIR), pp. 67–72 (2007)

28. Huq, A., Bello, J.P., Rowe, R.: Automated music emotion recognition: A systematic evaluation. Journal of New Music Research 39(3), 227–244 (2010)

29. Kim, J.H., Lee, S., Kim, S.M., Yoo, W.Y.: Music mood classification model based on Arousal-Valence values. In: Proc. of the 2nd International Conference on Advancements in Computing Technology (ICACT), pp. 292–295 (2011)

30. Kim, Y.E., Schmidt, E.M., Emelle, L.: Moodswings: A collaborative game for music mood label collection. In: Proc. of the International Society for Music Information Retrieval (ISMIR) Conference, pp. 231–236 (2008)

31. Kim, Y.E., Schmidt, E.M., Migneco, R., Morton, B.G.: Music emotion recognition: a state of the art review. In: 11th International Society for Music Information Retrieval (ISMIR) Conference, pp. 255–266 (2010)

32. Kolozali, S., Fazekas, G., Barthet, M., Sandler, M.: Knowledge representation issues in musical instrument ontology design. In: 12th International Society for Music Information Retrieval Conference (ISMIR), Miami, USA, Florida, pp. 465–470 (2011)

33. Krumhansl, C.L.: An exploratory study of musical emotions and psychophysiology. Canadian Journal of Experimental Psychology 51(4), 336–353 (1997)

34. Laukka, P., Elfenbein, H.A., Chui, W., Thingujam, N.S., Iraki, F.K., Rockstuhl, T., Althoff, J.: Presenting the VENEC corpus: Development of a cross-cultural corpus of vocal emotion expressions and a novel method of annotation emotion appraisals. In: Proc. of the LREC Workshop on Corpora for Research on Emotion and Affect, pp. 53–57. European Language Resources Association, Paris (2010)

35. Laurier, C., Grivolla, J., Herrera, P.: Multimodal music mood classification using audio and lyrics. In: Proc. of the Conference on Machine Learning and Applications (ICMLA), pp. 688–693 (2008)

36. LeDoux, J.E.: The emotional brain: the mysterious underpinnings of emotional life. Touchstone, New York (1998)

37. Lee, J.A., Downie, J.S.: Survey of music information needs, uses, and seeking behaviors: preliminary findings. In: Proc. of the 5th International Society for Music Information Retrieval (ISMIR) Conference, pp. 441–446 (2004)

38. Lee, S., Kim, J.H., Kim, S.M., Yoo, W.Y.: Smoodi: Mood-based music recommendation player. In: Proc. of the IEEE International Conference on Multimedia and Expo. (ICME), pp. 1–4 (2011)

39. Lesaffre, M., Leman, M., Martens, J.P.: A user oriented approach to music information retrieval. In: Proc. of the Content-Based Retrieval Conference (Published online), Daghstul Seminar Proceedings, Germany, Wadern (2006)
40. Li, T., Ogihara, M.: Detecting emotion in music. In: Proc. International Society of Music Information Retrieval Conference, pp. 239–240 (2003)
41. Lin, Y.C., Yang, Y.H., Chen, H.H.: Exploiting online music tags for music emotion classification. ACM Transactions on Multimedia Computing Communications and Applications 7S(1), 26:1–26:15 (2011)
42. Lin, Y.C., Yang, Y.H., Chen, H.H., Liao, I.B., Ho, Y.C.: Exploiting genre for music emotion classification. In: Proc. of the IEEE International Conference on Multimedia and Expo. (ICME), pp. 618–621 (2009)
43. Lu, L., Liu, D., Zhang, H.J.: Automatic mood detection and tracking of music audio signals. IEEE Trans. on Audio, Speech, and Language Proc. 14(1), 5–18 (2006)
44. Mann, M., Cox, T.J., Li, F.F.: Music mood classification of television theme tunes. In: Proc. of the 12th International Society for Music Information Retrieval (ISMIR) Conference, pp. 735–740 (2011)
45. McVicar, M., Freeman, T., De Bie, T.: Mining the correlation between lyrical and audio features and the emergence of mood. In: Proc. of the 12th International Society for Music Information Retrieval (ISMIR) Conference, pp. 783–788 (2011)
46. Meyer, L.B.: Emotion and meaning in music. The University of Chicago press (1956)
47. MIREX: Audio mood classification (AMC) results (2009), http://www.music-ir.org/mirex/wiki/2009:Audio_Music_Mood_Classification_Results
48. Mortillaro, M., Meuleman, B., Scherer, R.: Advocating a componential appraisal model to guide emotion recognition. International Journal of Synthetic Emotions 3(1), 18–32 (2012)
49. Myint, E.E.P., Pwint, M.: An approach for multi-label music mood classification. In: 2nd International Conference on Signal Processing Systems (ICSPS), vol. VI, pp. 290–294 (2010)
50. Ogihara, M., Kim, Y.: Mood and emotional classification. In: Music Data Mining. CRC Press (2011)
51. Osgood, C.E., May, W.H., Miron, M.S.: Cross-Cultural Universals of Affective Meaning. University of Illinois Press, Urbana (1975)
52. Osgood, C.E., Suci, G.J., Tannenbaum, P.H.: The measurement of meaning. University of Illinois Press, Urbana (1957)
53. Parke, R., Chew, E., Kyriakakis, C.: Quantitative and visual analysis of the impact of music on perceived emotion of film. Computers in Entertainment (CIE) 5(3) (2007)
54. Raimond, Y., Abdallah, S., Sandler, M., Frederick, G.: The music ontology. In: Proc. of the 7th International Conference on Music Information Retrieval (ISMIR), Vienna, Austria, pp. 417–422 (2007)
55. Raimond, Y., Giasson, F., Jacobson, K., Fazekas, G., Gangler, T.: Music ontology specification (November 2010), http://musicontology.com/
56. Roseman, I.J., Smith, C.A.: Appraisal theory: Overview, assumptions, varieties, controversies. In: Scherer, K.R., Schorr, A., Johnstone, T. (eds.) Appraisal Processes in Emotion: Theory, Methods, Research, pp. 3–19. Oxford University Press, New York (2001)
57. Russell, J.A.: A circumplex model of affect. Journal of Personality and Social Psychology 39(6), 1161–1178 (1980)

58. Saari, P., Eerola, T., Lartillot, O.: Generalizability and simplicity as criteria in feature selection: application to mood classification in music. IEEE Trans. on Audio, Speech, and Language Proc. 19(6), 1802–1812 (2011)
59. Sanden, C., Zhang, J.: An empirical study of multi-label classifiers for music tag annotation. In: Proc. of the 12th International Society for Music Information Retrieval (ISMIR) Conference, pp. 717–722 (2011)
60. Scherer, K.R., Brosch, T.: Culture-specific appraial biases contribute to emotion disposition. European Journal of Personality 288, 265–288 (2009)
61. Scherer, K.R., Schorr, A., Johnstone, T.: Appraisal processes in emotion: Theory, methods, research. Oxford University Press, New York (2001)
62. Schlosberg, H.: The description of facial expressions in terms of two dimensions. Journal of Experimental Psychology 44, 229–237 (1952)
63. Schmidt, E.M., Kim, Y.E.: Prediction of time-varying musical mood distributions from audio. In: Proc. of the 11th International Society for Music Information Retrieval (ISMIR) Conference, pp. 465–470 (2010)
64. Schmidt, E.M., Kim, Y.E.: Prediction of time-varying musical mood distributions using Kalman filtering. In: Proc. of the 9th International Conference on Machine Learning and Applications (ICMLA), pp. 655–660 (2010)
65. Schmidt, E.M., Kim, Y.E.: Modeling musical emotion dynamics with conditional random fields. In: Proc. of the 12th International Society for Music Information Retrieval (ISMIR) Conference, pp. 777–782 (2011)
66. Schmidt, E.M., Turnbull, D., Kim, Y.E.: Feature selection for content-based, time-varying musical emotion regression. In: Proc. of the 11th ACM SIGMM International Conference on Multimedia Information Retrieval (MIR), pp. 267–273 (2010)
67. Schubert, E.: Measuring emotion continuously: Validity and reliability of the two-dimensional emotion-space. Australian Journal of Psychology 51(3), 154–165 (1999)
68. Schubert, E.: Update of the Hevner adjective checklist. Perceptual and Motor Skills, pp. 117–1122 (2003)
69. Schubert, E.: Continuous self-report methods. In: Juslin, P.N., Sloboda, J.A. (eds.) Handbook of Music and Emotion, pp. 223–253. Oxford University Press (2010)
70. Schuller, B., Weninger, F., Dorfner, J.: Multi-modal non-prototypical music mood analysis in continous space: reliability and performances. In: Proc. of the 12th International Society for Music Information Retrieval (ISMIR) Conference, pp. 759–764 (2011)
71. Sloboda, J.A., Juslin, P.N.: Psychological perspectives on music and emotion. In: Juslin, P.N., Sloboda, J.A. (eds.) Music and Emotion Theory and Research. Series in Affective Science, pp. 71–104. Oxford University Press (2001)
72. Thayer, J.F.: Multiple indicators of affective responses to music. Dissertation Abstracts International 47(12) (1986)
73. Thompson, W.F., Robitaille, B.: Can composers express emotions through music? Empirical Studies of the Arts 10(1), 79–89 (1992)
74. Trohidis, K., Tsoumakas, G., Kalliris, G., Vlahavas, I.: Multi-label classification of music into emotions. In: Proc. International Society of Music Information Retrieval Conference, pp. 325–330 (2008)
75. Tsunoo, E., Akase, T., Ono, N., Sagayama, S.: Music mood classification by rhythm and bass-line unit pattern analysis. In: Proc. of the International Conference on Acoustics, Speech, and Signal Processing (ICASSP), pp. 265–268 (2010)
76. Turnbull, D., Barrington, L., Torres, D., Lanckriet, G.: Towards musical query by semantic description using the CAL500 data set. In: Proc. of the ACM Special Interest Group on Information Retrieval (SIGIR), pp. 439–446 (2007)

77. Vaizman, Y., Granot, R.Y., Lanckriet, G.: Modeling dynamic patterns for emotional content in music. In: Proc. of the 12th International Society for Music Information Retrieval (ISMIR) Conference, pp. 747–752 (2011)

78. Vuoskoski, J.K.: Measuring music-induced emotion: A comparison of emotion models, personality biases, and intensity of experiences. Musicae Scientiae 15(2), 159–173 (2011)

79. Waletzky, J.: Bernard Hermann: Music For the Movies. DVD Les Films d'Ici / Alternative Current (1992)

80. Wang, J., Anguerra, X., Chen, X., Yang, D.: Enriching music mood annotation by semantic association reasoning. In: Proc. of the International Conference on Multimedia, pp. 1445–1450 (2010)

81. Wang, X., Chen, X., Yang, D., Wu, Y.: Music emotion classification of Chinese songs based on lyrics using TF*IDF and rhyme. In: Proc. of the 12th International Society for Music Information Retrieval (ISMIR) Conference, pp. 765–770 (2011)

82. Wehrle, T., Scherer, K.R.: Toward computational modelling of appraisal theories. In: Scherer, K.R., Schorr, A., Johnstone, T. (eds.) Appraisal Processes in Emotion: Theory, Methods, Research, pp. 92–120. Oxford University Press, New York (2001)

83. Whissell, C.M.: The dictionary of affect in language. In: Plutchik, R., Kellerman, H. (eds.) Emotion: Theory Research and Experience, vol. 4, pp. 113–131. Academic Press, New York (1989)

84. Wieczorkowska, A., Synak, P., Ras, Z.W.: Multi-label classification of emotions in music. In: Proc. of Intelligent Information Processing and Web Mining, pp. 307–315 (2006)

85. Yang, Y.H., Chen, H.H.: Ranking-based emotion recognition for music organisation and retrieval. IEEE Trans. on Audio, Speech, and Language Proc. 19(4), 762–774 (2010)

86. Yang, Y.H., Chen, H.H.: Music emotion recognition. In: Multimedia Computing. Communication and Intelligence Series. CRC Press (2011)

87. Yang, Y.H., Chen, H.H.: Prediction of the distribution of perceived music emotions using discrete samples. IEEE Trans. on Audio, Speech, and Language Proc. 19(7), 2184–2195 (2011)

88. Yang, Y.H., Lin, Y.C., Su, Y.F., Chen, H.H.: A regression approach to music emotion recognition. IEEE Trans. on Audio, Speech, and Language Proc. 16(2), 448–457 (2008)

89. Yang, Y.H., Liu, C.C., Chen, H.H.: Music emotion classification: A fuzzy approach. In: Proc. of the 14th Annual ACM International Conference on Multimedia, Santa Barbara, CA, USA, pp. 81–84 (2006)

90. Yoo, M.J., Lee, I.K.: Affecticon: emotion-based icons for music retrieval. IEEE Computer Graphics and Applications 31(3), 89–95 (2011)

91. Zentner, M., Grandjean, D., Scherer, K.R.: Emotions evoked by the sound of music: Differentiation, classification, and measurement. Emotion 8(4), 494–521 (2008)

92. Zhao, Y., Yang, D., Chen, X.: Multi-modal music mood classification using co-training. In: International Conference on Computational Intelligence and Software Engineering (CiSE), pp. 1–4 (2010)

93. Zhao, Z., Xie, L., Liu, J., Wu, W.: The analysis of mood taxonomy comparison between Chinese and Western music. In: Proc. of the 2nd International Conference on Signal Processing Systems (ICSPS), vol. VI, pp. 606–610 (2010)

Predictive Modeling of Expressed Emotions in Music Using Pairwise Comparisons

Jens Madsen, Bjørn Sand Jensen, and Jan Larsen*

Department of Applied Mathematics and Computer Science,
Technical University of Denmark,
Matematiktorvet Building 303B, 2800 Kongens Lyngby, Denmark
{jenma,bjje,janla}@dtu.dk

Abstract. We introduce a two-alternative forced-choice (2AFC) experimental paradigm to quantify expressed emotions in music using the
arousal and valence (AV) dimensions. A wide range of well-known audio
features are investigated for predicting the expressed emotions in music
using learning curves and essential baselines. We furthermore investigate
the scalability issues of using 2AFC in quantifying emotions expressed
in music on large-scale music databases. The possibility of dividing the
annotation task between multiple individuals, while pooling individuals'
comparisons is investigated by looking at the subjective differences of
ranking emotion in the AV space. We find this to be problematic due
to the large variation in subjects' rankings of excerpts. Finally, solving
scalability issues by reducing the number of pairwise comparisons is analyzed. We compare two active learning schemes to selecting comparisons
at random by using learning curves. We show that a suitable predictive
model of expressed valence in music can be achieved from only 15% of
the total number of comparisons when using the Expected Value of Information (EVOI) active learning scheme. For the arousal dimension we
require 9% of the total number of comparisons.

Keywords: expressed emotion, pairwise comparison, Gaussian process,
active learning.

1 Introduction

With the ever growing availability of music through streaming services, and
with access to large music collections becoming the norm, the ability to easy-to-
navigate-and-explore music databases has become increasingly pertinent. This
problem has created the need to use alternative methods to organize and retrieve musical tracks, one being cognitive aspects such as emotions. The reasoning behind using emotions dates back to Darwin, who argued that music was a
predecessor to speech in communicating emotions or intents [6]. This alternative
seems appealing and a natural way of thinking about music, since most people
can relate to happy or sad music, for example. The aspects about music that

---

* This publication only reflects the authors' views.

M. Aramaki et al. (Eds.): CMMR 2012, LNCS 7900, pp. 253–277, 2013.
© Springer-Verlag Berlin Heidelberg 2013

express or induce emotions have been studied extensively by music psychologists [13]. The Music Information Retrieval (MIR) community has been building on their work with the aim to create automatic systems for recognition of emotions and organization of music based on emotion. The approach by music psychologists have been to exhaustively make experiments with human subjects/users to quantify emotions and analyze this data. To annotate the massive collections of music using a fully manual approach is not feasible and has resulted in the increased attention on automatic Music Emotion Recognition (MER).

The approach to automatically predict the expressed emotion in music has typically relied on describing music by structural information such as audio features and/or lyrics features. Controlled experiments have been conducted to obtain data describing the emotions expressed or induced in music. Machine learning methods have subsequently been applied to create predictive models of emotion, from the structural information describing music, predicting the emotional descriptors [1]. The reasoning behind using the emotions expressed in music and not induced (which describes how the subject feels as a result of the musical stimuli) has mainly been due to the availability of data. The mechanisms that are involved in the induction of emotions by music [12] are daunting. To potentially model this highly subjective aspect, a great deal of additional data about the user and context should be available in order to recognize the user's general state of mind. We see that to solve the MER, three main topics should be investigated: namely how to represent the audio using feature extraction; the machine learning methods to predict annotations, evaluations, rankings, ratings, etc.; and the method of quantifying and representing the emotions expressed in music. In the present work we want to look more closely into the aspect of quantifying the emotions expressed in music using an alternative experimental paradigm to gather more accurate ground truth data.

Music psychologists have offered different models to represent emotions in music, e.g., categorical [8] or dimensional [25], and depending on these, various approaches have been taken to gather emotional ground truth data [14]. When using dimensional models such as the well established *arousal* and *valence* (AV) model [25] the majority of approaches are based on different variations of self-report listening experiments using direct scaling [26].

Direct-scaling methods are fast ways of obtaining a large amount of data. However, they are susceptible to drift, inconsistency and potential saturation of the scales. Some of these issues could potentially be remedied by introducing anchors or reference points; hence, implicitly using relative rating aspects. However, anchors are problematic due to the inherent subjective nature of the quantification of emotion expressed in music, which makes them difficult to define, and the use of them will be inappropriate due to risks of unexpected communication biases [31]. Relative experiments, such as pairwise comparisons, eliminate the need for an absolute reference anchor, due to the embedded relative nature of pairwise comparisons, which persists the relation to previous comparisons. However, pairwise experiments scale badly with the number of musical excerpts. This was accommodated in [30] by a tournament-based approach that limits the number of comparisons. Furthermore they introduce chaining, that is, inserting additional comparisons based on subjects' judgments and disregarding potential noise on the subjects' decisions. Multiple participants' judgments are pooled to form a large data set that is transformed into rankings which are then used to model emotions expressed in music.

However, the connection between the artist expressing emotions through music and how each individual experiences it will inherently vary. This experience is to be captured using a model of emotions using an experiment. The setup of this experiment alone gives rise to subjective differences such as interpretation and understanding of the experimental instruction, understanding and use of the scales, and projection of the emotional experience into the cognitive AV representation. Besides this, a multitude of aspects and biases can effect the judgments by participants [31]. Most of these effects are almost impossible to eliminate, but are rarely modeled directly. The issue is typically addressed through outlier removal or simply by averaging ratings for each excerpt across users [11], thus neglecting individual user interpretation and user behavior in the assessment of expressed emotion in music. For pairwise comparisons this approach is also very difficult. In previous work [20] we showed the potentially great subjective difference in the ranking of emotions, both in valence and arousal, which is due to the inherently different subjective judgments by participants.

The main objective in this work is to propose and evaluate a robust and scalable predictive model of valence and arousal, despite the adverse noise and inconsistencies committed by the participants. Our solution to this challenge is based on a two-alternative forced-choice (2AFC) approach, with the responses modeled in a Thurstonian framework with a principled noise model and a flexible non-parametric Bayesian modeling approach. This provides a supervised model, which has previously been applied in [20,21] for analyzing the ranking of excerpts in the AV space. In this work, we do not focus on the ranking, but the predictive properties of the approach, i.e., whether the model can predict the pairwise relations for new unseen excerpts.

Firstly, the predictive setting requires structural information describing the audio excerpt, so-called features (or covariates) from which new unseen comparisons can be predicted based on observed audio excerpts. Audio features and the representation of audio excerpts are still an open question in many audio modeling domains and particularly in emotion recognition. In this work we investigate the effect of various common audio features in a single mean/variance representation, given the proposed predictive approach.

Secondly, to model and understand the complex aspects of emotion requires extensive and costly experimentation. In the 2AFC paradigm the number of comparisons scales quadratically with the number of excerpts. This is not a favorable property of the current methodology. Given the best set of features (selected from the feature set investigation) we investigate two solutions to this problem: we consider the common approach of dividing the rating task between multiple individuals and/or pooling individuals' ratings [30]. Based on the rankings, we show that such an approach is not recommendable in the predictive case, due to large subject variability. This is in line with previous work [20] on ranking. We furthermore propose and evaluate an alternative approach, namely sequential experimental design (or active learning) for reducing the number of comparisons required. In the Bayesian modeling approach deployed, this is an easy extension of the methodology. We show that faster learning rates can be obtained by applying a principled Bayesian optimal sequential design approach.

The investigation of the outlined aspects requires that all possible unique comparisons are made on both valence and arousal dimensions. Furthermore, to show variation across users, it is required to test on a reasonable number of subjects. Compared to previous work [20,21], the experimental part in this work is based on an extended data set using the 2AFC experimental paradigm quantifying the expressed emotion in music on the dimensions of valence and arousal. Finally, we discuss various extensions and open issues, outlining future research directions and possibilities.

Outline. In Sect. 2 the general methodology for examining the outlined aspects is introduced. This includes a relatively technical presentation of the modeling framework. The underlying experiment and data is described in Sect. 3, and Sect. 4 contains the experimental results including a description of the most important aspects. The results are discussed in Sect. 5, and finally Sect. 6 concludes the paper.

2   Methodology

Cognitive aspects, such as emotion, can be elicited in a number of ways which can be divided into self-report, observational indirect behavioral measures [29], psychophysiological [9] and functional neuroimaging [15]. Self-reporting approaches rely on human test subjects to actually be able to express the directed aspects, albeit using some experimental paradigm. This work focuses on self-report methods, thus asking direct questions to the user in order to elicit his or her understanding and representation of the cognitive aspect under investigation. This requires careful consideration regarding the experimental paradigm and subsequent analysis/modeling aspects.

When quantifying a cognitive aspect using either unipolar or bipolar scales, assuming that one can arrange the cognitive aspect in such a manner that we can ask the question if one element is more or less than the other. In this case we can use relative quantification methods to obtain a ranking of objects in that dimension. How the objects are arranged in the internal representation of the cognitive aspect is not being asked directly but acquired indirectly, i.e., indirect scaling. The question to the subject is not to place the object for evaluation on the scale, but cognitively a much simpler question, namely to compare objects. The argument is that simple questions about cognitive aspects provide a robust approach in obtaining information. The simplest of such indirectly scaling methods is the two-alternative forced-choice model (2AFC). Participants are simply asked which of the two objects presented has the most/highest (or least/lowest) of a given cognitive aspect, which is the approach we use in this work.

In the present setting, we look into the cognitive aspect of expressed emotion in music. To quantify this we use an experimental paradigm relying on the two-dimensional valence and arousal model, which consist of two bipolar dimensions, namely valence, ranging from happy to sad, and arousal ranging from excited to sleepy [25]. This dimensional approach naturally allows us to use the robust relative paradigm.

With this in mind, the general framework for the proposed 2AFC for eliciting and modeling general cognitive aspects is outlined in Fig. 1. Here we aim to elicit and model the users' cognitive representation of emotion, thus we present the user with a general set of instructions regarding the task and intent of the experiment. There are obvious elements of bias that can be introduced here and care has to be taken to ensure that the underlying idea of the experiment is understood to reduce bias.

The Thurstonian based paradigm in essence starts with **step A** in Fig. 1, where an experimental design mechanism will select two musical excerpts, indexed u and v, out of total of N. These two excerpts constitute a paired set for comparison indexed by k and denoted ε_k, out of K possible comparisons.

In **step B**, excerpts u_k and v_k are presented to the user through a user interface (UI), which provides instructions, asking the user to compare the two excerpts either on the valence or arousal dimension. Understanding and interpretation of the UI and the instructions given can vary between subjects and bias and variance can be introduced at this stage.

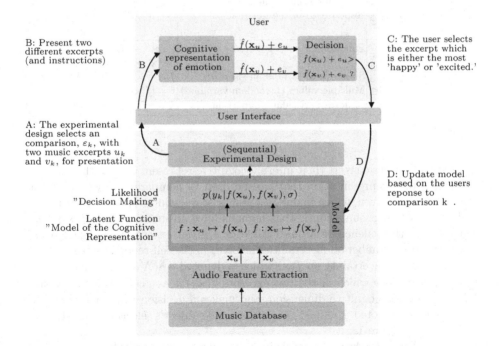

Fig. 1. Overview of the methodology from a system perspective

Table 1. Notation overview

System Element	Description	Notation
Music Database	Excerpt index	$u, v, r, s \in [1 : N]$
	Number of excerpts	N
Audio Features	Audio feature representation	$\mathbf{x} \in \mathbb{R}^D$
	of excerpt (model input)	e.g. $\mathbf{x}_u, \mathbf{x}_v$
	A test input (to model)	$\mathbf{x}_*$
	A set of inputs (to model)	$\mathcal{X} = \{\mathbf{x}_i \mid i = 1..N\}$
User	Comparison with two inputs	$\hat{\varepsilon}_k = \{u_k, v_k\}$
	Response to a comparison	$y_k \in \{-1, +1\}$
	Number of comparisons	K
	Internal 'value' of an object in respect to a given cognitive aspect.	$\hat{f}(\mathbf{x})$
	Internal noise (independent of other inputs)	$e \sim \mathcal{N}(0, \sigma)$
	Internal basis for decision making	$\hat{f}(\mathbf{x}) + e$
Model (non-parametric)	Comparison	$\varepsilon_k = \{\mathbf{x}_{u_k}, \mathbf{x}_{v_k}\}$
	A set of K comparisons	$\mathcal{E} = \{\varepsilon_i \mid i = 1..K\}$
	A set of responses	$\mathcal{Y} = \{(y_k; \varepsilon_k) \mid k = 1..K\}$
	Hyperparameters in the model	$\theta = \{\theta_{\mathcal{GP}}, \theta_{\mathcal{L}}\}$
Response	Likelihood ...of observing a particular response given the function.	$p(y_k \mid f(\mathbf{x}_{u_k}), f(\mathbf{x}_{v_k}), \theta_{\mathcal{L}}) = p(y_k \mid \mathbf{f}_k, \theta_{\mathcal{L}})$
Function	Function	$f : \mathbb{R}^D \to \mathbb{R}$ i.e. $\mathbf{x} \mapsto f(\mathbf{x})$
	Single value (a random variable)	$f(\mathbf{x})$
	Multiple values (L random variables) ...for a particular comparison	$\mathbf{f} = [f(\mathbf{x}_1), f(\mathbf{x}_2), ..., f(\mathbf{x}_L)]^\top$ $\mathbf{f}_k = [f(\mathbf{x}_{u_k}), f(\mathbf{x}_{v_k})]^\top$

In **step C** users convert their internal cognitive representation of the musical excerpts into a representation that can be used to compare the two based on the instructions given, which in our case comprise questions representing valence and arousal. Our assumption is that humans have an internal value $\hat{f}(\mathbf{x}_i) + e_i$ representing the valence or arousal value of a given excerpt $\mathbf{x}_i$ indexed by i. Given the great number of uncertainties involved in the self-report, we reasonably assume there is uncertainty on $\hat{f}(\mathbf{x})$ which is denoted $e \sim \mathcal{N}(0, \sigma)$. Prior to step C the user decides which of the two excerpts $\hat{f}(\mathbf{x}_u) + e_u$ and $\hat{f}(\mathbf{x}_v) + e_v$ is the largest given the cognitive dimension, and makes a decision which modelled by additive noise denoted $y_k \in \{-1, +1\}$, where the subject's selection is illustrated by step C in Figure 1.

In **step D** the analysis and modeling of the user's response takes place. With the aim of a predictive model, i.e., predicting the pairwise responses for unseen music excerpts, this calls for a special modeling approach. The method applies a principled statistical modeling approach, relying on a choice model taking into account the noise, e, on the (assumed) internal representation. Secondly, the modeling approach places this choice model (likelihood function) in a Bayesian modeling framework, allowing for predictive capabilities. This results in a mathematical representation of the assumed internal representation of emotion, denoted $f(\mathbf{x})$, for a given excerpt. This representation like the internal, only makes sense when compared to the representation of other excerpts. The technical aspect of the modeling approach is described in the following sub-sections.

2.1   Likelihood

The decision process underlying 2AFC was considered in the seminal paper of Thurstone [27]. The main assumption is that the choice between two excerpts is based on the internal 'value' for each object which has a particular additive noise element. The decision is then based on the probability of the noisy internal 'value' of u or v being larger. If the additive noise is assumed to be distributed according to a Normal distribution, and independent from object to object, then the well-know probit choice model is obtained [28]. The probit choice model defines the likelihood of observing a particular response $y_k \in \{-1, +1\}$ as

$$p\left(y_k | f\left(\mathbf{x}_{u_k}\right), f\left(\mathbf{x}_{v_k}\right), \boldsymbol{\theta}_\mathcal{L}\right) = \Phi\left(y_k \frac{f\left(\mathbf{x}_{u_k}\right) - f\left(\mathbf{x}_{v_k}\right)}{\sqrt{2}\sigma}\right) \qquad (1)$$

where $\Phi(\cdot)$ denotes the cumulative Normal distribution. The function values $f(\mathbf{x}_u)$ and $f(\mathbf{x}_v)$ are the model variables representing the assumed internal representation. However, the likelihood is seen to be dependent on the difference between the two (assumed) internal representations, in effect this means that the function itself has no absolute meaning and decisions are only based on differences. The noise variance on the (assumed) internal representation is denoted σ and provides a simple model of the internal noise process.

2.2   Latent Function

Given the response and likelihood function defined in Equ. (1), the remaining question relates to the latent function $f : \mathcal{X} \rightarrow \mathbb{R}$ defining the function values, $f(\mathbf{x})$, for each input, $\mathbf{x} \in \mathcal{X}$.

In this work we propose a non-parametric approach, in essence directly estimating values for individual $f(\mathbf{x})$'s, i.e., not through a parametric function (e.g. $f(\mathbf{x}) = \mathbf{w}^\top\mathbf{x}$). This is mainly motivated by the fact that the complexity of the underlying representation is virtually unknown, i.e., whether the problem is linear or non-linear is an open question which is best evaluated by allowing for very flexible function classes.

The non-parametric approach provides extreme flexibility, and we consider this in a Bayesian setting where we first assume that the likelihood factorizes, i.e., $p\left(\mathcal{Y}|\mathbf{f}\right) = \prod_{k=1}^{K} p\left(y_k|\mathbf{f}_k, \boldsymbol{\theta}_\mathcal{L}\right)$. This in effect means that, given the cognitive representation, represented by $f(\cdot)$, we assume that there are no dependencies between the responses to the different comparisons. Thus, it is essential that the experimental procedure does not introduce a particular order of comparisons which may cause dependencies and systematic errors.

Given the factorized likelihood and placing a prior on the individual function values, $p(\mathbf{f}|\mathcal{X})$, the Bayesian approach directly provides the inference schema via Bayes relation. I.e. when keeping the hyperparameters, $\boldsymbol{\theta}$, constant, the posterior is directly given by

$$p(\mathbf{f}|\mathcal{X},\mathcal{Y},\boldsymbol{\theta}) = \frac{p(\mathbf{f}|\mathcal{X},\boldsymbol{\theta}_{\mathcal{GP}}) \prod\limits_{k=1}^{K} p(y_k|\mathbf{f}_k,\boldsymbol{\theta}_{\mathcal{L}})}{p(\mathcal{Y}|\mathcal{X},\boldsymbol{\theta})} \tag{2}$$

The natural prior for the individual function values is a Gaussian Process (GP) [24]. This was first considered with the pairwise probit likelihood in [4]. A GP is defined as "a collection of random variables, any finite number of which have a joint Gaussian distribution" [24]. The GP provides a mean for each individual $f(x)$, and correlates the functional values through a correlation function which implies some notion of smoothness; the only constraint on the function. With a zero-mean function, such a GP is denoted by $f(\mathbf{x}) \sim \mathcal{GP}(\mathbf{0}, \mathrm{k}(\mathbf{x},\mathbf{x}'))$ with co-variance function $\mathrm{k}(\mathbf{x},\mathbf{x}')$. The fundamental consequence is that the GP can be considered a distribution over functions, which is denoted as $p(\mathbf{f}|\mathcal{X}) = \mathcal{N}(\mathbf{0},\mathbf{K})$ for any finite set of N function values $\mathbf{f} = [f(\mathbf{x}_1), ..., f(\mathbf{x}_N)]^{\top}$, where $[\mathbf{K}]_{i,j} = k(\mathbf{x}_i,\mathbf{x}_j)$. This means that the correlation between a function value is defined by the input $\mathbf{x}$, for example audio features. The correlation function allows prediction by calculating the correlation between a new input and already observed inputs in terms of their audio features.

A common covariance function is the so-called squared exponential (SE) co-variance function defined as $\mathrm{k}(\mathbf{x},\mathbf{x}') = \sigma_f^2 \exp\left(-\|\mathbf{x}-\mathbf{x}'\|_2^2 \big/ \sigma_l^2\right)$, where σ_f is a variance term and σ_l is the length scale, in effect, defining the scale of the correlation in the input space. This means that σ_ℓ defines how correlated two excerpts are in terms of their features. A special case arises when $\sigma_l \to 0$ which implies that the function values of two inputs are uncorrelated. In this case, knowing the functional of one input cannot be used to predict the function value of another due to the lack of correlation. On the other hand when $\sigma_l \to \infty$ the functional values are fully correlated i.e., the same.

For robustness, we provide a simple extension to the original model proposed in [4] by placing hyperpriors on the likelihood and covariance parameters, which act as simple regularization during model estimation. The posterior then yields $p(\mathbf{f}|\mathcal{X},\mathcal{Y},\boldsymbol{\theta}) \propto p(\boldsymbol{\theta}_{\mathcal{L}}|\cdot) p(\boldsymbol{\theta}_{\mathcal{GP}}|\cdot) p(\mathbf{f}|\mathcal{X},\boldsymbol{\theta}_{\mathcal{GP}}) p(\mathcal{Y}|\mathbf{f})$, where $p(\boldsymbol{\theta}|\cdot)$ is a fixed prior distribution on the hyperparameters and a half student-t is selected in this work.

Inference. Given the particular likelihood, the posterior is not analytically tractable. We therefore resort to approximation and in particular the relatively simple Laplace approximation [24], which provides a multivariate Gaussian approximation to the posterior.

The hyperparameters in the likelihood and covariance functions are point estimates (i.e., not distributions) and are estimated by maximizing the model evidence defined as the denominator in Equ. 2. The evidence provides a principled approach to select the values of $\boldsymbol{\theta}$ which provides the model that (approximately) is better at explaining the observed data (see e.g. [2,24]). The maximization is performed using standard gradient methods.

Predictions. To predict the pairwise choice y_* on an unseen comparison between excerpts r and s, where $\mathbf{x}_r, \mathbf{x}_s \in \mathcal{X}$, we first consider the predictive distribution of $f(\mathbf{x}_r)$ and $f(\mathbf{x}_s)$. Given the GP, we can write the joint distribution between $\mathbf{f} \sim p(\mathbf{f}|\mathcal{Y}, \mathcal{X})$ and the test variables $\mathbf{f}_* = [f(\mathbf{x}_r), f(\mathbf{x}_s)]^T$ as

$$\begin{bmatrix} \mathbf{f} \\ \mathbf{f}_* \end{bmatrix} = \mathcal{N}\left(\begin{bmatrix} \mathbf{0} \\ \mathbf{0} \end{bmatrix}, \begin{bmatrix} \mathbf{K} & \mathbf{k}_* \\ \mathbf{k}_*^T & \mathbf{K}_* \end{bmatrix}\right), \tag{3}$$

where $\mathbf{k}_*$ is a matrix with elements $[\mathbf{k}_*]_{i,2} = k(\mathbf{x}_i, \mathbf{x}_s)$ and $[\mathbf{k}_*]_{i,1} = k(\mathbf{x}_i, \mathbf{x}_r)$ with $\mathbf{x}_i$ being a training input.

The conditional $p(\mathbf{f}_*|\mathbf{f})$ is directly available from Equ. (3) as a Gaussian too. The predictive distribution is given as $p(\mathbf{f}_*|\mathcal{Y}, \mathcal{X}) = \int p(\mathbf{f}_*|\mathbf{f}) p(\mathbf{f}|\mathcal{Y}, \mathcal{X}) d\mathbf{f}$, and with the posterior approximated with the Gaussian from the Laplace approximation then $p(\mathbf{f}_*|\mathcal{Y}, \mathcal{X})$ will also be Gaussian given by $\mathcal{N}(\mathbf{f}_*|\boldsymbol{\mu}^*, \mathbf{K}^*)$ with $\boldsymbol{\mu}^* = \mathbf{k}_*^T \mathbf{K}^{-1} \hat{\mathbf{f}}$ and $\mathbf{K}^* = \mathbf{K}_* - \mathbf{k}_*^T (\mathbf{I} + \mathbf{W}\mathbf{K})^{-1} \mathbf{W} \, \mathbf{k}_*$, where $\hat{\mathbf{f}}$ and $\mathbf{W}$ are obtained from the Laplace approximation (see [24]). In this paper, are often interested in the binary choice y_*, which is simply determined by which of $f(\mathbf{x}_r)$ or $f(\mathbf{x}_s)$ is the largest.

2.3   Sequential Experimental Design

The acquisition of pairwise observations can be a daunting and costly task if the database contains many excerpts due to the quadratic scaling of the number of possible comparisons. An obvious way to reduce the number of comparisons is only to conduct a fixed subset of the possible comparisons in line with classical experimental design. In this work we propose to obtain the most relevant experiments by sequential experimental design, also known as active learning in the machine learning community. In this case comparisons (each with two inputs) are selected in a sequential manner based on the information provided when conducting the particular comparison. The information considered here is based on the entropy of the predictive distribution or change in the entropy.

We consider the set of comparisons conducted so far, $\mathcal{E}_a$, which gives rise to a set of unique inputs $\mathcal{X}_a$ and a response set $\mathcal{Y}_a$ which are all denoted as active set(s). Secondly, we consider a set of candidate comparisons, $\mathcal{E}_c$, , which gives rise to a set of unique inputs $\mathcal{X}_c$ and an unknown response set $\mathcal{Y}_c$. The task is to select the next comparison $\varepsilon_* = \{\mathbf{x}_{u_*}, \mathbf{x}_{v_*}\}$ from $\mathcal{E}_c$. The following three cases is considered for solving this task:

Random: The next pairwise comparison is selected at random from the set of candidate comparisons.

VOI (Value of Information): Selection of the next comparison with the maximum entropy (i.e., uncertainty) of the predictive distribution of the model[1], $S\left(\mathbf{f}_*|\varepsilon_*, \mathcal{E}_a, \mathcal{Y}_a, \boldsymbol{\theta}\right)$.

The next comparison is simply selected by $\arg\max_{\varepsilon_* \in \mathcal{E}_c} S\left(\mathbf{f}_*|\varepsilon_*, \mathcal{E}_a, \mathcal{Y}_a, \boldsymbol{\theta}\right)$.

The predictive distribution is a bivariate normal distribution which has the entropy [5], $S\left(\mathbf{f}_*|\varepsilon_*, \mathcal{E}_a, \mathcal{Y}_a, \boldsymbol{\theta}\right) = \frac{1}{2}\log\left((2 \cdot \pi \cdot e)^D |\mathbf{K}^*|\right)$. Where $|\mathbf{K}^*|$ denotes the determinant of the (predictive) covariance matrix.

EVOI (Expected Value of Information): In the Bayesian framework it is possible to evaluate the expected entropy change of the posterior which was suggested in the work of Lindley [18]. Hence, the information of conducting a particular comparison is the change in entropy of the posterior i.e.,

$$\Delta S\left(\mathbf{f}\right) = S\left(\mathbf{f}|y_*, \varepsilon_*, \mathcal{X}_a, \mathcal{Y}_a, \boldsymbol{\theta}\right) - S\left(\mathbf{f}|\mathcal{X}_a, \mathcal{Y}_a, \boldsymbol{\theta}\right)$$

The expectation in regards to y can be shown to yield [19]

$$\mathrm{EVOI}\left(\varepsilon_*\right) = \sum_{y \in \{-1,1\}} p\left(y_*|\varepsilon_*, \mathcal{X}_a, \mathcal{Y}_a, \boldsymbol{\theta}\right) \Delta S\left(\mathbf{f}|y_*, \varepsilon_*, \mathcal{X}_a, \mathcal{Y}_a, \boldsymbol{\theta}\right) \qquad (4)$$

$$= \sum_{y \in \{-1,1\}} \int p\left(y_*|\mathbf{f}_*, \mathcal{X}_a, \mathcal{Y}_a, \boldsymbol{\theta}\right) p\left(\mathbf{f}_*|\varepsilon_*, \mathcal{X}_a, \mathcal{Y}_a, \boldsymbol{\theta}\right) \log p\left(y_*|\mathbf{f}_*, \mathcal{X}_a, \mathcal{Y}_a, \boldsymbol{\theta}\right) d\mathbf{f}_*$$

$$- \sum_{y \in \{-1,1\}} p\left(y_*|\varepsilon_*, \mathcal{X}_a, \mathcal{Y}_a, \boldsymbol{\theta}\right) \log p\left(y_*|\varepsilon_*, \mathcal{X}_a, \mathcal{Y}_a, \boldsymbol{\theta}\right)$$

$$(5)$$

Thus, the next comparison is chosen as $\arg\max_{\varepsilon_* \in \mathcal{E}_c} \mathrm{EVOI}\left(\varepsilon_*\right)$. The (inner) integral is analytical intractable and requires numerical methods. This is feasibly only due to the low dimensionality (which is effectively only one, since considering the difference distribution). An analytical approximation has been proposed for standard classification [10]; however, here we rely on numerical integration based on adaptive Gauss-Kronrod quadrature.

2.4   Evaluation

In order to evaluate the performance of the proposed modeling approach, we use a specific Cross Validation (CV) approach and baselines for verification and significance testing. When dealing with pairwise comparisons the way the cross validation is set up is a key issue.

---

[1] Alternatively we may consider the predictive uncertainty on the response, y_*. See e.g. [3] for a general discussion of various information criterion.

Cross Validation

In previous work [21] we evaluated the ability of the GP framework to rank excerpts on the dimensions of valence and arousal using learning curves. To obtain the learning curves, Leave-One-Out CV was used and in each fold a fraction of comparisons was left out. These comparisons are potentially connected and thus, to evaluate the ability of the model to predict an unseen excerpts rank, all comparisons with an excerpt must be left out in each fold. Thus in the present work we use a Leave-One-Excerpt-Out (LOEO) method. Learning curves are computed as a function of the fraction of all available comparisons, evaluating the question of how many pairwise comparisons are needed to obtain a competitive predictive model. Each point on the learning curves is computed as an average of 50 randomly chosen equally-sized subsets from the complete training set. The reasoning behind this is that testing all unique possible combinations of e.g. choosing 8 out of 15 excerpts is exhausting, so random repetitions are used to obtain robust learning curves.

Baselines

Three basic baselines are introduced that consider the distribution of the pairwise comparisons, namely a random baseline ($Base_{rnd}$) and two that only predict one class ($Base_{+1}$ and $Base_{-1}$), i.e., excerpt u always greater than excerpt v, or vice versa. This takes into account that the data set is not balanced between the two outcomes of $+1$ and -1. An additional baseline ($Base_{upper}$) is introduced. Given a model type, a baseline model of same type is trained on both training and test data and evaluated on the test data for that given CV fold. This provides an upper limit of how well it is possible for that given model and features can perform. Furthermore, a baseline model $Base_{low}$ is introduced that only uses information from the comparisons available in each CV fold (not the audio features). The model ranks excerpts using a tournament approach, counting the number of times a specific excerpt has been ranked greater than another. The number of wins is assigned to each excerpt's f value. All excerpts that have no f assignment are given the average f value of all available f values. To predict the test data in each CV fold, the assigned f values are used, and for f values that are equal a random choice is made with equal probability of either class. This naive baseline model serves as a lower limit, which all models have to perform better than.

Significance Testing

To ensure that each of the trained models perform better than $Base_{low}$ we use the McNemar paired test with the $Null$ hypothesis that two models are the same, if $p < 0.05$ then the models can be rejected as equal on a 5% significance level.

AV-Space Visualization

In the principled probabilistic GP framework the latent function $f(\cdot)$ is directly available to compare rankings between models. However for visualization to compare the rankings we use a reference numerical space. The ranking of excerpts, given by $f(\cdot)$, is assigned the same functional value as the reference space, preserving the ranking of excerpts, but losing the relative distance given by $f(\cdot)$. This allows us to average rankings across users, folds and repetitions.

3   Experiment and Data

3.1   Experiment

A listening experiment was conducted to obtain pairwise comparisons of expressed emotion in music using the 2AFC experimental paradigm. A total of 20 different 15 second excerpts were chosen, in the middle of each track, from the USPOP2002[2] data set as shown in Table 2. The 20 excerpts were chosen such that a linear regression model developed in previous work [19] maps 5 excerpts into each quadrant of the two-dimensional AV space. A subjective evaluation was performed to verify that the emotional expression throughout each excerpt was considered constant. This fact, and using short 15 second excerpts, should reduce any temporal change in the expressed emotion thus making post-ratings applicable. A sound booth provided neutral surroundings for the experiment to

Table 2. Excerpts used in experiment

No.	Song name
1	311 - T and p combo
2	A-Ha - Living a boys adventure
3	Abba - Thats me
4	Acdc - What do you do for money honey
5	Aaliyah - The one I gave my heart to
6	Aerosmith - Mother popcorn
7	Alanis Morissette - These R the thoughts
8	Alice Cooper - I'm your gun
9	Alice in Chains - Killer is me
10	Aretha Franklin - A change
11	Moby - Everloving
12	Rammstein - Feuer frei
13	Santana - Maria caracoles
14	Stevie Wonder - Another star
15	Tool - Hooker with a pen..
16	Toto - We made it
17	Tricky - Your name
18	U2 - Babyface
19	Ub40 - Version girl
20	Zz top - Hot blue and righteous

[2] http://labrosa.ee.columbia.edu/projects/musicsim/uspop2002.html

reduce any potential bias of induced emotions. The excerpts were played back using closed headphones to the 13 participants (3 female, 10 male) age 16-29, average 20.4 years old, recruited from a local high school and university. Participants had a musical training of 0-15 years, on average 2 years, and listened to 0-15 hours of music every day, on average 3.5 hours. Written and verbal instructions were given prior to each session to ensure that subjects understood the purpose of the experiment and were familiar with the two emotional dimensions of valence and arousal. Furthermore instructions were given ensuring that participants focused on the expressed emotions of the musical excerpts. Each participant compared all 190 possible unique combinations. To reduce any systematic connection between comparisons, each comparison was chosen randomly. For the arousal dimension, participants were asked the question *Which sound clip was the most exciting, active, awake?*. For the valence dimension the question was *Which sound clip was the most positive, glad, happy?*. The reasoning behind these question lies in the communication of the dimensions of valence and arousal, pilot experiments showed a lack of understanding when fewer words were used. The two dimensions were evaluated independently and which of the two dimensions should be evaluated first was chosen randomly. The total time for the experiment was 4 hours, each session taking 1 hour in order to reduce any fatigue. After the experiments, participants rated their understanding of the experiment, the results can be seen in Table 3.

The understanding of the experiment and the scales was generally high, and it was noted that people rated the audio higher than the lyrics as a source of their judgments of the emotions expressed in music. The experiment had two atypical participants, one had low overall understanding of the experiment because he did not find the scales appropriate, and the other did understand the experiment, but did not understand the scales or found them inappropriate.

Table 3. Results of post-experiment questions to the 13 participants. All ratings were performed on a continuous scale, here normalized to 0-1. Results are presented as: minimum-maximum (average).

Question	Rating
General understanding	0.36-0.99 (0.70)
Understanding of scales	0.34-1.00 (0.84)
Appropriateness of scales	0.36-0.99 (0.78)
Lyrics, source of expressed emotion	0.00-0.74 (0.43)
Audio, source of expressed emotion	0.18-1.00 (0.69)

3.2 Audio Features

In order to represent the 15 second musical excerpts in later mathematical models, each excerpt is represented by audio features. These are extracted using four standard feature-extraction toolboxes, the MIR[17], CT[23], YAAFE[22], and

MA[3] toolboxes, and furthermore the Echonest API[4]. An overview is given in Table 4 of the features used from these toolboxes.

Due to the vast number of features used in MIR, the main standard features are grouped. In addition, the Echonest timbre and pitch features have been extracted, resulting in a total of 18 groups of features. The audio features have been extracted on different time scales, e.g., MFCCs result in 1292 samples for 15 seconds of audio data, whereas pitch produce 301 samples. Often the approach to integrate the feature time series over time is to assume that the distribution of feature samples is Gaussian and subsequently the mean and variance are used to represent the entire feature time series. In the present work, Gaussian distributions are fitted where appropriate and beta distributions are fitted where the distribution has a high skewness. The entire time series is represented by the mean and standard deviation of the fitted distributions.

4   Experimental Results

In this section we evaluate the ability of the proposed framework to capture the underlying structure of expressed emotions based on pairwise comparisons directly. We apply the GP model using the squared exponential (SE) kernel described in Sect. 2 with the inputs based on the groups of audio features described in Sect. 3.2 extracted from the 20 excerpts. The kernel was initialized with $\sigma_l = 1$ and $\sigma_f = 2$, furthermore the half student-t [7] hyperprior is initialized with $df = 4$ and $scale = 6$. We present three different investigations into the modeling of expressed emotions using the 2AFC paradigm. First a performance evaluation of the 18 groups of features is performed finding the best combination of features. These features are used in all subsequent results. Second, to investigate the scaling issues of 2AFC, the subjective variation in the model's predictive performance is investigated, along with a visualization of the subjective variation in rankings. Third, the question of how many pairwise comparisons are needed to obtain a predictive model of expressed emotions in music is investigated. This is evaluated using three different methods of selecting pairwise comparisons in an experimental setup, namely using the EVOI or VOI active learning methods or choosing comparisons randomly.

4.1   Performance of Features

The performance of the GP framework using the 18 different feature groupings is evaluated using LOEO learning curves. The predictive performance for the valence dimension is shown in Table 5. The single best performing feature, modeling the valence dimension is the Fluctuations feature resulting in a classification error of 0.2389 using the entire training set. For valence the Echonest pitch feature perform worse than Chroma and Pitch features from the CT toolbox although the timbre features perform slightly better than the MFCC features which are

---

[3] http://www.pampalk.at/ma/
[4] http://the.echonest.com/

Table 4. Acoustic features used for emotion prediction

Feature	Description	Dimension(s)
Mel-frequency cepstral coefficients (MFCCs)[1]	The discrete cosine transform of the log-transformed short-time power spectrum on the logarithmic mel-scale.	20
Envelope (En)	Statistics computed on the distribution of the extracted temporal envelope.	7
Chromagram CENS, CRP [23]	The short-time energy spectrum is computed and summed appropriately to form each pitch class. Furthermore statistical derivatives are computed to discard timbre-related information.	12 12 12
Sonogram (Sono)	Short-time spectrum filtered using an outer-ear model and scaled using the critical-band rate scale. An inner-ear model is applied to compute cochlea spectral masking.	23
Pulse clarity [16]	Ease of the perception by listeners of the underlying rhythmic or metrical pulsation in music.	7
Loudness [22]	Loudness is the energy in each critical band.	24
Spectral descriptors (sd) [22] (sd2) [17]	Short-time spectrum is described by statistical measures e.g., flux, roll-off, slope, variation, etc.	9 15
Mode, key, key strength [17]	Major vs. Minor, tonal centroid and tonal clarity.	10
Tempo [17]	The tempo is estimated by detecting periodicities on the onset detection curve.	2
Fluctuation Pattern [17]	Models the perceived fluctuation of amplitude-modulated tones.	15
Pitch [23]	Audio signal decomposed into 88 frequency bands with center frequencies corresponding to the pitches A0 to C8 using an elliptic multirate filterbank.	88
Roughness [17]	Roughness or dissonance, averaging the dissonance between all possible pairs of peaks in the spectrum.	2
Spectral Crest factor [22]	Spectral crest factor per log-spaced band of 1/4 octave.	23
Echonest *Timbre*	Proprietary features to describe timbre.	12
Echonest *Pitch* [17]	Proprietary chroma-like features.	12

Table 5. Valence: Classification error learning curves as an average of 50 repetitions and 13 individual user models, using both mean and standard deviation of the features. McNemar test between all points on the learning curve and $Base_{low}$ resulted in $p < 0.05$ for all models except results marked with *, with a sample size of 12.350.

Training size	5%	7%	10%	20%	40%	60%	80%	100%
MFCC	0.4904	0.4354	0.3726	0.3143	0.2856	0.2770	0.2719	0.2650
Envelope	**0.3733**	**0.3545**	0.3336	0.3104	0.2920	0.2842	0.2810	0.2755
Chroma	0.4114*	0.3966*	0.3740	0.3262	0.2862	0.2748	0.2695	0.2658
CENS	0.4353	0.4139	0.3881	0.3471	0.3065	0.2948	0.2901*	0.2824
CRP	0.4466	0.4310	0.4111	0.3656	0.3066	0.2925	0.2876	0.2826
Sonogram	0.4954	0.4360	0.3749	0.3163	0.2884	0.2787	0.2747	0.2704
Pulse clarity	0.4866	0.4357	0.3856	0.3336	0.3026	0.2930	0.2879	0.2810
Loudness	0.4898	0.4310	0.3684	0.3117	0.2854	0.2768	0.2712	0.2664
Spec. disc.	0.4443	0.4151	0.3753	0.3263	0.2939	0.2857	0.2827	0.2794
Spec. disc. 2	0.4516	0.4084	0.3668	0.3209	0.2916	0.2830	0.2781	0.2751
Key	0.5303	0.4752	0.4104	0.3370	0.2998	0.2918	0.2879	0.2830*
Tempo	0.4440	0.4244	0.3956	0.3559*	0.3158	0.2985	0.2933	0.2883
Fluctuations	0.4015	0.3584	**0.3141**	**0.2730**	**0.2507**	**0.2433**	**0.2386**	**0.2340**
Pitch	0.4022	0.3844	0.3602	0.3204	0.2926	0.2831	0.2786	0.2737
Roughness	0.4078	0.3974	0.3783	0.3313	0.2832	0.2695	0.2660	0.2605
Spec. crest	0.4829	0.4289	0.3764	0.3227	0.2994	0.2942	0.2933	0.2923
Echo. timbre	0.4859	0.4297	0.3692	0.3127	0.2859	0.2767	0.2732	0.2672
Echo. pitch	0.5244	0.4643	0.3991*	0.3275	0.2942	0.2841	0.2790	0.2743
$Base_{low}$	0.4096	0.3951	0.3987	0.3552	0.3184	0.2969	0.2893	0.2850

said to describe timbre. Including both mean and variance of the features showed different performance for the different features, therefore the best performing for valence and arousal was chosen resulting in both mean and variance for valence and only mean for arousal.

The learning curves showing the predictive performance on unseen comparisons on the arousal dimension are shown in Table 6. The single best performing feature, using the entire training set is Loudness resulting in an error rate of 0.1862. Here a picture of pitch and timbre related features seem to show a good level of performance.

Using a simple forward feature selection method. the best performing combination of features for valence are fluctuation pattern, spectral crest flatness per band, envelope statistics, roughness, CRP and Chroma resulting in an error of 0.1960 using the mean of the features. It should be noted that using only the 4 first produces an error of 0.1980. For arousal the best performing combination was Spectral descriptors, CRP, Chroma, Pitch, Roughness and Envelope statistics using mean and standard deviation of the features results in an error of 0.1688. All models trained for predicting valence and arousal are tested with McNemar's paired test against the $Base_{low}$, with the $Null$ hypothesis that two models are the same, all resulted in $p < 0.05$ rejecting the $Null$ hypothesis of being equal at a 5% significance level.

Table 6. Arousal: Classification error learning curves as an average of 50 repetitions and 13 individual user models, using only the mean of the features. McNemar test between all points on the learning curve and $Base_{low}$ resulted in $p < 0.05$ for all models except results marked with *, with a sample size of 12.350.

Training size	5%	7%	10%	20%	40%	60%	80%	100%
MFCC	0.3402	0.2860	0.2455	0.2243	0.2092	0.2030	0.1990	0.1949
Envelope	0.4110*	0.4032	0.3911	0.3745	0.3183	0.2847	0.2780	0.2761
Chroma	0.3598	0.3460	0.3227	0.2832	0.2510	0.2403	0.2360	0.2346
CENS	0.3942	0.3735	0.3422	0.2994	0.2760	0.2676	0.2640	0.2621
CRP	0.4475	0.4336	0.4115	0.3581	0.2997	0.2790	0.2735	0.2729
Sonogram	0.3325	0.2824	0.2476	0.2244	0.2118	0.2061	0.2033	0.2026
Pulse clarity	0.4620	0.4129	0.3698	0.3281	0.2964	0.2831	0.2767*	0.2725
Loudness	0.3261	0.2708	**0.2334**	**0.2118**	**0.1996**	**0.1944**	**0.1907**	**0.1862**
Spec. disc.	0.2909	0.2684	0.2476	0.2261	0.2033	0.1948	0.1931	0.1951
Spec. disc. 2	0.3566	0.3223	0.2928	0.2593	0.2313	0.2212	0.2172	0.2138
Key	0.5078	0.4557	0.4059	0.3450	0.3073*	0.2959	0.2926	0.2953
Tempo	0.4416	0.4286	0.4159	0.3804	0.3270	0.3043	0.2953	0.2955
Fluctuations	0.4750	0.4247	0.3688	0.3117	0.2835	0.2731	0.2672	0.2644*
Pitch	0.3173	0.2950	0.2668	0.2453	0.2301	0.2254	0.2230	0.2202
Roughness	**0.2541**	**0.2444**	0.2367	0.2304	0.2236	0.2190	0.2168	0.2170
Spectral crest	0.4645	0.4165	0.3717	0.3285	0.2979	0.2866*	0.2828	0.2838
Echo. timbre	0.3726	0.3203	0.2797	0.2524	0.2366	0.2292	0.2258	0.2219
Echo. pitch	0.3776	0.3264	0.2822	0.2492	0.2249	0.2151	0.2089	0.2059
$Base_{low}$	0.4122	0.3954	0.3956	0.3517	0.3087	0.2879	0.2768	0.2702

4.2   Subjective Variation

By letting multiple test participants rate the same musical excerpts and model these responses individually we can explore the subjective differences in greater detail.

Learning Curves

To evaluate the differences between subjects in how well the model predicts their pairwise comparisons, the LOEO learning curves for each individual are shown in Fig. 2. The $Base_{low}$ and $Base_{upper}$ described in Sect. 2.4 are shown, which indicate the window in which the proposed model is expected to perform. In Fig. 2(b) the individual learning curves are shown, computed by using the best performing combination of features as mentioned in Sect. 4.1. The difference in performance between the average of all individual models and the $Base_{upper}$ is 0.0919. Compared to the $Base_{low}$ we see a difference of 0.0982, showing a large improvement. The models trained in the data for participants 6 and 7 results in a classification error of 0.2553 and 0.2526 respectively, compared with the average of 0.1688 for the arousal dimension. Post-experiment ratings show that participant 6 rated a low rating of understanding and appropriateness of the scales of 0.3033 and 0.3172 respectively, although participant 7 rated a high understanding. In Fig. 2(a) the individual learning curves for the valence dimension are shown. Participants 1 and 5 have an error rate when using the whole training

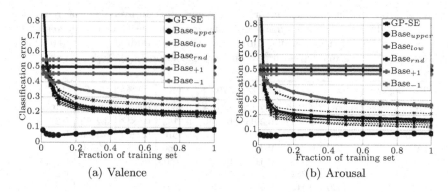

Fig. 2. Individual classification error learning curves; Dashed black lines: individually trained models, Bold black crosses: average across individual models

set of 0.2421 and 0.2447 respectively compared to the average of 0.2257. Participant 5 rated in the post questionnaire a lack of understanding of the scales used in the experiment and furthermore did not find them appropriate. Participant 1 on the other hand did not rate any such lack of understanding. To investigate if there is an underlying linear connection between the models' classification error and the participants' post-questionnaire ratings, simple correlation analysis was made for all questions, a correlation of 0.13 for the appropriateness of the scales and the arousal was found and even less for the other questions, so no significant correlation was found. Comparing the average performance of the individual models and $Base_{upper}$, the difference in performance is 0.1109 using the whole training set. Furthermore comparing it to $Base_{low}$ the difference in performance is 0.0887, showing an improvement of using audio features compared to only using comparisons.

AV Space

The Gaussian Process framework can, given the features, predict the pairwise comparisons given by each participant on unseen excerpts. This on the other hand does not necessarily mean that participants' rankings of excerpts on the dimensions of valence and arousal are the same, which was investigated in previous work [20]. These variations in rankings of excerpts between subjects are visualized in the AV space on Fig. 3 using the method mentioned in Sect. 2.4. Excerpts 5, 2, 7, 9 and 20 in the low-valence low-arousal quadrant of the AV space show a relatively low variation in ranking, both in the dimension of valence and arousal, whereas the excerpts in the low-valence high-arousal quadrant, namely excerpts 12 and 15, have a high variation in both dimensions. It is evident that participants agree on the ranking of some excerpts and fundamentally disagree on some.

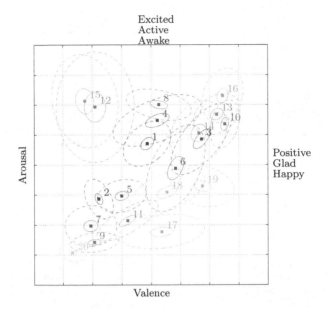

Fig. 3. Variation in ranking of excerpts in the valence and arousal space. Solid lines: 5% percentile, dashed line 50% percentile. Number refers to Table 2.

4.3   Reducing the Number of Required Comparisons

In this section we investigate how the model performs using only a fraction of available comparisons in predicting comparisons for unseen excerpts and to visualize the subsequent change in ranking of excerpts in the AV space.

Learning Curves

We investigate how many comparisons are needed to obtain a predictive model using LOEO learning curves. The traditional method of selecting a comparison in an experimental setup is simply to choose one at random from the comparisons defined by the experiment. This was the procedure in the listening experiment described in Sect. 3. But on the other hand this might not be the optimal way of choosing what comparisons should be judged by participants. Therefore we simulate if these comparisons can be chosen in alternative ways that can potentially improve the performance and decrease the number of comparisons needed to obtain a predictive model. As described in Sect. 2.3 we compare the procedure of using random selection of comparisons and the EVOI and VOI model. On Fig. 4 we see the three methods in detailed learning curves with a McNemar paired test between the model selecting comparisons at random and the EVOI and VOI models. The largest performance gains using the sequential design method EVOI are seen on the valence dimension using 4% of the training data, improving 0.105 and for arousal at 2.5% improving 0.106. Visually it is apparent that the EVOI model produces the largest improvement compared to selecting comparisons randomly. The difference after

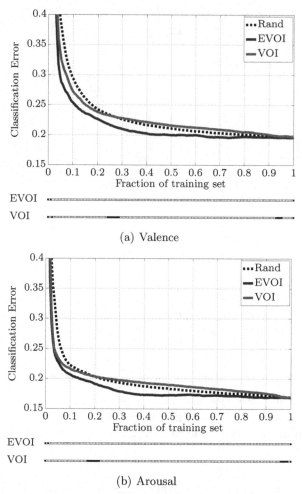

(a) Valence

(b) Arousal

Fig. 4. Classification error learning curves comparing the EVOI, VOI and Rand models. The secondary graph below the learning curves shows filled squares when $p > 0.05$ and white when $p < 0.05$ using the McNemar's paired test. The test is performed between the the Rand model and the two EVOI and VOI.

10% of the training data is 0.041 decreasing to 0.015 at 20% with the same performance gain until 40% and gain in performance is obtained until all comparisons are judged for the valence dimension. On the arousal dimension the improvement after 4 comparisons is 0.104 and from 10% to 50% an improvement is achieved around 0.015 and 0.010. For arousal the VOI model improves the performance around 0.08 in the beginning of the learning curve at around 2-3%. Using 20% of the training set and above, selecting comparisons at random results in a better performance than selecting with the VOI model for arousal.

To evaluate the number of comparisons needed to obtain a predictive model we set a 95% performance threshold, using the entire training set. The EVOI model

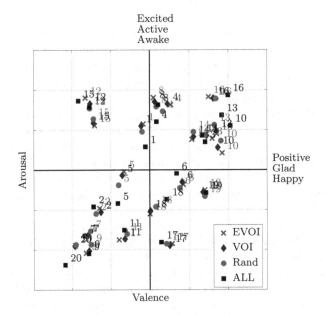

Fig. 5. AV space visualizing the change in ranking of the models trained on a fraction of available comparisons. EVOI model trained on 15.20% and 8.77% of the training set, VOI model trained on 21.64% and 14.04% and model selecting comparisons randomly (Rand) on 23.39% and 15.79% for valence and arousal respectively. Numbers refer to Table 2. Method of visualization in the AV space is described in Sect. 2.4.

achieves this performance corresponding to 0.2362 using only 15.2% of the training set, whereas the VOI model reaches this level using 21.64% and with random selection at 23.39% for the valence dimension. On the arousal dimension, the threshold performance corresponds to an error rate of 0.2104, choosing comparisons at random the model reaches this 95% performance level at 15.79% of the comparisons in the training set, the VOI model at 14.04% and the EVOI at 8.77%.

AV Space

Using a threshold we ensure that we reach a certain predictive performance, the consequence this has on the ranking of the excerpts in the AV space on the other hand could potentially be dramatic. Therefore we visualize the ranking of excerpts using the threshold discussed in the last section. The reference point to compare the change in rankings is the model trained on all comparisons for each subject individually. The rankings are visualized in the AV space on Fig. 5. Judging by the position of the excerpts in the AV space, the change in ranking is relative small, although on some excerpts the ranking does change, using the 95% performance threshold ensures that we have a good predictive performance and still reach the final ranking.

5   Discussion

The results clearly indicate that it is possible to model expressed emotions in music by directly modeling pairwise comparisons in the proposed Gaussian process framework. How to represent music using structural information is a key issue in MIR and the field of MER. In this work we use audio features and the optimal combination is found using learning curves and forward-feature selection. On the data set deployed, we find the gain of using audio features to predict pairwise comparisons on the dimensions of valence and arousal is 0.09 and 0.10, respectively. To make this comparison it is essential to have a proper baseline model which we introduce using the novel baseline $Base_{low}$. The baseline makes predictions solely by looking at the comparisons, and by disregarding any other information. The baseline performs similarly to a model with $\sigma_l \to 0$, resulting in no correlation between any excerpts as mentioned in Sect. 2.2. We can therefore ensure that we do capture some underlying structure represented in the music excerpts that describes aspects related to the expressed emotions in music.

Furthermore we observe a small gain in performance on the learning curves when including more comparisons for prediction. One aspect could be attributed to the pairwise comparisons, but the $Base_{upper}$ shows a very high performance, and given the flexibility of the GP model, it is plausible that this lower performance can be attributed to the audio feature representation.

The issue of scalability is addressed in the present work by investigating the possibility of using multiple participants to make judgments on subsets of a larger data set, and subsequently pooling this data to obtain one large data set. This is investigated by having 13 subjects make comparisons on the same data set and training individual models on their comparisons. The GP framework can model each individual well, although a few models show a relatively higher error rate than others. These can be attributed to lack of understanding of the experiment, scales and appropriateness of scales. Although no clear connection can be attributed solely to the post-questionnaire answers by participants as investigated by using simple correlation analysis. Either they reported incorrectly or the model and features do not capture their interpretation of the experiment. If one used comparisons from these subjects it could increase the noise in the larger data set. When visualizing the ranking in the AV space, as investigated in previous work, we furthermore see a large subjective difference in both valence and arousal for some excerpts. Even though individual models are trained, the difference in rankings would make the solution to the scalability of the 2AFC by pooling subsets of data sets problematic at best.

An alternative method in making 2AFC scalable for evaluating large music collections is to reduce the number of pairwise comparisons, which we investigate by detailed learning curves. The full Bayesian active-learning method EVOI shows the ability of potentially substantially reducing the required number of comparisons needed to obtain a predictive model down to only 15.2% of the comparisons for valence, resulting in 1.3 comparisons per excerpt, and 8.77%, resulting in 0.75 comparisons per excerpt. Although this result is obtained by sampling from the experimental data, the results are promising. Future work can look into the performance achieved by following the active learning principle applied in the experimental design. In addition, more efficient methods of relative experimental designs should be investigated to obtain multiple pairwise comparisons and still preserving the robustness that the 2AFC provides. Furthermore, based on the findings in present work, more extensive work should be done to find features or representations of features that describe and capture the aspects that express emotions in music.

6   Conclusion

We introduced a two-alternative forced-choice experimental paradigm for quantifying expressed emotions in music along the well-accepted arousal and valance (AV) dimensions. We proposed a flexible probabilistic Gaussian process framework to model the latent AV dimensions directly from the pairwise comparisons. The framework was evaluated on a novel data set and resulted in promising predictive error rates. Comparing the performance of 18 different selections of features, the best performing combination was used to evaluate scalability issues related to the 2AFC experimental paradigm. The possibility of using multiple subjects to evaluate subsets of data, pooled to create a large data set was shown to potentially be problematic due to large individual differences in ranking excerpts on the valence and arousal dimensions. Furthermore, the scalability of the 2AFC and the possibility of using only a fraction of all potential pairwise comparisons was investigated. By applying the active learning method, Expected Value of Information, we showed that a suitable predictive model for arousal and valence can be obtained using as little as 9% and 15% of the total number of possible comparisons, respectively.

Acknowledgments. This work was supported in part by the Danish Council for Strategic Research of the Danish Agency for Science Technology and Innovation under the CoSound project, case number 11-115328.

References

1. Barthet, M., Fazekas, G., Sandler, M.: Multidisciplinary perspectives on music emotion recognition: Implications for content and context-based models. In: 9th International Symposium on Computer Music Modeling and Retrieval (CMMR) Music and Emotions, pp. 19–22 (June 2012)
2. Bishop, C.M.: Pattern Recognition and Machine Learning. Springer (2006)
3. Chaloner, K., Verdinelli, I.: Bayesian experimental design: A review. Statistical Science 10(3), 273–304 (1995)
4. Chu, W., Ghahramani, Z.: Preference learning with Gaussian Processes. In: ICML 2005 - Proceedings of the 22nd International Conference on Machine Learning, pp. 137–144 (2005)
5. Cover, T., Thomas, J.: Elements of information theory. Wiley (1991)
6. Cross, I.: The nature of music and its evolution. In: Oxford Handbook of Music Psychology, pp. 3–13. Oxford University Press (2009)

7. Gelman, A.: Prior distributions for variance parameters in hierarchical models. Bayesian Analysis 1(3), 515–533 (2006)
8. Hevner, K.: Experimental studies of the elements of expression in music. American Journal of Psychology 48(2), 246–268 (1936)
9. Hodges, D.A.: Psychophysiology measures. In: Music and Emotion: Theory, Research, Applications, pp. 279–312. Oxford University Press, New York (2010)
10. Houlsby, N., Hernandez-Lobato, J.M., Huszar, F., Ghahramani, Z.: Collaborative Gaussian processes for preference learning. In: Bartlett, P., Pereira, F., Burges, C., Bottou, L., Weinberger, K. (eds.) Advances in Neural Information Processing Systems, vol. 25, pp. 2105–2113 (2012)
11. Huq, A., Bello, J.P., Rowe, R.: Automated Music Emotion Recognition: A Systematic Evaluation. Journal of New Music Research 39(3), 227–244 (2010)
12. Juslin, P.N., Vastfjall, D.: Emotional response to music: The need to consider underlying mechanism. Behavioral and Brain Sciences 31, 559–621 (2008)
13. Juslin, P.N., Sloboda, J.A. (eds.): Music and Emotion: theory, research, applications. Oxford University Press, New York (2010)
14. Kim, Y., Schmidt, E., Migneco, R., Morton, B., Richardson, P., Scott, J., Speck, J., Turnbull, D.: Music emotion recognition: A state of the art review. In: 11th International Conference on Music Information Retrieval (ISMIR), pp. 255–266 (2010)
15. Koelsch, S., Siebel, W.A., Fritz, T.: Functional neuroimaging. In: Music and Emotion: Theory, Research, Applications, pp. 313–346. Oxford University Press, New York (2010)
16. Lartillot, O., Eerola, T., Toiviainen, P., Fornari, J.: Multi-feature modeling of pulse clarity: Design, validation, and optimization. In: 9th International Conference on Music Information Retrieval (ISMIR), pp. 521–526 (2008)
17. Lartillot, O., Toiviainen, P., Eerola, T.: A matlab toolbox for music information retrieval. In: Preisach, C., Burkhardt, H., Schmidt-Thieme, L., Decker, R. (eds.) Data Analysis, Machine Learning and Applications, Studies in Classification, Data Analysis, and Knowledge Organization. Springer (2008)
18. Lindley, D.V.: On a measure of the information provided by an experiment. The Annals of Mathematical Statistics 27(4), 986–1005 (1956)
19. Madsen, J.: Modeling of Emotions expressed in Music using Audio features. DTU Informatics, Master Thesis (2011), http://www2.imm.dtu.dk/pubdb/views/publicationtextunderscoredetails.php?id=6036
20. Madsen, J., Jensen, B.S., Larsen, J., Nielsen, J.B.: Towards predicting expressed emotion in music from pairwise comparisons. In: 9th Sound and Music Computing Conference (SMC) Illusions (July 2012)
21. Madsen, J., Nielsen, J.B., Jensen, B.S., Larsen, J.: Modeling expressed emotions in music using pairwise comparisons. In: 9th International Symposium on Computer Music Modeling and Retrieval (CMMR) Music and Emotions (June 2012)
22. Mathieu, B., Essid, S., Fillon, T., Prado, J., Richard, G.: An easy to use and efficient audio feature extraction software. In: 11th International Conference on Music Information Retrieval, ISMIR (2010)
23. Müller, M., Ewert, S.: Chroma Toolbox: MATLAB implementations for extracting variants of chroma-based audio features. In: 12th International Conference on Music Information Retrieval (ISMIR), Miami, USA (2011)
24. Rasmussen, C.E., Williams, C.K.I.: Gaussian Processes for Machine Learning. MIT Press (2006)

25. Russell, J.: A circumplex model of affect. Journal of Personality and Social Psychology 39(6), 1161 (1980)
26. Schubert, E.: Measurement and time series analysis of emotion in music. Ph.D. thesis, University of New South Wales (1999)
27. Thurstone, L.L.: A law of comparative judgement. Psychological Review 34 (1927)
28. Train, K.: Discrete Choice Methods with Simulation. Cambridge University Press (2009)
29. Västfjäll, D.: Indirect perceptual, cognitive, and behavioral measures. In: Music and Emotion: Theory, Research, Applications, pp. 255–278. Oxford University Press, New York (2010)
30. Yang, Y.H., Chen, H.: Ranking-Based Emotion Recognition for Music Organization and Retrieval. IEEE Transactions on Audio, Speech, and Language Processing 19(4), 762–774 (2011)
31. Zentner, M., Eerola, T.: Self-report measures and models. In: Music and Emotion: Theory, Research, Applications, pp. 187–222. Oxford University Press, New York (2010)

Analyzing the Perceptual Salience of Audio Features for Musical Emotion Recognition

Erik M. Schmidt[1], Matthew Prockup[1], Jeffrey Scott[1], Brian Dolhansky[2], Brandon G. Morton[1], and Youngmoo E. Kim[1]

[1] Electrical and Computer Engineering, Drexel University
{eschmidt,mprockup,jjscott,bmorton,ykim}@drexel.edu
[2] Computer Science, University of Pennsylvania
bdol@seas.upenn.edu

Abstract. While the organization of music in terms of emotional affect is a natural process for humans, quantifying it empirically proves to be a very difficult task. Consequently, no acoustic feature (or combination thereof) has emerged as the optimal representation for musical emotion recognition. Due to the subjective nature of emotion, determining whether an acoustic feature domain is informative requires evaluation by human subjects. In this work, we seek to perceptually evaluate two of the most commonly used features in music information retrieval: mel-frequency cepstral coefficients and chroma. Furthermore, to identify emotion-informative feature domains, we explore which musical features are most relevant in determining emotion perceptually, and which acoustic feature domains are most variant or invariant to those changes. Finally, given our collected perceptual data, we conduct an extensive computational experiment for emotion prediction accuracy on a large number of acoustic feature domains, investigating pairwise prediction both in the context of a general corpus as well as in the context of a corpus that is constrained to contain only specific musical feature transformations.

Keywords: emotion, music emotion recognition, features, acoustic features, machine learning, invariance.

1 Introduction

The development of methods for automatic recognition of emotion in music is a topic of growing attention within the music information retrieval (Music-IR) research community [12,1]. While there has been much progress in machine learning systems for estimating human emotional response to music, very little progress has been made in terms of compact or intuitive feature representations. Current methods generally focus on combining several feature domains (e.g., loudness, timbre, harmony, rhythm), in some cases as many as possible, and performing dimensionality reduction techniques such as principal component analysis (PCA). Overall, these methods have not sufficiently improved performance and have done little to advance the field.

M. Aramaki et al. (Eds.): CMMR 2012, LNCS 7900, pp. 278–300, 2013.

In previous work, we looked closely at two of the most commonly used features in Music-IR: mel-frequency cepstral coefficients (MFCCs) and chroma [20]. The perceptual salience (or informativeness) of the two features was investigated using Amazon's Mechanical Turk[1] (MTurk) to analyze the relative emotion of two song clips, comparing human ratings of both the original audio and audio reconstructions from these features. By analyzing these reconstructions, we sought to directly assess how much information about musical emotion is retained in these features. Reasonably high agreement was found between original audio and reconstruction pairs, indicating emotional salience does exist to some degree within those domains. However, these types of experiments are limited to feature domains that allow reconstruction, and most do not. To address those challenges, we proposed identifying musical parameter invariances (e.g., key, mode, tempo) and relating them to feature space invariances. To this end, we ranked features in terms of their variance with respect to musical parameter shifts based on audio rendered from MIDI transformations of key, mode and tempo.

This new work expands on the previous experiments in several new directions. First, we employ a new metric for comparing the relative tempi of different pieces of music and create a new pair dataset that ensures an even distribution of musical parameters (e.g., key, mode, tempo) with a significantly increased number of pairs. We also analyze these results in terms of a variety of categorical and demographic types: gender, age, musical training, music listening habits and country.

Investigating invariance to musical parameters, we introduce a new perceptual evaluation asking human listeners to rate pairwise shifts of musical parameters on the same song. These experiments serve two main purposes. First, they provide the ability to more closely evaluate the perceptual weight of musical parameters by analyzing the relative ranking of MIDI generated audio. Second, we use the rankings to see if the relative changes are present in the feature domains as well.

Given our collected data on the weight of musical parameters in determining musical emotion, we seek to develop computational methods for selecting features. In order to properly assess a large variety of features, we investigate the features used in our perceptual study reconstructions, features used in our prior work [21,18,17,19] and 14 additional features from the *MIRtoolbox*[2]. These experiments are supported by a supervised machine learning task using a ranking based support vector machine classifier. In this problem, we predict the relative emotion between clips that were annotated in the first experiment.

In investigating feature salience, we seek to provide further insight into how to properly validate the feature domains used in music emotion recognition. By analyzing invariances, we hope to inform approaches that develop feature representations specifically optimized for the prediction of emotion. Combining these results, we provide a more grounded approach to feature selection in general.

---

[1] http://mturk.com

[2] http://www.jyu.fi/hum/laitokset/musiikki/en/research/coe/materials/ mirtoolbox

2 Background

This background section is dedicated to prior work on the relationships between musical parameters and emotion and to the use of Amazon's Mechanical Turk for human data collection. For an in-depth review on music emotion recognition the interested reader is referred to [12,1].

2.1 Perception of Emotion and Music Theory

A musical piece is made up of a combination of different attributes such as key, mode, tempo and instrumentation. While no single attribute fully describes a piece, each contributes to the listener's perception of the music. While these compositional parameters alone are not the sole contributors to the emotion in music (others include expression, performance style, etc.), they are easy to both measure and control when using symbolic data. The ability to measure and control these parameters facilitates more grounded studies of human judgments of emotional affect in music which are very subjective in nature [11].

Several independent experiments in psychology have looked at users' responses as they relate to musical attributes [7,16,26]. When discussing emotion, happy versus sad temperament is referred to as valence and higher versus lower intensity is referred to as arousal [25]. Mode and tempo have been shown to consistently elicit a change in perceived emotion. Mode is the selection of notes (scale) that form the basic tonal substance of a composition, and tempo is the speed of a composition [15]. Research shows that major modes tend to elicit happier emotional responses, while the inverse is true for minor modes [26,5,3,6]. Tempo also determines a user's perception of music, with higher tempi generally inducing stronger positive valence and arousal responses [16,26,5,3,4].

2.2 Mechanical Turk

Mechanical Turk (MTurk) is a service provided by Amazon to hire people to perform tasks online. Using MTurk's Human Intelligence Tasks (HITs), it is possible to obtain human judgements on almost any task for a small fee. These tasks are open to anyone on the web and therefore provide the ability to collect large amounts of data over a short period of time.

MTurk Workers

A recent study on the demographics of MTurk workers (Turkers) has indicated that respondents tend to be reasonably well-educated and most frequently located in the United States [8]. The study found that 62.8% of respondents had attained at least a four year college degree. Respondents were located in 66 countries, with the highest percentages in the US at 46.8% and India at 34%. Among US respondents, the majority were women (70%), and 65% had a household income below $60,000.

MTurk in Music-IR

The natural language processing (NLP) [22] and machine vision [27,23] communities have utilized MTurk extensively, but machine listening and Music-IR have just started to adopt its use. Lee found crowdsourcing music similarity judgments on MTurk to be less time-consuming than collecting data from experts in the research community [13]. Their experiment cost $130.90 and produced 6,732 similarity judgements, less than $0.02 per rating. HITs were rejected if workers rated songs too quickly or failed to assign high similarity to identical songs. While nearly half of all HITs were rejected, the dataset was obtained an order of magnitude more quickly than their previous attempts. Comparing the datasets yields a Pearson's correlation coefficient of 0.495, consistent with previous NLP work involving MTurk [22]. As the previous data collection was assembled for MIREX, Lee returned the submitted systems using MTurk data as ground truth and found no significant alterations to the outcome, scoring a 5.7% difference on the Friedman test.

Mandel *et al.* employed MTurk for collecting free form tags to study relationships between audio tags and content [14]. The group collected 2,100 unique tags across 925 clips, for a reported cost of approximately $100. To ensure data quality, they rejected a HIT if any tag had more than 25 characters, if less than 5 tags were provided or if less than half of tags were contained in a dictionary of commonly applied tags (Last.fm). All HITs by a particular worker were rejected if the worker used too small a vocabulary, if they used more than 15% "stop words" (e.g., "music" or "nice") or if half of their individual HITs were rejected for other reasons. The authors then trained a support vector machine (SVM) classifier for content-based autotagging. With smoothed labels, the MTurk version increased performance to 63.4% versus 63.09% with MajorMiner.

3   Constructing an Annotation Task for Perceptual Evaluation of Acoustic Features

MFCCs have been shown in previous work to be one of the most informative feature domains for music emotion recognition [21,18,17,19], but as MFCCs were originally designed for speech recognition, it is unclear why they perform well or how much information about emotion they actually contain. To evaluate the efficacy of common Music-IR features for modeling and predicting emotion in music, we present an annotation task where users rank short audio clips in terms of valence and arousal. The participant is presented with a web page that contains four clip pairs with one such pair depicted in Fig. 1. The user must select which song is 'happier' and which song is 'more intense' for the given pair. They are presented with a total of five clips per page and can listen to each clip as many times as they wish. The participants can also change their answers as many times as they choose prior to submission. Once they leave the page, they cannot return to change their annotations. Upon submission, the user is presented with a new page containing a different version of the same clip pairs. There are three pages, one for each set of audio types. The presentation of the clip pairs is listed in Table 1.

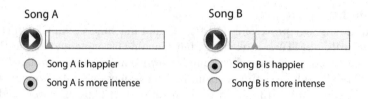

Fig. 1. An example of a single comparison in the annotation task

Table 1. Mechanical Turk HIT page ordering for clip pair presentation

Feature Type	Presentation Order
MFCC Reconstruction	First
Chroma Reconstruction	Second
Original Audio	Last

The participants are always comparing chroma reconstructions to chroma reconstructions, MFCC reconstructions to MFCC reconstructions or original audio to original audio. Subjects never compare a reconstruction to the original audio. The participants are presented with MFCCs first and original audio last since it is possible to discern what song the reconstruction is after listening to the original audio. We do not want people's familiarity with the original audio to influence their rating of the reconstruction clips. This is important due to the level of awareness many people have with our corpus, which consists of songs chosen from the Beatles catalog (see Sect. 3.1).

3.1   Dataset

Since we are studying changes in the acoustic feature domain, we require samples that can be easily manipulated in terms of key, mode and tempo. These transformations are most easily performed using symbolic MIDI data, which can be rendered using an instrument library to create audio files. Our dataset consists of 59 Beatles MIDI files obtained from EarlyBeatles[3], spanning 9 albums from the Beatles discography. There are 23 minor key songs and 36 key major songs in the dataset, and the tempi range from 75 bpm to 224 bpm.

The MIDI files contain arrangements for many instruments including voice, piano, guitar, bass, drums and percussion. In order to normalize instrumentation, the unpitched instruments (drums and percussion) are removed. All of the remaining voices are rendered to audio using the grand piano included in the Garritan Personal Orchestra[4] sample library. Chroma features are extracted and reconstructed using Dan Ellis' chroma features analysis and synthesis code[5],

---

[3] http://earlybeatles.com/

[4] http://www.garritan.com/

[5] http://www.ee.columbia.edu/~dpwe/resources/matlab/chroma-ansyn/

and MFCCs using his rastamat[6] library. The MFCC reconstructions sound like a pitched noise source, and the chroma reconstructions have an ethereal 'warbly' quality to them but sound more like the original audio than the MFCC reconstructions (examples are available online[7]). For each song, we select a 15 second clip that does not exhibit any significant change between the start and end of the clip.

3.2 Song Pair Selection Based on Musical Attributes

An important factor in the design of our experiment is the inclusion of control groups for the parameters that we wish to evaluate, namely tempo and mode. We generate 250 pairings broken up into five groups (50 pairs each), as shown in Table 2.

Table 2. The five possible combinations of mode and tempo are shown. Note there are no Major/Minor pairings of different tempi.

Pair Class	Song A Mode	Song B Mode	Tempo Similarity	Number of Pairs
1	Major	Major	Different	50
2	Major	Major	Similar	50
3	Minor	Minor	Different	50
4	Minor	Minor	Similar	50
5	Major	Minor	Similar	50

In each of the categories, one compositional attribute (tempo/mode) is varied over the set, while the other remains constant. For the major-minor pairs, we require songs to have similar tempi, and we do not create pairs that differ in mode and tempo simultaneously. For like-mode comparisons (major-major and minor-minor), the pairs are separated into two groups by tempo. Additionally, we constrain the pairings to be approximately uniformly distributed over the available number of songs. The number of major and minor songs in the dataset, as well as the unequal distribution of tempo across all of the song clips, results in some songs occurring in more pairs than others.

Average Inter-Onset-Interval (AIOI) Constraint

Two songs can be perceived as having different rhythmic pulses even if they are at the same tempo. A song played at a faster tempo with longer note values can feel slower than a song played at a slower tempo with shorter note values. This concept is illustrated in Fig. 2, where the tempo and average inter-onset-interval are both shown.

---

[6] http://www.ee.columbia.edu/~dpwe/resources/matlab/rastamat/
[7] http://music.ece.drexel.edu/research/emotion/invariance

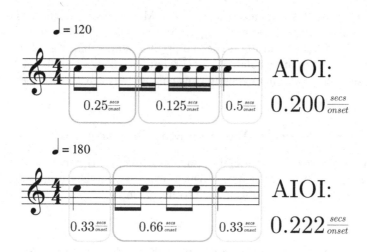

Fig. 2. Example of average inter-onset-interval calculations for two sequences. The top example has a slower tempo (120 bpm) but sounds faster due to the prominence of shorter note values. A lower average inter-onset-interval means the clip sounds faster.

The AIOI is computed for all clips in the dataset and used to inform pair selection according to the five groups outlined at the beginning of the section. For a given seed clip, k, we compute the absolute difference between the AIOI of the seed clip and the AIOI of all other clips. If we treat the set of distances between the seed clip and all other clips as $\mathcal{N}(\mu_k, \sigma_k^2)$, we describe all clips within $\mu_k \pm \frac{3}{8}\sigma_k$ as similar and all clips beyond the range $\mu_k \pm \frac{7}{4}\sigma_k$ as different. The coefficients for the standard deviation were found empirically by adjusting the parameters to avoid having songs over-represented in the dataset. From the pool of possible pairs, we select clips to avoid over-representation in the dataset as much as possible. Due to the distribution of AIOI in the dataset, some song clips have very few pair candidates. For instance, a very fast song will have few candidate songs that are also very fast, limiting the number of possible pairs. This difficulty is compounded by the restriction of pairing by major/minor mode as well. We set a hard maximum of 15 occurrences for a clip appearing in one of the five pair types. A histogram showing the number of times each song is used in a pair is shown in Fig. 3.

4   Mechanical Turk Annotation Task

To annotate our clip pairs, we use the Mechanical Turk online crowd-sourcing engine to gain input from a wide variety of subjects [24]. In our Human Intelligence Task (HIT), we ask participants to listen to four clip pairs. For each pair, they are required to label which song clip exhibits more positive emotion and which song clip is more intense. The three categories of audio sources are

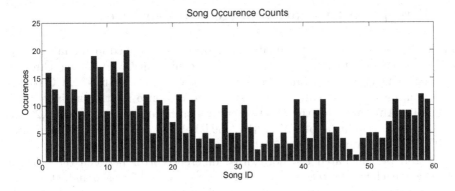

Fig. 3. Number of times each song clip is used in the dataset (250 pairs total)

presented on three separate pages, with MFCC reconstructions first, chroma reconstructions next and the original audio pairs last. Subjects never compare a reconstruction to the original audio.

In addition to the valence and arousal labels, we collect demographic information from the participants as well as details about their listening habits and musical training. The demographic and categorical fields are listed below:

- Age
- Gender
- Country

- Musical Training
- Listening Time

Although Mechanical Turk provides a platform to gather a large amount of data rather quickly and in a scalable manner, there are inherent difficulties in verifying whether a subject fully understands the task. We therefore employ a set of rejection criteria for the trials completed by each user, as well as some restrictions in the functionality of the task itself.

The first constraint is the time it takes a participant to complete the task. There are ten 15-second clips per page for a total of 150 seconds, and we require a participant to spend at least 90 seconds on the page or else they are prevented from completing the task. This ensures that the participant has listened to enough of each clip to make a rating of valence and arousal.

For each HIT, we randomly select a clip to repeat as a means of verification. If a user labels the duplicated verification clip differently during the round with the original audio, their data is removed from the dataset. We experimented with rejecting the user if they labeled any of the verification (MFCC and chroma reconstructions included) clips differently, but this constraint proved to be too stringent. This is due to the ambiguous nature of the reconstructed clips. Participants are allowed to complete many HITs with each HIT containing pairs randomly selected from the database. If we reject more than 5 of a user's attempts at a HIT, we reject all of that user's HITs.

5   Perceptual Evaluation of Acoustic Features

In this first experiment, we evaluate the information retained in the most ubiq-
uitous features used throughout the Music-IR community, MFCCs and chroma.
A participant labels the same clip pair three times, once for the MFCC reconstruction, once for the chroma reconstruction and once for the original MIDI
rendering. After applying the rejection criteria outlined above, we reject 6,294 of
14,850 labels, yielding a total of 11.41 ± 3.39 labels per clip pair with a maximum
of 22 labels and a minimum of 7 labels per pair.

In [20], we calculated the normalized difference error between the original
audio and each feature reconstruction. For each pair and for each audio type, we
compute the ratio of subjects that rated clip A as more positive (valence) and
the ratio that labeled clip A as more intense (arousal),

$$\rho_{valence} = \frac{1}{N} \sum_{n=1}^{N} \mathbb{1}\{\mathbb{A}_n = \text{HigherValence}\}, \tag{1}$$

$$\rho_{arousal} = \frac{1}{N} \sum_{n=1}^{N} \mathbb{1}\{\mathbb{A}_n = \text{HigherArousal}\}, \tag{2}$$

where N is the total number of annotations for a given pair, $\rho_{valence}$ is the
ratio of annotators that labeled clip A as higher valence, and $\rho_{arousal}$ is the
ratio of annotators that labeled clip A as higher arousal. We then compute the
absolute difference between $\rho_{valence}$ for the original clips and $\rho_{valence}$ for the
reconstructions and similarly for arousal. The mean absolute difference error
across all songs for the data in [20] and the new dataset is shown in Table 3.

Table 3. Normalized difference error between the valence/arousal ratings for the
reconstructions versus the originals

Experiment	Audio Source	Normalized Difference Error	
		Valence	Arousal
Past [20]	MFCC Reconstructions	0.133 ± 0.094	0.104 ± 0.080
	Chroma Reconstructions	0.120 ± 0.095	0.121 ± 0.082
Current	MFCC Reconstructions	0.189 ± 0.155	0.190 ± 0.138
	Chroma Reconstructions	0.160 ± 0.144	0.162 ± 0.124

Previously, we used each song only once in the pair generation process and
did not enforce tempo constraints on the clip pairs. In this experiment, we have
control groups for both tempo and mode and allowed each song to be used
multiple times in order to create the control groups. We collect data in a pairwise
fashion, where each participant labels the same clip pair for both reconstruction
types as well as the original audio. We can now directly compute the difference in

Table 4. Ratio of labels that were maintained between listening to the original audio and the reconstructed feature audio

Audio Type	Valence Agreement	Arousal Agreement
Original → Chroma	0.625	0.567
Original → MFCC	0.599	0.563

valence and arousal labels between the original audio and reconstructed feature audio. In Table 4, we show the results of this analysis where we compute,

$$\alpha_{valence} = \frac{1}{L} \sum_{l=1}^{L} \mathbb{1}\{V_l^{(original)} = V_l^{(reconstruction)}\}, \tag{3}$$

$$\alpha_{arousal} = \frac{1}{L} \sum_{l=1}^{L} \mathbb{1}\{A_l^{(original)} = A_l^{(reconstruction)}\}, \tag{4}$$

where L is the total number of pairwise annotations in the dataset and V and A represent valance and arousal respectively. We notice a significant decrease in the rating consistency between the original audio and reconstructed audio. This is due to the fact that modeling the difference as in Equation 1, the participants who change their label from song $\mathbb{A}$ to song $\mathbb{B}$ and those who change from song $\mathbb{B}$ to song $\mathbb{A}$ would cancel out.

5.1 Information Retained in Reconstructions

In Table 4, we observe that more people maintain their valence ratings for the chroma reconstructions than for the MFCC reconstructions. Listening to the audio clips, it is evident that there is more tonal information in the chroma reconstructions than in the MFCC reconstructions. This is the most likely reason that there is more correlation with the chroma reconstructions than the MFCCs. However, the ratios are rather close and overall fairly low, indicating that rhythmic information, which is still perceptible in the MFCC and chroma reconstructions, may be more important than tonal information.

We do not have any measurements of rhythmic information beyond tempo or AIOI as it is very difficult to quantify the rhythmic *feel* of a piece. Accents, syncopation and other attributes of rhythm are still somewhat present in both reconstruction types. This suggests that features that represent higher level characteristics like groove or feel, rather than the speed or rate at which a piece is played, would be informative about emotional affect. These ideas are further explored in Sect. 7.

5.2 Demographic and Musical Categories

We also analyze the retention of the labels based on demographic information and musical experience (Table 5). It is first important to note that the data

Table 5. Ratio of labels that were maintained between listening to the original audio and the reconstructed feature audio broken down by demographic and musical categories

			Valence		Arousal	
Category	Range	People	Chroma	MFCC	Chroma	MFCC
Gender	Male	140	0.627	0.556	0.598	0.573
	Female	148	0.614	0.571	0.585	0.547
Age (Years)	18-25	90	0.592	0.551	0.566	0.536
	26-35	118	0.600	0.561	0.569	0.561
	36-45	47	0.679	0.574	0.643	0.548
	46-55	32	0.680	0.607	0.657	0.610
	over 55	12	0.680	0.600	0.620	0.660
Musical Training (Years)	None	87	0.641	0.597	0.595	0.583
	Less than 5	143	0.576	0.551	0.568	0.563
	More than 5	27	0.707	0.570	0.693	0.543
Listening Time (Hours)	Less than 1	74	0.642	0.550	0.616	0.571
	1-2	123	0.620	0.569	0.581	0.543
	More than 2	89	0.616	0.583	0.591	0.596
Country	India	184	0.593	0.534	0.561	0.542
	USA	62	0.682	0.584	0.682	0.591

collected from Mechanical Turk is noisy, even after applying the constraints detailed in Sect. 4. There are some participants that have multiple demographic values associated with their unique identifier. In computing the values in Table 5, we remove any users who are not consistent in their responses for any of the attributes in the category column.

The trend of more ratings being maintained between chroma/original ratings than MFCC/original ratings for valence remains true over almost all categories. The tendency to retain the same valence rating between original and reconstructed clips increases with age for both chroma and MFCCs. While there is not a definite trend in respondents' level of musical training, one result does stand out. Those who have more than five years of training are more consistent in rating the chroma reconstructed clips than any others. Here, they may be latching on to harmonic and melodic cues that are present, but very distorted, in the chroma reconstructions.

Participants were asked to provide their country of residence, with most participants being from India or the United States. Other countries are not listed due to the limited number of participants residing in those nations. The ratio of people who changed their ratings for chroma/original pairs is significantly higher for those from the United States than those from India, while the ratings on MFCC reconstructions are very similar. This may be due to the difference in tonal organization between non-Western and Western music, especially since chroma provides an intuitive representation designed for Western music.

5.3 Comparison With Previous Experiments

In prior work, we observed that major songs were labeled more often as having higher valence (approximately 67 percent of the time) and higher arousal (57 percent of the time) [20]. The correlation between tempo and A/V was significantly weaker. We observe similar results regarding the relationships between arousal, valence, tempo and mode in the results presented in Table 6.

The correlation between positive valence and the major mode is weaker in this experiment, but the relationship between mode and arousal is stronger, with the major song being labeled as higher arousal only 38.9% of the time. An important distinction between the experiment in [20] and this trial is the pair selection process. In the previous experiment, we did not restrict major/minor pairs to contain similar tempos, which could have a significant impact on the correlation between mode and arousal. We also observe the difference in ratings based on AIOI or tempo. The correlation between speed and valence is stronger when measured by AIOI rather than tempo, but remains similar when analyzing the arousal dimension.

Table 6. Ratio of participants labeling a clip as higher arousal or valence according to musical parameters of AIOI, tempo and mode

Musical Relationship	Higher Valence	Higher Arousal
Faster AIOI	0.631	0.482
Faster Tempo	0.588	0.493
Major (vs minor) Song	0.606	0.389

6 The Effect of Musical Transformations on Emotional Affect

In previous work, we explored the concept of evaluating features by the amount they change in response to altering various musical parameters [20]. By changing the tempo, key and scale degrees of the MIDI data, we generated audio examples of the same clip varied by key, tempo and 'mode'. We ranked the features in terms of how much they changed in response to the various alterations of the musical parameters. In this study, we perform an additional labeling task in which participants listen to pairs of the same song varied by key and tempo.

6.1 Musical Transformation Labeling Task

The experimental setup for this labeling task is identical to the one outlined in Sect. 4. In this case, the pairs consist of a clip paired with a version of the same clip altered by key or tempo. A description of the pair types and the number of

Table 7. The transformations performed for each clip and the total number of pairs for each transformation

Pair Class	SongA	SongB	Number of Pairs
1	Original	Tempo Up	59
2	Original	Tempo Down	59
3	Original	Key Up	59
4	Original	Key Down	59

each pair type in the dataset is detailed in Table 7. For the tempo-up and tempo-down pairs, the tempo of the original clip is multiplied by $\frac{4}{3}$ or $\frac{3}{4}$ respectively. For the key-up and key-down transformations, the key of the piece is transposed up a perfect fifth or down a perfect fifth respectively. We choose these transformations to be of fairly high perceptual magnitude so we can observe trends in the data. Small trends in perceptual ratings may not be evident in the data collected from Mechanical Turk.

As an example, the song *While My Guitar Gently Weeps* is in A minor and is played at 120 beats per minute (bpm). We pair this song with versions at tempi of 160 bpm and 90 bpm. It is also paired with versions in E minor (5th above) and D minor (5th below). For each clip, we compute chroma and MFCCs and reconstruct audio from the features. These clips and pairs are used within the same pairwise comparison framework as Sect. 4.

6.2 Valence and Arousal Ratings for Transformations of Key and Tempo

This labeling task is also completed via Mechanical Turk, using the same criteria as the previous data collection round. We rejected 9405 of 17205 labels for a total of 9.01 ± 5.31 labels per pair over 236 total pairs.

Table 8 shows the arousal and valence labels for the clip pairs containing variations on key and tempo. These numbers are compiled from ratings of the original audio only; no feature reconstructions are included in this table. We observe a significant number of respondents labeling the clip that is transposed down a fifth as lower valence. There is also a strong correlation between the slower tempo clips and lower ratings of valence. It is surprising to see less correlation between lower arousal and slower tempo, given the results of previous experiments.

6.3 Information Retained in Feature Reconstructions with Transformations

Table 9 presents the ratio of participants whose labels for the original and reconstructed audio are in agreement. We observe similar results compared to Table 4 in terms of the ratio of people that maintain the same rating from chroma/MFCC

Table 8. Ratio of participants labeling a clip as higher arousal or valence according to musical parameters of key and tempo. This includes the original audio clips only.

Musical Relationship	Higher Valence	Higher Arousal
Key Up	0.574	0.430
Key Down	0.313	0.591
Faster	0.581	0.528
Slower	0.288	0.553

Table 9. Ratio of labels that were maintained between listening to the original audio and the reconstructed feature audio averaged over all transformations

Audio Type	Valence Agreement	Arousal Agreement
Original → Chroma	0.635	0.590
Original → MFCC	0.612	0.580

reconstructions to the original audio. Comparing the values in Table 4 to Table 9, each category differs by an average of 0.0158. One interpretation of this result is that users are able to latch onto tonal and rhythmic queues that remain in the reconstructed audio regardless of whether the piece is different or not.

Table 10 provides the results for the overall agreement of valence/arousal ratings between reconstructions by key and tempo transformations. Here, we note that when the tempo is decreased, participants are more likely to maintain their ratings than with other transformations.

Table 10. Agreement ratio of participants labeling the pair as higher arousal or valence according to transformations of key and tempo

Transformation	Chroma Valence	Arousal	MFCC Valence	Arousal
Tempo Up	0.690	0.680	0.583	0.610
Tempo Down	0.702	0.663	0.665	0.639
Key Up	0.546	0.527	0.542	0.530
Key Down	0.613	0.586	0.578	0.551

7   Computational Evaluation of Acoustic Features

In this section, we seek to identify salient acoustic feature domains for the prediction of musical emotion through computational experiments. In the first set of experiments, we try to find appropriate variances and invariances as they relate to a musical quality. For example, if emotion is invariant to key, and the key changes, the features should also be invariant to that key change. We desire correlation in variance as well. If the emotion of the audio changes, we want the features that describe it to change correspondingly. In order to investigate these variances and invariances, we use the transformed audio pairs from Sect. 6, as well as feature sets from prior work [21,18] and from the MIRtoolbox. A full list of audio features used in these experiments and their descriptions is available in Table 11.

In the later experiments, we seek to further validate features computationally, employing the pairwise collected data from Sect. 5 and 6. By analyzing the original pairs from Sect. 5, we investigate the salience of each feature in ranking emotion on pairwise data from different songs. In addition, we also look at the transformed pairs from Sect. 6 where participants compared versions of the same song that had modified musical attributes (e.g. key, tempo). In those experiments, we rank features based on performance in a supervised machine learning task and compare the results to the ranking based on feature change (F_c) in Equation 7. This correlates performance in a computational task with feature variance observed by changing tempo or key.

In all machine learning experiments, we employ a ranking support vector machine (SVM) [10,2] to learn a model for automatically ranking acoustic data in terms of emotion parameters. It is important to note that these SVMs are specifically designed for ranking problems (as opposed to binary classification), as it is possible that one song could be the higher valence song in one pair in which it is included, and the lower valence song in another.

Table 11. Acoustic feature collection

Short Name	Feature Class	Feature Origin	Feature Description
RMS	Dynamics	MIRtoolbox *mirrms*	Root-mean-square energy
Fluctuation	Rhythm	MIRtoolbox *mirfluctuation*	Spectrum summary showing rhythmic periodicities
Beat Spec.	Rhythm	MIRtoolbox *mirbeatspectrum*	Self-similarity as a function of time lag
Onsets	Rhythm	MIRtoolbox *mironsets*	Estimated position of notes in time
SSD	Statistics	Schmidt SSD [21]	Statistics of the spectrum related to timbral texture
MFCC	Timbre	Rastamat *melfcc*	Mel-frequency cepstral coefficients
Contrast	Timbre	Jiang spectral contrast [9]	Strength of peaks and valleys in spectral sub-bands
Attack Time	Timbre	MIRtoolbox *mirattacktime*	Temporal duration of the attacks
Attack Slope	Timbre	MIRtoolbox *mirattackslope*	Average slope of the attacks
Zerocross	Timbre	MIRtoolbox *mirzerocross*	Number of times the signal changes sign
Brightness	Timbre	MIRtoolbox *mirbrightness*	Measures the amount of energy above a cutoff frequency
Roughness	Timbre	MIRtoolbox *mirroughness*	Estimation of the sensory dissonance
Regularity	Timbre	MIRtoolbox *mirregularity*	Degree of variation of the successive peaks of the spectrum
Chroma	Tonality	Ellis *chromagram_IF*	Projection of spectrum into 12 semitone bins
xChroma	Tonality	Autocorrelation of chroma [18]	Autocorrelation of chroma in frequency
Key	Tonality	MIRtoolbox *mirkey*	Estimation of tonal center positions and their respective clarity
Mode	Tonality	MIRtoolbox *mirmode*	Estimate of major vs. minor
Tonal Cent.	Tonality	MIRtoolbox *mirtonalcentroid*	Projection along circles of fifths, minor thirds, and major thirds
HCDF	Tonality	MIRtoolbox *mirHCDF*	Harmonic change detection function, the flux of the tonal centroid

7.1 Relating Musical Parameter Invariances to Feature Space Invariances

Using the Beatles' transformation pairs from Sect. 6 we analyze feature space invariances for each of the features described in Table 11. Because the features contain different dimensions and have different ranges, looking at changes in their direct results does not allow for proper comparison between them. In order to draw proper comparisons, the features are normalized over dimension and range.

Given two feature vectors over time $F_1 \in \mathbb{R}^{N \times M_1}$ and $F_2 \in \mathbb{R}^{N \times M_2}$, we normalize the content over the vectors' shared range:

$$F_1' = \frac{F_1 - \min(F_1 \cup F_2)}{\max(F_1 \cup F_2 - \min(F_1 \cup F_2))}, \tag{5}$$

$$F_2' = \frac{F_2 - \min(F_1 \cup F_2)}{\max(F_1 \cup F_2 - \min(F_1 \cup F_2))}. \tag{6}$$

This operation scales the feature vectors to be in the range $[0, 1]$. The mean for each dimension is calculated, creating mean vectors $\mu_1 \in \mathbb{R}^{N \times 1}$ and $\mu_2 \in \mathbb{R}^{N \times 1}$. The average change across all feature dimensions is then computed,

$$F_c = \frac{1}{N} \sum_{n=1}^{N} |\mu_1(n) - \mu_2(n)|. \tag{7}$$

If this F_c value is low, it means that the feature is potentially invariant to the musical change being presented. In Table 12, we observe that features that exhibit higher variance to the specified change (i.e., tempo up/down, key up/down) may be more effective in computational models that are sensitive to these parameters. Several intuitive features, including onsets, RMS energy and beat spectrum, emerge as the most variant features to tempo. Conversely, it is intuitive that features like mode and tonal center do not vary much with tempo.

7.2 SVM-Based Ranking of Musical Emotion

To further validate our features for music emotion recognition, we develop an SVM based system for ranking the pairs of songs collected in Sect. 5. Pairwise ground truth annotations are generated by aggregating Mechanical Turk worker labels over each song. These pairs are selected because they contain different songs as opposed to transforms, and we desire to identify features which generalize to rank the emotional quality of different songs.

For each feature domain, we train a ranking SVM using the *pysvmlight*[8] Python binding for the *SVM-Light*[9] library [10]. Due to the limited size of the

---

[8] https://bitbucket.org/wcauchois/pysvmlight
[9] http://svmlight.joachims.org/

Table 12. Normalized feature change with respect to musical mode and tempo alterations

Tempo Up		Tempo Down		Key Up		Key Down	
Feature Domain	Feature Change	Feature Domain	Feature Change	Feature Domain	Feature Change	Feature Domain	Feature Change
Onsets	0.134	Beat Spec.	0.141	Beat Spec.	0.173	Beat Spec.	0.168
Beat Spec.	0.129	Onsets	0.131	Key	0.132	Tonal Cent.	0.110
RMS	0.067	RMS	0.053	Tonal Cent.	0.114	Key	0.085
xChroma	0.030	xChroma	0.025	MFCC	0.083	MFCC	0.074
HCDF	0.028	Roughness	0.021	Zerocross	0.064	Chroma	0.062
Zerocross	0.028	HCDF	0.021	Chroma	0.062	Regularity	0.061
Fluctuation	0.026	Fluctuation	0.021	RMS	0.060	xChroma	0.048
Roughness	0.025	SSD	0.019	S. Contrast	0.048	Brightness	0.048
MFCC	0.023	MFCC	0.018	SSD	0.047	Mode	0.044
SSD	0.022	Brightness	0.017	Brightness	0.047	S. Contrast	0.042
Brightness	0.021	Chroma	0.015	Regularity	0.037	Zerocross	0.040
Regularity	0.019	Regularity	0.014	Mode	0.037	SSD	0.036
Chroma	0.019	Zerocross	0.014	xChroma	0.032	RMS	0.033
S. Contrast	0.017	Key	0.013	Roughness	0.026	HCDF	0.022
Key	0.013	S. Contrast	0.011	Onsets	0.026	Roughness	0.021
Tonal Cent.	0.013	Mode	0.010	Attack Time	0.025	Onsets	0.021
Mode	0.010	Tonal Cent.	0.010	Fluctuation	0.017	Fluctuation	0.018
Attack Time	0.009	Attack Time	0.007	HCDF	0.017	Attack Time	0.018
Attack Slope	0.006	Attack Slope	0.005	Attack Slope	0.009	Attack Slope	0.008

dataset (250 song pairs) and the necessity to ensure the training and testing sets have a good sample of the musical differences in the dataset (see Table 2), we choose to do leave-one-out training. That is, we hold out testing pairs one at a time and train on the remaining data. During training, we employ a radial basis function (RBF) kernel and a grid search algorithm using 5-fold cross-validation to parameterize the kernel width γ and regularization parameter C. For each fold, we train an SVM on 10 logarithmically spaced values of γ ranging from 10^{-1} to 10^3, and 10 logarithmically spaced values of the regularization parameter C from 10^{-2} to 10^3. Given the parameter combination that performs best on average across all folds, we train the final SVM on all training data.

The results for SVM ranking are shown in Table 13. Tonal centroid and onsets tend to perform very well, showing results as good (or better) than MFCC and spectral contrast. In addition, an interesting result is that performance for the valence dimension is generally much higher than arousal. This is consistent with the perceptual results shown in Table 4.

Table 13. Results for SVM ranking

Feature Domain	Valence Accuracy	Feature Domain	Arousal Accuracy
Tonal Centroid	0.824	S. Contrast	0.676
Onsets	0.820	Fluctuation	0.652
MFCC	0.820	Onsets	0.636
Fluctuation	0.816	Tonal Centroid	0.632
Zerocross	0.812	Zerocross	0.628
Chroma	0.804	SSD	0.628
S. Contrast	0.792	Chroma	0.624
Key	0.788	Beat Spec.	0.624
Attack Slope	0.784	Attack Slope	0.620
Regularity	0.784	MFCC	0.612
SSD	0.780	Key	0.612
Roughness	0.776	HCDF	0.592
Mode	0.708	Mode	0.588
xChroma	0.676	RMS	0.588
Brightness	0.676	Roughness	0.584
HCDF	0.672	xChroma	0.560
Beat Spec.	0.648	Regularity	0.544
Attack Time	0.620	Attack Time	0.532
RMS	0.612	Brightness	0.520

7.3 SVM-Based Ranking of Transform Pairs

In these experiments, we employ the audio pairs from Sect. 6, where pairs were generated by modifying musical parameters. Refer to Table 7 for a full description of the transformed pairs. In each experiment, we train a ranking SVM on the dataset for a specific transform type (e.g., key up, tempo down). The goal of this experiment is to see if the SVM can perform as well as humans can, and also to look for relationships between the features that perform well and the musical parameters that may be responsible for the emotion shifts. For each transform type, we have a total of 59 pairs, so once again leave-one-out training is used following the identical training procedure as Sect. 7.2.

Shown in Table 14 are the results for the dataset containing pairs of the same songs at different tempi. In general, the system is better at predicting the correct label for the valence dimension for tempo down pairs, which is consistent with what was found with humans in Table 8. An interesting result is the relatively low performance of MFCCs on the valence dimension for the tempo up transformed set (0.610) versus the tempo down transformed set, where they performed among the best (0.881). These discrepancies are perhaps attributed the ambiguity imposed by the perceptual labeling (Table 8), where decreasing tempo seemed to be induce valence changes, but the effects of increasing tempo were less clear. However, a similar trend for MFCCs is seen when looking at the arousal dimension. In the tempo up pairs, MFCCs are the worst performing

Table 14. SVM ranking performance for tempo transformed pairs

Tempo Up				Tempo Down			
Feature Domain	Valence Accuracy	Feature Domain	Arousal Accuracy	Feature Domain	Valence Accuracy	Feature Domain	Arousal Accuracy
Roughness	0.797	Zerocross	0.729	Fluctuation	0.898	MFCC	0.695
xChroma	0.763	Regularity	0.661	HCDF	0.881	HCDF	0.678
SSD	0.763	Attackslope	0.661	Attackslope	0.881	Brightness	0.627
RMS	0.763	Mode	0.644	Onsets	0.881	RMS	0.627
Attackslope	0.746	Fluctuation	0.644	MFCC	0.881	Zerocross	0.593
HCDF	0.729	Beat Spec.	0.644	Zerocross	0.864	S. Contrast	0.593
Fluctuation	0.729	xChroma	0.644	SSD	0.847	Attackslope	0.576
Chroma	0.712	SSD	0.644	RMS	0.847	Key	0.559
Onsets	0.678	Key	0.627	Roughness	0.831	Regularity	0.559
Key	0.661	Roughness	0.627	xChroma	0.831	Mode	0.559
S. Contrast	0.644	RMS	0.627	Chroma	0.814	Beat Spec.	0.559
Brightness	0.610	HCDF	0.610	Brightness	0.797	Chroma	0.559
MFCC	0.610	Onsets	0.610	S. Contrast	0.797	Tonal Cent.	0.525
Tonal Cent.	0.559	S. Contrast	0.610	Tonal Cent.	0.763	Roughness	0.525
Zerocross	0.542	Tonal Cent.	0.593	Regularity	0.695	Fluctuation	0.525
Attacktime	0.542	Chroma	0.576	Attacktime	0.678	SSD	0.525
Beat Spec.	0.542	Brightness	0.525	Beat Spec.	0.610	Attacktime	0.508
Mode	0.525	Attacktime	0.508	Key	0.576	Onsets	0.508
Regularity	0.525	MFCC	0.508	Mode	0.508	xChroma	0.508

feature (0.508), performing essentially at chance, but in the tempo down category they are the highest performing feature (0.695).

Table 15 shows the ranking performance for pairs of the same song in different musical keys. Just as with tempo, the system is much better at predicting emotion changes on pairs where the key has been modified down as opposed to up. This is also consistent with Table 8, where it was found that humans much more commonly rated the key down as being related to an emotion change as opposed to key up. Another interesting result with MFCCs is that they perform among the best features for key down (0.949) on the valence dimension, but significantly lower for key up (0.627). Also, in nearly all columns the MIRtoolbox key feature performs in the bottom half and is the lowest performing feature on the valence dimension for key down, while human subjects reported high correlation between valence and key down (Table 8).

8   Discussion and Future Work

In this work, we have extended the scope of a set of experiments carried out in [20]. The size of the dataset was improved, as well as the pairwise distribution over the musical parameters we were evaluating. Differences between tempo and mode in each song were constrained to allow for more detailed analyses of the

Table 15. SVM ranking performance for key transformed pairs

Key Up				Key Down			
Feature Domain	Valence Accuracy	Feature Domain	Arousal Accuracy	Feature Domain	Valence Accuracy	Feature Domain	Arousal Accuracy
S. Contrast	0.797	RMS	0.763	Attackslope	0.949	S. Contrast	0.695
Attackslope	0.712	Roughness	0.729	Fluctuation	0.949	Attackslope	0.678
Fluctuation	0.712	Brightness	0.729	MFCC	0.949	Fluctuation	0.661
SSD	0.712	SSD	0.712	Zerocross	0.915	SSD	0.661
Attacktime	0.695	Tonal Cent.	0.678	SSD	0.915	Zerocross	0.644
xChroma	0.678	Attackslope	0.678	Tonal Cent.	0.847	xChroma	0.610
RMS	0.644	Fluctuation	0.678	xChroma	0.831	Chroma	0.610
Tonal Cent.	0.627	Zerocross	0.661	S. Contrast	0.831	HCDF	0.593
HCDF	0.627	xChroma	0.661	Chroma	0.831	Roughness	0.593
MFCC	0.627	MFCC	0.644	HCDF	0.797	Regularity	0.593
Roughness	0.610	Key	0.610	Regularity	0.712	Key	0.576
Key	0.593	Chroma	0.610	Mode	0.678	RMS	0.576
Brightness	0.593	S. Contrast	0.593	Attacktime	0.678	Attacktime	0.559
Mode	0.576	Onsets	0.576	Beat Spec.	0.593	Brightness	0.559
Onsets	0.576	HCDF	0.559	Roughness	0.576	Onsets	0.559
Chroma	0.559	Beat Spec.	0.542	RMS	0.576	Beat Spec.	0.559
Beat Spec.	0.559	Attacktime	0.525	Brightness	0.559	Mode	0.559
Regularity	0.542	Mode	0.508	Key	0.525	MFCC	0.525
Zerocross	0.508	Regularity	0.508	Onsets	0.525	Tonal Cent.	0.508

relationships in the data. The labels collected from Mechanical Turk showed significant correlation with the data we previously collected and provided more insight into the relationship between acoustic features and emotional content.

In Sect. 5, we built on the experiments from prior work, performing a pairwise analysis that showed a more mild correlation between participants' emotional ratings of original audio and feature reconstructions. We used the extended dataset to analyze the effect that various demographic categories and levels of musical experience have on a participant's ability to extract emotional information from audio. People with a significant amount of musical training were able to more consistently choose the same ratings for chroma reconstructed audio, which contains more harmonic information than MFCC reconstructed audio. We also note that there was an increased ambiguity with arousal labeling in general. This could be related to the demographics of the Turkers, which we believe to be highly non-stationary given the comparison between those of our dataset (see Table 5) and those found by others in previous work [8].

We also observed in Sect. 6 that an individual participant's valence and arousal agreement on the transformation clips was very similar to the clip pairs containing different songs, suggesting that features able to capture these phenomena would be useful for music emotion recognition. While some agreement does exist, it is not overwhelming, making it clear that simple musical parameter changes do not tell the whole story about musical emotion.

In Sect. 7, we analyzed the relative contribution of musical parameter modification to feature space invariance. We evaluated each feature domain in the context of a supervised machine learning problem for automatically ranking song pairs. In the experiments using the original pair dataset (Sect. 5), we find that features such as MFCC and spectral contrast perform the best. Additionally, tonal centroid, onsets and rhythm fluctuation, which generally receive much less attention, also performed well. Because these additional features are of different classes (e.g. timbre, rhythm), their use in combination may improve performance by incorporating information from multiple domains. In looking at the predictions of the transformed pairs (Sect. 6), there are very interesting changes in terms of the ranking of relative feature performance between tempo up and tempo down, as well as key up and key down. It was identified in Sect. 6 that the magnitude of emotion changes is significantly different for key up versus key down and tempo up versus tempo down, but the change in relative ranking is not necessarily expected.

Overall this work presents a comprehensive study of the relationships between musical parameters, the emotional responses they induce and the responses within acoustic feature domain. It provides a more grounded approach to feature selection and design than previous work, and has demonstrated that there is perceptual salience of musical emotion in many common Music-IR features. We see this work as providing grounding for those investigating them in future work, but maintain that they do not tell the whole story. There are correlations between musical parameter changes (e.g. key, tempo) and human emotion, but the relationships are complex and do not offer a simple answer to feature selection. Additionally, there is more to emotion in music than just these compositional building blocks. The individual expressions and articulations of a performance may also play a very large roll. In continuing to bring this complex picture into focus, future work may want to consider taking these relationships into account as well.

References

1. Barthet, M., Fazekas, G., Sandler, M.: Multidisciplinary perspectives on music emotion recognition: Implications for content and context-based models. In: Proceedings of the International Symposium on Computer Music Modeling and Retrieval (CMMR), London, UK (June 2012)
2. Cortes, C., Vapnik, V.: Support-vector networks. Machine Learning 20, 273–295 (1995)
3. Dalla Bella, S., Peretz, I., Rousseau, L., Gosselin, N.: A developmental study of the affective value of tempo and mode in music. Cognition 80(3) (July 2001)
4. Husain, G., Thompson, W., Glenn Schellenberg, E.: Effects of musical tempo and mode on arousal, mood, and spatial abilities. Music Perception 20(2), 151–171 (2002)
5. Gagnon, L., Peretz, I.: Mode and tempo relative contributions to happy-sad judgements in equitone melodies. Cognition & Emotion 17(1), 25–40 (2003)
6. Gerardi, G., Gerken, L.: The development of affective responses to modality and melodic contour. Music Perception 12(3), 279–290 (1995)

7. Hevner, K.: Experimental studies of the elements of expression in music. American Journal of Psychology 48, 246–268 (1936)
8. Ipeirotis, P.: Demographics of mechanical turk. In: CeDER Working Papers. NYU Stern School of Business (2010)
9. Jiang, D., Lu, L., Zhang, H., Tao, J., Cai, L.: Music type classification by spectral contrast feature. In: Proc. Intl. Conf. on Multimedia and Expo., vol. 1, pp. 113–116 (2002)
10. Joachims, T.: Optimizing search engines using clickthrough data. In: Proceedings of the ACM Conference on Knowledge Discovery and Data Mining, KDD (2002)
11. Juslin, P.N., Karlsson, J., Lindström, E., Friberg, A., Schoonderwaldt, E.: Play it again with feeling: Computer feedback in musical communication of emotions. Journal of Experimental Psychology: Applied 12(2), 79–95 (2006)
12. Kim, Y.E., Schmidt, E.M., Migneco, R., Morton, B., Richardson, P., Scott, J., Speck, J.A., Turnbull, D.: Music emotion recognition: A state of the art review. In: Proceedings of the International Society for Music Information Retrieval (ISMIR) Conference, Utrecht, Netherlands (2010)
13. Lee, J.H.: Crowdsourcing music similarity judgments using mechanical turk. In: Proceedings of the International Society for Music Information Retrieval (ISMIR) Conference, Utrecht, Netherlands (2010)
14. Mandel, M.I., Eck, D., Bengio, Y.: Learning tags that vary within a song. In: Proceedings of the International Society for Music Information Retrieval (ISMIR) Conference, Utrecht, Netherlands (2010)
15. Randel, D.M.: The Harvard dictionary of music, 4th edn. Belknap Press of Harvard University Press, Cambridge (2003)
16. Rigg, M.G.: Speed as a determiner of musical mood. Journal of Experimental Psychology 27, 566–571 (1940)
17. Schmidt, E.M., Kim, Y.E.: Prediction of time-varying musical mood distributions using Kalman filtering. In: Proc. of the 9th IEEE Intl. Conf. on Machine Learning and Applications (ICMLA), Washington, D.C (2010)
18. Schmidt, E.M., Kim, Y.E.: Prediction of time-varying musical mood distributions from audio. In: Proceedings of the International Society for Music Information Retrieval (ISMIR) Conference, Utrecht, Netherlands (2010)
19. Schmidt, E.M., Kim, Y.E.: Modeling musical emotion dynamics with conditional random fields. In: Proceedings of the International Society for Music Information Retrieval (ISMIR) Conference, Miami, FL (October 2011)
20. Schmidt, E.M., Prockup, M., Scott, J., Morton, B., Kim, Y.E.: Relating perceptual and feature space invariances in music emotion recognition. In: Proceedings of the International Symposium on Computer Music Modeling and Retrieval (CMMR), London, UK (2012)
21. Schmidt, E.M., Turnbull, D., Kim, Y.E.: Feature selection for content-based, time-varying musical emotion regression. In: ACM MIR, Philadelphia, PA (2010)
22. Snow, R., O'Connor, B., Jurafsky, D., Ng, A.: Cheap and Fast - But is it Good? Evaluating Non-Expert Annotations for Natural Language Tasks. In: Proc. Empirical Methods in NLP (2008)
23. Sorokin, A., Forsyth, D.: Utility data annotation with amazon mechanical turk. In: CVPR Workshops (2008)
24. Speck, J.A., Schmidt, E.M., Morton, B.G., Kim, Y.E.: A comparative study of collaborative vs. traditional annotation methods. In: Proceedings of the International Society for Music Information Retrieval (ISMIR) Conference, Miami, Florida (2011)

25. Thayer, R.E.: The Biopsychology of Mood and Arousal. Oxford Univ. Press, Oxford (1989)
26. Webster, G.D., Weir, C.G.: Emotional responses to music: Interactive effects of mode, texture, and tempo. Motivation and Emotion 29, 19–39 (2005)
27. Whitehill, J., Ruvolo, P., Wu, T., Bergsma, J., Movellan, J.: Whose vote should count more: Optimal integration of labels from labelers of unknown expertise. In: NIPS. MIT Press (2009)

Sample Identification in Hip Hop Music

Jan Van Balen[1], Joan Serrà[2], and Martín Haro[3]

[1] Dept of Information and Computing Sciences, Utrecht University, The Netherlands
j.m.h.vanbalen@uu.nl
[2] Artificial Intelligence Research Institute (IIIA-CSIC), Bellaterra, Barcelona, Spain
jserra@iiia.csic.es
[3] Music Technology Group, Universitat Pompeu Fabra, Barcelona, Spain
martin.haro@upf.edu

Abstract. Sampling is a creative tool in composition that is widespread in popular music production and composition since the 1980's. However, the concept of sampling has for a long time been unaddressed in Music Information Retrieval. We argue that information on the origin of samples has a great musicological value and can be used to organise and disclose large music collections. In this paper we introduce the problem of automatic sample identification and present a first approach for the case of hip hop music. In particular, we modify and optimize an existing fingerprinting approach to meet the necessary requirements of a real-world sample identification task. The obtained results show the viability of such an approach, and open new avenues for research, especially with regard to inferring artist influences and detecting musical reuse.

Keywords: Digital Sampling, Sample Recognition, Musical Influence, Content-based Music Retrieval.

1 Introduction

Digital sampling is a creative tool in composition and music production. It can be defined as the use of a fragment of another artist's recording in a new work. The practice of digital sampling has been ongoing for well over two decades. It has become widespread amongst mainstream artists and genres, including hip hop, electronic, dance, pop, and rock [20]. Information on the origin of samples holds valuable insights into the inspirations and musical resources of an artist. Furthermore, such information could be used to enrich music collections, e.g. for music recommendation purposes. However, in the context of music processing and retrieval, the topic of automatic sample identification has been largely unaddressed [8,21].

In this contribution we introduce automatic sample identification as a new line of research in Music Information Retrieval (MIR), and present a first approach to detecting whether a query song samples another song inside a given music collection. The next section of this article will state some of the motivations for developing a sample identification system and lists the requirements that such a system should meet, in relation to existing research in content-based

M. Aramaki et al. (Eds.): CMMR 2012, LNCS 7900, pp. 301–312, 2013.

music retrieval. Audio fingerprinting techniques are shown to be a good basis for experiments. In the third and fourth sections, experiments are presented and discussed.

1.1   Sampling in Popular Music

The Oxford Music Dictionary defines sampling as "the process in which a sound is taken directly from a recorded medium and transposed onto a new recording" [14]. As a tool for composition, it first appeared when *musique concrète* artists such as Pierre Schaeffer started assembling tapes of found field-recordings and in musical collages. Examples of the use of previously released music recordings are James Tenney's repurposing of Elvis Presley's *Blue Suede Shoes* in *Collage #1* (1961), and the Terry Riley composition *Bird of Paradise* (1965), which uses the song *Shotgun* by Junior Walker and his All-Stars as direct source material [15,16].

The phenomenon of sampling reappeared in the 1970's when New York DJs such as Kool DJ Herc started using their vinyl players to repeat and mix parts of popular recordings, to provide a continuous stream of music for the dancing crowd. The breakthrough of sampling followed the invention of the digital sampler around 1980. It allowed producers to isolate, manipulate, and combine portions of others' recordings to obtain entirely new sonic creations [10,23]. The possibilities that the sampler brought to the studio have played a role in the appearance of several new genres in electronic music, including hip hop, house music (from which a large part of electronic dance music originates), jungle (a precursor of drum&bass music), dub, and trip hop [22]. The first famous sample-based single was Sugarhill Gang's *Rapper's Delight* (1979), containing a looped sample taken from *Good Times* by Chic (1979) [14]. A famous example of sampling in rock music is the song *Bittersweet Symphony* by The Verve (1997), which looped a pattern sampled from a 1966 instrumental string arrangement of The Rolling Stones' *The Last Time* (1965) [14].

1.2   Motivations for Computational Research on Sampling

A first motivation to undertake the automatic identification of samples originates in the belief that the musicological study of popular music would be incomplete without the study of samples and their origins. Knowledge on the origin of samples provides a direct insight into the inspirations and musical resources of an artist, and reveals some details about his or her composition methods and production choices. At the level of popular music history, there has been an emerging interest to study how some of the particular musical properties of contemporary popular music may be traced back to the influence of the technology that has been used to produce it, such as song structures, groove (the activating quality of music), and rhythm [5,9,18][1]. To our knowledge, an extensive study of how

---

[1] Talking Heads singer David Byrne also devotes two insightful chapters of his recent book *How Music Works* (2012) to the influences of technology on the artistic process.

harmony, timbre, rhythm, groove and other qualities of sampled music may have descended from past cultural activity has yet to be performed.

Samples also hold valuable information on the level of genres and communities, revealing cultural influences and dependence. Many researchers have studied the way that hip hop has often sampled 60's and 70's African-American artists [10,18] and, more recently, Bryan and Wang [4] analysed musical influence networks in sample-based music, inferred from a unique dataset provided by the WhoSampled web project[2]. Such annotated collections exist, but they are assembled through hours of manual introduction in a collaborative effort of amateur enthusiasts. It is clear that an automated approach could both widen and deepen the body of information on sample networks, while at the same time bringing the freedom to individuals to perform their own analysis, so that they do not need to rely on the collaborative efforts of others, or the platforms that store them.

Equally interesting opportunities lie alongside recent advances in folk song [27] and version identification [25] research, where sample identification research can be applied within a larger effort to trace specific musical ideas and observe musical reuse in the recorded history of the last century.

As the amount of accessible multimedia and the size of personal collections continue to grow, sample identification from raw audio also provides a new way to bring structure to the organisation of large music databases, complementing a great amount of existing research in this direction [8,21]. Finally, sample identification could serve legal purposes. Copyright considerations have always been an important motivation to understand sampling as a cultural phenomenon; a large part of the academic research on sampling is focused on copyright and law [20].

1.3   Requirements for a Sample Identification System

The challenges of automatic sample recognition can be directly related to the way samples have been manipulated by producers. Typical parameters controlling playback in popular hardware and software samplers (e.g. AKAI, Yamaha, Ableton, Native Instruments) include filtering parameters, playback speed, and level envelope controls (attack, sustain, decay, release). Filtering can be used by producers to maintain only the most interesting part of a sample. Playback speed may be changed to optimise the tempo (time-stretching), pitch (transposition), and mood of samples. Naturally, each of these operations complicates the automatic recognition of affected samples. In addition, samples may be as short as one second or less, and do not necessarily contain tonal information, i.e. they may consist of only percussive sounds. Finally, given that it is not unusual for two or more samples to appear at the same time in a mix, the sample's energy may be low compared to that of the musical elements that obscure it. This further complicates recognition.

---

[2] www.whosampled.com

In the light of these observations, three important requirements for any sample recognition system should be that:

1. The system is able to identify heavily manipulated query audio in a given music collection. This includes samples that are filtered, time-stretched, transposed, very short, tonal and non-tonal, processed with audio effects, and/or appear underneath a thick layer of other musical elements.
2. The system is able to perform this task for large collections.
3. The system is able to perform the task in a reasonable amount of time.

These requirements allow us to introduce and situate the problem of sample identification in the field of content-based music retrieval. Like in other fields of information retrieval, performance in music retrieval is typically expressed in terms of precision (how good the retrieved results are) and recall (how many good results are retrieved). It should be noted that, in the context of the applications proposed above, a good recall is the more important requirement: a musicologist trying to identify source material in a composition can assess system output fairly easily. Regardless, we argue that the unseen difficulty of facing these three challenges at once is in itself an excellent motivation for the proposed research.

1.4 Content-Based Music Retrieval

Research in content-based music retrieval can be characterised in terms of the *specificity* [8] and *granularity* [17] of the task. Specificity refers to the degree of similarity between query and match. Tasks with a high specificity intend to retrieve almost identical documents; low specificity tasks look for more loosely associated matches that are similar with respect to some musical properties. Granularity refers to the difference between fragment-level and document-level retrieval: audio fingerprinting is an example of a fragment-level (low granularity) task, while version detection requires a more document-level (high granularity) approach. Automatic sample recognition has mid-specificity and very low granularity (i.e. very short-time matches that are similar with respect to some musical properties). Given these characteristics, it relates to audio fingerprinting.

Audio fingerprinting systems attempt to identify unlabeled audio by matching a compact, content-based representation of it, the fingerprint, against a database of labeled fingerprints [6]. Just like fingerprinting systems, sample recognition systems should be designed to be robust to additive noise and several transformations. However, the deliberate transformations possible in sample-based music production, especially changes in pitch and tempo, suggest that the problem of sample recognition is in fact a significantly more challenging task.

Audio matching and version identification systems are typical mid-specificity problems [17]. Version identification systems assess if two complete musical recordings are different renditions of the same musical piece, usually taking changes in key, tempo and structure into account [25]. Audio matching works on a more granular level and includes remix recognition, amongst other tasks [7,17]. Many of these systems use chroma features [8,21]. These descriptions of the pitch content of audio require the audio to be tonal and are generally not robust with respect to changes in tonality, as may occur with the addition of other musical layers. This may be problematic in the case of sampling. We therefore claim that sample recognition should be cast as a new problem with unique requirements, for which the right tools are still to be made.

Potential sample identification tools have been proposed by a small number of authors. A system capable of fingerprinting pitch-shifted audio is described by Fenet [13]. The system relies on an existing fingerprinting technique and, as we propose in [26], uses a logaritmic frequency representation to facilitate the search for pitch-shifted audio. It performs well on the recognition of radio broadcast audio, as intended in its design. As a result however, it does not provide robustness to time-stretching or to pitch shifts up to a semitone and more. More recently, Dittmar et. al. [11] explicitly addressed sample recognition in the context of plagiarism assessment. Two approaches are proposed: a brute-force comparison of spectrograms (again with logaritmically spaced frequencies), and a method based on non-negative matrix factorization (NMF). The techniques are claimed to be robust against time-stretching and pitch-shifting respectively, but have not been formally evaluated yet.

2 Experiments

2.1 Evaluation Methodology

We now present our first approach to the automatic identification of samples [26]. Given a query song in raw audio format, the experiments aim to retrieve a ranked list of candidate files with the sampled songs first. To narrow down the scope of experiments, only samples used in hip hop music were considered, as hip hop is the first and most widely known genre to be built on samples [10]. Regarding the origins of samples, there were no genre restrictions.

An evaluation collection was established using data from specialized internet sites[3]. The set consists of 76 query tracks and 68 sampled tracks [26]. It includes 104 sample relations (expert-confirmed cases of sampling). Additionally, 320 'noise' files, very similar to the candidates in genre and length, were added to challenge the system as suggested in [24]. This makes a total of 388 candidates. All examples are real-world cases of sampling. Aiming at representativeness, the ground truth was chosen to include both short and long samples, tonal and percussive samples, and isolated samples (the only layer in the mix) as well as background samples. So-called 'interpolations', i.e. samples that have been re-recorded in the studio, were not included, nor were non-musical samples (e.g. film dialogue).

Figure 1 shows a visualisation of sample relations between the artists appearing in the music collection established for the evaluation of our experiments. The orange nodes represent sampled artists, the blue nodes represent the artists

---

[3] WhoSampled (`www.whosampled.com`), accessed 02/2011 and Hip Hop is Read (`www.hiphopisread.com`, accessed 02/2011).

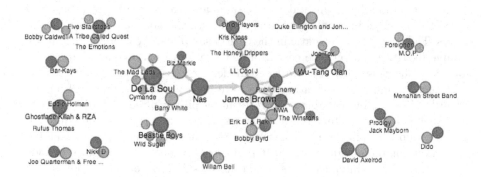

Fig. 1. Network visualisation of the connections between some of the artists in the music collection established for the evaluation of experiments. The light nodes (orange) represent sampled artists, the dark nodes (blue) represent the artists that sampled them.

Table 1. Example: two audio tracks and a sample relation as they are represented in the ground truth dataset. The sample relation S019 is identified by the associated query Q, the candidate C, and the times TC and TQ at which the sample occurs the first time. N counts the number of times the sample occurs in Q.

	Artist	Title	Year	Genre
T034	Pete Rock & C.L. Smooth	Straighten it Out	1992	Hip-hop
T035	Ernie Hines	Our Generation	1972	R&B/Soul

	C	Q	TC	TQ	N	Comments
S019	T035	T034	0:40	0:10	48	Vocals

that sampled them. The diagram shows how the emerging links between artists quickly give rise to a complex network of influence relations.

The mean average precision (MAP) was chosen as the experiment's evaluation metric [19]. The MAP is a common measure in information retrieval and has been used in several related tasks [12]. With the collection used in this study, a random baseline of 0.017 was found over 100 iterations, with a standard deviation of 0.007.

2.2   Optimisation of a State-of-the-Art Audio Fingerprinting System

In a first experiment, a state-of-the-art fingerprinting system was optimised to perform our task. We chose to work with the spectral peak-based audio fingerprinting system designed by Wang [28]. A fingerprinting system was chosen because of the chroma argument in Section 1.4. The landmark-based system was chosen because of its robustness to noise and distortions and the alleged 'transparency' of the spectral peak-based representation: Wang reports that, even with a large database, the system is able to correctly identify each of several tracks

Table 2. Strengths and weaknesses of spectral peak-based fingerprints in the context of sample identification

Strengths	Weaknesses
– High proven robustness to noise and distortions. – Ability to identify music from only a very short audio segment. – 'Transparent' fingerprints: ability to identify multiple fragments played at once. – Does not explicitly require tonal content.	– Not designed for transposed or time-stretched audio. – Designed to identify tonal content in a noisy context, fingerprinting drum samples requires the opposite. – Percussive recordings may not be representable using spectral peak locations only.

mixed together. The same system was used by Fenet et al. [13] and has previously also been adapted for use in version recognition [1]. Table 2 lists some of the system's strengths and weaknesses with respect to the current task.

As in most other fingerprinting systems, the landmark-based system consists of an extraction and a matching component [28]. Briefly summarized, the extraction component takes the short time Fourier transform (STFT) of audio segments and selects from the obtained spectrogram a uniform constellation of prominent spectral peaks. The time-frequency tuples with peak locations are paired in 4-dimensional 'landmarks', which are then indexed as a start time stored under a certain hash code for efficient lookup by the matching component. The matching component retrieves for all candidate files the landmarks that are identical to those extracted from the query. Query and candidate audio segments match if these corresponding landmarks show consistent start times [28].

An implementation of this algorithm was made available by Ellis[4]. It works by the same principles as [28], and features a range of parameters to control the implementation-level operation of the system. Important STFT parameters are the audio sample rate and the FFT size, determining the frequency and time resolution of the spectral analysis. Another important quantity is the number of spectral peaks to consider. It is governed by the Peak Density parameter (controlling the density of peaks in the time domain) and a Peak Spacing parameter (in the frequency domain). The number of resulting landmarks is governed by three more parameters: the peak pairing horizons in the frequency and time domain, and the maximum number of formed pairs per spectral peak.

A wrapper was written to slice the query audio into short fixed-length chunks, overlapping with a hop size of $1s$ and a length around the expected length of the longest samples. The same wrapper then feeds these chunks to the fingerprinting system as implemented by Ellis, and uses a distance function to sort the results

---

[4] http://labrosa.ee.columbia.edu/matlab/fingerprint/

into a ranked list. The distance that was used is

$$d_a = \frac{1}{m+1} \tag{1}$$

a function of the number of matching landmarks m.

As a complete optimisation of the system would have been too time-consuming, we have performed a large number of tests to optimise the most influential parameters. Table 3 summarizes the optimisation process, of which more details can be found in [26]. The resulting MAP was 0.218. Interestingly, better performance was achieved for lower sample rates. The optimal density of peaks and number of pairs per peak are also significantly larger than required in a standard fingerprinting context, resulting in many more extracted landmarks per second. This requires more computation time for both extraction and matching, and requires for a higher number of extracted landmarks to be stored in the system's memory.

The MAP of around 0.23 is low for a retrieval task but promising as a first result: it is well beyond the random baseline and the system retrieves a correct best match (top 1) for around 15 of the 76 queries. These matches include both percussive and tonal samples. However, due to the lowering of the sample rate, some frequency resolution is lost, and much of the spectral information remains unused. This may affect the scalability of the system: a sufficient number of frequency bins is needed to ensure that the landmarks allow differentiation between a high number of almost identical spectra.

Table 3. Some of the intermediate results in the optimisation of the audio fingerprinting system by Wang as implemented by Ellis [26]. The first row shows default settings with its resulting performance.

pairs/pk	pk density (s^{-1})	pk spacing (bins)	sample rate (Hz)	FFT size (ms)	MAP
3	10	30	8,000	64	0.114
10	10	30	8,000	64	0.117
10	36	30	8,000	64	0.118
10	36	30	4,000	64	0.193
10	36	30	2,000	64	0.176
10	36	30	2,000	128	0.228
10	36	30	2,000	256	0.144

2.3   Constant Q Fingerprints

As a second experiment, we did a number of tests using a constant Q transform (CQT) [2] instead of a Fourier transform (FT). We would like to consider all frequencies up to the default 8,000 Hz but make the lower frequencies more important, as they contributed more to the best performance so far. The constant Q representation, in which frequency bins are logarithmically spaced, allows us to do so. The CQT also suits the logarithmic representation of frequency in the human auditory system.

We integrated the fingerprinting system with Ellis' implementation[5] of Brown's fast algorithm to compute the CQT [3]. A brief optimisation of the new parameters returns an optimal MAP of 0.21 at a sample rate of 8,000 Hz, showing that similar precision as before can be obtained. With this sample rate and with an optimised resolution of 32 bins per octave, the information in the frequency domain is now restored: at 8000 Hz sample rate and 32 bins per octave, the CQT spans 224 bins, whereas a 128ms FT at 2000 Hz results in only 128. The use of the constant Q will also prove convenient for reasons explained in the next section.

2.4   Repitching Fingerprints

In a third and last experiment, a first attempt was made to deal with repitched samples. As laid out in section 1.3, artists often time-stretch and pitch-shift samples. This is typically done by changing the samples' playback speed. As a result, the samples' pitch and tempo rescale with the same factor. Algorithms for independent pitch-shifting and time-stretching without audible artifacts have only been around for less than a decade, after phase coherence and transient processing problems were overcome. Even now, repitching is still popular practice amongst producers, as inspection of the used music collection confirms.

The most straightforward, brute-force method to deal with repitching is to repitch query audio several times and perform a search for each of the copies. Alternatively, however, the extracted landmarks themselves can also be repitched through the appropriate scaling of time and frequency components. This way the extraction needs to be done only once. We have performed three tests in which both methods are combined: all query audio is resampled several times, to obtain N copies, all pitched ΔR semitones apart. For each copy of the query audio, landmarks are then extracted, duplicated and rescaled to include all possible landmarks repitched between $r = 0.5$ semitones up and down. This is feasible because of the CQT's finite resolution in time and frequency. Note that the use of the constant Q transform also provides us with a convenient advantage at this point: the difference between two peaks' logaritmic frequency is invariant to pitch-shifting. In more detail: one of the landmark's dimensions is rewritten as the logaritmic frequency difference between the peaks to exploit this property. The invariance of this component reduces the amount of landmarks needed to cover a range of repitch values.

The results for repitching experiments are shown in Table 4. We have obtained a best performance of MAP equal to 0.390 for the experiment with $N = 9$ repitched queries, all $\Delta R = 0.5$ semitones apart. This results in a total searched pitch range of 2.5 semitones up and down. A MAP of 0.390 is rather low, yet it is in the range of some early version identification systems, or even slightly

---

[5] See http://www.ee.columbia.edu/~dpwe/resources/matlab/sgram/ and
http://labrosa.ee.columbia.edu/matlab/sgram/logfsgram.m

Table 4. Results of experiments using repitching of both the query audio and its extracted landmarks to search for repitched samples

sample rate (Hz)	bins/octave	min. freq.	N	ΔR (st)	r (st)	MAP
8000	32	32	1	-	0.0	0.228
8000	32	32	1	-	0.5	0.288
8000	32	32	5	1.0	0.5	0.334
8000	32	32	9	5.0	0.5	0.390

better [24]. A total of 29 out of 76 queries now retrieve a correct song as their best match, examples now including several repitched samples, both percussive and tonal.

3   Discussion

We have introduced and detailed the first research to fully address the problem of automatic sample identification. The problem has been defined and situated in the broader context of sampling as a musical phenomenon and the requirements that a sample identification system should meet have been listed. A state-of-the-art fingerprinting system has been adapted, optimised, and modified to address the task. Many challenges have to be dealt with and not all of them have been met, but the obtained performance of MAP = 0.39 is promising and unmistakably better than the performance obtained without taking repitching into account. Overall, our approach is a substantial first step in the considered task.

A more detailed characterisation of the unrecognised samples is rather time-consuming but will make a very informative next step in future work. Furthermore, we suggest performing tests with a more extensively annotated dataset, in order to assess what types of samples are most challenging to identify, and perhaps a larger number of ground truth relations. This will allow us to relate performance and the established requirements more closely and lead to better results.

Advances in the presented research will eventually pave the road for reliable fingerprinting of percussive audio, sample recognition based on perceptual models, or the analysis of typical features of sampled audio. These can in turn support many of the proposed applications presented in this contribution, such as musicological research, music understanding and recommendation and perhaps even tools for providing musicians with new and inspiring resources. All this will hopefully allow a greater understanding of sampling as an artistic phenomenon and help musicologists make sense of the popular music of today.

Acknowledgments. This research was done between Jan. and Sept. 2011 at the Music Technology Group of Universitat Pompeu Fabra in Barcelona, Spain. The authors would like to thank Perfecto Herrera and Xavier Serra for their advice and support. JS acknowledges JAEDOC069/2010 from Consejo Superior de Investigaciones Científicas and 2009-SGR-1434 from Generalitat de Catalunya. MH acknowledges FP7-ICT-2011.1.5-287711.

References

1. Bertin-Mahieux, T., Ellis, D.P.W.: Large-scale Cover Song Recognition Using Hashed Chroma Landmarks. In: IEEE Workshop on Applications of Signal Processing to Audio and Acoustics, pp. 117–120 (2011)
2. Brown, J.C.: Calculation of a Constant Q Spectral Transform. Journal of the Acoustical Society of America 89(1), 425–434 (1991)
3. Brown, J.C., Puckette, M.: An efficient algorithm for the calculation of a constant Q transform. Journal of the Acoustical Society of America 92(5), 2696–2701 (1992)
4. Bryan, N.J., Wang, G.: Musical Influence Network Analysis and Rank of Sample-Based Music. In: 12th International Society for Music Information Retrieval Conference, pp. 329–334 (2011)
5. Butler, M.J.: Unlocking the groove: Rhythm, meter, and musical design in electronic dance music. Indiana University Press, Bloomington (2006)
6. Cano, P., Battle, E., Kalker, T., Haitsma, J.: A Review of Audio Fingerprinting. Journal of VLSI Signal Processing-Systems for Signal, Image, and Video Technology 41(3), 271–284 (2005)
7. Casey, M., Slaney, M.: Fast Recognition of Remixed Music Audio. IEEE International Conference on Acoustics Speech and Signal Processing 4(12), 300–304 (2007)
8. Casey, M., Veltkamp, R., Goto, M., Leman, M., Rhodes, C., Slaney, M.: Content-Based Music Information Retrieval: Current Directions and Future Challenges. Proceedings of the IEEE 96(4), 668–696 (2008)
9. Danielsen, A. (ed.): Musical Rhythm in the Age of Digital Reproduction. Ashgate, Farnham, Surrey (2010)
10. Demers, J.: Sampling the 1970s in Hip-Hop. Popular Music 22(1), 41–56 (2003)
11. Dittmar, C., Hildebrand, K.F., Gaertner, D., Winges, M., Müller, F., Aichroth, P.: Audio Forensics Meets Music Information Retrieval, A Toolbox for Inspection of Music Plagiarism. In: 20th European Signal Processing Conference, Bucharest, Romania, pp. 1249–1253 (2012)
12. Downie, J.S.: The Music Information Retrieval Evaluation EXchange (2005-2007): a Window into Music Information Retrieval Research. Acoustical Science and Technology 29(4), 247–255 (2008)
13. Fenet, S., Richard, G., Grenier, Y.: A Scalable Audio Fingerprint Method with Robustness to Pitch-Shifting. In: 12th International Society for Music Information Retrieval Conference, Miami, USA, pp. 121–126 (2011)
14. Fulford-Jones, W.: Sampling. In: Grove Music Online. Oxford Music Online (2011), http://www.oxfordmusiconline.com/subscriber/article/grove/music/47228
15. Grimshaw, J.: Bird of Paradise, Tape Collage. In: Allmusic (2013), http://www.allmusic.com/composition/bird-of-paradise-tape-collage-mc0002598825
16. Grimshaw, J.: Collage # 1 ("Blue Suede"). In: Allmusic (2013), http://www.allmusic.com/composition/collage-1-blue-suede-mc0002499059
17. Grosche, P., Müller, M., Serrà, J.: Audio Content-Based Music Retrieval. In: Müller, M., Goto, M., Schedl, M. (eds.) Multimodal Music Processing. Dagstuhl Publishing, Wadern (2012)
18. Katz, M.: Music in 1s and 0s: The Art and Politics of Digital Sampling. In: Capturing Sound: How Technology has Changed Music, pp. 137–157. University of California Press, Berkeley (2004)

19. Manning, C.D., Prabhakar, R., Schutze, H.: An Introduction to Information Retrieval. Cambridge University Press, Cambridge (2008)
20. McKenna, T.: Where Digital Music Technology and Law Collide - Contemporary Issues of Digital Sampling, Appropriation and Copyright Law. Journal of Information Law and Technology 1 (2000)
21. Müller, M., Ellis, D., Klapuri, A., Richard, G.: Signal Processing for Music Analysis. IEEE Journal of Selected Topics in Signal Processing 5(6) (2011)
22. Peel, I.: Dance Music. In: Grove Music Online. Oxford Music Online (2011), http://www.oxfordmusiconline.com/subscriber/article/grove/music/47215
23. Self, H.: Digital Sampling: A Cultural Perspective. UCLA Ent. L. Rev. 9(2), 347–359 (2001)
24. Serrà, J., Gómez, E., Herrera, P.: Audio Cover Song Identification and Similarity: Background, Approaches, Evaluation, and Beyond. In: Raś, Z.W., Wieczorkowska, A.A. (eds.) Advances in Music Information Retrieval. SCI, vol. 274, pp. 307–332. Springer, Heidelberg (2010)
25. Serra, J.: Identification of Versions of the Same Musical Composition by Processing Audio Descriptions. PhD Thesis, Universitat Pompeu Fabra, Barcelona, Spain (2011)
26. Van Balen, J.: Automatic Recognition of Samples in Musical Audio. Master thesis, Universitat Pompeu Fabra, Spain (2011), http://mtg.upf.edu/node/2342
27. Wiering, F., Veltkamp, R., Garbers, J., Volk, A., Kranenburg, P.: Modelling Folksong Melodies. Interdisciplinary Science Reviews 34(2-3), 154–171 (2009)
28. Wang, A.: An Industrial Strength Audio Search Algorithm. In: 4th International Society for Music Information Retrieval Conference, pp. 7–13 (2003)

Music Similarity Evaluation Using the Variogram for MFCC Modelling

Lorenzo J. Tardón and Isabel Barbancho

Dept. Ingeniería de Comunicaciones
E.T.S.I Telecomunicación, Universidad de Málaga
Campus Universitario de Teatinos s/n
29071, Málaga, Spain
lorenzo@ic.uma.es

Abstract. This chapter describes two different approaches using the variogram in the context of Mel Frequency Cepstral Coefficients (MFCCs) and the evaluation of music similarity. The first approach is referred to as the full variogram approach; in this case, all the lags of the variogram of the second coefficient of the MFCC are employed. The second choice is referred to as the reduced variogram approach; in this case, a subset of the lags of the variogram of the MFCC matrix is considered. Thus, the usage of the variogram is proposed as a tool to synthesize the timbre information contained in the MFCCs.

Also, four different weighting functions are tested for the calculation of the distance measure between songs. The performance of the methods proposed is evaluated by applying the pseudo-objective evaluation scheme of the MIREX AMS task. The results are compared against the scores obtained by other methods submitted to the MIREX AMS 2011.

Keywords: Music Similarity, Variogram, MFCCs, MIREX AMS task.

1 Introduction

The rapid evolution of the technology during the last years has allowed the creation of tons of new digital multimedia content. This fact has made the requirements for the distribution of music content grow. But also, proper storage schemes are necessary, together with the development of labelling and indexation techniques of the material in order to provide efficient access to the content.

In this context, a growing number of tasks concerning the Music Information Retrieval (MIR) community have been proposed over the years. Among them, one of the fields to which the MIR community is currently devoting resources is focused on the development of content-based music recommendation systems. Briefly, these systems are based on the calculation of a number of descriptors of the songs, extracted from the time and/or frequency domain, and the derivation of some kind of representative patterns based on those features that are used to create signatures of the songs. Then, these signatures must be compared to obtain measures of music similarity.

M. Aramaki et al. (Eds.): CMMR 2012, LNCS 7900, pp. 313–332, 2013.

So, a key concept of content-based music recommendation systems is the extraction of significant features from the songs to create meaningful signatures for each of the pieces that must be considered.

Some commonly used descriptors are based on the rhythm pattern of the song. Gouyon [9] demonstrated how using only the main tempo of the song, a music genre classification scheme attains an accuracy of 80%.

Melody extraction is the basis of other sets of algorithms aimed to exploit the tonal content of the song for music characterization and indexation. Gómez, in [8], described how the melody pattern (often symbolically represented using MIDI [20]) can be successfully employed for music recommendation.

Timbre is another important feature. Timbre is widely defined as the 'quality of sound'. It is a perceivable characteristic of the sound that cannot be rigorously described by a unique numeric descriptor. Conversely, it is rather qualitatively described as the sensation transmitted by the sound [2]. Although the nature of timbre is typically qualitative, a number of descriptors have been defined in an attempt to numerically resume some spectral features of the audio excerpts strictly related to the sensation transmitted to the listener [4].

Together with the musical features described above, a brief description of some of the most popular computational 'low-level features' follows:

- Spectral centroid - The spectral centroid [24] is defined as the centre of mass of the spectrum. It is related to the 'brightness' of the timbre.
- Spectral flatness - The spectral flatness defines the shape of the spectrum or, more specifically, how much the spectrum resembles a tonal or a noisy signal [13].
- Spectral flux - Tzanetakis [26] defines the spectral flux as a measure of the evolution of the spectrum over the time. Thus, this descriptor reveals the rate of musical variation along the time of the song.
- Spectral Rolloff - The spectral rolloff measures the accumulation of the energy of sound in the lower parts of the spectrum [10].

These and other low-level descriptors are rarely used individually but together to give rise to vectors of descriptors.

On the other hand, the whole spectrum is not actually considered as a descriptor itself. Hence, a simplified version of the spectrum, revealing most of the information on the distribution of the amplitude of the sinusoidal components, is widely employed in MIR. Such a descriptor is, in fact, a vector of components known as the *Mel Frequency Cepstral Coefficients* (MFCC). We will pay attention to this descriptor and the utilization of the variogram in the context of the application of MFCCs to define music similarity.

This chapter is organized as follows: a brief introduction to MFCCs will be given in the next section. In Section 3, the variogram will be presented. Then, in Section 4, the usage of the variogram in the contexts of MFCCs will be described. Distance measures for the evaluation of music similarity will be presented in Section 5. The results of the evaluation of the methods proposed will be presented in Section 6 and, finally, some conclusions will be drawn in Section 7.

2   Mel Frequency Cepstral Coefficients

One of the most successfully used features to describe the spectral content of an audio signal are the Mel Frequency Cepstral Coefficients (MFCC) [22]. These are short-time spectrum-based features often employed to summarize the timbre content of the songs. Thus, MFCCs are involved in many known algorithms for music similarity evaluation.

The MFCCs are calculated according to a known procedure [21] (although sometimes modifications are introduced):

1. The short-time spectrogram is obtained.
2. The spectrogram is mapped onto the Mel scale using (see Figure 1):

$$M = 1127.01048 \cdot \log_e(1 + f/700) \tag{1}$$

where f represents the frequency in Hz that will be converted into Mel units.

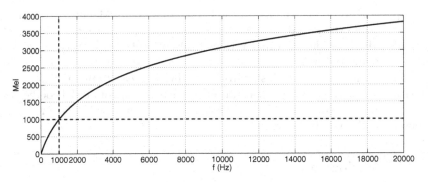

Fig. 1. The Mel scale. The reference value of 1000 Mel is highlighted.

To this end, a Mel filter bank (Figure 2) is applied.
3. The filtered spectrum is expressed in decibels.
4. The resulting data are compressed using the Discrete Cosine Transform (DCT).

A flow chart of the entire process is shown in Figure 3.

The entire process implies a lossy compression of the original spectrum. The descriptor obtained is a matrix with a size depending both on the number of coefficients (fixed a priori) and the set of chunks the song has been divided into during the windowing of the spectrogram.

Logan and Salomon [18], employed the popular K-means algorithm to cluster the MFCCs and then used the means and covariance matrices of the centroids to define the song signature that would be used to measure music similarity. A simple flowchart of a music similarity estimation process in shown in Figure 4.

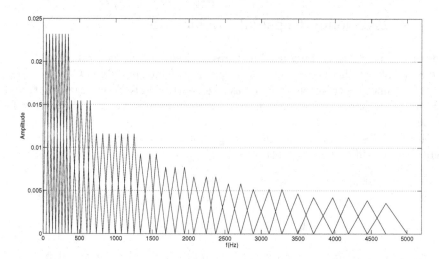

Fig. 2. The Mel filter bank

Pampalk [21] proposed the use of the Gaussian Mixture Models (GMMs) and the Expectation-Maximization (EM) approach [6] in this context, modelling the probability distribution functions of the vectors of coefficients. Aucouturier and Pachet [3] employed a Monte Carlo approach as clustering technique. Mandel and Ellis [19] used only one cluster from a GMM whereas Tzanetakis and Cook [26] simply extracted the mean and variance from each vector of Mel coefficients.

In this chapter, a discussion on the use of the variogram for MFCC modelling, proposed in [23], will be provided.

3   The Variogram

The variogram is a popular tool in Geostatistics. It is widely employed to model the spatial continuity of environmental variables. In this sense, Isaaks and Srivastava [12] affirm that 'Two data close to each other are more likely to have similar values than two data that are far apart'. This characteristic is quantitatively defined as *spatial continuity*, making reference to the spatial correlation of spatial variables.

Let z_x, with $x = 1, \ldots, n$ represent a set of n sampled observations of certain spatial phenomenon. The index x stands for the vector of coordinates of the samples, generally unidimensional in the case of temporal variables, but two- or three- dimensional in the case of spatial phenomena.

One way to measure the spatial continuity of the values of the samples is to observe their behaviour when considered in pairs related by their distance or separation. The h-scatter plot performs this task. It represents the scatter plot of samples paired by a specific value of distance h [12] (see Figure 5).

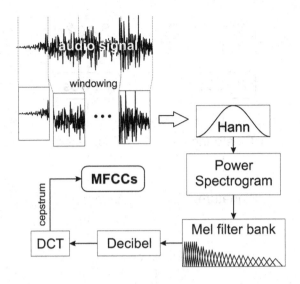

Fig. 3. Flow chart for the calculation of MFCC

We can draw two important considerations:

- The h-scatter plot of the paired samples at $h = 0$ (Figure 5(a)) is simply the comparison of each sample with itself. Thus, it will always be a straight line with slope 1.
- The widening of the cloud of samples in the h-scatter plot as h grows (Figure 5(b-d)), reveals the decrease of their pairwise correlation with the distance. The larger the distance, the lesser the degree of similarity between them. This makes the scatter cloud wider and more diffuse [12] with growing h.

Now, we need a quantitative measure of the spread of the cloud, and of its dependence on h. One popular measure of the spread of a scatter plot is the correlation coefficient.

The general definition of the correlation coefficient follows:

$$\rho_{x,y} = \frac{C_{x,y}}{\sigma_x \cdot \sigma_y} \tag{2}$$

where σ_x and σ_y are the standard deviations of x and y, respectively, and $C_{x,y}$ is the covariance of the variables x and y: $(E[x - E[x]])(E[y - E[y]])$. The sample covariance is defined as follows:

$$C_{x,y} = \frac{1}{n-1} \sum_{i=1}^{n} (x_i - \bar{x}) \cdot (y_i - \bar{y}) \tag{3}$$

where $\bar{x}$ and $\bar{y}$ are the sample mean values of the variables x and y, respectively. It is possible to find the sample correlation coefficient of the two subsets of the variable z separated h, generally $z(x)$ and $z(x + h)$, for each value of h.

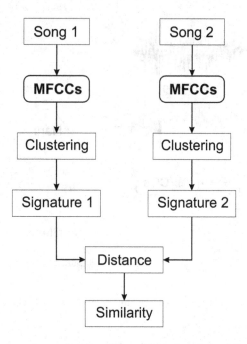

Fig. 4. Flow chart of a scheme for the automatic estimation of the similarity between two songs

The relationship between the correlation coefficient and the distance h is defined as the *correlation function*, or *correlogram* $(\rho(h))$ [12]:

$$\rho(h) = \frac{C_{z(x),z(x+h)}}{\sigma_{z(x)} \cdot \sigma_{z(x+h)}} \tag{4}$$

As has been shown, the degree of correlation of the paired samples typically decreases with the magnitude of h. This behaviour results in a rather clear asymptotic behaviour of the function as h grows. This is a crucial feature in geostatistics and can be easily related to the geometrical meaning of the h-scatter plot itself. In Figure 5, the cloud of the h-scatter plots spreads more and more with the magnitude of h. The spread can grow up to a certain limit, given by the meaning and the geometric extent of the h-scatter plot itself. This fact is related to the meaning of the correlation coefficient. When the samples are widely scattered on the plane, they reveal independence between the paired variables. Thus, when the plane tends to be uniformly filled, their correlation coefficient tends to zero. This asymptotic behaviour is properly reflected by the shape of the correlogram.

An alternative measure for the spatial continuity is the covariance of the paired variables. The sample covariance of the paired variables is defined as follows:

$$C(h) = \frac{1}{n(h) - 1} \sum_{i=1}^{n(h)} (z_i(x) - \bar{z}(x)) \cdot (z_i(x + h) - \bar{z}(x + h)) \tag{5}$$

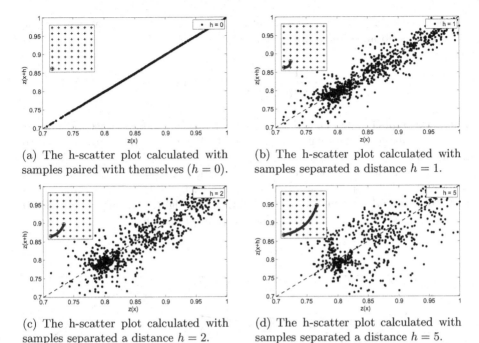

(a) The h-scatter plot calculated with samples paired with themselves ($h = 0$).

(b) The h-scatter plot calculated with samples separated a distance $h = 1$.

(c) The h-scatter plot calculated with samples separated a distance $h = 2$.

(d) The h-scatter plot calculated with samples separated a distance $h = 5$.

Fig. 5. h-scatter plots of a set of regularly separated spatial samples. The first plot resembles a straight line with slope 1. Note that $h = 0$ implies the comparison of each sample with itself. In the plots, the increase of the spread of the cloud of samples with h is evident. In each plot, a small graph showing the pairing of the first sample is shown. The analysed data are a subset of topography data, freely provided by the US National Geophysical Data Center (NOAA).

As seen in equations (4) and (5), the two functions refer to two closely related statistics

Another value for the measure of the spread of the h-scatter plot cloud is the *moment of inertia*. If the cloud of samples of Figure 5 is considered as a molecular mass spinning around its central axis (the geometrical locus of the paired samples at $h = 0$), then it is possible to measure the spread of the cloud as the moment of inertia of the mass. This parameter can be estimated as follows:

$$T = \frac{1}{2 \cdot n} \cdot \sum_{i=1}^{n} (x_i - y_i)^2 \tag{6}$$

The moment of inertia is a measure of the drift of the samples around the diagonal. As with the case of the correlogram and the covariance function, the moment of inertia can be related to the distance h. In this case, the function is referred to as *semivariogram*, or simply *variogram*.

The variogram of a pair of variables ($z(x)$ and $z(x + h)$) separated by the distance h is obtained as follows:

$$\gamma(h) = \frac{1}{2 \cdot n(h)} \cdot \sum_{i=1}^{n(h)} (z(x_i) - z(x_i + h))^2 \qquad (7)$$

where the number of pairs n is represented as a function of h, because the number of pairs available changes with the distance h. The term h is usually referred to as the *lag*.

A typical variogram curve reflects the empirical assumption made for the h-scatter plot. It is zero at the origin, it grows with the lag distance and starts to flatten around a certain value of variance. In Figure 6, a typical empirical variogram is shown, together with the covariance function.

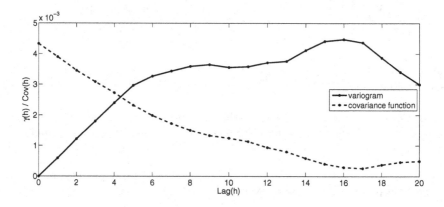

Fig. 6. A sample of an empirical variogram and its corresponding covariance function

The approximation of the law of spatial continuity for all the lags is often demanded. Then, some theoretical analytic models are often fitted to the empirical variogram.

In order to infer the theoretical behaviour of the experimental variogram, the samples of the spatial variable are considered realizations of a random variable, and a series of assumptions are applied. In particular, stationarity is assumed.

Under the hypothesis of second order stationarity [27], the empirical variogram can be conveniently approximated by a family of functions (bounded authorized models) that allow us to infer the information on the spatial continuity over the entire range. Two of the most popular models used to fit the sample variogram function are the exponential and the spherical models [12].

The fit of the sample variogram function with analytic models allows us to define simple parameters to characterize the behaviour of the variogram. The main features typically used to describe the shape of the variogram are:

- The *sill*: the asymptotic value that the variance curve tends to.
- The *range*: the lag value after which the sill is considered to be reached.
- The *nugget effect*: as already indicated, the theoretical value of the variogram at $h = 0$ is zero. However, in a practical experimental framework, a significant discontinuity in the sample variogram curve can be observed. This is called the nugget effect and this phenomenon is referred to as the *small scale variability* [16]. So, the model of the nugget effect is employed to take into account this observation to properly fit the theoretical models to the variogram curve by summing a certain offset to the main model. Thus, the first lag of the model is pushed to a level of variance larger than zero to cope with the small scale variability.

In Figure 7, a commonly used theoretical model (a spherical model) fitted to a real variogram curve is shown together with the main parameters described.

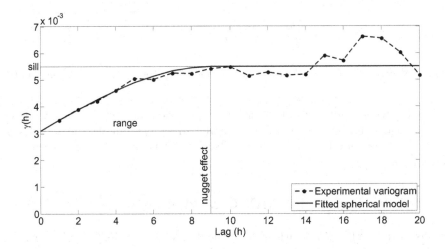

Fig. 7. An empirical variogram and the corresponding analytical spherical model fitted. Main variogram parameters are indicated.

Despite the fact that variogram was originally devised in a spatial statistics framework, it can be conveniently applied to time series. Many authors [15,11,14] have used the variogram, together with classic signal processing techniques, as a tool for the study of the periodicity of signals and for general time series analysis.

In the case of temporal signals, the distance parameter h becomes unidimensional and it simply represents the time lag between the samples.

The number of pairs available is a linearly decreasing function with its maximum at lag $h = 1$. For this reason, the reliability of the sample variogram values decreases with the lag. The variogram values estimated for the first lags are more reliable than the ones estimated for further lags. Fortunately, the most revealing part of the behaviour of a variogram is at the small scale, where it evolves faster, whereas a less interesting and rather constant behaviour is found at larger scales. In Figure 8, a typical temporal variogram that illustrates these observations is shown.

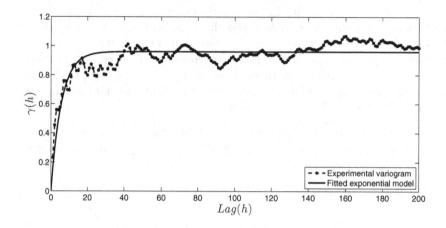

Fig. 8. A temporal variogram. An exponential model is fitted to the experimental data.

Finally, when applied to audio signals, the variogram curve typically shows a periodical behaviour. In fact, the squared difference among the samples is affected by the periodicity of the signal itself and it is faithfully reflected by the variogram.

4   The Variogram for MFCC Modelling

In this work, the temporal variogram is calculated on the MFCCs and is thereby used as a tool to model the variation of the cepstral descriptors over the time fragments. A modification of the variogram proposed in [23] and a series of choices for the calculation of the distance are tested.

For the calculation of the MFCC, the input signal is split into a series of non-overlapping chunks with 1024 samples each. A hamming function is applied to each chunk. The number of Mel filters employed (the triangular filter bank) is 40 and the number of DCT coefficients stored is 13. Thus, using this set of parameters, one minute of an audio signal is represented by an MFCC matrix of 13×2583 samples.

When the variogram is applied to the MFCCs, the lag values correspond to a temporal distance in terms of the number of chunks into which the song had been split. In order to define a standard measure for the quantitative comparison between the songs, each variogram is normalized by the global variance of the MFCC analysed. The result is an empirical variogram with asymptotic tendency towards a reference variance of one. This is called the *standardized variogram* [23].

The variogram approach is applied to the 2004 Audio Description Contest (pre-MIREX) database for genre classification. This is a set of about 700 songs, whose duration is between 5 seconds and 5 minutes.

For the analysis, two different options related to the usage of the variogram are considered: the *full variogram* and the *reduced variogram*.

4.1   The Full Variogram

The so-called *full variogram* is the variogram of the second MFCC, calculated from lag 1 to 200. That is, the temporal separation between the pairs of sampled considered ranges from 1 chunk (1024 samples, about 23 ms) to 200 chunks (about 4.6 seconds). The resulting unidimensional vector of 200 elements corresponds to the song signature.

This approach implies a compression rate, regarding the data employed for the evaluation of music similarity, of about 93% in the case of the shortest audio fragment (5 seconds): the process converts about 2800 samples of the original MFCC matrix (with size 215×13) into 200 samples of the variogram vector. In the case of the largest audio fragment (with a maximum duration of 5 minutes), the compression rate is about 99.8%: 168000 samples from the original MFCC matrix (with size 12919×13) are converted into the 200 samples of the variogram vector.

In Figure 9, two examples of the full variogram are shown, calculated on the second MFCC of two different songs from the sets of songs corresponding to the classical and electronic genres. The large differences expected when comparing these two songs of very different genres are reflected by the variogram functions obtained.

The second MFCC of the two songs is rather different: that of the classical piece shows a more structured and smoother variability than that of the electronic piece. Also, the classical piece shows few high-frequency components and a hidden (or missing) periodicity, unlike the electronic piece. On the other hand, the variogram function obtained for the electronic piece looks much fuzzier and with a larger contribution of high frequencies than the classical one. Also, a clear periodical behaviour is found for the electronic piece.

Furthermore, the variogram function obtained for the classical piece reveals a high pairwise continuity at the small scale (the nugget effect is null) and a smoothly increasing variance with a clear asymptotic trend towards the range. Conversely, the variogram of the electronic piece is much more unstructured, with continuous periodic oscillations coupled with a weak asymptotic trend. Also, the nugget effect in this latter case is large.

4.2   The Reduced Variogram

The *reduced variogram* is calculated using 12 MFCCs (from the second MFCC to the last one), on a reduced bunch of lags.

A total amount of 20 lags are sampled with a logarithmically varying density, from 1 to 200. Thus, the number of lags considered is concentrated at the small

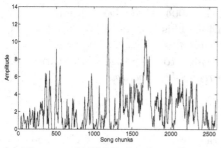

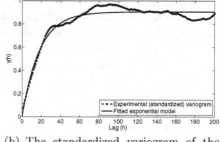

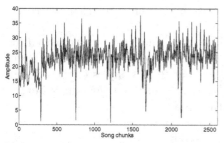

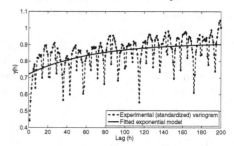

(a) The second MFCC of a classical piece.

(b) The standardized variogram of the second MFCC of the classical piece.

(c) The second MFCC of an electronic piece.

(d) The standardized variogram of the second MFCC of the electronic piece.

Fig. 9. Two examples of the full standardized variogram function obtained for the second MFCC of two different songs of the classical (top) and electronic (bottom) genres (respectively). The excerpts analysed have a duration of 1 minute.

scale, where most of the relevant information should be found (see Figure 10). The signature matrix found is of dimensions 12×20.

In Figure 11, the reduced versions of the full variogram of Figure 9 are shown.

The conclusions drawn for the reduced variograms are the same as the ones found for the full variogram. The classical piece shows a smoother variogram, a more structured variability and a higher small-scale pairwise continuity than the electronic piece. Conversely, the electronic track reveals a larger variability of its structure and a marked periodical behaviour. In both cases, the reduction of the number of lags does not substantially affect the representation of the original full variogram.

5   Distance Measures

In order to obtain an estimation of the degree of similarity between songs, the signatures extracted from them have to be quantitatively compared. To this end, a distance or separation measure must be defined. In this work, a weighted Euclidean distance is used.

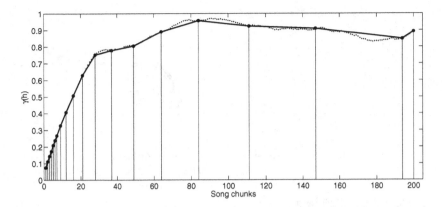

Fig. 10. The reduced variogram function (solid line) for the classical piece of Figure 9(b) obtained by the logarithmic lag subsampling process. The samples employed to define the reduced variogram are marked by stems.

The distance is calculated as follows:

$$D_{i,j} = \sqrt{\sum_{k=1}^{n} \left((V_i(k) - V_j(k)) \cdot w(k) \right)^2} \tag{8}$$

where $V_i(k)$ and $V_j(k)$ are the values of the k-th lag of the variograms of the songs i and j. $w(k)$ is the weight of the k-th lag. The maximum number of lags n is 240 for a bi-dimensional reduced variogram and 200 for a full unidimensional variogram. Note that the bi-dimensional variogram is reordered into a unidimensional vector to simplify the calculations.

As previously observed, the variogram stores most of its information (in terms of quality and reliability) at the small scale. The most meaningful measures come from the first lags, until the range is reached. Remember that beyond the range, the values of the variogram function loose significance. For this reason, three different sets of weights are proposed: a set of exponentially decreasing weights, a set of logarithmically decreasing weights and, finally, a set of linearly decreasing weights. Additionally, the Euclidean distance (unweighted) is also considered.

In Figure 12, the three sets of weights selected are compared. Note that the vectors of weights represented correspond to the stacked vectors obtained when the reduced variogram (20 lags) is considered. In all cases, the weights are normalized so that their sum is 1.

6 Evaluation of the Performance of the Algorithms

Using each of the two options described for the usage of the variogram in the context of MFCCs and music similarity evaluation, a set of four different weighting configurations for the definition of the weighted Euclidean distance have been

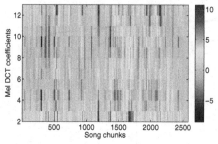

(a) Whole MFCCs matrix of a classical piece.

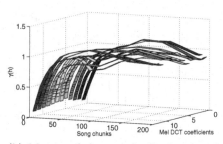

(b) Matrix of the standardized reduced variogram of the whole MFCCs matrix. Classical piece.

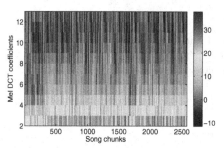

(c) Whole MFCCs matrix of an electronic piece.

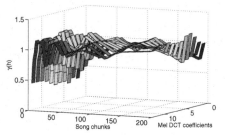

(d) Matrix of the standardized reduced variogram of the whole MFCCs matrix. Electronic piece.

Fig. 11. The matrices of the standardized reduced variogram of the whole MFCC matrices for two different songs. The songs correspond to the classical and electronic genre, at the top and the bottom of the figure, respectively. The excerpts analysed have a duration of 1 minute.

defined, as previously stated: the three weighting vectors previously defined and a fourth one, corresponding to the unweighted configuration.

The evaluation of the performance of the methods is done on the basis of the genre classification music database of the 2004 Audio Description Contest of the ISMIR2004 conference [5]. Undoubtedly, ISMIR is, nowadays, a reference in this context.

The only real freely available music collection for these purposes is limited to the Magnatune dataset released in 2004 in the first (pre-) MIREX contest on audio description. This database is under Creative Commons license and it is currently freely downloadable from the MIREX website. The collection is part of the whole database employed in the task devoted to the classification of music genres during the ISMIR2004 conference. It consists of a series of more than 700 pieces unequally grouped into six music genres: classical, electronic, jazz/blues, metal/punk, rock/pop and world. The audio waveforms are sampled at 44100 Hz.

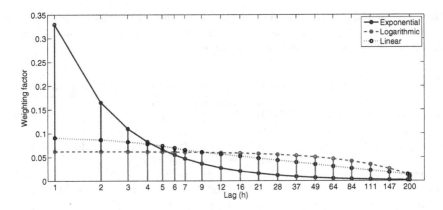

Fig. 12. The three vectors of weights employed for the calculation of the distance measure: exponentially decreasing weights, logarithmically decreasing weights and linearly decreasing weights. Note that the observed shape of the linear weights is due to the fact that the lag axis is logarithmic.

The pseudo-objective evaluation [7], currently employed in the MIREX music similarity tasks, is performed. The matching rates of artist, album and (artist-filtered) genre for the first 5, 10, 20 and 50 songs are calculated. The matching values are expressed as a function of the number of available pieces per artist, album and genre. In this way, the unequal distribution of pieces in the database is taken into account.

In Table 1, the matching scores of the music similarity evaluation scheme for the two different strategies of utilization of the variogram described are shown.

The performance obtained using the reduced variogram is globally better than the one attained using the full variogram, for any kind of weighting configuration. Remember that although the full variogram contains a more complete information of the second (and most representative) MFCC than the reduced model, the reduced model is calculated on a smaller but more reliable (globally) bunch of lags. Apparently, the loss of information due to the reduction of the lags considered is compensated more than necessary by the improvement derived from the utilization of the more reliable samples.

Different trends of the variation of the scores for the three different categories (artist, album and genre) are observed. In particular, the artist- and album-based scores increase with the number of items considered; however, the genre scores evolve with opposite tendency.

The best results found using the full variogram (e.g. 43.62%, obtained for the genre coincidence of the first 5 items of the list) have been obtained with the set of exponentially decreasing weights. Using this set of weights, the contribution of the first lags to the distance measure is more important than in the other cases. Surprisingly, the result found when the reduced variogram is used is different: the best scores obtained correspond to the utilization of the raw Euclidean distance. However, in this latter case, the trend is not as clear as in the former one.

Table 1. Pseudo-objective evaluation of the music similarity estimation strategy proposed using both the full variogram and the reduced variogram. Note that the genre scores are calculated on the artist-filtered subset.

	Full variogram				Reduced variogram			
	Euclidean distance							
Artist	4.50	5.47	8.40	16.43	15.23	16.32	21.59	32.38
Album	3.42	5.65	9.23	17.97	13.03	17.55	25.23	36.07
Genre	38.19	38.08	37.63	37.25	48.48	47.68	46.18	43.70
	Exponential weights							
Artist	7.24	9.12	13.01	23.63	16.99	18.47	23.11	34.26
Album	5.29	8.52	14.23	26.20	13.25	19.14	26.30	37.69
Genre	43.62	42.46	41.85	40.16	46.43	45.29	44.17	43.23
	Logarithmic weights							
Artist	5.20	5.94	9.37	18.05	15.81	16.70	21.88	32.86
Album	3.86	5.70	10.43	19.40	12.62	17.83	25.72	37.03
Genre	38.72	38.48	38.41	37.65	48.07	46.66	45.51	42.84
	Linear weights							
Artist	5.14	5.81	8.90	18.45	16.51	17.70	22.40	33.77
Album	3.79	5.47	9.64	19.44	12.93	19.15	26.74	38.68
Genre	39.25	38.44	38.40	37.79	47.84	46.94	44.81	42.73
	First 5	First 10	First 20	First 50	First 5	First 10	First 20	First 50

The scores obtained by the two possibilities of the utilization of the variogram described, for the different genres, show a non-uniform behaviour for both choices. See Figure 13.

It is important to observe the correlation of this set of scores with the unequal number of songs available per genre in the database employed in the experiments (see Table 2). This seems to be a further confirmation of the necessity of a more representative database whose structure does not influence the results.

In this analysis, it can be observed that the distribution of scores is not equal for the two methods. The method that uses the reduced variogram seems to perform rather better than the one that uses the full variogram on the genres with the largest number of pieces available. On the other hand, the usage of the reduced variogram seems to lead to worse performance than the full variogram

Table 2. Percentages of the number of songs available per genre in the database

Genre	Songs available per genre (%)
Classical	43.9
Electronic	15.8
Jazz/Blues	3.6
Metal/Punk	6.2
Rock/Pop	13.8
World	16.7

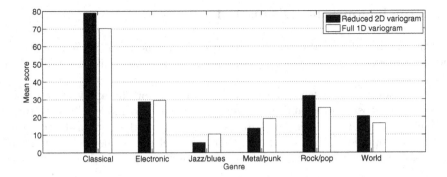

Fig. 13. The artist-filtered genre scores for the first 5 items, calculated for the two best configurations of the two variogram-based approaches: the exponentially weighted distance measure for the full variogram and the Euclidean distance for the reduced variogram

Table 3. Average artist-filtered genre scores of the algorithms proposed for the MIREX 2011 contest [1]. The method acronyms correspond to the standard coding employed in the MIREX contest.

Method	First 5	First 10	First 20	First 50
STBD1	24.19	23.34	22.14	20.57
STBD2	23.55	22.56	21.61	19.98
STBD3	23.07	22.55	21.78	20.47
DM2	46.02	44.14	42.22	39.28
DM3	46.08	44.20	42.33	39.37
GKC1	23.45	22.55	21.57	20.01
HKHLL1	34.91	33.81	32.72	31.39
ML1	41.77	39.86	38.09	35.53
ML2	40.19	38.45	36.28	33.62
ML3	41.06	38.99	36.80	33.85
PS1	54.11	52.17	50.13	46.74
SSKS3	54.65	53.15	51.52	48.98
SSPK2	54.24	52.75	51.19	48.56
YL1	37.40	35.43	33.01	29.54

on the two genres with the smaller number of songs: the Jazz/blues and the Metal/punk genres. In these two genres, the full variogram attains better results.

For comparison purposes, the results of the pseudo-objective evaluation of the algorithms proposed for the Audio Music Similarity contest of the MIREX 2011 [1] are reported in Table 3 (only artist-filtered genre scores).

As shown, the scores obtained for the variogram-based approaches are in the same range as the references found in the results of the MIREX Audio Music Similarity task.

7   Conclusions and Discussion

In this chapter, the utilization of an analysis technique from the spatial statistics field has been proposed for the development of music similarity evaluation algorithms.

The variogram represents the most popular tool for the analysis of spatial variables in geostatistics, and is commonly employed to model the structured variability for spatial prediction utilities. The usage of the temporal variogram has been proposed in this work, as a tool to model the temporal variability of the Mel Frequency Cepstral Coefficients in the context of the evaluation of music similarity.

A brief description of the theory of variogram analysis has been given. The idea for the adaptation of the variogram to a temporal framework has also been presented. Then, two different alternatives for the calculation of the variogram to define song signatures have been proposed: the full variogram and the reduced variogram. Four related distance measurement functions for the calculation of the distance between the song signatures have been evaluated.

The two approaches developed have been tested on a reference database of songs divided into six different genres. A pseudo-objective analysis has been computed in order to achieve a quantitative evaluation of the performance of the methods. Also, a comparison with a known reference, in terms of the evaluation of algorithms for the measurement of music similarity, has been shown.

The reduced variogram obtained better scores than the full variant. The method does not seem to be actually influenced by the kind of weighting function used for the calculation of the distance between signatures. The results attained by the approaches proposed are in the range of the reference scores found in the Audio Music Similarity contest of the MIREX 2011.

All the variograms analysed are obtained by the application of the estimation equation (7). In the future developments, the theoretical models to fit the variogram can be employed to model the variogram function with a series of parameters. In particular, the nugget effect, the range and the sill of the theoretical models could be employed as low-level descriptors for classification purposes.

In order to test this concept, a simple approach has been evaluated. A least square fit algorithm for the exponential model has been implemented. It has been applied to the variograms of the songs of the collection used in this chapter in order to produce an initial estimation of the nugget effect. Then, it has been employed as a low-level descriptor, together with other popular MIR descriptors [25], and evaluated in a music genre classifier. The classifier employed was a simple knn-classifier, with $k = 5$. The results are rather encouraging. The performance of the usage of the nugget effect is similar to that of other popular features or better in some specific cases as in the genre world.

The process of fitting models to the empirical variograms is actually a matter of discussion and the issue is far from being solved [17]. However, these preliminary results encourage to focus on the development of automatic fitting processes for the variogram models in order to obtain robust descriptors for MIR tasks.

Acknowledgments. This work has been funded by the Ministerio de Ciencia e Innovación of the Spanish Government under Project TIN2010-21089-C03-02.

References

1. Audio music similarity and retrieval result (2011), http://www.music-ir.org/mirex/wiki/2011:Audio_Music_Similarity_and_Retrieval_Results (last viewed February 2013)
2. American Standard Association: Acoustical Terminology. American National Standards Institute (1960)
3. Aucouturier, J.J., Pachet, F.: Improving timbre similarity: How high is the sky? Journal of Negative Results in Speech and Audio Sciences 1(1) (2004)
4. Aucouturier, J.J., Pachet, F., Sandler, M.: "The way it sounds": timbre models for analysis and retrieval of music signals. IEEE Transactions on Multimedia 7(6), 1028–1035 (2005)
5. Cano, P., Gómez, E., en Gouyon, F., Herrera, P., Koppenberger, M., Ong, B., Serra, X., Streich, S., Wack, N.: Ismir 2004 audio description contest. Tech. rep., Music Technology Group, UPF (2006)
6. Dempster, A.P., Laird, N.M., Rubin, D.B.: Maximum likelihood from incomplete data via the EM algorithm. Journal of the Royal Statistical Society, series B 39(1), 1–38 (1977)
7. Downie, S.J.: The music information retrieval evaluation exchange (mirex). D-Lib Magazine 12(12) (2006)
8. Gómez, E.: Melodic Description of Audio Signals for Music Content Processing. Master's thesis, Doctoral Pre-Thesis Work. UPF (2002), www.files/publications/Phd-2002-Emilia-Gomez.pdf
9. Gouyon, F.: A Computational Approach to Rhythm Description — Audio Features for the Computation of Rhythm Periodicity Functions and their use in Tempo Induction and Music Content Processing. Ph.D. thesis, University Pompeu Fabra, Barcelona, Spain (November 2005), http://www.iua.upf.es/~fgouyon/thesis/
10. Guaus, E.: Audio content processing for automatic music genre classification: descriptors, databases, and classifiers. Ph.D. thesis, Universitat Pompeu Fabra (2009), http://www.dtic.upf.edu/~eguaus/phd/eguaus_phd_2009_genre_classification_A4.pdf
11. Haslett, J.: On the sample variogram and the sample autocovariance for nonstationary time series. The Statistician 46(4), 475–485 (1997)
12. Isaaks, E.H., Srivastava, M.R.: An Introduction to Applied Geostatistics. Oxford University Press, USA (January 1990)
13. Izmirli, O.: Using Spectral Flatness Based Feature for Audio Segmentation and Retrieval. Tech. rep., Department of Mathematics and Computer Science, Connectucut College (1999)
14. Kacha, A., Grenez, F., Schoentgen, J., Benmahammed, K.: Dysphonic speech analysis using generalized variogram. In: Proceedings of the IEEE International Conference on Acoustics, Speech, and Signal Processing (ICASSP 2005), vol. 1, pp. 917–920 (2005)
15. Khachatryan, D., Bisgaard, S.: Some results on the variogram in time series analysis. Quality and Reliability Engineering International (March 2009)
16. Krige, D.G.: A statistical approach to some basic mine valuation problems on the witwatersrand. Journal of the Chemical, Metallurgical and Mining Society of South Africa 52(6), 119–139 (1951)

17. Li, S., Lu, W.: Automatic fit of the variogram. In: Third International Conference on Information and Computing (ICIC), vol. 4, pp. 129–132 (June 2010)
18. Logan, B., Salomon, A.: A music similarity function based on signal analysis. In: IEEE International Conference on Multimedia and Expo., ICME 2001, pp. 745–748 (2001)
19. Mandel, M.I., Ellis, D.P.W.: Song-Level Features and Support Vector Machines for Music Classification. In: Reiss, J.D., Wiggins, G.A. (eds.) Proceedings of the 6th International Conference on Music Information Retrieval (ISMIR), pp. 594–599 (September 2005)
20. Manufacturers, A.M.: The Complete MIDI 1.0 Detailed Specification. MIDI Manufacturers Association Incorporated (1996)
21. Pampalk, E.: Computational Models of Music Similarity and their Application to Music Information Retrieval. Ph.D. thesis, Vienna University of Technology, Vienna (March 2006)
22. Rabiner, L., Juang, B.H.: Fundamentals of speech recognition. Prentice-Hall, Inc., Upper Saddle River (1993)
23. Sammartino, S., Tardón, L.J., de la Bandera, C., Barbancho, I., Barbancho, A.M.: The standardized variogram as a novel tool for music similarity evaluation. In: Proc. of Int. Symposium on Music Information Retrieval (ISMIR 2010), pp. 559–564 (2010)
24. Scheirer, E.D.: Tempo and beat analysis of acoustic musical signals. Journal of the Acoustical Society of America 103(1), 588–601 (1998), http://www.ncbi.nlm.nih.gov/pubmed/9440344
25. Tardón, L.J., Sammartino, S., Barbancho, I.: Design of an efficient music-speech discriminator. Journal of the Acoustical Society of America 127(1), 271–279 (2010)
26. Tzanetakis, G., Cook, P.: Musical genre classification of audio signals. IEEE Transactions on Speech and Audio Processing 10(5), 293–302 (2002)
27. Wackernagel, H.: Multivariate Geostatistics: An Introduction With Applications. Springer-Verlag Telos (January 1999)

Automatic String Detection
for Bass Guitar and Electric Guitar

Jakob Abeßer

Fraunhofer IDMT,
Ehrenbergstr. 17, 98693 Ilmenau, Germany
abr@idmt.fraunhofer.de
http://www.idmt.fraunhofer.de

Abstract. In this paper, we present a machine learning-based approach to automatically estimate the fretboard position (string number and fret number) from recordings of the bass guitar and the electric guitar. We perform different experiments to evaluate the classification performance on isolated note recordings. First, we analyze how the separation of training and test data in terms of instrument, playing-style, and pick-up setting affects the algorithm's performance. Second, we investigate how the performance can be improved by rejecting implausible classification results and by aggregating the classification results over multiple time frames. The algorithm showed highest string classification f-measure values of $F = .93$ for the bass guitar (4 classes) and $F = .90$ for the electric guitar (6 classes). A listening test with 9 participants with classification scores of $F = .26$ and $F = .16$ for bass guitar and electric guitar confirmed that the given tasks are very challenging to human listeners. Finally, we discuss further research directions with special focus on the application of automatic string detection in music education and software.

Keywords: string classification, fretboard position, fingering, bass guitar, electric guitar, inharmonicity coefficient.

1   Introduction

On string instruments such as the bass guitar or the guitar, most notes within the instrument's pitch range can be played at multiple positions on the instrument fretboard. The *fretboard position* of a note is defined by the string number n_s and the fret number n_f. Common music notation such as the *score* does not provide any information about the fretboard positions to be applied. Instead, musicians often have to choose appropriate fretboard positions based on their musical experience and stylistic preferences. The *tablature* notation, on the other hand, is specialized for the geometry of fretted string instruments such as the guitar or the bass guitar. It specifies the string and fret number for each note and thus resolves the ambiguity between note pitch and fretboard position. Figure 1 shows a bass-line both as score and tablature notation.

M. Aramaki et al. (Eds.): CMMR 2012, LNCS 7900, pp. 333–352, 2013.
© Springer-Verlag Berlin Heidelberg 2013

Fig. 1. Score and tablature notation of a bass-line. The four horizontal lines in the tablature notation correspond to the four strings with the tuning E1, A2, D2, and G2 (from bottom to top). The numbers correspond to the fret numbers on the strings that are to be played.

Conventional automatic music transcription algorithms only extract *score-related note parameters* such as pitch, onset, and duration. In order to analyze recordings of string instruments, the string and fret number need to be estimated as additional *instrument-related note parameters*. Algorithms for automatic tablature generation from an audio recordings can be applied in music assistance and music education software. Tablature notations are especially helpful to novices who are not familiar with reading musical scores.

As will be discussed in Section 3, various methods for estimating the fretboard position were proposed in the literature so far, ranging from pure audio-based methods to methods that exploit the visual modality or methods that use attached sensors on the instrument. However, the exclusive focus on audio analysis methods for this purpose bears several advantages: in music performance scenarios involving a bass guitar or an electric guitar, the instrument signals are directly accessible from the instrument's output jack. In contrast, video recordings of performing musicians and the instrument neck are often limited in quality due to movement, shading, and varying lighting conditions on stage. Additional sensors or cameras that need to be attached to the instrument are often obtrusive to the musicians and affect their musical performance. Therefore, we focus on audio-based analysis in this paper.

This paper is structured as follows: In Section 2, we outline the goals and challenges of this work. In Section 3, we discuss existing methods for estimating the fretboard position from string instrument recordings. We introduce a novel audio-based approach in Section 4, starting with the spectral modeling of recorded bass and guitar notes in Section 4.1. Based on the audio features explained in Section 4.2, we illustrate how the fretboard position is automatically estimated in Section 4.3. In Section 5, we present several experiments to evaluate the algorithm's performance and discuss the obtained results. This section also includes the results of a listening test with human participants for the task of string classification. Finally, we conclude our work in Section 6 and give an outlook in Section 7 on future research.

2   Goals and Challenges

In this paper, we aim to estimate the string number n_s from notes recorded with bass guitars and electric guitars. Based on the note (MIDI) pitch P and the string number, we can apply knowledge on the instrument tuning to derive the fret number n_f. In the evaluation experiments described in Section 5, we investigate how the classification results are affected by separating the training and test data according to different criteria such as the instruments, the pick-up (PU) settings, and the applied playing techniques. Furthermore, we analyze if a majority voting scheme that combines multiple string classification results for each note can improve the classification performance. Finally, the obtained results are compared to the human performance for the same task.

The main challenge of this work is to identify suitable audio features that allow to discriminate between notes that, on the one hand, have the same fundamental frequency f_0 but, on the other hand, are played on different strings. The automatic classification of the played string is difficult since the change of fingering alters the sonic properties of the recorded music signal only subtly. This was confirmed in the human listening test presented in Section 5.2.

Classic non-parametric spectral estimation techniques such as the Short-time Fourier Transform (STFT) are affected by the spectral leakage effect: the Fourier Transform of the applied window function limits the achievable frequency resolution to resolve the exact frequency position of spectral peaks. In order to achieve a sufficiently high frequency resolution for estimating the harmonic frequencies of a note, rather larger time frames are necessary. The decreased time resolution is disadvantageous if notes are played with frequency modulation techniques such as bending or vibrato, which cause short-term fluctuations of the harmonic frequencies [1]. This problem is especially impeding in lower frequency bands.

Thus, a system based on non-parametric spectral estimation techniques is only applicable to analyze notes with no or only slow pitch variation. This can be a severe limitation for a real-world application scenario such as music education software. Since we focus on the bass guitar and the electric guitar, frequencies between 41.2 Hz and 659.3 Hz need to be investigated as potential f_0-candidates[1].

3   Related Work

In this section, we discuss previous work on the estimation of the played string and the fretboard position from bass and guitar recordings. First, we review methods that solely focus on analyzing the audio signal. Special focus is given to the analysis of inharmonicity. Then, we compare different hybrid methods that incorporate computer vision techniques, instrument enhancements, and sensors.

---

[1] This corresponds to the most commonly used bass guitar string tunings E2 to G3 and electric guitar string tuning E3 to E5, respectively, and a fret range up to the 12th fret position.

3.1 Audio Analysis

Penttinen et al. estimated the plucking point on a string by analyzing the delay times of the two waves on the string, which travel in opposite directions after the string is plucked [22]. This approach solely focuses on a time-domain analysis and is limited to monophonic signals.

In [3], Barbancho et al. presented an algorithm to estimate the string number from isolated guitar note recordings. The instrument samples used for evaluation were recorded using different playing techniques, different dynamic levels, and guitars with different string material. After the signal envelope is detected in the time-domain, spectral analysis based on STFT is applied to extract the spectral peaks. Then, various audio features related to the timbre of the notes are extracted such as the spectral centroid, the relative harmonic amplitudes of the first four harmonics, and the inharmonicity coefficient (see also Section 3.1). Furthermore, the temporal evolution of the partial amplitudes is captured by fitting an exponentially decaying envelope function. Consequently, only one feature vector can be extracted for each note. As will be shown in Section 4.2, the presented approach in this paper allows us to extract a single feature vectors for each time frame. This allows us to accumulate classification results from multiple feature vectors that were obtained from the same note recording to improve the classification performance (compare Section 4.3). The authors of [3] reported diverse results from the classification experiments. However, they did not provide an overall performance measure to compare against. The performance of the applied classification algorithm strongly varied for different note pitch values as well as for different compilations of the training set in their experiments.

In [2], Barbancho et al. presented a system for polyphonic transcription of guitar chords, which also allows estimation of the fingering of the chord on the guitar. The authors investigated 330 different fingering configurations for the most common three-voiced and four-voiced guitar chords. A Hidden Markov Model (HMM) is used to model all fingering configurations as individual hidden states. Based on an existing multi-pitch estimation algorithm, harmonic saliency values are computed for all possible pitch values within the pitch range of the guitar. Then, these saliency values are used as observations for the HMM. The transitions between different hidden states are furthermore constrained by two models—a musicological model, which captures the likelihood of different chord changes, and an acoustic model, which measures the physical difficulty of changing the chord fingerings. The authors emphasized that the presented algorithm is limited to the analysis of solo guitar recordings. However, in that scenario, the algorithm clearly outperformed a state-of-the-art chord transcription system. The applied dataset contained instrument samples of electric guitar and acoustic guitar.

Maezawa et al. proposed a system for automatic string detection from isolated bowed violin note recordings in [17]. Similar to the bass guitar, the violin has 4 different strings, but within a higher pitch range. The authors analyzed monophonic violin recordings of various classical pieces with given score information. First, the audio signal is temporally aligned to the musical score. For the string classification, filterbank energies are used as audio features and a Gaussian mixture model (GMM) is applied as classifier. The authors proposed two additional steps to increase the robustness of the classification. First, feature averaging and feature normalization are used. Then, a context-dependent error correction is applied, which is based on empirically observed rules describing how musicians choose the string number. The authors investigated how training and testing with the same and different instruments and string types affect the classification scores (similar to Section 5). The highest F-measure value that was achieved for the string classification with 4 classes is $F = .86$.

In [4], Barbancho et al. presented an algorithm for automatic tablature generation from audio recordings of guitar. First, one or multiple fundamental frequencies are detected by investigating the most prominent peaks as f_0-candidates. Each candidate is rated based on the fitness of the corresponding partial peaks to a given model that incorporates inharmonicity. The string and fret number of the detected notes are taken from the best fitting model parameters. Multiple notes are obtained by iteratively removing detected fundamental frequency and harmonic components from the spectrum. For the analysis of guitar chords, the authors focus on two scenarios: guitar chords of arbitrary shape with up to 4 chord notes, and guitar chords with a known (template) shape such as barré chords with up to 6 chord notes. The authors also use constraints to avoid note combinations that exceed the hand span of a musician and thus cannot be played on the guitar neck. The presented algorithm performed well for the fretboard detection of single notes with error rates between 0 and 0.11 for instrument samples of the RWC database and samples recorded by the authors themselves.

Inharmonicity. For musical instruments such as the piano, the guitar, or the bass guitar, the equation describing the vibration of an ideal flexible string is extended by a restoring force caused by the string stiffness [8]. Due to dispersive wave propagation within the vibrating string, the effect of inharmonicity occurs, i.e., the purely harmonic frequency relationship of an ideal string is distorted and the harmonic frequencies are stretched towards higher values as

$$f_k = k f_0 \sqrt{1 + \beta k^2}; \ k \geq 1 \tag{1}$$

with k being the harmonic index of each overtone and f_0 being the fundamental frequency. The inharmonicity coefficient β depends on different properties of the vibrating string such as Young's Modulus E, the radius of gyration K, the string tension T, the cross-sectional area S, as well as the string length L. With the string length being approximately constant for all strings of the bass guitar and the electric guitar, the string diameter usually varies from 0.45 mm to 1.05 mm for electric bass and from 0.1 mm to 0.41 mm for electric guitar[2]. The string tension T is proportional to the square of the fundamental frequency of the vibrating string. Järveläinen et al. performed different listening tests to investigate the audibility of inharmonicity towards humans [13]. They found

---

[2] These values correspond to commonly used string gauges.

that the human audibility threshold for inharmonicity increases with increasing fundamental frequency.

Hodgekinson et al. observed a systematic time-dependence of the inharmonicity coefficient if the string is plucked hard [11]. The authors found that β does not remain constant but increases over time for an acoustic guitar note. In contrast, for a piano note, no such behavior was observed. In this paper, we aim to estimate β within single spectral frames and therefore do not take the temporal evolution of β into account.

Different methods have been applied in the literature to extract the inharmonicity coefficient such as the cepstral analysis, the harmonic product spectrum [9], or inharmonic comb-filter [10]. For the purpose of sound synthesis, especially for physical modeling of string instruments, inharmonicity is often included into the synthesis models in order to achieve a more natural sound [25].

3.2   Hybrid Approaches and Visual Approaches

Different methods for estimating the fretboard position from guitar recordings have been presented in the literature including analysis methods from computer vision as a multi-modal extension of audio-based analysis.

A combined audio and video analysis was proposed by Hybryk and Kim to estimate the fretboard position of chords that were played on an acoustic guitar [12]. The goal of this paper was to first identify a played chord on the guitar in terms of its chord style, i.e., root note and musical mode such as minor or major. For this purpose, the Specmurt [23] algorithm was used for spectral analysis in order to estimate a set of fundamental frequency candidates that can be associated with different note pitches. Based on the computed chord style (e.g., E minor), the chord voicing was estimated by tracking the spatial position of the hand on the instrument neck. The chord voicing is similar to the chord fingering as described in [2].

Another multi-modal approach for transcribing acoustic guitar performances was presented by Paleari et al. in [20]. In addition to audio analysis, the visual modality was analyzed to track the hand of the guitar players during their performance to estimate the fretboard position. The performing musicians were recorded using both two microphones and a digital video camera. The fretboard was first detected and then spatially tracked over time.

Other approaches solely used computer vision techniques for spatial transcription. Burns and Wanderley presented an algorithm for real-time finger-tracking in [5]. They used *attached cameras* on the guitar in order to get video recordings of the playing hand on the instrument neck. Kerdvibulvech and Saito used a stereo-camera setup to record a guitar player in [14]. Their system for finger-tracking requires the musician to wear *colored fingertips*. The main disadvantage of all these approaches is that both the attached cameras as well as the colored fingertips are unnatural for the guitar player. Therefore, they likely limit and impede the musician's expressive gestures and playing style.

Enhanced music instruments are equipped with additional sensors and controllers in order to directly measure the desired parameters instead of estimating

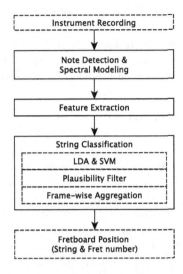

Fig. 2. Algorithm overview

them from the audio or video signal. On the one hand, these approaches lead to a high detection accuracy. On the other hand, these instrument extensions are obstructive to the musicians and can affect their performance on the instrument [12]. In contrast to regular electric guitar pickups, *hexaphonic pickups* separately capture each vibrating string. In this way, spectral overlap between the string signals is avoided, which allows a fast and robust pitch detection with very low latency and very high accuracy, as shown for instance by O'Grady and Rickard in [19].

4   Proposed System

Figure 2 provides an overview over the string classification algorithm proposed in this paper. All processing steps are detailed in the next sections.

4.1   Spectral Modeling

Non-parametric spectral estimation methods such as the Periodogram make no explicit assumption on the type of signal that is analyzed. In order to obtain a high frequency resolution for precise f_0-detection, relatively large time frames of data samples are necessary in order to compensate the spectral leakage effect, which is introduced by windowing the signal into frames. In contrast to the percussive nature of its short attack part (between approx. 20 ms and 40 ms), the decay part of a plucked string note can be modeled by a sum of decaying sinusoidal components. Their frequencies have a nearly perfectly harmonic relationship. Since the strings of the bass guitar and the electric guitar have a certain amount of stiffness, the known phenomenon of inharmonicity appears (compare Section 3.1).

Parametric spectral estimation techniques can be applied if the analyzed signal can be assumed to be generated by a known model. In our case, the power spectral density (PSD) $\Phi(\omega)$ can be modeled by an auto-regressive (AR) filter such as

$$\Phi(\omega) \approx \Phi_{AR}(\omega) = \sigma^2 \left| \frac{1}{1 + \sum_{l=1}^{p} a_l e^{-jl\omega}} \right|^2 \tag{2}$$

with σ^2 denoting the process variance, p denoting the model order, and $\{a_l\} \in \mathbb{R}^{p+1}$ being the filter coefficients. Since auto-regressive processes are closely related to linear prediction (LP), both a *forward prediction error* and a *backward prediction error* can be defined to measure the predictive quality of the AR filter. We use the *least-squares method* (also known as *modified covariance method*) for spectral estimation. It is based on a simultaneous least-squares minimization of both prediction errors with respect to all filter coefficients $\{a_l\}$. This method has been shown to outperform related algorithms such as the Yule-Walker method, the Burg algorithm, and the covariance method (See [18] for more details). The size of the time frames N is only restricted by the model order as $p \leq 2N/3$.

First, we down-sample the signals to $f_s = 5.5$ kHz for the bass guitar samples and $f_s = 10.1$ kHz for the electric guitar samples. This way, we can detect the first 15 harmonics of each note within the instrument pitch ranges, which is necessary for the subsequent feature extraction as explained in Section 4.2. In Figure 3, the estimated AR power spectral density for a bass guitar sample (E1) as well as the estimated partials are illustrated. Within this paper, we compute the fundamental frequency f_0 from the known fretboard position of all notes in the dataset. The separate evaluation of fundamental frequency estimation is not within the scope of this paper.

By using overlapping time frames with a block-size of $N = 256$ and a hop-size of $H = 64$, we apply the spectral estimation algorithm to compute frame-wise estimates of the filter coefficients $\{a_l(n)\}$ in the frames that are selected for analysis (compare Section 4.2). In order to estimate the harmonic frequencies $\{f_k\}$, we first compute the pole frequencies of the AR filter by computing the roots of the numerator in Equation (2). Then, we assign one pole frequency to each harmonic according to the highest proximity to its theoretical frequency value as computed using Equation (1).

4.2   Feature Extraction

Note Detection. In Section 4.1, we discussed that notes played on the bass guitar and the guitar follow a signal model of decaying sinusoidal components, i.e., the partials. In this section, we discuss how we extract audio features that capture the amplitude and frequency characteristics. We first detect the first frame shortly after the note attack part of the note is finished and the harmonic decay part begins. As mentioned in Section 4.1, signal frames with a percussive

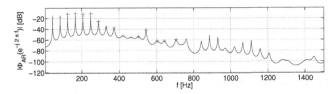

Fig. 3. Estimated AR power spectral density for the bass guitar sample with pitch E1 ($f_0 = 44.1 Hz$). The estimated first 15 partials are indicated with red crosses.

characteristic are indicated by high values of the process variance $\sigma^2(n)$ obtained the AR spectral estimation. We found that time frames after

$$n^\star = \arg\max_n \sigma^2(n) \tag{3}$$

are suitable for feature extraction. If the aggregation of multiple frame-wise results is used, we extract features in the first 5 frames after $n^\star$. If the aggregation is not applied, one feature vector is computed for each note in the first frame after $n^\star$.

Inharmonicity Estimation. In each analyzed frame, we estimate the discrete frequencies f_k of the first 15 partials. Then, we estimate the inharmonicity coefficient β_k as follows. From Equation (1), we obtain

$$(f_k/f_0)^2 = k^2 + \beta k^4 \tag{4}$$

We use polynomial curve fitting to approximate the left-hand side of Equation (4) by a polynomial function of order 4 as

$$(f_k/f_0)^2 \approx \sum_{i=0}^{4} p_i k^i \tag{5}$$

and use the coefficient p_4 as an estimate of the inharmonicity coefficient β:

$$\hat{\beta} \approx p_4 \tag{6}$$

Partial-Based Features. In addition to the inharmonicity coefficient β, we compute various audio features that capture the amplitude and frequency characteristics of the first 15 partials of a note. First, we compute the relative amplitudes

$$\{\hat{a}_{r,k}\} = \{a_k/a_0\} \tag{7}$$

of the first 15 partials related to the amplitude of the fundamental frequency. Then, we approximate the relative partial amplitude values $\{\hat{a}_{r,k}\}$ as a linear function over k as

$$\hat{a}_{r,k} \approx p_1 k + p_0 \tag{8}$$

Table 1. Overview of all applied audio features

Feature	Number of dimensions
Inharmonicity coefficient $\hat{\beta}$	1
Relative partial amplitudes $\{\hat{a}_{r,k}\}$	15
Statistics over $\{\hat{a}_{r,k}\}$	8
Normalized partial frequency deviations $\{\Delta\hat{f}_{norm,k}\}$	15
Statistics over $\{\Delta\hat{f}_{norm,k}\}$	8
Partial amplitude slope $\hat{s}_a$	1
All features	$\sum = 48$

by using linear regression. We use the feature $\hat{s}_a = p_1$ as estimate of the *spectral slope* towards higher partial frequencies.

Based on the estimated inharmonicity coefficient $\hat{\beta}$ and the fundamental frequency f_0, we compute the theoretical partial frequency values $\{f_{k,theo}\}$ of the first 15 partials based on Equation (1) as

$$f_{k,theo} = k f_0 \sqrt{1 + \hat{\beta}k^2}. \tag{9}$$

Then, we compute the deviation between the theoretical and estimated partial frequency values and normalize this difference value as

$$\Delta\hat{f}_{norm,k} = \frac{f_{k,theo} - \hat{f}_k}{\hat{f}_k}. \tag{10}$$

Again, we compute $\{\Delta\hat{f}_{norm,k}\}$ for the first 15 partials and use them as features. In addition, we compute the statistical descriptors: maximum value, minimum value, mean, median, mode (most frequent sample), variance, skewness, and kurtosis over both $\{\hat{a}_{r,k}\}$ and $\{\Delta\hat{f}_{norm,k}\}$. Table 1 provides an overview over all features and their dimensionality.

4.3   Estimation Of the Fretboard Position

String Classification. In order to automatically estimate the fretboard position from a note recording, we first aim to estimate the string number n_s. Therefore, we compute the 48-dimensional feature vector $\{x_i\}$ as described in the previous section. We use Linear Discriminant Analysis (LDA) to reduce the dimensionality of the feature space to $N_d = 3$ dimensions for bass guitar (4 string classes) and to $N_d = 5$ dimensions for guitar (6 string classes)[3], respectively. Then we train a Support Vector Machine (SVM) classifier using a Radial Basis Function (RBF) kernel with the classes defined by notes played on each string. SVM is a binary discriminative classifier that attempts to find an optimal

---

[3] The number of dimensions N_d is chosen as $N_d = N_{strings} - 1$.

decision plane between feature vectors of the different training classes [26]. The two kernel parameters C and γ are optimized based on a three-fold grid search. We use the LIBSVM library for our experiments [6].

The SVM returns the posterior probability $\{p\}$ for each string class. We estimate the string number $\hat{n}_s$ by maximizing p_i as

$$\hat{n}_s = \arg\max_i p_i. \tag{11}$$

We derive the fret number $\hat{n}_f$ from the estimated string number $\hat{n}_s$ by using knowledge of the instrument tuning as follows. The common tuning of the bass is E1, A2, D2, and G2; the tuning of the guitar is E2, A2, D3, G3, B3, and E4. The string tunings can be directly translated into a vector of corresponding MIDI pitch values as $\{P_S\} = [28, 33, 38, 43]$ and $\{P_S\} = [40, 45, 50, 55, 59, 64]$, respectively.

In order to derive the fret number $\hat{n}_s$, we first obtain the MIDI pitch value P that corresponds to the fundamental frequency $\hat{f}_0$ as

$$\hat{P} = \lfloor 12 \log_2(\hat{f}_0/440) - 69 \rfloor \tag{12}$$

Given the estimated string number $\hat{n}_s$, the fret number can be computed as

$$\hat{n}_f = \hat{P} - P_S(\hat{n}_s). \tag{13}$$

A fret number of $\hat{n}_f = 0$ indicates that a note was played by plucking an open string.

Plausibility Filter. As mentioned earlier, most note pitches within the frequency range of both the bass guitar and the guitar can be played on either one, two, or three different fret positions on the instrument neck. The total instrument pitch range is E2 to G3 for the bass guitar and E3 to E5 for the electric guitar[4]. Based on knowledge about the instrument string tunings, we can derive a set of MIDI pitch values that can be played on each string. Therefore, for each estimated MIDI pitch value $\hat{P}$, we can derive a list of strings on which this note can theoretically be played. If the plausibility filter is used, before estimating the string number as shown in Equation (11), we set the probability values in $\{p_i\}$ to zero for all strings, on which this note can not be played on.

Aggregation of Multiple Classification Results. If the result aggregation is used, all class probability values $\{p\}$ are summed up over 5 adjacent time frames and then again normalized to unit sum. The string number is then estimated by applying Equation (11) on the accumulated probability values.

---

[4] Here, a limited fret range up to the 12th fret position is considered in the database.

5   Evaluation and Results

5.1   Dataset

For the evaluation experiments, a dataset of 1034 audio samples was used. These samples are isolated note recordings, which were taken from the dataset previously published in [24].[5] The samples were recorded using two different bass guitars and two different electric guitars, each played with two different plucking styles (plucked with a plectrum and plucked with the fingers) and recorded with two different pick-up settings (either neck pick-up or body pick-up).

5.2   Experiments and Results

Experiment 1: Feature Selection for String Classification. In the first experiment, we aim to identify the most discriminatory features for the automatic string classification task as discussed in Section 4.3. For this purpose, the feature selection algorithm Inertia Ratio Maximization using Feature Space Projection (IRMFSP) [16, 21] was applied to all feature vectors and their corresponding class labels. This experiment was performed separately for both instruments. Table 2 lists the five most discriminatory features that were first selected by the IRMFSP algorithm for the bass guitar and the electric guitar.

The features $\Delta \hat{f}_{norm}$, $\hat{\beta}$, and $\hat{a}_{r,k}$ as well as the derived statistic measures were selected consistently for both instruments. These features measure frequency and amplitude characteristics of the partials and show high discriminative power between notes played on different strings independently of the applied instrument. The boxplots of the two most discriminative features $\Delta f_{norm,9}$ for bass and $\Delta f_{norm,15}$ for guitar are illustrated separately for each instrument string in Figure 4.

Since the deviation of the estimated harmonic frequencies from their theoretical values seems to carry distinctive information to discern between notes on different instrument strings, future work should investigate whether Equation (1) could be extended by higher order polynomial terms in order to better fit to the estimated harmonic frequency values.

Experiment 2: String Classification in Different Conditions. In this experiment, we aim to investigate the influence of

- the separation of the training and test set according to the applied instrument, playing technique, and pick-up setting,
- the instrument / the number of string classes,
- the use of a plausibility filter (compare Section 4.3),
- and the use of a aggregation of multiple classification results for each sample (compare Section 4.3).

on the performance of the automatic string classification algorithm.

---

[5] This dataset contains isolated notes from bass guitar and electric guitar processed with various audio effects. In this work, only the non-processed note recordings were used.

Table 2. Most discriminative audio features for the string classification task as discussed in Section 5.2. Features are given in order as selected by the IRMFSP algorithm.

Rank	Bass Guitar	Electric Guitar
1	$\Delta\hat{f}_{norm,9}$	$\Delta\hat{f}_{norm,15}$
2	$\hat{\beta}$	$\text{mean}\{\hat{a}_{r,k}\}$
3	$\Delta\hat{f}_{norm,3}$	$\text{var}\{\Delta\hat{f}_{norm,k}\}$
4	$\text{var}\{\Delta\hat{f}_{norm,k}\}$	$\text{max}\{\hat{a}_{r,k}\}$
5	$\hat{a}_{r,4}$	$\text{skew}\{\Delta\hat{f}_{norm,k}\}$

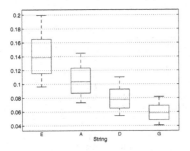 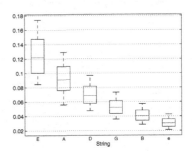

(a) Boxplot of feature $\Delta f_{norm,9}$ for bass.　(b) Boxplot of feature $\Delta f_{norm,15}$ for guitar.

Fig. 4. Boxplots of the two most discriminative features for bass guitar and electric guitar

The different experiment conditions are illustrated in Table 3 for the bass guitar and in Table 4 for the electric guitar. The colums "Separated instruments", "Separated playing techniques", and "Separated pick-up setting" indicate which criteria were applied to separate the samples from training and test set in each configuration. The fifth and sixth columns indicate whether the plausibility filter (compare Section 4.3) and the frame result aggregation (compare Section 4.3) were applied. In the seventh column, the number of folds for the configuration 1.6 and 2.6 and the number of permutations for the remaining configurations are given. The evaluation measures precision, recall, and F-measure were always averaged over all permutations and all folds, respectively.

After the training set and the test set were separated, the columns of the training feature matrix were first normalized to zero mean and unit variance. The mean vector and the variance vector were kept for later normalization of the test data. Subsequently, the normalized training feature matrix was used to derive the transformation matrix via LDA. The SVM model was then trained using the projected training feature matrix and a two-dimensional grid search is performed to determine the optimal parameters C and γ as explained in 4.3. For the configurations 1.6 and 2.6, none of the criteria to separate the training

Table 3. Mean Precision $\bar{P}$, mean Recall $\bar{R}$, and mean F-Measure $\bar{F}$ for different evaluation conditions (compare Section 5.2) for the bass guitar

Experiment	Separated instruments	Separated playing techniques	Separated pick-up settings	Plausibility filter (see Section 4.3)	Result aggregation over 5 frames (see Section 4.3)	No. of Permutations° / No. of CV folds*	Precision $\bar{P}$	Recall $\bar{R}$	F-Measure $\bar{F}$
1.1.a	x					2°	.85	.85	.85
1.1.b	x			x		2°	.87	.87	.87
1.1.c	x			x	x	2°	.78	.78	.78
1.2.a	x	x				8°	.86	.86	.86
1.2.b	x	x		x		8°	.87	.87	.87
1.2.c	x	x		x	x	8°	.88	.88	.88
1.3.a	x	x				8°	.57	.50	.49
1.3.b	x	x		x		8°	.71	.69	.69
1.3.c	x	x		x	x	8°	.88	.88	.88
1.4.a	x					8°	.60	.54	.54
1.4.b	x			x		8°	.73	.71	.72
1.4.c	x			x	x	8°	**.93**	**.93**	**.93**
1.5.a		x				8°	.62	.55	.54
1.5.b		x		x		8°	.74	.71	.71
1.5.c		x		x	x	8°	.92	.92	.92
1.6.a						10*	.92	.92	.92
1.6.b				x		10*	.93	.93	.93
1.6.c				x	x	10*	**.93**	**.93**	**.93**

and the test set was applied. Instead, here we used a 10-fold cross-validation and averaged the precision, recall, and F-measure over all folds.

The results shown in Table 3 and Table 4 clearly show that both the plausibility filter as well as the result aggregation step significantly improved the classification results in most of the investigated configurations. Furthermore, it can be seen that the separation of training and test samples according to instrument, playing technique, and pick-up setting has a strong influence on the achievable classification performance. In general, the results obtained for the bass guitar and the electric guitar show the same trends. We obtain the highest classification scores—$\bar{F} = .93$ for the bass guitar (4 classes) and $\bar{F} = .90$ for the electric guitar (6 classes)—for the configurations 1.6 and 2.6. These results indicate that the presented method can be successfully applied in different application tasks that require an automatic estimation of the played instrument string. In contrast to [17], we did not make use of any knowledge about the musical context such as that which may be derived from a musical score.

Experiment 3: Baseline Experiment Using MFCC Featues. We performed a baseline experiment separately for both instruments using Mel Fre-

Table 4. Mean Precision $\bar{P}$, mean Recall $\bar{R}$, and mean F-Measure $\bar{F}$ for different evaluation conditions (compare Section 5.2) for the electric guitar

Experiment	Separated instruments	Separated playing techniques	Separated pick-up settings	Plausibility filter (see Section 4.3)	Result aggregation over 5 frames (see Section 4.3)	No. of Permutations° / No. of CV folds*	Precision $\bar{P}$	Recall $\bar{R}$	F-Measure $\bar{F}$
2.1.a	x					2°	.64	.64	.63
2.1.b	x			x		2°	.70	.70	.70
2.1.c	x			x	x	2°	.76	.75	.75
2.2.a	x	x				8°	.69	.69	.68
2.2.b	x	x		x		8°	.71	.71	.70
2.2.c	x	x		x	x	8°	.78	.77	.77
2.3.a	x	x	x			8°	.61	.57	.56
2.3.b	x	x	x	x		8°	.68	.66	.66
2.3.c	x	x	x	x	x	8°	.74	.74	.73
2.4.a	x					8°	.64	.61	.60
2.4.b	x			x		8°	.71	.69	.69
2.4.c	x			x	x	8°	.80	.79	.79
2.5.a		x				8°	.69	.65	.65
2.5.b		x		x		8°	.74	.72	.72
2.5.c		x		x	x	8°	.84	.84	.84
2.6.a						10*	.72	.69	.70
2.6.b				x		10*	.81	.81	.81
2.6.c				x	x	10*	.90	.90	.90

quency Cepstral Coefficients (MFCC) as features. Again, LDA and SVM were applied for feature space transformation and classification respectively, as explained in Section 4.3. The same experimental conditions as in configuration 1.6. and 2.6. (see 5.2) were used. The classification results were performed and evaluated on a frame level. A 10-fold stratified cross-validation was applied and the results were averaged over all folds. We achieved classification scores of $\bar{F} = .46$ for the bass guitar and $\bar{F} = .37$ for the electric guitar.

Experiment 4: Human Performance on String Classification. In the final experiment, we aim to investigate the performance of human listeners for the given task of classifying the string number based on isolated bass guitar and electric guitar notes. The study comprised 9 participants, most of them being semi-professional guitar or bass players. To allow for a comparison between the algorithm performance and the human performance, similar test conditions must be guaranteed. Based on the results shown in Table 3 and Table 4, the conditions of Experiments 1.6.c and 2.6.c are used for the listening test. The samples are randomly assigned to training and test set—no separation based on playing technique, pick-up setting, or instrument is performed.

During the training phase, the participants could listen to as many notes from the training set for each string class as they wanted to. Afterwards, they were asked to assign randomly selected samples from the test set to one of the 4 or 6 string classes, respectively. Overall, 578 guitar notes and 522 bass notes were annotated with a string number.

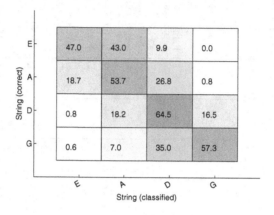

(a) Bass guitar notes.

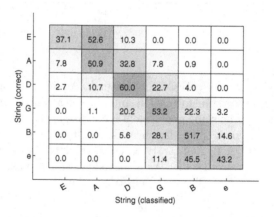

(b) Electric guitar notes.

Fig. 5. Confusion matrix from human performance for string classification. All values are given in percent.

As it can be seen in the two confusion matrices in Figure 5, human listeners tend to confuse notes between adjacent strings on the instrument. In total, classification scores of $\bar{F} = .27$ for the bass guitar and $\bar{F} = .16$ for the electric guitar were achieved.

6   Conclusions

In this paper, we performed several experiments geared towards the automatic classification of the string number from given isolated note recordings. We presented a selection of audio features that can be extracted on a frame-level. In order to improve the classification results, we first applied a plausibility filter to avoid non-meaningful classification results. Then, we used an aggregation of multiple classification results obtained from adjacent frames of the same note. Highest string classification scores of $\bar{F} = .93$ for the bass guitar (4 string classes) and $\bar{F} = .90$ for the electric guitar (6 string classes) were achieved. As shown in a baseline experiment, classification systems based on commonly-used audio features such as MFCC were clearly outperformed for the given task. The task of automatic string detection is very challenging for human listeners as the results of a listening tests confirmed: F-measure values of only $\bar{F} = .27$ and $\bar{F} = .16$ could be achieved for the bass guitar and the electric guitar, respectively.

7   Outlook

7.1   String Detection for Melodies and Chords

As mentioned in Section 2, guitar players and bass players usually choose the fingering to play a given music score in such a way that the overall physical strain is minimized. One major characteristic of this behavior is the preference of vertical play over horizontal play on the instrument neck: instead of playing melodies only on one or two adjacent strings with a strong vertical hand movement over the instrument neck, musicians prefer to stay in a fixed fretboard position as long as possible and try to use the whole possible pitch range, available there. This knowledge could be used to implement a temporal modeling of fretboard position changes over time using a Hidden-Markov Model (HMM) or a comparable method.

Secondly, polyphonic music signals such as chords played on a guitar were not covered in this paper. Multi-pitch estimation is still one of the most challenging tasks in Music Information Retrieval [7, 15]. In order to apply the feature-based approach for string detection as presented in this paper, several challenges need to be overcome. Guitar chords often contain up to 6 simultaneous sounding notes and furthermore include many octave intervals. As a consequence, many of the harmonics overlap in the frequency domain. This impedes the precise estimation of the harmonic frequency values and the computation of meaningful audio features (compare 4.2). Fortunately, all notes in guitar chords are always played within a fixed fret range on the instrument neck due to the limited span of the human hand. Thus, even if the string classification results are erroneous for some notes of a chord, the use of a majority voting scheme could be applied over all single string classification results to get a robust estimate of the overall fretboard position of an analyzed chord.

7.2 Application of String Classification for Music Education Software

In the context of music education software, the main application of string classification is to automatically evaluate how well a musician follows a given tablature. String classification can therefore be interpreted as an extension to conventional music transcription systems that is tailored for the analysis of string instrument performances. Assuming that the system can initially be trained with a dataset comparable to the one used in this paper, the system performance on notes from a different instrument[6] will likely be as in Experiment 1.1. or 2.1. since in these experiments, different instruments are used for training and testing.

In order to improve classification results, the *online learning* paradigm can be applied here: by using the software with his or her instrument, the user will continuously provide new training data to the system. The program can adapt to the timbre of the applied instrument by taking a selection of the recorded instrument notes. The class label of each new note can be taken from the corresponding playing instruction in the program. After adapting to the new instrument, the classification results will likely achieve values comparable to Experiment 1.6. or 2.6. In the context of a music learning application, no strict separation between training and test data is necessary, and "overfitting" to the player's instrument is reasonable and beneficial for the system's overall performance. However, occasional playing errors that involve playing on the wrong string could lead to the selection of training samples with erroneous string class labels. Those training samples could corrupt the improvements gained from using online learning.

Another challenge that was not covered in this paper is that in practice, strings with different material and gauges are used for different music styles. The string gauge directly affects the string inharmonicity coefficient and thus the features used for string classification. If the training samples for each string class are recorded with instruments having too many different string gauges, the class distributions in the feature space will overlap more and the classification performance is expected to decrease.

Acknowledgements. The author author would like to thank all participants of the listening tests as well as Michael Stein for the use of his data set. The Thuringian Ministry of Economy, Employment and Technology supported this research by granting funds of the European Fund for Regional Development to the project *Songs2See*[7], enabling transnational cooperation between Thuringian companies and their partners from other European regions.

---

[6] Since the musician uses his or her own instrument, it is most likely that this instrument is not incorporated in the initial training set.

[7] http://www.songs2see.net

References

1. Abeßer, J., Dittmar, C., Schuller, G.: Automatic Recognition and Parametrization of Frequency Modulation Techniques in Bass Guitar Recordings. In: Proc. of the 42nd Audio Engineering Sociery (AES) International Conference on Semantic Audio, Ilmenau, Germany, pp. 1–8 (2011)
2. Barbancho, A.M., Klapuri, A., Tardón, L.J., Barbancho, I.: Automatic Transcription of Guitar Chords and Fingering from Audio. IEEE Transactions on Audio, Speech, and Language Processing, 1–19 (2011)
3. Barbancho, I., Barbancho, A.M., Tardón, L.J., Sammartino, S.: Pitch and Played String Estimation in Classic and Acoustic Guitars. In: Proceedings of the 126th Audio Engineering Society (AES) Convention, Munich, Germany (2009)
4. Barbancho, I., Member, S., Tardón, L.J., Sammartino, S., Barbancho, A.M.: Inharmonicity-Based Method for the Automatic Generation of Guitar Tablature. IEEE Transactions on Audio, Speech, and Language Processing 20(6), 1857–1868 (2012)
5. Burns, A., Wanderley, M.: Visual Methods for the Retrieval of Guitarist Fingering. In: Proceedings of the 2006 International Conference on New Interfaces for Musical Expression (NIME 2006), Paris, France, pp. 196–199 (2006), http://portal.acm.org/citation.cfm?id=1142263
6. Chang, C.C., Lin, C.J.: LIBSVM: A Library for Support Vector Machines. Tech. rep., Department of Computer Science, National Taiwan University, Taipei, Taiwan (2011)
7. Christensen, M.G., Jakobsson, A.: Multi-Pitch Estimation. Synthesis Lectures on Speech and Audio Processing, Morgan & Claypool Publishers (2009)
8. Fletcher, N.H., Rossing, T.D.: The Physics of Musical Instruments, 2nd edn. Springer, New York (1998)
9. Galembo, A., Askenfelt, A.: Measuring inharmonicity through pitch extraction. Speech Transmission Laboratory. Quarterly Progress and Status Reports (STL-QPSR) 35(1), 135–144 (1994)
10. Galembo, A., Askenfelt, A.: Signal representation and estimation of spectral parameters by inharmonic comb filters with application to the piano. IEEE Transactions on Speech and Audio Processing 7(2), 197–203 (1999)
11. Hodgkinson, M., Timoney, J., Lazzarini, V.: A Model of Partial Tracks for Tension-Modulated Steel-String Guitar Tones. In: Proc. of the 13th Int. Conference on Digital Audio Effects (DAFX 2010), Graz, Austria, pp. 1–8 (2010)
12. Hrybyk, A., Kim, Y.: Combined Audio and Video for Guitar Chord Identification. In: Proc. of the 11th International Society for Music Information Retrieval Conference (ISMIR), Utrecht, Netherlands, pp. 159–164 (2010)
13. Järveläinen, H., Välimäki, V., Karjalainen, M.: Audibility of the timbral effects of inharmonicity in stringed instrument tones. Acoustics Research Letters Online 2(3), 79 (2001)
14. Kerdvibulvech, C., Saito, H.: Vision-Based Guitarist Fingering Tracking Using a Bayesian Classifier and Particle Filters. In: Mery, D., Rueda, L. (eds.) PSIVT 2007. LNCS, vol. 4872, pp. 625–638. Springer, Heidelberg (2007)
15. Klapuri, A.: Multipitch analysis of polyphonic music and speech signals using an auditory model. IEEE Transactions on Audio, Speech, and Language Processing 16(2), 255–266 (2008)
16. Lukashevich, H.: Feature selection vs. feature space transformation in automatic music genre classification tasks. In: Proc. of the AES Convention (2009)

17. Maezawa, A., Itoyama, K., Takahashi, T., Ogata, T., Okuno, H.G.: Bowed String Sequence Estimation of a Violin Based on Adaptive Audio Signal Classification and Context-Dependent Error Correction. In: Proc. of the 11th IEEE International Symposium on Multimedia (ISM 2009), pp. 9–16 (2009)
18. Marple, S.L.: Digital Spectral Analysis With Applications. Prentice Hall, Australia (1987)
19. O'Grady, P.D., Rickard, S.T.: Automatic Hexaphonic Guitar Transcription Using Non-Negative Constraints. In: Proc. of the IET Irish Signals and Systems Conference (ISSC), Dublin, Ireland, pp. 1–6 (2009)
20. Paleari, M., Huet, B., Schutz, A., Slock, D.: A Multimodal Approach to Music Transcription. In: Proc. of the 15th IEEE International Conference on Image Processing (ICIP), pp. 93–96 (2008)
21. Peeters, G., Rodet, X.: Hierarchical gaussian tree with inertia ratio maximization for the classification of large musical instruments databases. In: Proc. of the Int. Conf. on Digital Audio Effects (DAFx), London, UK (2003)
22. Penttinen, H., Siiskonen, J.: Acoustic Guitar Plucking Point Estimation in Real Time. In: Proc. of the IEEE International Conference on Acoustics, Speech, and Signal Processing (ICASSP), pp. 209–212 (2005)
23. Saito, S., Kameoka, H., Takahashi, K., Nishimoto, T., Sagayama, S.: Specmurt Analysis of Polyphonic Music Signals. IEEE Transactions on Audio, Speech, and Language Processing 16(3), 639–650 (2008)
24. Stein, M., Abeßer, J., Dittmar, C., Schuller, G.: Automatic Detection of Audio Effects in Guitar and Bass Recordings. In: Proceedings of the 128th Audio Engineering Society (AES) Convention, London, UK (2000)
25. Välimäki, V., Pakarinen, J., Erkut, C., Karjalainen, M.: Discrete-time modelling of musical instruments. Reports on Progress in Physics 69(1), 1–78 (2006)
26. Vapnik, V.N.: Statistical learning theory. Wiley, New York (1998)

Using Oracle Analysis for Decomposition-Based Automatic Music Transcription

Ken O'Hanlon[1], Hidehisa Nagano[1,2], and Mark D. Plumbley[1]

[1] Queen Mary University of London
[2] NTT Communication Science Laboratories, NTT Corporation
{keno,nagano,Mark.Plumbley}@eecs.qmul.ac.uk

Abstract. One approach to Automatic Music Transcription (AMT) is to decompose a spectrogram with a dictionary matrix that contains a pitch-labelled note spectrum atom in each column. AMT performance is typically measured using frame-based comparison, while an alternative perspective is to use an event-based analysis. We have previously proposed an AMT system, based on the use of structured sparse representations. The method is described and experimental results are given, which are seen to be promising. An inspection of the graphical AMT output known as a piano roll may lead one to think that the performance may be slightly better than is suggested by the AMT metrics used. This leads us to perform an oracle analysis of the AMT system, with some interesting outcomes which may have implications for decomposition based AMT in general.

Keywords: Automatic Music Transcription, Sparse representations, Oracle analysis.

1 Introduction

In Automatic Music Transcription (AMT) a machine understanding of a musical piece is sought. While many different methods have been proposed for AMT, the most popular methods in current AMT research are based on spectrogram decompositions, where the non-negative magnitude spectrogram $\mathbf{S} \in \Re^{M \times N}$ is decomposed such that

$$\mathbf{S} \approx \mathbf{DT} \tag{1}$$

where $\mathbf{D} \in \Re^{M \times K}$ is a dictionary matrix containing a note spectrum in each column and $\mathbf{T} \in \Re^{K \times N}$ is a coefficient matrix containing, in each row, the activations of a corresponding dictionary atom. Often a data-driven approach is taken, where the dictionary and the activation matrix are learnt together using algorithms such as Non-negative Matrix Factorisation (NMF) [6] or sparse dictionary learning [8]. Alternatively a dictionary may be learnt offline, with each atom learnt from a relevant signal containing an isolated note. In this case the decomposition can be performed using methods like P-LCA [9], sparse coding [4], or using the coefficient update from the NMF algorithm [15].

M. Aramaki et al. (Eds.): CMMR 2012, LNCS 7900, pp. 353–365, 2013.

While a complete transcription system would produce a musical score from an input musical signal, the output from AMT systems is usually communicated through a graphical representation known as a piano roll. A piano roll is a pitch-time representation showing the activations of each pitched note in time, and possibly other information such as the onsets and offsets of note events. AMT performance is measured by comparing a ground truth against the output piano roll, and different metrics have been proposed for this purpose. Regardless of the metric, two modes of evaluation are seen to be common in AMT research. The most prevalent of these is a frame-based approach, where the ground truth and computed piano rolls are compared at each pitch-time point, with true positives, true negatives and false positives being denoted, before metrics which exploit these annotations are calculated. While frame-based detection can give a reasonable indication of the performance of an AMT system, it may be more relevant, in some cases, to use an event-based analysis [5], whereby the comparison between ground truth and computed transcription is expressed in terms of correctly-pitched detections, with onsets aligned to the ground truth within a time-based tolerance.

Previously, we proposed an AMT system using a NMF-based decomposition, followed by a thresholding and subsequent clustering into molecules of adjacent pitch-time points seen to be still active after the thresholding. Following this clustering a greedy method, based on the Orthogonal Matching Pursuit (OMP) [11] performed a second decomposition, by iteratively selecting molecules from this set of clusters. The proposed method was seen to be competitive with other state-of-the-art AMT methods based on spectrogram decompositions, both in frame- and event- based transcription performance analysis. Visual inspection of the coefficient matrices confirmed that the transcription performed well, however limitations were noted. While early energetic parts of notes were captured well, sustained elements of notes often remained undetected. A simple threshold-based onset detection system, common to other decomposition based AMT methods, was used. However, visually some common errors were noticeable in the onset detection. While missing sustained elements of notes of longer duration may be an inevitable limitation of simple decomposition based AMT systems, or a side effect of spectral leakage in the Short-Time Fourier Transform (STFT), it may be questionable how much a transcription might suffer due to the omission of these low energy elements. Furthermore, undetected or incorrectly detected note onsets may have a large effect on the quality of a transcription, particularly if the end goal of the AMT system is the resynthesis of a musical piece. From a visual point of view, as seen in Figure 1, it seems that while many notes would seem to be correctly detected, the onset detection used in the event based analysis did not appear to reflect this accurately. These observations led us to perform an oracle analysis, simply effected as a ground truth was available for the dataset used for these transcription experiments.

In the rest of this paper, we first revisit the methods proposed in [7], before introducing the oracle transcription and its analysis of the oracle. We then conclude with some suggestions to future work.

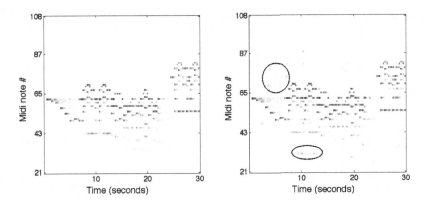

Fig. 1. Oracle coefficient matrix (left) compared with AMT output using M-NN-NS-OMP algorithm (right)

2 Transcription Using Structured Sparse Representations

Given a signal $\mathbf{s}$, and a dictionary matrix $\mathbf{D}$, a sparse approximation method seeks a coefficient vector $\mathbf{t}$ such that $\mathbf{s} \approx \mathbf{Dt}$ with the constraint that $\mathbf{t}$ contains few non-zero coefficients. Many algorithms have been proposed for performing sparse approximation, with greedy and convex optimisation-based methods being the most popular. Greedy methods, such as Orthogonal Matching Pursuit (OMP) [11], outlined in Algorithm 1, build up a representation by iteratively selecting the atom that is most correlated with the residual error, $\mathbf{r}$. This atom is added to the sparse support, the collection of currently selected atoms, and these supported atoms are backprojected onto the initial signal, giving interim coefficients and a new residual. The algorithm stops when a predefined stopping condition is met, which may be based on the number of atoms to be selected or the size of the error relative to the signal.

Another approach to sparse approximation is Basis Pursuit [12], an optimisation problem for which many algorithms can be used. Basis Pursuit seeks to solve

$$\min \|\mathbf{t}\|_1 \quad s.t \quad \mathbf{s} = \mathbf{Dt} \tag{2}$$

and a variant of this problem, used when there is noise in the signal is known as Basis Pursuit Denoising:

$$\min_t \|\mathbf{s} - \mathbf{Dt}\|_2^2 + \lambda\|\mathbf{t}\|_1 \tag{3}$$

which is seen to be a Least Squares solution with a sparsity promoting penalty applied where λ is a parameter used to control the sparsity level.

Several variants on the sparse approximation problem exist and our proposed method uses non-negative sparse representations, as we seek to decompose a magnitude spectrogram, and structured sparse representations, which allow the

---

Algorithm 1 Orthogonal Matching Pursuit [11]

Input
   $\mathbf{D} \in \Re_+^{M \times N}; \mathbf{s} \in \Re_+^M$
Initialise
   $i = 0; \quad \mathbf{r}^0 = \mathbf{s}; \quad \mathbf{t}^0 = 0; \quad \Gamma^0 = \{\};$
repeat
   $i = i + 1$
   $\hat{n} = \arg\max_n |\langle \mathbf{d}_n, \mathbf{r}^{i-1} \rangle|$
   $\Gamma^i = \Gamma^{i-1} \cup \hat{n}$
   $\mathbf{t}^i = \mathbf{D}_{\Gamma^i}^\dagger \mathbf{s}$
   $\mathbf{r}^i = \mathbf{s} - \mathbf{D}_{\Gamma^i} \mathbf{t}^i$
until stopping condition met

---

incorporation of prior knowledge. In particular two forms of structured sparsity are exploited. In group sparsity, the assumption is made that certain groups of atoms tend to be active simultaneously, a fact that can be used in AMT [7], affording the representation of a note with a subspace rather than a single atom. Using a subspace rather than one atom to represent a note may reduce the modelling error in the spectrogram decomposition by better capturing the dynamics in the spectral shape of a note.

In this work each block of atoms, or subspace, used to represent a note was made of a fixed number, P, of atoms which were placed adjacent in the dictionary $\mathbf{D} \in \Re^{M \times K}$. Here $K = L \times P$ where L is the number of groups, thereby allowing us to define a set of indices G for the group-based dictionary:

$$G = \{G_l \mid G_l = \{P \times (l-1) + 1, ..., P \times l\}\} \quad \forall l \in \{1, ..., L\}.$$

A variant of the Non-Negative Basis Pursuit (NN-BP) algorithm [1] was proposed in [7] which we called NN-BP(GC) and is outlined in Algorithm 2. The algorithm uses the multiplicative update from the Non-Negative Sparse Coding (NNSC) algorithm [14], which incorporates a sparse penalisation term λ into the multiplicative update of the NMF [15] algorithm. This variant differs from the NN-BP algorithm only through the calculation of a group coefficient, **GC**, on which the thresholding step is performed. Transcriptions using this method had high recall at the threshold used, as many true positives were recovered, while displaying low precision as many false positives were also found, though many of the false positives were seen to be of low energy. While better transcription results may be derived from this method by using a higher threshold, it is noted that using group sparsity in this way did not improve AMT performance, as the groups are not penalised. In [16] a similar algorithm called Group Non-Negative Basis Pursuit (G-NN-BP) was proposed which differed in using a group sparse penalty in the multiplicative update

$$t_{k,n} \longleftarrow t_{k,n} \frac{[\mathbf{D}^T \mathbf{S}]_{k,n}}{[\mathbf{D}^T \mathbf{D} \mathbf{T}]_{k,n} + \lambda \Psi_{k,n}} \tag{4}$$

where $\Psi_{k,n}$ is the gradient information for the group sparse penalty. G-NN-BP was shown to afford better AMT performance than NN-BP(GC). However, for the purpose of providing an initial estimate in order to supply an input for the molecular clustering step, little or no improvement was found in comparison to the NN-BP(GC), which suffices for this purpose, while remaining more computationally attractive.

A greedy method was also proposed; a non-negative group variant of OMP, referred to as Non-Negative Nearest Subspace OMP (NN-NS-OMP). The NN-NS-OMP functions in a similar manner to the OMP algorithm. However, at each iteration, the nearest subspace (in a non-negative sense) is selected rather than the nearest neighbour, as in OMP, and all atoms from the selected group are added to the sparse support. While results showed that using group sparsity captured the structure of the musical signal better than using sparsity alone, harmonic jumping was still seen to have a negative effect on time continuity in note events in the piano roll, and a difficulty in selecting low-energy signal elements was noted. As the method is iterative, a stopping condition needs to be selected, and it was found that selection of an apt stopping condition was tricky. The algorithm was also computationally expensive; however a fast version was proposed in [17], in which it was also shown that the use of alternative transforms to the STFT could drastically improve the AMT results using this method.

Algorithm 2 NN-BP(GC)

Input
  $\mathbf{D} \in \Re_+^{M \times K}$, $\mathbf{S} \in \Re_+^{M \times N}$, δ, $\mathbf{T}^0 = \mathbf{D}^\mathrm{T}\mathbf{S}$, $\Gamma = 1^{L \times N}$
repeat

$$t_{k,n} \longleftarrow t_{k,n} \frac{[\mathbf{D}^\mathrm{T}\mathbf{S}]_{k,n}}{[\mathbf{D}^\mathrm{T}\mathbf{D}\mathbf{T}]_{k,n} + \lambda}$$

until a fixed number of iterations
  $\mathbf{GC}_{l,n} = \sum \mathbf{T}_{G_l,n} \ \forall(l,n)$
  $\mathbf{GC}_{l',n'} = 0$; $\Gamma_{l',n'} = 0 \ \forall\{l',n'\}$ $s.t.$ $\mathbf{GC}_{l',n'} < \delta \times \max \mathbf{GC}$

Often in musical signal processing applications, it is desirable to exploit the structure found in the spectrogram. One such structure is the time-persistence seen in frequency elements belonging to a note. Another form of structured sparsity, known as molecular sparsity, can be used to extract these structured elements simultaneously. Molecular sparsity [2] is an extension of greedy sparse methods, allowing several atoms to be selected together. Unlike the group sparse assumption, the grouping of atoms is performed on the fly, according to some expected outcome. An example of this approach is the Molecular Matching Pursuit (MMP) [2], in which a molecule of time-persisting tonal elements is extracted from the spectrogram at each iteration. An initial atom is selected, as in typical Matching Pursuit algorithms, and tracking in a narrow frequency window is performed in both directions until the onset and offset of the tonal element were found, with all interim atoms forming a molecule which is added to the sparse support.

Initially, we proposed to construct a molecular AMT system built on the same tracking concept. However, these efforts were found to fail as early molecular extractions were seen to significantly overestimate the length of notes, as high projection values were often seen to be present beyond the onset and offset points of a note, particularly when similarly-pitched or harmonically-related notes were active there. Hence, a two-step approach was developed. As high recall and reasonable time continuity were observed in the NN-BP(GC) transcriptions, it was proposed to first decompose the spectrogram using the NN-BP(GC), and for the molecule supports to be estimated simultaneously from the output piano roll, after a thresholding step. All time-continuous pitch supports in the piano roll, Γ, were clustered into one molecule, and the molecules were input to a greedy method called Molecular Non-Negative Nearest Subspace OMP (M-NN-NS-OMP), outlined in Algorithm 3, which selects at each iteration one of these predetermined molecules. As time continuity was found to be reasonable using the NN-BP(GC), it was possible to use a threshold lower than optimal for AMT. This was possible as it was expected that spurious elements exceeding the threshold would be omitted from the final piano roll, as they were less likely to form a molecule with large energy. In this way the M-NN-NS-OMP affords higher recall values than other decomposition based AMT methods.

2.1 Experiments

Transcription experiments were run using the molecular approach on a set of pieces played on a Disklavier piano from the MAPS [3] database which includes a MIDI-aligned ground truth. A subdictionary was learnt for each MIDI note in the range $21-108$ from isolated notes also included in the MAPS database, and $\mathbf{D}$ was formed by concatenating these subdictionaries. Transcription was performed using the two-step NN-BP(GC) followed by the M-NN-NS-OMP approach.

The M-NN-NS-OMP algorithm returns a sparse group coefficient matrix, $\mathbf{T}$, and the transcription performance using this approach was measured with both frame-based and onset-based analysis. The frame-based analysis is performed by comparing a ground truth and the derived transcription. Each frame which is found to be active in both the ground truth and the transcription denotes a *true positive - tp* while frames which are active only in the ground truth and transcription denote *false negatives - fn* and *false positives - fp*, respectively.

For event-based analysis, onset detection was performed on $\mathbf{T}$. A simple threshold-based onset detector was used, based upon the one used in [10] which registered a note onset when a threshold value was surpassed and subsequently sustained for a given number of successive frames for a note in the coefficient matrix $\mathbf{T}$. A *tp* was registered when the onset was detected within one time bin of a similarly-pitched onset in the ground truth. Similar to the frame-based analysis, an onset found only in the ground truth registered a *fn*, and an onset found only in the transcription registered a *fp*.

Algorithm 3 M-NN-NS-OMP

Input

$\mathbf{D} \in \Re_+^{M \times K}$, $\mathbf{S} \in \Re_+^{M \times N}$, $\Gamma \in \{0,1\}^{L \times N}$, G, α

Initialise

$i = 0$; $\Phi = 0^{L \times N}$; $B = \{\beta_n | \beta_n = \{\} \forall n \in \{1, .., N\}\}$

repeat

   $i = i + 1$

   Get group coefs Θ and smoothed coefs $\bar{\Theta}$

   $\mathbf{x}_{G_l,n} = \arg\min_x \|\mathbf{r}_n^i - \mathbf{D}_{G_l}\mathbf{x}\|_2^2$ $s.t.$ $\mathbf{x} \geq 0$ $\forall l \in \Gamma_n$

   $\Theta_{l,n} = \|\mathbf{x}_{G_l,n}\|_1$; $\quad \bar{\Theta}_{l,n} = \displaystyle\sum_{n'=n}^{n+\alpha-1} \Theta_{l,n'}/\alpha$

   Select initial atom and grow molecule

   $\{\hat{l}, \hat{n}\} = \arg\max_{l,n} \bar{\Theta}_{l,n}$

   $n_{min} = \min \bar{n}$ $s.t.$ $\Gamma_{\hat{l},\Xi} = 1$, $\Xi = \{\bar{n}, ..., \hat{n}\}$

   $n_{max} = \max \bar{n}$ $s.t.$ $\Gamma_{\hat{l},\Xi} = 1$, $\Xi = \{\hat{n}, ..., \bar{n}\}$

   $\beta_n = \beta_n \cup \hat{l}$ $\forall n \in \Xi = \{n_{min}, ..., n_{max}\}$

   Calculate current coefficients and residual

   $\mathbf{t}_{G_{\beta_n},n} = \min_t \|\mathbf{s}_n - \mathbf{D}_{G_{\beta_n}}\mathbf{t}\|_2^2$ $\forall n \in \Xi$

   $\mathbf{r}_n^{i+1} = \mathbf{s}_n - \mathbf{D}_{G_{\beta_n}}\mathbf{t}_{G_{\beta_n}}$ $\forall n \in \Xi$

until stopping condition met

Using these markers the following metrics are defined for both frame- and event-based transcription;

$$\mathcal{P} = \frac{\#tp}{\#tp + \#fp} \tag{5}$$

relates the precision of the system in finding correct frames; the recall

$$\mathcal{R} = \frac{\#tp}{\#tp + \#fn} \tag{6}$$

defines the performance in terms of the amount of correct frames found relative to the number of active frames in the ground truth, and the $\mathcal{F}$-measure

$$\mathcal{F} = 2 \times \frac{\mathcal{P} \times \mathcal{R}}{\mathcal{P} + \mathcal{R}} \tag{7}$$

defines overall performance, considering both the precision and recall in the measure.

The results for the transcriptions are given in Table 1 where it is seen that the performance for both onset-based and frame-based metrics improves as the group size P increases, thereby validating the use of group sparse representations for AMT. A deterioration in performance was seen in further experiments with larger group sizes, which was considered an overfitting phenomenon. The experiments were run with a common value used as the stopping condition for all group sizes.

Table 1. Frame-based and onset-based transcription results for the proposed molecular approach, relative to the block size, P

P	Onset-based			Frame-based		
	$\mathcal{P}$	$\mathcal{R}$	$\mathcal{F}$	$\mathcal{P}$	$\mathcal{R}$	$\mathcal{F}$
1	78.3	74.3	76.3	69.1	73.6	71.3
2	78.8	76.2	77.5	69.0	76.4	72.5
3	77.6	77.1	77.4	69.5	78.7	73.8
4	78.8	77.3	78.1	71.8	79.3	75.3
5	78.6	77.8	78.2	72.9	80.0	76.3

3   Transcription Oracle for Sparse Methods

While the results shown in the last section show that this transcription method performs well, observation of the output coefficient matrix would indicate that, in an event based analysis, the true performance could actually be higher. This observation is not isolated to our proposed method and may also be extended to other decomposition based AMT methods. Hence, an oracle for transcription performance was proposed in order to ascertain the source of these errors.

As the MAPS [3] database comes with a standardised ground truth, it is easy to produce an oracle transcription for a given dictionary. At each time bin the Non-Negative Least Squares projection was calculated using only the groups of atoms G_n^{oracle}, known from the ground truth to be active at the time bin n.

$$\mathbf{t}_{G_n^{oracle}} = \min_t \|\mathbf{s}_n - \mathbf{D}_{G_n^{oracle}}\mathbf{t}\|_2^2 \quad s.t. \quad \mathbf{t} > 0 \quad \forall n \in \{1, ...N\} \tag{8}$$

The oracle group coefficient matrix $\mathbf{E}$ is formed by calculating the total energy in the coefficients of the individual group members

$$\mathbf{E}_{l,n} = \|\mathbf{D}_{G_l}\mathbf{t}_{G_l,n}\|_2 \tag{9}$$

4   Oracle Analysis

Using an oracle affords a hypothetical transcription and as this is a best case transcription, it is easy to observe deficiencies in an AMT system using this tool. It is possible that these problems are innate to using decomposition methods for AMT. In particular two noted observations were made, both of which are relevant to decomposition-based AMT in general; firstly there is often very low energy in supported atoms in $\mathbf{E}$, which may explain how the thresholding in the NN-BP(GC) effected the possible recall rate; secondly, using the oracle transcription provides an insight into the effectiveness of the onset detection system used.

Table 2. Analysis of effect of δ on precision and recall of NN-BP(GC) and the recall of the oracle

	STFT			ERB		
δ	$\mathcal{P}$	$\mathcal{R}$	$\mathcal{R}^{oracle}$	$\mathcal{P}$	$\mathcal{R}$	$\mathcal{R}^{oracle}$
0.1	88.6	38.2	44.1	84.4	37.3	44.6
0.01	38.5	84.6	90.7	36.4	85.0	90.6
0.001	19.2	92.8	96.5	17.7	93.5	96.4
0.0001	12.7	95.2	97.1	12.2	95.6	97.0

4.1 Energy-Based Thresholding

A thresholding factor δ is used in the NN-BP(GC) algorithm, which is multiplied by the maximum value of the group sparse coefficients **GC**. This is a common step in AMT, and other research [13] has suggested an optimum value of $c.27\,dB$ for this threshold. For the experiments in [7], a value of $\delta = 0.01$ was used, which allows a greater recall to be extracted, while it is hoped that the molecular method will omit many of the false elements detected at this level. A recall rate of 87% was observed using this value of δ for the NN-BP(GC) algorithm in these experiments. This recovery rate effectively sets an upper bound on the possible recall rate of the M-NN-NS-OMP. A closer analysis afforded the observation that the false negatives tended to exist at the tail of sustained notes, where it is expected that low energy is displayed. Indeed it is a relevant question to AMT as to what can be extracted, and possibly more importantly, what needs to be extracted to elicit a good transcription. Indeed, the definition of a good transcription may actually be dependent on the subsequent application of the transcription. For instance, if one is using a transcription in order to ascertain the key that a piece is set in, extraction of reliable high energy signal elements may suffice. If the transcription is being used as part of a source separation system, neglect of low energy elements may lead to artefacts being introduced.

The oracle energy matrix **E** was calculated for each piece from the MAPS dataset used in the transcription experiments [7]. Both Equivalent Rectangular Bandwidth (ERB) and STFT spectrograms were decomposed, using dictionaries learnt from the same dataset of isolated notes in MAPS. The signals were under-sampled to 22.05 kHz, and the ERB spectrogram used 250 frequency bin scale with a 23 ms time window. The STFT used a 1024 frequency bin spectrogram, with a a 75% overlap, in order to use the same time resolution as the ERB. The NN-BP(GC) was also run for both transforms to compare the effects of the δ thresholding.

The results are displayed in Table 2. Here it is seen that the recall of the oracle, $\mathcal{R}^{oracle}$, is similar across transforms, at all values of delta A similar pattern is also seen for the recall rate, $\mathcal{R}$, of the NN-BP(GC), which is slightly smaller than $\mathcal{R}^{oracle}$, but again is similar in both transforms. This similarity across transforms suggests, as might be expected, that the problem here is related to the signal itself, rather than the approach taken or the dictionary used, being energy related. However, any temptation to use a smaller threshold is easily

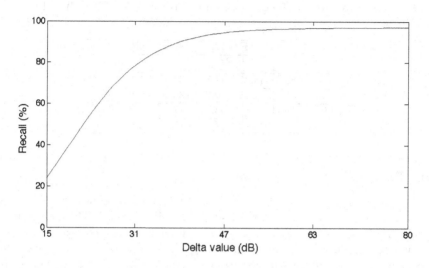

Fig. 2. Oracle recall based on varying values of thresholding parameter δ

tempered by the observation that as δ decreases and the recall of NN-BP(GC) increases, the precision is greatly reduced. If a piano roll of lower precision is input to the molecular approach, this may effect the transcription performance by introducing oversized molecules. The oracle recall relative to δ is shown in Figure 2. It is worth noting that, even at 80 dB, perfect recall is not achievable.

4.2 Onset Analysis

In the prior work, a simple threshold-based onset detection system was used, which triggered an onset when a threshold value was surpassed and sustained for a minimum length of time. A true positive was flagged when this trigger happened within one time frame of a ground truth onset of the same note. Using the optimal transcription **E** we can test the effectiveness of this onset detection system. Experiments were run using the same parameters as in [7] and the results are presented in Table 3.

Table 3. Onset analysis of oracle transcription **E** for different values of P

P	1	2	3	4	5
$\mathcal{R}$	76.2	78.5	79.5	80.1	80.1
$\mathcal{P}$	86.4	87.1	87.0	87.3	86.8

The results are not promising given that an oracle transcription is given to the onset detector. Closer inspection of the individual results reveal systematic flaws in the onset detection. False positives are often found when a sustained note is retriggered by oscillation around the threshold value, behaviour which is often found in the presence of other note onsets and may be due to transient signal elements effecting the smoothness of the decomposition across time. Several common types of false negative were found. It is found that a note replayed with minimal time between the offset of the original event and the onset of the following event may produce a false negative where the observed coefficient has not already fallen below the threshold value. When several notes onset simultaneously, onsets may not be detected for all of these notes. A tendency for lower pitched notes not to trigger an onset event in the detection system is also noticed. Further to this we find some timing errors, where a false negative and a false positive are closely spaced.

5   Conclusion

We have previously proposed an AMT system based on group sparse representations which is relatively fast and shows promising results. An oracle transcription has been presented here, which gives some insight into some weaknesses in the AMT system, as currently exists. While it would seem difficult to capture very low-energy elements from a musical signal, it is questionable how important capturing these elements might be to a transcription. However, other authors have proposed post-processing a decomposition based AMT with Hidden Markov Models in order to better ascertain the offsets of given notes [9]. It is also possible that the use of other tools may help to alleviate this problem. The spectrogram itself may be a blunt tool when presented with different signal elements, particularly in the presence of harmonic overlaps which are a common feature of musical signals, and possessing largely varying amplitudes.

In terms of onset detection, it would appear that the onset detection system used here is not sophisticated enough in order to capture many note events in the signal, even when an oracle analysis is used. However, it may be important to consider this further, as it is possible that simple decomposition-based methods themselves may not be able to capture the onset information clearly. Decomposition-based methods assume a certain level of linearity in the spectrogram in relationship to the dictionary. Whilst this is convenient and may work sufficiently well when the spectrogram is dominated by tonal elements, the onset of a piano note is known to have a percussive, transient element, displaying a more broadband spectrum. Coupled with this reaction of the piano body, the spectrogram itself is seen to react to the larger energy levels, with broader sidelobes on spectral peaks. These two facts may lead to errors in the decomposition, as many notes are often seen to become active on the occasion of an onset. While the molecular method presented is capable of erasing many of these false detections around note onsets, the energy in the spectrogram when shared between several simultaneous note onsets may be unevenly distributed or even insufficient to trigger the correct number of note events, as the energy transferred to the piano body may not differ much relative to whether two notes or five notes are played synchronously, thereby making it more difficult to capture the onsets in the case of many notes. Most of the other types of onset errors described in the last section also occur in the vicinity of other onsets, and can be hypothesised to happen as a result of these inaccuracies in the linear assumption, and spectrogram leakage.

Further work will need to incorporate a parallel onset detection system in order to improve on these results. Methods which seek to perform AMT on an onset-only basis have been proposed, such as that of Bock [18] which uses neural networks to classify onsets. Indeed, with an accurate onset detection system, it may be possible to improve the frame-based transcription metrics as well through incorporation as a discriminative event detector.

Acknowledgments. This research is supported by ESPRC Leadership Fellowship EP/G007144/1 and EU FET-Open Project FP7-ICT-225913 "SMALL".

References

1. Aharon, M., Elad, M., Bruckstein, A.M.: K-SVD and its Non-negative Variant for Dictionary Design. In: Proceedings of the SPIE Conference Wavelets, pp. 327-339 (2005)
2. Daudet, L.: Sparse and Structured Decompositions of Signals with the Molecular Matching Pursuit. IEEE Transactions on Audio, Speech and Language Processing 14(5), 1808–1816 (2006)
3. Emiya, V., Badeau, R., David, B.: Multipitch Estimation of Piano Sounds using a New Probabilistic Spectral Smoothness Principle. IEEE Transactions on Audio, Speech and Language 18(6), 1643–1654 (2010)
4. Leveau, P., Vincent, E., Richard, G., Daudet, L.: Instrument-Specific Harmonic Atoms for Mid-Level Music Representation. IEEE Transactions on Audio, Speech and Language 16(1), 116–128 (2008)
5. Poliner, G., Ellis, D.: A Discrimative Model for Polyphonic Piano Transcription. EURASIP Journal Advances in Signal Processing (8), 154–162 (2007)
6. Smaragdis, P., Brown, J.C.: Non-negative Matrix Factorization for Polyphonic Music Transcription. In: IEEE Workshop on Applications of Signal Processing to Audio and Acoustics (2003)
7. O'Hanlon, K., Nagano, H., Plumbley, M.D.: Structured Sparsity for Automatic Music Transcription. In: IEEE International Conference on Audio, Speech and Signal Processing (2012)
8. Abdallah, S.A., Plumbley, M.D.: Polyphonic Transcription by Non-negative Sparse Coding of Power Spectra. In: Proceedings of ISMIR, pp. 318–325 (2004)
9. Benetos, E., Dixon, S.: Multiple-Instrument Polyphonic Music Transcription using a Convolutive Probabilistic Model. In: Proceedings of the Sound and Music Computing Conference (2011)
10. Bertin, N., Badeau, R., Vincent, E.: Enforcing Harmonicity and Smoothness in Bayesian Non-negative Matrix Factorization applied to Polyphonic Music Transcription. IEEE Transactions on Audio, Speech, and Language Processing 18(3), 538–549 (2010)
11. Pati, Y.C., Rezaiifar, R.: Orthogonal Matching Pursuit: Recursive Function Approximation with Applications to Wavelet Decomposition. In: Proceedings of the 27th Annual Asilomar Conference on Signals, Systems and Computers, pp. 40–44 (1993)

12. Chen, S.S., Donoho, D.L., Saunders, M.A.: Atomic Decomposition by Basis Pursuit. SIAM Journal on Scientific Computing 20, 33–61 (1998)
13. Vincent, E., Bertin, N., Badeau, R.: Adaptive Harmonic Spectral Decomposition for Multiple Pitch Estimation. IEEE Transactions on Audio, Speech and Language Processing 18(3), 528–537 (2010)
14. Hoyer, P.O.: Non-negative sparse coding. In: Proceedings of the 2002 IEEE Workshop on Neural Networks for Signal Processing, pp. 557–565 (2002)
15. Lee, D.D., Seung, H.S.: Algorithms for Non-negative Matrix Factorization. In: Advances in Neural Information Processing Systems (NIPS), pp. 556–562 (2000)
16. O'Hanlon, K., Nagano, H., Plumbley, M.D.: Group Non-negative Basis Pursuit for Automatic Music Transcription. In: Proceedings of the Workshop on Music and Machine Learning (MML) at ICML (2012)
17. O'Hanlon, K., Plumbley, M.D.: Greedy Non-negative Group Sparsity. In: Proceedings of the 3rd IMA Conference on Numerical Linear Algebra and Optimisation (2012)
18. Bock, S., Schedl, M.: Polyphonic Piano Note Transcription with Recurrent Neural Networks. In: Proceedings of the 2012 International Conference on Acoustics, Speech and Signal Processing, pp. 121–124 (2012)

The Influence of Music on the Emotional Interpretation of Visual Contexts

Designing Interactive Multimedia Tools for Psychological Research

Fernando Bravo

University of Cambridge. Centre for Music and Science
nanobravo@fulbrightmail.org

Abstract. From a cognitive standpoint, the analysis of music in audiovisual contexts presents a helpful field in which to explore the links between musical structure and emotional response.

This work emerges from an empirical study that shows strong evidence in support of the effect of tonal dissonance level on interpretations regarding the emotional content of visual information.

From this starting point the article progresses toward the design of interactive multimedia tools aimed at investigating the various ways in which music may shape the semantic processing of visual contexts. A pilot experiment (work in progress) using these tools to study the emotional effects of sensory dissonance is briefly described.

Keywords: Music, emotions, film-music, interactive multimedia, algorithmic composition, dissonance, tonal tension, interval vector, Max/MSP/Jitter.

1 Introduction and Background

Although research in music cognition has been growing steadily during the past four decades, we still lack a significant body of empirical studies concerning the higher levels of musical response, including the emotional and aesthetic aspects. From a cognitive standpoint, the analysis of music in audiovisual contexts presents a helpful field in which to explore the affective and connotative aspects of musical information [1-3]. The purpose of my research is to investigate the effects of music upon the emotional processing of visual information. This work is directed towards understanding the influence of music in film and other electronic multimedia from a cognitive/neuroscientific perspective. In particular, my research is focused on analysing how alterations of specific aspects within the musical structure may influence the emotional interpretation of visual scenarios.

This paper describes a work in progress to investigate the influence of tonal dissonance on the emotional interpretation of visual information.

M. Aramaki et al. (Eds.): CMMR 2012, LNCS 7900, pp. 366–377, 2013.
© Springer-Verlag Berlin Heidelberg 2013

The objectives of this paper are:

- To report the results of an experiment showing the effect of tonal dissonance on interpretations of the emotional content of an animated short film (Section 2).
- To describe a series of interactive multimedia tools designed to investigate the various ways in which music may shape the semantic processing of visual contexts (Section 3).
- To show an example of how these tools could be used in experimental cognition research. In this example, I employ stochastically generated music to empirically study the links between sensory dissonance and emotional responses to music in a strictly controlled audiovisual setting (Section 3.2).

Consonance and dissonance refer to specific qualities that a musical interval can posses [4]. Tonal and sensory dissonance are sometimes used as equivalent concepts. However, as Krumhansl [5] has suggested, these two notions have different shades of meaning. Sensory dissonance designates, first of all, a psychoacoustic sensory property associated with the presence/absence of interaction between the harmonic spectra of two pitches [6]. Tonal dissonance generally includes sensory dissonance but it also captures a more cognitive or conceptual meaning beyond psychoacoustic effects that is typically expressed with terms such as tension or instability. The term "tonal dissonance", as employed here, refers both to sensory and cognitive dissonance.

Meyer [7] proposed that the confirmation, violation or suspension of musical expectations elicits emotions in the listener. Following this theory, researchers found associations between specific musical structures, precise neural mechanisms and certain neurophysiological reactions that are strongly connected with emotions [29-33]. In addition, studies focusing on the perception of tonal dissonance have shown that unexpected chords and increments in dissonance have strong effects on perceived tension [5, 8-10], which has been linked to emotional experience during music listening [11].

Tonal dissonance can be described by a number of variables [9], which have already been the subject of much historical study by music theorists and scientists: the tonal function of chords in a musical context [12-16], their acoustic or sensory consonance [6, 17], and melodic organization, usually referred to as "horizontal motion" [18].

Cognitive approaches usually emphasize the importance of melodic organization and tonal function while sensory-perceptual theories tend to focus on psychoacoustical aspects. In this paper, I use the term "tonal dissonance" as a synonym for "tonal tension", to refer to the effects of tonal function, sensory dissonance and horizontal motion on perceived musical tension.

2   Experimental Investigation

This paper emerges from an experiment entitled "The influence of tonal dissonance on emotional responses to film" [19]. The main experimental hypothesis predicted that, for the same film sequence (visual context), musical settings incorporating different levels of tonal dissonance would systematically elicit different interpretations of and expectations about the emotional content of the same movie scene.

2.1 Experimental Design

This experiment was aimed at addressing the particular emotional effect of tonal dissonance induced by chord changes, controlling for other elements within musical structure such as tempo, intensity, rhythm, timbre (instrumentation), etc. This was achieved by working with a precise experimental design similar to that used by Blood *et al.* in their neuroscientific research (which investigated the cerebral activations elicited by tonal dissonance) [20]. It is important to note that this study excludes other kinds of musical tension. Empirical evidence has shown that musical tension can be induced by many factors, such as rhythm, dynamics, tempo, gesture, textural density and tone timbre [25, 26, 27]. This work focuses on musical tension induced by tonal dissonance in the specific sense of tension created by melodic and harmonic motion.

A choral piece, specifically composed for the experiment, was made to sound more or less consonant or dissonant by modifying its harmonic structure, producing two otherwise-identical versions of the same music passage. These two contrasting conditions, in terms of tonal dissonance, were used as background music for the same passage of an animated short film ("Man with pendulous arms" - 1997, directed by Laurent Gorgiard).

Fig. 1. A frame from "Man with pendulous arms" – 1997, directed by Laurent Gorgiard

A total of 120 healthy volunteers with normal hearing took part in this experiment. The participants were randomly sampled from students at Argentine Catholic University. Two independent samples were used (60 participants each). The subjects were randomly assigned to two groups, one of which saw an animated short film with the "consonant music" condition and the other saw the same film with the "dissonant music" condition. At the end participants were asked to answer a survey about their associations and expectations towards the main character and the overall story of the film. The survey used 9 single-selection questions, asking participants to choose only one item from two items given. Table 1 shows participants' answers within each music condition.

Table 1. Cross-classification of music condition and response variable (number of participants and percentage of participants within condition)

The character...	feels confident		is scared	
consonant	37	61.7%	23	38.3%
dissonant	25	41.7%	35	58.3%
The mood of the story is...	nostalgic		sinister	
consonant	58	96.7%	2	3.3%
dissonant	26	43.3%	34	56.7%
The character is trying...	to create something		to destroy something	
consonant	45	75%	15	25%
dissonant	27	45%	33	55%
The character...	is a fantasy character		is monstrous	
consonant	53	88.3%	7	11.7%
dissonant	39	65%	21	35%
Genre of the short film...	Drama		Horror	
consonant	59	98.3%	1	1.7%
dissonant	42	70%	18	30%
The character...	is alienated		is sad	
consonant	11	18.3%	49	81.7%
dissonant	35	58.3%	25	41.7%
Character's actions...	directed by his own will		directed by external influence	
consonant	50	83.3%	10	16.7%
dissonant	35	58.3%	25	41.7%
The end of the short film...	will probably be hopeful		will probably be tragic	
consonant	41	68.3%	19	31.7%
dissonant	29	48.3%	31	51.7%
The character is trying...	to protect himself		to search for something	
consonant	47	78.3%	13	21.7%
dissonant	44	73.3%	16	26.7%

2.2 Experimental Results

Eight out of nine response variables were found to be associated with the explanatory variable (tonal dissonance level). The variable related to the character's objective (at the bottom of Table 1) was the only variable that did not reach significant association with tonal dissonance level.

For the eight response variables where an association was found, two ways to summarize the strength of the association are presented: the *difference of proportions*, forming confidence intervals to measure the strength of the association in the population, and the *odds ratio* (Table 2).

When measuring the strength of the association, variables related to the mood in the story, the emotional state of the character and the interpreted genre of the short film were found to have the strongest association with dissonance level in background music (see grey cells in Table 2).

Table 2. $\chi 2$, Difference of proportions and Odds Ratio

Variable	$\chi 2(p\ value)$	Differ. of proportions		Odds Ratio	Odds	
		$p1$-$p2$	95% CI	OR	Con	Dis
Intentions (create/destroy)	11.2(<.01)	0.3	[.133, .467]	3.667	3	0.8
Feeling (confident/scared)	4.80(<.05)	0.2	[.025, .035]	2.252	1.6	0.7
Mood (nostalgic/sinister)	40.6(<.01)	0.53	[.401, .667]	37.92	29	0.7
Emot. state (sad/alienated)	20.3(<.01)	0.4	[.241, .559]	6.236	4.4	0.7
Actions (own will/external)	9.07(<.01)	0.25	[.094, .406]	3.571	5	1.4
Class (fantasy/monstruous)	9.13(<.01)	0.23	[.087, .379]	4.077	7.5	1.8
Genre (drama/horror)	18.0(<.01)	0.28	[.163, .403]	25.28	59	2.3
Ending (hopeful/tragic)	4.93(<.05)	0.2	[.027, .373]	2.307	2.1	0.9

For example, Table 2 shows that there was a rise of 0.4 in the proportion that interpreted the emotional state of the character as sad among participants who saw the film with consonant music. Also, we may infer, with 95% confidence, that $p1$ (the proportion of people seeing the film with consonant music and interpreting the character's emotional state as sad) may be as much as between [0.241, 0.559] larger than $p2$ (the proportion of people seeing the film with dissonant music and interpreting the character's emotional state as sad).

In addition, from Tables 1 and 2, we observe that for the consonant music condition the proportion of people who interpreted the character's emotional state as sad equals 49 / 11 = 4.4545. The value of 4.45 means that, for participants who saw the film with consonant music, there were 4.45 participants who interpreted the character's emotional state as sad for every 1 person in the dissonant condition. On the other hand, for the dissonant music condition the proportion of people who interpreted the character's emotional state as sad equals 25 / 35 = 0.7143. Equivalently, since 35 / 25 = 1 / 0.7143 = 1.4, this means that there were 1.4 participants in the dissonant condition who interpreted the character's emotional state as alienated for every 1 person in the consonant condition. For the consonant music condition, the odds of interpreting the character's emotional state as sad were about 6.2 times the odds of the same interpretation for the dissonant music condition.

The results of this experiment offer strong evidence in support of the effect of tonal dissonance level (in film music) on interpretations regarding the emotional content of visual information.

2.3   Discussion of Experimental Results

The empirical research described here supports and confirms previous research on mood congruency effects [1], and can be interpreted within Annabel Cohen's Congruence-Associationist framework of the mental representation of multimedia [2, 3].

In this work, tonal dissonance level was experimentally isolated in order to analyze a particular feature within the overall musical structure that may elicit musical emotions. As noted in section 2.1, this study was focused on musical tension induced by chord changes. Other important factors that contribute to the building and release of musical tension, such as timbre, dynamics, textural density, etc., which were controlled in the experiment, are not addressed here.

Results revealed that the background music significantly biased the affective impact of the short film. Generally, the consonant music condition guided participants toward positive emotional judgments, while dissonant music guided participants toward negative judgments. In addition, the dissonant background music seems to have rendered the interpretation more ambiguous when compared to the higher percentages of positive judgments in the consonant condition. However, additional research is needed to further examine this hypothesis since the present experiment did not include a visual-alone condition, which would be necessary to control for the effects of visual content by itself.

Music theory provides technical descriptions of how styles organize musical sounds and offers insights about musical structures that might underlie listeners' interpretations. Within the general perspective of post-tonal music theory, Allen Forte has introduced the notion of interval-class content [21]. This concept, widely used in the analysis of atonal twentieth-century music, offers an interesting approach to qualifying sonorities. A pitch interval is simply the distance between two pitches, measured by the number of semitones. The ordered pitch intervals (ascending or descending) focus attention on the contour of the line. The unordered pitch intervals ignore direction of motion and concentrate entirely on the spaces between the pitches. An unordered pitch-class interval is the distance between two pitch classes, and is also called interval class [28]. Because of octave equivalence, compound intervals (intervals larger than an octave) are considered equivalent to their complements in mod 12. In addition, pitch-class intervals larger than six are considered equivalent to their complements in mod 12. The number of interval classes a sonority contains depends on the number of distinct pitch classes in the sonority. For any given sonority, we can summarize the interval content in scoreboard fashion by indicating, in the appropriate column, the number of occurrences of each of the six interval classes (occurrences of interval class 0, which will always be equal to the number of pitch classes in the sonority, are not included). Such a scoreboard conveys the essential sound of a sonority.

Table 3 summarizes interval class content for the first measure of the experimental transformation used in this study to create contrasting conditions (Figure 2). The comparative dissonant condition was obtained by lowering, by a semitone, the second violin, viola and violoncello lines, while keeping the other instruments in their original position (at their original pitch). Thus, the level of dissonance was uniform throughout a given version. The analysis, therefore, can generally represent the comparative level of dissonance throughout.

Table 3. Interval Content of the two music conditions

Consonant condition - Interval Class content					
Interval Class	1	2	3	4	5	6
No. of occurrences	0	0	3	6	5	0
Dissonant condition - Interval Class content					
Interval Class	1	2	3	4	5	6
No. of occurrences	4	2	2	3	6	2

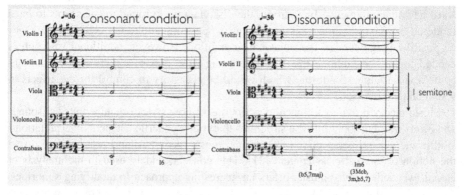

Fig. 2. Score of the consonant and dissonant music conditions (first measure)

The consonant condition is primarily governed by collections of intervals considered to be consonant (thirds, fourths and fifths). In contrast, the use of dissonant intervals in the dissonant version (major second, minor second and tritone) has a very specific emotional effect that is reflected in the participants' interpretations.

3   Future Work: Interactive Multimedia Tools for Experimental Research on Interval Content and Musical Emotions

The described experiment stimulated the investigation of tonal [15] and post-tonal [21] interval theory, and the parallel design of interactive multimedia tools to empirically analyze the effects of interval content on musical emotions.

3.1   Background Elements

From a tonal perspective, Paul Hindemith's work is especially noteworthy [15]. According to Hindemith, the overtone series system (see Figure 3) gives a complete proof of the natural basis of tonal relations. In general, as new intervals are introduced, the stability decreases and the two tones involved are considered more distant in their relation. All music theories have a general agreement with this model.

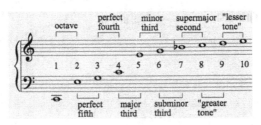

Fig. 3. Overtone series with intervals labeled

This theory has several links with the concept of sensory dissonance as studied in psycho-acoustic literature [6, 22-24]. According to this model, the most consonant intervals would be the ones that could be expressed with simple frequency ratios, which has been supported by psychological study. Intervals such as the unison (1:1), octave (2:1), perfect fifth (3:2), and perfect fourth (4:3) are regarded as the most consonant. Intermediate in consonance are the major third (5:4), minor third (6:5), major sixth (5:3), and minor sixth (8:5). The most acoustically dissonant intervals (comprised of fundamental frequencies between which the ratios are not simple) are the major second (9:8), minor second (16:15), major seventh (15:8), minor seventh (16:9), and the tritone (45:32).

From the perspective of atonal theory, Allen Forte's work provided a general theoretical framework from which to begin the exploration of intervals in a new way, a way that was intimately concerned with the idea of sonority [21]. He explained that different types of sonorities could be generally defined by listing their constituent intervals. In the previous experiment, I showed how the two music conditions could be described in terms of interval content. Forte introduced the basic concept of "interval vector" to analyze the properties of pitch class sets and the interactions of the components of a set in terms of intervals. An interval vector is an array that expresses the intervallic content of a set. It has six digits, with each digit standing for the number of times an interval class appears in the set [21]. According to Forte, such interval vector conveys the essential sound (color, quality) of a sonority.

3.2   'Intermedia Patch'. Cross-Modal Research on Intervals and Visuals

The interactive multimedia tools presented in this section, called 'Intermedia patch', were built to explore the interval vector theory in a practical and strictly controlled setting, in order to experimentally study the links between sonority and emotional response. The patch works with an initial supply of intervals and allows to experiment with different algorithmic composition techniques, allowing a detailed control over many coincident variables such as loudness, rhythm, timbre, melody, intensity and instrumentation.

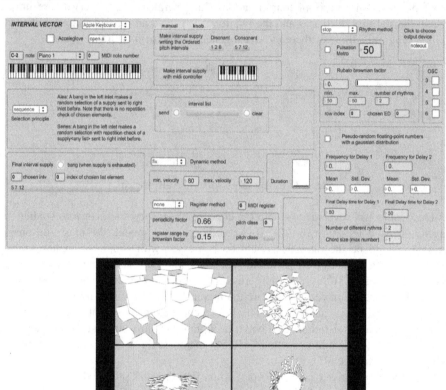

Fig. 4. Intermedia patch built with Cycling'74 Max/MSP/Jitter (top) that allows it to simultaneously work with images created with Maxon Cinema 4D software (bottom)

The patch not only provides a programming environment for analyzing different types of sonorities based on interval selection (Figure 4 top), it also allows it to simultaneously work with images (Figure 4 bottom), enabling the study of mood congruency effects between sound and visuals.

The tool is currently being tested in a pilot study (in progress), which employs the patch for the creation of sound stimuli. In this experiment I opted to analyze the emotional reactions induced by interval content. Participants are asked to see a short animation created for this study, with stochastically generated background music.

Participants are randomly assigned to three independent groups; one control group sees the animation without music, a second group sees the animation with a consonant interval content as background music (interval set: 5-7-12, all perfect consonances), and a third group sees the same animation with a dissonant interval content (1-2-6, all dissonances). Immediately after viewing the clip, participants are asked to complete a series of bipolar adjective ratings representing the three connotative dimensions: activity, potency and valence.

The question posed in this study is whether two contrasting examples of background music, solely in terms of interval content, can selectively bias observers' emotional interpretation of visual information. People who have internalized the Western tonal music conventions normally respond to certain sonorities in a specific manner. The main experimental hypothesis predicts that, in particular, the valence dimension should differ significantly under these two conditions. Positive results would confirm mood congruency effects induced exclusively by interval content (surface or sensory consonance).

4   Conclusions

The empirical research included in this paper supports and confirms previous studies that have examined, from a cognitive perspective, the role of music on the interpretation of a film or a video presentation [1-3]. The results offer strong evidence in support of the effect of tonal dissonance level on interpretations regarding the emotional content of visual information. Moreover, it gives insights to the richness and potentiality of the aural "palette", since extensive effects on the emotional interpretation of visual contexts may be achieved by the manipulation of a single musical structure feature (tonal dissonance).

Studies such as this demonstrate associations between aspects of musical structure and musical meaning, which then becomes automatically attached to the visual content or implied narrative that is in the focus of the spectator's attention.

The positive results of this study indicate that further research that systematically examines the multiple and subtle ways in which music performs elaborative functions in the comprehension of visual contexts should be pursued. The interactive multimedia tools introduced in section 3 are aimed at exploring this path. These tools incorporate a variety of potential variables in both musical sound and transformations of the visual stimuli for experimental purposes, providing a foundation on which future research could build.

Acknowledgments. Thanks to Prof. Ian Cross, Prof. Sarah Hawkins and to all the researchers at the Centre for Music and Science (University of Cambridge). Thanks to Dr. Christopher Hopkins, Prof. Anson Call and Prof. Steve Herrnstadt for their constant support. Thank you to the anonymous reviewers for their suggestions that improved the paper considerably. This work was conducted at the University of Cambridge and is supported by a Queens' College Walker Studentship.

References

1. Boltz, M.G.: Musical Soundtracks as a Schematic Influence on the Cognitive Processing of Filmed Events. Music Perception 18, 427–454 (2001)
2. Cohen, A.J.: Music as a source of emotion in film. In: Juslin, P., Sloboda, J. (eds.) Music and Emotion, pp. 249–272. Oxford University Press, Oxford (2001)
3. Cohen, A.J.: How music influences the interpretation of film and Video: Approaches from experimental psychology. In: Kendall, R.A., Savage, R.W. (eds.) Selected Reports in Ethnomusicology: Perspectives in Systematic Musicology, vol. 12, pp. 15–36 (2005)
4. Bharucha, J.J.: Anchoring effects in music: The resolution of dissonance. Cognitive Psychology 16, 485–518 (1984)
5. Lerdahl, F., Krumhansl, C.L.: Modeling tonal tension. Music Perception 24, 329–366 (2007)
6. Helmholtz, H.L.F.: On the Sensation of Tone as a Physiological Basis for the Theory of Music. Dover, New York (1954) (Original German work published 1863)
7. Meyer, L.B.: Emotion and meaning in music. University of Chicago Press, Chicago (1956)
8. Bigand, E., Parncutt, R., Lerdahl, F.: Perception of musical tension in short chord sequences: The influence of harmonic function, sensory dissonance, horizontal motion, and musical training. Perception & Psychophysics 58, 124–141 (1996)
9. Bigand, E., Parncutt, R.: Perception of musical tension in long chord sequences. Psychological Research 62, 237–254 (1999)
10. Krumhansl, C.L.: A perceptual analysis of Mozart's Piano Sonata, K. 282: Segmentation, tension and musical ideas. Music Perception 13, 401–432 (1996)
11. Steinbeis, N., Koelsch, S., Sloboda, J.A.: The role of harmonic expectancy violations in musical emotions: Evidence from subjective, physiological, and neural responses. Journal of Cognitive Neuroscience 18(8), 1380–1393 (2006)
12. Riemann, H.: Harmony simplified. Augener, London (1896); Bewerung, H. (Trans.) (Original work published 1893)
13. Koechlin, C.: Traité de l'harmonie. Max Eschig, Paris (1930)
14. Schenker, H.: Free Composition. Longman, New York (1979); Oster, E. (Trans.) (Original work published 1935)
15. Hindemith, P.: UnterweisungimTonsatz, vol. 3. Schott, Mainz (1937-1970); English edition, as The Craft of Musical Composition, vol. 1: Theoretical Part. Associated Music Publishers, London (1942); Mendel, A. (Trans.)
16. Costère, E.: Lois et styles des harmonies musicales. Presses Universitaires de France, Paris (1954)
17. Rameau, J.P.: Treatise of Harmony. Dover, New York (1971); Gosset, P. (Trans.) (Original work published 1722)
18. Ansermet, E.: Les fondements de la musiquedans la consciencehumaine. Delachaux et Niestle, Neuchâtel (1961)
19. Bravo, F.: The influence of music on the emotional interpretation of visual contexts. Master's Thesis, AAT 1494771, Iowa State University, United States (2011)
20. Blood, A.J., Zatorre, R.J., Bermudez, P., Evans, A.C.: Emotional responses to pleasant and unpleasant music correlate with activity in paralimbic brain regions. Nat. Neurosci. 2, 382–387 (1999)
21. Forte, A.: The Structure of Atonal Music. University Press, Yale (1973)
22. Plomp, R., Levelt, W.J.M.: Tonal consonance and the critical bandwidth. Journal of the Acoustical Society of America 38, 548–560 (1965)

23. Vos, J., Vianen, B.G.: Thresholds for discrimination between pure and tempered intervals: The relevance of nearly coinciding harmonics. Journal of the Acoustical Society of America 77, 76–187 (1984)
24. DeWitt, L.A., Crowder, R.G.: Tonal fusion of consonant musical intervals. Perception & Psychophysics 41, 73–84 (1987)
25. Barthet, M., Depalle, P., Kronland-Martinet, R., Ystad, S.: From clarinet control to timbre perception. Acta Acustica United with Acustica 96, 678–689 (2010)
26. Barthet, M., Depalle, P., Kronland-Martinet, R., Ystad, S.: Acoustical correlates of timbre and expressiveness in clarinet performance. Music Perception 28, 135–153 (2010)
27. Paraskeva, S., McAdams, S.: Influence of timbre, presence/absence of tonal hierarchy and musical training on the perception of tension/relaxation schemas of musical phrases. In: Proceedings of the 1997 International Computer Music Conference, Thessaloniki, pp. 438–441 (1997)
28. Strauss, J.N.: Introduction to Post-Tonal Theory. Prentice-Hall, Cliffs (1990)
29. Sloboda, J.A.: Music structure and emotional response: Some empirical findings. Psychology of Music 19, 110–120 (1991)
30. Krumhansl, C.L.: An exploratory study of musical emotions and psychophysiology. Canadian Journal of Experimental Psychology 51(4), 336–352 (1997)
31. Gabrielsson, A., Juslin, P.N.: Emotional expression in music. In: Goldsmith, H.H., Davidson, R.J., Scherer, K.R. (eds.) Handbook of Affective Sciences, pp. 503–534. Oxford University Press, New York (2003)
32. Gomez, P., Danuser, B.: Affective and physiological responses to environmental noises and music. International Journal of Psychophysiology 53(2), 91–103 (2004)
33. Koelsch, S., Fritz, T., von Cramon, Y., Müller, K., Friederici, A.: Investigating emotion with music: an fMRI study. Human Brain Mapping 27(3), 239–250 (2006)

The Perception
of Auditory-Visual Looming in Film

Sonia Wilkie and Tony Stockman

Queen Mary University of London, UK
{sonia.wilkie,tony.stockman}@eecs.qmul.ac.uk

Abstract. Auditory-visual looming (the presentation of objects moving in depth towards the viewer) is a technique used in film (particularly those in 3D) to assist in drawing the viewer into the created world. The capacity of a viewer to perceptually immerse within the multidimensional world and interact with moving objects can be affected by the sounds (audio cues) that accompany these looming objects. However the extent to which sound parameters should be manipulated remains unclear. For example, the amplitude, spectral components, reverb and spatialisation can all be altered, but the degree of their alteration and the resulting perception generated need greater investigation. Building on a previous study analysing the physical properties of the sounds, we analyse people's responses to the complex sounds which use multiple audio cues for film looming scenes, reporting which conditions elicited a faster response to contact time, causing the greatest amount of underestimation.

Keywords: Auditory-Visual Looming, Sound Design, Psychoacoustics.

1   Introduction

A feature of film and gaming is interacting with objects that move in space, particularly objects that move in depth towards the viewer. Examples can be seen in 3-D presentations where objects appear to leap out of the screen towards the viewer; and in gaming where judgements are made to avoid or attack approaching objects.

The sound that accompanies these looming objects can affect the extent to which a viewer can perceptually immerse within the multidimensional world and interact with the moving objects. To accurately generate a dynamic and rich perception of the looming objects, the design of such complex sounds should be based on a firm scientific foundation that encompasses what we know about how we visually and aurally perceive events and interactions.

2   Previous Research and Practice

Previous research on auditory looming has revealed that people associate an approaching object with at least three attributes of sound, including interaural temporal differences, frequency change, and amplitude change [1].

M. Aramaki et al. (Eds.): CMMR 2012, LNCS 7900, pp. 378–386, 2013.

In addition to finding that all three attributes of sound were associated with a looming object, they found that the change in amplitude elicited the fastest response to contact time, at the point in which the object passed, whilst the change in frequency prompted a response before the object had passed [1]. This underestimation of the contact time of a looming object implies that the object is approaching at a faster rate and is anticipated to contact sooner.

Later studies on auditory looming showed that people overestimate the magnitude of intensity when presented with increasing stimuli [2,3]. This implies that the increasing intensity of the approaching object is more dramatic than the extent of its physical approach.

In an evolutionary context for both the physical and virtual worlds, these overestimations of magnitude and underestimation of contact time provide an advantage to the observer, giving them more time to prepare (an increased safety margin) for the object's arrival, and to initiate the appropriate response (being fight or flight), therefore increasing the chance of survival.

However, many of these previous auditory looming perception experiments [1,2,3,4] have been conducted in extremely controlled conditions, with the aural stimuli consisting of simple tones (often a sine or triangle wave at 400 - 1000 Hz), and sound parameter manipulations such as an amplitude increase (between 10 - 30 dB), frequency change (using 804 Hz - 764.6 Hz, and 602.9 Hz - 572 Hz, which in musical terms equates to the tone and deviation of G5 $\pm$ 43 cents, and D5 $\pm$ 45 cents), and interaural temporal differences (a delay between the channels from 0.557 ms to 0.00 ms).

Limiting these variables used in experimental conditions compromises the ecological validity of the results, sound parameters manipulated, and real world application.

In contrast however, the film and gaming industries require sound designers to manipulate complex sounds, with the purpose of maximising the viewers' experience, immersiveness, responsiveness to onscreen action, and overall perception of the virtual environment.

Examination of the sound manipulation techniques that sound designers and post-production technicians use as cues for an approaching object in looming scenes provides a basis for a broader range of variables that can then be used in psychological studies on the perception of approaching objects.

Building upon our previous research [5] that examined the audio cues and techniques that sound designers use to generate the perception of an object moving in depth (looming), this research examines the percepts generated by complex sounds.

3   Feature Analysis Studies

A feature analysis study was previously conducted on the audio track of the 27 film looming scene samples used in this study, to understand which features the sound designers and post-production technicians were using as cues for auditory looming, how the features were manipulated, and the degree of the manipulation. Features that were analysed include: amplitude change; amplitude levels;

amplitude slope; interaural amplitude differences; pan position; spectral centroid; spectral spread; spectral flux; roll-off; and image motion tracking of the object.

In summary, our findings showed a number of similar techniques existed between the variety of samples. This includes:

- An average amplitude increase of 62.68 dB ($SD = 15.49$) on a linear / near-linear slope.
- The pan position centrally placed, and close to the image position, however fluctuates more than the image position. This fluctuation emphasises the spatial movement without having to hard pan to a single channel.
- An average spectral centroid increase of 1673.36 Hz.
- An average spectral flux increase of 167.0 Hz (with an average amount of flux of 13.8 Hz at the start of the sample, and 180.8 Hz at the peak).

In contrast to the previous auditory looming studies, the feature analysis of the film samples showed that they have:

- A greater range of variables used simultaneously to form complex looming stimuli (compared to the simple waves in the psychoacoustic studies).
- A greater increase in the levels that the variables were manipulated (i.e. 62.68 dB amplitude increase in the film samples, versus 10 - 30 dB in the psychoacoustic studies).

4   An Investigation of Responses to Complex Looming Sounds

This study is an extension of our previous research which examined the sound features in the looming samples, and will examine subjects' responses to the looming stimuli that uses complex sounds produced by the sound designers and technicians.

4.1   Aim

The aim of this study is to determine if a subject's response to a looming object differs with the inclusion of complex designed sounds that use multiple audio cues, as opposed to looming scenes with no sound.

4.2   Hypothesis

It is hypothesised that the combination of the multimodal (auditory-visual) presentation (with the greater number of cues used, and the greater amount of stimuli change) will cause people to underestimate the contact time of the approaching object, thereby eliciting a faster response time than the looming scenes with no sound.

4.3   Method

Participants. A sample of 15 participants oblivious to the study purpose were recruited. They were Ph.D students and Postdoc. researchers from Queen Mary, University of London aged between 20 and 36 years ($\mu = 27.07$ years, $SD = 4.70$), with more male participants than female participants (11 males, 4 females).

Stimuli. The stimuli consisted of 27 scenes that presented objects moving towards the viewer, and comprised both auditory and visual components. The scenes used are listed in Table 1. They were presented via computer with the visual stimulus presented on the monitor, and the auditory stimulus output through a pair of headphones.

The 27 scenes were presented in each of the three conditions - the multimodal (*sound and image*) condition, and the two unimodal conditions (*sound only* or *image only*). Each trial condition was presented once only (totaling 81 trial presentations) and in a randomised order.

Apparatus. Participants were located at a computer workstation with their head distanced approximately 40 cm from the computer monitor and eyes level with the centre of the monitor. A Mac Pro 1.1 with a NEC MultiSync EA221WM (LCD) monitor was used. The screen size was 22 inches with the resolution set to 1680 x 1050 pixels and the display was calibrated to a refresh rate of 60 Hz. The auditory stimulus was presented through Sennheiser HD515 headphones. The program MAX / MSP / Jitter version 4.6 was used to construct the software application that presented the auditory and visual stimuli, presented the trials in a randomised and collected order, timed the participants' responses using the computer's internal clock, and collected the participant responses in a text file.

Procedure. Participants sat at the computer workstation and were informed of the experiment procedure. They were given an information sheet summarising both the procedure and the ethics approval, signed a consent form, and completed a background questionnaire asking questions on gender, age, and whether they have had corrections made to their vision or hearing.

Before commencing the experiment, the participants completed a practise test using 6 looming scenes (that were not additionally presented in the experiment). It was conducted as a supervised learning procedure to enable the participants to comprehend the experiment, the procedure, the micro time scale of the stimulus, and how to complete the task.

Participants were then instructed to start the experiment when ready. The task required participants to watch and/or listen to the scene of an approaching object, and to press the keyboard 'space bar' when they thought the object was closest to them. Each trial lasted for a total duration of 0.5 - 3.0 seconds (depending on the looming scene presented) and a 6 second break was given between each trial. With a total of 81 trial presentations, the experiment lasted for approximately 25 minutes. Participants were not given any information implying there might be correct, incorrect or preferred responses.

Table 1. List of film scenes that were used in the experiment

#	Title	Year	Chapter, Time (min : sec)
1	The Matrix	1999	Chapter 1, 1:22 - 1:25
2	Star Wars (*Return of the Jedi*)	1983	Chapter 3, 0:20 - 0:24
3	Star Wars (*Revenge of the Sith*)	2005	Chapter 31, 3:08 - 3:09
4	X-men (*The Last Stand*)	2006	Chapter 15, 0:35 - 0:36
5	The Day After Tomorrow	2004	Chapter 12, 2:29 - 2:33
6	King Arthur	2004	Chapter 7, 10:46 - 10:48
7	Sherlock Holmes	2009	Chapter 22, 4:36 - 4:38
8	Van Helsing	2004	Chapter 17, 1:52 - 1:54
9	I Am Legend	2007	Chapter 17, 0:00 - 0:03
10	Troy	2007	Chapter 27, 2:22 - 2:24
11	Beowulf	2007	Chapter 2, 4:03 - 4:05
12	The Bourne Identity	2002	Chapter 12, 2:10 - 2:12
13	Charlie & the Chocolate Factory	2005	Chapter 15, 1:24 - 1:26
14	Mr and Mrs Smith	2005	Chapter 20, 0:40 - 0:44
15	Sin City	2005	Chapter 18, 1:06 - 1:07
16	28 Days Later	2002	Chapter 11, 0:01 - 0:04
17	Gattaca	1997	Chapter 21, 2:39 - 2:40
18	Alice in Wonderland	2010	Chapter 15, 0:19 - 0:20
19	Avatar	2009	Chapter 22, 1:42 - 1:45
20	Clash of the Titans	2010	Chapter 13, 4:11 - 4:13
21	Despicable Me	2010	Chapter 18, 2:23 - 2:24
22	Kill Bill vol2	2004	Chapter 6, 0:03 - 0:06
23	Mission Impossible 3	2006	Chapter 4, 1:06 - 1:08
24	Yogi Bear	2010	Chapter 1, 1:25 - 1:27
25	Final Destination	2009	Chapter 15, 0:06 - 0:07
26	Salt	2010	Chapter 9, 3:13 - 3:14
27	Saving Private Ryan	1998	Chapter 19, 3:17 - 3:21

4.4   Results

Image motion tracking was previously performed on each scene to determine the approaching object's position, size, and area, over time. For the purpose of this study, the time (of the frame) in which the object encompassed the greatest area was considered the contact point and is called the 'peak'.

Participants' responses to the stimuli (by pressing the keyboard 'space bar' when they thought the object was closest) was timed. This time was subtracted from the 'peak' time, to give the amount of time that was underestimated or overestimated, and for the purpose of this study is called the 'time to contact'.

Presentation Condition × Time to Contact. The time to contact was averaged across all of the participants responses, for each sample presentation condition, and is plotted in Figure 1.

Looking at the spread of the data, the majority of the trials caused participants to underestimate the contact time, rather than overestimate it, with the conditions that contained sound (being the *sound only* condition and the *sound + image* condition) having a greater underestimation than the condition with no sound (the *image only* condition).

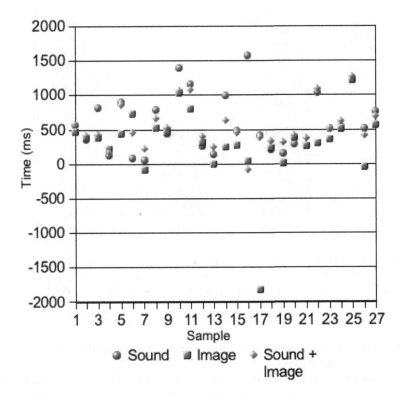

Fig. 1. Time to Contact × Sample × Presentation Condition The time to contact for each sample condition was averaged across all of the participants, and is plotted. The contact time occurs at 0ms, with any underestimation shown in the positive range of the scale, and overestimation shown in the negative range.

The time to contact was then averaged across all of the participants and samples, for each presentation condition, and is plotted in Figure 2.

The condition which generated the least 'time to contact' (least amount of underestimation, and was closest to the 'peak' time), was the *image only* condition ($M = 302.16$ ms, $SE = 100.62$), followed by the *sound + image* condition ($M = 534.75$ ms, $SE = 59.81$); and the *sound only* condition ($M = 591.74$ ms, $SE = 81.62$).

Clustered Results. Because certain samples caused people to overestimate the contact time, which could affect the analyses, the results were separated into

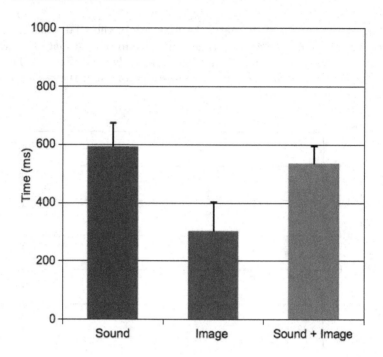

Fig. 2. Presentation × Time to Contact The results are plotted for each presentation condition (*sound only, image only, sound + image*) were averaged across all of the all of the samples and participants. The error bars indicate the standard error for each condition.

two clusters - those samples which caused an underestimation, and those which caused an overestimation.

This separation will allow us to obtain the average time to contact per condition, based on the samples which prompted people to underestimate or overestimate the contact time.

No trials had an average contact time during the image 'peak' (which had a duration of 41.67 ms, or one frame at 24 fps), with no individual participants indicating contact during this time.

Presentation Condition × Time to Contact (underestimation cluster). The condition that had the most number of trials in which the 'time to contact' was before the 'peak' time (therefore underestimating the contact time) was the *sound only* condition (with all 27 trials, totaling 100.00% of the trials presented for that condition; weighted mean = 591.74 ms, weighted standard deviation = 424.11); and the *sound + image* condition, (with 26 trials, totaling 96.30% of the trials presented for that condition; weighted mean = 537.91 ms, weighted standard deviation = 279.86); followed by the *image only* condition (with 23 trials, totaling 85.19% of the trials presented for that condition; weighted mean = 375.06ms, weighted standard deviation = 241.36).

Presentation Condition × Time to Contact (overestimation cluster).
The condition that had the most number of trials in which the 'time to contact' was after the 'peak' time (therefore overestimating the contact time) was the *image only* condition (with 4 trials, totaling 14.81% of the trials presented for that condition; weighted mean = -72.90 ms, weighted standard deviation = 131.94); followed by the *sound + image* condition (with 1 trial, totaling 3.70% of the trials presented for that condition; weighted mean = -3.16 ms); the *sound only* condition, when averaged across all of the participants, did not have any trials after the image peak.

4.5   Discussion

The results indicate that the *image only* condition had the slowest response to the contact time both before and after the peak time, with the least amount of underestimation before the 'peak' time and greatest amount of overestimation after the 'peak'.

In contrast, the *sound only* condition, which still only provided unimodal information about the approaching object, prompted participants to have the greatest amount of underestimation of the contact time, and furthermore, all of the samples generated an underestimation in the contact time (and none generating an overestimation).

This suggests that the addition of sound and looming audio cues (in both the *sound only* condition and the *sound + image* condition) prompted people to underestimate the contact time more often, and with a greater time frame, than the scenes that had no sound.

5   Conclusion

Although the individual sound parameters that act as the audio cues for an approaching object were not controlled and varied in this study, this investigation of the complex sounds in their original form as recorded or created by the sound designers has shown that the addition of sound, and the multiple techniques used to create audio cues, cause people to underestimate the contact time of an approaching object. This result suggests that further investigation is warranted, with future research on the complex stimuli's individual sound parameters, as independent variables, and the perception generated as a result.

References

1. Rosenblum, L., Carello, C., Pastore, R.: Relative effectiveness of three stimulus variables for locating a moving sound source. Perception 16, 175–186 (1987)
2. Neuhoff, J.G.: An adaptive bias in the perception of looming auditory motion. Ecological Psychology 13(2), 87–110 (2001)
3. Neuhoff, J.G., Heckel, T.: Sex differences in perceiving auditory "looming" produced by acoustic intensity change. In: Proceedings of ICAD 2004-Tenth Meeting of the International Conference on Auditory Display, Sydney, Australia (2004)

4. Cappe, C., Thut, G., Romei, V., Murray, M.M.: Selective integration of auditory-visual looming cues by humans. Neuropsychologia 47(4), 1045–1052 (2009)
5. Wilkie, S., Stockman, T., Reiss, J.D.: Amplitude Manipulation For Perceived Movement in Depth. In: 132nd Convention of the Audio Engineering Society, Budapest (2012)
6. Ghazanfar, A.A., Neuhoff, J.G., Logothetis, N.K.: Auditory looming perception in rhesus monkeys. Proceedings of the National Academy of Sciences 99(24), 15755–15757 (2002)
7. Maier, J.X., Chandrasekaran, C., Ghazanfar, A.A.: Integration of Bimodal Looming Signals through Neuronal Coherence in the Temporal Lobe. Current Biology 18, 963–968 (2008)
8. Maier, J.X., Ghazanfar, A.A.: Looming biases in monkey auditory cortex. Journal of Neuroscience 27(15), 4093–4100 (2007)
9. Maier, J., Neuhoff, J., Logothetis, N., Ghazanfar, A.: Multisensory integration of looming signals by rhesus monkeys. Neuron 43, 177–181 (2004)
10. Neuhoff, J.G.: Ecological psychoacoustics: introduction and history. Ecological Psychoacoustics. Elsevier Academic Press, California (2004)
11. Rosenblum, L., Wuestefeld, A., Saldana, H.: Auditory looming perception: Influences on anticipatory judgements. Perception 22, 1467–1482 (1993)

Maximum a Posteriori Estimation of Piecewise Arcs in Tempo Time-Series

Dan Stowell and Elaine Chew

Centre for Digital Music, Queen Mary, University of London
dan.stowell@eecs.qmul.ac.uk

Abstract. In musical performances with expressive tempo modulation, the tempo variation can be modelled as a sequence of tempo arcs. Previous authors have used this idea to estimate series of piecewise arc segments from data. In this paper we describe a probabilistic model for a time-series process of this nature, and use this to perform inference of single- and multi-level arc processes from data. We describe an efficient Viterbi-like process for MAP inference of arcs. Our approach is score-agnostic, and together with efficient inference allows for online analysis of performances including improvisations, and can predict immediate future tempo trajectories.

Keywords: tempo, expression, Viterbi, time series.

1 Introduction

In various types of musical performance, one component of the musical expression is conveyed in the short-term manipulation of tempo, with tempo modulation reflecting musical phrase structure [7,9]. This has motivated various authors to construct automatic analyses of the arc-shaped tempo modulations in recorded musical performances, with or without score-derived information to supplement the analysis [7,9,5]. (See also [6] who fit piecewise linear arcs to rock and jazz data, applying similar techniques but to genres in which the underlying tempo is held more fixed.)

Machine understanding of tempo, including its variability, can be useful in live human-machine interaction [1,8]. However most current online tempo-tracking systems converge to an estimate of the current tempo, modelling expressive variations as deviations rather than as components of an unfolding tempo expression. In this paper we work towards the understanding of tempo arcs in a real-time system, paving the way for automatic accompaniment systems which follow the expressive tempo modulation of players in a more natural way.

We also consider tempo arcs within a probabilistic framework. Previous authors have approached piecewise arc estimation using Dynamic Programming (DP) with cost functions based on squared error [5,6]. These are useful and can provide efficient estimation, but by setting the problem in a probabilistic framework (and providing the corresponding Viterbi-like DP estimator), we gain some

M. Aramaki et al. (Eds.): CMMR 2012, LNCS 7900, pp. 387–399, 2013.

advantages: prior beliefs about the length and shape of arcs can be expressed coherently as prior distributions; measurement noise is explicitly modelled; and the goodness-of-fit of models is represented meaningfully as posterior probabilities, which allows for model comparison as well as integration with other workflow components which can make use of estimates annotated with probability values. Note that while we describe a fully probabilistic model, for efficient inference we will develop a Maximum A Posteriori (MAP) estimator, which returns only the maximum probability parameter settings given the priors and the data.

In the following we will describe our model of arcs in time-series data, and develop an efficient MAP estimation technique based on least-squares optimisation and Viterbi-like DP. The approach requires some kind of unsmoothed instantaneous tempo estimate as its input, which may come from a tempo tracker or from a simple measurement such as inter-onset interval (IOI). We will then discuss how the estimator can be used for immediate-future tempo prediction, and how it can be applied to multiple levels simultaneously. Finally we will apply the technique to tempo data from three professional piano performances, and discuss what the analysis reflects in the performances.

2   Modelling and Estimation

For our basic model, we consider tempo to evolve as a function of metrical position (beat number) x in a musical piece as a series of connected arcs, where each arc's duration, curvature and slope are independently drawn from prior distributions (to be described shortly). Our model is deliberately simple, and agnostic of any score information that might be available. To sample from this model, we pick an initial tempo at the starting time, then define a single upwards tempo arc which starts from that point, and the tempo trajectory (speeding up and then slowing down) over a number of measures. Any tempo data which may be measured during this interval is modelled as being drawn from the arc plus some amount of gaussian noise. Once the ending breakpoint of this arc is reached, the next arc is sampled from the same priors, using the ending tempo as the new starting tempo. Hence each tempo arc is conditionally independent of all previous observations once the starting tempo is determined, i.e. once the previous arc's parameters are fixed. This assumption of conditional independence is slightly unrealistic, since it ignores long-range relationships between tempo arcs, but it accounts for the most important interactions and makes inference tractable.

Our basic model is also only single-level, assuming that a single arc contributes to the current tempo at any moment, rather than considering for example contributions from multiple timescales such as piece-level, movement-level, phrase-level and bar-level combined. In Section 2.4 we will consider a simple multi-scale extension of our technique, which we will apply in our analysis of piano performance data. (For an alternative approach in which various components can be simultaneously active see [7].)

2.1 Fitting a Single Arc

To fit a single arc shape to data, one can use standard quadratic regression, fitting a function of the form

$$f(x) = a + bx + cx^2, \tag{1}$$

and minimising the L_2 prediction error over the supplied data for $y \approx f(x)$. In the Bayesian context, we wish to incorporate our prior beliefs about the regression parameters (here a, b and c), which is related to the optimisation concept of *regularisation*, the class of techniques which aims to prevent overfitting by favouring certain parameter settings. In fact, a gaussian prior on a regression parameter can be shown to be equivalent to the conventional L_2-norm regularisation of the parameters [2, p. 153], summarised as:

$$\text{regularisation coefficient} = \frac{\text{variance of gaussian noise}}{\text{variance of gaussian prior}}. \tag{2}$$

This equivalence is useful because it allows us to use common convex optimisation algorithms to perform the equivalent regularised least squares optimisation, and they will yield the MAP estimate for the probabilistic model.

However, in this context a standard gaussian prior is not exactly what we require, since we are expecting upwards arcs and not troughs – we are expecting c in Equation 1 to be negative. A more appropriate choice of prior might be a negative log-gaussian distribution, which allows us to specify a "centre of mass" for the arc shapes (expressed through the log-mean and log-standard-deviation parameters), yet better represents our expectation that tempo arcs will always have negative curvature, (almost) flat and extremely strongly curved arcs being equally rare.

The unconventional choice of prior might seem to remove the equivalence of the MAP regression technique with standard regularised least squres. Yet if we rewrite our function to be

$$f(x) = a + bx - e^c x^2, \tag{3}$$

then our prior belief about this modified parameter c becomes a gaussian, yielding a negative-log-gaussian in combination with our function. In addition, we will use a standard gaussian prior on b. We could do the same for a but instead we will use an improper uniform prior, for reasons which will be described in Section 2.2. Therefore, our priors for Equation 3 will be gaussian priors on b and c, which can easily be converted to the equivalent L_2-regularisation terms for optimisation.

The strength of the regularisation (the value of the regularisation coefficient) reflects the specificity of our priors versus our data – specifically, the regularisation parameter is given by the noise variance divided by the prior variance [2, p. 153]. Again, we see how the probabilistic setting helps to ground our problem, connecting the strength of the regularisation directly to our prior beliefs about the model and the data rather than manually-tuned parameters.

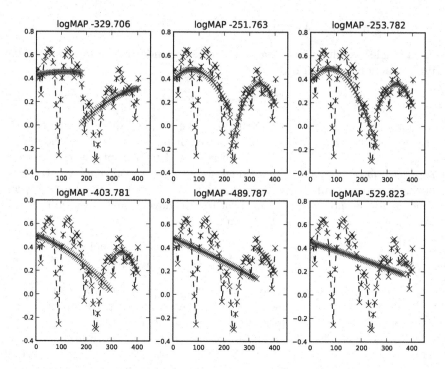

Fig. 1. A selection of piecewise arc fits performed on a synthetic dataset. For illustration purposes, we have manually specified a sequence of possible breakpoint locations, and then performed a single-arc fit within each subsection. The "logMAP" (log of MAP probability) values quoted with each plot indicate the relative likelihood assigned to the depicted fit, given the prior parameters chosen. Prior parameters are the same for each of these plots. The best-fitting plots have correspondingly higher (less negative) logMAP values.

2.2   Fitting Multiple Arcs

If a time-series is composed of multiple arcs and the breakpoints are known, then fitting multiple arcs is as simple as performing the above single-arc fit for each subsection of the time series (as in Figure 1). Additionally, one should take care of the arc's dependence upon its predecessor (to enforce that they meet up), which is not shown in these plots. In our case, we want to estimate the breakpoint locations as well as the arc shapes between those breakpoints. This can be performed by iterating over all possible combinations of one breakpoint, two breakpoints, three (...) for the dataset, and choosing the result with the lowest cost (the highest posterior likelihood).

The Bayesian setting makes it possible to compare these different alternatives (e.g. one single arc vs. one arc for every datapoint) without having to add arbitrary terms to counter overfitting; instead, we specify a prior distribution over the arc durations, which in combination with the other priors and data likelihoods yields a MAP probability for any proposed set of arcs. In this paper we choose a log-normal prior distribution over arc durations. See Figure 1 for some examples of different sets of arcs fitting to a synthetic dataset, and the posterior (log-)probabilities associated.

In order for only a single tempo value to exist at each breakpoint (and not a discontinuous leap from one tempo to another), we fit each arc under the constraint that its starting value equals the ending value of the previous arc. This removes one degree of freedom from the function to be fit (Equation 3) which otherwise has three free parameters. We implement this by constraining the value of a in the optimisation so that the function evaluates to the predetermined value at the appropriate time-point. The least-squares optimisation therefore only operates on b and c.

2.3   Viterbi-Like Algorithm

The number of possible combinations of arcs for even a small time-series (such as Figure 1) grows quickly very large, and so it is impractical to iterate all combinations. This is where Dynamic Programming (DP) can help. Here we describe our DP algorithm, which, like the well-known Viterbi algorithm, maintains a record of the most likely route that leads to each of a set of possible states. Rather than applying it to the states of a Hidden Markov Model, we apply it to the possibility that each incoming datum represents a breakpoint.

Assume that the first incoming datum is a breakpoint. (This assumption can be relaxed, in a similar way to the treatment of the final datum which we consider later.) Then, for each incoming datum (x_n, y_n), we find what would be the most likely path *if it were certainly* a breakpoint. We do this by finding the most appropriate past datum (x_{n-k}, y_{n-k}) which could begin an arc to the current datum – where the appropriateness is judged from the MAP probability of said arc, combined with the MAP probability of the whole multiple-arc history that leads up to that past datum (recursively defined).

With our lognormal prior on the arc lengths (and with many common choices of prior), the probability mass is concentrated at an expected time-scale, and very long arcs are highly improbable *a priori*. Hence in practice we truncate the search over potential previous arc points to some maximum limit K (i.e. $k \leq K$).

Thus, for every incoming data point we perform no more than K single-arc fits, then store the details of the chosen arc, the MAP probability so far, and a pointer back to the datapoint at the start of the chosen single arc. The simplest way to choose the overall MAP estimate is then to pick another definite breakpoint (for example, the last datum if the performance has finished) and backtrack from there to recover the MAP arc path.

Complexity. The time complexity of the algorithm depends strongly on that of the convex optimisation used to perform a single-arc fit. Assume that the complexity of a single-arc fit is proportional to the number of data points k included in the fit, where $k \leq K$. Then for each incoming data point a search is performed for one subset each of 2, 3, . . . K data points, which essentially yields an order $\mathcal{O}(K^2)$ process. For online processing this is manageable if K is not too large. Analysing a whole dataset of M points then has time complexity $\mathcal{O}(K^2 M)$. (Compare this to the broadly similar complexity analysis of [6].) The space complexity is simply $\mathcal{O}(M)$, or $\mathcal{O}(K)$ if the full arc history since the very beginning does not need to be stored. This is because a small fixed amount of data is stored per datapoint.

Predicting Immediate Future Arcs. As discussed, if we know the performance has finished then we can find the Viterbi path leading to a breakpoint at the final data point received. However, we would also like to determine the most likely set of arcs in cases where the performance might not have finished (e.g. for real-time interactive systems), and thus where we do not wish to assert that the latest datum is a breakpoint. We wish to be able to estimate an arc which may still be in progress. If we can, this has a specific benefit of predicting the immediate future evolution of the tempo modulations (until the end of the present arc), which may be particularly useful for real-time interaction.

We can carry this out in our current approach as follows. Since an arc's duration (as well as the curve-fit) affects its MAP probability, in the case where the latest arc may or may not be terminating we must iterate over the arc's possible durations and pick the most likely. To do this we choose a set of future time-points as candidate breakpoints, $x_{n+1} \ldots x_{n+J}$ (e.g. an evenly-spaced tatum grid of $J = K$ future points). Then we supply these data to the Viterbi update process exactly as is done with actual data, but with no associated y values. These "hypothetical" Viterbi updates will use these time-points to determine the arc-lengths being estimated, and in normalising the data subset, but will not include them in the arc-fitting process. It will therefore yield a MAP probability estimate for each of the time-points as if an arc extended from the real data as far as this hypothetical breakpoint. Out of these possibilities, the one with the highest MAP probability is the MAP estimate for an arc which includes the latest real datum and some portion of the hypothetical future points. (The hypothetical Viterbi updates are not preserved: if more data comes in, it is appended to the Viterbi storage corresponding only to the actual data.)

2.4   Multi-scale Estimation

The model we describe operates at one level, with expected arc durations given by the corresponding prior. Our model is adaptable to any time-scale by simply adapting the prior. It does not however automatically lend itself to simultaneous consideration of multiple active timescales.

Multi-scale analysis can be carried out by analysing a dataset with one timescale, then analysing the residual at a second timescale. This residual-based decomposition has been used previously in the literature (e.g. [9]); it requires a strong hierarchical assumption that the arcs at the first timescale do not depend at all on those at the second timescale, while the second is subordinate to the first. We consider this to be unrealistic, since there may well be interactions between the different timescales on which a performer's expression evolves. However this assumption leads to a tractable analysis.

Note also that this approach to multi-scale estimation requires the first analysis to be completed (so that the residual is known) before the second scale can be analysed. Some DP approach may be possible to enable both to be calculated online, but we have not developed that here. For the present work, the single-scale Viterbi tracking is applicable and useful for online tracking, while multi-scale analysis is an offline process, which we will next apply to modelling of pre-recorded tempo data.

3   Analysis of Expressive Piano Performance

We applied our analysis to an existing set of annotations of three performances of Beethoven's *Moonlight Sonata*. The annotations by Elaine Chew have previously been analysed by Chew with reference to observations noted by Jeanne Bamberger [4]. For each of three well-known performances of the piece—by Daniel Barenboim (1987), Maurizio Pollini (1992) and Artur Schnabel (2009)—the first 15 bars have been annotated with note onset times, which correspond to regular triplet eighth-note timings.

We implemented the algorithm in Python, using the `scipy.optimize.fmin` optimiser to solve individual regressions. Source code is available.[1] (Note that this development implementation is not generally fast enough for real-time use.)

Instantaneous tempo was derived from these inter-onset intervals, then analysed using a two-pass version of our algorithm: first the data was analysed using an arc-duration prior centred on four bars; then the residual was analysed using an arc-duration prior centred on one bar. This choice of timescales is a relatively generic choice which might reasonably be considered to reflect a performer's short-term and medium-term state; however it might also be said to be a form of basic contextual information about the relevant timescales in the current piece. For the current study, we confine ourselves to priors with log-normal shapes, though an explicitly score-derived or corpus-derived prior could have a more tailored and perhaps multimodal shape.

Figure 2 shows a set of manual annotations of hierarchically embedded phrases, and Figure 3 shows the automatically computed results. The automatic analyses show some notable similarities with the manual one at the shorter time scale, and significant differences at the longer time scale. The difficulty of the longer time scale analysis may be explained by Figure 5, which shows one plausible set of phrase groupings for this excerpt; the overlapping {5,5,7} bar phrases do not fit easily into a four-bar duration framework.

Nevertheless, the longer time scale analysis (centred on four bars) highlights differences between the performances: Pollini's performance appears to contain relatively little variation on this level, as the fit yields long and shallow arcs, with breakpoints near positions 48, 96 and 168 (structurally important positions; 96

---

[1] https://code.soundsoftware.ac.uk/projects/arcsml

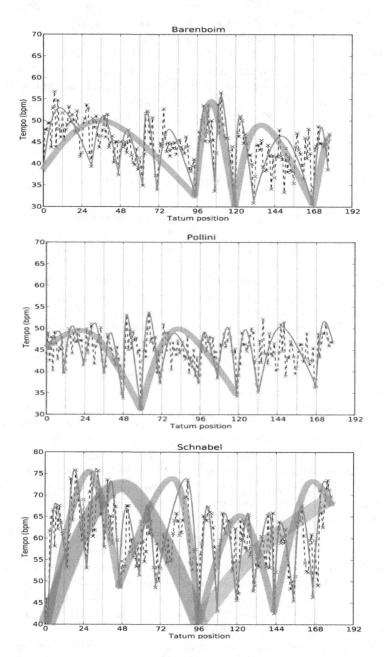

Fig. 2. Manual analyses of performances by each of three pianists (Barenboim, Pollini, Schnabel). Two to three levels of arcs are drawn by visual inspection for each tempo time series. No higher level arcs are drawn when it is uncertain that one exists.

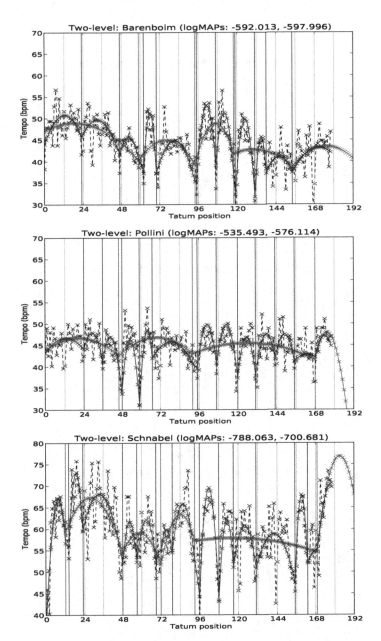

Fig. 3. Two-level analysis of performances by each of three pianists (Barenboim, Pollini, Schnabel). In each plot, the first long-scale fit (centred on the four-bar timescale) is depicted in red, and the second shorter-scale fit (centred on the one-bar timescale) is given in blue. The second fit is pre-offset by the first, meaning the blue arcs display the combined model produced by both timescales combined. Annotated data finish at tatum 180; where the MAP choice extends beyond that, we show the predicted immediate future arc.

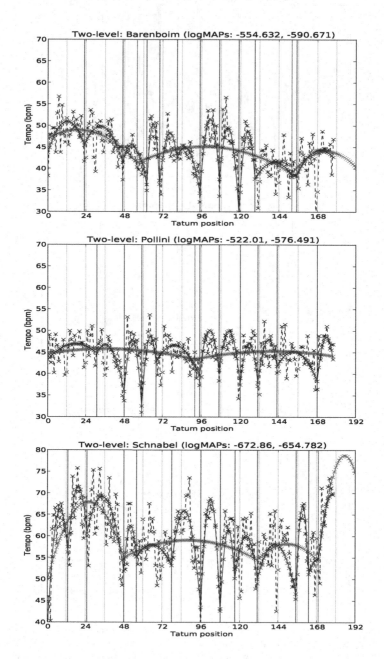

Fig. 4. As Figure 3 but with the standard deviation of the noise prior set at 4.0 rather than 3.0

Fig. 5. Possible set of overlapping phrases in the first 15 bars of the Moonlight Sonata

is where the key-change occurs). On the other hand, both Barenboim and Schnabel's tempo curves exhibit fairly deep and varied arcs. Schnabel's performance exhibits the most dramatic variation in the first four bars until around measure 48: this first four-bar section corresponds to the opening statement of the basic progression, before the melody enters in the fifth bar (and the underlying progression repeats). Bamberger described Schnabel as performing them "as if in one long breath" (quoted in [4]), not quite reflected in our automatic analysis.

On the shorter time scale, the analysis tends to group phrases into one-bar or two-bar arcs. Aspects of the musical structure are reflected in the arcs observed. Sections of the melody which lend themselves to two-bar phrasing (e.g. 72–96) are generally reflected in longer arcs crossing bar lines. Conversely, in the region 96–132 the change to the new key unfolds as each new chord enters at the start of a bar, and the tempo curves for all three performers reflect an expressive focus on this feature, with one-bar arcs which are more closely locked to the bar-lines than elsewhere. Note that in this section Schnabel matches Pollini in exhibiting a long and shallow arc on the slow timescale, with all the expressive variation concentrated on the one-bar arcs.

Over the excerpt generally, the breakpoints for Schnabel are further away from the barline than the others, as was observed in Chew's manual analysis. We can quantify this by measuring the mean deviances of arc endpoints from the barlines in each performance. The resulting mean deviances confirm our observations (Table 1).

We have extended the plots slightly beyond the 180 annotated data points, to illustrate the immediate-future predictions made by the model. (This is done for both timescales, though only the longer timescale (in red) shows noticeable extended arcs.) All the performers, and especially Schnabel, exhibit an acceleration towards the end of the annotated data, reflected in the predictions of an upward arc followed by a gradual slowing over the next bar. This type of prediction is plausible for such expressively-timed music.

Table 1. Mean deviance from the barlines of the arc endpoints inferred for each performance, averaged over the short-timescale arcs in each case

Performer	Mean deviance (bars)
Barenboim	13.9%
Pollini	8.3%
Schnabel	15.5%

To illustrate the effect that the prior parameters have upon the regression, Figure 4 shows the same analysis as Figure 3 but with the standard deviation of the noise prior set at 4.0 rather than 3.0. The increase in the assumed noise variance leads the algorithm to "trust" the data less and the prior slightly more (cf. Equation 2). In our example, some of the breakpoints for the long-term arcs (in red) have changed, losing some detail, though most of the detail of the second-level analysis (in blue) is consistent.

4   Conclusions

We have described a model with similarities to some previous piecewise-arc models of musical expression, but with a Bayesian formulation which facilitates model comparison and the principled incorporation of prior beliefs. We have also described an efficient Viterbi-like Dynamic Programming approach to estimation of the model from data. The approach provides scope to apply the model to real-time score-free performance tracking, including prediction of immediate future tempo modulation. Source code for the algorithm (in Python) is available.

We have applied the model in a two-level analysis to data from expressive piano performance, illustrating the algorithm's capacity to operate at different time-scales, and to recover expressive arc information that corresponds with some musicological observations regarding phrasing and timing.

Further research would be needed to develop a model of multiple simultaneously-active levels of expression which can be applied online as with our single-level Viterbi-like algorithm. Similar arcs have been observed and analysed in loudness information extracted from performances [3]. It would also be useful to combine loudness information with tempo information in this model.

References

1. Allen, P.E., Dannenberg, R.B.: Tracking musical beats in real time. In: Proc. International Computer Music Conference (ICMC), Hong Kong, pp. 140–143 (1990)
2. Bishop, C.M.: Pattern Recognition and Machine Learning, vol. 4. Springer, New York (2006)
3. Cheng, E., Chew, E.: Quantitative analysis of phrasing strategies in expressive performance: computational methods and analysis of performances of unaccompanied bach for solo violin. Journal of New Music Research 37(4), 325–338 (2008), doi:10.1080/09298210802711660

4. Chew, E.: About time: Strategies of performance revealed in graphs. Visions of Research in Music Education 20(1) (January 2012), http://www-usr.rider.edu/~vrme/v20n1/

5. Chuan, C.H., Chew, E.: A dynamic programming approach to the extraction of phrase boundaries from tempo variations in expressive performances. In: Proceedings of the International Conference on Music Information Retrieval (ISMIR), Vienna, Austria URL, pp. 305–308 (2007), http://ismir2007.ismir.net/proceedings/ISMIR2007_p305_chuan.pdf

6. Dannenberg, R.B., Mohan, S.: Characterizing tempo change in musical performances. In: Proceedings of the International Computer Music Conference (ICMC), pp. 650–656 (2011)

7. McAngus Todd, N.P.: The dynamics of dynamics: A model of musical expression. Journal of the Acoustical Society of America 91(6), 3540–3550 (1992), doi:10.1121/1.402843

8. Robertson, A., Plumbley, M.D.: B-Keeper: A beat-tracker for live performance. In: Proc. International Conference on New Interfaces for Musical Expression (NIME), New York, USA, pp. 234–237 (2007), doi:10.1145/1279740.1279787

9. Widmer, G., Tobudic, A.: Playing Mozart by analogy: Learning multi-level timing and dynamics strategies. Journal of New Music Research 32(3), 259–268 (2003), doi:10.1076/jnmr.32.3.259.16860

Structural Similarity Based on Time-Span Tree

Satoshi Tojo[1] and Keiji Hirata[2]

[1] Japan Advanced Institute of Science and Technology
tojo@jaist.ac.jp
[2] Future University Hakodate
hirata@fun.ac.jp

Abstract. The *time-span tree* is a dependable representation of musical structure since most experienced listeners deliver the same one, almost independently of context and subjectivity. In this paper, we pay attention to the reduction hypothesis of the tree structure, and introduce a notion of distance as a promising candidate of stable and consistent metric of similarity. First, we design a feature structure to represent a time-span tree. Next, we regard that when a branch is removed from the tree, that is, its corresponding pitch event is reduced, the amount of information comparable to its time-span is lost. Then, we suggest that the sum of the length of those removed spans is the distance between two trees. We will show mathematical properties of the distance, including that the distance becomes unique in multiple shortest paths. Thereafter, we illustrate how the distance works in a set of reductions. We consider a metric of similarity both from human cognition and from set operation, and discuss the relation of distance and similarity. Also, we discuss such other related issues as flexible tree matching and music rendering.

Keywords: Similarity, time-span reduction, feature structure, join, meet.

1 Introduction

As is remarked in [26], *an ability to assess similarity lies close to the core of cognition.* Music similarity is multi-faceted as well [16], and inevitably raises a context-dependent, subjective behavior [15]. As to context dependency, similarity cannot be perceived in isolation from the musical context in which it occurs. Volk stated in [23]: *Depending on the context, similarity can be described using very different features.* For instance, the impact of cultural knowledge may degrade a stable similarity assessment. As to subjectivity, similarity is perceived differently from person to person, even within a person, depending on listening style, preference, and so on.

Thus far, many research initiatives have explored stable and consistent similarity metrics as a central topic in music modelling and music information retrieval [9,4]. Some of them are motivated by engineering demands such as music retrieval, classification, and recommendation [16,7,20], and others are by modelling the cognitive processes as reported in the Discussion Forum on music similarity [5,6]. In this paper, we also seek for a stable and consistent similarity, avoiding context-dependency and subjectivity. We regard that similarity is stable in the sense that similarity assessment is performed only on a score of music, disregarding such context-dependent factors as

M. Aramaki et al. (Eds.): CMMR 2012, LNCS 7900, pp. 400–421, 2013.
© Springer-Verlag Berlin Heidelberg 2013

timber, artist, subject matter of lyrics, and cultural factors. Also, we regard that similarity assessment is consistent in the sense that most experienced listeners can deliver same results, as long as the western-tonal-classical music is targeted. To propose a stable and consistent similarity, we rely on the assumption that the cognitive reality or the perceptual universality reside in music. As addressed in [24], *systems which aim to encode musical similarity must do so in a human-like way.* Our approach is parallel to this research direction. Note that such cognitive reality may depend on a category of music that each music theory targets, which is prescribed by a genre, style, and other features.

Now, we take the stance that *tree* structure underlies such cognitive reality. Bod claimed in his DOP model [1] that there lies cognitive plausibility in combining a rule-based system with a fragment memory when a listener parses music and produces a relevant tree structure, like a linguistic model. Lerdahl and Jackendoff presumed that perceived musical structure is internally represented in the form of hierarchies, which means *time-span tree* and *strong reduction hypothesis* in the Generative Theory of Tonal Music (GTTM, hereafter) [13, p.2, pp.105-112, p.332]. Dibben argued that the experimental results show that pitch events in tonal music are heard in a strictly hierarchical manner and provide evidence for the internal cognitive representation of time-span tree of GTTM [3]. Wiggins et al. deployed discussions on the tree structures and argued that they are more about semantic grouping than about syntactic grouping [25]. We basically follow their views, under which we assume the time-span tree of a music piece represents its meaning. Here, we need to admit that GTTM has its inherent problem, that is, those ambiguous preference rules may result in multiple time-span analyses; however, we have solved this issue, assigning a parametric weight to each rule, and have implemented an automatic tree analyzer [8].

Among the properties of time-span tree, in particular, we consider the concept of *reduction* essential, when a time-span tree subsumes a reduced one. Selfridge-Field also claimed that a relevant way of taking deep structures (meaning) into account is to adopt the concept of reduction [21]. The subsumption relation between time-span trees is defined as a partial order, and this fact implies that we can treat time-span trees (i.e., the meaning of a music piece) as mathematical entities. Our objective is to derive a notion of distance from the reduction and the subsumption relation, to employ it as a metric of similarity. In this paper, we attempt to formally design the similarity based on the time-span reduction. At this stage, our attitude toward the design is strictly computational; that is, there must lie a reliable logical and algebraic structure so that we will be able to implement the similarity onto computers.

In effect, tree representation has contributed to the study on similarity. Here, we briefly summarize the related works concerning the tree representation of music structures. Marsden proposed a representational framework for polyphony, employing not only ternary but also n-ary ($n \geq 4$) relations in pitch events [14]. Marsden began with conventional tree representations and allowed joining of branches in the limited circumstances with the directed acyclic graph (DAG) to express information dependency [14]. As a result, high expressiveness was achieved, though it was difficult to define consistent similarity between music pieces. Rizo Valero proposed a representation method dedicated to a similarity comparison task, called *metrical tree* [18]. He used a binary tree representing the metrical hierarchy of music and avoided the necessity of explicitly encoding onsets and duration; only pitches were needed to be encoded. For ease of a similarity comparison, he also gave several procedures concerning propagating pitch labels from the leaves upward to those at the internal nodes in a metrical tree. As a measure to compare metrical trees, he adopted the tree edit distance with many parameters, such as the cost for each edit operation, for the label-propagation procedure, and for the pruning level to control the metrical resolution. Metrical tree was intuitive, easy to automatize, and had a wide range of applicability. The parameter setup, however, was justified by the best performance in experiments, not by the theoretical point of view.

In the following Section 2, we translate a time-span tree into a feature structure, carefully preventing the other factors from slipping into the structure, to guarantee stability. In Section 3, we define a notion of distance between time-span trees and then show that the notion enjoys several desirable mathematical properties, including the triangle inequality. In Section 4, we illustrate our analysis. Then, we try to position our distance in other criteria in Section 5. In Section 6 we discuss open problems concerning how we can apply our notion of distance to music similarity, and in Section 7 we summarize our contribution.

2   Time-Span Tree in Feature Structure

In this section, we develop the representation method for time-span tree in [11,10], in terms of feature structure. First we introduce the general notion of feature structure, and then we propose a set of necessary features to represent a time-span tree. The set of feature structures are partially ordered, and thus we define such algebraic operations as *meet* and *join* and show that the set becomes a *lattice*. Since this section and the following section include mathematical foundation, those who would like to see examples first may jump to Section 4 and come back to technical details afterward.

2.1   Time-Span Tree and Reduction

A music piece is considered to be a sequence of pitch events, i.e., notes or chords, in a temporal order. Time-span reduction [13] assigns structural importance to each pitch events in the hierarchical way. The structural importance is derived from the *grouping analysis*, in which multiple notes compose a short phrase called a group, and from the *metrical analysis*, where strong and weak beats are properly assigned on each pitch event. As a result, a time-span tree becomes a binary tree constructed in a bottom-up manner by comparison between the structural importance of adjacent pitch events at different hierarchical levels.

Fig. 1 shows an excerpt from [13] demonstrating the concept of reduction. In the sequence of reductions, each level should sound like a natural simplification of the previous level.[1] In other words, the more reductions proceed, each sounds dissimilar

---

[1] Once a music piece is reduced, each note with onset and duration properties becomes a virtual note that is just a pitch event being salient during the corresponding time-span, omitting onset and duration. Therefore, to listen to a reduced melody, we assume that it needs to be rendered by regarding a time-span as a real note with such onset timing and duration.

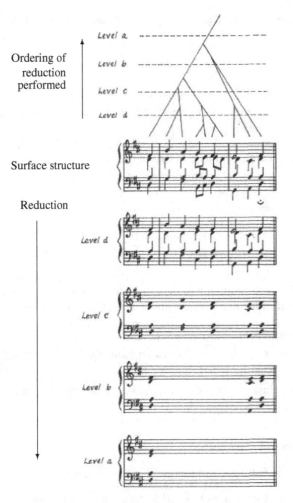

Ordering of reduction performed

Surface structure

Reduction

Fig. 1. Time-span reduction in GTTM (Lerdahl and Jackendoff [13, page 115])

to the original. Reduction can be regarded as abstraction, but if we could find a proper way of reduction, we can retrieve a basic melody line of the original music piece. The key idea of our framework is that reduction is identified with the subsumption relation, which is one of the most fundamental relations in knowledge representation.

2.2 Feature Structure and Subsumption Relation

Feature structure (*f-structure*, hereafter) [2] has been mainly studied for applications to linguistic formalism based on unification and constraint, such as Head-driven Phrase Structure Grammar (HPSG) [19]. An f-structure is a list of feature-value pairs where a value may be replaced by another f-structure recursively. Below is an f-structure in attribute-value matrix (AVM) notation where σ is a structure, the label headed by ' $\sim$ '

(tilde) is the *type* of the whole structure, and f_i's are feature labels and v_i's are their values:

$$\sigma = \begin{bmatrix} \tilde{~}type \\ f_1 \; v_1 \\ f_2 \; v_2 \end{bmatrix} .$$

Each type requires its indispensable features. When all these intrinsic features are properly valued, the f-structure is said to be *full-fledged*.

Now we define the notion of *subsumption*. Let σ_1 and σ_2 be f-structures. σ_2 subsumes σ_1, that is, $\sigma_1 \sqsubseteq \sigma_2$ if and only if for any $(f \; v) \in \sigma_1$ there exists $(f \; v) \in \sigma_2$. Here '$\sqsubseteq$' corresponds to the so-called Hoare order of sets (e.g., $\{b, d\} \sqsubseteq \{a, b, c, d\}$).[2] For example, σ_1 below is subsumed by the following σ_2 but not by σ_3 unless v_1 is another f-structure such that $v_1 \sqsubseteq [f_3 \; v_3]$.

$$\sigma_1 = \begin{bmatrix} \tilde{~}type1 \\ f_1 \; v_1 \end{bmatrix} , \qquad \sigma_2 = \begin{bmatrix} \tilde{~}type1 \\ f_1 \; v_1 \\ f_2 \; v_2 \end{bmatrix} , \qquad \sigma_3 = \begin{bmatrix} \tilde{~}type1 \\ f_1 \begin{bmatrix} \tilde{~}type2 \\ f_3 \; v_3 \end{bmatrix} \end{bmatrix} .$$

Since there is no direct subsumption relation between σ_2 and σ_3, ordering '$\sqsubseteq$' is a partial order, not a total order like integers and real numbers. Equivalence $a = b$ is defined as $a \sqsubseteq b \wedge b \sqsubseteq a$.

To denote value v of feature f in structure σ, we write $\sigma.f = v$. Thus, $\sigma_1.f_1 = v_1$ and $\sigma_1.f_2$ is undefined while $\sigma_3.f_1.f_3 = v_3$. We call a sequence of features $f_1.f_2.\cdots.f_n$ a *feature path*. Structure sharing is indicated by boxed tags such as $\boxed{i}$ or $\boxed{j}$. The set value $\{x, y\}$ means the choice either of x or y, and $\bot$ means that the value is empty. Even for $\bot$, any feature f_i is accessible though $\bot.f_i = \bot$.

2.3 Time-Span Trees in F-Structures

We defin type $\tilde{~}tree$ of an f-structure, to represent a time-span tree.

Definition 1 (Tree Type F-structure). *A full-fledged $\tilde{~}tree$ f-structure possesses the following features.*

- *head represents the most salient pitch event in the tree.*
- *span represents the length of the time-span of the whole tree, measured by the number of quarter notes.*
- *dtrs (daughters) are subtrees, whose left and right are recursively $\tilde{~}tree$. This dtrs feature is characterized by the following two conditions.*
  - *The value of span must be the addition of two spans of the daughters.*
  - *The value of head is chosen from either that of left or of right daughter.*

If $head = dtrs.left.head$, it is right-branching, while if $head = dtrs.right.head$, left-branching. If $dtrs = \bot$ then the tree consists of a single branch with a single pitch event at its leaf.

---

[2] When a subsumption relation is also defined in atomic values, e.g., $v_1 \sqsubseteq v_2$, $\sigma_1 \sqsubseteq \sigma_2$ if and only if for any $(f \; v_1) \in \sigma_1$ there exists $(f \; v_2) \in \sigma_2$.

Fig. 2 shows the examples. Such bold-face letters as **C4**, **E4** and **G4** are trees for pitch events, in which the value of *head* feature is occupied by ˜*event* f-structure with *pitch*, *onset*, and *duration* features, where *duration* of ˜*event* coincides with that of *span* in its upper ˜*tree*.

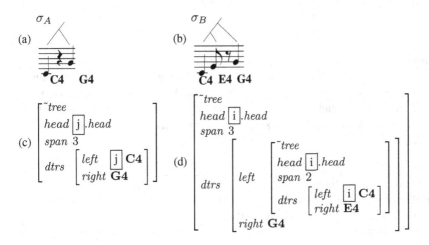

Fig. 2. Melodies (a) and (b) and their f-structures (c) and (d), respectively

The value of *head* feature is occupied by ˜*event* f-structure; a full-fledged one should include *pitch*, *onset*, and *duration* features. For example,

$$
\mathbf{C4} = \begin{bmatrix} \tilde{\ }tree \\ head \begin{bmatrix} \tilde{\ }event \\ pitch \quad C4 \\ onset \quad \cdots \\ duration\ 1 \end{bmatrix} \\ span \ \cdots \\ dtrs \ \perp \end{bmatrix}.
$$

2.4 Unification, *Join* and *Meet*

We introduce the set notation of an f-structure using the set of feature-path-value pairs: $\{(f_{11}\cdots.f_{1n}\ v_1), (f_{21}\cdots.f_{2m}\ v_2), \cdots\}$. Unification is the consistent union of f-structures in the set notation, results in another f-structure. Unification fails only if there exists an inconsistency in any feature-path-value pair.

Now, when we compare two f-structures for unification, if there is a missing feature f_i on one f-structure let us complement it with $(f_i\ \perp)$. For example, we identify

$$
\sigma_4 = \begin{bmatrix} \tilde{\ }type1 \\ f_1\ v_1 \end{bmatrix} \text{ and } \sigma_5 = \begin{bmatrix} \tilde{\ }type1 \\ f_2\ v_2 \end{bmatrix},
$$

with

$$
\begin{bmatrix} \tilde{\ }type1 \\ f_1\ v_1 \\ f_2\ \perp \end{bmatrix} \text{ and } \begin{bmatrix} \tilde{\ }type1 \\ f_1\ \perp \\ f_2\ v_2 \end{bmatrix},
$$

respectively. Here, we extend the definition of unification in two different ways. If the unification of two values of v_i and $\perp$ is redefined as v_i, we call *join* operation; if the same two becomes $\perp$, we call *meet* operation. Then,

$$join(\sigma_4, \sigma_5) = \begin{bmatrix} \tilde{}type1 \\ f_1 \ v_1 \\ f_2 \ v_2 \end{bmatrix}.$$

while $meet(\sigma_4, \sigma_5) = \perp$.

The *join* tree is composed by Algorithm 1, that is, when a subtree matches with a single branch with a single pitch event, the subtree would be chosen (see lines 4–7).

The *meet* of two time-span trees is composed by Algorithm 2, that is, when a subtree matches with a single branch with a single pitch event, the single branch would be chosen (see lines 4–7).

Input: two time span trees σ_1, σ_2
Output: $\sigma_1 \sqcup \sigma_2 = join(\sigma_1, \sigma_2)$
1 **if** $\sigma_1.\{head, span\} = \sigma_2.\{head, span\}$ **then**
2 $\quad$ **if** $\sigma_1 = \sigma_2$ **then**
3 $\quad\quad$ **return** σ_1;
4 $\quad$ **else if** $\sigma_1.dtrs = \perp$ **then**
5 $\quad\quad$ **return** σ_2;
6 $\quad$ **else if** $\sigma_2.dtrs = \perp$ **then**
7 $\quad\quad$ **return** σ_1;
8 $\quad$ **else**

$$\text{return} \begin{bmatrix} \tilde{}tree \\ head\ \sigma_1.head \\ span\ \sigma_1.span \\ dtrs \begin{bmatrix} left & join(\sigma_1.dtrs.left, \sigma_2.dtrs.left) \\ right & join(\sigma_1.dtrs.right, \sigma_2.dtrs.right) \end{bmatrix} \end{bmatrix};$$

9
10 **else**
11 $\quad \perp$;

Algorithm 1. join algorithm

Because there is no alternative action in composing f-structures by recursive functions in Algorithm 1 and Algorithm 2, $\sigma_1 \sqcup \sigma_2$ and $\sigma_1 \sqcap \sigma_2$ exist uniquely. Thus, the partially ordered set of time-span trees becomes a *lattice*.

Although we have given procedures of *join/meet*, we should emphasize their intrinsic property in the lattice. Here, we redefine *join* and *meet* operations in terms of the subsumption relation in f-structures.

Input: two time span trees σ_1, σ_2
Output: $\sigma_1 \sqcap \sigma_2 = meet(\sigma_1, \sigma_2)$

1 **if** $\sigma_1.\{head, span\} = \sigma_2.\{head, span\}$ **then**
2   **if** $\sigma_1 = \sigma_2$ **then**
3   **return** σ_1;
4   **else if** $\sigma_1.dtrs = \bot$ **then**
5   **return** σ_1;
6   **else if** $\sigma_2.dtrs = \bot$ **then**
7   **return** σ_2;
8   **else**

$$
\text{return} \begin{bmatrix} \tilde{\ } tree \\ head\ \ \sigma_1.head \\ span\ \ \sigma_1.span \\ dtrs\ \begin{bmatrix} left\ \ \ \ meet(\sigma_1.dtrs.left, \sigma_2.dtrs.left) \\ right\ \ meet(\sigma_1.dtrs.right, \sigma_2.dtrs.right) \end{bmatrix} \end{bmatrix} ;
$$

9

10 **else**
11   **return** $\bot$;

Algorithm 2. meet algorithm

Definition 2 (Join). *Let σ_A and σ_B be full-fledged f-structures representing the time-span trees of melodies A and B, respectively. If we can fix the least upper bound of σ_A and σ_B, that is, the least y such that $\sigma_A \sqsubseteq y$ and $\sigma_B \sqsubseteq y$ is unique, we call such y the join of σ_A and σ_B, denoted as $\sigma_A \sqcup \sigma_B$.*

Carpenter [2] provides that the unification of f-structures A and B is the least upper bound of A and B, which is equivalent to *join* in this paper. Similarly, we regard the intersection of the unifiable f-structures as *meet*.

Definition 3 (Meet). *Let σ_A and σ_B be full-fledged f-structures representing the time-span trees of melodies A and B, respectively. If we can fix the greatest lower bound of σ_A and σ_B, that is, the greatest x such that $x \sqsubseteq \sigma_A$ and $x \sqsubseteq \sigma_B$ is unique, we call such x the meet of σ_A and σ_B, denoted as $\sigma_A \sqcap \sigma_B$.*

Obviously from Definitions 2 and 3, we obtain the absorption laws: $\sigma_A \sqcup x = \sigma_A$ and $\sigma_A \sqcap x = x$ if $x \sqsubseteq \sigma_A$. Moreover, if $\sigma_A \sqsubseteq \sigma_B$, for any x $x \sqcup \sigma_A \sqsubseteq x \sqcup \sigma_B$ and $x \sqcap \sigma_A \sqsubseteq x \sqcap \sigma_B$.

We show a music example in Fig. 3. The '$\sqcup$' (*join*) operation takes quavers in the scores to fill *dtrs* value, so that missing note in one side is complemented. On the other hand, the '$\sqcap$' (*meet*) operation takes $\bot$ for mismatching features, and thus only the common notes appear as a result.

Since time-span tree T is rigidly corresponds to f-structure σ, we identify T with σ and may call σ a tree in the following sections as long as no confusion.

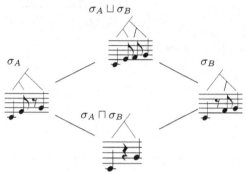

Fig. 3. *Join* and *Meet* operations of time-span trees

3   Strict Distance in Time-Span Reduction

In this section, we introduce the notion of distance between two time-span trees. We propose that:

> *If a branch with a single pitch event is reduced, the amount of information corresponding to the length of its time-span is lost.*

Thus, we regard the accumulation of such lost time-spans as the distance of two trees in the sequence of reductions, called *reduction path*. Thereafter, we generalize the notion to be feasible, not only in a reduction path but in any direction in the lattice. Finally in this section, we show the distance suffices the triangle inequality. Again as this section includes technical details, those who would like to see examples earlier may skip this section and can come back later.

We presuppose that branches are reduced only one by one, for the convenience to sum up distances. A branch is *reducible* only in the bottom-up way, i.e., a reducible branch possesses no other sub-branches except a single pitch event at its leaf. In the similar way, we call the reverse operation *elaboration*; we can attach a new sub-branch when the original branch consists only of a single event.

The *head* pitch event of a tree structure is the most salient event of the whole tree, and the temporal duration of the tree appears at *span* feature. Though the event itself retains its original duration, we may regard its saliency is extended to the whole tree. The situation is the same as each subtree. Thus, we consider that each pitch event has the maximal length of saliency.

Definition 4 (Maximal Time-span). *Each pitch event has the maximal time-span within which the event becomes most salient, and outside the time-span the salience is lost.*

The *head* pitch event of a tree structure is the most salient event of the whole tree, and the temporal duration of the tree appears at *span* feature. Though the event itself retains its original duration, we may regard its saliency is extended to the whole tree. The situation is the same as each subtree. Thus, we consider that each pitch event has the maximal length of saliency.

Definition 5 (Maximal Time-span). *Each pitch event has the maximal time-span within which the event becomes most salient, and outside the time-span the salience is lost.*

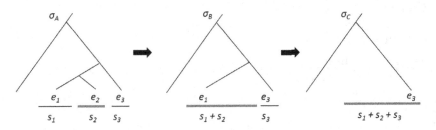

Fig. 4. Reduction by maximal time-spans; gray thick lines denote maximal time-spans while thin ones pitch durations

In Fig. 4, a reducible branch on pitch event e_2 has the time-span s_2. After e_2 is reduced, branch on e_1 becomes reducible and the connected span $s_1 + s_2$ becomes e_1's maximal time-span, though its original duration was s_1. Finally, after e_1 is reduced, e_3 dominates the length of $s_1 + s_2 + s_3$.

Prior to *join/meet* operations, if either two heads or their time-spans of time-span trees are different, the comparison itself is futile. Therefore, we impose *Head/Span Equality Condition (HSEC, hereafter)*:

$$\sigma_A.head = \sigma_B.head \ \& \ \sigma_A.span = \sigma_B.span.$$

on the operations. Note that if $\sigma.dtrs = \bot$, i.e., the tree consists of a single pitch event, we do not need to care this head/span equality, as $\sigma \sqcup \bot = \sigma$ and $\sigma \sqcap \bot = \bot$. We have included this restriction in the following algorithm, so as to avoid any futile comparison; if the identity of two heads and their time-spans is disregarded, the distance between them is meaningless.

Let $\varsigma(\sigma)$ be a set of pitch events in σ, $\sharp\varsigma(\sigma)$ be its cardinality, and s_e be the maximal time-span of event e. Since reduction is made by one reducible branch at a time, a reduction path $\sigma_B = \sigma^n, \sigma^{n-1}, \ldots, \sigma^2, \sigma^1, \sigma^0 = \sigma_A$ suffices $\sharp\varsigma(\sigma^{i+1}) = \sharp\varsigma(\sigma^i) + 1$. For each reduction step, when a reducible branch on event e disappears, its maximal time-span s_e is accumulated as distance.

Definition 6 (Reduction Distance). *The distance $d_\sqsubseteq$ of two time-span trees such that $\sigma_A \sqsubseteq \sigma_B$ in a reduction path is defined by*

$$d_\sqsubseteq(\sigma_A, \sigma_B) = \sum_{e \in \varsigma(\sigma_B) \backslash \varsigma(\sigma_A)} s_e.$$

For example in Fig. 4, when e_2 and e_1 are reduced in this order, the distance between σ_A and σ_C becomes $s_2 + (s_1 + s_2)$, since the reduction of e_2 yields s_1 and e_1 yields $(s_1 + s_2)$. Although the distance is a simple summation of maximal time-spans at a glance, there is a latent order in the addition, for reducible branches are different in each reduction step. In order to give a constructive procedure on this summation, we introduce the notion of total sum of maximal time-spans.

Input: two time span trees σ_1, σ_2 such that $\sigma_1 \sqsubseteq \sigma_2$
Output: $d_{\sqsubseteq}(\sigma_1, \sigma_2)$
1 **if** $\sigma_1 = \sigma_2$ **then**
2 $\quad$ **return** 0;
3 **else if** $\sigma_1 = \bot$ **then**
4 $\quad$ **if** $\sigma_2.dtrs = \bot$ **then**
5 $\quad\quad$ **return** $\sigma_2.span$;
6 $\quad$ **else**
7 $\quad\quad$ **return** $d_{\sqsubseteq}(\bot, \sigma_2.dtrs.left) + d_{\sqsubseteq}(\bot, \sigma_2.dtrs.right)$;
8 **else if** $\sigma_1.head = \sigma_2.head$ & $\sigma_1.span = \sigma_2.span$ **then**
9 $\quad$ **if** $\sigma_1.dtrs = \bot$ **then**
10 $\quad\quad$ **case** $\sigma_1.head = \sigma_2.dtrs.left.head$
11 $\quad\quad\quad$ **return** $d_{\sqsubseteq}(\bot, \sigma_2.dtrs.right)$;
12 $\quad\quad$ **case** $\sigma_1.head = \sigma_2.dtrs.right.head$
13 $\quad\quad\quad$ **return** $d_{\sqsubseteq}(\bot, \sigma_2.dtrs.left)$;
14 $\quad$ **else**
15 $\quad\quad$ **return**
   $\quad\quad d_{\sqsubseteq}(\sigma_1.dtrs.left, \sigma_2.dtrs.left) + d_{\sqsubseteq}(\sigma_1.dtrs.right, \sigma_2.dtrs.right)$;
16 **else return** ∞;

Algorithm 3. Distance in reduction path

Definition 7 (Total Maximal Time-span). *Given ˜tree f-structure* σ,

$$tms(\sigma) = \sum_{e \in \varsigma(\sigma)} s_e.$$

We present $tms(\sigma)$ as a recursive function in Algorithm 4.

Input: a ˜tree f-structure σ
Output: $tms(\sigma)$
1 **if** $\sigma = \bot$ **then**
2 $\quad$ **return** 0;
3 **else if** $\sigma.dtrs = \bot$ **then**
4 $\quad$ **return** $\sigma.span$;
5 **else**
6 $\quad$ **case** $\sigma.head = \sigma.dtrs.left.head$
7 $\quad\quad$ **return** $tms(\sigma.dtrs.left) + tms(\sigma.dtrs.right) + \sigma.dtrs.right.span$;
8 $\quad$ **case** $\sigma.head = \sigma.dtrs.right.head$
9 $\quad\quad$ **return** $tms(\sigma.dtrs.left) + tms(\sigma.dtrs.right) + \sigma.dtrs.left.span$;

Algorithm 4. Total Maximal Time-span

In Algorithm 4, Lines 1–2 are the terminal condition. Lines 3–4 treat the case that a tree consists of a single branch. In Lines 6–7, when the right subtree surrender to the left, the left extends the domination rightward by $\sigma.dtrs.right.span$. Ditto for the case the right-hand side overcomes the left, as Lines 8–9.

When $\sigma_A \sqsubseteq \sigma_B$, from Definition 6 and 7,

$$d_\sqsubseteq(\sigma_A, \sigma_B) = \sum_{e \in \varsigma(\sigma_B) \backslash \varsigma(\sigma_A)} s_e = \sum_{e \in \varsigma(\sigma_B)} s_e - \sum_{e \in \varsigma(\sigma_A)} s_e$$
$$= tms(\sigma_B) - tms(\sigma_A).$$

As a special case of the above, $d_\sqsubseteq(\bot, \sigma) = tms(\sigma)$.

Next, we consider the notion of distance that can be applicable to two trees reside in different paths.

Lemma 1. *For any reduction path from $\sigma_A \sqcup \sigma_B$ to $\sigma_A \sqcap \sigma_B$, $d_\sqsubseteq(\sigma_A \sqcap \sigma_B, \sigma_A \sqcup \sigma_B)$ is unique.*

Proof: As there is a reduction path between $\sigma_A \sqcap \sigma_B$ and $\sigma_A \sqcup \sigma_B$, and $\sigma_A \sqcap \sigma_B \sqsubseteq \sigma_A \sqcup \sigma_B$, $d_\sqsubseteq(\sigma_A \sqcap \sigma_B, \sigma_A \sqcup \sigma_B)$ is computed by the difference of total maximal time-span in Algorithm 4. Because the algorithm returns a unique value, the distance is unique. ∎

Theorem 1 (Uniqueness of Reduction Distance). *If there exist reduction paths from σ_A to σ_B, $d_\sqsubseteq(\sigma_A, \sigma_B)$ is unique.*

Lemma 2. $d_\sqsubseteq(\sigma_A, \sigma_A \sqcup \sigma_B) = d_\sqsubseteq(\sigma_A \sqcap \sigma_B, \sigma_B)$ *and* $d_\sqsubseteq(\sigma_B, \sigma_A \sqcup \sigma_B) = d_\sqsubseteq(\sigma_A \sqcap \sigma_B, \sigma_A)$.

Proof: From set-theoretical calculus, $\varsigma(\sigma_A \sqcup \sigma_B) \backslash \varsigma(\sigma_A) = \varsigma(\sigma_A) \cup \varsigma(\sigma_B) \backslash \varsigma(\sigma_A) = \varsigma(\sigma_B) \backslash \varsigma(\sigma_A) \cap \varsigma(\sigma_B) = \varsigma(\sigma_B) \backslash \varsigma(\sigma_A \sqcap \sigma_B)$. Then, by Definition 6, $d_\sqsubseteq(\sigma_A, \sigma_A \sqcup \sigma_B) = \sum_{e \in \varsigma(\sigma_A \sqcup \sigma_B) \backslash \varsigma(\sigma_A)} s_e = \sum_{e \in \varsigma(\sigma_B) \backslash \varsigma(\sigma_A \sqcap \sigma_B)} s_e = d_\sqsubseteq(\sigma_A \sqcap \sigma_B, \sigma_B)$. ∎

Definition 8 (Meet and Join Distances).

- $d_\sqcap(\sigma_A, \sigma_B) = d_\sqsubseteq(\sigma_A \sqcap \sigma_B, \sigma_A) + d_\sqsubseteq(\sigma_A \sqcap \sigma_B, \sigma_B)$ *(meet distance)*
- $d_\sqcup(\sigma_A, \sigma_B) = d_\sqsubseteq(\sigma_A, \sigma_A \sqcup \sigma_B) + d_\sqsubseteq(\sigma_B, \sigma_A \sqcup \sigma_B)$ *(join distance)*

Lemma 3. $d_\sqcup(\sigma_A, \sigma_B) = d_\sqcap(\sigma_A, \sigma_B)$.

Proof: Immediately from Lemma 2. ∎

Lemma 4. *For any σ', σ'' such that $\sigma_A \sqsubseteq \sigma' \sqsubseteq \sigma_A \sqcup \sigma_B$, $\sigma_B \sqsubseteq \sigma'' \sqsubseteq \sigma_A \sqcup \sigma_B$, $d_\sqcup(\sigma_A, \sigma') + d_\sqcap(\sigma', \sigma'') + d_\sqcup(\sigma'', \sigma_B) = d_\sqcup(\sigma_A, \sigma_B)$. Ditto for the meet distance.*

Now the notion of distance, which was initially defined in the reduction path as $d_\sqsubseteq$ is now generalized to $d_{\{\sqcap, \sqcup\}}$, and in addition we have shown they have the same values. From now on, we omit $\{\sqcap, \sqcup\}$ from $d_{\{\sqcap, \sqcup\}}$, simply denoting 'd'.

Theorem 2 (Uniqueness of Distance). $d(\sigma_A, \sigma_B)$ *is unique among shortest paths between σ_A and σ_B.*

Note that shortest paths can be found in ordinary graph-search methods, such as *branch and bound*, Dijkstra's algorithm, best-first search, and so on.

Corollary 1. $d(\sigma_A, \sigma_B) = d(\sigma_A \sqcup \sigma_B, \sigma_A \sqcap \sigma_B)$.

Proof: From Lemma 2 and Lemma 3. ∎

Theorem 3 (Triangle Inequality). *For any σ_A, σ_B and σ_C, $d(\sigma_A, \sigma_B) + d(\sigma_B, \sigma_C) \geq d(\sigma_A, \sigma_C)$.*

Proof: From Corollary 1 and by definition,

$$d(\sigma_i, \sigma_j) = d(\sigma_i \sqcup \sigma_j, \sigma_i \sqcap \sigma_j) = \sum_{e \in \varsigma(\sigma_i \sqcup \sigma_j) \backslash \varsigma(\sigma_i \sqcap \sigma_j)} s_e.$$

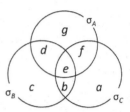

Since we employ the set-notation of f-structure (cf. Section 2.4), the relationship between $\sigma_{\{A,B,C\}}$ can be depicted in Venn diagram. Then, $d(\sigma_A, \sigma_B) + d(\sigma_B, \sigma_C)$ becomes the sum of maximal time-spans in $\varsigma(\sigma_A \sqcup \sigma_B) \backslash \varsigma(\sigma_A \sqcap \sigma_B)$ plus those in $\varsigma(\sigma_B \sqcup \sigma_C) \backslash \varsigma(\sigma_B \sqcap \sigma_C)$, which corresponds to $(f + g + b + c) + (a + c + d + f) = a + b + 2c + 2f + d + g$ in the diagram. On the contrary, $d(\sigma_A, \sigma_C)$ becomes the sum of $a + b + d + g$. Since $(a + b + 2c + 2f + d + g) - (a + b + d + g) = 2c + 2f \geq 0$, we obtain the result. ∎

In the above proof, c and f are counted twice because branches in these areas are once reduced and later added, or once added and later reduced. This implies that these reduction/addition can be skipped and there exists a short cut between σ_A and σ_C without visiting σ_B.

In Fig. 5, we have laid out various reductions originated from a piece. As we can find three reducible branches in A we possess three different reductions: B, C, and D. In the figure, C (shown diluted) lies behind the lattice where three back-side edges meet.

The distances, represented by the length of edges, from A to B, D to F, C to E, and G to H are same, since the reduced branch is common. Namely, the reduction lattice becomes parallelepiped,[3] and the distances from A to H becomes uniquely $2 + 2 + 2 = 6$, which we have shown as Theorem 1. We exemplify the triangle inequality (Theorem 3); from A through B to F, the distance becomes $2 + 2 = 4$, and that from F through D to G is $2 + 2 = 4$, thus the total path length becomes $4 + 4 = 8$. But, we can find a shorter path from A to G via either C or D, in which case the distance becomes $2 + 2 = 4$. Notice that the lattice represents the operations of *join* and *meet*; e.g., $F = B \sqcap D$, $D = F \sqcup G$, $H = E \sqcap F$, and so on. In addition, the lattice is locally Boolean, being A and H regarded to be $\top$ and $\bot$, respectively. That is, there exists a complement,[4] and $E^c = D$, $C^c = F$, $B^c = G$, and so on.

Finally in this section, we suggest that the distance can be a metric of similarity between two music pieces. As long as we stay in the lattice of reductions under *HSEC*, the distance exactly reflects the similarity. However, even though *head*s and *span*s are different in two pieces of music, we can calculate the similarity with our notion of distance. We show such examples in Section 4.

---

[3] In the case of Fig. 5, as all the edges have the length of 2, the lattice becomes equilateral.

[4] For any member X of a set, there exists X^c and $X \sqcup X^c = \top$ and $X \sqcap X^c = \bot$.

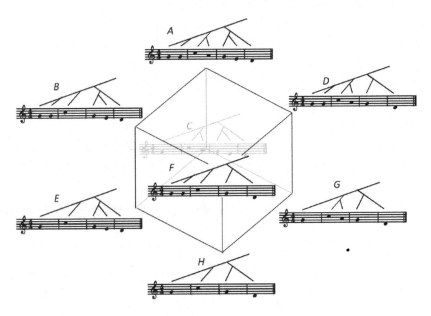

Fig. 5. Reduction lattice

4 Examples

In this section, we illustrate our analyses. The first example is Mozart's K265, *Ah! vous dirais-je, maman*, equivalent to *Twinkle, Twinkle, Little Star*. The melody in the left-hand side of Fig. 6 is the theme, while those in the right-hand side are the third variation and its reduced melodies in downward order. The horizontal lines below each score are the maximal time-spans of pitch events though we omit explicit connection between events and lines in the figure. The lines drawn at the bottom level in each score correspond to reducible branches (i.e., reducible pitch events) at that step. For example, from Level c in the right-hand side of Fig. 6 to Level b, eight maximal time-spans of 1/3-long disappear by reduction, thus, according to Algorithm 4 the distance is $1/3 \times 8 = 8/3$. The configuration of maximal time-spans at Level a in the right-hand of Fig. 6 quite resembles that in the left-hand side, which is the theme of the variation. Actually, since the difference between (1) and Level a is the rightmost quarter note in the 4-th measure, the distance between these two is so close as just 1. This implies that we can retrieve the theme by reducing the variation.

In the next example, we compare two time-span trees in reduction. The left-hand side in Fig. 7 is *Massa's in De Cold Ground* (Stephen Collins Foster, 1852) and the right-hand side is *Londonderry Air* (transposed to C major). The vertical distance is strictly computable in each reduction, but in addition, we may notice that these two pieces are quite near in their skeletons in the abstract levels. Especially, we should compare the configurations of maximal time-spans in the bottom three levels and find them topologically equal to each other. Note, however, that we cannot calculate the distance between two arbitrary music pieces yet under the strict *HSEC*. Thus, the demonstrated comparison in this section is approximate and/or intuitive in some sense.

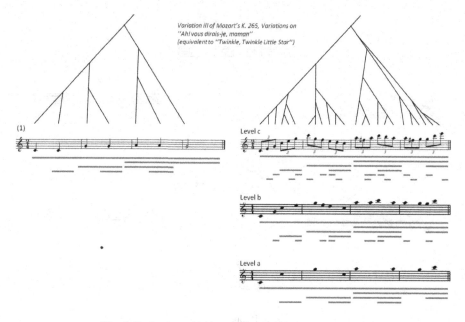

Fig. 6. Reduction of *Mozart: Ah! vous dirais-je, maman*

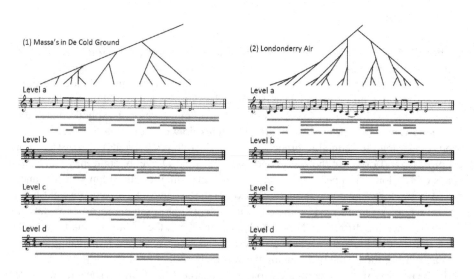

Fig. 7. Reduction processes of *Massa's in De Cold Ground* and *Londonderry Air*

5   Similarity Revisited

In Section 1, we have mentioned that similarity plays an intrinsic role in human recognition of music. Thereafter in Section 3, we have defined the distance in time-span trees. In this section, we look back on the general criteria of similarity both from the viewpoint of equivalence relation and from that of set.

5.1 From Equivalence Relation to Similarity

The prime objective to model our cognition is to model the real world, to give an abstract representation of them. Here, we argue that the representation methods should properly segment the target domain by equivalence relations. In human recognition, however, the equivalence relations do not appear directly; instead, they are perceived as similarity indirectly. According to the MIT Encyclopedia of the Cognitive Sciences [26], various approaches to modeling similarity can be employed, such as geometric, featural, alignment-based, and transformational ones. What we would emphasize here is the fact that every approach to similarity is underlain by the equivalence relations. That is, whatever similarity we think of, it is determined by the extent to which the equivalence relations hold recursively for substructures of music. In other words, we think that a consistent and stable equivalence relation yields a consistent and stable similarity.

Now the question is how we can obtain such a similarity, or an appropriate equivalence relation, in the representation of musical objects. Marsden [14] addresses the requirements of a representation system: musical objects must be well-defined and be all grounded to relevant ones in the real world. We think these requirements play an important role in mechanizing music theory. Note that these requirements are almost parallel to formalizing intelligence and representing knowledge. Since a music piece contains notes, passages, chords, rhythms, and so on, we can consider various kinds of equivalence relations between them. We show examples of equivalence relations between the two melodies in Fig.8, which shows (a) the incipit of Bach's Invention No.1 and (b) its fake that is transposed a perfect fifth above and notes B are lowered by a semitone. If (a) and (b) are compared on the note-wise basis in the literal representation, they

Fig. 8. Three Equivalence Relations of Melodies

are not equal to each other at all. Next, we consider the pitch-interval representations of (a) and (b); for (a) we have $+2, +2, +1, -3, +2, -4$ and (b) $+2, +1, +2, -3, +1, -3$ (unit: semitone). Thus, we find the two elements out of six are identical (the first $+2$ and the fourth -3). Furthermore, when we employ the Parsons code [17], where up (u) if a note is higher than the previous note, $down$ (d) if lower, and $repeat$ (r) if the same, then we get u, u, u, d, u, d for both (a) and (b). The difference in resolution among these equivalence relations are determined by an interpretation of musical phenomena or practical requirements.

We have employed tree representation in this paper, and its hierarchical structure is considered to reflect such segmentation. Namely, in a lower level of hierarchy a music piece is segmented minutely while in a upper level the piece is seen as a sequence of groups. Therefore, we contend that the assessment of similarity by tree structure should correctly show our intuition on resemblance.

5.2 Similarity of Set

The similarity measures widely used in data mining and information retrieval include Jaccard index, Simpson index, Dice's coefficient, and Point-wise mutual information (PMI) [22]. For instance, the Jaccard index (also known as Jaccard similarity coefficient) is defined as

$$sim(A, B) = \frac{|A \cap B|}{|A \cup B|}$$

for set A and B; the similarity value lies between 0.0 to 1.0. If we apply the index to our f-structure,

$$sim(\sigma_A, \sigma_B) = \frac{|\sigma_A \sqcap \sigma_B|}{|\sigma_A \sqcup \sigma_B|},$$

where we may naïvely interpret '$|\sigma|$' as the number of pitch events in the tree as '$\sharp_\varsigma(\sigma)$'. However, the number of notes does not fully reflect the internal structure. Then, it may be appropriate to weight an individual note by its time-span, and the content of a structure hence amounts to the total maximal time-span $tms(\sigma)$ in Definition 7, as

$$sim(\sigma_A, \sigma_B) = \frac{tms(\sigma_A \sqcap \sigma_B)}{tms(\sigma_A \sqcup \sigma_B)}.$$

Since the value of $tms(\sigma)$ represents the complexity of the whole structure, we can also consider the *density* of notes in the music piece. Similarly, we may make use of Simpson index with tms as follows:

$$sim(\sigma_A, \sigma_B) = \frac{tms(\sigma_A \sqcap \sigma_B)}{min(tms(\sigma_A), tms(\sigma_B))}.$$

However, we need to scrutinize the general tendency of these similarities with the larger database including more complicated examples.

We have treated the maximal time-spans evenly, independent of their lengths and levels at which they occur. However, suppose we listen to two melodies of the same length; one is with full of short notes while the other with a few long notes, then the psychological lengths of these two melodies may be different. This effect is actually well known as the Weber-Fechner law; the relationship between stimulus and perception is logarithmic in auditory and visual psychology. Since our initial purpose of this paper has been to present a stable and consistent similarity, we could not reflect such perceptional aspects, which should be considered in our future research.

6 Discussion

In this section, we discuss several open problems.

6.1 Why Time-Span Tree?

In GTTM, *prolongational tree* has been introduced as well as time-span tree, and we understand that there are researchers paying more attention to prolongational tree rather than time-span tree. However, a prolongational tree is composed from a time-span tree, and thus inherits the problems that the time-span tree has. The resultant time-span reduction may not be always reliable because the contradiction between multiple preference rules may obstruct a deterministic proper reduction. Thus, utilizing the prolongational tree does not seem to improve the situation.

In this work, we prefer time-span tree to prolongational tree, since the former is the raw objective structure retrieved from original music data while the latter includes human perception/interpretation of music. Our attitude in this paper is to avoid context-dependency and subjectivity, and thus we adopted the time-span tree. In future, however, as long as the reduction process is formally defined, we can treat prolongational trees in the similar way to time-span trees.

6.2 Flexible Matching

In Section 2, we have introduced the representation of time-span tree in f-structure and *join* and *meet* operations, which however only work properly under *HSEC*. From a practical point of view, this condition is too restrictive. We found that *Massa's in De Cold*

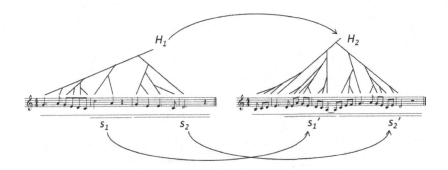

Fig. 9. flexible matching

Ground and *Londonderry Air* do not share strictly common time-span trees, but are somewhat similar as a result of reduction as in Fig. 7. Since we actually recognize a flavor of similarity in them, we have a good reason to seek for a more flexible mechanism to map *heads* and *spans* as in Fig. 9 in *join* and *meet* computation. The situation is same for the comparison of pitch events residing at *head* feature. For the purpose, we have to provide the subsumption relations in time-spans and in pitch events, grounded to cognitive reality; if these partial orders truly coincide with our intuition or perception, we can tolerate the condition of unification.

6.3 Melodic Rendering

As was mentioned in Footnote 1, after several reductions from the time-span tree of an original music piece, we obtain a reduced time-span tree together with remaining pitch events. As a result of reduction, pitch events becomes sparse in general. Since those remaining pitch events through join and meet operations possess only the original durations/locations, we need to fill the gaps. Namely, to obtain a properly rendered music score, we have to insert extra rests, shift their durations, or lengthen them. We call such a transformation from a tree to an audible music *melodic rendering*.

Here, according to the hypothesis introduced in Section 3 (the information that a time-span possesses is proportional to its length), a possible way of melodic rendering would be:

(i) In *join*, the duration of the rendered pitch event is the maximal temporal union of the durations of the head pitch events in two input time-spans, if they have common time (overlap). But, the rendered head should not trespass into the maximal time-spans of the secondary branches.

(ii) In *meet*, the duration of the rendered pitch event is the minimal temporal intersection of the durations.

Following the above idea, Fig. 10 exemplifies melodic rendering of the results of *join/meet* operations. In the figure, gray thick lines denote maximal time-spans in the piano roll manner, while black line segments the durations of head pitch events. As depicted, the duration occurs anywhere in the maximal time-span. The left-hand side

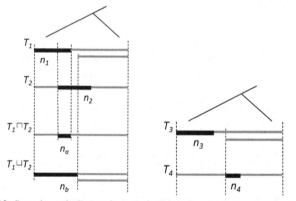

Fig. 10. Sample melodic rendering of the results of join/meet operations

of Fig. 10 shows that *join/meet* operations take T_1 and T_2 and generate $T_1 \sqcup T_2$ and $T_1 \sqcap T_2$, respectively. Since original heads n_1 and n_2 overlap, for the result of *meet*, we obtain n_a. On the other hand, for *join*, n_b because the duration of the head of $T_1 \sqcup T_2$ cannot extend into the maximal time-span of the right branch of T_1. In the right-hand side of Fig. 10, since heads n_3 and n_4 do not have common time in their durations, the result of melodic rendering is null duration, although *join/meet* can generate time-spans themselves from T_3 and T_4 like T_1 and T_2. We inductively apply this way of melodic rendering to a time-span tree as long as *HSEC* holds.

Note that the rendering strategy may include multiple options; in the above, we have shown only one possible consistent way to render each maximal time span to audible note.

6.4   Application to Melodic Morphing Algorithm

We have presented the melodic morphing algorithm, using *join/meet* operations, in a formal way [11]. However, as we have introduced a more rigid f-structure to represent a time-span tree in this paper, and in addition, we have given the actual procedures for *join/meet* operations in Section 2.4, we can define the morphing algorithm in a more rigorous style, as follows:

Definition 9 (Melodic Morphing Algorithm). *The algorithm consists of the following steps (Fig. 11):*
   Step 1: Calculate $T_A \sqcap T_B$ (meet).
   Step 2: Select melody T_C on the reduction path from T_A to $T_A \sqcap T_B$, and select T_D on the reduction path from T_B to $T_A \sqcap T_B$.
   Step 3: Calculate $T_C \sqcup T_D$ (join), and the result is morphing melody μ.

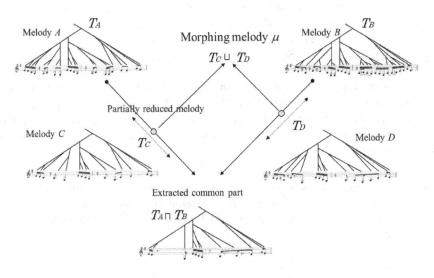

Fig. 11. Melodic morphing algorithm

Now we have obtained the morphing as a genuine mathematical operation, which is composed by *join* and *meet*, and thus we can locate the algorithm within our algebraic framework.

Besides this morphing algorithm, we are now considering multiple application systems with our *join/meet* methodology, together with various rendering strategies. In future, we would evaluate the feasibility of our distance with such actual applications.

7   Conclusions

In this paper, we relied on the strong reduction hypothesis of the tree structure in GTTM, and presented a notion of distance in music pieces. In order to do that, we first designed an f-structure to represent a time-span tree, and we showed that its *head* feature and *span* feature properly reflected the original structure proposed in GTTM. Thereafter, we regarded that a reduction was the loss of information, and the loss was quantified by the length of time-span of a reduced event. We defined the distance by the lost time-span. We have shown several mathematical properties concerning the metric, including uniqueness of distance in any shortest paths as well as the triangle inequality. Furthermore, we have discussed a possibility for the distance to be a metric of similarity.

At present, we have the following five open problems entangled each other. First, (i) if we are to apply our unification mechanism such as *join* and *meet* operations to practical problems, e.g., melodic morphing, we need to ease *HSEC*. For example, if we apply our methodology to morphing algorithm to produce a new melody, taking two music pieces, we are obliged to loosen the time-span matching. Also, (ii) we need more statistical witness in comparison of such existing metrics as Jaccard/Simpson indices, referring to a large-scale music database. As was mentioned in Section 6, (iii) we have treated the maximal time-spans evenly, disregarding the psychological length of music. Since we have postponed such subjective and context-dependent metric, we are obliged to face this aspect from now. Incidentally, (iv) we still have various alternatives to render each remaining pitch event in a reduction tree on actual staff. As we have mentioned this in the footnote 1 and in Section 6.3, we need to develop the strategy furthermore. Finally, (v) the more fundamental problem is the reliability of the time-span tree. We admit that some processes in the time-span reduction is still non-deterministic and the validity of reduction is not promised yet. Thus far we have tackled the automatic reduction system, and even from now on we need to improve the system performance. All in all, to apply such an objective metric to practical cases we need further consideration, which would be our future works.

Acknowledgments. The authors would like to thank the all anonymous reviewers for their fruitful comments, which helped us to develop the contents and to improve the readability. This work was supported by KAKENHI 23500145, Grants-in-Aid for Scientific Research of JSPS.

References

1. Bod, R.: A Unified Model of Structural Organization in Language and Music. Journal of Artificial Intelligence Research 17, 289–308 (2002)
2. Carpenter, B.: The Logic of Typed Feature Structures. Cambridge University Press (1992)
3. Dibben, N.: Cognitive Reality of Hierarchic Structure in Tonal and Atonal Music. Music Perception 12(1), 1–25 (1994)
4. Downie, J.S., Byrd, D., Crawford, T.: Ten Years of ISMIR: Reflections of Challenges and Opportunities. In: Proceedings of ISMIR 2009, pp. 13–18 (2009)
5. ESCOM: 2007 Discussion Forum 4A. Similarity Perception in Listening to Music. Musicæ Scientiæ (2007)
6. ESCOM: 2009 Discussion Forum 4B. Musical Similarity. Musicæ Scientiæ (2009)
7. Grachten, M., Arcos, J.-L., de Mantaras, R.L.: Melody retrieval using the Implication/Realization model, MIREX (2005),
   http://www.music-ir.org/evaluation/mirexresults/articles/
   similarity/grachten.pdf

8. Hamanaka, M., Hirata, K., Tojo, S.: Implementing "A Generative Theory of Tonal Music". Journal of New Music Research 35(4), 249–277 (2007)

9. Hewlett, W.B., Selfridge-Field, E.: Melodic Similarity. Computing in Musicology, vol. 11. The MIT Press (1998)

10. Hirata, K., Tojo, S.: Lattice for Musical Structure and Its Arithmetics. In: Washio, T., Satoh, K., Takeda, H., Inokuchi, A. (eds.) JSAI 2006. LNCS (LNAI), vol. 4384, pp. 54–64. Springer, Heidelberg (2007)

11. Hirata, K., Tojo, S., Hamanaka, M.: Melodic Morphing Algorithm in Formalism. In: Agon, C., Andreatta, M., Assayag, G., Amiot, E., Bresson, J., Mandereau, J. (eds.) MCM 2011. LNCS, vol. 6726, pp. 338–341. Springer, Heidelberg (2011)

12. Lartillot, O.: Multi-Dimensional Motivic Pattern Extraction Founded on Adaptive Redundancy Filtering. Journal of New Music Research 34(4), 375–393 (2005)

13. Lerdahl, F., Jackendoff, R.: A Generative Theory of Tonal Music. The MIT Press (1983)

14. Marsden, A.: Generative Structural Representation of Tonal Music. Journal of New Music Research 34(4), 409–428 (2005)

15. Ockelford, A.: Similarity relations between groups of notes: Music-theoretical and music-psychological perspectives. MusicæScientiæ, Discussion Forum 4B, Musical Similarity, 47–98 (2009)

16. Pampalk, E.: Computational Models of Music Similarity and their Application in Music Information Retrieval. PhD Thesis, Vienna University of Technology (March 2006)

17. Parsons, D.: The Directory of Classical Themes. Piatkus Books (2008)

18. Rizo Valero, D.: Symbolic Music Comparison with Tree Data Structure. Ph.D. Thesis, Universitat d' Alacant, Departamento de Lenguajes y Sistemas Informatícos (2010)

19. Sag, I.A., Wasow, T.: Syntactic Theory: A Formal Introduction. CSLI Publications (1999)

20. Schedl, M., Knees, P., Böck, S.: Investigating the Similarity Space of Music Artists on the Micro-Blogosphere. In: Proceedings of ISMIR 2011, pp. 323–328 (2011)

21. Selfridge-Field, E.: Conceptual and Representational Issues in Melodic Comparison. Computing in Musicology 11, 3–64 (1998)

22. Tan, P.N., Steinbach, M., Kumar, V.: Introduction to Data Mining. Addison-Wesley (2005)

23. Volk, A., Wiering, F.: Music Similarity. In: Proceedings of ISMIR 2011 Tutorial on Musicology (2011), http://ismir2011.ismir.net/tutorials/ISMIR2011-Tutorial-Musicology.pdf

24. Wiggins, G.A.: Semantic Gap?? Schematic Schmap!! Methodological Considerations in the Scientific Study of Music. In: 2009 11th IEEE International Symposium on Multimedia, pp. 477–482 (2009)

25. Wiggins, G.A., Müllensiefen, D., Pearce, M.T.: On the non-existence of music: Why music theory is a figment of the imagination. MusicæScientiæ, Discussion Forum 5, 231–255 (2010)

26. Wilson, R.A., Keil, F. (eds.): The MIT Encyclopedia of the Cognitive Sciences. The MIT Press (May 1999)

Subject and Counter-Subject Detection for Analysis of the Well-Tempered Clavier Fugues

Mathieu Giraud[1], Richard Groult[2], and Florence Levé[2,1]

[1] LIFL, CNRS, Université Lille 1 and INRIA Lille, France
mathieu@algomus.fr
[2] MIS, Université Picardie Jules Verne, Amiens, France
{richard.groult,florence.leve}@u-picardie.fr

Abstract. Fugue analysis is a challenging problem. We propose an algorithm that detects subjects and counter-subjects in a symbolic score where all the voices are separated, determining the precise ends and the occurrence positions of these patterns. The algorithm is based on a diatonic similarity between pitch intervals combined with a strict length matching for all notes, except for the first and the last one. On the 24 fugues of the first book of Bach's *Well-Tempered Clavier*, the algorithm predicts 66% of the subjects with a musically relevant end, and finally retrieves 85% of the subject occurrences, with almost no false positive.

Keywords: symbolic music analysis, contrapuntal music, fugue analysis, repeating patterns.

1   Introduction

Contrapuntal music is a polyphonic music where each individual line bears interest in its own. Bach fugues are a particularly consistent model of contrapuntal music. The fugues of Bach's *Well-Tempered Clavier* are composed of two to five voices, appearing successively, each of these voices sharing the same initial melodic material: a subject and, in most cases, a counter-subject. These patterns, played completely during the exposition, are then repeated all along the piece, either in their initial form or more often altered or transposed, building a complex harmonic network. We focus here on the 24 fugues of the first book of Bach's *Well-Tempered Clavier*. Musical analysis of this corpus can be found in many sources [27,3].

To analyze symbolic scores with contrapuntal music, one can use generic tools detecting repeating patterns or themes, possibly with approximate occurrences. Similarity between a pattern and several parts of a piece may be computed by the Mongeau-Sankoff algorithm [23] and its extensions or by other methods for approximate string matching [9,10], allowing a given number of restricted mismatches. Several studies focus on finding *maximal repeating patterns*, limiting the search to *non-trivial* repeating patterns, that is discarding patterns that are a

M. Aramaki et al. (Eds.): CMMR 2012, LNCS 7900, pp. 422–438, 2013.

sub-pattern of a larger one with the same frequency [16,17,19,20]. Other studies try to find musically significant *themes*, with algorithms considering the number of occurrences [29], but also the melodic contour or other features [21].

Some MIR studies already focused on contrapuntal music. The study [30] builds a tool to decide if a piece is a fugue or not, but no details are given on the algorithm. The bachelor thesis [2] contains a first approach to analyze fugues, including voice separation. For sequence analysis, it proposes several heuristics to help the selection of repeating patterns inside the algorithms of [16] which maximizes the number of occurrences. The website [13] also produces an analysis of fugues, extracting sequences of some repeating patterns, but without precise formal analysis nor precise bounds. Finally, we proposed in [12] a study on episodes focusing on harmonic sequences.

One can take advantage of the apparently simple structure of a fugue: as the main theme – the subject – always begins at only one voice, this helps the analysis. But a good understanding of the fugue requires to find *where the subject exactly ends*. In this work, we start from a symbolic score which is already voice-separated, and we propose an algorithm to sketch the plan of the fugue. The algorithm tries to retrieve the *subjects* and the *counter-subjects*, precisely determining the *ends* of such patterns. We tested several substitution functions to have a sensible and specific approximate matching. Our best results use a simple *diatonic similarity* between pitch intervals [5] combined with a strict length matching for all notes, except for the first and the last one.

The paper is organized as follows. Section 2 gives definitions and some background on fugues, Section 3 details the problem of the bounds of such patterns, Section 4 presents our algorithm, and Section 5 details the results on the 24 fugues of the first book of Bach's *Well-Tempered Clavier*, as well as first results on Shostakovitch fugues (op. 87). The results on Bach fugues were evaluated against a reference musicological book [3]. The algorithm predicts two thirds of the subjects with a musically relevant end, and finally retrieves 85% of the subject occurrences, with almost no false positives.

2   Preliminaries

A *note* x is described by a triplet (p, o, ℓ), where p is the pitch, o the onset, and ℓ the length. The pitches can describe diatonic (based on note names) or semitone information. We consider ordered *sequence of notes* $x_1 \ldots x_m$, that is $x_1 = (p_1, o_1, \ell_1), \ldots, x_m = (p_m, o_m, \ell_m)$, where $0 \le o_1 \le o_2 \le \ldots \le o_m$ (see Fig. 1). The sequence is *monophonic* if there are never two notes sounding at the same onset, that is, for every i with $1 \le i < m$, $o_i + \ell_i \le o_{i+1}$. In such a sequence, there is a *rest* between two notes x_i and x_{i+1} if $o_i + \ell_i < o_{i+1}$, and the length of this rest is $o_{i+1} - (o_i + \ell_i)$. To be able to match transposed patterns, we consider relative pitches, also called *intervals*: the interval sequence is defined as $^\Delta x_2 \ldots {}^\Delta x_m$, where $^\Delta x_i = (^\Delta p_i, o_i, \ell_i)$ and $^\Delta p_i = p_i - p_{i-1}$.

We now introduce some notions about fugue analysis (see for example [3,27] for a complete musicological analysis). These concepts are illustrated by an example on Fugue #2, which has a very regular construction.

pitch p		72	71	72	67	68		72	71	72	74		67
interval Δp			-1	1	-5	1		4	-1	1	2		-7
onset o		2	3	4	6	8		10	11	12	14		16
length l		1	1	2	2	2		1	1	2	2		2

Fig. 1. A monophonic sequence of notes (start of Fugue #2, see Fig. 2), with the corresponding values of p, Δp, p and ℓ. In this example, onsets and lengths are counted in sixteenths, and pitches and intervals are counted in semitones through the MIDI standard.

A *fugue* is given by a set of *voices*, where each voice is a monophonic sequence of notes. In Bach's *Well-Tempered Clavier*, the fugues have between 2 and 5 voices, and Fugue #2 is made of 3 voices.

The fugue is built on a theme called *subject* (S). The first three *occurrences* of the subject in Fugue #2 are detailed in Fig. 2: the subject is *exposed* at one voice (the alto), beginning by a C, until the second voice enters (the soprano, measure 3). The subject is then exposed at the second voice, but is now transposed to G. Meanwhile, the first voice continues with the first *counter-subject* (CS) that combines with the subject. Fig. 3 shows a sketch of the entire fugue. The fugue alternates between other instances of the subject together with counter-subjects (8 instances of S, 6 instances of CS, and 5 instances of the *second counter-subject* CS2) and development on these same patterns called *episodes* (E).

All these instances are not exact ones – the patterns can be transposed or altered in various ways. As an example, Fig. 4 shows the five complete occurrences of CS. For these occurrences, the patterns can be (diatonically) transposed, and the lengths are conserved except for the first and last note.

3   Where Does the Subject End?

A fundamental question concerns the precise *length* of the subject and of any other interesting pattern. The subject is heard alone at the beginning of the first voice, until the second voice enters. However, this end is generally not exactly at the start of the second voice.

Formally, let us suppose that the first voice is $x_1, x_2, ...$, and the second one is $y_1, y_2, ...$, with $x_i = (p_i, o_i, \ell_i)$ and $y_j = (p'_j, o'_j, \ell'_j)$. Let x_z be the last note of the first voice heard before or at the start of the second voice, that is $z = \max\{i \mid o_i \leq o'_1\}$. The end of the subject is roughly at x_z.

For example, in the Fugue #2, the soprano voice starts at note x_{22} of the alto voice, thus $z = 22$. However, the actual subject has 20 notes, ending on alto note x_{20} (the first sixteenth of the third measure, E♭, first circled note on Fig. 2), that

Fig. 2. Start of Fugue #2 in C minor (BWV 847) indicating subjects, counter-subjects and numbers of notes

is 2 notes before the start of the soprano voice. This can be deduced from many observations:

- metrically, the phrase ends on a strong beat;
- harmonically, the five preceding notes "F G A♭ G F" suggest a 9th dominant chord, which resolves on the E♭ suggesting the C minor tonic;
- moreover, the subject ends with a succession of sixteenths with small intervals, whereas the following note x_{21} (C) belongs to CS with the line of falling sixteenths.

Let g_s be the integer such that the *true* subject ends at x_{z+g_s}: for Fugue #2, we have $g_s = -2$. Thus g_s is the *relative position* of the true subject compared to the beginning of the second voice: it is negative if the subject ends before the start of the second voice, and positive otherwise. Table 1 lists the values of g_s in the 24 fugues of the first book of Bach's *Well-Tempered Clavier*: g_s is always between -8 and $+6$, and, in the majority of cases, between -4 and $+1$.

Determining the precise end of the subject is thus an essential step in the analysis of the fugue: it will help to localize the counter-subject and build the structure with all occurrences of these patterns, but also to understand the rhythm, the harmony and the phraseology of the whole piece.

We could use generic algorithms to predict the subject end. For example, the "stream segment detection" described in [28] considers melody, pitch and rhythm information. Many different features are also discussed in [21] for theme

Table 1. Results of the proposed algorithm on the 24 fugues of the first book of Bach's *Well-Tempered Clavier*. We take as a truth the analysis of [3], keeping here only the complete occurrence of each pattern. The values s and cs indicate the index of the note ending the true subject and the counter-subject, whereas s' and cs' are the values predicted by the algorithm. See Section 3 and Section 4 for a definition of g_s and g_{cs}.

The columns "occ" lists the number of occurrences of Subjects and Counter-Subjects found by our method compared to the number of occurrences in the ground truth. All false positives (FP) are counted in the remarks.

#	BWV	tonality	voices	S				CS				remarks
				s	g_s	s'	occ.	cs	g_{cs}	cs'	occ.	
1	846	C major	4	14	−2	14	21/23					
2	847	C minor	3	20	−2	20	8/8	40	0	40	5/6	
3	848	C# major	3	17	−5	17	12/12	44	0	42	7/11	wrong CS
4	849	C# minor	5	5	0	5	14/29	19	+4	19	2/2	
5	850	D major	4	13	−2	9	35/11	19	0	15	8/9	wrong S, S: 24 FP / wrong CS, CS: 4 FP
6	851	D minor	3	12	0	12	11/11 $3^i/5^i$	29	0	33	2/3	wrong CS
7	852	Eb major	3	16	−8	16	9/9	40	0		0/6	no CS found
8	853	D# minor	3	13	0	9	18/19 $7^i/7^i\ (+\ 2^i)$ $3^a/3^a$					wrong S
9	854	E major	3	6	−6	18	10/12	22	0		0/★	wrong S
10	855	E minor	2	26	+1	26	8/8	36	−2		0/7	no CS found
11	856	F major	3	15	−4	15	10/14	34	0	34	3/5	CS: 1 FP
12	857	F minor	4	11	−3	10	10/10	37	0	37	4/8	wrong S, good CS end
13	858	F# major	3	16	−1	16	7/8	41	0	41	2/4	
14	859	F# minor	4	18	0	18	6/7 $2^i/2^i$	44	0	38	5/6	wrong CS
15	860	G major	3	31	0	31	4/10 $2^i/3^i$	65	0		0/1	no CS found
16	861	G minor	4	11	0	11	14/16	22	0	22	3/10	
17	862	Ab major	4	7	0	7	15/15			23	3/0	wrong CS, CS: 3 FP
18	863	G# minor	4	15	−2	15	12/12	30	0	30	5/7	
19	864	A major	3	13	+6	11	12/8	21	0		0/2	wrong S, S: 5 FP
20	865	A minor	4	31	0	31	14/14 $5^i/14^i$	44	−12		0/3	no CS found
21	866	Bb major	3	38	0	38	8/8	65	0	65	7/7	
22	867	Bb minor	5	6	0	10	11/21			16	2/0	wrong S / wrong CS, CS: 2 FP
23	868	B major	4	14	0	13	10/10 $2^i/2^i$	34	+1	31	3/4	wrong S, wrong CS
24	869	B minor	4	21	0	19	11/13	45	0		0/3	wrong S, no CS found
							288/306 (29 FP) (85% occ.) $23^i/33^i$ $3^a/3^a$				61/104 (10 FP) (49% occ.)	

^{i} : inverted subject   – ^{a} : augmented subject

#8: Two incomplete inverted subjects (also noted in [3]) are detected on measure 54.

#9: The values for CS (★) are not counted in the total, as the CS is presented in a segmented form in almost all measures of the fugue [3].

#14: The first true CS exactly finishes on note 38, but the following occurrences correspond to note 44.

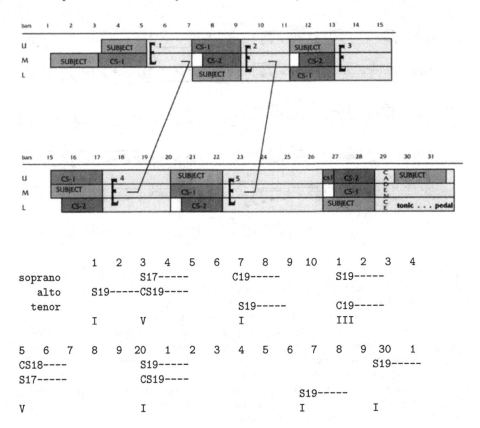

Fig. 3. Analysis of Fugue #2 in C minor (BWV 847). Top: diagram summarizing the analysis by S. Bruhn, used with permission [3], [4, p. 80]. Bottom: output of the proposed algorithm, retrieving all occurrences of S (and their degrees in roman numerals) and all but one occurrences of CS. The numbers indicate the pitch intervals exactly matching (in a diatonic way) those of the patterns (out of 19 for S). The two S17 occurrences correspond thus to approximate matches of the subject (tonal answers).

extraction. However, in the following, we will show that a simple algorithm, only based on similarities, is able to detect precisely most of the subject ends.

4 Algorithm

Starting from voice-separated data, we propose here to detect the subject as a repeating pattern finishing approximatively at the start of the second voice, under a substitution function considering a diatonic similarity for pitch intervals, and enforcing length equalities of all notes except the first one and the last one.

The similarity score between a pattern and the rest of the fugue piece can be computed via dynamic programming by the Mongeau-Sankoff equation [23].

Fig. 4. The 5 complete occurrences of the first counter-subject into Fugue #2 in C minor (BWV 847). (Note that this counter-subject actually has a latter occurrence, split between two voices.) In these occurrences, all notes – except the first and the last ones – have exactly the same length. The values in the occurrences indicate the intervals, in number of semitones, inside the counter-subject. Only occurrences #2 and #5 have exactly the same intervals. The occurrence #4 is almost identical to occurrence #1, except that it lacks the octave jump (+3 instead of +15). Between groups {#1, #4}, {#2, #5}, and {#3}, the intervals are not exactly the same. However, all these intervals (except the lack of the octave jump in #4) are equal when one considers only diatonic information (bottom small staff): clef, key and alterations are here deliberately omitted, as semitone information is not considered.

The alignment can then be retrieved through backtracking in the dynamic programming table.

As almost all the content of a fugue is somewhat derived from a subject or some counter-subject, any part will match a part of the subject or of another base pattern within a given threshold. Here, we will use very conservative settings – only substitution errors, and strict length requirements – to have as few false positives as possible, still keeping a high recognition rate.

Subject Identification. To precisely find the end of the subject, we want to test patterns finishing at notes x_{z+g}, where $g \in [g_s^{\min}, g_s^{\max}] = [-8, +6]$. Each of these candidates is matched against all the voices. In this process, we use a substitution cost function able to match the first and the last notes of the subject independently of their lengths.

Let $S(a, b)$ be the best number of matched intervals when aligning the start of a given pattern $x_1 \ldots x_a$ (the subject) against a part of a given voice y finishing at b, and let $S_f(a, b)$ be the best number of matched intervals when aligning the complete pattern $x_1 \ldots x_a$ (the complete candidate subject) against the same part. These tables S and S_f may be computed by the following dynamic programming equation:

$$
\begin{cases}
\qquad S(1,b) = 0 \\[4pt]
\forall a \ge 2, S(a,b) = S(a-1,b-1) + \delta(^\Delta x_a, {}^\Delta y_b) \qquad \text{(match, substitution)} \\[4pt]
\forall a \ge 2, S_f(a,b) = S(a-1,b-1) + \delta_f(^\Delta x_a, {}^\Delta y_b) \qquad \text{(finishing)}
\end{cases}
$$

where the substitution functions δ and δ_f are the following:

$$
\delta((^\Delta p, o, \ell),(^\Delta p', o', \ell')) =
\begin{cases}
+1 & \text{if} \quad {}^\Delta p \approx {}^\Delta p' \quad \text{and} \quad \ell = \ell' \\
0 & \text{if} \quad {}^\Delta p \not\approx {}^\Delta p' \quad \text{and} \quad \ell = \ell' \\
-\infty & \text{otherwise}
\end{cases}
$$

$$
\delta_f((^\Delta p, o, \ell),(^\Delta p', o', \ell')) =
\begin{cases}
+1 & \text{if} \quad {}^\Delta p \approx {}^\Delta p' \\
0 & \text{otherwise}
\end{cases}
$$

Notice that δ checks pitch intervals and lengths, whereas δ_f only considers pitch intervals. The relation $\approx$ is a similarity relation on pitch intervals (see below for some similarity models). The actual comparison of length ($\ell = \ell'$) also checks the equality of the rests that may be immediately before the compared notes. Neither of the lengths of the first notes (x_1 and y_1) is checked, as the algorithm actually compares ${}^\Delta x_2 \ldots {}^\Delta x_a$ against ${}^\Delta y_2 \ldots {}^\Delta y_b$. Finally, notice that these equations only use substitution operations, but can be extended to consider other edit operations.

As in [16], we compute each table only once (for a given voice), then we scan the table S_f to find the occurrences: given a sequence x and a threshold τ, the candidate finishing at x_{z+g} occurs in the sequence y if for some position i in the text, $S_f(z+g, i) \ge \tau$. The best candidate g'_s is selected on the total number of matched intervals in all occurrences. The algorithm outputs thus the pattern $x_1...x_{s'}$ as a subject, where $s' = z + g'_s$. The whole algorithm is in $O(mn)$, where $m = z + g_s^{\max}$.

For example, on the Fugue #2, the algorithm correctly selects the note x_{20} as the end of the subject (see Table 2).

Table 2. Occurrences and scores when matching all candidate subjects in Fugue #2. The score is the sum of the $S_f(z+g, i)$ values at least equal to τ: it is the total number of intervals exactly matched on all occurrences. Here this end corresponds to the "non-trivial maximal-length repeating pattern" for most occurrences, but it is not always the case.

$z+g$	14	15	16	17	18	19	**20**	21	22	23	24	25	26	27	28
g	-8	-7	-6	-5	-4	-3	**-2**	-1	0	$+1$	$+2$	$+3$	$+4$	$+5$	$+6$
occ.	8	8	8	8	8	8	**8**	3	3	3	3	2	2	2	2
score	100	108	116	124	132	140	**148**	59	61	63	65	48	50	52	54

Interval Similarities and Diatonic Matching. The preceding equations need to have a similarity relation $\approx$ on pitch intervals. Fig. 5 depicts some similarity models. Between a strict pitch equality and very relaxed "up/down" classes defining the contour of some melody [11], some intermediary interval classes may be defined as "step/leap intervals" [6] or "quantized partially overlapping intervals" (QPI) [18].

We use here a similarity on *diatonic pitches*. Such a pitch representation is often mentioned [24,25] and was studied in [5,7,15]. A diatonic model is very relevant for tonal music: it is sensible enough to allow mode changes, while remaining specific enough – a scale will always match only a scale. For example, with diatonic similarity, all occurrences but one of the counter-subject on the Fig. 4 can be retrieved exactly, and the occurrence #4 with only one substitution.

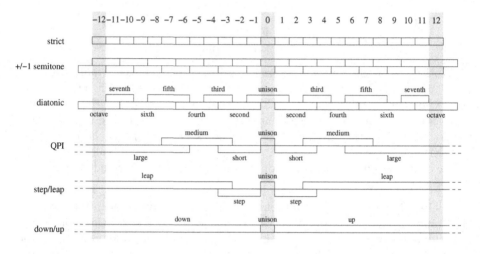

Fig. 5. Interval similarity models, from the most stringent one (strict equality, top) to the most relaxed one (down/up, bottom). When one starts from semitone information (as MIDI pitches), some interval classes may be overlapping in some models. However, in a pure diatonic similarity model, the interval classes are not overlapping: C – G# is an (augmented) fifth and C – A♭ is a (minor) sixth, both of them having +8 semitones. The Base40 encoding [14] enables to encode such enharmonically different pitches and intervals in a pleasant arithmetic way. (Note that intervals for diatonic can be even larger, if one considers some less frequent diminished or augmented intervals.)

Counter-subjects Identification. The same method as for subject identification is used to retrieve the first counter-subject, which starts right after the subject[1]. Usually, this counter-subject has roughly the same length than the subject: we thus have a rough end of the counter-subject at x_w, the last note of the first voice heard before or at the end of the *true* subject on the second voice.

Let g_{cs} be the integer such that the *true* counter-subject ends at $x_{w+g_{cs}}$. This value is negative if the counter-subject ends before the end of the second occurrence of the subject, and positive otherwise. For Fugue #2, we have $g_{cs} = 0$,

---

[1] Very unfrequentky, there can be additional notes between the end of S and the beginning of CS, such as in the Fugue #16. We do not handle these cases.

Fig. 6. Some subject occurrences in Fugue #8 in D# minor. The occurrence #1 is the first one, and is similar to 16 occurrences, sometimes with diatonic transpositions. In the occurrence #2, the last but one note of the subject (circled E) has not the same length than in the other occurrences (and this is forbidden by our substitution function δ). In the occurrence #3, a supplementary note (circled G) is inserted before the end of the subject, again preventing the detection if the true length of the subject is considered. Moreover, the occurrences #3, #4 and #5 are truncated to the head of the subject, and lead to a false detection of subject length.

as the counter-subject exactly ends at the end of the second occurrence of the subject (the first quarter of the fifth measure, G, circled on Fig. 2). It reinforces the perception of closure of the S/CS couple (and helps to mark transition between exposition and episodic material). The same $g_{cs} = 0$ value can be found in the majority of the 24 fugues of the first book of Bach's *Well-Tempered Clavier*, and, more generally, we have $g_{cs} \in [-12, +4]$ (see Table 1).

Hence, to precisely find the end of the counter-subject, we test patterns starting at note $x_{s'+1}$ and finishing at notes x_{w+g}, where $g \in [-12, +4]$, and select the best candidate g'_{cs}. The algorithm outputs thus the pattern $x_{s'+1}...x_{cs'}$ as a counter-subject, where $cs' = w + g'_{cs}$. Note that we start from our detected end of subject (s') which can differ from the actual value (s) in some cases. To prevent detection of non-relevant patterns, the counter-subject is marked as not detected if the above procedure leads to more occurrences than the subject occurrences.

5   Results and Discussion

We tested the algorithm of the previous section on the 24 fugues of the first book of Bach's *Well-Tempered Clavier*, starting from Humdrum files where the voices are separated, available for academic purposes at `http://kern.humdrum.org/`. The pitches were encoded according to two frameworks: MIDI encoding, and Base40 encoding [14]. While the first one only counts semitones, the second one allows to discriminate enharmonic pitches, thus allowing a precise diatonic match as described in the previous section.

Table 3. Comparison between several interval similarity models on the recognition of Subjects and Counter-subjects. The last two columns show the total number of occurrences on the 24 fugues. The strict equality does not allow to match for transposed occurrences. More relaxed models allow to find more occurrences, but may generate also more false positives.

interval similarity	subject lengths	occurences of S			total S /306	total CS /104
		#2	#17	#21		
strict	16/24	7/8	9/15	6/8	220	59
± 1 semitone	16/24	8/8	15/15	8/8	291	67
diatonic [5]	16/24	8/8	15/15	8/8	288	61
QPI [18]	15/24	8/8	16/15	8/8	292	68
step/leap [6]	15/24	8/8	24/15	8/8	300	69
down/up [11]	16/24	8/8	31/15	8/8	404	97

We ran the algorithm on the 24 fugues[2], and manually checked all results and occurrences. Results (with diatonic similarity) are summarized on Table 1. We fixed a minimum threshold of $\tau = 0.9z - 3$, where z is the number of notes defined in Section 3.

Subject lengths. We searched for end of subjects in the range $[g_s^{\min}, g_s^{\max}] = [-8, +6]$, that are the observed values. In 16 of the 24 fugues, the algorithm retrieves precisely the ends of the subjects. To our knowledge, this is the first algorithm able to correctly detect the ends of most subjects: In [2], the subjects found are said to be "missing or including an extra 1 to 4 notes", and the ends of the subjects on [13] are also very approximate.

Fugue #8 shows why the proposed algorithm does not always find the correct length of the subject. In this fugue, a subject of length 9 notes is found instead of 13 notes: there are several truncated occurrences of the subject, and the algorithm chooses the end that provides the best match throughout the piece (Fig. 6).

The algorithm already considers the last note in a special way (and the former notes can be handled through substitution errors in the pitch intervals). It is possible to adapt the matching to be even more relaxed towards the end of the pattern, but we did not see a global improvement in the detection of subject lengths.

False Positives. There are very few false positives among the subjects found (specificity of 90%), even when the length of the subject is badly predicted. The false positives appear in only two fugues:

- in Fugue #19, the 5 false positives correspond to 4 extended subjects [3], and one almost complete subject. There are no differences at the beginning of these pattern, so that these occurrences are considered as normal subjects.

---

[2] A part of the output of the algorithm is shown at the bottom of Fig. 3, and the full output on all the fugues used in this paper is available at http://www.algomus.fr/fugues.

Table 4. Results of the proposed algorithm on the 24 fugues of Shostakovitch Op. 87. We take here as a truth the analysis of the website [1] for the length of subjects and counter-subjects. The values s and cs indicate the index of the note ending the true subject and the counter-subject, whereas s' and cs' are the values predicted by the algorithm. See Section 3 and Section 4 for a definition of g_s and g_{cs}.

The columns "occ" lists the number of occurrences of Subjects and Counter-Subjects. found by our method, but we have no ground truth information to evaluate this number of occurrences. The analysis of [1] also gives a "number of occurrences" of these patterns, but without precise position nor completeness information.

#	tonality	voices	S					CS			
			s	g_s	s'	occ.	occ. [1]	cs	g_{cs}	cs'	occ.
1	C major	4	14	0	14	11	13	39	+3	38	7
2	A minor	3	20	0	17	9	10	36	+9		
3	G major	3	26	+2	21	9	15	48	+2	44	4
4	E minor	4	12	0	6	9	15	27	+3		
5	D major	3	24	−1	24	9	17	36	0	34	8
6	B minor	4	8	−18	–	–	23	36			
7	A major	3	23	−1	24	9	15	39	0	39	7
8	F# minor	3	39	−1	34	10	14	66	+6	64	2
9	E major	2	22	−3	22	11	15	51	+3	52	4
10	C# minor	4	13	0	13	21	22	23	0	23	1
11	B major	3	23	−3	18	14	14	76	+4		
12	G# minor	4	22	−3	17	23	15	43	+3		
13	F# major	5	7	0	5	23	26	17	+1	16	4
14	Eb minor	3	22	−2	22	11	10	55	+2	57	2
15	Db major	4	21	−1	21	15	22	34	+1	33	5
16	Bb minor	3	56	0	60	7	12	98	0	98	5
17	Ab major	4	37	−1	37	12	15	88	+2	88	9
18	F minor	4	13	0	13	16	20	31	+3	31	4
19	Eb major	3	14	0	14	10	13	22	0	20	6
20	C minor	4	12	−1	12	16	17	21	0	21	8
21	Bb major	3	23	−1	–	–	18	46	0		
22	G minor	4	13	−1	13	11	17	37	+1	38	2
23	F major	3	20	−3	20	14	15	72	+5	71	4
24	D minor	4	14	−1	14	16	20	27	0	27	4

#6: The first exposition of S is doubled in octave, so our algorithm fails to detect him.
#12: The CS ends at +3 even if the first occurrence of the CS is not the one kept by [1]. This first occurrence is altered (by consolidations) but the length is the same as the other occurrences.

- in Fugue #5, the length of the subject is selected to the first 9 notes (8 first thirty-second notes and a final note), and this head of the subject matches the 11 true occurrences, but also 24 false positives compared to the analysis of [3]. Nevertheless, this shorter subject exactly corresponds to the one choosen by the analysis of [8].

False Negatives. The algorithm correctly retrieves about 85% of the subject occurrences. The false negatives are occurrences that are too much altered: insertions, deletions, or too many substitutions compared to the threshold.

Inverted and Augmented Subjects. In some fugues, the subject appears upside down (all its intervals are reversed) or augmented (all lengths are doubled). Once the subject is known, the same matching algorithm can thus be applied to the inversion or the augmentation of the subject. This method never produced a false positive, and was able to recover 72% (26/36) of the complete inverted and augmented subjects reported in [3].

Counter-subjects. Counter-subjects were detected with the same algorithm within the range $[g_{cs}^{\min}, g_{cs}^{\max}] = [-2, +4]$. In 40% of the fugues, the algorithm correctly detects the exact length of the CS or the absence of a CS.

In 9 fugues, the algorithm predicts the absence of CS. This was expected for Fugues #1, #8 (no CS), #15 (the CS occurs completely only once) #19 (late exposition of CS) and #20 (there is no real "characteristic and independent counter-subject" according to [3]). As in the case of the subjects, there are false negatives due to the bad recognition of altered patterns. Moreover, when the subject is badly detected, the detection of the counter-subject end fails in the majority of the cases.

The algorithm retrieves correctly about the half of the CS occurrences, with more than 80% specificity.

Pitch Interval Similarities. Table 3 compares different interval similarity models. We compared the diatonic matching against a strict matching on MIDI semitones, possibly adapting the error threshold. As expected, diatonic similarity has a better performance, because such a relaxed similarity is able to match approximate occurrences as the counter-subjects shown on Fig. 4.

Starting from MIDI pitches, an idea could be thus to use pitch spelling methods as [22]: such methods are almost perfect and provide the diatonic spelling of some pitches. However, we also tested a pseudo-diatonic matching on semitone information – considering as similar the intervals that differ from at most 1 semitone. The results are very similar to those with true diatonic matching.

Other Edit Operations. Finally, we also tested other edit operations. The equations of Section 4 consider only substitutions, and can be simply extended to include the full Mongeau-Sankoff edit operations [23]. For instance, using insertions and allowing rhythm substitutions will, starting from the true subject, retrieve the occurrences #2 and #3 in Fig. 6. However, in the general case, insertions or deletions destroy the measure, leading to bad results on the predicted subject lengths.

More musical operations (fragmentation, consolidation), with fine-tuned costs, give a slight advantage in some of the 24 fugues, but this has not been reported here to keep the simplicity of the algorithm.

Results on Other Fugues. Shostakovitch's *24 Preludes and Fugues* (Op. 87), though written more than 200 years later than Bach's *Well-Tempered Clavier*, are clearly inspired from Bach's work. Shostakovitch even cites some of his themes. We tested our algorithm on Shostakovitch fugues. As we started from MIDI files, we used a pitch equivalence of ±1 semitone. The algorithm found 13 correct lengths of subjects out of 24, using [1] as a ground truth (Table 4). Concerning the numbers of occurrences, it is now difficult to estimate the real accuracy of our

Fig. 7. Subjects of the Fugues #1 to #12 of the first book of Bach's *Well-Tempered Clavier*. Circled notes show the end of subject, as reported in [3], with g_s as defined in Section 3. Boxed notes shows the ends found by the proposed method. On Fugues #9 and #10, there are several possible ends depending on the source consulted [3,27].

Fig. 8. Subjects of the Fugues #13 to #24 of the first book of Bach's *Well-Tempered Clavier*. On Fugue #19, there are several possible ends depending on the source consulted [3,27].

algorithm on this corpus, since this reference only gives a number of occurrences without their precise positions. Among other references on these fugues, there is one systematic study on their interpretation [26], but we found no detailed ground truth with positions of S/CS.

6   Conclusions

A complete fugue analysis tool should use any available information, including pattern repetition, harmonic analysis and phrasing considerations. In this work, we focused only on pattern repetition. Our simple algorithm, based on the total number of matched intervals in all occurrences of patterns, allows to find precise ends of subjects and first counter-subjects in the majority of cases. This model considers a unique substitution operation with a diatonic similarity, enforcing the equality of lengths for all notes except the first and the last ones.

Extensions could include a study on the second counter-subject and on other inferred patterns. Combined with other techniques, this algorithm could lead to a more robust and complete automatic fugue analysis tool.

The current algorithm works on voice-separated data. Starting from plain MIDI files, we could use voice separating algorithms. Although it would be a challenging problem to adapt our algorithm to directly treat standard poly-phonic MIDI files, we first want to improve the current approach to complete our comprehension of any fugue.

Finally, it could be interesting to continue the analysis on Shostakovitch fugues, and as well to study the efficiency of our algorithm on other baroque or classical fugues, keeping in mind some practical limitations (availability of voice-separated files, ground truth). As far as the fugues keep the strict struc-ture with a clear subject exposition, we are confident that our algorithm should give good results.

References

1. 24 Jewels, http://www.earsense.org/Earsense/WTC/Shostakovich
2. Browles, L.: Creating a tool to analyse contrapuntal music. Bachelor Dissertation, Univ. of Bristol (2005)
3. Bruhn, S.: J. S. Bach's Well-Tempered Clavier. In-depth Analysis and Interpre-tation (1993) iSBN 962-580-017-4, 962-580-018-2, 962-580-019-0, 962-580-020-4, http://www-personal.umich.edu/~siglind/text.htm
4. Bruhn, S.: J. S. Bachs Wohltemperiertes Klavier, Analyse und Gestaltung. Edition Gorz (2006) iSBN 3-938095-05-9
5. Cambouropoulos, E.: A general pitch interval representation: Theory and applica-tions. Journal of New Music Research 25(3), 231–251 (1996)
6. Cambouropoulos, E., Crochemore, M., Iliopoulos, C.S., Mohamed, M., Sagot, M.F.: A pattern extraction algorithm for abstract melodic representations that allow partial overlapping of intervallic categories. In: Int. Society for Music Information Retrieval Conf. (ISMIR 2005), pp. 167–174 (2005)
7. Cambouropoulos, E., Tsougras, C.: Influence of musical similarity on melodic seg-mentation: Representations and algorithms. In: Sound and Music Computing, SMC 2004 (2004)
8. Charlier, C.: Pour une lecture alternative du Clavier bien tempéré. Jacquart (2009)
9. Clifford, R., Iliopoulos, C.S.: Approximate string matching for music analysis. Soft. Comput. 8(9), 597–603 (2004)
10. Crawford, T., Iliopoulos, C., Raman, R.: String matching techniques for musical similarity and melodic recognition. Computing in Musicology 11, 71–100 (1998)

11. Ghias, A., Logan, J., Chamberlin, D., Smith, B.C.: Query by humming: musical information retrieval in an audio database. In: ACM Multimedia, pp. 231–236 (1995)
12. Giraud, M., Groult, R., Levé, F.: Detecting Episodes with Harmonic Sequences for Fugue Analysis. In: Int. Symp. for Music Information Retrieval, ISMIR 2012 (2012)
13. Hakenberg, J.: The Pirate Fugues, http://www.hakenberg.de/music/music.htm
14. Hewlett, W.B.: A base-40 number-line representation of musical pitch notation. Musikometrika 4(1-14) (1992)
15. Hiraga, Y.: Structural recognition of music by pattern matching. In: Int. Computer Music Conference (ICMC 1997), pp. 426–429 (1997)
16. Hsu, J.L., Liu, C.C., Chen, A.: Efficient repeating pattern finding in music databases. In: Int. Conference on Information and Knowledge Management, CIKM 1998 (1998)
17. Karydis, I., Nanopoulos, A., Manolopoulos, Y.: Finding maximum-length repeating patterns in music databases. Multimedia Tools Appl. 32, 49–71 (2007)
18. Lemström, K., Laine, P.: Musical information retrieval using musical parameters. In: Int. Computer Music Conference (ICMC 1998), pp. 341–348 (1998)
19. Liu, C.C., Hsu, J.L., Chen, A.L.: Efficient theme and non-trivial repeating pattern discovering in music databases. In: Int. Conf. on Data Engineering (ICDE 1999), pp. 14–21 (1999)
20. Lung Lo, Y., Yu Chen, C.: Fault tolerant non-trivial repeating pattern discovering for music data. In: Int. Workshop on Component-Based Software Engineering, Software Architecture and Reuse (ICIS-COMSAR 2006), pp. 130–135 (2006)
21. Meek, C., Birmingham, W.P.: Automatic thematic extractor. Journal of Intelligent Information Systems 21(1), 9–33 (2003)
22. Meredith, D.: Pitch spelling algorithms. In: 5th Triennal ESOM Conference, pp. 204–207 (2003)
23. Mongeau, M., Sankoff, D.: Comparaison of musical sequences. Computer and the Humanities 24, 161–175 (1990)
24. Orpen, K.S., Huron, D.: Measurement of similarity in music: A quantitative approach for non-parametric representations. Computers in Music Research 4, 1–44 (1992)
25. Perttu, S.: Combinatorial pattern matching in musical sequences. Master Thesis, University of Helsinki (2000)
26. Plutalov, D.V.: Dmitry Shostakovich's Twenty-Four Preludes and Fugues op. 87: An Analysis and Critical Evaluation of the Printed Edition Based on the Composer's Recorded Performance. Ph.D. thesis, University of Nebraska (2010)
27. Prout, E.: Analysis of J.S. Bach's forty-eight fugues (Das Wohltemperierte Clavier). E. Ashdown, London (1910)
28. Rafailidis, D., Nanopoulos, A., Manolopoulos, Y., Cambouropoulos, E.: Detection of stream segments in symbolic musical data. In: Int. Society for Music Information Retrieval Conf. (ISMIR 2008), pp. 83–88 (2008)
29. Smith, L., Medina, R.: Discovering themes by exact pattern matching. In: Int. Symp. for Music Information Retrieval (ISMIR 2001), pp. 31–32 (2001)
30. Weng, P.H., Chen, A.L.P.: Automatic musical form analysis. In: Int. Conference on Digital Archive Technologies, ICDAT 2005 (2005)

Market-Based Control
in Interactive Music Environments

Arjun Chandra[1], Kristian Nymoen[1], Arve Voldsund[1,2],
Alexander Refsum Jensenius[2], Kyrre Glette[1], and Jim Torresen[1]

[1] fourMs, Department of Informatics, University of Oslo, Norway
{chandra,krisny,kyrrehg,jimtoer}@ifi.uio.no
[2] fourMs, Department of Musicology, University of Oslo, Norway
{ arve.voldsund,a.r.jensenius}@imv.uio.no

Abstract. The paper presents the interactive music system SoloJam, which allows a group of participants with little or no musical training to effectively play together in a "band-like" setting. It allows the participants to take turns playing solos made up of rhythmic pattern sequences. We specify the issue at hand for enabling such participation as being the requirement of *decentralised coherent circulation* of playing solos. Satisfying this requirement necessitates some form of intelligence within the devices used for participation, with each participant being associated with their respective enabling device. Markets consist of *buyers* and *sellers*, which interact with each other in order to trade commodities. Based on this idea, we let devices enable buying and selling, more precisely *bidding* and *auctioneering*, and assist participants trade in musical terms. Consequentially, the intelligence in the devices is modelled as their ability to help participants trade solo playing responsibilities with each other. This requires them to possess the capability of assessing the *utility* of the associated participant's deservedness of being the soloist, the capability of holding *auctions* on behalf of the participant, and of enabling the participant *bid* within these auctions. We show that holding auctions and helping bid within them enables decentralisation of co-ordinating solo circulation, and a properly designed utility function enables coherence in the musical output. The market-based approach helps achieve decentralised coherent circulation with artificial agents simulating human participants. The effectiveness of the approach is further supported when human users participate. As a result, the approach is shown to be effective at enabling participants with little or no musical training to play together in SoloJam.

Keywords: active music, collaborative performance, conflict resolution, market-based control, decentralised control, algorithmic auctions.

1 Introduction

In many musical cultures and genres there is often a large gap between those who *perform* and those who *perceive* music. In such ecosystems, the performers

M. Aramaki et al. (Eds.): CMMR 2012, LNCS 7900, pp. 439–458, 2013.

(musicians) *create* the music, while the perceivers (audience) *receive* the music [14]. Even though perceivers may have some control of the music creation in a concert situation, by means of cheering, shouting, etc., this only indirectly changes the musical output. The divide between performer and perceiver is even larger in the context of recorded music, which is typically mediated through some kind of playback device (CD, MP3 file, etc.). Here the perceiver has very limited possibilities in controlling the musical content besides starting/stopping the playback and adjusting the volume of the musical sound.

The last decades have seen a growing interest in trying to bridge the gap between the performance and the perception of music [8]. Examples of this can be seen as interactive art/museum installations, music games (e.g. Guitar Hero) [9], keyboards with built-in accompaniment functionality [2], "band-in-a-box" types of software, mash-up initiatives of popular artists [13], sonic interaction designs in everyday devices [11], mobile music instruments [4], active listening devices [6,10], etc. An aim of all such *active music* systems is to give the end user control of the sonic/musical output to a greater or lesser extent, and to allow people with little or no training in traditional musicianship or composition to experience the sensation of "playing" music themselves [7].

There are numerous challenges involved in creating such active music experiences: everything from low-level microsonic control (timbre, texture), mid-level organisation (tones, phrases, melodies) to large-scale compositional strategies (form). In addition comes all the challenges related to how one or more participants can control all of these sonic/musical possibilities through mappings from various types of human input devices. In this paper we will mainly focus on creating a system that is flexible enough for the participants' interaction, yet bound by an underlying compositional idea.

Our approach in SoloJam is to allow for a group of participants with little or no musical training to come together and behave as a "band" of musicians, wherein, they play their respective solos in turn. Thus, the responsibility of playing solos circulates around the band and continues to do so until an indefinite period. To solve the problem of co-ordinating the circulation of responsibility of playing these solos autonomously and effectively, we propose an approach inspired by the economic sciences, in particular markets. Specifically, we borrow the concepts of *auctions* and *utility* to address the problem. Our investigation shows that trading the responsibility of being the soloist via auctions does indeed help decentralised, thus autonomous, circulation of solos within the group. In addition, a careful consideration of the utility function helps participants produce coherent musical output.

We start by introducing the interactive musical scenario that we refer to as SoloJam in Section 2, specifying the issue with enabling participation within it. We then describe our proposed market-based approach to tackling the issue, and the implementation details for the same, in Section 3. Section 4 then looks at the application of the approach within SoloJam, investigating the approach for its effectiveness in enabling participation by artificial agents (who simulate participants with little or no musical training) and human users. This section also discusses typical modes of communication in bands in relation to SoloJam. This is followed by a discussion on the flexibility offered by SoloJam. We conclude in Section 5.

2   The Musical Scenario

In our current context we are interested in creating a system that allows for a group of participants with little or no musical training to get the feeling of being involved with creating music, yet defined in such a way that a certain level of musicality is ensured in the final sounding result. The participants are to play music using a device that assists them for the same. Such a device, together with the participant using it, is what we call a *node* in this paper. The participant may either be a human user using the device, or an artificial agent behaving in a specified manner simulating a user, and as such associated with the device. Multiple participants would thus aim at controlling various musical features within the composition. As such, we will need the devices to help co-ordinate the participants' intentions. Situations might arise where multiple participants intend on controlling the same musical feature, giving rise to a conflict with regards to who might eventually control. This would be more prevalent when participants have little or no musical training, as they are not likely to be conversant with the typical modes of communication that trained musicians use when facing this problem. Thus, the devices will have to resolve these conflicts. For such interactive compositions, conflict resolution should be a necessary constituent part of the system, but indeed, not necessarily the only thing.

In this paper, we focus our attention on this conflict resolution aspect of compositions. As such, we imagine a band of musicians who want to play their respective solos pertaining to the same musical feature. Only one musician ever plays their respective solo at a time. We call this musician the *soloist*. However, over time, the playing of solos circulates across the band, as and when other musicians become soloists. The control of circulation of solos happens in a decentralised manner.

The musical space within the system considered in this paper is made up of rhythmic patterns. A sequence of rhythmic patterns when played by one node, is viewed as a *solo* in the context of this paper, until another node commences playing rhythmic patterns. Each rhythmic pattern has a specified number of beats, which we consider as one bar. Thus the musical output is supposed to be a series of rhythmic patterns, one in each bar. Each bar in a sequence can either be a repetition of the rhythmic pattern in the previous bar or not, specifically when played by one node as a solo. And, the next solo, which would be played by another node, should start with a rhythmic pattern that is not exactly the same as, and ideally only slightly different to, the one played by the soloist in the previous bar. The composition is specified by the aforementioned elements, which also describe the boundaries or constraints to which the musical output should adhere to.

As such, SoloJam can be seen as a compositional idea, or *musical scenario*, where a group of nodes acting in a decentralised fashion come together and take turns in playing a piece based on rhythmic solos. Though nodes act in a decentralised fashion, they must also be able to produce a coherent musical result.

2.1   The Issue with Enabling Participation

Given the scenario mentioned above, if a group of participants are to play music, the devices that they use for this participation cannot be traditional instruments. Instead, the devices need to possess some form of artificial intelligence which might allow the group to produce a coherent musical output, and help the participants do so via decentralised interactions with other participants, i.e. without requiring an expert to direct their interactions. Devices helping with coherence are required due to the assumption that the participants do not possess sufficient musical knowledge to produce a satisfactory result on their own. As such, what gets played should be influenced by the devices to some extent, whilst making sure that the participants are still able to explore the musical space themselves. Devices helping with decentralised interaction are required in order to adhere to the vision of a "band" where members organise themselves into taking turns playing solos, without a central authority directing them. Moreover, participants not possessing sufficient musical knowledge also renders them to be unfamiliar with the modes of communication used by trained musicians to a large extent. Thus, deciding who plays the solo next should be dealt with by the devices interacting intelligently with each other on behalf of the participants. Such intelligence in the devices forms the crux of the issue with making participants play together effectively within our musical scenario.

We define *decentralised coherent circulation* as giving us a yardstick against which to evaluate the effectiveness of the solution to the issue of allowing participants to effectively play together in SoloJam. *Decentralisation* means that there is no central control over the circulation of playing of solos by participants. *Coherence* in our case means for nodes to be playing slight variations of each others rhythmic patterns over time as and when they become soloists, such that the next soloist plays a slight variation of the rhythmic pattern played by the current soloist. Thus, our goal is to design an intelligent system that allows for both decentralised control and coherent musical output. It should enable participants who do not possess much musical knowledge to play together without requiring an expert to direct their interaction with other participants.

3   Market-Based Approach for Enabling Participation

In recent years, there has been a surge of ideas being borrowed from the economic sciences for designing systems with interacting autonomous components. In the context of our work, a node can be seen as an autonomous component interacting with other nodes. A family of such ideas, known as market-based control, is aimed at applying economic principles to tackling resource allocation problems in distributed computing systems [3]. One of the key characteristics that markets possess, which market-based systems benefit from, is that of rendering the interacting components as being part of a decentralised system.

A typical market-based system consists of software agents representing components of the system, where each component has its own task to perform. These agents act and make decisions autonomously on behalf of the components, yet interact with each other based on a defined market mechanism, e.g. auctions or bargaining. Taking on roles of buyers and sellers of resources as and when needed, or indeed bidders for and auctioneers of such resources, they are able to engage in trades. Such resources may be needed by them in order for the components they represent be able to perform their respective tasks. Typically, virtual money is introduced in the system to facilitate exchanges as the agents interact in accordance with the market mechanism. As they interact with each other to trade, they attempt at maximising their utility function, which is usually derived from task requirements, the higher the utility, the better they enable performing individual tasks. With buyers paying more for resources they value more, and sellers charging what they are able to get away with, resources tend to go to components that value them most, all in a decentralised way.

A wide range of application domains have applied this concept since its inception [3]. We envisage software agents, as described above, as modelling the intelligence in the devices which form part of a node in our context. Thus, we take this concept into the domain of music in order to tackle the issue described in Section 2.1. A detailed specification of the market-based approach now follows.

3.1   Specification of the Approach

One can see the problem of decentralised control of circulation of solos as a resource allocation problem, where the resource can be viewed as a metaphor for *having the responsibility of playing a solo*. This responsibility is what needs to be continuously allocated to the node who may be *most deserving* of being the soloist within SoloJam at any point in time.

The concept of auctions has a long standing history in human society, where the idea is to have a mechanism in place that allows for the allocation of resources/goods/services via the exchange of these resources/goods/services with other resources/goods/services, or indeed some currency. Anything that may be exchanged has some value for the parties between which the exchange happens. This is where the concept of utility comes in. Utility [5,15], as a concept, has a long history in the economic sciences as being an idea that allows for expressing the value of a choice or decision that one needs to make. For example, how much may one be willing to spend on buying a type of guitar amongst other choices, is the value of the guitar for the individual. This value can, with certain assumptions about the preferences of the individual with respect to making choices, be quantified in the form of a mathematical function. Such numerical expression of value makes exchanging resources/goods/services practical.

Assuming that it may be possible to compute the deservedness of being the soloist, at every time step, whilst the soloist is playing its solo, we make it also hold (broadcast) an *auction*, in which all other nodes can *bid* in order to become the next soloist. We thus design the node such that every node can evaluate the deservedness of itself being the soloist. This is computed as the viability, or in economic terms, *utility* of its current rhythmic pattern being played in the next bar. The utility values derived from their respective rhythmic patterns are what the nodes use as their respective bids. As such, at any given time, the node with the highest utility must be the soloist, provided this value is computed truthfully (or honestly). At every time step, a bidder node can also change its respective rhythmic pattern, in order to come up with a new rhythmic pattern from which a higher utility may be derived, as compared to the utility derived from its current rhythmic pattern. The transfer of responsibility happens when a bidder node wins the auction held by the soloist. This necessitates a gain for the soloist, i.e. the auction can only be won if the soloist gains from handing over the responsibility to the highest bidder. This implies that the utility derived from the rhythmic pattern that the soloist is currently playing, must, at the time of the transfer, be lower than the highest bid it receives. We now detail the auction mechanism used for node interaction, helping achieve decentralised circulation of responsibility, and elaborate on the computation of utility which quantifies deservedness and helps garner coherence in the musical output.

Auction Mechanism. The soloist takes the role of an auctioneer and holds a second-price sealed-bid auction, in particular, the *Vickrey auction* [16] in every bar. This is done in order that the soloist receive bids from the bidders, which then are used to decide whether or not there is a winner to whom the responsibility of playing the solo would pass in the next bar. The reason for this design choice is that Vickrey auctions deem truthful bidding to be the dominant bidding strategy. In our case, this means that a bidder can do no better than bidding with the true utility value derived from its rhythmic pattern. The second-price nature of the auction suggests for the winner of the auction to make a payment equal to the value of the second highest bid to the soloist. The second price aspect of this auction mechanism makes truthful bidding a dominant bidding strategy. However, in the current setup we do not exchange money[1] (in the form of such payments by bidders to the soloist). This means that, although the transfer of responsibility necessitates a gain for the soloist, as mentioned above, the soloist only ever compares the received bids and the current utility derived from its own rhythmic pattern, in order to ascertain whether or not it should hand over the responsibility to the highest bidder. Ties in bids, when the bids are higher than the soloist's rhythmic pattern utility, are broken randomly. The sealed-bid nature of the auction requires that the bids are not public and only known to the bidder and soloist. We leave the consideration of exchange of money and other possibilities offered by this auction mechanism to the future, when dealing with more complex variants of SoloJam.

---

[1] The auction and bidding setup in SoloJam allow for money (or virtual money), in the form of bid values to be exchanged. But, we only consider monitoring the utilities for now.

Utility. To participate in the auction effectively, each node must have a way of evaluating and communicating a value that it considers playing its current rhythmic pattern in the next bar to be worth. A rhythmic pattern in SoloJam is represented as a bit string parsed from left to right, whereby, a 1 indicates 'triggering a beat' and a 0 represents 'not triggering a beat'. For each node, we define a utility function which the node uses to evaluate the value its current rhythmic pattern can yield, both in relation to itself and to the soloist, knowing its role as either a bidder or the auctioneering soloist. The following equation specifies part of this utility function:

$$u_i = \frac{c}{(1 + aD_l)(1 + bT_l)} \tag{1}$$

Here, D_l is the hamming distance of a node's current rhythmic pattern with respect to the soloist's current rhythmic pattern, T_l is the length of time a node has been playing the solo, i.e. the number of bars a node has played rhythmic patterns as a soloist, the coefficient a is the importance (in terms of a weighting) given to D_l, the coefficient b is the importance (in terms of a weighting) given to T_l, and c is a normalisation constant. In addition to this, two more conditions completely specify the utility function. These clauses being:

1. The utility is *zero* for a bidder node if D_l goes below $\epsilon\lambda$, where ϵ is a small percentage of the length of the rhythmic pattern (λ).
2. The utility is *zero* for a bidder node if the node has handed over control to a new soloist node in the previous time step.

According to the utility function above, the longer (in terms of bars) a node is the soloist, the lesser it values its current rhythmic pattern, indicating boredom or fatigue, of which the node is made aware via the utility function. The node also possesses knowledge about the hamming distance between its own and the soloist's respective rhythmic patterns. This knowledge can be used by the node to come up with rhythmic patterns that yield higher value, given the soloist's rhythmic pattern. The closer a node can match its rhythmic pattern against the soloist's pattern, the more is the value it can derive from its pattern. This remains true as long as the match does not get closer than or equal to $\epsilon\lambda$, allowing for the node to stir clear of intending to play a rhythmic pattern that may be very similar to or exactly the same as that of the soloist (as per the first clause above). Additionally, we can see that this specification of utility, taking the soloist's rhythmic pattern into consideration, also provides the node with a gradient (i.e. the closer the rhythmic pattern to that of the soloist, the higher the value it yields), which it may make available to the participant in order for them to come up with rhythmic patterns which are slight variations (at least $\epsilon\lambda$ different) of the soloist's rhythmic pattern. As such, in addition to computing deservedness, we see the utility function as a means of instilling coherence in the musical output from SoloJam. Note that D_l forms the main link between nodes (the node in question and the current soloist node), and the coefficient a associated with D_l emphasises or otherwise, the strength of this link. We will put this coefficient to use for the investigation carried out in this paper in Section 4. The clauses above further indicate a way of carefully considering designing the utility function in order for a globally coherent piece of music to result from decentralised interactions within SoloJam. The first clause suggests for there not to be a perpetual repetition of the same rhythmic pattern by all the nodes of SoloJam, which would be monotonous. The second clause allows for a node to not take over the responsibility soon after it released it, which may happen otherwise, since the node's rhythmic pattern would already be a slight variation of the new soloist that took over the responsibility from this node. Not considering this clause may thus reduce the variations that may occur in the music performance in the global sense.

3.2   Implementation

Fig. 1 shows the building blocks of the implementation of SoloJam. Fig. 1(a) outlines the schematic of the implementation of SoloJam. The current SoloJam scenario has been implemented on a Macintosh computer, in conjunction with iOS devices for human interaction within the scenario. The setup can be broken down into 4 modules: the Computation module, the Interaction module, the Sound interfacing module, and the Sound synthesis module.

The Computation module is implemented in Python and simulates our market-based approach for effective participation described in Section 3.1, with a thread representing each node. These threads interface with the Interaction module as well as the Sound interfacing module. The Interaction module can function in two ways. If an artificial agent is to be part of the node, the thread in the Computation module representing this node is made to implement the functionality of the agent in terms of the manner in which this agent comes up with rhythmic patterns. If a human user is to be part of the nodes, iOS devices (specifically iPod Touch) are used for sensing the shaking of the device (using the built-in inertial sensors). The signals from shaking are sent as Open Sound Control (OSC) [17] messages to a thread in the Computation module associated with the device, which are then converted into rhythmic patterns within this thread. The bit strings representing rhythmic patterns are further sent as OSC messages to the Sound interfacing module, together with the utilities/bids (computed within the Computation module) that the soloist/bidder nodes derive from their respective rhythmic patterns in every bar.

The Sound interfacing module is implemented as a Max/MSP patch. It serves as a control module for the SoloJam scenario, accepting strings of rhythmic patterns, synchronising and converting them to control signals for the Sound synthesis module. The audio streams from the Sound synthesis module are channeled back to the Sound interfacing module for mixing and effects processing. The Sound interfacing module also performs a visualisation of various aspects of the system, such as node utilities. The Sound synthesis module is currently instantiated as a virtual sound module rack in Reason. A drum kit synthesiser module is used for each node. Reason is controlled by the Sound interfacing

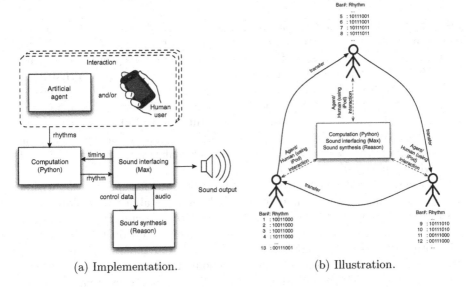

(a) Implementation.   (b) Illustration.

Fig. 1. Building blocks of the implementation of SoloJam showing (a) a schematic of the implementation of SoloJam, and (b) an illustration of the SoloJam scenario within the context of this implementation

module through ReWire. MIDI signals are sent to the synthesisers, and the audio streams are sent back to the Sound interfacing module.

Fig. 1(b) illustrates the SoloJam scenario within the context of the aforementioned implementation. It shows 3 agents or human users participating in the scenario. The rhythmic patterns associated with each participant at various bars are shown. These rhythmic patterns are fed in to our market-based approach for effective participation simulated by the Computation module. As per the rhythmic patterns shown, one possibility for the transfers of responsibility of playing solos is indicated in the figure.

4 SoloJam with Participants

We now look at how the market-based approach proposed in this paper, consisting of auctions and a properly designed utility function, enables effective participation within the composition. We primarily look at the case where artificial agents are considered as simulating the behaviour of participants with little or no musical training, and act within SoloJam as participants. The case where SoloJam involves human participants is also discussed.

4.1 SoloJam with Artificial Agents: Enabling Participation

Although SoloJam involves human interaction, in order for behavioural equivalence across the participants, we consider experimenting with artificial agents in this section. Moreover, an artificial agent can be designed to behave as a participant with little or no musical training with little effort. As such, we get artificial participants behaving in a specified manner operating the respective nodes similarly. This allows for evaluating a base line system, which is a system that must work when all the nodes are operated by participants with little or no musical training. Otherwise, one could argue that a human operator may influence the system towards having the requisite functionality, even if the system did not work. Thus, artificial agents allow for controlling the nature of the interaction of the operator, removing human induced functionality into the circulation of solos, which may be hard to account for.

We primarily investigated the effects of the utility function specification within SoloJam, considering the manner in which knowledge about the soloist node affects the circulation of solos within the group of participating nodes. Since we are only interested in the effect of the utility function on the circulation, fixing other factors which may influence the circulation, makes a plausible case for using artificial agents with a fixed behaviour. In this study, these artificial agents use the notion of mutation to generate the bit strings that represent rhythmic patterns. This mutation is such that the agents can flip each bit in their bit string with a probability $1/\lambda$, where λ is the length of the rhythmic pattern. In so doing, the agent generates a new rhythmic pattern, which is a mutation of its old rhythmic pattern. This mutation based rhythmic pattern generation process is essentially used by bidder nodes in every bar they have to bid in, as they search for slight variations of the soloist's rhythmic pattern. We limit our study with agents to the case where, once the soloist starts playing their solo, they do not change their rhythmic pattern for the duration of the solo (which should be some bars long), i.e. a solo is made up of repetitions of the same rhythmic pattern. This limitation allows us to clearly observe if the bidder nodes are indeed able to search for slight variations of the soloist's rhythmic pattern, which, upon winning the auction, they eventually play.

Note that the coefficient a, within Equation 1, signifies the importance (in terms of a weighting) that a node gives to the distance D_l between its current rhythmic pattern and the soloist's current pattern. Setting the value of this coefficient to 0.0 within a node, allows for switching off knowledge about the soloist node. In essence, the node then only knows its own rhythmic pattern and the duration it has played a rhythmic pattern when acting as a soloist. Setting a to a positive value makes the node consider knowledge about the soloist. We take $a = 0.0$ and $a = 1.0$ in order to explicitly investigate the effects of not disclosing and disclosing respectively, the knowledge about the soloist node to other nodes. Note that the soloist node remains unaffected from a change in the value of a, because D_l is zero for it, thus making a irrelevant.

We can now detail the effects of such knowledge within the workings of Solo-Jam, specifically looking at the nature of the decentralised circulation of solos and also the coherence that can be achieved in the generated piece of music. We first look at the piece resulting from the system, and then provide a discussion based on the evolution of the utilities of the nodes, both with respect to such knowledge. For our study, we use the following parameter settings: *Rhythmic pattern length* (λ) = 8, ϵ = 0.1, *Node count* = 3, c = 2, b = 0.05.

Observations about the Resultant Piece. Figs. 2 and 3 show snapshots of rhythmic patterns that are generated when the agents play SoloJam, under two specific cases, one where bidder nodes do not consider using knowledge about the soloist's rhythmic pattern when evaluating the utility derived from their own rhythmic patterns, and the other where they do so. These two cases are realised by $a = 0.0$ (Fig. 2) and $a = 1.0$ (Fig. 3) respectively within the part of the utility function (Equation 1) used by each node for this evaluation.

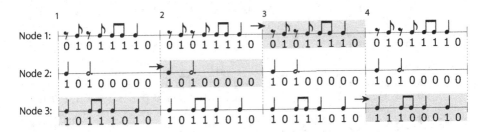

Fig. 2. Snapshot of the rhythmic patterns when $a = 0.0$. There is maximal circulation of responsibility of playing solos (at every bar). The musical output is incoherent as there is no mutation towards closer rhythmic patterns by bidders. In effect, there is no active participation via mutation. Enabling participation is not effective.

These figures show the rhythmic patterns as bit strings and in music notation, for each node in the system. Since we have 3 nodes, 3 lines with bit strings and music notation correspond to each node, as indicated. These lines can be read from left to right for each node. At the end of the 3 lines, the reader can continue at the left of the next 3 lines (see Fig. 3), and so on. Each bar is clearly marked as enclosing the respective rhythmic patterns (of length 8 bits) for each node. The shaded regions denote the current soloist. An arrow between bars denotes a rhythmic pattern being sufficient for a transfer to happen. Mutations within a pattern from a previous bar for a node are denoted by dotted circles. The numbers above bars are bar numbers, wherein a range means that the rhythmic pattern is repeated for all the bars in that range, without any mutations or transfers.

For the case with $a = 0.0$, the 3 nodes do not mutate their respective rhythmic patterns over successive bars. Moreover, the transfer of control of responsibility for the solo happens in every bar, as indicated by the shaded regions in the figure. For the case with $a = 1.0$, we can see a more interesting final result: it can be seen that at bar 21, the rhythmic pattern with which Node 1 bids in the auction held by Node 3 (the then soloist), differs less (different by 1 bit) from Node 3's rhythmic pattern, as compared to the rhythmic pattern associated with Node 2 (different by 2 bits). Node 1 wins this auction in this bar, and from bar

Fig. 3. Snapshot of the rhythmic patterns when $a = 1.0$. Decentralised coherent control is exhibited. The transfer of responsibility of playing solos happens after the soloist having played their rhythmic pattern for some bars. Coherence results from the nodes actively searching for closer variants, via mutation, of the soloist's rhythmic pattern, and the closest rhythmic pattern being played by the respective bidder, provided the bidder wins the auction. Enabling participation is effective.

22 onwards until bar 42, plays its rhythmic pattern. At bar 23, Node 2 and 3 mutate their rhythmic patterns, a further mutation happening at bar 29 for Node 3. Note that in bar 23, Node 3 comes up with a rhythmic pattern that is 2 bits different from the soloist, as compared to its rhythmic pattern in bar 22. This is because the rhythmic pattern in bar 22 has its value reduced to zero in the following bar in accordance with the utility function. Thus, any mutation of that rhythmic pattern in the bar following that will have a value greater than zero. As such, this mutation will replace the previous rhythmic pattern. Other than such a situation, the mutations that are generated over time take the nodes closer to the rhythmic pattern of the soloist, as can be seen in the figure. In bar 42, there is a tie between Node 2 and Node 3, which is broken randomly and Node 2 takes over the responsibility of playing its rhythmic pattern as a solo. In bar 44, and then in 46, Node 1 mutates towards a closer variant of Node 2. This is followed by a tie again in bar 63, which is then broken randomly in favour of Node 3. In bar 65, Node 2 mutates away from Node 3, again due to the

nature of our utility function, as described above. It is clear from Fig. 3 that the nodes actively search for closer variations of the soloist's rhythmic pattern via mutation, and the node (that is sometimes decided upon by a tie break) with the closest match, becomes the soloist in the next bar, provided this node wins the auction.

Discussion Based on the Utilities of Nodes. Fig. 4 plots the utilities that each node derives from its respective rhythmic pattern in each bar, as individually evaluated by these nodes using the utility function described in Section 3.1, and the sum of these utilities. These figures correspond to the snapshots of the pieces from the system (Figs. 2 and 3).

As observed with the corresponding piece (Fig. 2), for the case when $a = 0.0$, the transfer of control happens at every time step, thus a soloist node only ever plays its rhythmic pattern for one bar. The auction held by the soloist immediately leads to the bidder who was not the previous soloist, to take over the control from the soloist, thus becoming the new soloist, but for only one bar. This happens due to the nodes not considering using the knowledge about the soloist's rhythmic pattern, and thus having a utility and bid of $u = c = 2.0$, if they were not the soloist in the immediate previous time step. The process of such transfers of control carries on. Note that all possible mutations of rhythmic patterns for a bidder who was not the soloist in the previous bar, have the same value of 2.0. Thus, the agent has no pressure towards coming up with bids of higher value. We see however, that there is not enough time for the bidders to search (via mutation) for new rhythmic patterns. This is because when a mutation results in a new rhythmic pattern, the previous rhythmic pattern has its value equal to the value of this new rhythmic pattern at all times, be it in the round after the round in which the node was the soloist (the value for both rhythmic patterns is 0.0 in this case), or the rounds after this (value is 2.0). As such, the rhythmic patterns with which the nodes started with in the first bar, either as a soloist or bidder, remain as the rhythmic patterns associated with these nodes forever, as can also be observed in the corresponding piece for the $a = 0.0$ case (Fig. 2). In effect, coherence remains an issue, since the initial rhythmic patterns of the nodes will not necessarily be slight variations of each other. Moreover, the fact that nodes play their rhythmic patterns for only one bar, goes against the whole idea behind playing solos, unless of course playing for only one bar were to be a requirement from the composition. Most importantly, however, the agents are not able to actively participate to explore the composition. The current utility function with $a = 0.0$ is thus not suitable for being used when participants are to play rhythmic solos within a band-like setting. Using this, there would be maximal circulation of control (at every bar, thus no solo being played), the musical output will be incoherent, and there would be no active participation.

For the case when $a = 1.0$ however, the playing of solos and transfer of control over time happens in a more favourable manner with respect to the envisaged goal of decentralised interactions producing a resultant globally coherent piece of music, or decentralised coherent circulation. Fig. 4(b) shows spikes in the node

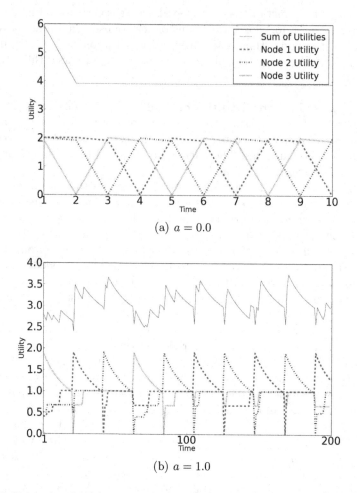

(a) $a = 0.0$

(b) $a = 1.0$

Fig. 4. Utilities of nodes (a) without ($a = 0.0$) and (b) with ($a = 1.0$) knowledge about the soloist's rhythmic pattern

utilities, which indicate the start of nodes playing their rhythmic pattern as solos, and these utilities depleting over time. Whilst the soloist node's rhythmic pattern utility depletes, the bidder nodes have their artificial agents search towards slight variations of the soloist's rhythmic pattern, as indicated by the increase in their utilities over time. As a result, the soloist gets to play its rhythmic pattern as a solo for some time and then hands over control to the bidder managing to search and bid to play the closest variation of the soloist's rhythmic pattern, as observed with the corresponding piece in Fig. 3. The flat regions in the utility graphs (Fig. 4) indicate agents associated with bidder nodes having found rhythmic patterns at a distance D_l of $\epsilon\lambda$ from the soloist's rhythmic pattern. Note that there are always multiple rhythmic patterns that the agent could come up with, all of which differing by distance $\epsilon\lambda$, or indeed differing by a given distance from the soloist's rhythmic pattern, which can be seen as the flexibility in the composition that may be explored by a participant based on their preferences, e.g. preferring one rhythmic pattern over another, even though these rhythmic patterns yield the same utility as assigned to them by the device. The artificial agents mimicking participants have thus been enabled to play rhythmic solos in a decentralised and coherent fashion via the consideration of a utility function that takes the knowledge of the soloist's rhythmic pattern into account. The agents must now, as compared to the case where $a = 0.0$, actively participate to search for a rhythmic pattern, and upon being the soloist, play them. The solos that get played adhere to the composer defined boundaries as defined in Section 2, and the system maintains a decentralised coherent circulation. As mentioned before, having a decentralised coherent circulation shows that the system enables the agents to play through the composition effectively.

It would be interesting to consider how the increase in the number of nodes affects the resultant behaviour of the system, with nodes possessing a utility function such as the one defined in this paper, for the case with $a = 1.0$. We leave this as future work.

4.2   SoloJam with Human Users

SoloJam with human participation has also been implemented. As mentioned before, human participation involves a human user using a device that allows for the exploration of the composition. The iPod Touch devices that we use for human participation, one for each human user, have a thread each in the Computation module representing them. Upon shaking the device, the signals from this shaking are received by the associated thread and converted into a rhythmic pattern, which becomes the candidate rhythmic pattern for the next bar for the node in question. The human user, unlike the agent, may change the rhythmic pattern in any bar when part of a soloist node.

A video of SoloJam with human participation can be found online[2]. The video shows three people using iPod Touch devices to play through the piece, playing rhythmic solos as soloists, and bidding for playing slight variations of the soloist's current rhythmic pattern as bidders, whenever a conflict arises. Fig. 5 shows a labelled screenshot of this video. The Max/MSP patch (our Sound interfacing module described in Section 3.2) in the background visualises the utilities (three horizontal bars at the top right part of the patch) for each node. The top horizontal bar is the utility associated with the person on the right (Node 1). The middle horizontal bar is associated with the person on the left at the back (Node 2). The lower horizontal bar is associated with the person on the left in the front (Node 3). The reader is advised to focus on the rhythmic patterns resulting from the users shaking their devices and the horizontal bars representing utility for each node. In the video, it is possible to see that the transfer of responsibility happens when the soloist node's utility goes below the

---

[2] http://fourms.uio.no/downloads/video/SoloJam.mov

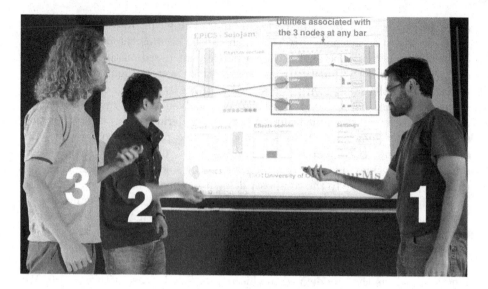

Fig. 5. Labelled screenshot of the video of SoloJam with human participation

utility of the highest bidder node. Furthermore, the bidder nodes have their utilities increased, as and when they come up with closer (in terms of hamming distance) variations (but not exact copies) of the soloist's rhythmic pattern.

The circulation of solos in this particular video follows the sequence: *Node 1 → Node 2 → Node 3 → Node 2*. Node 1 starts off with the control of the rhythmic feature in the music as a soloist and sets a rhythm. The node then joins in with the others in influencing some other musical features not needing conflict resolution[3]. In every bar, the soloist holds an auction. Thus, the device which is part of Node 1 holds an auction, as long as Node 1 is a soloist. At some point during the course of the piece, Nodes 2 and Node 3 individually decide on controlling the rhythmic feature, whilst Node 1 still has control, resulting in a conflict. The conflict gets resolved as Node 1 receives Node 2's bid with a utility value higher than that offered by Node 3, making Node 2 the soloist. After becoming the soloist and setting the rhythm, Node 2 joins in with the others to influence other musical features. While Node 2 still is the soloist, Node 3 feels the urge to become the soloist and starts shaking the device. This leads to Node 3 producing rhythmic patterns which are closer matches to Node 2's rhythmic pattern, increasing Node 3's bids for becoming the soloist. Node 3 takes over eventually, while the others continue influencing other musical features. Moving further with Node 3 as the soloist, others then decide to control the rhythm as well, with Node 2 again taking over as the soloist. This is followed by all participants playing other musical features. Thus, our approach encourages human users to come up with rhythmic patterns that are slight variations of the

---

[3] These other features are part of an extension to the work being presented in this paper, so we limit their discussion.

soloist. The closest bidder is then aptly rewarded by this bidder becoming the next soloist, once this bidder wins the auction held by the current soloist.

4.3   The Relationship between SoloJam and Typical Modes of Communication in Bands

Avoiding conflicts in a band with trained musicians can take various forms. Consider the case of a jazz band. In such a band, the band members communicate both before and during the performance [12]. Communication that occurs during the performance is primarily non-verbal, which may refer to bodily gestures, such as lifting the instrument, or even a barely noticeable nod or a glance. Further, non-verbal communication between musicians occurs through the musical sound, e.g. by responding to phrases by other musicians with a "matching" phrase, or by adjusting the intensity, for instance to signal the transition to a new section.

One particular communication task in a jazz band is to signal the beginning of a solo. The order of soloists and/or the start time and duration of each solo may be pre-planned, but this is not necessarily the case always — another possibility is that the soloist and the time of the solo is decided during the performance. In this case, it is quite common that a band leader decides when the next solo be played and who might play it, and signals this through an indicative gesture [1]. This can be seen as a form of centralised control, and is indeed a predominant mode of communication. It is clear that this mode of communication violates the fundamental requirement of decentralised control within the interactive musical scenario considered in the paper. If indeed one participant were to control the circulation of solos, that participant would need greater musical training than the others, which further violates our assumption about the participants of our system having little or no musical training.

On the other hand, there are bands with trained musicians which have no pre-defined leader. In this case, the selection of the next soloist may be based on a musical or gestural initiative of the current or would be soloist, or based on the initiative of one or more (e.g. forming a consensus) of the other members of the group. It is also possible for certain members in the band to have a greater impact on the choice of the next soloist, as compared to others. In addition to such gestural cues, the notion of "empathetic attunement" [12] can also be a possibility. This notion suggests that people can get musically attuned to each other in time, and can thus seamlessly and coherently play solos, as if they individually know what the group wants, thus spending very little time in explicit communication. One can view these modes of communication between band members, as a decentralised way of resolving conflicts which could arise if such communication were not present. Such decentralised control requires musical training. However, a group that is not trained musically will need assistance for decentralised interactions, which is where our work comes in.

Remarkably, the modes of communication mentioned above have much in common with interaction mechanisms that have thoroughly been investigated in the social and economic sciences, and indeed markets, albeit not within a musical setting. For example, if gestural initiatives represent expressions of interest in performing solos, one could see them as equivalent to bidding for the position of soloist. If the initiatives are a form of consensus, they can be seen as votes resulting in a socially acceptable choice of soloist. Thus, the commonalities between the social setup of a band, and social interaction schemes studied in the social and economic sciences, have much to offer towards formulating interaction schemes for a band consisting of members with little or no musical training, in order to realise decentralisation. Such schemes forming part of the intelligence in devices helps enable the requisite type of participation, as we show via market-based control. It would indeed be interesting to explore other interaction schemes, for example, voting to choose a soloist, or indeed other auction types, as part of future work.

4.4   Flexibility of SoloJam

The presented system is extendable beyond the currently presented implementation, both in terms of musical output and the type of responsibility for which conflict resolution via auctions may be useful. For example, the solos in the present system could take the more traditional form of melodic phrases rather than a sequence of rhythmic patterns. This would require small changes in the representation of musical output, and correspondingly in the utility function, e.g. replacing the bit-string by a string of integer midi notes, or real-valued frequencies. Further, instead of bidding for the position of soloist, the bid could be for the control of some larger structure in the music. For example, bidding to decide a chord progression with a duration of multiple bars, or to decide the downbeats of a drum-pattern. We have already implemented the latter as one extension to the SoloJam system presented in this paper. An online video example[4] shows three agents bidding for control of a single drum module. As in the system presented throughout this paper, the musical output is represented by bit-strings, but rather than controlling each individual beat directly, the bit-strings are mapped to downbeats in the rhythm. A heuristic is implemented to generate full drum patterns from the downbeat pattern. As a consequence, a dynamic musical output is obtained, while SoloJam ensures coherence in the downbeat patterns as the control circulates across nodes.

5   Conclusions

We have outlined and discussed the issue with enabling participants with little or no musical training to play together in the interactive music system SoloJam. An approach inspired by the economic sciences, in particular markets, specifically considering the concepts of auctions and utility, is proposed in order to address this issue. Nodes that possess the capability of evaluating the deservedness of being able to take on the responsibility of playing the solo starting in the next bar (via a utility function), and auctioning and bidding capabilities,

---

[4] http://fourms.uio.no/downloads/video/SolojamDownbeat.mov

are shown to exhibit decentralised co-ordination when circulating solos in Solo-Jam. Furthermore, a careful design of the utility function enables participants (simulated by artificial agents) to come up with an output that is musically coherent. This is highlighted by the manner in which the agents, as bidders, search towards higher utility deriving variants of the soloist node's rhythmic pattern. These variants, in fact, are slight variations of the soloist node's rhythmic pattern. We further exhibit human user participation within SoloJam supporting our approach. In effect, decentralised coherent circulation that results from our market-based approach, demonstrates the effectiveness of the approach towards enabling participation within SoloJam. Having proven the concept, our next step will be to conduct usability tests with human participants. In addition to testing the system with participants with little or no musical training, we are also interested in seeing how music students and professional musicians interact with the system.

Acknowledgments. The research leading to these results has received funding from the European Union Seventh Framework Programme under grant agreement n° 257906 and the Norwegian Research Council through the project Sensing Music-related Actions (project n° 183180).

References

1. Bastien, D.T., Hostager, T.J.: Jazz as a process of organizational innovation. Communication Research 15(5), 582–602 (1988)
2. Bunce, G.: Electronic Keyboards: their use and application in Secondary School Music teaching. Master's thesis, Royal Holloway, University of London (2005)
3. Clearwater, S.H. (ed.): Market-based Control: A Paradigm for Distributed Resource Allocation. World Scientific, Singapore (1996)
4. Essl, G., Rohs, M.: Interactivity for mobile music-making. Organised Sound 14(2), 197–207 (2009)
5. Fishburn, P.C.: Utility theory. Management Science 14(5), 335–378 (1968)
6. Goto, M.: Active music listening interfaces based on signal processing. In: IEEE International Conference on Acoustics, Speech and Signal Processing, vol. 4, pp. 1441–1444 (2007)
7. Jennings, K.: Toy symphony: An international music technology project for children. Music Education International 2, 3–21 (2003)
8. Leman, M.: Embodied Music Cognition and Mediation Technology. MIT Press, Cambridge (2008)
9. Miller, K.: Schizophonic performance: Guitar hero, rock band, and virtual virtuosity. Journal of the Society for American Music 3(4), 395–429 (2009)
10. Moens, B., van Noorden, L., Leman, M.: D-jogger: Syncing music with walking. In: Sound and Music Computing Conference, Barcelona, Spain, pp. 451–456 (2010)
11. Rocchesso, D.: Explorations in Sonic Interaction Design. Logos Verlag, Berlin (2011)
12. Seddon, F.A.: Modes of communication during jazz improvisation. British Journal of Music Education 22(1), 47–61 (2005)

13. Shiga, J.: Copy-and-persist: The logic of mash-up culture. Critical Studies in Media Communication 24(2), 93–114 (2007)
14. Small, C.: Musicking: The Meanings of Performing and Listening. Wesleyan University Press, Hanover (1998)
15. Stigler, G.J.: The development of utility theory, Parts I and II. Journal of Political Economy 58, 307–327, 373–396 (1950)
16. Vickrey, W.: Counterspeculation, auctions, and competitive sealed tenders. The Journal of Finance 16(1), 8–37 (1961)
17. Wright, M.: Open Sound Control: an enabling technology for musical networking. Organised Sound 10(3), 193–200 (2005)

(Re)Shaping Musical Gesture:
Modelling Voice Balance and Overall Dynamics Contour

Regiane Yamaguchi[1,2] and Fernando Gualda[3,4]

[1] School of Music, Federal University of Rio Grande do Norte (UFRN),
Av. Passeio dos Girassóis, Campus Universitário, Lagoa Nova, Natal - RN, Brazil
[2] Department of Music, Federal University of Paraíba (UFPB),
Cidade Universitária, João Pessoa - PB, Brazil
yamaguchiregiane@hotmail.com
[3] Sonic Arts Research Centre, School of Creative Arts, Queen's University Belfast
BT7 1NN Belfast, Northern Ireland
[4] Music Department, Federal University of Rio Grande do Sul (UFRGS)
Rua Sr. dos Passos, 248, Centro Histórico, Porto Alegre - RS, Brazil
gualda@ufrgs.br

Abstract. This research focuses on identifying and modelling performers' preferred strategies for achieving expressive performances. This paper reports on the results of analysis of a professional pianist's practice session of Chopin's 2nd Ballade, Op. 38. The analysis focused on his approach to balance voices within polyphonic texture. The model for balance of voices is a weighted average of several renditions of the excerpt. Differences of average balance of voices are statistically significant, which suggests that each voice varies around a preferred, overall balance. Tukey HSD reveals that each of the four voices of the excerpt (beginning of the musical work) had been performed within an independent dynamic range. New models representing similar renditions were created using clustering techniques. Those models can then be transformed into new, reshaped performances.

Keywords: Musical Gesture, Music Performance, Expressiveness, Piano, Deliberate Practice.

1   Introduction

From a creative perspective, music encompasses thoroughly crafted structures and patterns, which we call here *organised sound*. From an interpretative perspective, those structures are recognised by performers as graphic *signs* in the musical score and by listeners as *sonic signs*, from which symbols (complex meaning) may arise [1]. The process of interpreting a score has been studied as *immanent* analysis (of those signs), *poietics* (composer and meaning), and *esthesics* (listeners and cognition) [2].

Within this paper, the balance among voices and the overall contour of dynamics are, thus, the *signs* being analysed. The research focuses on modelling the manner

M. Aramaki et al. (Eds.): CMMR 2012, LNCS 7900, pp. 459–468, 2013.
© Springer-Verlag Berlin Heidelberg 2013

through which contours of dynamics are reshaped in each new performance. Thus, this research follows the approach suggested by literature on musical expression as behaviour, which recommends to study differences among performances [3].

1.1   Musical Gesture, Melody Lead, and the Performance of Polyphonic Texture

The theory of Musical Gesture proposes that a rhetorical construction of musical meaning emerges from humans' "ability to recognize the significance of energetic shaping through time" [4]. Polyphonic texture presents concurrent melodic lines that can be emphasised at will by the performer. It was, thus, assumed in this paper that the performer may change the emphasis of melodic lines within the polyphonic texture whilst practising. Within the scope of this paper, only differences in dynamics were utilised to compare melodic lines. Therefore, the performer's reshaping of the balance among voices was studied here in regard to differences in dynamics measured as MIDI-velocity values of notes within the melodic lines of a polyphonic texture.

In addition to differences in dynamics, louder melodic lines may usually be anticipated as a result of piano hammer action on the strings as well as performers' intentional use of asynchronous playing as expressive strategy [5], [6]. The amount of overlap has also been reported as an expressive strategy adopted by organists [7].[1] The ability to perform polyphonic textures is highly relevant for keyboard musicians. New approaches include deliberate practice to identify strategies to enhance the necessary skills to perform polyphonic texture [8].

1.2   Deliberate Practice along with Ecological Validity

A professional pianist with more than 20 years of performance experience has recorded the first bars of Chopin's Ballade Op. 38 on a digital piano eleven times.[2] In order to seek ecological validity [9], the only direction given to the performer was to practise these bars as he would normally do. He was allowed to define his own goals, and to practise the preferred excerpt as many times as he wished [10].[3] No specific information about the goal of the research was given. The performer could listen to the recorded excerpts, and was asked to choose his preferred one. According to the performer, the goal of his deliberate practice was to intuitively find "the ideal balance of dynamics and phrasing to communicate the desired expression" during each rendition of the excerpt. He preferred his last performance, recording session 11.

---

[1] "Variations in the amount of overlap appear to be the most widespread and consistent strategy used by organists to emphasize a voice, at least in the experiment described here. Specifically, a voice was played in a more detached manner when it was emphasized than when it was not." (pp. 57-8) [7].

[2] The same excerpt has also been utilised for researching asynchronous playing [5].

[3] At first sight, the concepts of *ecological validity* and *deliberate practice* seem to be mutually exclusive for one is actively observing oneself during the deliberate practice session.

2   Methods

The main hypothesis of this paper is that the pianist segregates melodic lines within different dynamic ranges. In order to compare performances, two models were devised: one containing score data, and another representing MIDI Δvelocities.

Three kinds of differences in dynamics were considered in this study: (1) within voices, (2) between voices, and (3) centered in relation to all other notes. In case of comparisons within a voice, each note velocity value is subtracted from all other note velocities in that voice, as in Table 2, whereas in comparisons between voices, each note velocity value is subtracted from all concurrent notes, as in Figure 2.

The statistical significance of differences in average Δvelocity have been computed using ANOVA, and Tukey HSD post-hoc tests. Distances between clusters of overall dynamics contour were computed using Ward's agglomerative hierarchical clustering method [11].[4] Ward's method considers the minimal variance within the cluster before including members [12]. The minimal variance produces clusters formed by samples more similar to one another than those produced by other clustering techniques.

2.1   Score Model

The score model included the first 73 notes from the excerpt. It contains information regarding pitches and onset times, as organised into four voices. Information regarding metric accents and durations has not been considered. The voices are labelled as Upper/Lower voice (melodic line) on the Right/Left Hand.

Table 1. Score model - initial 73 pitches on the score, organised into four voices

Voice	0.3	0.4	0.6	1.1	1.3	1.4	1.6	2.1	2.3	2.4	2.6	3.1	3.2	3.3	3.4	3.6	4.1	4.3	4.4	4.6	5.1	5.3	5.4
URH	C_4	C_4	C_4	C_4	C_4	C_4	C_4	C_4	C_4	C_4	C_4	E_4	D_4	C_4	F_4	D_4	C_4	A_4	F_4	G_4	G_4	—	A_4
LRH					A_3	A_3	Bb_3	Bb_3	Bb_3	—	Bb_3	A_3	F_3	F_3	E_3	C_3	F_4 E_4 D_4 Bb_2 Bb_2 Bb_2			C_4			
ULH	C_3	C_3	C_3	C_3	C_3	C_3	C_3	C_3	C_3	C_3	C_3	C_3	—	C_3	C_3	Bb_2	A_2	A_2	A_2	D_2			F_2
LLH					F_2	F_2	F_2	F_2	F_2	—	F_2	F_2			C_2	D_2	G_1	C_2	C_2	F_1			

Fig. 1. Data from the score model, represented as a score. Note stems are presented as follows: URH upward on G-clef, LRH downward on G-clef, ULH upward on F-clef, LLH downward on F-clef. Editions [14] and [16] present a single slur (phrasing arch) over this excerpt.

---

[4] Ward's *distance* is "an ultrametric, or tree distance, which defines a hierarchical clustering (and also an ultrametric topology, which goes beyond a metric geometry) (...) differs from a distance in that the strong triangular inequality is instead satisfied." [12].

As discussed earlier, the fundamental hypothesis is that melodic lines were performed within distinct dynamic ranges. The recognition of melodic lines in the score, however, depends upon interpretation [13]. In this research, a four-voice model has been devised, and notes were organised as presented in Table 1 and Figure 1.

Nevertheless, melodic lines that may arise from rules of counterpoint and voice-leading (four-part writing) do not necessarily conform with any four-voice model. This is the case of the beginning of Op. 38. Just after the highest point (both as pitch height and dynamic level), in measure 3.6, only three notes continue their melodic path (4.1 and 4.4). In 4.6, five pitches occur at the same time. Moreover, from 4.6 to 5.4, another melodic line could be recognised (f-e-d-c), which are slurred in [15], which suggests their independence and facilitates their recognition by the performer.

2.2   Empirical Models of Each Rendition

The empirical model of each rendition of the excerpt consists of two values for each note, namely onset velocity minus the mean velocity for the entire excerpt,[5] and a proportional onset time. Thus, velocities are centred and onset times become invariant to overall musical tempo. The proportional onset time is a (L1) normalisation in which the entire proportions of onset add up to one. The value of each bar (measure) is 0.004. Table 2 presents a model with velocities centred on each voice, instead of the entire excerpt. Also, the proportional onset time is multiplied 100 times in Table 2 which eases reading. Thus, in Table 2, each bar is located around multiples of 0.4. Rubato and gogic accents may change the exact position in time.

3   Results

This paper reports three kinds of results: (1) Analysis of Variance (ANOVA) suggests that each voice has been performed in distinct dynamic ranges (mean MIDI-velocity); (2) Hierarchical Clustering reveals 4 cluster centres with average renditions, which can be rendered as new, reshaped performances; and (3) a representation based on interpolation of Δvelocities is offered as a visual feedback for performers.

3.1   Balance Among Voices

The model for balance of voices is an average of the first ten renditions of the excerpt. ANOVA (F = 128.43, df = 3, $p < 0.001$) resulted in statistically significant differences between average Δvelocities, which suggests that voices vary around a preferred, overall balance. Tukey HSD confirms that each of the four voices had been performed within an independent dynamic range. The differences between all voices were statistically significant ($p < 0.01$, and LRH x LLH $p < 0.05$).

---

[5] MIDI velocities range from 0 to 127. Δvelocity values are defined as the MIDI velocity value of a note subtracted from the mean of the velocities of the set of all notes to which the note belongs. Thus, Δvelocity values can be negative.

Table 2. Empirical model for each voice of all recording sessions. Below are presented the average Δvelocity and the proportional onset time (t) of the first 43 pitches of the excerpt. The actual model includes all 73 pitches from the excerpt. MIDI velocity values are centered on each voice by subtracting the mean velocity, then values are averaged on each note.

	0.3	0.4	0.6	1.1	1.3	1.4	1.6	2.1	2.3	2.4	2.6	3.1	3.2	3.3	3.4
URH	C4	C4	C4	C4	C4	C4	C4	C4	C4	C4	C4	E4	D4	C4	F4
$\overline{\Delta v}$	-24.6	-19.1	-16.8	-9.84	-7.93	-4.84	-4.20	-3.20	0.62	2.80	6.43	10.3	7.89	12.8	16.8
t	0.001	0.090	0.230	0.314	0.452	0.537	0.679	0.787	0.944	1.031	1.172	1.263	1.364	1.397	1.490
LRH								A3	A3	Bb3	Bb3	Bb3		Bb3	A3
$\overline{\Delta v}$								-11.0	-6.52	-0.79	-2.25	-1.34		-8.70	9.21
t								0.789	0.946	1.032	1.173	1.263		1.396	1.491
ULH	C3	C3	C3	C3	C3	C3	C3	C3	C3	C3	C3	C3		C3	C3
$\overline{\Delta v}$	-4.89	-6.07	-4.34	2.0	4.57	5.02	1.57	-6.62	-6.16	-3.16	-0.52	0.57		4.29	1.75
t	0.002	0.092	0.230	0.315	0.453	0.540	0.683	0.792	0.948	1.036	1.175	1.270		1.400	1.493
LLH								F2	F2	F2	F2	F2		F2	F2
$\overline{\Delta v}$								-7.42	-4.88	-4.15	-4.06	-3.42		0.40	1.03
t								0.793	0.948	1.036	1.176	1.269		1.400	1.493

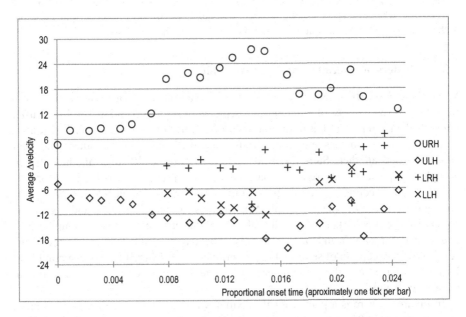

Fig. 2. Average model for Δvelocity of the first ten performances. In this model, the average velocity for each simultaneous set of notes is subtracted, which separates the balance of voices from the overall contour of dynamics. The model includes all 73 pitches from the excerpt.

When the pitch difference between an inner voice and the main melody became small (e.g. major second, in 3.3), the balance among voices changed completely. The pitch of the secondary voice that comes closer in pitch to the main melody becomes much softer. This sudden change of dynamics is soon reverted as the pitch difference increases. This exception to the model can be explained by the Gestalt principle of pitch proximity [17]. In order to maintain their independence, the pitch proximity needed to be compensated with a change of balance among voices.

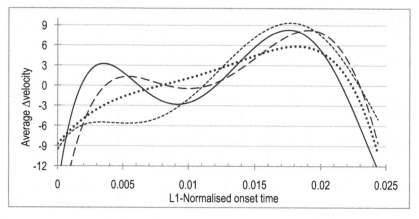

Fig. 3. The four curves represent clusters of averages of overall contour of dynamics of practice sessions. Cluster 1 (dotted) and Cluster 2 (small dashed) represents sessions 3, 6 and 1, 2, 5 respectively, whereas Cluster 3 (long dashed), sessions 7, 8, 10; and Cluster 4 (solid) sessions 4, 9, 11. Session 11 was the preferred rendition, according to the performer.

3.2   Clusters of Overall Contour of Dynamics

Ward's agglomerative hierarchical clustering reveals at least four cluster centres in regard to overall contour of dynamics, as depicted in Figures 3 and 4. The first cluster contains data samples representing the overall contour of dynamics from sessions 4, 9, and 11. Those three samples are, thus, very different from all others and very similar to one another. Samples from sessions 7, 8, and 10 form another cluster. Sample M represents the average of data samples from sessions 1 to 10. Therefore, all samples with exception to the preferred one (sample 11). Samples 4, 7, 8, 9, and 10 clearly differ from the mean (sample M), whereas samples 1, 2, 3, 5, and 6 seem, in comparison, closer to the mean. The other two clusters are formed by samples 1, 2, and 5, and samples 3 and 6, respectively. Thus, in the first half of the recording session, with exception of session 4, the overall contour differed from the second half. It can be inferred that the performance of sample 4 may have influenced the contour of samples 9 and 11.

In Figure 3, there is a pair of local maxima, with the first local maximum situated between 0 and 0.005; and another between 0.015 and 0.020 of the proportional onset time. Arguably, it can be inferred that Clusters 1 and 2 tended to present strong difference between the first and second local maxima, whereas Clusters 3 and 4, seem to exhibit two local maxima with a local minima between them. Those results suggest that in earlier renditions the performer sought a different contour from the later ones.

3.3   Representation of Combined Contours for Each Voice

The model that represents the contour of each voice consists of four polynomial fittings on note velocities and normalised onset times. This representation provides an overview that may serve as visual feedback for performers. In this particular study, the performer preferred the smoothest, most gradual crescendo, contour in the main melodic line, along with the most accentuated pair of local maxima in overall contour.

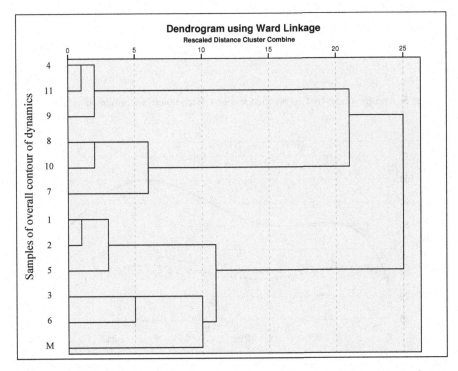

Fig. 4. Hierarchical clustering of samples of overall dynamics contour using Ward's *distance.* Cluster 4 (formed by samples 4, 9, and 11) presents the closest samples to one another, at the maximal distance of 2; distance 21 to the Cluster 3 (samples 7, 8, and 10); and distance 25 to the other Clusters.

Figures 5, 6, and 7 depict the three representations of the four-voice model of dynamic contour. The top, bold line represents the main melodic line (URH), which was the most prominent (loudest) in all samples. The dotted line represents the voice performed by the lower pitches of the right hand (LHR, often played by the thumb and index finger), and this voice was usually the softest in dynamics among all voices. The small dotted lines represent the upper and lower voices performed by

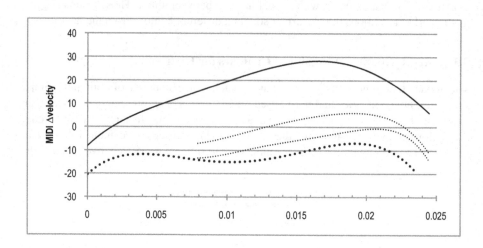

Fig. 5. Average of the first 10 practice sessions. Each voice is represented by a curve.

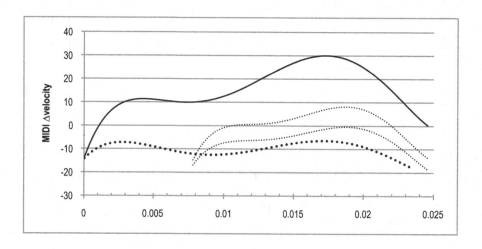

Fig. 6. Practice session 4, which exhibited the similar patterns of dynamic contour

the left hand (ULH and LLH, respectively). The ULH was slightly louder than LLH. The differences in overall average Δvelocity are +16.6 URH, -12.0 ULH, -0.6 LRH, -5.9 LLH. Those differences are statistically significant (as discussed earlier), and thus it can be inferred that voices were performed in distinct dynamic ranges.

The largest differences in dynamics occur between URH and ULH, and the most subtle differences occur between LRH and LLH. This seems to indicate that the pianist performed the lines consistently maintaining this balance, for it occurs independently from the overall dynamic contour.

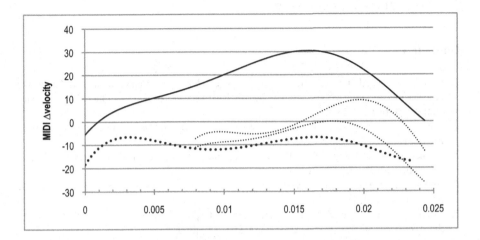

Fig. 7. Practice session 11, which was the preferred sample by the performer

4   Conclusion

Results suggest that (1) the pianist performed each voice in a different dynamic range; (2) the preferred contour sought during deliberate practice can be traced with the four cluster centres and that it favours higher variation in overall dynamic range; (3) the preferred performance may combine minimal variation in the main melody with maximal variation in the overall dynamic contour; (4) the pianist follows a pattern by keeping the balance among the four voices (URH > ULH > LRH > LLH) independently from the overall dynamic contour.

5   Discussion and Applications

The approach presented in this study could be used to follow the evolution of deliberate practice and, thus, be used both as pedagogical tool and as a resource of interpretative possibilities for the professional performer. For the teacher and the developing musician, it can be used as an aid to refine listening and interpretive skills for it allows the visualization of subtle differences in phrasing that are generated by different balances among voices and dynamic contours. In each new performance, by (re)shaping the dynamic balance of voices and visualizing the resulting dynamic contours, pianists can receive immediate feedback on the differences among his various attempts in search of his ideal interpretative version. The software interface also allows reshaping the balance of note velocities by the user. It serves as a theoretical feedback for understanding subtle changes within the balance among voices and of overall dynamic contour.

Acknowledgements. The authors are very thankful for support from PROPESQ/UFRGS and SARC/QUB.

References

1. Gualda, F.: Subtleties of Inflection and Musical Noesis: Computational and Cognitive Approaches to Aural Assessment of Music Performance. PhD. diss. Queen's University Belfast, Belfast (2011)
2. Nattiez, J.J.: Music and Discourse: Toward a Semiology of Music. Princeton University Press, Princeton (1990); Abbate, C. (Trans.)
3. Palmer, C.: Anatomy of a Performance: Sources of Musical Expression. Music Perception 13(3), 433–453 (1996)
4. Hatten, R.: Interpreting Musical Gestures, Topics, and Tropes. Indiana University Press, Bloomington (2004)
5. Goebl, W.: Melody lead in piano performance: Expressive device or artifact? Journal of the Acoustical Society of America 110(1), 563–752 (2001)
6. Widmer, G., Goebl, W.: Computational Models of Expressive Music Performance: The State of the Art. Journal of New Music Research 33(3), 203–216 (2004)
7. Gingrass, B.: Expressive Strategies and Performer-Listener Communication in Organ Performance. PhD. diss. McGill University, Montreal (2008)
8. Carvalho, A.R., Barros, L.C.: Using the organ as a practice strategy while learning a fugue on the piano: An experimental study focusing on polyphonic listening. In: Performa 2009 Conference on Performance Studies (2009)
9. Clarke, E.: Ways of Listening. Oxford University Press, Oxford (2004)
10. Ericsson, K.A.: The Influence of Experience and Deliberate Practice on the Development of Superior Expert Performance. In: Ericsson, K.A., Charness, N., Feltovich, P., Hoffman, R.R. (eds.) Cambridge Handbook of Expertise and Expert Performance, pp. 685–706. Cambridge University Press, Cambridge (2006)
11. Murtagh, F., Legendre, P.: Ward's Hierarchical Clustering Method: Clustering Criterion and Agglomerative Algorithm. arXiv:1111.6285 (p.2) Cornell University Library (2011)
12. Ward Jr., J.H.: Hierarchical Grouping to Optimize an Objective Function. Journal of the American Statistical Association 48, 236–244 (1963)
13. Winold, A.: Music Analysis: Purposes, Paradigms, and Problems. Journal of Music Theory Pedagogy 7, 29–40 (1993)
14. Chopin, F.: 2ème ballade. Beitkopf&Härtel, Leipzig (1840)
15. Chopin, F.: Dzielawszystkie Fryderyka Chopina. In: Paderewsky, I.J., Bronarski, L., Turczynski, J. (eds.) Ballades, vol. III. Institut Pryderyka Chopina, Warsaw (1949)
16. Chopin, F.: Oeuvres complètes de Frédéric Chopin. Bote&Bock, Berlin (1880); Klindworth, K. (ed.)
17. Bregman, A.S.: Auditory Scene Analysis: The Perceptual Organization of Sound. MIT Press, Cambridge (1990)

Multimodal Analysis of Piano Performances Portraying Different Emotions

Kristoffer Jensen and Søren R. Frimodt-Møller

Aalborg University Esbjerg, Denmark
krist@create.aau.dk, soren@frimodt-moller.dk

Abstract. This paper discusses the role of gestural vs auditive components of a piano performance when the performer is prompted to portray a specific emotion. Pianist William Westney was asked to perform a short passage from a specific piece of music 6 times, 3 times without making any deliberate changes, and 3 times where the music was intended to portray the emotions *happy*, *sad* and *angry*, respectively. Motion-capture data from all of the performances was recorded alongside the audio. We analyze differences in the data for the different emotions, both with respect to the size and shape of the pianist's movements and with respect to the sonic qualities of the performances. We discuss probable explanations of these differences. Although differences are found in both the gestural and auditive components of the performance, we argue that the gestural components are of particular importance to the performer's shaping of a musical expression.

Keywords: Music Informatics, Music Performance, Aesthetics, Gesture, Motion Capture.

1 Introduction

Several studies have been concerned with how music communicates emotions. According to Juslin [1], music elicits emotional responses in listeners, and performers are able to communicate anger, sadness, happiness and fear to listeners through tempo, sound level, frequency spectrum, articulation and articulation variability. It has also been shown [2] that the gestures of musicians communicate emotions efficiently. The current study proposes to compare the auditive aspects of a music performance with the gestural, analyzing how both vary across different music performances intended to communicate different emotions.

While the present study concerns piano performance, the movements described here have a lot in common with the movements of performers playing percussive instruments and to a large extent with the movements of musicians in general. Gestures are by definition movements that are expressive, but the way they are expressive varies. In relation to music, some gestures, which we will denote as *expressive gestures*, express something in addition to the produced musical sounds, they may emphasize certain moods or add a dramatic pathos to the performance. Gestures in a performance can, however, also be *effective* in the sense defined by Wanderley [3]:

M. Aramaki et al. (Eds.): CMMR 2012, LNCS 7900, pp. 469–479, 2013.
© Springer-Verlag Berlin Heidelberg 2013

An effective gesture participates in defining the sound. (In this sense, one can say that it is not an expressive movement in itself, but the movement participates in producing music, which is, strictly speaking, a means of expression) As an example of effective gestures, Dahl [4] has investigated the preparatory gestures of drummers and showed that the drummers move the hand and the tip of the drumstick in a fishtail movement in order to gain the necessary height to perform certain notes. Many performance gestures, e.g. the movements of the pianists' arms and hands, are at the same time expressive and effective in the sense that they are both practically needed for the performance of certain notes and give the impression of being infused with a certain energy or emotion. Other gestures, such as head and facial ones may, however, primarily be regarded as expressive - they are apparently mainly part of a visual communication process with the audience. In the work of Davidson [5] (as well as the related work she provides a review of), facial gestures are argued to be an 'added value' on the emotions expressed by the pianist's entire torso, which, however, also seems to trace the phrase structure, dynamics and rhythm of the piece played. In this study, we consider gestures that may be both expressive and effective, but also comment on certain gestures that are arguably only expressive.

In February 2010, the Nordic Network for the Integration of Music Informatics, Performance and Aesthetics[1] held a workshop in Oslo, involving a session at the fourMs laboratory (Department of Musicology, University of Oslo) hosted by Professor Rolf Inge Godøy and postdoctoral researcher Alexander Refsum Jensenius. During this session, Pianist William Westney was prompted by the workshop participants (including the authors of this paper) to perform a short passage from "That Old Black Magic" (written by Harold Arlen, arranged for the piano by Cy Walter[2]) 6 times, 3 times without making any deliberate changes (denoted *normal* in the following), and 3 times where the music was intended to portray the emotions *happy*, *sad* and *angry*, respectively[3]. The performances were made on a Yamaha Disklavier. Motion-capture data from all of the performances was recorded alongside the audio. In this paper, we analyze differences in the data for the different emotions, both with respect to the pianist's movements, with the hand movements as an example, and with respect to the sonic qualities of the performances. When relevant, the emotions chosen are classified according to a two dimensional model [6], with arousal (the level of energy in the emotion) and valence (whether the emotion is positive or negative).

The motion capture equipment was a Qualisys motion capture system consisting of a nine-camera Oqus 300 system and a 200 fps grayscale Point Grey camera. Data was streamed in real time through OSC-protocol via UDP/IP to MAX/MSP/Jitter software and synchronized through a MOTU timepiece allowing synchronous playback of

---

[1]　See www.nnimipa.org for more information on this research network.

[2]　Sheet music for this passage can be found here: http://www.cywalter.com/archives/SheetMusic/ThatOldBlackMagic/HTMLs/Page2.htm (retrieved by April 29, 2013).

[3]　Videos, alongside MoCap visuals of the three emotion-laden performances can be found under part 3 of [11], http://nnimipa.org/JWG.html

analog, motion, video and audio data [7,8]. MoCap data of 23 different points[4] on Westney's head, torso, arms and lower body are available.

2   Audio Analysis

For the analysis of the audio, 4 different features were estimated from the sound files: the sound pressure level (SPL), according to the ISO-226 standard (2003); the dynamics, calculated as 90% of the max volume minus the median, divided by the median; the spectral centroid (SC) - a relative measure of the strength of the higher partials (related to brightness); and the sensory dissonance (SD), calculated as the sum of all overtone pairs that cause fluctuations, weighted with the amplitude of the overtones [9]. The latter is related to musical tension.

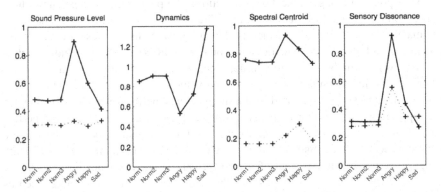

Fig. 1. Mean (solid) and standard deviation (dotted) of Sound Pressure Level (left), Dynamics, Spectral Centroid and Sensory Dissonance (right). Dynamics are calculated globally, so the value has no mean or standard deviation.

In Figure 1, the four features, as calculated from the six performances are shown. It can be seen that the three *normal* performances have very much the same values of these features, while the 'emotional' performances have varying values. In particular, the *angry* and, to a lesser degree, the *happy* performances have higher sensory dissonance, sound pressure level and spectral centroid, but less dynamics, while the *sad* performance has lower dissonance, loudness and brightness and more dynamics than the *normal* performances. The lower degree of dynamics in the *angry* and *happy* performances is obtained because very little of the audio has low loudness, thus restraining the dynamic range. Similarly, the *sad* performance has more dynamics, because even though most of the audio has low loudness, a few very loud notes occurred. In addition, the tempo of the six performances were estimated, showing that the *angry* and, to a lesser degree, the *happy* performances were played significantly faster (154 & 138 BPM respectively), and the *sad* performance slower (94 BPM) than the

---

[4] http://fourms.wiki.ifi.uio.no/MoCap_marker_names. Some of these are omitted in the current study.

normal performances (all three at 104 BPM). (All tempi given as measured at start of piece.)

3 Video Analysis of Hand Movements

As an example of how the movements of a performer can be analyzed, we consider the movement of two points on William Westney's body (out of the 23 that were mapped by the Motion Capture system), namely the right and left hand inwards markers (RHAI and LHAI), placed on upper part of the hand under the index finger of each hand. (The movement of Westney's head will be discussed in section 4.) The movements of these are shown in Figure 2 for the six performances. (The y-axis indicates the horizontal distance from the keyboard, whereas values on the x-axis indicate the horizontal position along the keyboard direction. The path of each graph shows how the position of the hands shifts over time.) The three *normal* performances have approximately the same gestures, which is shown below. Some of these are simply related to the performance of specific notes, others are effective, e.g. the movement of one hand away from the keyboard in order to make room for the other hand.

For the emotion-laden performances, the movements seem (in Figure 2) to be larger for *angry* and *happy* compared to the three *normal* performances, but smaller for *sad*, supporting the idea that *angry* and *happy* prompt larger gestures in the performance than *sad* does. The *angry* and *happy* performances also seem to have more preparatory movements (made before starting the performance, at the vicinity of 'start' in Figure 2) at the start and end of the performances, again supporting the idea of *angry* and *happy* as more lively gestures than *sad*. Some of the differences (such as the lack of the arc in the *normal* performances) may be attributed to the performer changing his approach. The more detailed analysis given in the sections below reveals interesting differences between the movements made during the different emotions. When reading the following sections, it is, however, important to keep in mind that the standard deviation is generally too large, and varies too much between different conditions, to allow for any statistical significance of the differences between the emotions. More data, i.e. more musicians and more pieces of music would be necessary in order to perform a study with statistically significant differences.

3.1 Height, Width and Depth of Movements

In order to measure the relative size of the hand movements in the different performances, we detect the positions in each of the three spatial dimensions where the performer changes direction. For all positions, we measure the distance between the lower and higher points. Finally we calculate the mean of these distances for each of the three dimensions.

Figure 3 shows the mean movement distances along the x- y- and z-axes for each of the six performances.

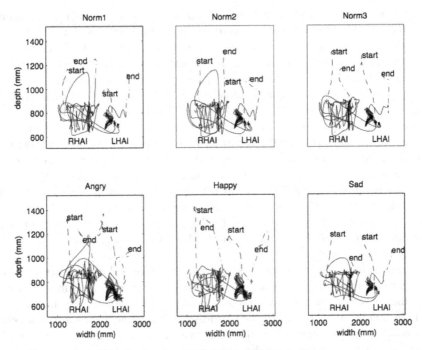

Fig. 2. Movement of RHAI and LHAI markers

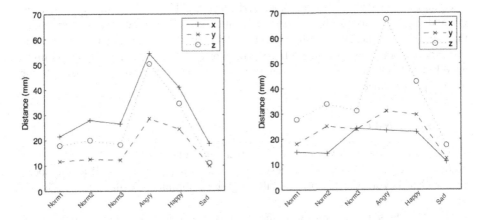

Fig. 3. Mean movement distances along the x- y- and z-axes for each of the six performances. The left figure shows the values for the LHAI markers, the right figure for the RHAI markers. The standard deviation (not shown) is generally as high as or higher than the means.

In all of the performances, the right hand displays larger movements than the left if measured along the vertical dimension (the y-axis), whereas the left hand in general has 'wider' movements, i.e. the largest movements when measured along the x-axis. Both of these facts can be explained in relation to the piece of music being played:

The left hand mainly plays accompanying chords, whereas the right hand mainly plays the melody. The left hand moves to the right of the right hand at one passage, while the right hand typically stays within the same octave on the keyboard. The left hand stays closer to the keyboard to make the transitions between chords easier, whereas the right hand has more freedom to move upwards, away from the keys, in the small pauses between notes. For the same reason, the values for movement along the z-axis (height), are also slightly smaller for the left hand than for the right.

Movements along the x-axis are in general tied to which notes are being played. It is, however, worth noting that the values for movements in the left hand along the x-axis are in fact higher for *angry* and *happy* than for the other performances. In fact, when the distance values for one dimension increase, the other two dimensions follow suit. This may indicate that the pianist is not able to isolate the expressive energy he infuses his gestures with to just one spatial dimension - or even one limb. Put differently, if he wants to move, say, his right hand more violently up and down, this character spreads to all of his movements, so that left hand movements from side to side also become more intense.

As seen in Figure 3, *angry* has larger movement distances along the y-axis than the other performances (for both right and left hand), indicating that the pianist in general plays the notes more violently when trying to capture this emotion. This is caused (as found in data not shown here) by the performer starting from a greater height before each attack for *angry* than in the other performances. *Angry* and *happy* both display larger movement distances in all three dimensions for the left hand and along the y- and z-axes for the right hand, whereas *sad* has lower distance values for all of the three dimensions than any of the other performances. This supports the idea that *angry* and *happy* involve a *high arousal level*, meaning that they are types of emotions that have a lot of energy in them, whereas *sad* prompts a more timid and calm attitude of the performer. This mirrors the finding in Figure 2, that *angry* and *happy* has higher SPL, brightness and sensory dissonance, and *sad* has lower, when compared to the *normal* performances.

3.2   Speed and Curvature

The size of the hand movements is, however, only one parameter of a performer's gestures. The actual shape of the gestures is just as important, as well as the speed with which they are carried out, e.g. the degree of abruptness with which the hands move.

'Pointy' edges in the graphs in Figure 2 suggest that the pianist plays more staccato, that is, moves his hand away fast after the attack, whereas softer edges indicate a gentler movement. In order to assess this trait of the motion capture data, the Euclidean speed and the curvature (how bent the gesture is; calculated as the length of the vector cross product of the first and second time derivative of the positions divided by the length of the time derivative to the power of 3) has been calculated for the different markers (low curvature corresponds to a high degree of 'pointiness' in the graph). The mean and standard deviation of the speed and curvature is shown in Figure 4. With regards to the speed, it is clear that the emotions *angry* and *happy* have higher speed in comparison with the *normal* performances, while the *sad* performance has lower speed. The curvature values are markedly lower for the *angry* and *happy* performances than for the other performances. While there is much noise in the curvature values (c.f. the standard deviations), intuitively, the curvature values seem reciprocal to the speed. This is related to the 1/3 power law [10], which states that, for a specific gesture, the angular speed is equal to a constant (k) multiplied with the radius to the power of one third. As the curvature is the reciprocal of the radius, it is normal to expect the curvature to be inversely proportional to the speed. The constant (k) is calculated as the mean of the speed multiplied by the curvature to the power of one-third and found to be proportional to the arousal value of the emotion, as the *high arousal*-emotions *angry* and *happy* [6] are found to have a constant (k) higher than in the *normal* performances while the *low arousal*-emotion *sad* has a constant (k) below the one in the *normal* performances. It is interesting to observe how the speed and the one-third power law constant (k) (not shown in figure) are systematically lower for the left hand. This is probably related to the fact that the left hand has less general movement, but whether this is further related to the music performed here, or a potential right-handedness of the performer is a matter for further studies beyond the reach of this work. In short, when Westney plays *happy* or *angry*, the speed is higher, and the curvature is lower. Speed is then correlated to the audio features SPL, brightness and sensory dissonance, i.e. when the speed is higher then the audio features is also higher.

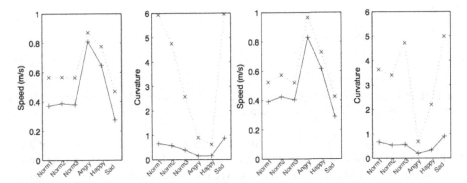

Fig. 4. Mean values (solid) and standard deviations (dotted) for Euclidian speed and curvature. Left hand (left) and right hand (right)

4   Exclusively Expressive Gestures

So far, we have only considered how differences with respect to how the pianist shapes his hand gestures in the performance coincide with his attempt to infuse the performances with particular emotions. Gestures involving other parts of the body might, however, also be important parts of the musician's expressive means. In the following we look first at the role of the pianist's head in his performance gestures and postures, and then proceed to consider the role of his facial gestures. These gestures have in common that they do not seem to be effective, although in theory part of the movement of the pianist's head might intuitively follow other movements in his torso which are caused by effective gestures in the arms and hands.

4.1   Head Posture

When studying the movements of the trackable points on William Westney's head, we found that while the movement of Westney's head were not significantly large or different enough to warrant any conclusions with respect to their expressivity, the *position* of his head was in fact quite different from performance to performance. More specifically, we found interesting differences in how high Westney holds his head over the piano in the different performances, and also in the slope of his head, that is, how it is inclined. The results for the 6 video recordings are showed in Figure 5 below.

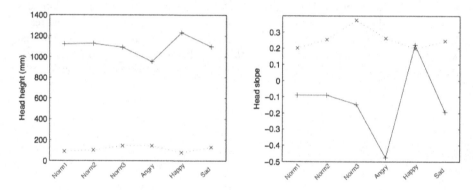

Fig. 5. Head height (left) and slope (right) for the six performances. Mean values are indicated with solid '+' and standard deviation with dotted 'x'.

The head height is measured using four head markers (left and right and front and back), and calculated as the mean of the front left and right head height, and the slope is calculated by dividing the differences between the front and back height and depth values. It is clear that the head is lower and more inclined forward in the *angry* performance, and higher and more inclined backwards in the *happy* performance. These results points to a significant correlation between the valence of the intended infused emotions and the position of the head: Positive valence corresponds to a positively inclined head held high, while negative valence coincides with a negatively inclined head held low. Camurri et al [12], in an observation study of a pianist's gestures and their role in the interaction with the audience, show that the pianist moves his head more in a markedly expressive performance than in a *normal* performance. Our result above expands on this observation in the sense that we are able to distinguish between different kinds of expressivity and their relation to different head postures. Camurri et al also hypothesize that the back contracts along with heightened arousal or build-up of tension while opening when this tension is released. Our study (deduced from head position in Figure 5, and confirmed by C7 marker depth, not shown) shows that this process goes in both directions dependent on the valence: the body leans forward and the head lowers with negative valence and the body leans backwards and the head rises with positive valence. This differs from the audio analysis, in which *angry* and *happy* generally had larger feature values, and thus it does not seem to be related to the sound production, at least not to the features estimated from the audio.

4.2   Facial Gestures

In ensemble performances, facial gestures are important parts of the interaction between the players, e.g. in a string quartet, in the sense that they tend to communicate very specific information (e.g. "it is your turn to play now" or "play softer"). Isabella Poggi [13] has described how a conductor's facial gestures during symphony orchestra performances even constitute an almost unambiguous sign system (in relation to the orchestra musicians). In the case of one person performing, i.e. a solo performance, the role of facial gestures seems less well-defined. Thorough observation of the 6 video recordings of William Westney showed that there was little connection between the intended emotion to be conveyed and the facial expression of the pianist. In the three *normal* performances, one sees an inkling of a smile on the pianist's face 32 seconds into the first video, and in the other two videos, a solemn look at the start and again at about 15-18 seconds into the performance. In the *angry* performance, Westney looks down so much that it is not possible to see his facial expressions properly. In the *happy* video, the performer displays a solemn smile throughout, while the *sad* performance has the performer looking downwards a lot. Other than these subtle differences, the pianist keeps a fairly expressionless face throughout the performances.

Our tentative conclusion regarding facial gestures in Westney's solo performance is that they do not play any important part in his communication with the audience, given that they do not seem to display any of the emotions that Westney is trying to portray in the situation. All that can be observed is a solemn smile that is not properly speaking *happy*.

5   Conclusions and Further Perspectives

We have shown specific differences between the *normal* and the *angry*, *happy*, and *sad* performances of one piece of music played by a pianist with respect to sound level, spectral centroid, dynamics and sensory dissonance in the audio, and for the hand movement sizes, speed and curvature. We have also shown that the pianist's head posture seems to follow changes in the intended infused emotions. While the size, speed and curvature are directly correlated with the audio features, the head slope is not, as it accounts for valence changes that are not found in the audio features.

We also looked for differences across the different performances with respect to the pianist's facial gestures, and found that the pianist was smiling in the *happy* performance. To sum up, while there are also marked differences between the audio from the 6 performances, gesture (as observed for the hands and head) seems to be a very important component for the pianist, when prompted to shape his expression according to a specific emotion.

Given that the study only uses data from one pianist and one piece of music, the findings only give a general idea with respect to tendencies in the expressive means of a performer. We have also not considered whether the gestures of the performer actually give the audience an experience of the different emotions the performer intends to portray. Possible expansions of this study thus includes repeated experiments with more pianists, different pieces of music, and data from the audience (e.g. collected via questionnaires) with respect to how they experience the performance.

With respect to the shape of gestures, a further analysis of the movements of the other 21 points on Westney's body might yield more nuanced results. Nonetheless, this study shows interesting observations on the differences in both audio and gestures for different emotional expressions, indicating how performances rely on both modalities when conveying emotions.

References

1. Juslin, P.: Cue Utilization in Communication of Emotion in Music Performance: Relating Performance to Perception. Journal of Experimental Psychology: Human Perception and Performance 26(6), 1797–1813 (2000)
2. Dahl, S., Friberg, A.: Visual Perception of Expressiveness in Musicians' Body Movements. Music Perception: An Interdisciplinary Journal 24(5), 433–454 (2007)
3. Wanderley, M.M.: Non-obvious performer gestures in instrumental music. In: Braffort, A., Gibet, S., Teil, D., Gherbi, R., Richardson, J. (eds.) GW 1999. LNCS (LNAI), vol. 1739, pp. 37–48. Springer, Heidelberg (2000)
4. Dahl, S.: Measurements of the motion of the hand and drumstick in a drumming sequence with interleaved accented strokes: A pilot study. In: Report Speech, Music and Hearing, Quarterly Progress and Status Report, 4/1997, pp. 1–6. Royal Institute of Technology, Stockholm (1997)
5. Davidson, J.W.: Bodily movement and facial actions in expressive musical performance by solo and duo instrumentalists: Two distinctive case studies. Psychology of Music 40(5), 595–633 (2012)
6. Russell, J.A.: A Circumplex Model of Affect. Journal of Personality and Social Psychology 39(6), 1161–1178 (1980)
7. Morander, C.: FourMs - Music, Mind, Motion, Machines: How Can Knowledge About Movement & Sound Create Better Technologies? Qualisys Newsletter (1), 4 (2010)
8. Jensenius, A.R., Glette, K.H., Godøy, R.I., Høvin, M.E., Nymoen, K., van Dorp Skogstad, A., Tørresen, J.: FourMs, University of Oslo - Lab Report. In: Rowe, R., Samaras, D. (eds.) Proceedings of the International Computer Music Conference, New York, June 1-5 (2010)
9. Sethares, W.A.: Local Consonance and the Relationship between Timbre and Scale. Journal of the Acoustical Society of America 94(3), 1218–1228 (2003)
10. Lacquaniti, F., Terzuolo, C., Viviani, P.: Global Metric Properties and Preparatory Processes in Drawing Movements. In: Kornblum, S., Requin, J. (eds.) Preparatory Processes in Drawing Movements, pp. 357–370. Lawrence Erlbaum, Hillsdale (1984)

11. Jensenius, A.R., Nymoen, K., Grund, C.M., Westney, W., Skogstad, S.A.: Video Suite – in Three Movements: Jensenius-Westney-Grund on Motion-capture, Music and Meaning. Multimodal webpage presentation (2010), http://www.nnimipa.org/JWG.html

12. Camurri, A., Mazzarino, B., Ricchetti, M., Timmers, R., Volpe, G.: Multimodal Analysis of Expressive Gesture in Music and Dance Performances. In: Camurri, A., Volpe, G. (eds.) GW 2003. LNCS (LNAI), vol. 2915, pp. 20–39. Springer, Heidelberg (2004)

13. Poggi, I.: The Lexicon of the Conductor's Face. In: McKevitt, P., Nuallin, S., Mulvihil, C. (eds.) Language, Vision and Music: Selected papers from the 8th International Workshop on the Cognitive Science of Natural Language Processing, Galway, Ireland 1999, pp. 271–284. John Benjamins Publishing Company, Philadelphia (2002)

Focal Impulses and Expressive Performance

John Paul Ito

Carnegie Mellon University, School of Music, Pittsburgh, PA, USA
itojp@cmu.edu

Abstract. This paper presents an overview of a theory of motor organization in the performance of music, the theory of focal impulses, and it draws out implications for use in modeling expressive performance. According to the theory of focal impulses, motor organization is chunked by means of the placement of focal impulses, usually on the beats at some chosen main beat level. Focal impulses are bodily motions that often involve larger and more proximal effector segments and that, by recruiting stable resonance frequencies of the body, create a motional context that facilitates the production of the hierarchically-subordinate motions that follow. Several issues are discussed: the sonic traces of focal impulses; focal impulses that are inflected to suggest motion either with or against the pull of gravity; the different character of accents aligned with focal impulses vs. not; and the effects of choosing a metrical interpretation when multiple interpretations are possible.

Keywords: performance, motor control, meter, embodiment, modeling.

1   Introduction and Overview

This paper presents an overview of a large theory [1] and [2], giving glimpses of main ideas rather than explicating or defending them in detail. Its main goal is to suggest new possibilities for researchers who want to model (in the sense of imitate) subtle sonic aspects of expressive performance, and it does this by suggesting ways in which physical coordination is organized in the performance of music.

In the dynamic systems approach to motor control, which builds on foundational work by Kelso and Turvey [3-6], motor behavior exploits stable resonance properties of musculoskeletal and neuronal systems. Simple period and phase relationships do not need to be constructed; they are an available groove that the system naturally finds. In the dynamic systems approach, a large part of constructing complex motion sequences is a matter of recruiting and exploiting stable, periodic resonance patterns.

Under the present theory of coordination in performance, the theory of focal impulses, musicians exploit these natural resonance periods in performance, inscribing the detailed, aperiodic or quasi-periodic motions of performance within larger, periodic motions, almost like a physically enacted version of Fourier synthesis. The larger periodic motions often involve larger portions of the body and are often driven by larger and more proximal joints or even by the spine and/or legs, so that the larger, more central parts of the body move more slowly while more distal effectors

M. Aramaki et al. (Eds.): CMMR 2012, LNCS 7900, pp. 480–489, 2013.
© Springer-Verlag Berlin Heidelberg 2013

(e.g. fingers) make the aperiodic motions involved in playing individual notes. The larger periods tend to align with the stable periodicities of the music, that is with the meter, and musicians talk about the choice of a specific periodicity in terms of feeling a beat, e.g. feeling the music in two vs. in four. Video Example 1 presents a selection of passages from DVDs of music performance, passages that illustrate the slower motions of larger portions of the body that are often involved in performance.[1] Figure 1 illustrates one possible way in which focal impulses might help to organize the performance of a passage of music.

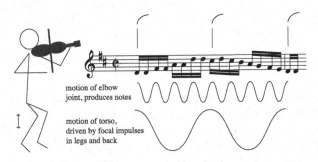

Fig. 1. One possible instantiation of focal impulses

Even at this very basic level, this understanding of motor organization already sheds light on expressive performance, as this hierarchical organization of motion is a developmental precondition for musical expressivity. Novice performances are often deadpan in part because many novices do not employ any kind of hierarchical organization; instead they string together individual motions to produce individual notes. The lack of fluidity that this engenders usually renders the performance inexpressive. In contrast, the goal-directedness inherent in the motor organization of experts (even at the simple level of playing from larger beat to larger beat instead of from note to note) is already a step toward greater expressiveness. Videos of this kind of novice performance are widely available (though also ephemeral) on the internet.

In this theory, felt beats of the kind described above are called *focal impulses*. It is helpful to name the individual beats instead of a level of beat (such as the quarter-note beat) because these basically periodic motions can shift in and out of phase with the beat levels they track; while it is a default to have focal impulses align with some level of beat, a variety of contextual factors can lead a musician to shift the focal impulses to some other metrical position.[2] Furthermore, it is a standard option in triple meter to have a pattern of motion in which only one of the two weak beats receives a focal impulse, for example hearing the meter as "*one two* three *one two* three," where the italics indicate the use of a focal impulse. Triple meter was often understood as

---

[1] For media examples, please see the following directory of my personal website: <http://www.andrew.cmu.edu/user/johnito/research/FocalImpulses/CMMR>

[2] Most commonly this happens when the heard meter and the notated meter are in conflict, as discussed below. For another example, it can also happen when an attack point on a weak beat is understood – and performed – as an anticipation of a strong beat ([1], pp. 116-119).

uneven duple in the renaissance and baroque periods [7], and many compositional techniques make this a reasonable approach to performance, for example the emphasis on the second beat in the sarabande. Robert Port has also made parallel observations regarding the use of two positions within a three-beat cycle in the rhythmic organization of language [8].

An analogy with halfpipe skateboarding and snowboarding may help convey the main idea: the focal impulses are like the pushes off from the surface, as they set basic motional parameters for the aerial phase, especially momentum and angular momentum. In addition to determining flight time, these parameters determine which maneuvers can be done during the flight and which cannot. There remains much active motion to be made during the flight, but the push off from the surface establishes a crucial context of motion and imposes constraints on the motion to follow. Video Example 2 gives examples of halfpipe sports and illustrates the relationship with musical performance.

From discussion with motor control scientists, it seems that this theory is quite consonant with the dynamic systems approach, but that the discipline has not yet advanced to a point at which the theory could be directly tested. It is also not entirely clear how this might best be modeled, but one simple possibility would be to treat some large portion of the body (head and torso, for example) as a damped mass-spring system that is tuned to the periodicity of one of the prominent beat levels in the music. This could affect easily measurable parameters such as loudness and timing as well as more subtle aspects of articulation, envelope, and timbre. This possibility for modeling is elaborated in the second half of the paper, together with more detailed aspects and consequences of the theory of focal impulses.

2   Possibilities for Modeling

There are number of ways in which the theory of focal impulses both offers new perspectives on expressive performance and opens new possibilities for modeling. The selection discussed here begins with the most generally applicable implications and proceeds to more specific cases.

2.1   The Sonic Profile of Focal Impulses

Focal impulses can affect the sound in a number of ways that are holistic and therefore difficult to decompose, but there are also three straightforward common effects. Focal impulses can lead to: 1) a loudness accent on the note that receives the focal impulse, as a result of the stronger muscular contractions involved; 2) lengthening of the duration immediately following the focal impulse, as a result of leaning on the note with the focal impulse; 3) lengthening of the duration immediately preceding the next focal impulse, as a result of rushing through the intervening notes because of a strong sense of release of tension accompanying the focal impulse. In thirteen papers dating as far back as 1937, each often describing multiple experiments, researchers report finding at least one of these cues to meter, and only two papers have looked at both loudness and timing and failed find these patterns ([1], pp. 182—189; for representative examples see [9-14]). Because of these sonic traces, choosing a focal impulse placement (e.g. feeling the music in two vs. in four) leads to global expressive differences.

Because focal impulses have to do with the performer's organization of physical motion, determining their placement in a sound recording, i.e. with no motion data, is always conjectural to some degree; this is because many other factors can result in similar loudness accents and note lengthenings. Recordings can, however, feature very strong clues to focal impulse placement. Figure 2 comes from the Gigue from Bach's First Suite for Unaccompanied Cello, and Audio Example 1 is Yo-Yo Ma's 1983 recording of this passage. In the example, the vertical lines with the beginnings of slurs are the notation for focal impulses. Here the clues to focal impulse placement are the strong accents on the dotted-quarter beats, some noticeable lengthening of the note that is on the beat (especially in mm. 1 and 5), and in m. 3 a noticeable lengthening of the duration that precedes the beat (a lengthening that arises because preceding notes came early, not because the main beat arrives late). These cues furthermore project a very strong gestural sense, making it seem quite plausible that the passage was indeed performed from dotted-quarter beat to dotted-quarter beat.

Fig. 2. Bach, First Suite for Unaccompanied Cello, mm. 1-12, with focal impulse notations describing Yo-Yo Ma's recording

Figure 3 shows the beginning of the Allemande from Bach's Sixth French Suite, and Audio Example 2 is Gustav Leonhardt's 1975 recording of the passage. The harpsichord cannot, of course, produce dynamic accents, but Leonhardt's recording does have both of the timing traces of focal impulses (placed at the level of the half-note beats): an often quite noticeable lengthening of the duration that falls on the beat; and sometimes a smaller but still noticeable lengthening of the duration that directly precedes the beat. Again, these project a strong gestural sense of motion organized in half-note spans.

Fig. 3. Bach, Sixth French Suite, mm. 1-4, with focal impulse notations describing Gustav Leonhardt's recording

2.2   Upward and Downward Focal Impulses

Focal impulses can be correlated with a sense of motion either with or against gravity. This sense of motion in relation to gravity is more a matter of imagined character than of actual orientation of motion in a gravitational field, but it trades on basic physiological distinctions (e.g. the greater potential for force and explosiveness of elbow extension in comparison to flexion) and on very well established tendencies in the organization of motion (e.g. when lifting a heavy object vs. letting it drop) ([1], pp. 82-89). Taking extreme cases to illustrate tendencies, upward pulls against gravity have a gentler attack and a more sustained sound, while motions downward with gravity have sharper attacks followed by rapid release of the sound. Upward and downward focal impulses are focal impulses that are given a special shape in performance, inflecting them with senses of motion either with or against gravity. If the standard conducting pattern for measures in two is performed with a strong sense of pulling on the upbeat and with a strong sense of release for the downbeat, this will convey the gestural character of upward and downward focal impulses.

Figure 4 shows a passage in which the contrast can be quite salient, the first section from the Sarabande from Bach's Fifth Suite for Unaccompanied Cello. The example indicates two focal impulse placements, one from Yo-Yo Ma's 1983 recording (Audio Example 3) and the other from Anner Bylsma's 1979 recording (Audio Example 4); the downward and upward arrows indicate downward and upward focal impulses. Both performances give a sense of alternation between upward and downward motion, but one places the upward impulse on beat 2 and the other on beat 3; as a result the downward character predominates in one performance, the upward in the other. This contributes to a strong affective contrast; the performance in which the longer span is governed by the upward impulse (Bylsma's) has a more positive and hopeful character, while the performance in which the longer span is governed by the downward impulse (Ma's) has a heavier and more lamenting character. To most clear-ly appreciate the contrast, it is helpful to conduct along in two with the examples, with a downward releasing motion for the downward arrow and an upward pulling motion for the upward arrow.

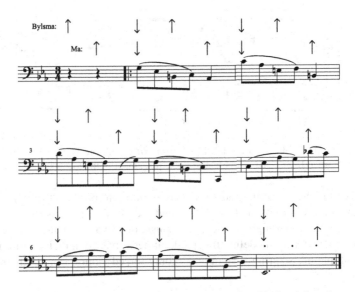

Fig. 4. Bach, Fifth Suite for Unaccompanied Cello, mm. 1-8, with focal impulse notations describing Yo-Yo Ma's and Anner Bylsma's recordings

This contrast between downward and upward focal impulses could be modeled in terms of the dynamic contrasts between allowing an object to fall (with an impact on the beat) and pulling it upwards non-ballistically. This would probably involve a con-trast between sharper attacks and quicker releases versus gentler attacks and more insistent sustain phases, with these contrasts applying not only to the notes coinciding with the focal impulses but also being distributed through the span until the next focal impulse.

2.3   Qualitative Differences between Accents Based on Focal Impulse Alignment

Strong accents played on the beat (with focal impulses) are more straightforward to perform than strong accents off the beat, and the physical difference in the manner of production leads to audible differences in the sound. Thus the near-canonic rhythms in the passage from Stravinsky's *Rite of Spring* in Figure 5 and Audio Example 5 are quite different both performatively and sonically. The basses' attack points coincide with focal impulses, so that their performance has an economy of movement that helps it to be stable and grounded, while the winds are much more active and energet-ic, as they must produce both the strong focal impulses (silently, in order to keep the body synchronized with the meter) and the strong accents that follow them. These contrasting modes of performance are best appreciated by miming the parts in turn along with the recording, imagining playing them on any familiar instrument.

Fig. 5. Stravinsky, "Glorification de l'Élue" from *Rite of Spring*, mm. 1-3, with focal impulse notations. Dashed lines clarify the focal impulse placement in the lower staff.

This extra level of activity and intensity required to produce the syncopated notes will leave traces in the sound produced, and the physicality of performance is likely part of the reason that highly syncopated music often has such an active and unstable rhythmic character. In modeling this mode of performance, a first attempt might be to use a multiple mass-spring system undergoing forced motion from both ends simultaneously.

2.4   Performative Consequences of Different Metrical Interpretations

Some pieces of music can be heard under multiple metrical interpretations, and in such cases the metrical interpretation of the performer, though not determinative of that of the listener, can nonetheless strongly influence the sound of the performance through determining which notes will receive focal impulses. Figure 6 shows a passage from Schumann in which surface rhythms often conflict with the notated meter.

In Figure 7 this passage is rebarred to fit surface rhythms more closely, drawing on an analysis of the passage by Harald Krebs [15]. Figure 7 indicates focal impulses placed in accord with the meter, and pianist David Keep was instructed to use this focal impulse placement when recording Audio Example 6. (That is, Keep understood the theory, he believed he was placing focal impulses in this way, and the resulting sound was judged to fit this intention/belief.)

While Figure 7 captures many surface rhythms well, the underlying harmonic motion supports the notated meter; as illustrated in Figure 8, the passage can be generated through a three-stage process, first presenting main harmonies at a rate of one per dotted half note, then adding embellishing harmonies, and finally adding anticipations to create the actual passage.

In Audio Example 7, Keep plays the passage as in Figure 9, with focal impulses that follow the notated meter until the hemiola of mm. 69-70. It is instructive to compare the two performances; because the performance as in Figure 9 makes so many more of the attacks into syncopations, it makes sense that this performance sounds more dynamic, the performance as in Figure 7 sounding much more stable and grounded. In metrically malleable music, choice of a metrical interpretation may be expected to bring with it gestalt changes in the expressive details of a performance.

Fig. 6. Schumann, "Grillen" from the *Phantasiestücke*, mm. 61-72

Fig. 7. The same passage from "Grillen," rebarred to follow surface rhythms, with focal impulses that follow the (new) meter

Fig. 8. Two successive stages in the derivation of mm. 61-66 from "Grillen"

Fig. 9. "Grillen," focal impulses with notated meter except for hemiola in mm. 69-70

2.5   Conclusion

The placement of focal impulses influences the sound produced, as does choice of type (upward or downward); but as mentioned above, this influence is not unambiguously recoverable from the sound produced. Though in the clearer cases there may be a convincing best fit, if the listener is hearing in terms of a different beat level or a different metrical interpretation, the performance will not make that hearing impossible. Rather, a different performance will often be understood in terms of the listener's mental framework, as features that might point to a different framework can instead be interpreted as an unusual musical shaping, even as a trace of an unusual posture, or of an unusual way of organizing physical motion in performance [16]. The kind of one-to-one correlation that would be most convenient for scientific testing of the theory is absent, and in its absence tests that measure aspects of the motion itself will be necessary.

For the performer, however, the theory of focal impulses illuminates a number of ways in which changes in the mode of performance may be expected to have systematic effects on the sound produced. And those who attempt to model the human performance of music may find helpful new ways to approach the design of their models, ways that capture aspects of the performer's embodiment, aspects of the complex dynamic system that is the human body in motion.

References

1. Ito, J.P.: Impulse Structure in Tonal Music: A Theory of the Metrical Coordination of Motor Behavior in Performers. PhD diss., Columbia Univ (2004)
2. Ito, J.P.: Musical Expression, Meter, and the Body (in preparation)
3. Turvey, M.T.: Preliminaries to a Theory of Action with Reference to Vision. In: Shaw, R., Bransford, J. (eds.) Perceiving, Acting, and Knowing: Toward an Ecological Psychology, pp. 211–265. Erlbaum, Hillsdale (1977)
4. Kugler, P.N., Kelso, J.A.S., Turvey, M.T.: On the Concept of Coordinative Structures as Dissipative Structures: I. Theoretical Lines of Convergence. In: Stelmach, G., Requin, J. (eds.) Tutorials in Motor Behavior, pp. 3–47. North-Holland, Amsterdam (1980)
5. Kelso, J.A.S., Holt, K.G., Kugler, P.N., Turvey, M.T.: On the Concept of Coordinative Structures as Dissipative Structures: II. Empirical Lines of Convergence. In: Stelmach, G., Requin, J. (eds.) Tutorials in Motor Behavior, pp. 49–70. North-Holland, Amsterdam (1980)
6. Kelso, J.A.S.: Dynamic Patterns: The Self-organization of Brain and Behavior. MIT Press, Cambridge, MA (1995)
7. Houle, G.: Meter in Music, 1600-1800: Performance, Perception, and Notation. Indiana University Press, Bloomington (1987)
8. Port, R.F.: Meter and Speech. J. Phonetics 31, 599–611 (2003)
9. Clarke, E.F.: Structure and Expression in Rhythmic Performance. In: Howell, P., Cross, I., West, R. (eds.) Musical Structure and Cognition, pp. 209–236. Academic Press, London (1985)
10. Drake, C., Palmer, C.: Accent Structures in Music Performance. Music Perception 10, 343–378 (1993)
11. Sloboda, J.: The Communication of Musical Metre in Piano Performance. Q. J. Exp. Psych. 35A, 377–396 (1983)
12. Sloboda, J.: Expressive Skill in Two Pianists: Metrical Communication in Real and Simulated Performances. Can. J. Psych. 39, 273–293 (1985)
13. Povel, D.J.: Temporal Structure of Performed Music: Some Preliminary Observations. Acta Psych. 41, 309–320 (1977)
14. Repp, B.H.: Patterns of Expressive Timing in Performances of a Beethoven Minuet by Nineteen Famous Pianists. J. Acous. Soc. Am. 88, 622–641 (1990)
15. Krebs, H.: Fantasy Pieces: Metrical Dissonance in the Music of Robert Schumann. Oxford, New York (1999)
16. Clarke, E.F.: Imitating and Evaluating Real and Transformed Musical Performances. Music Perception 10, 317–343 (1993)

Learning to Make Feelings: Expressive Performance as a Part of a Machine Learning Tool for Sound-Based Emotion Control

Alexis Kirke[1], Eduardo R. Miranda[1], and Slawomir J. Nasuto[2]

[1] Interdisciplinary Centre for Computer Music Research, Plymouth University, Plymouth, UK
{alexis.kirke,eduardo.miranda}@plymouth.ac.uk
[2] Cybernetics Research Group, University of Reading, Reading, UK
s.j.nasuto@reading.ac.uk

Abstract. We propose to significantly extend our work in EEG-based emotion detection for automated expressive performances of algorithmically composed music for affective communication and induction. This new system involves music composed and expressively performed in real-time to induce specific affective states, based on the detection of affective state in a human listener. Machine learning algorithms will learn: (1) how to use biosensors such as EEG to detect the user's current emotional state; and (2) how to use algorithmic performance and composition to induce certain trajectories through affective states. In other words the system will attempt to adapt so that it can – in real-time - turn a certain user from depressed to happy, or from stressed to relaxed, or (if they like horror movies!) from relaxed to fearful. Expressive performance is key to this process as it has been shown to increase the emotional impact of affectively-based algorithmic composition. In other words if a piece is composed by computer rules to communicate an emotion of happiness, applying expressive performance rules to humanize the piece will increase the likelihood it is perceived as happy. As well as giving a project overview, a first step of this research is presented here: a machine learning system using case-based reasoning which attempts to learn from a user how themes of different affective types combine sequentially to communicate emotions.

Keywords: Music, Emotion, Bio-signals, Affective Computing, Music Therapy, Medicine, Machine Learning, Algorithmic Composition, Computer Expressive Performance.

1 Introduction

The aim of our research is to develop technology for implementing innovative intelligent systems that can monitor a person's affective state and induce a further specific affective state through music, automatically and adaptively. [1] investigates the use of EEG to detect emotion in an individual and to then generate emotional music based on this. These ideas have been extended into a 4.5 year EPSRC research project [2] in which machine learning is used to learn, by EEG emotional feedback, what types of

M. Aramaki et al. (Eds.): CMMR 2012, LNCS 7900, pp. 490–499, 2013.
© Springer-Verlag Berlin Heidelberg 2013

music evoke what emotions in the listener. If the positive affective state inducing capacity of music could be harnessed in a more controlled way, it would make a significant impact in various recreational and medical areas. The economic impact of a system that would enable users to enter a desired affective state using music would contribute to (a) the UK's burgeoning entertainment industry and (b) the health sector (e.g., preventive medicine). Such a system could help to enhance our quality of life and contribute towards the wellbeing of the population (e.g., help reducing levels of stress and/or anxiety). This chapter introduces the key background elements behind the project: Music and Emotion, Emotional Expressive Performance and Algorithmic Composition, and EEG Affective Analysis; then details some preparatory work being undertaken, together with the future project plans.

2   Music and Emotion

Music is commonly known to evoke various affective states (popularly referred to as "emotions"); e.g., elation, calm or cheerfulness [3]. There have been a number of questionnaire studies supporting the notion that music communicates affective states (e.g., [4, 5]) and that music can be used for affect regulation and induction (e.g., [6, 7]). However the exact nature of these phenomena is not fully understood. The literature makes a distinction between perceived and induced emotion with music being able to generate both types [4]. The differences between induced affective state and perceived affective state have been discussed by Juslin and Sloboda [3]. For example a listener may enjoy a piece of music like Barber's Adagio, which most people would describe as a "sad" piece of music. However, if they gain pleasure from listening, the induced affective state must be positive, but the perceived affective state is sadness; i.e., a negative state. Despite the differences between perceived and induced affective state, they are highly correlated [4, 8]. Zentner et al. [9] reported on research into quantifying the relationship between perceived and induced affective state in music genres. Scherer [10] discussed the underlying physical mechanisms of musically induced emotions.

3   Emotion-Based Algorithmic Composition

One area of algorithmic composition which has received more attention recently is affectively-based computer-aided composition. A common theme running through some of the affective-based systems is the representation of the valence and arousal of a participant's affective state [11]. Valence refers to the positivity or negativity of an affective state; e.g., a high valence affective state is joy or contentment, a low valence one is sadness or anger. Arousal refers to the energy level of the affective state; e.g., joy is a higher arousal affective state than happiness. Until recently the arousal-valence space was a dominant quantitative two-dimensional representation of emotions in research into musical affectivity. More recently, a new theory of emotion with the corresponding scale, referred to as GEMS (Geneva Emotional Musical Scale) has been proposed [9].

Many of the affective-based systems are actually based around re-composition rather than composition; i.e. they focus on how to transform an already composed piece of music to give a different emotional effect – e.g. make it sadder, happier, etc. This is the case with the best known and most thoroughly tested system - the Computational Music Emotion Rule System (CMERS) [11]. The rules for expressing emotions map valence and arousal onto such elements as modes and pitch class. These rules were developed based on the combining a large number of studies by psychologists into music and emotion. However it was found these needed to be supplemented by rules for expressive performance of the transformed music to express the emotion successfully. Hence CMERS is actually an integrated composition and expressive performance system. CMERS key limitation as a composition system is that it is designed for re-composition, not for generating new material.

Oliveira and Cardoso [13] also perform affective transformations on MIDI music, and utilize the valence-arousal approach to affective specification. These are to be mapped on to musical features: tempo, pitch register, musical scales, and instrumentation. A knowledge-base of musical features and emotion was developed based on musical segments with a known affective content. This knowledge-base was then used to train a generalized mapping of affective state to required music and a model was then generated based on Support Vector Machine regression. The model was tested for transforming the emotion of classical music – the current results are not as good as CMERS. One reason for this may be that Oliveira and Cardoso has the limitation that it is unable to generate expressive performances.

Although Legaspi et al. [14] utilize pre-composed music as its heart, it is more focused on composing new music. An affective model is learned based on score fragments manually labeled with their appropriate affective perception – this maps a desired affective state on to a set of musical features. The model is learned based on the machine learning approaches Inductive Logic Programming and Diverse Density Weighting Metric. This is then used as a fitness function for a Genetic Algorithm – however the GA is also constrained by some basic music theory. The GA is then used to generate the basic harmonic structure, and a set of heuristics are used to generate melodies based on the harmonic structure. The system was trained with emotion label dimensions "favourable-unfavourable", "bright-dark", "happy-sad", and "heartrending-not heartrending". Listening tests were done on a series of eight bar tunes and the results obtained were considered promising, but indicated that more development was needed. Once again, the system is lacking the ability to generate expressive performances.

4   Expressive Music Performance

The introduction of MIDI led to an explosion in the use of sequencers and computers, thanks to the new potential for connection and synchronization. These computers and sequencers performed their stored tunes in perfect metronomic time, a performance which sounded "mechanical". They sounded mechanical because human performers normally perform expressively – for example speeding up and slowing down while playing, and changing how loudly they play. The performer's changes in tempo and dynamics, and other subtle musical features, allow them to express a fixed score – hence the term expressive performance. Publications on computer expressive performance of music have lagged behind computer-aided composition by almost quarter of a century. But from the end of the 1980s onwards there was an increasing interest in automated and semi-automated Computer Systems for Expressive Music Performance (CSEMP). A CSEMP is a computer system which – given a score in some form – is able to generate expressive performances of music [15]. For example software for music typesetting will often be used to write a piece of music, but some packages play back the music in a relatively mechanical way – the addition of a CSEMP enables a more "human sounding" playback, giving a better idea of how the final performance may sound. Computer expressive music performance is used in this chapter to make performances sound less mechanical to the user, and thus increase the affective impact, as demonstrated by [11]. The particular system to be utilized is now described.

Director Musices (DM) [2] has been an ongoing project since 1982. Researchers including violinist Lars Fryden developed and tested performance rules using an analysis-by-synthesis method (later using analysis-by-measurement and studying actual performances). Currently there are around 30 rules which are written as relatively simple equations that take as input music features such as height of the current note pitch, the pitch of the current note relative to the key of the piece, or whether the current note is the first or last note of the phrase. The output of the equations defines the performance actions. For example the higher the pitch the louder the note is played, or during an upward run of notes, play the piece faster. Another DM rule is the Phrase Arch which defines a "rainbow" shape of tempo and dynamics over a phrase .The performance speeds up and gets louder towards the centre of a phrase and then tails off again in tempo and dynamics towards the end of the phrase. Each rule in DM can be weighted to give it a greater or lesser relative effect on the performance, by changing a parameter known as its k-value.

DM has also been developed to enable emotion-based expression [16]. Listening experiments were used to define the k-value settings on the DM rules for expressing emotions. The music used was a Swedish nursery rhyme and a computer-generated piece. Six rules were used from DM to generate multiple performances of each piece. Subjects were asked to identify a performance emotion from the list: fear, anger, happiness, sadness, solemnity, tenderness or no-expression. As a result parameters were found for each of the 6 rules which mould the emotion-communicating expression of a piece. For example for "tenderness": inter-onset interval is lengthened by 30%, sound level reduced by 6dB, and two other rules are used: the Final Ritardando rule (slowing down at the end of a piece) and the Duration Contrast rule (if two adjacent notes have contrasting durations, increase this contrast).

5   EEG and Emotion

EEG measurements have been found to be useful in a clinical setting for diagnosing brain damage, sleep conditions and epilepsy; e.g. [17]. It is well known in the literature that it is possible to relate different EEG spectral bandwidths (often referred to as

"EEG rhythms") to certain characteristics of mental states, such as wakefulness, drowsiness, etc. As early as the 1970s researchers have reported on the relationship between EEG asymmetry and affective state. Reviews of EEG asymmetry and affective state can be found in [18, 19] and one of the most recent sets of results can be found in [20]. Davidson [21] proposed a link between asymmetry of frontal alpha activation and the valence and arousal of a participant's affective state.

Musha and co-workers [22] developed one of the earliest computer EEG affective state detection systems and a number of detection methods have been investigated since then; e.g., [23]. More recently detection and analysis of weak synchronization patterns in EEG have been shown to be indicators of cognitive processing; growing evidence suggests that synchronization may be a carrier of information about the information processing in the brain [24]. There are different ways in which signals may co-vary. For instance, there is the hypothesis that information about many cognitive phenomena is preserved not necessarily in the intensity of the activation, but rather in the relationship between different sources of activity. There are an increasing number of studies investigating the role of synchronization in cognitive processing using various techniques, e.g. [25]. A particularly promising form of synchronization is called Phase–locking, which has been studied extensively by the third author and co-workers, e.g. [26]. Moreover, there is growing evidence supporting the role of synchronization in music perception [27] and also in response to affectively charged non-musical stimuli [28].

6   Emotional Feedback EEG Music

The above sections show that there is increasing evidence in the literature that musical traits such as rhythm, melody and tonality, can communicate specific affective states. There is also increasing evidence (e.g. [12]) that these states are detectable in the EEG of the listener. There are fewer studies into establishing which musical traits are useful for implementing a system to *induce* affective states. Amongst the techniques available, the analysis of synchronisation patterns in the EEG signal is a promising option for detecting affective states induced by music. Other techniques (such as frontal asymmetry) will also be considered in the project and the most suitable will be adopted. Thus the detection of affective state by EEG is a research area which this project will contribute to as well.

As was mentioned earlier, [1] investigates the use of EEG to detect emotion in an individual and to then generate emotion-inducing music based on this. The work done previously in [1] was not real-time and did not involve any machine learning process. The research and implementation of a real-time version of a more advanced detection method would allow us to monitor affective states induced by music on the fly. We hypothesise that once we establish – for a given context - specific musical traits associated with specific affective states, then we will be able to parameterise such traits in order to exert control in a musical composition; e.g., speed up the tempo to induce affective state X, use a "harsher" timbre to induce state Y, etc. The parameterisation of musical traits will allow for the design of algorithms capable of generating music (e.g., rule-based) embodying musical traits aimed at inducing specific EEG-observed trajectories correlated to affective states. Such a generative system can be rendered intelligent and adaptive by means of machine learning techniques (e.g., case-based reasoning and reinforcement learning) that are able to learn to recognize complex patterns and make decisions based on detected patterns in real-time.

Our initial results will be driven by more universal musical determinants of emotional response than context-specific. Thus, they will be based on results averaged across a test population. The later stages of the project will extend the former to include context-specific emotional responses. Later stages will also include the more real-time approach to learning and detection. The move towards more on-going assessment of affective state will be important because it will enable us to extend the system beyond the music composition based on manipulation of the musical traits eliciting generic affective responses, to a more adaptive individual-oriented system taking into account participants' states; thus utilising also the contextual effects of an individual and the environment.

7   Affective Structure Prototype

It has been discussed how expressive performance and various compositional musical elements will be tested for their affective impact based on context. On the music and machine learning side of the project, a Matlab prototype has been produced for investigating the effects of one musical element on emotional communication. This element is musical structure. (Communicated emotion analysis is a first step towards induced emotional analysis.)

At the heart of this prototype is a phrase generator that uses random walk with jumps [29] to generate the basic motifs. The phrases produced by the generator are then transformed in pitch height, loudness level and global tempo to investigate affective features. They can also be transformed between major and minor key modes. Once these transforms have been done Director Musices rules are applied. The following rules are utilized: Duration Contrast, Duration Contrast Articulation, Punctuation, High Loud, Phrase Arch, and Motor Errors. Although DM is capable of mimicking emotional expression, the rules are being used here to make the performances sound less mechanical to the user, and thus increase the affective impact [11].

The prototype is embedded in a test-bed which uses a pairs comparison system for ascertaining communicated valence, which is correlated to induced emotion [4, 8]. The user is presented with a piece of monophonic expressively performed music and the user is asked "Which of the following two tunes reminds you of more positive feelings?" This question is designed to ascertain the communicated valence of the tune. The user is given the options of selecting tune 1 or 2, selecting a "don't know" option, or asking to have the tunes played again. Thus at the end of the experiment a series of locally-ordered parameter set pairs (a1, a2) (b1, b2) ... etc. will have been generated. Each pair will be ordered by valence, thus leading to series of inequalities. If sufficient pairs are available for valence, then the inequalities can be used to infer a global ordering for which parameters communicate a greater valence for the user.

An algorithm for inferring the global ordering from the local ordering is incorporated into the test-bed.

The structure-based testing currently involves the following procedure. Benchmark transformations have been assigned for Happy, Sad, Stressed, and Relaxed – based on past research into the area of musical affective communication [11][30]. To initiate a structure test, two phrases are generated. Two benchmark states are randomly selected from the four above. The first phrase is transformed using the first benchmark and the second using the second. Thus a tune consisting of two affective parts is played – for example one Happy and one Sad, or one Stressed and one Happy, etc. It was found that this created a perceptible discontinuity between the two halves, so an interpolation system was developed which approximately interpolated pitches, loudness, tempo and key between the two halves – thus perceptually smoothing the transition. The whole combined theme is then also transformed using the expressive performance algorithms of DM. The original two generated phrases can then be used again and transformed to create a different affective interpolated structure. So there will now be two themes, built from the same initially generated phrases, but with different affective structures. These are then presented to the test subject one after the other, who orders them by communicated valence.

Due to the correlation between induced and communicated affect, this system will help to generate an initial core rule-set for the machine learning algorithm which we are developing. However it is also useful in learning more about the effects of musical structure on affective communication.

8   Conclusions

A new method for utilizing the emotion-inducing nature of music and sound has been introduced. The background elements have been detailed, including affective representation, computer expressive performance, affective algorithmic composition and EEG-based machine learning. Some initial steps in this research have been the development of a test-bed which utilizes computer expressive performance, and investigates the testing of musical structure effects on affective communication. The system uses a pairs-based analysis approach and structural emotion interpolation. This test-bed enables the development of a core rule-set linking musical structure and valence.

Future work in the broader project includes characterising synchrony patterns corresponding to different induced affective states from the EEG recordings while participants listen to music stimuli. Initially, the analysis and the system for learning the emotional control music generation will be developed based on the valence arousal emotional scale, due to its widespread acceptance and availability of tagged databases. We will subsequently develop a GEMS representation and will evaluate the usefulness of the two scales for developing our system.

Then, we shall progressively move towards the final goal of real-time assessment of affective states using reinforcement learning (RL). Initially, the affective state estimation will be updated at a slower time scale consistent with the computational demands of the synchronisation analysis. However, our aim is to create a system for a fast real-time assessment of affective state based on efficient analysis using feature selection and dimensionality reduction.

We plan to develop further algorithms for generating music featuring the various musical traits that have been discussed in the literature. Some musical features are more universal determinants of affective response, invariant across populations with common cultural background [9]. Other features may show more variation dependent on contextual effects of culture, personality and environment. Our initial results will be driven by more universal musical determinants of emotional response than context-specific. Thus, they will be based on results averaged across a test population. The later stages of the project will extend the former to include context-specific emotional responses.

We plan to test our initial generative music algorithms for inductive effects using an offline EEG affective state detector. The results of these tests will be used to initialize a case-based reasoning (CBR) system for affective induction by music. Then, we will extend the CBR system by investigating specific musical genres. A recent study [9] also suggested the importance of genre selection for the induction of certain affective states. The benchmark will be a classical solo piano genre, as classical music has well known computational approaches for eliciting certain affective states, but expansions on this will be investigated utilizing ideas from pop and electroacoustic music genres.

In order to have a real-time, dynamic assessment of the affective state – so as to increase accuracy and effectiveness - we will use the CBR system to initialise an automatic music generation system based on reinforcement learning (RL). RL has been successfully used in optimising the stimulation patterns in deep brain stimulation therapy of the epileptic seizures [31]. The RL system we plan to build will be used in action selection optimizing a desired affective response of this participant. The move towards more on-going assessment of affective state will be important because it will enable us to extend the system beyond the music composition based on manipulation of the musical traits eliciting generic affective responses, to a more adaptive individual-oriented system taking into account participants' states; thus utilising also the contextual effects of an individual and the environment.

Acknowledgements. This research was supported by EPSRC grant EP/J003077/1 "Brain-Computer Interface for Monitoring and Inducing Affective States".

References

1. Kirke, A., Miranda, E.R.: Combining EEG Frontal Asymmetry Studies with Affective Algorithmic Composition and Expressive Performance Models. In: Proceedings of International Computer Music Conference (ICMC 2011), Huddersfield, UK (2011)
2. Nasuto, S.J., Miranda, E.R.: Brain-Computer Interface for Monitoring and Inducing Affective States, EPSRC Grant EP/J002135/1 (2012)
3. Juslin, P., Sloboda, J.: Music and Emotion: Theory and Research. Oxford University Press (2001)

4. Juslin, P., Laukka, P.: Expression, perception, and induction of musical emotion: a review and a questionnaire study of everyday listening. Journal of New Music Research 33, 216–237 (2004)
5. Minassian, C., Gayford, C., Sloboda, J.A.: Optimal experience in musical performance: A survey of young musicians. Annual General Meeting of the Society for Education, Music and Psychology Research (2003)
6. Goethem, A.: The Functions of Music for Affect Regulation. In: International Conference on Music and Emotion, Durham, UK (2009)
7. Juslin, P.: Five Facets of Musical Expression: A Psychologist's Perspective on Music Performance. Psychology of Music 31, 273–302 (2003)
8. Bigand, E., Vieillard, S., Madurell, F., Marozeau, J., Dacquet, A.: Multidimensional scaling of emotional responses to music: The effect of musical expertise and of the duration of the excerpts. Cognition and Emotion 19(8), 1113–1139 (2005)
9. Zentner, M., Grandjean, D., Scherer, K.R.: Emotions evoked by the sound of music: characterization, classification, and measurement. Emotion 8(4), 494–521 (2008)
10. Scherer, K.R.: Which Emotions Can be Induced by Music? What are the Underlying Mechanisms? And How Can we Measure Them? Journal of New Music Research 33(3), 239–251 (2004)
11. Livingstone, S., Muhlberger, R., Brown, A., Thompson, W.F.: Changing Musical Emotion: A Computational Rule System for Modifying Score and Performance. Computer Music Journal 34(1), 41–64 (2010)
12. Schmidt, L.A., Trainor, L.J.: Frontal brain electrical activity (EEG) distinguishes valence and intensity of musical emotions. Cognition and Emotion 15(4), 487–500 (2001)
13. Oliveira, A.P., Cardoso, A.: Automatic Manipulation of Music to Express Desired Emotions. In: Proceedings of the 6th Sound and Music Computing Conference, Porto, Portugal, pp. 265–270 (2009)
14. Legaspi, R., Hashimoto, Y., Moriyama, K., Kurihara, S., Numao, M.: Music Compositional Intelligence with an Affective Flavor. In: Proceedings of the 2007 International Conference on Intelligent User Interfaces, Honolulu, Hawaii, USA, pp. 216–224 (2007)
15. Kirke, A., Miranda, E.R.: Guide to Computing for Expressive Music Performance. Springer, UK (2012) (in print)
16. Bresin, R., Friberg, A.: Emotional Coloring of Computer-Controlled Music Performances. Computer Music Journal 24(4), 44–63 (2000)
17. Sheerani, M., Hassan, A., Jan, A., Zaka, R.: Role of Video-EEG Monitoring in the Management of Intractable Seizures and Non-epileptic Spells. Pakistan Journal of Neurological Sciences 2(4), 207–209 (2007)
18. Silberman, E.K., Weingarter, H.: Hemispheric lateralization of functions related to emotion. Brain and Cognition 5(3), 322–353 (1986)
19. Allen, J.J.B., Kline, J.P.: Frontal EEG asymmetry, emotion, and psychopathology: the first, and the next 25 years. Biological Psychology 67(1), 1–5 (2004)
20. Wyczesany, M., Kaiser, J., Coenen, A.M.L.: Subjective mood estimation co-varies with spectral power EEG characteristics. Acta Neurobiologiae Experimentalis 68(2), 180–192 (2008)
21. Davidson, R.J.: The neuropsychology of emotion and affective style. In: Lewis, M., Haviland, J.M. (eds.) Handbook of Emotion. Guilford Press (1993)
22. Musha, T., Terasaki, Y., Haque, H.A., Ivamitsky, G.A.: Feature extraction from EEGs associated with emotions. Art. Life Robotics 1(1), 15–19 (1997)

23. Bos, D.O.: EEG-based Emotion Recognition: The Influence of Visual and Auditory Stimuli (2007), `http://hmi.ewi.utwente.nl/verslagen/capita-selecta/CS-Oude_Bos-Danny.pdf`

24. Fries, P.: A mechanism for cognitive dynamics: neuronal communication through neuronal coherence. Trends in Cognitive Sciences 9(10), 474–480 (2005)

25. Sauseng, P., Klimesch, W., Doppelmayr, M., Pecherstorfer, T., Freunberger, R., Hanslmayr, S.: EEG alpha synchronization and functional coupling during top-down processing in a working memory task. Hum. Brain Map. 26(2), 148–155 (2005)

26. Sweeney-Reed, C.M., Nasuto, S.J.: A novel approach to the detection of synchronization in EEG based on empirical mode decomposition. Journal of Computational Neuroscience 23(1), 79–111 (2007)

27. Bhattacharya, J., Petsche, H., Pereda, E.: Long-range synchrony in the gamma band: role in music perception. Journal of Neuroscience 21, 6329–6337 (2001)

28. Hu, M., Li, J., Li, G., Tang, X., Freeman, W.J.: Normal and Hypoxia EEG Recognition Based on a Chaotic Olfactory Model. In: Wang, J., Yi, Z., Żurada, J.M., Lu, B.-L., Yin, H. (eds.) ISNN 2006. LNCS, vol. 3973, pp. 554–559. Springer, Heidelberg (2006)

29. Kirke, A., Miranda, E.R.: An Instance Based Model for Generating Expressive Performance During Composition. In: Proceedings of International Computer Music Conference (ICMC 2008), Belfast, UK (2008)

30. Kirke, A., Miranda, E.R.: Artificial Social Composition: A Multi-Agent System for Composing Music Performances by Emotional Communication. In: Klouche, T. (ed.) Mathematical and Computational Musicology. Springer (2010)

31. Guez, A., Vincent, R.D., Avoli, M., Pineau, J.: Adaptive Treatment of Epilepsy via Batch-mode Reinforcement Learning. In: Proceedings of the 20th Innovative Applications of Artificial Intelligence Conference, pp. 1671–1678 (2008)

Author Index